ROUTLEDGE LIBRARY EDITIONS:
PSYCHOLOGY OF EDUCATION

Volume 15

THE DELIVERY OF PSYCHOLOGICAL SERVICES IN SCHOOLS

THE DELIVERY OF PSYCHOLOGICAL SERVICES IN SCHOOLS
Concepts, Processes, and Issues

Edited by
STEPHEN N. ELLIOTT AND JOSEPH C. WITT

LONDON AND NEW YORK

First published in 1986 by Lawrence Erlbaum Associates, Inc.

This edition first published in 2018
by Routledge
2 Park Square, Milton Park, Abingdon, Oxon OX14 4RN

and by Routledge
711 Third Avenue, New York, NY 10017

Routledge is an imprint of the Taylor & Francis Group, an informa business

© 1986 Lawrence Erlbaum Associates, Inc.

All rights reserved. No part of this book may be reprinted or reproduced or utilised in any form or by any electronic, mechanical, or other means, now known or hereafter invented, including photocopying and recording, or in any information storage or retrieval system, without permission in writing from the publishers.

Trademark notice: Product or corporate names may be trademarks or registered trademarks, and are used only for identification and explanation without intent to infringe.

British Library Cataloguing in Publication Data
A catalogue record for this book is available from the British Library

ISBN: 978-1-138-24157-2 (Set)
ISBN: 978-1-315-10703-5 (Set) (ebk)
ISBN: 978-1-138-06965-7 (Volume 15) (hbk)
ISBN: 978-1-138-06972-5 (Volume 15) (pbk)
ISBN: 978-1-315-11554-2 (Volume 15) (ebk)

Publisher's Note
The publisher has gone to great lengths to ensure the quality of this reprint but points out that some imperfections in the original copies may be apparent.

Disclaimer
The publisher has made every effort to trace copyright holders and would welcome correspondence from those they have been unable to trace.

THE DELIVERY OF PSYCHOLOGICAL SERVICES IN SCHOOLS

Concepts, Processes, and Issues

Edited by

Stephen N. Elliott
Joseph C. Witt
Louisiana State University

LAWRENCE ERLBAUM ASSOCIATES, PUBLISHERS
1986   Hillsdale, New Jersey   London

Copyright © 1986 by Lawrence Erlbaum Associates, Inc.
All rights reserved. No part of this book may be reproduced in
any form, by photostat, microform, retrieval system, or any other
means, without the prior written permission of the publisher.

Lawrence Erlbaum Associates, Inc., Publishers
365 Broadway
Hillsdale, New Jersey 07642

Library of Congress Cataloging-in-Publication Data

The Delivery of psychological services in schools.

   Includes indexes.
   1. School children—Mental health services.
2. School psychologists.   I. Elliott, Stephen N.
II. Witt, Joseph C.
LB3430.D45   1986   371.4'6   86-11543
ISBN 0-89859-581-9

Printed in the United States of America
10 9 8 7 6 5 4 3 2 1

Contents

List of Contributors vii

Acknowledgments ix

Preface xi

1. Fundamental Questions and Dimensions of Psychological
   Service Delivery in Schools
   Stephen N. Elliott and Joseph C. Witt 1

2. Current Practice in School Psychology
   James E. Ysseldyke 27

3. Psychology and Schooling: The Interrelationships Among
   Persons, Processes, and Products
   Jack I. Bardon 53

4. Disentangling the Complexities of Clientage
   Krista J. Stewart 81

5. The Organization and Structuring of Psychological Services
   Within Educational Settings
   Michael J. Curtis and Joseph E. Zins 109

6. Models of School Psychological Service Delivery
   Jonathan Sandoval 139

7. Conceptual and Logistical Hurdles: Service Delivery to
   Urban Schools
   John H. Jackson — 171

8. Service Delivery to Rural Schools: Conceptual and
   Logistical Hurdles
   Jack J. Kramer and Glenda J. Peters — 203

9. School Psychology in Bicultural Settings: Implications for
   Service Delivery
   Ed N. Argulewicz — 227

10. The Effectiveness of School Psychological Services
    *Thomas R. Kratochwill, Jason K. Feld, and
    Kurt R. Van Someren* — 249

11. The Connections Among Educational and Psychological
    Research and the Practice of School Psychology
    Maurine A. Fry — 305

12. The Impact of Education and Training on School
    Psychological Services
    Beeman N. Phillips — 329

13. An Alternative Model for the Delivery of Psychological
    Services in the School Community
    Sandra Christenson, Brian Abery, and Richard A. Weinberg — 349

14. School Psychology: A Reconceptualization of Service
    Delivery Realities
    Jane Close Conoley and Terry B. Gutkin — 393

Author Index — 425

Subject Index — 437

Contributors

Brian Abery, Department of Psychoeducational Studies, University of Minnesota, Minneapolis

Ed Argulewicz, Ph.D.,* Department of Educational Psychology, Arizona State University, Tempe

Jack I. Bardon, Ph.D., Department of Psychology, University of North Carolina, Greensboro

Sandra Christenson, Department of Psychoeducational Studies, University of Minnesota, Minneapolis

Jane Close Conoley, Ph.D., Department of Educational Psychology, University of Nebraska-Lincoln

Michael J. Curtis, Ph.D., Department of School Psychology, University of Cincinnati

Stephen N. Elliott, Ph.D., Department of Psychology, Louisiana State University, Baton Rouge

Jason K. Feld, Department of Educational Psychology, University of Arizona, Tucson

*deceased

CONTRIBUTORS

Maurine Fry, Ph.D., Department of Educational Psychology, Arizona State University, Tempe

Terry B. Gutkin, Ph.D., Department of Educational Psychology, University of Nebraska-Lincoln

John H. Jackson, Ph.D., Division of Exceptional Education and Supportive Services, Milwaukee Public Schools

Jack J. Kramer, Ph.D., Educational Psychology, University of Nebraska-Lincoln

Thomas R. Kratochwill, Ph.D., School Psychology Program, University of Wisconsin, Madison

Glenda J. Peters, Norman Public Schools, Norman, OK

Beeman N. Phillips, Ph.D., Department of Educational Psychology, University of Texas, Austin

Jonathan Sandoval, Ph.D., Department of Education, University of California, Davis

Krista J. Stewart, Ph.D., Department of Psychology, Tulane University, New Orleans, LA

Kurt R. Van Someren, Department of Educational Psychology, University of Wisconsin-Madison

Richard Weinberg, Ph.D., Department of Psychoeducational Studies, University of Minnesota, Minneapolis

Joseph C. Witt, Ph.D., Department of Psychology, Louisiana State University, Baton Rouge

James E. Ysseldyke, Ph.D., Department of Psychoeducational Studies, University of Minnesota, Minneapolis

Joseph E. Zins, Ed.D., Department of School Psychology, University of Cincinnati

Acknowledgments

This book has come about because of the gifts and energies of many people. We are hopelessly in debt to so many who, individually and collectively, have dramatically influenced the quality of this volume. Although it is difficult to know where to start and end in acknowledging the many who have contributed in innumerable ways, the listing here should make it abundantly clear that this volume is the result of the efforts of many people.

Our most immediate gratitude must go to the contributors themselves. Their dedication to scholarship and academic craftsmanship made our task a pleasure. We extend a warm thank you to the authors for their cooperation, persistence, and patience during the writing, editing, and revision process. Their scholarship and friendship are valued.

A number of dedicated professionals gave their time and talents to review and provide comments on the chapters of this book. Thus, we gratefully acknowledge Jim Carroll, Jack Cummings, Terry Gutkin, Jerry Harris, Nadine Lambert, and Walter Pryzwansky. In addition, two of our students, Lester Andrews and Mary Von Brock, provided helpful editorial assistance.

As psychologists who recognize the importance of the environment on behavior, we wish to acknowledge the Department of Psychology at Louisiana State University as well as James Geer (Department Head) and Henry Snyder (Dean of Arts and Sciences), who continue to make it possible for us to work productively and efficiently. We are also grateful for the opportunity to work with Frank Gresham and other members of the Driftwood Association who not only stimulate us intellectually, but infuse the process of doing our work with enjoyment.

Finally, but most especially, we want to thank our families for their patience, understanding, and encouragement during the completion of this volume.

Preface

Seymour Sarason, of Yale University, has wondered aloud about how a being from outer space would react if allowed to observe our schools for a few days. What would a being with no preconceptions notice if given the opportunity to hover above the organized chaos of our schools? Sarason posits that certain processes and procedural regularities would very soon become apparent to the being (e.g., small people sit in orderly rows and listen while one larger person stands in front of a room and talks to them). Once these regularities are identified, it then becomes possible to question whether that particular regular way of doing things is the best way to do things. For example, perhaps learning can occur more effectively when children sit in a circle, work at home, or are taught by peers rather than teachers.

Although the contributors to this volume were not provided with a space craft, their task was somehow to rise above the day-to-day activities of school psychologists and examine the larger process-oriented issues that influence our field. The task is analogous to examining a river from different vantage points. If we look at a small stretch of river from the bank, we will notice whatever is within sight. However, the amount of river that we see is controlled by our perspective and by the circumstances that cause us to see that particular part of the river. If that section of the river is very narrow and the water runs quickly over rapids, then we may assume the entire river looks that way. However, if we observe the river from the air, we get a much wider perspective of not only what the river looks like, but where it is going and the many tributaries contributing to it. Similarly, with this volume, our goal was to obtain the collective wisdom and perspective of some of the freshest thinkers in school psychology concerning the most forceful currents influencing the delivery of psychological services in schools. It is our hope that this examination of the existing *process* regularities will provoke questions about their workability.

This book grew out of a perception that *process* issues within school psychology have not received the attention they deserve. For the most part, school psychologists have been most concerned with the *content* of what they do. Thus, there has been a great deal written about the actual, desired, and ideal roles and functions of school psychologists. This book is emphatically *not* about those roles and functions. Rather, it is about the major *concepts, processes, and issues* that serve as foundations for the field.

The volume is organized into three parts: Basic Issues, Models and Settings, and Evaluation and Development. Elliott and Witt begin with a description of the major conceptual dimensions and the fundamental questions that affect the practice of school psychology. This chapter was provided to all contributors to the volume before they commenced writing and, in many ways, serves as an advanced organizer for the text. In Chapter 2, Ysseldyke reviews the current status of school psychology practice. Bardon, in Chapter 3, presents a detailed review of the considerations and issues that determine *how* school psychologists should carry out their work, with an emphasis on the vast knowledge base which has been accumulated within psychology and educational psychology. Finally, Stewart, in Chapter 4, provides an illuminating discussion of clientage and service delivery in the schools.

Part 2 focuses on psychological service delivery issues as they are affected by particular models of service delivery and the settings in which service is provided. In Chapter 5, Curtis and Zins elucidate organizational factors known to influence the structuring of service delivery. Sandoval, in Chapter 6, presents a detailed comparative discussion of various models of service delivery. The remaining three chapters in this section discuss conceptual and logistical hurdles encountered when delivering psychological services in various settings. Specifically, Jackson (Chapter 7) describes hurdles confronting service delivery in urban settings, Kramer and Peters (Chapter 8) cover services in rural settings, and Argulewicz (Chapter 9) reviews services in bicultural settings.

Part 3 consists of various evaluation and development issues that influence school psychology. In Chapter 10, Kratochwill, Feld, and Van Someren describe numerous issues and methodologies for the evaluation of school psychological services. Chapter 11, by Fry, examines the impact of educational and psychological research on the practice of school psychology, and Chapter 12, by Phillips, discusses the impact of education and training on practice. In Chapter 13, Christenson, Abery, and Weinberg argue cogently for an ecological model of service delivery and emphasize the interface between school, home, and community settings. Finally, Conoley and Gutkin, in Chapter 14, offer a reconceptualization of school psychology as an indirect service delivery model and discuss the training and practice ramification of such a model.

Taken together, the chapters provide a comprehensive view of major service delivery issues within school psychology. In addition, virtually all of the chapters offer suggestions about needed directions for the field and many identify avenues by which these new directions can be accomplished.

SNE
JCW

1 Fundamental Questions and Dimensions of Psychological Service Delivery in Schools

Stephen N. Elliott
Joseph C. Witt
Louisiana State University

Schools provide an ideal setting for the delivery of psychological services. This supposition is based on the belief that schools are relatively predictable environments where children spend hundreds of hours during formative years interacting with significant adults and peers. It is estimated that collectively 67 million children, parents, and teachers are directly involved with kindergarten through high school (Hummel & Humes, 1984). In addition to the favorable setting and large number of potential clients, many of the goals and processes of education are highly consistent with those of psychology. Both professions want to see children develop cognitively, emotionally, and physically to their fullest potential. In sum, no other social system provides a more comprehensive opportunity to impact children and parents. Yet, psychology is a "guest" in education's house, which is akin to living with friends who frequently fight and also occasionally are targets of public criticism. Thus in addition to its own shortcomings, psychology runs the risk of additional public criticism through association with education. We believe, however, it is a risk well worth taking!

This book, and particularly this chapter, focuses on concepts and processes that influence the delivery of psychological services in schools. To date, relatively little has been written specially about the delivery of school psychological services even though it was a major topic at the Thayer Conference (Cutts, 1955) and the Spring Hall Symposium (Ysseldyke & Weinberg, 1981). Instead of focusing on delivery systems, previous authors have examined related areas such as the roles of school psychologists (Bardon, 1965; Monroe, 1979; Reger, 1965; Valett, 1965) and the administrative organization of psychological services (Cutts, 1955; Elkin, 1963; Herron, Green, Guild, Smith, & Kantor, 1970; Rettke, 1971). The primary purpose here is to examine *concepts, processes,* and *issues* involved in delivering psychological services to school children.

FUNDAMENTAL QUESTIONS FOR SERVICE DELIVERY

As a means of analyzing present arrangements for delivering psychological services in schools, we will pose and explore answers to four basic questions: What are the major service goals of school psychologists? Who is the client when psychologists work in schools? What are the major theoretical orientations of service delivery systems? Are school psychological services socially valid and effective? In an earlier volume entitled *School Psychology: Essentials of Theory and Practice* (Reynolds, Gutkin, Elliott, & Witt, 1984), we examined similar questions and found it a useful heuristic for conceptualizing service delivery practices and issues. We hope that by revisiting the first three questions and initiating an exploration of the fourth, we will foster further understanding of concepts and processes central to successful school psychological services.

What are the Major Service Goals of School Psychologists?

Education has been characterized as the major path to personal development and success. Consequently, the public has high and varied expectations for schools. In many ways, it is the result of this public concern for education that applied psychology is present in schools. Psychologists' entree to schools was initiated by educators concerned about assessing the learning potential of children. By now, most everyone knows the story of Alfred Binet and Theophile Simon and their work in France during the early 1900s to develop a test that could accurately assess the cognitive functioning of children. Even earlier (in the 1800s), Galton had begun to keep systematic records of students' performances on tests of vision, hearing, reaction time, and discrimination. In fact, White and Harris (1961) cited Galton's work as the first example of school psychological services. Regardless of who was first, it seems accurate to conclude that psychological services in schools started in the form of testing with the intent to classify children as capable or not capable of benefiting from education. The testing movement, originally given impetus by educators, served to promote many changes in educational practices (Murphy, 1929).

The form in which psychology appears in schools today varies, with testing providing a baseline and other activities such as family counseling, teacher and system-level consultation, and direct intervention providing examples of more advanced forms of school psychological services. Ysseldyke, in Chapter 2 of this volume, provides a more comprehensive examination of the scope and nature of the psychological services provided in school today. To identify the major service goals of school psychology, however, we believe the American Psychological Association's (1982) *Guidelines for the Delivery of Services by School Psychologists* provides the best summary. According to the Specialty Guidelines (APA, 1982):

School Psychological Services refers to one or more of the following services offered to clients involved in educational settings from pre-school through higher education for the protection and promotion of mental health and facilitation of learning: a. Psychological and psychoeducational evaluation and assessment of the school functioning of children and youth through the use of screening procedures, psychological and educational tests (particularly individual psychological tests of intellectual functioning, cognitive development, affective behavior, and neuropsychological status), interviews, observation, and behavioral evaluations with explicit regard for the context and the setting in which the professional judgments based on assessment, diagnosis and evaluation will be used.
b. Interventions to facilitate the functioning of individual or groups with concern for how schooling influences and is influenced by their cognitive, conative, affective, and social development. Such interventions may include, but are not limited to, recommending, planning, and evaluating special education services, psychoeducational therapy, counseling, affective educational programs, and training programs to improve coping skills.
c. Interventions to facilitate the educational services and child-care functions of school personnel, parents, and community agencies. Such interventions may include, but are not limited to, in-service school personnel education programs, parent-education programs, and parent counseling.
d. Consultation to and collaboration with school personnel and/or parents concerning specific school-related problems of pupils and students and the professional problems of staff. Such services may include, but are not limited to, assistance with the planning of educational programs from a psychological perspective; consultation to teachers and other school personnel to enhance their understanding of the needs of particular pupils; modification of classroom instructional programs to facilitate children's learning; . . . and the creation, collection, organization and provision of information from psychological research and theory to educate staff and parents.
e. Program development services to individual schools, to school administrative systems, and to community agencies in such areas as needs assessment and evaluation of regular and special education programs; . . . coordination, administration, and planning of specialized educational programs; the generation, collection, organization, and dissemination of information from psychological research and theory to educate staff and parents.
f. Supervision of school psychological services.

More specific goals could be added to this list, but items *a* through *f* capture the essence of most school psychologists' service goals.

A recent proposal from the National School Psychology Inservice Network, entitled "School Psychology: A Blueprint for Training and Practice" (Yesseldyke, Reynolds, & Weinberg, 1984), identified 16 domains of school psychology leadership and function. These domains extend the list of service goals for school psychologists and emphasize educational relevance within the mission of school psychology. Briefly, it was proposed the following domains represent parts of the knowledge base in psychology that can be applied to the solution of educational problems:

1. Class Management,
2. Interpersonal Communication and Consultation,
3. Basic Academic Skills,
4. Basic Life Skills,
5. Affective/Social Skills,
6. Parental Involvement,
7. Classroom Organization and Social Structure,
8. Systems Development and Planning,
9. Personnel Development,
10. Individual Differences in Development and Learning,
11. School-Community Relations,
12. Instruction,
13. Legal/Ethical and Professional Issues,
14. Assessment,
15. Multicultural Concerns, and
16. Research

The 16 domains of knowledge identified in "School Psychology: A Blueprint for Training and Practice" represent challenging "goals" *within* the profession of school psychology. The goals of the School Psychology profession are similar to the goals of any other organization: that is, self-preservation and growth. But at some point, we must begin to ask hard questions about the ends (i.e., the goals) which this expansion in activities will allow us to accomplish. Many of the calls for role expansion are made without any reference to how, for example, children would be better served. Those who write about expansion seem to believe that because a skill (e.g., system development) is taught in a graduate school psychology program, that fact alone is reason enough to add it to the list of activities that school psychologists *should* perform. Where are the data supporting the virtually infinite list of activities school psychologists *want* to perform? Unfortunately, school psychologists should spend less time writing about what they want to do and more time conducting efficacy studies on what they can do. With very few exceptions, there are no organized bodies of knowledge in school psychology (i.e., area of systematic research) and the field is relatively devoid of any conceptual (i.e., theoretical) unification.

Who Is The Client When Psychologists Work in Schools?

Traditionally, clients for school psychologists have included children and youth, both normal and abnormal; parents and occasionally entire families; and teachers and other significant educational personnel. The current emphasis on school psychological consultation research and evaluation services has served to increase this list of clients to include organizational units such as classrooms, schools, curriculum tracks within schools, and even entire school districts (e.g., see Snapp & Davidson, 1982). Thus, potential clients for psychologists working in educational settings range from one child and a teacher and/or parent to an entire school district composed of hundreds of children and educational personnel.

We believe one's general conceptualization of clients is influenced by several factors including (a) a psychologist's model of human behavior; (b) a psychologist's training or spectrum of competent services; (c) a psychologist's philosophy about preventive mental health; (d) legal mandates; and (e) financial remuneration. The extent to which these factors actually affect client selection and services may be influenced most by the work load or psychologist-to-student ratio within a given school district.

Our answer to the question of "Who is the client?" is "It depends!" This seemingly ambiguous response is based on the recognition that several factors can influence psychologists' conceptions of their target population. Some of the factors, such as one's model or theory of human behavior, training, and spectrum of competent services, are controlled by the individual psychologist. Other factors, such as legal mandates, workload, financial remuneration, and educational philosophy, are more externally controlled. To the extent that psychologists influence these factors, they can determine who their clients will be. Handicapped children traditionally have been and will likely continue to be a high-needs population for school psychologists. However, with the recent increased interest in education for the gifted and preschool-age children, and the consistently increasing number of requests for inservice and consultation services, school psychologists' clients are increasing in number and variety. Clearly, the question of clientage has theoretical as well as pragmatic implications for the actions of psychologists working in schools. A more comprehensive examination of this topic is presented by Stewart in Chapter 4 of this volume.

What Are the Major Theoretical Orientations of Service Delivery Systems?

Theoretical models of human behavior influence how psychologists and educators view and interact with children, especially exceptional children. Lambert (1981) has argued the necessity of theoretical models or conceptual frameworks for the healthy practice of school psychology. Quoting Lambert:

> One quality that differentiates the professional from the technician is that the professional knows the reason for a practice whereas the technician knows only how to practice. . . . School psychologists who have theoretical frames of reference, sets of theories and concepts that they employ in their practices, and reference sources of useful empirical evidence to support their frames of reference, are not easily taken in by the latest fads but test them out before moving ahead. Also,

school psychologists whose training has provided them with a conceptual framework as the foundation for continued professional development continue to experience growth and change and thus are less likely to "burn out." (p. 204)

A brief examination of three models of human behavior will provide a foundation for understanding what and how theoretical models can influence the delivery of psychological services in schools. These models include the medical model, the behavioral-ecological model, and the reciprocal determinism model.

The medical model in psychology emerged from psychoanalytic theory (Stuart, 1970). A central postulate of this model is that psychological disturbances are best understood and modified through the intensive study of intrapsychic life. The medical model assumes (a) behavior that deviates in a negative direction from normative standards is a reflection of a personal disease and (b) behavior classified as deviant must be changed within the individual by a curative process (Reger, 1972). The first assumption implies children who cannot be maintained or accommodated in a regular education program are suffering from an *internal* psychoeducational disorder. The second assumption also has practical implications that influence educational programs. Once children are classifed as deviant or "diseased," the educational system must respond to cure them. Educational "cures" seem to come most frequently in the form of special classes which tend to isolate the "diseased" child from normal or healthy children. The medical model of psychological and educational services for children experiencing learning and behavior problems has been critically challenged on conceptual, empirical, and practical grounds (Reger, 1972; Szasz, 1960; Zubin, 1967).

Alternative models of human behavior that acknowledge the role other people and environmental factors have in shaping a child's behavior are currently prominent in the eyes of many educators and psychologists. Chief among these are the behavioral and the ecological models. The major postulate of those espousing the behavioral model is that human behavior is primarily a function of environmental events (Skinner, 1953). The ecological model is built on a similar supposition, that is, human behavior results from a complex interaction between environmental factors and the individual characteristics of people (Barker, 1965, 1968; Hunt, 1967; Levin, 1951; Reilly, 1974). Both the behavioral and ecological models provide an alternative approach to understanding human behavior that is responsive to the criticisms directed at the medical model. For example, pathology is viewed as behavior that is deemed inappropriate (generally, excessive or deficient) when compared to subjective norms and values, rather than as an "illness" in any absolute sense (Ullmann & Krasner, 1969). Advocates of the behavioral-ecological approach reject a "mental illness" or intrapsychic causal explanation of psychopathology and instead are oriented toward the belief that human problems are primarily the result of interactions between people and their environments.

1. FUNDAMENTAL QUESTIONS AND DIMENSIONS 7

An ecologically oriented model of behavior that also takes individuals' cognitions into consideration would be the most suitable model for analyzing the problems of all children, not just potentially abnormal children. Therefore, we believe the reciprocal determinism model (Bandura, 1974, 1977, 1978) of human behavior is the model of choice for school psychologists, as well as other psychologists since it provides the most comprehensive view of children and youth who experience a wide range of problems.

The reciprocal determinism model, deduced from social learning theory, conceptualizes human behavior as a continuous reciprocal interaction between an individual's thoughts and behaviors, and environmental factors. The term *determinism* is used by Bandura (1978) "to signify the production of effects by events, rather than in the doctrinal sense that actions are completely determined by a prior sequence of causes independent of the individual" (p. 345). Schematically (see Fig. 1.1), Bandura represents reciprocal determinism as a triadic or three-way interaction among behavior (B), cognitions and other internal events that affect perceptions and actions (P), and external environment (E). Thus, the reciprocal determinism model extends the basic interactionist formula of behavioral and ecological models (i.e., $B = f(P,E)$ or behavior is a function of the interaction between person and environment factors) to include internal personal factors such as beliefs, values, and perceptions. The reciprocal interaction between an individual's personal factors (P) and behavior (B), although conceptually simple, is the dimension that makes this model different and more heuristic than previous models of human behavior.

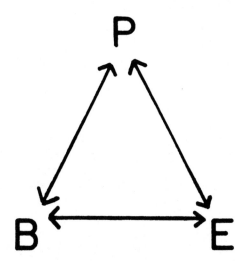

FIG. 1.1. Schematic representation of Bandura's reciprocal determinism model of human behavior.

The question of theoretical orientation and subsequent service delivery models is a complex one. The interested reader will find more comprehensive treatments of this topic in Chapter 6 by Sandoval, Chapter 13 by Christenson, Abery, and Weinberg, and in Chapter 14 by Conoley and Gutkin.

Are School Psychological Services Socially Valid and Effective?

This two-part question is the hardest to answer and thus has elicited much interest but relatively little empirical evidence. Before delving into an answer, however, some definitions and contextual information are warranted.

First, the issue of social validity. The notion here is that one's work can be evaluated by society (i.e., teachers, parents, children) on several levels (Wolf, 1978). Wolf identified three levels: (a) the social significance of *goals,* (b) the social appropriateness of *procedures,* and (c) the social importance of *effects.* Although Wolf's work with social validity focused on behavioral treatments, the definitional structure he developed easily generalizes to a broader range of psychological services. Thus, one can ask: Are the service delivery *goals* of school psychology really what society wants? Do the consumers and participants consider the service delivery *procedures* acceptable? Are the consumers satisfied with the *effects* or results of services? These questions are posed primarily for rhetorical value, but it should be noted several groups of researchers are beginning to amass data relevant to answering questions about the social validity of school psychological services. For example, Witt and his associates (Witt, Elliott, & Martens, 1984; Witt & Martens, 1984; Witt & Robbins, 1985; Witt, Moe, Gutkin, & Andrews, 1984) have investigated the social validity of different teacher-initiated interventions and influence of different philosophical orientations (e.g., behavioral vs. humanistic) as used during consultation and in psychological reports. Another line of social validity research focusing on school children has been initiated by Elliott and his associates (Elliott, 1986; Elliott, Witt, Galvin, & Moe, in press; Turco & Elliott, in press). This research with children has focused on their acceptability of various treatment procedures for classroom misbehavior. Gresham's work (1985) in social skills assessment and intervention is perhaps one of the best illustrations of how the social validity of service *goals, procedures,* and *effects* impact the conceptualization of a problem and delivery of services to remediate the problem. Other examples of social validity research that can influence the practice of school psychology include investigations by Kazdin (1980) and McMahon and Forehand (1983).

We are not of the opinion that a detailed set of socially valid services can or should ever be prescribed for everyone. The treatment situation is obviously more complex, requiring an appreciation for at least the individual differences of one's consumers (e.g., parents, teachers, children), the demands and resources in a setting, and the skills and orientation of the service provider. The point we want to stress is that social validity *can* and *should* be assessed *prior to* and *after* the delivery of psychological services. Although we cannot say that high social validity is a necessary but not sufficient condition for effective outcomes, we do believe services that meet the tests (goals, procedures, effects) of social validity have a higher probability of changing behavior in a desired direction.

The reader should not interpret our position on socially valid services to mean school psychologists simply provide the services requested. One could argue the profession has done just that in the case of testing and placement of children. Instead, it behooves psychologists to foster a problem-solving mindset *with* their consumers so dialogue about alternative services can be established. In fact, high social validity for a particular service may only be established *after* a service has been deemed effective. Thus, when psychologists are armed with effectiveness evidence for a particular service, they may want to proceed (within the context of law and ethics) to implement the service.

This point brings us to the second part of our major question: How effective are school psychology services? To begin answering the question of service effectiveness, we suggest that one investigate the knowledge base of school psychology. As noted earlier in this chapter, Ysseldyke et al. (1984) have identified what they described as 16 domains of "a well-confirmed knowledge base for practice of psychology in the schools" (p. 10). We agree that these domains embody knowledge and techniques directly relevant to the delivery of effective services. Thus, some of the *means* to an effective *end* have been identified. The development of systems that allow for use of such means remains a major challenge.

Kratochwill, Feld, and Van Someren (in Chapter 10 of this volume) cogently discuss issues that impact upon the evaluation of the effectiveness of school psychological services. Briefly, these issues include (a) the wide scope of services available which need evaluating, (b) the manner in which psychological service efficacy questions are posed, (c) the type and scope of measurement strategies used to determine effectiveness, and (d) the wide variety of design and evaluation strategies available. These and other relevant issues are explored in detail by Kratochwill and his associates. Of particular relevance here, however, is the manner in which we have posed the question of effectiveness. Paraphrasing Paul (1967, p. 111), questions of service delivery effectiveness become, What service, by whom, is most effective with the individual experiencing a specific concern under which set of circumstances?

Our point here is not to discourage the evaluation of service effectiveness; rather, we encourage a focused approach to the evaluation of effectiveness so as to avoid many of the pitfalls and controversies experienced by researchers interested in the effectiveness of psychotherapy (Garfield, 1983). We believe the question of service effectiveness is dependent upon one's answers to our questions concerning service goals, clients, and models of human behavior. Thus, posing questions about effectiveness can serve as a valuable heuristic for organizing one's thoughts about features and dimensions of psychological services. With this comment, we depart from posing questions to examine conceptual dimensions of psychological service delivery in schools.

ORGANIZATIONAL AND CONCEPTUAL DIMENSIONS OF SCHOOL PSYCHOLOGICAL SERVICES

Historically, administrators of progressive schools found it impractical to assign regular teachers and supervisors all the functions implied in adequate psychological services (Hildreth, 1930). In large school systems, provisions for such services were made through the organization of bureaus of research, psychological clinics, or departments of child study and guidance. Similar bureaus were maintained by the leading state universities and by a number of state departments of education. The services of these latter bureaus were especially useful to small communities that were unable to support an independent bureau.

Today, the organization and administration of psychological services within educational systems seems to assume at least four forms: a department of psychological services, a department of pupil personnel services, a department of special education, or an outside agency developed and operated by a state department of education or mental health. Detailed information has not been collected about differences in actual services provided by psychologists from each of the four types of organizational forms. In fact, relative differences in the organizational forms may be more semantic than anything else, with the possible exception of those services housed in an outside agency under the direction of a state department.

Cutts (1955), in her summarization of the Thayer Conference, described each of the four major organizational forms of school psychological services. Basically, her descriptions, although quite general, are still appropriate today. The major features she used to differentiate the four organizational forms were the personnel or staff background (training) and functions of the department.

The organizational form assumed for the provision of school psychological services would seem to be influenced by a variety of factors. Certainly, the number of psychologists on staff would be a major factor, along with the perceived importance of psychological services in the eyes of school administrators. Our experiences suggest the more staff members and the greater the perceived importance, the more likely the organizational form will be a separate department of school psychological services. The perceived recipients of psychological service may also affect the organizational placement of such services. For example, if all students are perceived as potential recipients of school psychological services, then the possibility of being organized as a separate department or being embedded with a pupil personnel department would seem conceptually more likely than becoming part of a special education department. Interpersonal working relationships and professional turf issues may also influence the organizational form of services. The relationship between school psychologists and special educators is particularly complex and has become a focal issue for many professionals in both fields. Hence, the pairing of these two groups should be planned well to maximize cooperation and minimize friction and duplication of services.

In 1970, Herron and his associates stated, "There seems to be no universal plan for the organization of [school] psychological services. The current picture is one of disturbing diversity. There are highly organized services and there are very unorganized services" (1970, p. 211). Diversity is still an appropriate descriptor for school psychological services in the 1980s; however, we believe they are diversified less than in 1970. Major factors acting to reduce the variance among psychological service systems have been the increase in special education legislation (e.g., P.L. 94–142, The Educational Rights for all Handicapped Children Act, 1975), litigation concerning psychological testing and psychological treatment (e.g., *Larry P.*, 1979; *PASE*, 1980), and the continued development of service delivery standards by APA Division 16 and NASP. Curtis and Zins, in Chapter 5, provide a detailed examination of these and other forces impinging on the organizing of school psychological services.

Each of the aforementioned factors has been a significant force in defining the legal and ethical boundaries of psychological practice in the schools. Within such boundaries, however, there is still wide latitude for organizing and delivering psychological services. Thus, at this point, it is not possible to single out a best system of psychological service delivery; therefore, we examine four major conceptual dimensions along which services vary: direct-indirect, centralized-decentralized, proactive-reactive, and rural-urban.

Direct-Indirect Services

Traditionally, psychological services have been conceptualized as direct services. In other words, a psychologist personally worked with an individual referred for services. This approach is characteristic of the medical model of psychology. Types of services that require direct contact between a psychologist and the referred individual include testing, counseling, and some forms of cognitive or behavioral treatments.

Indirect service delivery has begun to be used more frequently by psychologists, particularly those working in schools (Gutkin & Curtis, 1982). Psychologists working in an indirect service model interact primarily with other professionals (e.g., teachers) paraprofessionals (e.g., teacher aides), and lay persons (e.g., parents) who in turn work directly with clients. Consultation is an exemplar of this method of service delivery. Other types of services that illustrate an indirect service approach include inservice training for educators, parent training, curriculum advisement, and some behavioral interventions. Conoley and Gutkin, in Chapter 14, discuss the trend toward indirect services.

Monroe (1979) has used a direct-indirect service continuum concept as a means of characterizing five major roles or functions of school psychologists. The functions she identified were counseling/therapy, psychoeducational assessment, consultative child study, inservice, and research. Although admittedly oversimplified, Monroe believed that counseling/therapy was the strongest example of direct service to children, and research represented the most extreme example of indirect service. Her schema for characterizing the relative relationships along the direct-indirect service continuum of the five primary functions of school psychologists is reproduced in Fig. 1.2.

A common goal of both direct and indirect service models is to provide remedial services for problems. An additional important goal or objective of an indirect service model is to increase the consultees' knowledge and intervention skills so they can prevent or respond more effectively to similar problems in the *future*. Thus, theoretically, indirect service systems may have a greater capability for dealing with larger numbers of individuals than direct service systems because they utilize more persons in the treatment or remediation of problems.

Realistically, psychologists who wish to provide comprehensive services to children and youth will utilize both direct and indirect services. An exclusive

Direct Influence on Child	Counseling / Therapy – Psychologist works with individual child or small groups of children to enhance adjustment or development.
	Psychoeducational Assessment – Psychologist uses formal and informal data collection devices with individual children to obtain information needed for decisions about screening, classification, placement, and interventions.
	Consultative Child Study – Psychologist works with parents or teachers to enhance adjustment or development of child.
	Inservice – Psychologist works to increase knowledge or skills or to change attitudes of groups of school personnel.
Indirect Influence on Child	Research – Psychologist systematically gathers data to aid in decision making regarding groups of children and their educational programs.

FIG. 1.2. Influences of school psychological services on children. From "Roles and Status of School Psychology" by V. Monroe. In G. D. Phye and D. J. Reschly (Eds.), *School Psychology: Perspectives and Issues* (pp. 25–47). New York: Academic Press. Copyright 1979. Reprinted by permission.

reliance on either direct or indirect service techniques is probably indicative of an incomplete service model and should be avoided; certain cases demand the direct attention and skills of a psychologist; others can be handled effectively by teachers, parents, or even peers.

Centralized-Decentralized Services

The organizational structure through which psychological services are administered and the physical location of the primary service providers are two major factors that influence the delivery of school psychological services. These two factors seem to have a strong effect on the actual, as well as perceived, coordination and proximity of services. In general, we believe centralized organization structures are characterized as more coordinated, yet more distal, to the majority of clientele. Decentralized organizations are characterized as less coordinated but more proximal to the majority of clientele. Thus, in theory, the organization and delivery of school psychological services can be meaningfully conceptualized along a centralized-decentralized continuum. This continuum is a summation of characteristics such as degree of administrative coordination and physical location of service providers.

Few writers or researchers, with the exception of Elkin (1963) and Phillips (1968), have examined the centralized-decentralized dimensions of school psychological services. Therefore, one is left to theorize about the actual functionality of such a continuum until future investigators establish an empirical base. Theorizing and hypothesizing about the centralization or decentralization of school psychological services can, nevertheless, shed valuable light on the organization and utilization of such services.

Elkin (1963) in a chapter titled, "Structuring School Psychological Services: Internal and Interdisciplinary Considerations," strongly advocated the centralization of such services. He argued that a centralized office under a Chief of Service was essential for efficient utilization of school psychologists administratively and professionally. Elkin believed the trend toward centralization of psychological services was based on practical experiences of psychologists and educators and could be attributed to five categories of factors, which he labeled (a) benefits to children, (b) needs of the educational community, (c) confidentiality of communication, (d) supervisory requirements, and (e) utilization of professional staff.

Elkin believed there were three major, direct benefits of centralized services for children. First, he argued that continuity of contact and communication between any individual child and a given psychologist who had been involved previously with the child was desirable and highly probable within a centralized service mode. In fact, a psychologist could follow a child from school entry through high school graduation if need be. Such case flexibility may allow for quicker actions and less redundancies in services (e.g., developmental histories, parent interventions, etc.). A second benefit of centralized services results from the availability of organized and centralized record keeping systems. Such systems, according to Elkin, provide for more efficient storage and retrieval of critical information, as well as increased confidentiality of such information. A third benefit to children of centralized services may be the increased flexibility of staff utilization. Elkin elaborated upon this with an example whereby psychologists could be assigned to high need schools temporarily to alleviate problems.

The final component of Elkin's rationale for centralized services concerned issues of supervision of staff by a "qualified" chief of service and optimal staff utilization (or accountability). Many of the same examples used with the previous two features were also used as support for these final two components.

In sum, Elkin identified several major strengths of a centralized model of school psychological services. Several of these identified strengths are not, however, idiosyncratic to a centralized model of psychological services. For example, confidentiality of communications and record keeping can probably be carried out with equal effectiveness in a decentralized service system. One must be aware that other factors such as psychologist/student ratio, number of schools within a district, perceived nature of psychologists (i.e., administrator- or teacher-like), and interest in preventive mental health will also influence decisions concerning the administrative structure of school psychological services.

To date, no writer has published a parallel article to Elkin's in support of a decentralized mode of psychological services, although Phillips (1968) designed a model for psychological service which stressed a decentralized or school-based organization. Specifically, Phillips' model featured a diagnosis-intervention class and a teacher-psychological specialist. Decentralized service systems would appear to have several advantages. First, in a relatively decentralized system of psychological services, the service providers would be housed within the school or schools where they work, thus increasing the number of contacts with potential consumers. Such an arrangement would seem to be particularly helpful in establishing consultation and preventive mental health activities. Specialized service units for particular populations of students (e.g., retarded, physically handicapped, etc.) have also been an impetus for the decentralization of school psychological services. A final common reason experienced by both urban and rural school districts has been travel distance between central office and the various schools desiring service. As a result, many psychologists have elected to increase their direct service hours by relocating to field offices in the various schools they serve.

In practice, we have observed a variety of service delivery systems that have a combination of centralized and decentralized features. The majority of psychological service models probably can be characterized at different points on the centralized-decentralized continuum with respect to various service features.

Proactive-Reactive Services

School psychologists' actions should be guided by *anticipated* or perceived mental health and educational problems. Reaction to an anticipated problem is proactive, whereas reaction to an *existing* problem is characterized as reactive. In general, most school psychological activities such as assessment, consultation, and intervention are in response to identified problems (and thus reactive). These same activities can be used within a preventive framework as well. Krischenbaum's (1983) review of early behavioral intervention programs for children testifies to this point.

An analysis of psychological interventions that directly correspond with the proactive-reactive continuum of services was explicated by Cowen (1977). According to Cowen, a comprehensive system of mental health requires a three-level model of intervention. He refers to the first level as primary prevention. Basically, primary prevention refers to lowering the rate of emotional, behavioral, and learning disorders in a given population and building psychological health and resources in people. Healthy children are the main targets for primary prevention within schools, whereas secondary preventions have high-risk children or youngsters whose problems are just beginning as their targets. Early identification of and intervention with children who are just beginning to have academic and/or behavior difficulties are the major objective of secondary prevention. The final level of prevention is referred to as tertiary. Tertiary prevention services are concentrated on children and youth having "full-blown" academic or behavior problems. The fundamental goal of this third level of intervention is to remediate or repair psychologically damaged individuals so they will be able to function productively.

When moving through the levels of Cowen's prevention models, from primary prevention to secondary prevention to tertiary prevention, actions become more reactive and less proactive with regard to planning and delivering psychological services. To the chagrin of most school psychologists, a majority of services are delivered within the secondary and tertiary levels of prevention with tertiary services taking the lion's share of the psychologists' time (Benson & Hughes, 1985; Smith, 1984).

A number of school and community psychologists have championed the call for preventive mental health services within schools (Allen, Chinsky, Larcen, Lochman, & Selinger, 1976; Alpert, 1985; Clarizio, 1979a; Kirschenbaum, 1983); however, a number of factors seem to mitigate against the ready acceptance of proactive or preventive services for school children. The foremost problem is one of perception. Many educators seems to want immediate solutions to current problems and there is a perception that efforts directed toward prevention are a luxury that schools cannot afford. Also, psychologists and educators seem generally to be overwhelmed by the complexities involved in designing and establishing preventive programs. Thus, a lack of know-how coupled with a relative paucity of prepackaged programs seems to be a significant limiting factor. Other deterrents to prevention include invasion-of-privacy and the difficulty of specifying and evaluating the goals of prevention (Clarizio, 1979b).

Rural to Urban Services

Herron and his associates (1970) emphasized the differential influence of an urban, suburban, or rural setting on the organization of school psychological services. According to these writers and to Jackson (Chapter 7 in this volume), city schools have pressing social and family difficulties, and violence in and around schools is also common. Thus, they believe family services are absolutely necessary, along with prevention programs, group therapy, and inservice training for teachers. Because of the complexity and significance of the problems encountered within urban schools, Herron et al. recommended a service structure where there was a director of pupil personnel, and all service providers (e.g., psychologists, counselors, social workers, etc.) reported to him/her.

In a suburban school, psychological services were reported to be characterized by two types of organizational structures, both of which are more decentralized than in urban schools (Herron et al., 1970). One organizational approach used psychologists on a specialized basis for such things as handling of early admissions or readiness programs. In the other type of organization, psychologists were assigned to a single school where they did everything from prevention to placement. With both of these service approaches, psychologists appeared to be housed within a separate department of psychology rather than as a section of a pupil personnel department.

Herron and his associates (1970) characterized rural school psychological services as primarily a "one-person operation" where a psychologist usually functions under the direction of a state board of education or a county agency. In actuality, a rural psychologist is not usually a part of a particular department within a school district and functions with a high degree of autonomy. Kramer and Peters in Chapter 8 of this volume provide an up-to-date examination of the major service delivery issues facing rural school psychologists.

A TAXONOMY FOR THE DELIVERY OF PSYCHOLOGICAL SERVICES

In an earlier volume (Reynolds et al., 1984), Elliott developed a taxonomy of psychological services from the work of Catterall (1970). Briefly, Catterall's taxonomy of interventions included two interactive dimensions which he referred to as *directness of approach* and *focus of approach*. Directness of approach referred to a continuum of contact, direct or indirect, between a service provider and a client. Focus of approach referred to the primary target for change, the environment or an individual, and characterized whether the service provider was attempting change in the total environment or trying to focus on an individual in a more personal way. Schematically (see Fig. 1.3), the interaction of the directness and focus dimensions results in four types of service: indirect environmental, direction environmental, indirect personal, and direct personal. When viewed from the reciprocal determinism perspective of human behavior, direct and indirect environmental services focus on the E of the PBE triad, whereas direct and indirect personal services focus on the P and B components of the model.

Using this taxonomy of services, one can examine, from a child-as-client perspective, the directness and focus of four major psychological services generally provided by school psychologists. These four major psychological services are assessment, consultation, intervention, and research.

Assessment

Assessment is a process that is characterized by the collection of information to aid in making several possible types of decisions about an individual. School psychologists use a variety of techniques to collect information about an individual, as well as aspects of his/her environment. Typical techniques include interviewing parents, teachers, or students; reviewing student records; testing with standardized instruments and informal inventories; and observing an individual's behavior in several situations.

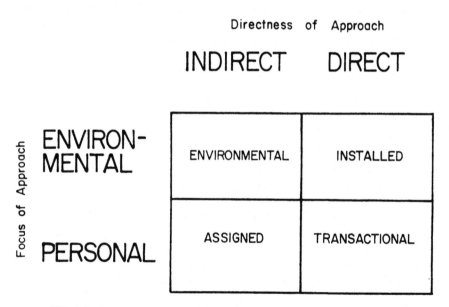

FIG. 1.3. Taxonomic dimensions of school psychological services.

Traditional assessment is considered a direct personal service because such practices are test-oriented, requiring a client to interact directly with a psychologist. Parental or teacher interviews do not directly involve the child, but rather significant others. Hence, interviewing can be considered an indirect environmental service. Similarly, the review of a child's records and classroom observations during the assessment process also would be considered indirect environmental services because such services do not directly involve the child and are focused on other persons or objects within the child's daily environment.

Assessment services characterized as direct environmental or indirect personal are used relatively infrequently. An example of a direct environmental assessment service could involve diagnostic teaching in an area proven difficult as a result of a child's test performance. An example of an indirect personal assessment service could involve a child's filling out a personality or careers inventory on his/her own and returning it to the psychologist for scoring and interpretation.

Assessment is truly a multifaceted process because it is possible to identify four categories of assessment services that differentially involve a psychologist, a child, and significant others in the child's environment. In general and in concert with current school practice, most assessment services are direct personal or indirect environmental in nature.

Some have argued convincingly (see Conoley and Gutkin, Chapter 14 in this volume) that the assessment activities of psychologists are *not* services at all. Instead, they are activities that can lead to services but they are not services per se. This point becomes more obvious if we ask simply; What benefits does a child derive from most of the assessment activities conducted by psychologists? For example, is there any inherent benefit for the child who spends over an hour responding to the WISC-R? Typically, the benefit comes to the child in the form of linking the child up with an appropriate service. Within this context, assessment serves the system and has very little direct benefit to a child.

Intervention

Interventions can be defined as strategic reactions by psychologists, educators, and/or parents to children's "inappropriate" behavior or "unsuccessful" learning. A brief review and update of Catterall's (1970) work can provide a conceptual overview of various school psychology intervention services.

Traditionally, school psychologists' interventions with children involved talk or play therapies primarily and were intended as a means by which a child could gain insights into his/her feelings and behaviors (Barbanel, 1982). Recently, most psychologists and educators have had a stronger affinity for behavioral therapies than "talk" therapies. A number of factors have contributed to such a large-scale adoption of behavioral intervention techniques. Important factors include enhanced clarity of communication and utilization of behavioral techniques in everyday classroom teaching and management.

As demonstrated by Catterall in 1970, interventions utilized by school psychologists could be classified in all four of the basic categories of service. With the addition of a few recent interventions such as self-monitoring (an indirect personal service) and biofeedback (a direct environmental service), Catterall's taxonomy would be up-to-date. From our experience as school psychology practitioners and trainers, we believe indirect environmental and direct environmental services are used most frequently. Although with the current research interest in self-monitoring (Kazdin, 1982; Shapiro, 1984) and social skills training (Gresham, 1981), we predict increased utilization of both indirect personal and direct personal services, and when accomplished in concert with environmental intervention, such services will epitomize the reciprocal determinism model of behavior and its changes.

Consultation

Consultation is defined frequently as a process of "collaborative problem-solving between a mental health specialist (the consultant) and one or more persons (the consultees) who are responsible for providing some form of psychological assistance to another (the client)" (Medway, 1979, p. 276). To a large degree, consultative services developed in response to dissatisfaction with traditional approaches to mental health services for both children and adults (Carter, 1975; Meyers, Parsons, & Martin, 1979). Primary among the targets of dissatisfaction was the medical model approach to psychology.

To classify consultation according to our taxonomy of services, we must examine its core characteristics briefly. The major distinguishing characteristics of consultation include (a) the provision of services to children and (b) the development of a relationship between a consultant and consultee that is voluntary and collaborative in nature. Hence, from the perspective that a child is the client, consultation activities can best be classified as indirect environmental services, for they are done around the client. In comparison to assessment and intervention services, consultation is a more focused or defined service. This does not imply that it is more important, effective, or efficient. In fact, such a classification is largely the result of consultation services conceptually preceding and subsuming assessment and intervention services.

Research

Research is characterized as an empirical, fact-finding process that should inform individuals' decisions and actions. The domain of school psychology research is vast, for it can be argued that all of the behavioral sciences are an appropriate research base. Although such a view has legitimacy given the trend toward integraton of school, family, and social services, the obstacles of truly integrating such a large body of research are probably insurmountable. One way to scale down the research domain of school psychology is to allow major service functions to guide the development of research. Fry, in Chapter 11 of this volume, discusses the connections between research and practice in educational and school psychology.

In general, research activities of school psychologists are not made explicit to children, if children are involved directly at all. Therefore, most research happens around children and to children without their prior knowledge. As a result, most school psychology research can be categorized as indirect environmental or direct environmental services.

ASSUMPTIONS AND PROCEDURES OF SCHOOL PSYCHOLOGICAL DELIVERY SYSTEMS

No single best model of school psychological services has been identified. A major reason for this is that service providers must be sensitive to the needs of consumers and aware of environmental constraints (e.g., organizational structure of services, financial ability to pay for staff and services, and legal guidelines concerning services). Because the needs of consumers and environmental constraints vary across school districts and states, school psychological service models also vary. Such variability of services does not, however, negate an analysis and discussion of the typical processes by which school psychological services are delivered. On the contrary, a common core of consultation, assessment, and intervention procedures is identifiable in most states. This is due primarily to the implementation in the mid-70s of federal legislation such as P.L. 94–142 and its corollary state mandates, which in many ways have functioned to standardize the process of providing services for handicapped children and youth.

Two delivery system models for school psychological services have been most prevalent in the literature. They are the diagnostic or assessment model (Catterall, 1972; Sabatino, 1972) and the consultation or problem-solving model (Bergan, 1977; Lambert, 1974, Meyers, Parsons, & Martin, 1979). In practice, a third, less discrete model exists that is a combination of the diagnostic and consultation models. Sandoval, in Chapter 6 of this volume, provides an integrated examination of these models, and in subsequent chapters Christenson, Abery, and Weinberg (Chapter 13) and Conoley and Gutkin (Chapter 14) effectively champion particular models for the future. Rather than advocate any one model here, we wish to focus on the development of a generic model of school psychological services that integrates components from both the assessment and the consultation models.

A Generic Model of School Psychological Service Delivery

The development of a generic model for the delivery of psychological services has much instructional value, but is certainly subject to modification upon implementation within any given school district because of numerous factors already discussed in this chapter. The generic service delivery model we espouse is premised on six basic assumptions about work with potentially handicapped or troubled individuals. The six assumptions and brief elaborative comments about each one follow:

1. *Behavior and learning problems of children are functionally related to the setting in which they are manifest.* This assumption does not mean educational settings such as schools necessarily cause the psychoeducational problems children manifest in such settings; however, it does suggest that the relationship may be primarily causal or that behavior is triggered by a factor(s) in the school environment. Thus, it is necessary to evaluate an educational environment, as well as a particular child.

2. *A primary goal of psychoeducational assessment is to determine what a child does and does not know, and how the child learns best so successful interventions can be designed.* This assumption stems logically from the required end-product of assessment; in other words, *what* and *how* information is prerequisite to the development of a valid individual education plan. Such a supposition is consistent with a thorough consultative problem-solving and a skills-training approach to assessment.

3. *Techniques for individual diagnosis and intervention need to be supplemented with techniques for diagnosing and intervening in specific school settings and in the school as a social system.* Generally, it is not sufficient to intervene only at the level of an individual student. In order to enhance the probability of meaningful and long-term behavior change, it is necessary to intervene on a broader level.

4. *The greater the proximity in place and time of psychological services to educational settings, the greater the utilization of these services.* This assumption is based on the premise that problem-solving communications among professionals working with an individual will be enhanced if they work in the same environment. In addition, psychologists who work in and are a part of a particular ecology (e.g., a school) will be more knowledgeable of the resources and constraints of the system. In this situation, proximity does not breed contempt; rather, proximity breeds accessibility.

5. *Psychological services should be directed toward the development and utilization of resources indigenous to schools.* The essence of a consultation-oriented service system is for consultants to work indirectly with children through a consultee (i.e., teachers and parents), and thus enhance the consultee's ability to solve future problems. By focusing on indigenous resources, we increase the likelihood of designing interventions that are socially valid and that can realistically be implemented in a classroom or other settings.

6. *Psychoeducational interventions require the ongoing attention of the person(s) who implemented them because over time a child's response to a particular intervention will change.* If we had to choose one fatal flaw of education (relative to business or other fields), it is that it fails to evaluate and to periodically follow up on suggested interventions with children. Such follow-ups allow for refinement of a particular intervention and provide feedback concerning the effectiveness of previous actions.

A procedural flowchart illustrating our generic service model is displayed in Fig. 1.4. The step-by-step sequence of this service model was influenced strongly by a presentation given by Grimes and Reschly (1980). In fact, the procedural flowchart illustrating the core of our consultation-assessment-intervention service system was adapted from a similar flowchart developed by Grimes and Reschly. Persons seeking a detailed description of each procedural step in this model are referred to Reynolds et al. (1984).

This 15-step model of school psychological services for referred students should not be viewed as a rigid process. Rather, it is an attempt to organize typical services in a logical, temporal order. In addition, readers should note

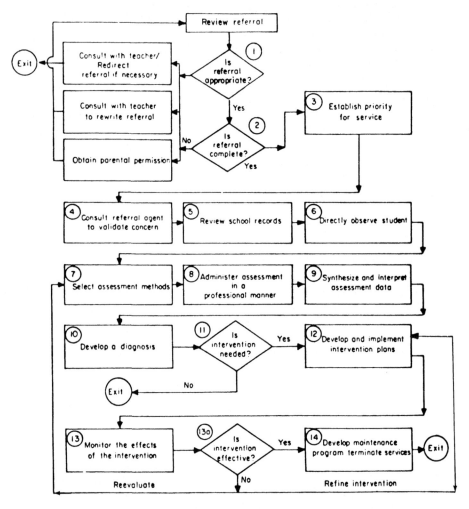

FIG. 1.4. Flowchart of consultation-assessment-intervention service system.

that feedback or refinement loops are available at each major decision point, thus allowing for redefinition of a problem, further assessment of a student, or redesigning of an intervention.

CONCLUSIONS

John Dewey (1917) has encouraged us to nourish our science in two ways and his wisdom seems as fresh and applicable today as ever. In the most typical way, knowledge advances in an additive sense whereby new information (usually data) is added to what is already known in an existing area of inquiry. A second, less common, but nonetheless important method demands qualitative rather than quantitative change in the way we think about problems and the addition of knowledge. In other words, these two alternatives can be summed up by considering the first as looking for new answers to old questions and the second as looking for ways to ask new questions. This chapter (and this book) is concerned with both of these approaches to service delivery issues within school psychology.

When a field of endeavor is really understood, it is possible for our actions to be governed by a knowledge that forces us beyond the preconception into a new or renewed awareness of the infinite possibilities. Dewey (1917) put it this way:

> A being which can use given and finished facts as signs of things to come, which can take given things as evidence of absent things, can, in that degree, forcast the future; it can form reasonable expectations. It is capable of achieving ideas; it is possessed of intelligence. For use of the given or finished to anticipate going on is precisely what is meant by 'ideas,' by 'intelligence.' (p. 21)

For school psychology, what are the possibilities? For that matter, what are the major themes which run through our profession and guide our actions? A knowledge of the latter question will help us to answer the former. A major goal of this chapter (and the book) has been to illuminate the major *process* and *conceptual* dimensions impinging on service delivery. Our intent has been to rise above the murky quagmire of day-to-day *activities* and to identify and discuss the major conceptual regularities that influence school psychology. We have done this in an attempt to see not only where we are but also where we are going. Perhaps our current efforts to "take stock" will aid future writers in the development of a plan or plans for the desired direction for the future. Without an overall plan of the desired directions for the future, development and advancement would be relegated to a haphazard status. Such a status is incompatible with the goals of science.

REFERENCES

Allen, G. J., Chinsky, J. M., Larcen, S. W., Lochman, J. E., & Selinger, H. V. (1976). *Community psychology and the schools: A behaviorally oriented multilevel preventive approach.* Hillsdale, NJ: Lawrence Erlbaum Associates.

Alpert, J. L. (1985). Change within a profession: Change, future, prevention, and school psychology. *American Psychologist, 40,* 1125–1130.

American Psychological Association (1982). Specialty guidelines for the delivery of services by school psychologists. *American Psychologist, 36,* 670–681.

Bandura, A. (1974). Behavior theory and the models of man. *American Psychologist, 29,* 859–869.

Bandura, A. (1977). Self-efficacy: Toward a unifying theory of behavioral change. *Psychological Review, 84,* 191–215.

Bandura, A. (1978). The self-system in reciprocal determinism. *American Psychologist, 33,* 344–358.

Barbanel, L. (1982). Short-term dynamic therapies with children. In C. R. Reynolds & T. B. Gutkin (Eds.), *The handbook of school psychology* (pp. 554–569). New York: Wiley.

Bardon, J. I. (Ed.). (1964–1965). Problems and issues in school psychology—1964: Proceedings of a conference on "new directions in school psychology" sponsored by the National Institute of Mental Health. *Journal of School Psychology, 3,* 1–44.

Barker, R. G. (1965). Explorations in ecological psychology. *American Psychologist, 20,* 1–14.

Barker, R. G. (1968). *Ecological psychology.* Stanford, CA: Stanford University Press.

Benson, A. J., & Hughes, J. (1985). Perceptions of role definition processes in school psychology: A national survey. *School Psychology Review, 14-1,* 64–74.

Bergan, J. R. (1977). *Behavioral consultation.* Columbus, OH: Charles E. Merrill.

Carter, B. D. (1975). School mental health consultation: A clinical social work interventive technique. *Clinical Social Work Journal, 3,* 201–210.

Catterall, C. D. (1970). Taxonomy of prescriptive interventions. *Journal of School Psychology, 8-1,* 5–12.

Catterall, C. D. (1972). Special education in transition—implications for school psychology. *Journal of School Psychology, 10,* 91–98.

Clarizio, H. F. (1979a). Primary prevention of behavioral disorders in the schools. *School Psychology Digest, 8,* 434–445.

Clarizio, H. F. (1979b). School psychologists and the mental health needs of students. In G. D. Phye & D. J. Reschly (Eds.), *School psychology: Perspectives and issues.* New York: Academic Press.

Cowen, E. L. (1977). Baby-steps toward primary prevention. *American Journal of Community Psychology, 5,* 1–22.

Cutts, N. E. (Ed.). (1955). *School psychologists at mid-century.* Washington, D.C.: American Psychological Association.

Dewey, J. (1917). *Creative intelligence: Essays in the pragmatic attitude.* New York: Henry Holt.

Elliott, S. N. (1986). Children's acceptability ratings of classroom interventions for misbehavior: Findings and methodological considerations. *Journal of School Psychology, 24,* 23–35.

Elliott, S. N., Witt, J. C., Galvin, G. A., & Moe, G. (in press). Children's suggestions and acceptability ratings of classroom interventions for misbehavior. *Professional Psychology: Research and Practice.*

Elkin, V. B. (1963). Structuring school psychological services: Internal and interdisciplinary considerations. In M. G. Gottsegen & G. B. Gottsegen (Eds.), *Professional school psychology.* New York: Grune & Stratton.

Garfield, S. L. (1983). Effectiveness of psychotherapy: The perennial controversy. *Professional Psychology, 14,* 35–43.

Gresham, F. M. (1981). Social skills training with handicapped children: A review. *Review of Educational Research, 51,* 139–176.

Gresham, F. M. (1985). The assessment of social behavior/competence in children. In P. Strain, M. Guralnick, & H. Walker (Eds.), *Children's social behavior: Development, assessment, and modification.* (pp. 143–179). New York: Academic Press.

Grimes, J., & Reschly, D. J. (1980, September). *Standards and competencies for psychological assessment, intervention, and follow-up.* Paper presented to the Nebraska School Psychologists Association, Lincoln, NE.

Gutkin, T. B., & Curtis, M. J. (1982). School-based consultation: Theory and techniques. In C. R. Reynolds and T. B. Gutkin (Eds.), *The handbook of school psychology* (pp. 796–828). New York: Wiley.

Herron, W., Green, M., Guild, M., Smith, A., & Kantor, R. (1970). *Contemporary school psychology.* Scranton, PA: International Textbook.

Hildreth, G. H. (1930). *Psychological service for school problems.* Yonkers, NY: World.

Hummel, D. L., & Humes, C. W. (1984). *Pupil services: Development, coordination, administration.* New York: Macmillan.

Hunt, J. M. (1967). Traditional personality theory in light of recent evidence. In E. P. Hollander & R. G. Hunt (Eds.), *Current perspectives in social psychology* (2nd ed., pp. 157–184). New York: Oxford University Press.

Kazdin, A. E. (1980). Acceptability of alternative treatment for deviant child behavior. *Journal of Applied Behavior Analysis, 13,* 259–273.

Kazdin, A. E. (1982). Applying behavioral principles in the schools. In C. R. Reynolds & T. B. Gutkin (Eds.), *The handbook of school psychology.* New York: Wiley.

Kirschenbaum, P. S. (1983). Toward more behavioral early intervention programs: A rationale. *Professional Psychology, 14,* 159–169.

Lambert, N. M. (1974). A school based consultation model. *Professional Psychology, 5,* 267–276.

Lambert, N. M. (1981). School psychology training for the decades ahead, on rivers, streams, and creeks—currents and tributaries to the seas. *School Psychology Review, 10,* 194–205.

Larry, P. et al. v. Wilson Riles et al. No. C 71 2270. United States District Court for the Northern District of California, San Francisco, October 1979, slip opinion.

Lewin, K. (1951). *Field theory in the social sciences.* New York: Harper & Row.

McMahon, R. J., & Forehand, R. L. (1983). Consumer satisfaction in behavioral treatment of children: Types, issues, and recommendations. *Behavior Therapy, 14,* 209–225.

Medway, F. J. (1979). How effective is school consultation: A review of recent research. *Journal of School Psychology, 17,* 275–282.

Meyers, J., Parsons, R. D., & Martin, R. (1979). *Mental health consultation in the schools.* San Francisco: Jossey-Bass.

Monroe, V. (1979). Roles and status of school psychology. In G. D. Phye & D. J. Reschly (Eds.), *School psychology: Perspectives and issues* (pp. 25–47). New York: Academic Press.

Murphy, G. (1929). *An historical introduction to modern psychology.* New York: Harcourt, Brace.

Paul, G. P. (1967). Outcome research in psychotherapy. *Journal of Consulting Psychology, 31,* 109–118.

PASE: *Parents in action on special education et al. v. Hannon et al.* No. c 74 3586. United States District Court for the Northern District of Illinois, Eastern Division, July 1980, slip opinion.

Phillips, B. N. (1968). The diagnostic-intervention class and the teacher-psychological specialist: Models for the school psychological services network? *Psychology in the Schools, 5,* 135–139.

Reger, R. (1965). *School psychology.* Springfield, IL: Charles C Thomas.

Reger, R. (1972). The medical model in special education. *Psychology in the Schools, 9,* 8–12.

Reilly, D. H. (1974). A conceptual model for school psychology. *Psychology in the Schools, 11,* 165–170.

Rettke, G. H. (1971). Psychological services: A developing model. In F. D. Holt & R. H. Kicklighter (Eds.), *Psychological services in the schools* (pp.   ). Dubuque, IA: Wm. C. Brown.
Reynolds, C. R., Gutkin, T. B., Elliott, S. N., & Witt, J. C. (1984). *School psychology: Essentials of theory and practice.* New York: Wiley.
Sabatino, D. A. (1972). School psychology—special education: To acknowledge a relationship. *Journal of School Psychology, 10,* 99–105.
Shapiro, E. S. (1984). Self-monitoring. In T. H. Ollendick & M. Hersen (Eds.), *Child behavior assessment: Principles and procedures* (pp. 148–165). New York: Pergamon Press.
Skinner, B. F. (1953). *Science and human behavior.* New York: Free Press.
Smith, D. K. (1984). Practicing school psychologists: Their characteristics, activities, and populations served. *Professional Psychology: Research and Practice, 15-6,* 798–810.
Snapp, M., & Davidson, J. L. (1982). Systems intervention for school psychologists: A case study approach. In C. R. Reynolds & T. B. Gutkin (Eds.), *The handbook of school psychology* (pp. 858–870). New York: Wiley.
Stuart, R. B. (1970). *Trick or treatment: How and when psychotherapy fails.* Champaign, IL: Research Press.
Szasz, T. S. (1960). The myth of mental illness. *American Psychologist, 15,* 113–118.
Turco, T. L., & Elliott, S. N. (in press). Assessment of students' acceptability of teacher-initiated interventions for classroom behavior. *Journal of School Psychology.*
Ullman, L., & Krasner, L. (1969). *A psychological approach to abnormal behavior.* Englewood Cliffs, NJ: Prentice-Hall.
Valett, R. E. (1965). A formula for providing psychological services. *Psychology in the Schools, 11,* 326–329.
White, M. A., & Harris, M. (1961). *The school psychologist.* New York: Harper.
Witt, J. C., Elliott, S. N., & Martens, B. K. (1984). The influence of amount of teacher time, severity of behavior problem, and type of intervention on teacher judgments of intervention acceptability. *Behavioral Disorders, 9,* 95–104.
Witt, J. C., & Martens, B. K. (1983). Assessing the acceptability of behavioral interventions. *Psychology in the Schools, 20,* 510–517.
Witt, J. C., Moe, G., Gutkin, T. B., & Andrews, L. (1984). The effect of saying the same thing in different ways: The problem of language and jargon in school-based consultation. *Journal of School Psychology, 22,* 361–367.
Witt, J. C., & Robbins, J. (1985). Acceptability of reductive interventions for the control of inappropriate child behavior. *Journal of Abnormal Child Psychology, 13,* 59–68.
Wolf, M. M. (1978). Social validity: The case for subjective measurement or how applied behavior analysis is finding its heart. *Journal of Applied Behavior Analysis, 11,* 203–214.
Ysseldyke, J. E., Reynolds, M. C., & Weinberg, R. A. (1984). *School psychology: A blueprint for training and practice.* Minneapolis: National School Psychology Inservice Training Network.
Ysseldyke, J. E., & Weinberg, R. (1981). Editorial comment: An introduction to the Spring Hill Symposium. *School Psychology Review, 10,* 116–120.
Zubin, J. (1967). Classification of behavior disorders. *Annual Review of Psychology, 18,* 373–406.

2 Current Practice in School Psychology

James F. Ysseldyke
University of Minnesota

School psychology is a relatively young profession that has expanded rapidly over the last decade. Currently, there are probably over 25,000 school psychologists. There are 211 programs at colleges and universities that offer graduate training in school psychology, that educate personnel for the practice of psychology in the schools.

My task in this chapter is to provide the reader with a description of what school psychologists actually do. When I agreed to write the chapter, I naively envisioned providing such a description as a relatively easy undertaking. Yet, I soon found that trying to describe the practice of school psychology is like trying to describe the practice of farming, law, architectual engineering, or nearly any other profession. One is faced initially with defining school psychology, and then with describing what school psychologists do. *And, there are few good accounts of what school psychologists actually do in practice.* There are formal records of the practice of law, yet few descriptions of the practice of school psychology. School psychologists simply do not do a very good job of writing about, or in other ways recording formally, what they do.

There are, of course, many (most would argue too many) *opinions about*, or accounts of *perceptions of*, the role and function of the school psychologist. In addressing issues of role and function, school psychologists have been asked for their own views of what they do (Barbanel & Hoffenberg-Rutman, 1974; Cook & Patterson, 1977; Farling & Hoedt, 1971; Giebink & Ringness, 1970; Goldwasser, Meyers, Christenson & Graden, 1983; Keogh, Kukic, Becker, McLaughlin & Kukic, 1975; Martin & Meyers, 1980; Meacham & Peckham, 1978; Ramage, 1979). Sometimes efforts have been made to understand what psychologists do by asking other professionals their perceptions of the functioning of school psychologists. Several have reported teachers' perceptions (Ford & Migles, 1979; Gilmore & Chandy, 1973; Grubb, Petty & Flynn, 1976; Medway, 1977; Roberts, 1970). Still others have reported administrators' perceptions of the roles and functioning of school psychologists (Hughes, 1979; Kaplan, Clancy & Chrin, 1977; Lesiak & Lounsbury, 1977). Researchers who have surveyed school psychologists' perceptions of their role and function have generally concluded there is a considerable disparity between how school psychologists say they spend their time and how they say they would like to spend their time. In general, school psychologists report that they spend their time primarily in psychoeducational assessment functions, but that they would prefer to spend their time on other functions like consultation, intervention, and inservice training.

Although laws and guidelines on the practice of psychology in the schools are more specific, current practice is more diverse than ever before in the history of the profession. For that reason, it is virtually impossible to describe "typical" current practice. One must, rather, address the issue of diversity in practice and try in some way to account for it or at least describe it.

Why is there so much diversity in current practice, and what are the factors that result in such diversity? Even a cursory reading of the professional literature in school psychology will reveal a kind of overwhelming preoccupation with the extent to which, and the ways in which, external, environmental, or systems factors control the behavior of school psychologists (Bersoff, 1979; Brown, Cardon, Coulter, & Meyers, 1982; Ysseldyke, 1978; Ysseldyke & Weinberg, 1981). School psychologists have been especially quick to say that they are not in control of their own functioning and destiny. Before proceeding to an analysis of current practice, I would like to propose a model for viewing the practice of school psychology.

A MODEL FOR VIEWING THE PRACTICE OF SCHOOL PSYCHOLOGY

Efforts to understand the behavior of school psychologists are comparable to efforts to explain any human behavior. Bandura (1978) described three different models for explaining factors that influence human behavior. These are shown in Fig. 2.1. Bandura states that the most frequent model of viewing the causes of human behavior is a unidirectional model: $B = f(P,E)$. From such a view, behavior is seen as determined by one of two factors—the person or the environment. According to Bandura, such a causal model of explaining human behavior should be questioned, because "personal and environmental factors do not function as independent determinants [of behavior]; rather, they determine each other" (p. 345). Bandura proposes an alternative view, stating that "it is

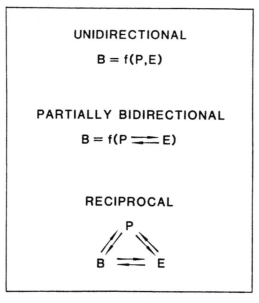

FIG. 2.1 Schematic representation of three alternative conceptions of interaction. B signifies behavior, P the cognitive and other internal events that can affect perceptions and actions, and E the external environment. From "The Self System in Reciprocal Determination" by A. Bandura, 1978, *American Psychologist, 33,* 345. Copyright 1978 by the American Psychological Association. Reprinted by permission of the author.

largely through their actions that people produce the environmental conditions that affect their behavior in a reciprocal fashion" (p. 345).

A second model of viewing the causes of human behavior is described by Bandura as a partially bi-directional model: $B = f(P,E)$. Within this model, persons, situations, and events are seen as interdependent causes of behavior. Yet, behavior itself is viewed only as a by-product of interactions between the person and the environment; it is seen as having no influence on the person, the environment, or the person's behavior.

The third model of viewing the causes of human behavior is labeled by Bandura the reciprocal determinism model: $B^P E$. According to this model, behavior is seen as determined by a continuous reciprocal interaction between behavioral, cognitive, and environmental influences. Within this view, behavior is seen as influenced by the environment, but the environment is seen as partly a function of the person's own making.

I believe the behavior of individual school psychologists (what they do) can best be understood from the perspective of the model of reciprocal determinism. In their functioning in schools, school psychologists are not merely reactors to external stimuli or events, nor are they merely reactors to external constraints.

In describing the causes of behavior, Bandura stated that "cognitive factors partly determine which external events will be observed, how they will be perceived, whether they have any lasting effects, what valence and efficacy they have, and how the information will be organized for future use" (p. 345).

In viewing what psychologists do in schools and how they react to environmental events, it is clear there is much diversity. People working in the same environment (e.g., school system) behave differently. Individual school psychologists react differently to the same environmental event. Take, for example, a major environmental event like passage and signing of Public Law 94–142. Some psychologists state that passage of that law had a major impact on their behavior and practices (see Brown et al., 1982). Others report that passage of PL 94–142 has had no impact on their practice (see Goldwasser et al., 1983). Some readers may have had the experience of conducting an inservice workshop for school psychologists. No matter what the topic, it is perceived differently by different school psychologists. In fact, the content of a workshop does not register for some, whereas it has a lasting impact on the practice of others.

Bandura observes that behavior is influenced by the environment, but that the environment is partly determined by behavior. Certainly, this is true in school psychology. To become school psychologists, individuals must attend a training institution to earn a degree in school psychology. Individuals are not assigned randomly to training institutions; they determine where they would like to attend, and an institution decides to accept them. Training differs from setting to setting. Yet, even within the same setting, training differs. Students choose different major advisors who have differing competencies and interests. Students in the same training program may select different coursework. There is much within-program and across-program variation. Different school psychologists practice differently because they hold different perspectives and have had different kinds of training and experiences.

School psychologists choose to be employed in different settings, and personnel in the settings choose to employ different people as school psychologists. The act of deciding to take a job, to be employed in a setting, quite obviously determines the setting in which one is employed. Within settings, individuals choose to work closely with some colleagues, and not at all with others. They choose to get excited about, or to ignore, certain environmental events. As you think about the practice of school psychology, recognize that although there is much commonality in practice, there is also considerable diversity. This diversity is best understood as a function of reciprocal interaction among the person (his or her characteristics, beliefs, training, experiences), the environment in which the person functions (both the day-to-day environment and the larger social system), and the ways in which the person behaves or acts in that environment.

At the same time, recognize that the practice of psychology in the schools changes over time. It changes because the demands of settings change. It changes because those who practice psychology in the schools change. These facts—

diversity in practice, and change over time—make it difficult to describe current practice. Whose practice will we describe? In what settings and at what point in time will we describe a diverse, dynamic profession? Obviously, then, what is presented here is but one perspective on the practice of psychology in the schools.

THE ENVIRONMENT FOR THE PRACTICE OF SCHOOL PSYCHOLOGY

The practice of school psychology is determined in part by the expectations that school personnel and parents hold for the behavior of school psychologists, and in part by social, political, economic, and educational factors.

School System Expectations

Bardon (1982) described the perceptions of people about school psychologists when he said:

> If you ask teachers or parents what school psychologists do, chances are good that you will get one of three responses: they will not know what a school psychologist is; they will say that school psychologists give tests to atypical children; or they will describe functions commonly attributed to psychiatrists or clinical psychologists. If you ask clinical or counseling psychologists what school psychologists do, they will most likely talk about testing of children for special education by an assortment of persons certified as school psychometrists. If you ask school psychologists what they do, you can expect to receive detailed information about the many functions school psychologists could perform, given an opportunity to do so. These functions will include virtually everything that can be done by professional psychologists of any kind or persuasion, but with emphasis on their performance in schools or with school-age children and their families. If you press further and insist that you be told what school psychologists actually do rather than what they could do if permitted, your respondents reluctantly will describe functions that are less encompassing than they would like them to be and inevitably involve substantial attention to the administration of individual tests to children referred by school personnel either for special education classification or because of untoward behavior or poor school performance in a classroom. (p. 3)

In the majority of school settings today, school psychologists are expected to behave as technicians. In some settings they are expected to behave as professionals. This distinction is an important one. People call upon the services of a technician when there are known solutions to a problem and someone is needed to "fix the problem." Think, for example, of the times you call a person to repair something in your home. You call a plumber, an electrician, or an appliance repair person when you have a problem for which there is a known solution. The nature of the problem is diagnosed, and an action is taken to remedy the problem. Professionals, on the other hand, are called on when there is no known solution to a problem, but when someone is needed to apply the knowledge base in a discipline to solution of the problem. Most school psychologists have been trained as professionals and are capable of working as professionals rather than as technicians. In fact, though, most school personnel act as if the problems they face are technical problems, problems for which there is a known solution, and expect psychologists to behave as technicians. Yet, sometimes school personnel expect psychologists to work as professional problem solvers, applying the knowledge base from psychology and education to the solution of educational problems.

Social, Political, and Economic Factors that Influence the Practice of School Psychology

The practice of school psychology and the behavior of individual school psychologists are influenced by a variety of social, political, and economic factors. One would hardly expect otherwise. School psychologists who practice their profession in schools function in an environment that is ever-changing, one influenced significantly by social, political, and economic factors. Below, I describe some of these. It is impossible to consider all factors because they change daily.

William Bevan (1981), in his keynote address at the Spring Hill Symposim on the Future of Psychology in the Schools, described major social, political, and economic changes that are having an impact on the practice of psychology in the schools. Bevan called attention to economic problems (a 20% inflation rate and 8% unemployment), to shrinking public school enrollments, and to growing federal intervention in the affairs of schools. He called attention to the fact that education is extremely vulnerable when the fiscal climate becomes restrictive. Yet, he addressed economic concerns in the context of public displeasure with schools and the outcomes of schooling. Bevan (1981) stated, "Our problems of funding and enrollment intensify precisely when the lay public is increasingly displeased with the schools. It looks back at two decades of rising costs without convincing improvement of academic quality. Indeed it believes strongly that academic quality has significantly deteriorated." (p. 127)

Bevan described the huge educational system with its more than 107,000 public schools, more than 3 million staff, and an annual budget of more than $107.5 billion, and stated that students' test scores are declining. The public questions the accountability of the current system.

Two years after Bevan's statements at Spring Hill, the U.S. Commission on Excellence on Education (1983) issued a report entitled *A Nation at Risk*. The Commission called attention to major problems in education, and concluded that "The educational foundations of our society are presently being eroded by a rising tide of mediocrity that threatens our very future as a nation and a people. Our society and its educational institutions seem to have lost sight of the basic purposes of schooling, and of the high expectations and disciplined effort needed to attain them" (pp. 5–6).

The Commission called attention to declines in pupil achievement, high rates of functional illiteracy, and the need for military and business leaders to spend much time and money on remedial and training programs. They cited major problems in American secondary education, reporting that secondary school curricula have been homogenized, diluted, and diffused to the point they no longer have a central purpose, that schools are offering a curricular smorgasbord with extensive student choice, a decrease in homework, grade inflation, and declines in the number of math and science courses required for graduation, and that the minimum competency has become the maximum.

According to Bevan, the most worrisome problem facing schools and school psychologists is the wholesale intrusion of the federal government into public education. He observed that we now have a massive set of rules and regulations to guide practice, and that these have "diverted the professionals—teachers, psychologists, and others—from their appointed rounds and have forced them to become clerks, bookkeepers, and petty managers" (p. 128).

The schools have become increasingly bureaucratic, and professionals have been forced to function in a rigid system of formal controls and contractual arrangements. "What is dangerous is not that there is regulation but that there is an inevitable accelerating over-regulation" (Bevan, 1981, p. 128).

School psychologists work in an environment (schools) that is considered to be troubled or in trouble. Recent reports from Commissions (e.g., Education Commission, 1983; National Commission, 1983), Task Forces (e.g., Knitzer, 1978; Peterson et al., 1983), and public opinion polls (Elam, 1983) highlight the very significant problems evident in current educational practice. Yet, the problems may well be bigger and require more fundamental analysis for solution than described in the reports. Consider the kinds of major problems schools and school personnel face and that school psychologists are called upon to help solve.

Schools reflect society, and all of the problems afflicting society became apparent in schools. Packard (1983) observed that "the schools and their personnel are affected not only by giantism, urbanization, community fragmentation, ethnic shifts, union rules, and a decline in parental involvement—but by a tendency of our society to push more child-care and child-socialization roles upon the school" (p. 33). Schools and school personnel clearly are expected to do more than ever before, and they are criticized when they fail to deliver with excellence.

Many children are troubled and experience significant problems at school and in the community. This is reflected by widespread slacking off in scholastic effort, decline in achievement, drops in school attendance, crime, precocious sexual behavior, increased drug use, and alcoholism. The devaluation of children by parents and the society in general is evidenced by the rapid rise in instances of child abuse and the rise in sentiment against children.

Packard (1983) highlighted problems evidenced by children out of control. Decline in scholastic effort is reflected in lowering SAT scores, especially in language, problem-solving ability, and reasoning ability. It is highlighted by the fact that more than 12% of students approaching their final year in high school are functionally illiterate. Crime involving students under 18 years of age is significant. A pupil in a typical secondary school has a one in nine chance of being a victim of theft in any given school month. Half of all burglaries nationwide are committed by persons under 18. The arrest rate of young females is rising three times faster than that of young males. Arrests for children are rising three times faster than for adults. There is a "rise in pandemonium"—violence, mass disobedience, and resistance in the classroom. School vandalism costs schools one-half billion dollars per year. In 1969 American school children committed 100 murders, 12,000 armed robberies, 9,000 rapes, 204,000 aggravated assaults, and 270,000 school burglaries. Each year, 65,000 teachers are victims of assault. Students are seldom excluded from school, but are required to attend—no matter how unscholarly they are.

The fact that children's lives are in disorder and out of control is evidenced in precocious sexual behavior and drug use. Each year, 400,000 girls under 15 years of age become pregnant. In the last 15 years the arrest of youngsters for use of drugs or trafficking in drugs rose 4,600%. Drug use, especially of marijuana and cocaine, is rampant in Junior High Schools. Youngsters say they are bored and lonely.

That children's lives are in disorder and out of control is evidenced by the fact that they are abusing alcohol, drinking harder, and starting earlier. The *average* student now has the first drink by age 12. It is estimated that 1,300,000 youngsters between 12 and 17 have serious drinking problems, serious enough to result in run-ins with police or school personnel (Packard, 1983).

Parents are also out of control. Packard (1983) reported that there are 625,000 cases of serious child abuse each year. Each year 40,000 children are so seriously battered that they require hospitalization.

Within society, there is a rapid rise in sentiment against children. Children often are viewed as obstacles to personal fulfillment, as obstacles to the careers of parents, as economic burdens, and as barriers to marital happiness. Many children enter school and/or spend much of their school years with a feeling of isolation that results from fragmentation of families and communities due to high mobility. Children who move a lot must learn to cope with new schools, friends, and neighborhoods.

Packard (1983) identifies 12 descriptors of what it is like to be a child today. He lists the following stresses on children.

1. Wondering if your parents are going to split—or, if they have, living in a one-parent home.
2. Being alone a lot of the time.
3. Seeing a lot of "No Children" signs on apartment houses while on your way to school.
4. If you are small, the possibility of being left every weekday with some kind of caretaker, usually outside your home.
5. Being home a lot in an empty house.
6. Having little real contact with adults.
7. Feeling you are a burden and being given few ways to make yourself useful.
8. Living in a neighborhood that makes you apprehensive.
9. Adjusting to newcomers in the home.
10. Eating a lot of food that has been left for you—or food you must go out and get at some fast-food place.
11. Most of the talk you hear coming from machines rather than from people you know.
12. Often coping with parents who are pretty self-absorbed, or uncertain about their proper role in life.

School Responses to Problems

Schools and school personnel have responded to the problems of low achievement, truancy, discipline problems, exceptional children, and social/emotional problems in a number of ways. I argue that the responses have largely ignored the contributions school psychologists could make, and that school personnel have misused the services of school psychologists.

There have always been a large number of students who failed to profit to the extent thought necessary from their educational experiences. Early in our educational history such students were simply excluded from school. When exclusionary practices were ruled illegal and unconstitutional, school personnel responded to the problem of low achievement by developing or creating a number of set-aside programs, classes and settings where students could be put (Ysseldyke & Algozzine, 1984). At about the time of World War II, with increased sophistication in the development of measurement technologies, school personnel began to use tests in the process of making decisions about eligibility for enrollment in set-aside programs. School psychologists were employed for the primary purpose of testing children and declaring them eligible/ineligible for enrollment in special education.

School personnel have responded to discipline problems in a number of ways. In some schools, police and/or guard dogs are used to avert discipline problems. In other settings students who trouble school personnel are simply suspended or excluded from school. In some settings, standards have been lowered, but in still others, standards have been raised and minimal competency testing used to make promotion, retention, or graduation decisions. And, as described above, schools have responded to problems by creating set-aside structures for the purpose of educating troublesome students.

A number of problems have arisen as a direct result of the ways in which school personnel have chosen to deal with low achievement, truancy, discipline problems, exceptional students, and social/emotional problems. Reynolds and Wang (1983) described some of these. They pointed out that school personnel have created a wide variety of set-aside structures for educating disruptive, disadvantaged, and bilingual children as well as those who perform poorly in school. Each program, in turn, has its own bureaucracy, funding system, and system for demonstrating accountability. This has led to what Reynolds and Wang (1983) called "disjointed incrementalism." Programs and services are ever expanding, but programs must compete with one another for monies, personnel, and so on. In addition, school personnel, tied to funding leashes, develop and disband programs in response to the crisis of the moment or the latest instructional whim.

The rapid expansion of categorical approaches to educating students who experience academic difficulties has not been across-the-board. Over the last decade there has been almost no change in the number of students labeled severely handicapped and served by special education. There has been a decline in the number of students called mildly mentally retarded, and a geometric increase in the number of students served in programs for the learning disabled. As the number of students enrolled in classes for the learning disabled has increased dramatically, there has been considerable questioning and criticism of the validity of the concept of learning disabilities (Algozzine & Ysseldyke, 1983; Shepard & Smith, 1981; Ysseldyke, Algozzine & Epps, 1983; Ysseldyke, Algozzine, Shinn, & McGue, 1982).

In efforts to provide appropriate educational services to all handicapped students, school personnel have become burdened by a rapidly expanding number of procedural requirements. School psychologists now operate as members of teams of school personnel in making decisions about students. They participate in the preparation of IEPs, in formal meetings with parents and other school personnel, and in periodic reevaluation of individual students. School psychologists complain of increasing paper work and bureaucracy. A kind of dysfunctional funding system in which funding of programs is directly contingent on number of students identified has led to a bounty hunting mentality in schools.

Summary

School psychologists find themselves working in an environment (schools) in which there are very big problems. The problems of low achievement, truancy, discipline, exceptional students, and social/emotional dysfunction were highlighted briefly. School personnel *could* call upon school psychologists to be of help in solving those problems, and in some instances they have. Yet, more often than not, school personnel have responded to problems inappropriately in ways that simply create serious new problems. And, in most settings, they have misused the services of school psychologists.

WHAT DO SCHOOL PSYCHOLOGISTS DO?

School psychologists bring to the educational setting a number of competencies derived from their training and experiences. There are a set of assumptions that ought to guide the delivery of psychological services in schools. School psychologists function in diverse ways. These points are elaborated below.

What Do School Psychologists Bring to the Educational Setting?

In the very broadest sense, school psychologists bring to the educational setting a knowledge base derived from theory and research in clinical, experimental, educational, and general psychology that can be applied to the solution of educational problems. Yet, clearly, not all school psychologists are competent in all aspects of applying psychology to the solution of educational problems, and not all school psychologists apply what they know. Each individual school psychologist exhibits a set of skills, competencies, motivations, attitudes, and understandings derived for the most part from training and experience. It is important, therefore, to digress briefly here, and consider the differing ways in which school psychologists are trained.

Components of Training Programs. Most often, training programs are characterized as either doctoral programs or sixth-year specialist programs. Standards for training programs reflect this kind of orientation (e.g., National Association of School Psychologists, 1984). People describe the activities of school psychologists as a function of their level of training. I argue that it is more appropriate to think of the kind of educational experiences provided to students, of the philosophy of the program, than of the level of training provided. I believe that some programs, in spite of the levels at which they train people, train professionals, whereas others, again in spite of levels of training, train technicians. College and university training programs differ considerably in the ways the practice of school psychology is viewed and in the ways they prepare people to practice school psychology. All school psychology training programs provide training in assessment or diagnosis. Some educate professionals; that is, individuals are educated to bring the knowledge base in psychology to bear on the solution of educational problems. Yet, in many training programs, school psychologists are prepared to function as technicians. They learn to function essentially as psychometric robots, to administer tests to students, and to write reports describing pupil performance on tests. In some programs graduate students learn to diagnose learners, whereas in a few, they learn to diagnose the nature of instruction being given to learners. In a few training programs, school psychologists learn to function in an integrated manner, learning to ascertain the extent to which specific kinds of instruction are appropriate for specific learners as a function of the level of those learners' skill development.

Either directly or indirectly school psychologists are educated in interpersonal functioning. For years, school psychologists functioned as loners in school systems; they were given considerable autonomy in making decisions about students. More recently, because of legislative mandates, they are required to function as members of interdisciplinary teams. Although all training programs recognize that school psychologists must work as team members, much of the training in school psychology still occurs in isolation. I speak regularly with school psychologists whose training has been relatively recent, who report they received no training in interpersonal functioning, and who state that they never received training in team decision making. Some report that all of their courses were taken with others who were learning to be school psychologists; they state they never took courses with individuals preparing to function as regular or special educators.

College and university training consists of at least some training in intervention. Here, clearly, different perspectives on the nature of school psychological services are apparent. In some programs, graduate students receive training in instructional intervention. In most programs they learn to function as mental health experts. Still other programs provide an integrated set of experiences in both instructional intervention and mental health services.

College and university programs vary considerably in the extent to which those learning to be school psychologists are given training in theory. In many programs, there is an absence of training in the theory that underlies practice; people are trained as technicians. In most programs there is at least some training in theory, and in some programs that training is extensive.

How Do School Psychologists View Themselves?

School psychologists view themselves differently, largely as a function of the ways in which they were educated and the ways in which they are allowed to function. Many view themselves as diagnosticians. They are highly trained in the administration and scoring of individual psychometric measures. Others view themselves as therapists and mental health experts who function as counselors and therapists in school settings. Still others consider themselves teacher consultants and facilitators of children's learning. They are trained to function, and do function, as teacher consultants.

How Do School Psychologists View Their Training?

Graden, Christenson, Ysseldyke and Meyers (1984) asked 232 graduating school psychology students and 195 practicing school psychologists to rate the quality of their training in a variety of functional areas. Both groups said they were best trained for communication/interpretation, assessment, and consultation roles. Yet, their ratings of the quality of their training was above average for only one role: communication/interpretation. More than 30% of those in both groups reported *no* training in the following areas:

- developing school system programs
- consulting on school curricula
- organizational consultation
- writing grant proposals
- evaluating service delivery
- evaluating educational programs
- advocating for school changes
- testifying as an expert witness
- communicating about services
- training in decision making

What Competencies Do School Psychologists Have?

Ideally, school psychologists demonstrate competence in reasonably distinct domains. In reality, few demonstrate competence in all areas. Most are better in some areas than in others. Competency areas are listed below because they describe current practice and are areas in which good school psychologists reasonably can be expected to be competent and to deliver. Description of competency areas (the state of the art) will be helpful later as I describe current practice. Knowledge of competency areas will assist in thinking about the considerable disparity between the state of practice and the state of the art.

Classroom Management. School personnel experience much difficulty in managing classes. There is well-confirmed knowledge on class management in the psychological literature. Much is known about the effectiveness of alternative approaches to discipline and class management. There is a knowledge base on such matters as starting the school year, structuring settings effectively, and dealing with crisis situations. School psychologists can be expected to have expertise on class management and to be able to consult with teachers on effective class management.

Interpersonal Communication and Consultation. Many of the problems currently confronted in education are the direct result of problems in interpersonal communication. Often, teachers do not communicate effectively with students, other teachers, related services personnel, administrators, or parents. Psychologists know much, or should know much, about the development of interpersonal skills and their use in the consultation process.

Basic Academic and Life Skills. Much has been written on the decline in students' acquisition of basic academic and life skills. In school settings school psychologists are the persons who ought to know the most about learning theory and its application to the educational process. There is much in the knowledge base in psychology that has direct relevance to teaching basic academic and life skills and developing study skills and practice. There is a considerable knowledge base on the development of self-dependence and adaptive behavior.

Affective/Social Skills. The school psychologist should be prepared to give leadership in developing instructional programs for students and to conduct inservice instruction in dealing with special problems of affective development and social skills. There are major systems for teaching affective and social skills. There is a knowledge base on deliberate psychological education that can be delivered to schools.

Parent Involvement. Over the last decade, parents have become increasingly involved in determining the educational program for their children. It is required that parents be present at IEP meetings, and that school personnel and parents work together in efforts to help children. School psychologists are in a very good position to help school personnel with parents and to facilitate home-school cooperation and communication. There is a good knowledge base in psychology that can be applied to the development of training programs for parents and to parent and family counseling.

Classroom Organization and Structure. The literature on social psychology has much information that can be applied to problems in organizing and structuring classrooms. Literature on cooperative goal structuring, peer and cross-age tutoring, planning and use of space, facilities and equipment, and the effective use of classroom aides and volunteers can be applied to the solution of problems.

Systems Development and Planning. As some have looked at the failure of large numbers of students, they have attributed failure to the ways in which schools are organized. Clearly, many problems are "systems problems." School psychologists can contribute much to school organization and program planning. The knowledge base in psychology can be applied to development of effective measurement systems, effective systems for personnel development, the use of technology to manage information and instruction, and formal and informal approaches to evaluation and planned change.

Personnel Development. Many teachers are now inadequately trained to perform many of the most important tasks with which they are confronted. Psychologists should be able to help in the selection of staff and in putting together professional development programs. Assuming that the knowledge base in psychology is relevant to the problems in schools, the possibilities for continuing education are many and diverse.

Individual Differences in Development and Learning. We noted earlier that services provided by school psychologists are based on an appreciation and understanding of differences among individuals in the characteristics they bring to the educational setting and the extent to which they draw from it. The knowledge base in psychology contains much of direct relevance to school personnel's understanding of individual differences.

School-Community Relations. At least a portion of the literature in psychology is on the topic of inter-agency coordination and cooperation. School psychologists should be able to draw on that knowledge base to assist school personnel in coordinating activities with outside agencies like community mental health centers and institutions.

Instruction. The knowledge base on learning and instructional psychology includes much of direct relevance to teachers' instructional efforts. Through systematic application of principles of learning, school psychologists should be of considerable assistance to teachers. Specifically, psychologists can help teachers increase academically engaged time, set reasonable expectations for learners, motivate learners, and improve direct instruction.

Legal/Ethical Issues. The knowledge base is sufficiently well developed to enable school psychologists to meet appropriate ethical, professional, and legal standards. They can assist schools in enhancing the quality of services and in protecting the rights of all parties. The knowledge base specific to this domain of competence is derived from laws, regulations, and guidelines (for example, due process). It is also derived from standards documents, like *Standards for Educational and Psychological Tests,* and *Ethical Standards for Psychologists.*

Assessment. School psychologists must sometimes collect data to verify and specify problems and make decisions about individuals or groups. There is a considerable knowledge base on measurement and on technically adequate assessment. School psychologists can be expected to have this information and to engage in appropriate psychoeducational assessment.

Multicultural Concerns. More than ever before, students enrolled in today's schools come from a variety of cultural, racial, and ethnic backgrounds. There is much information in the psychological literature on effectively working with diverse cultural groups. School psychologists can reasonably be expected to have this knowledge and to use it to promote effective functioning.

Research. School psychologists are skilled in conducting and interpreting research. They bring to education the knowledge base on application of research to educational practice.

What Assumptions Should Guide the Practice of Psychology in the Schools?

A number of general assumptions ought to guide the practice of psychology in the schools. These assumptions apply based on the state of society, on the state of knowledge in psychology and in education, and on the areas of concern not adequately addressed now by human services personnel in schools. It is assumed that:

1. Psychology is relevant to education. School is an important place for psychology to be delivered, and when it is delivered at the *state of the art* level, it is highly relevant.

2. All children should be eligible for services that enhance learning. Recent policies on education of handicapped students (e.g., education is a right of all students, the right to be educated in the least restrictive environment, the need for explicit goal setting, collaboration with parents, due process) are important for them, but have also set an agenda for meeting the needs of *all* students.

3. Schools do not educate alone. Education takes place in many ways and in many settings (agencies, families, etc.). All of these settings and ways must be considered in planning optimal education for students.

4. Children cannot be competent individuals in our society unless and until they are provided the basic cultural imperatives of skill in reading, writing, and arithmetic and are given social experiences in learning how best to relate to others. The education of children goes beyond academic instruction; schools are critical determinants of the social competence of individuals and groups.

5. To understand the ways in which students function in school, the school context (its social nature and its objectives) must be understood.

6. It is necessary for professionals offering services to children in schools to state clearly what they can and cannot do. They must also know and state what society can legitimately expect them to do.

7. Decisions about students should be based on data. Assessment is a process of collecting data for the purpose of making decisions about students. The only legitimate purpose of assessment is to plan, establish, improve, or evaluate educational interventions for students.

8. Psychology is a specialized profession, and within the profession itself there are many areas of specialization. No one profession can be expected to know and do everything encompassed by a discipline; no one professional can be expected to know and do everything associated with a profession. The end point of training is to provide professional psychologists for the educational arena who can fill diverse roles, with varying degrees of specialization.

9. To serve schools well, psychological services must be offered at all levels of the system.

10. Psychological services to children in schools must be based on a clear code of ethics and principles of professional conduct.

11. The professional school psychologist should approach his/her work with an appreciation for rigorous scientific methods of study and an understanding that sound practice is based on objective, reliable data collection.

12. Offering adequate psychological services in schools requires self-study and understanding of one's competencies and personal strengths and weaknesses.

13. Training and credentialing mechanisms related to professional services in the schools are responsible for acknowledging and respecting professional codes of ethics and of professional conduct.

14. Services provided by school psychologists are based on an appreciation and understanding of differences among individuals in the characteristics they bring to the educational settings and to the extent to which they draw from it.

15. To understand the needs of the student, psychologists need to understand and be able to impact those social, political, economic, and educational factors that influence child development and services to children.

Current Practice

Early in this chapter I made the point that the behavior of individual school psychologists is in reciprocal relationship to their personal characteristics, training, and experiences and to the environment in which they are employed. Different school psychologists perform different kinds of functions in schools. It is impossible, in the scope of this chapter, to describe all of the diversity in practice and to describe all of the ways in which school psychologists function. Rather, I will borrow from Sidney Bijou's 1970 analysis of "What Psychology Has to

Offer Education—Now" and describe the functioning of the "vast majority" and the "small minority" of school psychologists.

The Vast Majority. Clearly the primary practice in which the majority of school psychologists function is in psychoeducational assessment and decision making. It is, at the same time, the practice school psychologists most dislike and say they must get away from (Peterson, 1981). What does that practice look like?

Over the last 6 years, the Institute for Research on Learning Disabilities at the University of Minnesota conducted an extensive set of investigations on the assessment and decision-making process. I have chosen here to highlight some of the findings of that research effort, as they illustrate nicely what current practice looks like.

Each year, personnel in this nation's public schools refer between 3% and 5% of school-age children for psychoeducational evaluation. Ninety-two percent of those who are referred are tested, and 73% of those who are tested are declared eligible for special education services (Algozzine, Christenson, & Ysseldyke, 1982). There are two alternative explanations for this finding. It could be argued that teachers are incredibly accurate in spotting students who are in need of special education services and who ought to be referred. Algozzine et al. (1982) instead concluded that the psychoeducational assessment and decision-making process operates as a "search for pathology" (Sarason & Doris, 1979) in which members of child study teams, and specifically school psychologists, function to find something wrong in students referred by teachers and find was to remove students from regular education programs.

It has been demonstrated that teachers refer students who bother them (Christenson, Ysseldyke, Wang, & Algozzine,1983; Ysseldyke & Algozzine, 1981; Ysseldyke, Christenson, Pianta & Algozzine, 1983) and that teachers' desires at the time of referral are to have students (a) tested and (b) removed from their classrooms. School psychologists are *expected* to test students and declare them eligible for special education. School psychologists *do* precisely that.

School psychologists function as parts of teams, called child study teams, special education placement teams, IEP planning teams, or what not. In the team decision-making process, where eligibility and instructional decisions are made, school psychologists have considerable power and authority. Or, at least other team members say the psychologists are the most influential members of the team (Ysseldyke, Algozzine, & Mitchell, 1982). Yet, when asked, school psychologists say they have very little power in the team decision-making process.

Many tests are used in the process of making decisions about students. In fact, it has been demonstrated that the more mildly handicapped a student is, the more tests are administered to the student (Regan & Ysseldyke, 1980). School psychologists do most of the testing, and the majority of the tests used are technically inadequate for making decisions about students (Ysseldyke, Algozzine, Regan, & Potter, 1981).

A considerable amount of test information is presented at placement team meetings. Yet, it has been demonstrated that there is little relationship between the decisions teams make and the extent to which the data support those decisions (Ysseldyke, Algozzine, Richey, & Graden, 1982). Similarly, it has been shown that there are few reliable differences between students classified as eligible for different kinds of special education services (Ysseldyke, Algozzine & Epps, 1983; Ysseldyke et al., 1982). School psychologists are required to participate in giving tests to students to determine their eligibility for placement in set-aside programs. Yet, there is little empirical support for the process by which those decisions are made.

The Small Minority. In most public school settings, school psychologists have recognized the difficulties inherent in engaging in norm-referenced assessment to try to make decisions about student eligibility for placement in set-aside programs. In some settings they have chosen to do something about the situation and have developed alternative practices. All of these cannot be described. I have chosen to illustrate alternative practice by describing model programs in three Minnesota school districts: Olympia, Washington; Pine County; and Anoka-Hennepin.

In September, 1981, school psychologists in the Olympia, Washington School District began the use of a consulting model to integrate more fully remedial and special education (Hauser et al., 1982). They instituted this model in response to a number of concerns, among which were the very rapid increase in the number of students being placed in special education, especially in classes for the learning disabled, and the fact that it was nearly impossible to differentiate these students from those enrolled in remedial programs or Title I. A consultant model was implemented and involved (a) inservice training or staff development, and (b) instructional support. Psychologists and educational specialists acquired the knowledge and process skills necessary to function as consultants to regular classroom teachers on strategies and techniques for maintaining low-performing students in their classes. School psychologists were given training in curriculum-based assessment, concept analysis, consultation techniques, direct instruction (reading, math, spelling), classroom organization and behavior management, and adult learning. During the academic year, school psychologists and educational specialists provided a variety of forms of direct and indirect instructional support. For example, they assisted teachers by helping adapt and modify parts of the curriculum, introducing direct instruction methods to be used by aides in teaching reading to low-performing students, establishing a contingency contracting system (Homme, 1970) for some students, adjusting students' overall programs, establishing study procedures for low-functioning students, assisting secondary teachers in monitoring pupil behavior, and assisting building administrators with instructional leadership.

Implementation of the model enabled 81.7% of the students referred to remain in regular education programs. Teachers were initially resistant to implementation of the model, but as time went on, they not only were receptive, but indicated considerable support for the approach used.

In the Pine County, Minnesota, Schools a data-based system has been implemented for making decisions about delivery of special education services (Tindal, Wesson, Germann, Deno, & Mirkin, 1982). The model is based on the use of simple, curriculum-based assessment strategies. Diagnostic personnel gather student performance data at each stage of the assessment and decision-making process, and use these data rather than scores on norm-referenced tests to make decisions about students. The model involves continuous measurement, use of comparative information across decisions, and formative evaluation.

In establishing this model of making service delivery decisions, Tindal et al. (1982) used the measurement system developed by Deno and Mirkin. The following academic and social behaviors are assessed using the procedures described.

Academic Areas

Reading—one-minute reading aloud from randomly selected passages from the basal curriculum and/or one minute reading aloud from a list of vocabulary words selected at random from the basal curriculum: Number of words read correct and incorrect (Deno, Mirkin, Chiang, & Lowry, 1980).

Spelling—two-minute spelling samples using dictation of a random selection of words from the basal spelling curriculum: Number of words or letter sequences spelled correct and incorrect (Deno, Mirkin, Lowry, & Kuehnle, 1980).

Written Expression—three-minute writing sample in response to story starters or topic sentences: Number of words or letters written or the number of words spelled correct (Deno, Mirkin, & Marston, 1980).

Math—two-minute samples of computation problems appearing in the basal text, one for each function (addition, subtraction, multiplication, and division): Number of digits computed correct and incorrect (Tindal, Germann, & Deno, 1983; Tindal, Germann, Marston, & Deno, 1983).

Social Behavior

Noise—Any sounds created by the child which distract either another student or the teacher from the business at hand. The noise may be generated vocally (including "talk outs" by unintelligible sounds) or nonvocally ("tapping a pencil" or "snapping fingers").

Out of place—Any movement beyond the explicitly or implicitly defined boundaries in which the child is allowed movement. If the child is seated at his/her desk, then movement of any sort out of the seat is "out of place."

Physical contact—Any contact with another person or another person's property which is unacceptable to that person. Kicking, hitting, pushing, tearing, breaking, taking, are categorized as physical contact.

Off task—Any movement off of a prescribed activity that does not fall into one of the three previously defined categories. "Looking around," "staring into space," "doodling," or any observable movement off of the task at hand is included (Deno, 1979).

The Pine County Model has been implemented for 3 years. Primary components of the program have included a focus on environmental/curriculum-based assessment, direct and frequent measurement of student performance within the curriculum, and systematic modification of students' instructional programs based on student performance data. A noncategorical delivery system is used in which special educational services are delivered to students who are severely discrepant from their local peers and/or environmental expectations on educationally relevant behaviors: academic behaviors, tool behaviors, social behaviors, communication behaviors, self-help behaviors, and physical behaviors. Special education services are not delivered to students based on implied inner disturbances or federal categorical labels. Micro-computer monitoring of student performance is used to make instructional evaluation decisions.

A third example of an approach being used by a minority of psychologists is illustrated by the work of Graden and her colleagues in the Anoka-Hennepin School District, a suburban/rural district in Minnesota. During 1983, psychologists in that district implemented a system of prereferral interventions in an effort to divert the more traditional referral to placement syndrome. Staff instituted a process of consultation and intervention prior to formal psychometric assessment. In this district teachers did not refer students *to* psychologists for testing. Rather, they requested consultation and assistance in planning interventions for students who were experiencing academic and social problems. Psychologists responded to requests for consultation and assistance by meeting with the classroom teacher. At that initial meeting, and as a result of the meeting, the following occurred:

1. Referring teachers were asked to specify in observable terms the reason(s) for referral.
2. Reasons for referral were ranked in order of importance for action.
3. Teachers were asked to specify ways in which the student's behavior affected them and the extent to which the behavior was incongruent with the teacher's expectations.
4. An intervention was designed by the referring teacher.

5. The intervention was implemented and evaluated.

The activities listed enabled staff to verify the existence and specify the nature of problems, to intervene in an effort to alleviate them, and to evaluate the effectiveness of the interventions. Much of the data collection in this district involved observation of pupils in the natural environment, the classroom. School psychologists observed students to note the frequency and duration of occurrence of behaviors of concern. They collected data on the curriculum being used with the student, the tasks the student was being asked to accomplish, the ways in which the teacher interacted with or responded to the student, specifically what the student did, grouping structures, interactions between the student and his/her classmates, and the causes and consequences of the student's behaviors. Data obtained through observation were used to plan prereferral intervention. Within the model, students do end up being referred for psychoeducational evaluation, but only after a number of prereferral interventions have been attempted and data collected on their effectiveness. Those who eventually assess and make decisions about students are at a decided advantage, for they have available a set of data on the extent to which a number of instructional interventions are effective in alleviating the student's difficulties.

PERSPECTIVE

The practice of psychology in the schools is both diverse and dynamic. I have illustrated only a few of the ways in which school psychologists currently practice. I have argued that the majority of school psychologists choose to function, or have been required to function as psychometric robots, as gatekeepers for special education. Most school psychologists view such a role as limited and indeed undesirable. Yet, clearly they continue to so function. A small minority of school psychologists have shed the psychometric robot role in favor of functioning as consultants to teachers and either directly or indirectly work to intervene in students' instructional programs in regular class settings. Three examples of such practices were briefly reviewed.

Earlier, I used Bandura's reciprocal determination paradigm to describe determinants of the practice of school psychology. The model helps us understand why school psychologists function as they do; it also gives us considerable hope for the future.

The behavior of a school psychologist is to a certain extent determined by that individual's personal characteristics, attitudes, beliefs, knowledge base, competencies, and experience. It is also determined in part by the demands and characteristics of the environment in which one is employed. Yet, at the same time, the behavior of school psychologists influences (changes) both the environment in which they work and their own personal characteristics. Some have continued to behave passively, as if their behavior does not or cannot change or have an impact on the environment in which they function. Others have behaved actively in new and innovative ways to change their environment and to improve the practice of school psychology. And therein lies hope for the future of the profession.

REFERENCES

Algozzine, B., Christenson, S., & Ysseldyke, J. (1982). Probabilities associated with the referral to placement process. *Teacher Education and Special Education, 5,* 19–23.

Algozzine, B., & Ysseldyke, J. E. (1983). Learning disabilities as a subset of school failure: The oversophistication of a concept. *Exceptional Children, 50,* 242–246.

Bandura, A. (1978). The self system in reciprocal determinism. *American Psychologist, 33,* 344–351.

Barbanel, L., & Hoffenberg-Rutman, J. (1974). Attitudes toward job responsibilities and training satisfaction of school psychologists: A comparative study. *Psychology in the Schools, 11,* 425–429.

Bardon, J. I. (1982). The psychology of school psychology. In C. Reynolds & T. Gutkin (Eds.), *The handbook of school psychology.* New York: Wiley.

Bersoff, D. N. (1979). Regarding psychologists testily: Legal regulation of psychological assessment in the public schools. *Maryland Law Review, 39,* 27–120.

Bevan, W. (1981). On coming of age among the professions. In J. Ysseldyke & R. A. Weinberg (Eds.), The future of psychology in the schools: Proceedings of the Spring Hill Symposium. *School Psychology Review, 10,* 127–137.

Bijou, S. (1970). What psychology has to offer education—now. *Journal of Applied Behavior Analysis, 3,* 65–71.

Brown, D. T., Cardon, B. W., Coulter, W. A., & Meyers, J. (1982). Introduction and historical background. In D. T. Brown, B. W. Cardon, W. A. Coulter, & J. Meyers (Eds.), The olympia proceedings. *School Psychology Review, 11,* 107–111.

Christenson, S., Ysseldyke, J. E., Wang, J. J., & Algozzine, B. (1983). Teachers' attributions for problems that result in referral for psychoeducational evaluation. *Journal of Educational Research, 76,* 174–180.

Cook, V., & Patterson, J. G. (1977). Psychologists in the schools of Nebraska: Professional functions. *Psychology in the Schools, 14,* 371–376.

Dansinger, S. S. (1969). A five year follow-up survey of Minnesota school psychologists. *Journal of School Psychology, 7,* 47–53.

Deno, S. L. (1979). *A direct observation approach to measuring classroom behavior: Procedures and application* (Research Report No. 6). Minneapolis: University of Minnesota Institute for Research on Learning Disabilities.

Deno, S. L., Mirkin, P. K., Chiang, B., & Lowry, L. (1980). *Relationships among simple measures of reading and performance on standardized achievement tests.* Minneapolis: University of Minnesota Institute for Research on Learning Disabilities.

Deno, S. L., Mirkin, P. K., Lowry, L., & Kuehnle, K. (1980). *Relationships among simple measures of spelling and performance on standardized achievement tests.* Minneapolis: University of Minnesota Institute for Research on Learning Disabilities.

Deno, S. L., Mirkin, P. K., & Marston, D. (1980). *Relationships among simple measures of written expression and performance on standardized achievement tests* (Research Report No. 22). Minneapolis: University of Minnesota Institute for Research on Learning Disabilities.

Education Commission of the States, Task Forces on Education for Economic Growth. (1983). *Action for excellence: A comprehensive plan to improve our nation's schools.* Denver, CO: The Commission.

Elam, S. M. (1983). The Gallup education surveys: Impressions of a poll watcher. *Phi Delta Kappan, 65*(1), 26–32.

Farling, W. H., & Hoedt, K. C. (1971). *National survey of school psychologists.* Akron, OH: U.S. Department of Health, Education, and Welfare.

Ford, J. D., & Migles, M. (1979). The role of the school psychologists: Teachers' preferences as a function of personal and professional characteristics. *Journal of School Psychology, 17,* 372–378.

Giebink, J. W., & Ringness, T. A. (1970). On the relevancy of training in school psychology. *Journal of School Psychology, 3,* 43–47.

Gilmore, G., & Chandy, J. (1973). Educators describe the school psychologists. *Psychology in the Schools, 10,* 397–403.

Goldwasser, E., Meyers, J., Christenson, S., & Graden, J. (1983). The impact of PL 94–142 on the practice of school psychology: A national survey. *Psychology in the Schools, 20,* 153–165.

Graden, J., Christenson, S., Ysseldyke, J., & Meyers, J. (1984). A national survey on students' and practitioners' perceptions of training. *School Psychology Review.*

Grubb, R. D., Petty, S. Z., & Flynn, D. (1976). A strategy for delivery of accountable school psychological services. *Psychology in the Schools, 13,* 39–44.

Hauser, G., Hertlein, W., Radonovich, J., Ramsey, S., Sulek-Dommis, B., & Thomas, J. (1982). *Initial report: Consultation model for delivery of psychological services.* Olympia, WA: Olympia Public Schools.

Homme, L. (1970). *How to use contingency contracting in the classroom.* Champaign, IL: Research Press.

Hughes, J. (1979). Consistency of administrators' and psychologists' actual and ideal perceptions of school psychologists' activities. *Psychology in the Schools, 16,* 22–29.

Kaplan, M. S., Clancy, B., & Chrin, M. (1977). Priority roles for school psychologists as seen by superintendents. *Journal of School Psychology, 15,* 75–80.

Keogh, B. K., Kukic, L. D., Becker, L. D., McLaughlin, R. J., & Kukic, M. B. (1975). School psychologists' services in special education programs. *Journal of School Psychology, 13,* 142–148.

Knitzer, J. (1978). *Unclaimed children: The failure of public responsibility to children and adolescents in need of mental health services.* Washington, DC: Children's Defense Fund.

Lesiak, W. J., & Lounsbury, E. (1977). Views of school psychology services: A comparative study. *Psychology in the Schools, 14,* 185–188.

Martin, R., & Meyers, J. (1980). School psychologists and the practice of consultation. *Psychology in the Schools, 17,* 478–484.

Meacham, M. L., & Peckham, P. D. (1978). School psychologists at three-quarters century: Congruence between training, practice, preferred role and competence. *Journal of School Psychology, 16,* 195–206.

Medway, F. (1977). An approach to training school psychologists in career education. *Psychology in the Schools, 15,* 243–245.

National Commission on Excellence in Education. (1983). *A nation at risk: The imperative for educational reform.* Washington, DC: U.S. Government Printing Office.

Packard, V. (1983). *Our endangered children.* New York: Free Press.

National Association of School Psychologists (1984). *Standards for School Psychology Training Programs.* Washington, DC: National Association of School Psychology.

Peterson, D. R. (1981). Overall synthesis of the Spring Hill Symposium on the Future of Psychology in the Schools. *School Psychology Review, 10*(2), 307–314.

Peterson, P. E., et al. (1983). *Making the grade: Report of the twentieth century fund task force on federal elementary and secondary education policy.* Unpublished paper (ERIC Document Reproduction Service No. ED 233 112).

Ramage, J. (1979). National survey of school psychologists: Update. *School Psychology Digest, 8,* 153–161.

Regan, R., & Ysseldyke, J. E. (1980). Individual differences among professionals in the process of making psychoeducational decisions. *Academic Psychology Bulletin, 2,* 157–168.

Reynolds, M. C., & Wang, M. C. (1983). Restructuring "special" school programs: A position paper. *Policy Studies Review, 2,* 189–212.

Roberts, R. D. (1970). Perceptions of actual and desired role functions of school psychologists by psychologists and teachers. *Psychology in the Schools, 7,* 175–178.

Sarason, S., & Doris, J. (1979). *Educational handicap, public policy, and social history.* New York: Free Press.

Shepard, L., & Smith, M. L. (1981). *Evaluation of the identification of perceptual-communicative disorders in Colorado.* Final Report. Laboratory of Educational Research, University of Colorado.

Tindal, G., Germann, G., Marston, D., & Deno, S. (1983). *The effectiveness of special education: A direct measurement approach.* (Research Report No. 123). Minneapolis: University of Minnesota Institute for Research on Learning Disabilities.

Tindal, G., Germann, G., & Deno, S. (1983). *Descriptive research on the Pine County norms: A compilation of findings.* (Research Report No. 132). Minneapolis, MN: University of Minnesota Institute for Research on Learning Disabilities.

Tindal, G., Wesson, C., Germann, G., Deno, S. L., & Mirkin, P. K. (1982). *The Pine County model for special education delivery: A data-based system* (Monograph No. 19). Minneapolis: University of Minnesota Institute for Research on Learning Disabilities.

U.S. Commission on Excellence in Education (1983). *A nation at risk.* Washington, DC: Author.

Ysseldyke, J. E. (1978). Who's calling the plays in school psychology? *Psychology in the Schools, 15,* 373–378.

Ysseldyke, J. E., & Algozzine, B. A. (1981). Diagnostic classification decisions as a function of referral information. *Journal of Special Education, 15,* 429–435.

Ysseldyke, J. E., & Algozzine, B. A. (1984). *Introduction to special education.* Boston: Houghton-Mifflin.

Ysseldyke, J. E., & Weinberg, R. A. (1981). The future of psychology in the schools: Proceedings of the Spring Hill Symposium. *School Psychology Review, 10.*

Ysseldyke, J. E., Algozzine, B. A., & Epps, S. (1983). A logical and empirical analysis of current practice in classifying students as handicapped. *Exceptional Children, 50,* 160–166.

Ysseldyke, J. E., Algozzine, B. A., & Mitchell, J. (1982). Special education team decision making: An analysis of current practice. *Personnel and Guidance Journal, 60,* 308–313.

Ysseldyke, J. E., Algozzine, B., Regan, R., & Porter, P. (1981). Technical adequacy of tests used by professionals in simulated decision making. *Psychology in the Schools, 17,* 202–209.

Ysseldyke, J. E., Algozzine, B. A., Richey, L., & Graden, J. (1982). Declaring students eligible for learning disability services: Why bother with the data? *Learning Disability Quarterly, 5,* 37–44.

Ysseldyke, J. E., Algozzine, B. A., Shinn, M. R., & McGue, M. (1982). Similarities and differences among low achievers and students labeled learning disabled. *Journal of Special Education, 16,* 73–85.

Ysseldyke, J. E., Christenson, S., Pianta, B., & Algozzine, B. (1983). An analysis of teachers reasons and desired outcomes for students referred for psychoeducational evaluation. *Journal of Psychoeducational Assessment, 1,* 73–83.

3 Psychology and Schooling: The Interrelationships Among Persons, Processes, and Products

Jack I. Bardon
University of North Carolina at Greensboro

What do school psychologists do all day? A *content analysis* of their activities informs us that they give tests; write reports; talk to teachers, parents, and administrators; contribute information and opinions to team and staff meetings; and sometimes, but not often, do research (Carroll, Harris, & Bretzing, 1979; Lacayo & Sherwood, 1981; Ramage, 1979). A *process analysis,* however, provides another less well understood and more compelling picture of school psychologists' daily activities. In carrying out their various and highly divergent duties, school psychologists interact with other people, form judgments about these people which influence their decisions and recommendations, and are in turn judged in ways that influence whether school psychologists' decisions and recommendations are taken seriously and acted upon. They move about in a system called a school that both restricts and enhances what they can do. They are seen by outsiders as part of that system and are judged according to whatever positive or negative values are associated with schools.

It is not surprising from a process point of view that school psychologists are often misunderstood by others (Bardon, 1982; Grimley, 1978; Howell, 1983). School psychologists are people with particular personality characteristics, educated in particular training programs, interacting with others who are themselves different from each other, all in a particular school system. They try to contribute to understanding or to resolving incredibly diverse and complex problems, often in a team arrangement in which "rules have already been predetermined by others and superimposed on schools which often reluctantly accept them, with team members who have different agendas as they participate and often do not have full commitment or even understanding of the team or of the dangers involved in misdirected team decisions" (Bardon, 1983b, p. 187). What is surprising is that school psychologists succeed as often as they do in helping to implement wise educational decisions and are regarded by many in the schools as useful (Dappen, 1979; Elliott, Piersel, & Galvin, 1983; Gutkin, Singer, & Brown, 1980; Senft & Snider, 1980).

When school psychologists are considered as processors, observers, and reporters of events, inter-actors, intermediaries between the concerned and the troubled, members of teams of others who share joint responsibility for the welfare of children and youth, the question "*What* do school psychologists do all day?" changes to "*How* do school psychologists do whatever they do all day?" The latter question lends itself well to the social learning perspective of reciprocal determinism (Bandura, 1978) taken by the editors of this book in their introductory chapter. It may no longer be productive to delineate the multiple roles that school psychologists take. It is well known that many do a few things consistently and that some do many things intermittently (Bardon, 1982). It may be more productive to consider how school psychologists deal with the continuous interrelated interactions among thought, behaviors, and environmental factors that occur as an integral part of their work; how they, in effect, understand what others are doing and thinking and how they behave in ways that permit them to accomplish their various assignments and tasks, whatever they may be. This chapter attempts to present in brief and selective form some of the considerations and issues that influence how school psychologists carry out their work. A number of theoretical positions have been selected for presentation at the outset because they appear to offer useful perspectives on the work of school psychologists. They include attribution theory, the self-efficacy mechanism, organization and group theory, and aptitude-treatment interaction. In addition to knowing something about how we come to make judgments and decisions in interaction with others, it is also important to consider both the personal and professional attributes of the school psychologists themselves. We also should understand something about the institutions in which school psychologists work and be able to discriminate among different elements of the process of education. Finally, two philosophical or value systems governing our professional behavior—education and mental health—are examined. Concluding remarks attempt to bring together central elements and points made throughout the chapter.

THEORETICAL CONSIDERATIONS

Four approaches compatible with reciprocal determinism seem especially appropriate to the work of school psychologists: attribution theory, affectance, organizational and group theory, and the concept of aptitude-treatment interaction.

Attribution Theory

Attribution theory has its roots in the study of person perception as developed by Heider (1958), in which concern was given to such matters as what people think about each other and how such judgments are formed. When theorists began also to consider what *causes* persons to think the way they do about themselves and others, attribution theory came into its own. As the idea took hold that it is the meaning of behavior rather than the behavior itself to which people attend (Bronfrenbrenner, 1979; de Charms, 1972; Harré & Secord, 1972; Nisbett & Valins, 1971), a vast literature developed in what has been termed social cognition. Social cognition refers to the belief that "much of our behavior can be understood by comprehension of how the world is cognitively represented: our impressions, inferences, and causal attributions" (Weiner, Graham, Taylor, & Meyer, 1983, p. 109). Throughout this literature, central themes have included locus of control and how ascriptions about ability level, praise and blame, help and neglect each influence the motivation to achieve and to persist and also how they affect reactions to specific events. At this time, for our purposes, the following extractions from the literature may provide a useful basis for consideration of what social cognition—especially attribution theory—has to offer to understanding the process of school psychological activity.

The world "out there" does not exist without taking on personal meaning. A person's processes are "psychologically channelized by the ways in which he [*sic*] anticipates events" (Bannister & Salmon, 1975, p. 28). In other words, behavior is understood as a function of its anticipated consequences (Bandura, 1974; Mischel, 1973) and also by how we then interpret or assign causes to behavior after it has occurred (Weiner, 1976).

The central purpose of the school is to help pupils progress in all ways, but especially in academic achievement. The success and failure of pupils to progress according to the objectives of the school become important factors in the lives of those who work in and attend them. In schools, all concerned with helping pupils learn—psychologists, other team members, administrators, teachers, and parents—have some part to play in whether children and youth behave and learn. When pupil behavior occurs, it is evaluated by all parties. Attributions are made about who was or was not helpful in furthering or detracting from anticipated pupil progress. In addition, all educators, including parents, have different responsibilities in their mutual involvement in the education of children and youth. Those involved in the day-to-day events of school life anticipate the consequences of their behavior and the behavior of others and account (seek causal explanations) for their part in what has happened. ("When this event took place, did it succeed? Why or why not? Did I have anything to do with its success or failure? How do I know? Why did I succeed? Why did I fail?") These are questions of importance in the daily lives of educators. The answers they give themselves influence what they do next and how they do it.

Weiner (1972) proposed that ability, effort, task difficulty, and luck are the main causal factors people use to explain success and failure. These four attributions can more broadly be considered as having either an internal or an external referent. If we attribute the cause of our behavior to internal factors (ability or effort), we experience ourselves as having originated the intention to behave a certain way and are said to be intrinsically motivated (Nichols, 1979).

An intrinsically motivated person has been termed an "origin" (deCharms, 1972). On the other hand, if the cause of our behavior is experienced as external (task difficulty or luck), we are said to be extrinsically motivated and are "impelled from without" and termed a "pawn" (deCharms, 1972, p. 96).

Although it seems logical to consider origins as better off than pawns—more in control of themselves—other factors influence the effectiveness of the results of external or internal causation. Internal causation is preferred to external causation when one experiences success. External causation may be preferable to internal causal attribution when one experiences failure. ("I succeeded because I tried hard." "I failed because the principal wouldn't cooperate.") People who attribute success to internal causes experience pride, competence, confidence, and satisfaction. Those who attribute failure to internal causes experience feelings of guilt and resignation (Weiner, 1980). Other factors that modify causal attributions are controllability and stability (Rogers, 1982). A stable cause is one that is thought to be relatively unchanging over time ("I always try hard"). A controllable cause is one that is believed to be within one's control ("I can make my classroom as attractive as I want it to be").

When making attributions about one's own behavior or the behavior of others, there is a tendency to distinguish between the attributions of observers, those who are not directly involved in a behavior, and actors, those who are directly involved. According to Jones and Nisbett (cited in Antaki, 1982), people tend to explain their behavior as due to the opportunities or demands of the situation, but see other people's actions as due to their dispositions. One takes into account one's own motives, attitudes, intentions, and knowledge of the situation when one is the actor, but may fail to do so when making attributions from the point of view of an observer. The actor (parent) believes his/her child failed because of bad teaching, leading to a poor attitude on the part of the child. The observer (teacher) believes the child failed because he/she wasn't bright enough to do the work, and didn't try. For the observer, behavior is the figure against the ground of the situation. For the actor, the situational cues are figural and are seen to elicit behavior.

It is not possible to be a school psychologist for long without coming to realize that attributions made about children and youth by adults in the school and community can affect the ways they think about pupils, for good or for ill. The sometimes pernicious effects of labeling on children classified for special education (Ysseldyke & Algozzine, 1982; Ysseldyke & Foster, 1978); the so-called self-fulfilling prophesy (Rosenthal & Jacobson, 1968) and the more generalized effects of bias and prejudice are well known. Less well understood is the possibility that at least some educators can change expectancies about the meaning of a special education label if sufficient opportunity is provided to observe behaviors that are inconsistent with the meaning of the label (Palmer, 1979; Reschly & Lamprecht, 1979). For some educators, attributions are based on lack of information and are subject to change if corrective information is provided. School psychologists who have evidence or information that can help alter opinion and attributions and also know how to offer useful information are in the best position to shift attributions in ways that help others view children positively.

When school psychologists present their findings in team meetings, when they write recommendations to teachers as part of their reports, and when they discuss their findings about a child with the child's parents, according to social cognition concepts—especially attribution theory—they are enveloped in interchanges strongly influenced by the meanings given to what each participant says and does. There is an expression seen on wall posters that says "I know you believe you understand what you think I said, but I'm not sure you realize that what you heard is not what I meant!" Without attention to the attributions that are part of professional interchange in psychological services, opportunities for creating the conditions for successful communication are diminished.

The Self-Efficacy Mechanism

Prior to ascribing meaning to one's own behavior and the behavior of others, people make judgments about how well they can "execute courses of action required to deal with prospective situations" (Bandura, 1982, p. 122). The basis for making such judgments derives from information acquired from the cumulative effects of rewards and punishments that followed teacher behavior (Estes, 1972). People process information by assigning meaning to these past experiences in order to make predictions about the course of future events. The ways predictions are made are not simple. They are made on the bases both of enduring judgments about one's capabilities and opportunities and on situation-specific assessment of possible outcomes. "People avoid activities that they believe exceed their coping capabilities, but they undertake and perform assuredly those that they judge themselves capable of managing" (Bandura, 1982, p. 123).

Bandura (1977) differentiates between outcome expectancy and efficacy expectation. Outcome expectancy involves a person's estimate that a given behavior will lead to certain outcomes. ("If I keep a record of Johnny's seat work, I can learn how well my plan to improve his arithmetic performance is succeeding.") If a favorable outcome expectancy is not anticipated, there is no reason to undertake any activity toward resolution of a problem. On the other hand, even if people know what to do and anticipate favorable outcomes if action is taken, they may still fail to act. Efficacy expectation is concerned with the conviction that one can successfully execute the behavior required to produce an outcome. ("I can't keep such records and take care of my other responsibilities to the other children in the room. I just don't have the skills. It has always been a problem for me to do too many things at once.") Perceived self-efficacy will determine how much effort people will put forth and also how long they will persist when faced with obstacles. It is important but not sufficient to know what are the possible consequences of an act. It is important to anticipate a favorable outcome expectancy. In addition, the strength of people's convictions about their own effectiveness will affect whether they will even try to cope with a given situation as well as how long they will persist in trying. The stronger the perceived self-efficacy, the more active and persistent will be effort. In turn, sustained effort can result in corrective experiences that further reinforce the sense of efficacy.

Optimum self-efficacy includes some degree of uncertainty. "In approaching learning tasks, those who perceive themselves to be supremely self-efficacious in the undertaking feel little need to invest much preparatory effort in it" (Bandura, 1982, p. 123). Therefore, when self-efficacy is so well established that it provides little reason to mobilize efforts to produce an outcome, it is useful to try to raise the level of uncertainty sufficiently so that effort and persistence occur. When self-efficacy is lacking, a number of studies suggest that there are different modes of influence that can strengthen and raise self-percepts of efficacy (Bandura, 1982). Nothing succeeds like success that is perceived as authentic and therefore serves to strengthen the conviction that one can, in fact, execute the behavior. Less powerful, but still influential, are vicarious experiences; verbal persuasion or encouragement if they lead people to try hard enough to succeed; and changes in people's reading of their physiological state used in their judgment of their capabilities; for example, tension, stamina, fatigue, aches, and pains.

With the self-efficacy mechanism in mind, consider what happens when a teacher refers a child to a school psychologist because of concern about the child's classroom behavior and receives back a report, written or verbal, that says certain teacher behaviors will lead to certain pupil outcomes. Further, the report goes on to offer suggestions about how the teacher might go about producing these outcomes. Without consideration of the teacher's efficacy expectations and how they can be raised, if low, the net result of the school psychologist-teacher interaction is left to chance. The often baffling and frustrating experience of having sound recommendations ignored or revised in such ways that hoped-for outcomes do not take place may well be a function of neglect or lack of understanding of how others process the information provided by the school psychologist and what may be needed in order to make that information both palatable and useful. It has been customary to consider rejection of recommendations and plans proferred by school psychologists as defensive reaction. The self-efficacy mechanism offers an alternative basis for understanding why some ideas are acceptable and acted upon, others are acceptable but not.acted upon, and still others are not acceptable and therefore not acted upon.

Organization and Group Theory

School districts are systems. Schools are subsystems within a larger organizational framework. Systems theory in general (Rogers & Rogers, 1976) and change strategies for organizational self-development and renewal are applicable to schools as they are to any other kind of complex organizational system (Fullan, Miles, & Taylor, 1980). However, it is unusual for school psychologists to be in position in which they can either participate in or modify large-scale organizational self-development and renewal. Instead, school psychologists typically function in a number of different school buildings or through a central office that is itself a subsystem of a system. Although influenced by decisions that affect the larger macrosystem (the district), the direct day-to-day within-system interrelationships are more pervasive forces in the work of school psychologists. Those aspects of the organizational system within the direct purview of school psychologists are most amenable to intervention and change. For instance, school psychologists may change teachers' attitudes, alter team procedures, and help to organize special programs. They are less likely directly to influence attendance policies, system organizational patterns, or employment policies and procedures. This more narrow view of systems operation and intervention may require that school psychologists who like to think of themselves as system change agents reconsider their sphere of influence. Perhaps they "might need to change the organization of . . . [their] . . . thinking in order to think about how we change our organizing" (Smith, 1982, p. 316).

School psychologists experience schools as systems in at least two ways:

1. Their activities are directed by how schools are organized. The results of rules, constraints, and mores that have been developed from within and from outside the school, and the established boundaries that serve to divide people into subgroups are directly experienced by school psychologists. Schools identify employees as line or staff, special education or pupil services, teachers or supervisors, and so on. The organizational divisions used determine who meets with whom, under what circumstances, and how they are expected to relate to one another. There are also physical properties to schools. People are put into buildings, and kept together or separated from each other in ways that modify interactions.

2. School psychologists are often asked to be part of a team that makes group decisions about the lives of children with special needs. This particular subsystem has a life of its own and is deeply affected by the direct person-to-person relationships among those involved (Maher & Pfeiffer, 1983).

Systems are not experienced directly; that is, they are not seen or heard. Rather, what is observed are behaviors and physical properties from which the "system" or organizational properties are inferred. Likewise, we do not see or hear relationships. We can only look at the behaviors of persons—the parts or elements through which relationships are expressed (Smith, 1982). Thinking and talking are amenable to modification but systems themselves are not. The logic of this position is that we are able to modify the system or organization in which we are *directly* involved by the way we think and talk about it and by the way we help others to think and talk about it.

The School as a Loose Coupling System. Weick (1982) has described school as a loosely coupled system with certain properties that result in certain system effects. A loosely coupled system is one in which any two components of the system affect one another (a) suddenly rather than continuously, (b) occasionally rather than constantly, (c) negligibly rather than significantly, (d) indirectly rather than directly, and (e) eventually rather than immediately. Although not invariate, it is most likely, for example, that the school psychologist and any other person in the system will interact because of a particular occurrence rather than on a continuing basis, infrequently, without significant impact, through channels and procedures, and by appointment or with some time lag. When change in schools occurs it is most likely to be "continuous rather than episodic, small scale rather than large, improvisational rather than planned, accommodative rather than constrained, and local rather than cosmopolitan" (Weick, 1982, p. 390).

In loosely coupled systems such as schools, change occurs at the macrocosmic level if it does at all, slowly and with difficulty. Loosely coupled systems are often adaptable in that units accommodate and learn to live within the larger system, but they also suffer from inability to make major changes that could improve the entire system itself.

According to Weick (1982), those who function in a loosely coupled system "rely on trust and presumption, persist, are often isolated, find social comparison difficult, have no one to borrow from, seldom imitate, suffer pluralistic ignorance, maintain discretion, improvise, and have less hubris because they know they cannot change the universe because it is not sufficiently connected to make this possible" (p. 405). Weick has described some important aspects of the lives of school psychologists. It is of some comfort to recognize that some of our behaviors and feelings are attributable to the qualities of the system we serve and are not entirely of our own making. And Weick adds, "A loosely coupled system is not a flawed system. It is a social and cognitive solution to constant environmental change, to the impossibility of knowing another mind, and to limited information processing capabilities . . . loose coupling is to social system as compartmentalization is to individuals, a means to achieve cognitive economy and a little peace" (1982, p. 405). School psychologists who understand the properties of the system and how system organization affects the behavior and feelings of those who work in the system are in positions to assist others with problems engendered by the nature of the system and also to assist others to understand and to live with those problems that are built into the system itself.

Influencing Others Through Working in Small Groups. Within a loosely coupled system—the school—change comes about in large part through language and communication (Weick, 1982). Everything school psychologists do culminates in communication. School psychologists' efforts are made effective by how words and actions are put together toward designated goals. In a loosely coupled system, the critical links usually take place among small groups of people. Therefore, small-group models and theories are useful to school psychologists who work with parents, teachers, and administrators together in some combination and as members of child study or special education teams.

What is known about small-group productivity that might help us understand how best school psychologists can work effectively in schools? The most productive groups, according to Hare (1976), are those in which the members are able to carry out effectively the problem-solving procedures needed to solve tasks *and* also to deal well with the social and emotional problems of groups and their individual members. Small groups cannot be considered solely as problem-solving groups. The social and emotional needs of group members are major factors in group process and cannot be ignored. Although the deleterious effects on group process of disordered personalities cannot be discounted, it is more likely that social and emotional needs in the work setting will be expressed through the attributions made about individual group members and by differences in orientation and styles as group members exchange views and information and try to work toward ostensible group goals. Issues of import to group harmony and teamwork include attributions of equality, the extent to which knowledge is shared and understood, the differences in levels and kinds of competencies among group members, the marginality of some group members in relation to the others, and territoriality, or domain; i.e., which areas are claimed by group members as their own and jealously protected from infringement by others (New, 1968).

Team operation often occurs at two levels: (a) the accepted reasons why persons come together in teams (e.g., to classify children for special education), which New calls the *functional rationality* of assembling a team; and (b) the other reasons that abound in team activity (e.g., the attributions made about self and others, the preservation of self-esteem, the enhancement of favorable position in the school hierarchy, the desire for power over others), which New calls the *substantive rationality*. According to Bardon and Bennett (1974), one example of how the two levels might work follows:

> The team members assume equality by recognizing that some are more "equal" than others. The psychologist has a doctorate, whereas the social worker is a recently upgraded visiting teacher. The learning disability specialist has been in the school for many years and knows all aspects of school functioning, but the school psychologist is an occasional consultant who hardly knows his [sic] way around the building. . . . Each professional specialty supposedly has some clear areas of competency; but in fact . . . the school nurse on the team is a better counselor than the guidance counselor or . . . the school social worker is a better diagnostician than the school psychologist. (p. 156)

Group productivity and harmony are increased whenever dissonance between functional and substantive rationalities can be lessened. Dissonance is lessened when group members are able to talk freely, become task oriented in that they are primarily interested in the achievement of the group effort itself, view their associates as helpful, try to assist colleagues with their work, and come to view the group as "we" and others as "they" (Zander, 1982). Certain events can sometimes be arranged to increase the chances of productive and harmonious group interaction and problem solving. Zander (1982) suggested a number of ways that group feeling is enhanced: (a) proximity—placing persons physically close to one another in offices and through social events that bring people together under pleasant circumstances, (b) homogeneity—encouragement of the likeness among members through orientation, development of mutual goals, reinforcement of similarities and, if necessary, transferring out individuals who persist in inappropriate behavior, (c) group distinction—creation of an aura of special or social identity through such means as providing special space for meetings, a special name, special resources or equipment and evidence of group usefulness to others. Still other ways of promoting group cohesiveness include having "satisfied members make certain sacrifices for the group" (Zander, 1982, p. 7). According to Zander, a participant who gives up something of value for the group becomes more attractive to that group. Also, members who invest their own resources in a group thereafter perceive their having a stake in its future success.

Other things being equal, member satisfaction is more likely in a democratic group organization using group problem-solving methods, but there probably is no group task-solving approach that is uniformly better than any other if productivity is the major consideration. "In an authoritarian setting the most productive group will tend to be authoritarian, whereas in a more democratic situation, the equalitarian group will be more productive" (Hare, 1976, pp. 355–356).

There is no way school psychologists can avoid communication and interaction with others. From a process point of view, the professional task is to determine how to make such communication as effective as possible through understanding the nature of the school system and its effects on interactions and by contributing in positive and helpful ways to diadic, triadic, and small-group communication so that all involved better understand the tasks at hand and work toward their resolution with correct information and concern for how people think about and talk about the tasks and each other.

Aptitude-Treatment Interaction

What is true for some children is not true for other children. What is true for one child at one time is not necessarily true for the same child at another time. The fact that research findings indicate a high probability that a particular treatment will be more effective than another does not guarantee that it will work for Mary Smith in Jones Elementary School with Mr. Diamond as the teacher in a room of *these* 24 children. Even though research findings suggest that a particular aptitude-treatment interaction is significantly more effective than other aptitude-treatment interactions may or may not have any relationship to what actually goes on in planning a sound education or management program for *this* child in *that* situation populated by *these* people under *those* circumstances.

This seemingly discouraging view of the relationship between knowledge and practice is really not as discouraging as it may seem. There are ways in which knowledge and practice can be brought together so that one complements the other, but the process is not automatic and it is not easy. Phillips (1982) presented a strong case that "research should *inform our actions as school psychologists*" (p. 24), and that interactive research is more likely to be compatible with school psychology practice than research that seeks main effects. Barclay (1981) agreed that "Given what we know about the differences in educational treatments and individual differences, the logical conclusion for instruction is that we match up individuals with the kind of educational treatment which will maximize their development in terms of the valued outcomes" (p. 26). Both Phillips and Barclay emphasize the importance of information from research, but they also point toward the need for individual attention to how information is interpreted and used in particular situations.

The voluminous research stemming from Cronbach's (1975) aptitude-treatment interaction (ATI) paradigm has not yet indicated that systematic matching between individual and environment is possible (Cotterell, 1982; Hessler & Sosnowsky, 1979). But optimism for the eventual usefulness of ATI research remains nevertheless, with recognition that at least part of the research problem lies in the need for research methodology that can better be used to investigate interactions (Cronbach & Snow, 1977; Hunt, 1975; Miller, 1981).

School psychologists who must work directly with the interrelationships among persons, processes, and products in order to make decisions about children and youth face the dilemma that, although research should inform actions, research usually offers only hazy guidelines and does not *determine* actions. School psychologists are ultimately left to their own resources when reaching decisions about the match between characteristics of individuals and interactions that may be beneficial. In this delicate balance between knowledge and judgment, three approaches are possible:

1. One approach follows from Phillips' dictum that action stems from a "personal acquisition-of-knowledge system" (1982, p. 32). Professional psychologists continuously build and refine bases of knowledge that serve as a first screen for determining what might be the most reasonable approach to the interaction of person characteristics and environmental factors. Superimposed on a research base, psychologists then consider other factors that are active in the actual situation, and make tentative "best guesses" about what might work, or why one decision might in this instance be better than another. Decisions are then followed by monitoring of subsequent events so that the psychologist can

begin to build a base of knowledge about what works best in that particular situation. Using this approach, psychologists use a knowledge base and also use themselves as scientific problem solvers (Burke, Haworth, & Brantley, 1980).

2. A second approach is a more technical one. School psychologists apply a body of certain knowledge to problems, using information derived from research or clinical wisdom in such a way that results are invariable (Rodgers cited in Bardon, 1983a). For example, the use of state guideline formulas for the determination of learning disability—a stated discrepancy between achievement and mental ability—used consistently may result in a classification of learning disability regardless of any other personal or environmental factors that are operating. When a classification is then made, it results invariably in a placement in a resource room for children with learning disabilities.

3. A third approach is an idiosyncratic and personal one. School psychologists make up their own rules, using only their inclinations and values as guides in forming judgments, justifying decisions on the bases of professional authority and privilege.

Of the three approaches the first describes professional school psychologists who struggle mightily to understand and to apply what is known, what they can learn, and what they can verify. The second describes a technician whose "hit and miss" rate may be no better or worse than the scientific problem-solving psychologist, but whose judgment is based on bureaucratic means-to-an-end rather than on tempered reason. Only when the knowledge base is so firm that highly predictable consequences result from certain data is this approach useful, and then one must wonder if school psychologists are needed here at all. The third approach describes behavior that is unethical and potentially dangerous, for it offers personal biases in the name of psychology and is built on ignorance parading as knowledge.

The state of knowledge in psychology is not likely in the foreseeable future to allow us to make precise predictions about person-environment match, although there is reason to believe we will learn more about general aptitude-treatment interactions that will increase the probability that our initial best guesses are better ones. Professional judgment will remain an indispensable tool when decisions are made about what happens to people in real-life situations.

PERSONAL AND PROFESSIONAL ATTRIBUTES OF SCHOOL PSYCHOLOGISTS

The literature about school psychology deals extensively with role and function, service delivery models, decision-making processes, methods, and techniques. Implicit in much of the literature is the assumption that school psychologists' personal and professional attributes are such that they present no special problems; i.e., that all school psychologists are well put together and have the requisite knowledge, skills, and personal characteristics to do what they are supposed to do. In fact, it is possible the effectiveness of school psychologists is determined as much, if not more, by the way they function and interact than by what they know and what duties they perform. School psychologists, like all others, vary in their styles, manifestations of their personalities, and ability to communicate well.

Personal Factors

No research literature could be found that relates explicitly to the personality characteristics and attitudes of successful and unsuccessful school psychologists. A commonality of expert opinion does exist, occasionally interspersed with research findings, that sheds some light on the qualities that may make for good professional functioning in school psychology.

High intelligence, or, better, the perception by others of high intelligence, appears to be a paramount characteristic that differentiates accepted and valued professionals from others (Hare, 1976; Peterson & Bry, 1980). How one concludes that a school psychologist has high intelligence is not clear. Presumably, the perception derives from a number of other factors that are discussed later concerning credibility and knowledge dissemination. It also seems related to perception of concomitant qualities and interactions that influence whether one is thought to be intelligent. "We tend to trust the judgment of others who agree with us. After all, how can their judgment be bad if they come to the same conclusions we do?" (Kuhn & Beam, 1982, p. 171). To agree with others presumably helps to create an aura of intelligence and trustworthiness. "In consequence, we tend to make our stated agreements with others stronger, or our disagreements weaker, than our actual ones. Hence . . . (people seen as intelligent) . . . seem to agree more than is actually the case" (Kuhn & Beam, 1982, p. 171). What is referred to here is the assumption of similarities, which helps the perceiver to view the perceived as "like me" in some critical respects. Also related to positive perception is what has variously been described as interpersonal warmth (Peterson & Bry, 1980), that complex of qualities long regarded in therapy and counseling as essential ingredients in good helping relationships; empathy, positive regard, genuineness, concreteness, and self-disclosure (Truax & Carkhuff, 1967).

Positively valued psychologists have also been described as having flexibility, sensitivity, stress resistance, objectivity, circumspection, ethical and social responsibility, wisdom, and maturity (American Board of Professional Psychology, 1976), creativity, eagerness to learn, and dedication (Peterson & Bry, 1980). Reflective judgment—the capacity for metacognition (Welfel, 1982)—

and what Bardon and Bennett (1974) described as an attitude of positive skepticism seem to be useful attributes of successful school psychologists. Positive skepticism includes a willingness to suspend judgment long enough to consider relevant information and to "try new approaches and to persist even in the face of disappointments, lack of immediate results, apparent lack of cooperation, and sheer frustration" (Bardon & Bennett, 1974, p. 2). Still another difficult-to-achieve personal posture includes the willingness to demonstrate concern for others through multiple means: to be seen as a decision processor more than a decision maker, to be viewed as having sincere and overriding concern for the welfare of others, to be willing to give psychology away in the interest of educating others (Bardon & Bennett, 1974).

One might wish that such virtuous and ideal school psychologists existed! Given that none of us achieve the ideal, what may matter most is school psychologists' recognition of the influence of personality and attitudinal factors on the perception of performance, an attempt to work toward the ideal whenever possible, conveying the intent to be helpful, and persisting and cooperating long enough to allow others to form positive impressions.

Professional Attributes

Personal characteristics are intertwined with professional skills and knowledge. Together they serve to modify how others react to the efforts of school psychologists to be helpful. Whatever this combination of factors may be, it works well when it results in reciprocal liking, respect, and trust (Goldstein, 1980). It is impossible to provide a prescription for the production of liking, respect, and trust, but certain professional components that help induce positive reactions are well known.

Credibility. School psychologists can be competent at what they do, but their efforts come to naught if others do not think the school psychologists are "good" (Schowengerdt, Fine, & Poggio, 1976). Basic to the perception of being good—meaning useful, interested, or whatever else the receiver values in the verbal or written interchange with the school psychologist—is the answer to the following question: Assuming that I know what the school psychologist means, how much reliance can I place in the message given to me (Kuhn & Beam, 1982)? This question has three subsidiary parts: (a) Does the school psychologist know what he or she is talking about? (b) Is this school psychologist providing a clear and useful rendition of that knowledge? (c) Does this school psychologist behave in ways that make me feel comfortable during the transaction?

Credibility, the degree to which one can be trusted and, therefore, considered worth listening to, is related to whether one is seen as an expert and also to whether one is able to convey that expertness in useful ways. The distinction between knowing and being able to deliver that knowledge is an area of special interest and significance to school psychologists and others who serve to bridge the gap between a knowledge base and the practice of a specialty emerging from that base.

The two major components of credibility have been referred to as expert and referent power (Martin, 1978). The interplay between expert and referent powers that lends itself to the creation of maximum credibility is something that cannot directly be taught. Martin (1978) hypothesized that school psychologists who serve as consultants are more or less effective depending on how certain aspects of expert and referent power occur. Based on his analysis, it seems likely that:

1. Those with high status will achieve greater success than those with low status. Status refers to external factors that affect the perception of the one receiving assistance, such as the amount of experience or education, or fee charged, or association with prestigious organizations.
2. Age will influence success. Young professionals will be less effective with older people than they will be with people their own age or younger.
3. The amount of contact will influence how one works. The less contact one has, the more one relies on the use of expertise, as referent power requires time to build.
4. The most successful professionals will strike a balance between expert and referent power.
5. The longer one works with another, the more successful the results of such contact are likely to be.

Although specific reference to outcome studies is not available here, these assertions drawn from Martin's work are in accord with the theoretical positions mentioned earlier in this chapter and receive verification from experience, always, of course, with acknowledgment that every rule has its exceptions.

Espoused Theories and Theories-in-Use. Credibility is also determined by some less obvious factors. Agyris (1976) offered a useful distinction between espoused theories and theories-in-use. Espoused theories are those "microtheories of action . . . people . . . hold in their heads . . . which they use to design and carry out their actions" (p. 638). For example, a school psychologist may think, "If you want to improve classroom behavior under these circumstances with those results, then you should behave this way." Theories-in-use describe the ways people *actually* behave.

Theories-in-use may or may not reflect the microtheories of action in which people believe. When someone acts as though there is congruence between words used and actions, but instead, the receiver of both the message and the behavior views them as discrepant, credibility is greatly diminished. The discrepancy can occur because advice given or recommendations offered are not in keeping with the way the school psychologist behaves in other contexts. The discrepancy can also come about from immediate mixed messages as well (Edinger & Patterson, 1983). Person-to-person or person-to-group behavior includes both verbal messages and body behavior including such mundane nonverbal media as distance, gaze, touch, paralinguistic cues, and facial expression. According to Kuhn and Beam (1982), most people assume that the body message "being unconscious, is the more truthful" (p. 169). Even in situations in which face-to-face contact is not made, such as in memos, letters, and psychological reports, the medium can convey either congruent or mixed messages, resulting in increased credibility when the message is congruent with the content and both are viewed positively, or it can result in decreased credibility when the content and the message form reflect a discrepancy between espoused theory and theory-in-use. The use of good or poor quality paper, neat or careless typing, good or poor spelling, good or poor organization (Kuhn & Beam, 1982) can influence how the content of a message is received and reflect on the credibility of the sender.

Edinger and Patterson (1983) concluded on the basis of a review of research on nonverbal behavior and social control that, in many instances, nonverbal behavior can be managed to influence the behavior of others. If school psychologists are aware of differences between their verbal and nonverbal behavior that lower their credibility, deliberate training in improvement of nonverbal behavior is possible. As we know, education and training in use of human relations skills often include exactly such considerations. It is also possible, however, that people can be overtrained in how to act to the extent that nonverbal behavior is seen as artificial and incongruent with other behaviors, resulting in an impression of insincerity. Self-scrutiny and use of supervisors or process consultants who assist with analysis of professional behavior are ways for school psychologists to learn more about how others react to them so that they can make appropriate behavioral adjustments.

A more subtle and difficult to control aspect of the difference between theories-in-use and espoused theories occurs when school psychologists purport to hold particular points of view about human behavior that are offered as explanation for pupil conduct and in recommendations for action, and then act in ways that belie the professed beliefs. A school psychologist who advises democratic classroom procedures, but is autocratic in team meetings, will be less credible than a school psychologist who advises behavior that is palatable to the receiver and also behaves in different situations as the receiver is advised to do. A behaviorist who is not positively reinforcing or a humanist who is not especially humane conveys discrepancies that will influence his or her credibility.

School psychologists are born, and they are also made. They come to their work as mature adults whose personal characteristics are relatively fixed but who also have been shaped by their training and other occupational experiences. They have a view of themselves as experts. They hold to certain persuasions and views about human behavior and tend not to use others. They also have some ideas—better than most—about how they influence others and some more or less clear conceptions about why they are doing what they do for a living. Their personal and professional characteristics provide a unique blend of knowledge, skills, and the ways both are delivered to others that cannot easily be described and certainly cannot be taught in exact form to any other person. Although there is increasing knowledge about factors that enhance human interchange and make for cooperative and effective communication, each school psychologist must work out how these generally accepted ways of functioning combine with "self" to lead to professional effectiveness as well as to professional satisfaction.

SCHOOLS, SCHOOLING, AND EDUCATION

Schools engage in schooling in order to educate children and youth. School psychologists assist schools in their efforts (schooling) to produce educated children and youth. These statements seem simple and clear enough. But anyone who has worked in schools soon understands that the simplicity is deceptive and that the distinctions among these terms and the multiple meanings they have are not at all clear.

Education is the broadest of these terms. It is most often used to describe the results, or products, of a process of teaching and learning, formal or informal, that takes place in the lives of everyone from birth on. It is not uncommon, though, for people to think of education as that which results solely from participation in formal schools. More generally, it is considered the way society passes on its values and skills. It takes place through the family, the press, the church, the workplace, the media, and also the schools (Cremin, 1980).

Schools in our culture are highly organized, formal, social, and cultural institutions that reflect the communities in which they exist. They are influenced by federal, state, and local laws and take on characteristics that differentiate them from other schools, even in the same school district, because of styles of leadership, the interaction among those who work there, and the characteristics of the children who attend (Bardon, 1982; Goodlad, 1977). One important distinction between school psychologists and other kinds of professional psychologists is school psychologists' recognition that schools must be understood as special places, and that each school has unique qualities that must be understood and taken into consideration if psychologists are to be most useful in helping those who work in and are served by schools.

Schooling usually refers to what actually happens to children and youth in schools, whether it be instruction or life as it is lived in the schools (Macdonald, 1975; Rogers, 1982). However, a more encompassing conception of schooling is emerging that has import for the practice of school psychology. This conception considers schooling to be the way a person interacts with any setting in which learning is to take place (Bardon, 1983a). Stephens in his classic text "The process of education: A psychological examination" (1967) wrote that, according to his theory of spontaneous schooling, "the mechanisms actually responsible for academic growth reside in humble, spontaneous tendencies which are always in operation when an adult consorts with maturing children" (p. 10), and that the concept of schooling should not "be limited to the highly elaborate institutions of the present day but the concept involved should be seen as extending, although with diminished force, to the very doorstep of the parent-child dyad" (p. 25). More recently, Bailey (1976) pointed out that "with or without our formal educational system, people would in fact learn. They always have" (p. 104). White and Duker (1973) indicated the many ways that schooling, formal and informal, can take place. Schooling is done privately in the home, in public places, between people in dyads and groups, between a technological apparatus and a person or group. They pointed out that it is done for short-term and immediate goals and for long-term and lifelong goals. They said that schooling is done by experts, peers, assistants, and nonexperts. Coleman (1972) also argued that children's needs for learning have outgrown the formal school experience as currently construed and that schooling must be a community-wide and multidimensional process.

Schooling, viewed as the interaction of a person who needs to learn something, in contact with a person or materials by which such learning can take place, in a setting with particular properties, takes on meaning that is not necessarily related to function within the sociocultural institution we now call school. Schooling as herein defined parallels Bandura's concept of reciprocal determinism, but considers the interactive elements as they are especially concerned with the task of predesignated learning and teaching.

In the continuing controversy in the United States about the quality of American education, the focus of concern appears to be on the quality of schools and their effectiveness in producing the competencies required for effective living in modern society. The issues of what should we educate toward—the ultimate values and knowledges that result from attendance in schools—remain unresolved. For some there is concern that our educational institutions "confer few educational benefits to those who pass through them" (Raven, 1983, p. 249). The controversies have not directly addressed the process of schooling except to confuse this process with the more narrow view that schooling is something confined to and synonymous with formal schools. The question of how best certain educational goals can be achieved has received little attention. The issues dealing with schools and schooling in America are better seen as having two parts: (a) One part addresses the need to improve the conditions under which schools operate so that their role in schooling can be improved, and (b) The other, not yet well understood, is that the axiom that "education best takes place in classrooms in school buildings" is "both unfounded and self-defeating" (Sarason, 1983, p. 5). Attention must be given both to the improvement of schools and to the alternative conditions, settings, and interactions that increase the chances that learning will take place.

It is important to clarify that schooling as defined here is definitely a part of what takes place in the formal school setting. To understand how a teacher teaches, what takes place in that classroom, what a pupil in that classroom brings to learning, what constraints are imposed by the system, and then to work out a way to enhance that teaching and learning involves schooling in a school. But schooling also is a way to describe what takes place in other settings when people learn from others or from materials and methods devised by others. Schooling also takes place in mental hospitals, in institutions of higher education, in homes, in day care centers, in industry, and in business.

If school psychologists are experts in helping educators to improve teaching and learning through individual assessment of particular teaching-learning situations, a strong case can be made that their major area of expertise—what distinguishes them from other psychologists—is, or could be, or should be, schooling. Such a conception of function does not require that school psychologists necessarily work in schools, although that is a natural setting. Instead, they can work in any situation in which they can help others to understand and to improve schooling through study of the learner, the teacher, and the setting interactively contributing toward a specified educational goal; the quintessential interrelationship of persons, processes, and products.

Needless to say, this view of school psychologists' function and purpose is not broadly accepted. There is some evidence that a gradual movement in this direction is taking place (Bardon, 1983a). The promotion of the idea that school psychologists are psychological experts in the understanding and improvement of schooling helps to shift conception of role and function in school psychology so that school psychology can become a major rather than a minor contributor to the process of education wherever it may occur.

EDUCATION AND MENTAL HEALTH

What we are asked to do as school psychologists, how our activities are interpreted, and to what extent they are then valued or disregarded are not only functions of how others perceive us, as already indicated, but they are also functions of what we tell others we are and what they make of our messages. Perception and communication are not identical. A perception occurs when we see or hear something happen and then interpret the meaning of that happening even though no direct message is necessarily involved. A communication occurs when someone sends an intended message, someone else receives that message, and decodes it, and then the receiver has a pattern in mind that is in some degree similar to the pattern in the sender (Kuhn & Beam, 1982).

Ineffective communications may suffer from misperception of meaning, but that misperception is superimposed on the initial intent to convey something to someone so that mutuality of understanding takes place. In communicating with others, miscommunication can occur because the sender and the receiver do not use words or concepts that convey the same meaning from one to the other or because the receiver's expectancy about the message is sufficiently different from what the sender intends so that confusion results. The language used in communication and the intention of the communication—its purposes—are both important if accurate communication is to take place.

In school psychology, communication with educators has suffered from the gradual development of bifurcated goals and exceptations that have taken place between school psychologists and those who use their services. School psychology has had two major foci: the improvement of mental health in the schools and school learning (Bardon, 1983a). Although both are important goals, they are not always identical or compatible, and, as been noted elsewhere, the match between the goals and methods of professional educators and of mental health specialists is not always harmonious (Cohen, 1975). There are differences between mental health specialists and educators in outcomes sought, terminology used, methods used, and sources of satisfaction along the way, leading to problems in communication and ultimately to problems in professional relationships.

The modern practice of school psychology has been influenced greatly by the dominant themes and techniques of other areas of psychology, especially clinical psychology (Bardon, 1976). The mental health movement has had a profound effect on language, methods, and purposes in school psychology. This movement has been a major force in the improvement of conditions for those suffering from mental illness and has served as impetus, at least since the 1940s, for the creation of a body of knowledge and techniques that has been helpful in alleviating human suffering. The movement has been strongly influenced by a medical model of human behavior and continues to reflect the values and purposes of the medical model.

Within recent years, research in educational, developmental, and social psychology in particular has led to application of research findings in schools and other settings in which people are educated. Interest in and application of approaches from behavioral and cognitive psychology have led to advances in practice far beyond that conceivable even 20 years ago. Yet, terminology adopted largely from medical and public health practices and theories has continued to be used to describe processes and activities that do not always fit well what is actually transpiring in attempts to help people deal with problems or to enhance different aspects of their lives.

Problems in Definition

Mental health is difficult to define. It is most often defined in terms that convey the message that good mental health is either the absence of mental illness or else a way of talking about and dealing with behaviors, attitudes, and values that can prevent people from becoming mentally ill or suffering from mental pathology. Terms related to mental health reflect this basic point of view. Primary prevention, a positive term, usually refers to the intention "to reduce the incidence, or number of new cases during a period of time, of psychological disorders of all kinds in a community" (Conyne, 1983, p. 331). It appears to be most closely related to community mental health theory which places strong emphasis on adopting a public health approach to the "widespread prevalence of mental illness" (Broskowski & Baker, 1974). In relation to schools, Lambert (1964) expressed well the difference posed by the two views of how school pupils can be helped: by strength through learning and by "preventing learning and behavior problems in children" (p. vii) through mental health approaches. Lack of attention to the subtle but important differences in approach and purposes between these two ways of helping has confused communications in school psychology and has added to the problem of how best to use the services of school psychologists.

The literature in professional psychology in its several fields has added to the confusion by continuing to mix terminology and purposes related to these two views: that maladjustment can be prevented by early action, and that people can be taught new things and can also be taught to do things well or better than they are now doing. The result of this inadvertent mixing is that the mental health view has often subsumed educational approaches as though they were merely subsidiary ways of accomplishing mental health goals rather than serving as distinctive approaches to solving particular kinds of problems.

For instance, White (1980) wrote about the importance of early education but titled his paper "Primary prevention: Beginning at the beginning," thereby confusing the desirability of early education in its own right with the purpose of keeping young children from failing later on. Henry (1981) described a program of parent training—an educational process—and called it "therapeutic intervention with children" (p. 4). Cognitive tutoring (teaching) is considered a mental health service when it is applied to children who do not learn easily (Chin, 1976). Albee (1982) wrote about primary prevention of mental and emotional disturbance through a variety of means, including the enhancement of self-esteem and social competence, these last two perhaps better indicative of educational processes and outcomes.

Does it make a difference whether one tries to enhance self-esteem and social competence of individuals in the present as part of the way education takes place or whether the purpose is to keep people from being maladjusted in later life? It is held here that there is considerable difference between these two approaches. One views the child as a learner entitled to the best education possible and defects as variables to be taken into account in teaching and learning. The other views the child at risk and approaches the situation as tentatively pathological unless "methods" are used to change the way the child or others think, feel, and act.

Ross (1981) expressed the dilemma and the most used current solution when he said: "The word *therapy*, in its traditional use, applies to only a limited number of . . . potential applications; helping a child who has difficulty learning to read, for example, was not considered therapy but an aspect of teaching. Yet one must ask whether helping a child acquire more appropriate ways of interacting with peers or siblings is not also a form of teaching, particularly when one uses psychological principles of learning" (p. 7). In writing particularly about behavior therapy, he went on to say "Indeed, behavior therapy is an unfortunate term to use for all of this and we adhere to it . . . only because the term has found such wide acceptance by now that it would be folly to write on this topic using a different, though more appropriate expression . . . well-established usage precludes the introduction of a more felicitous expression with which to label the application of psychology to the varied problems of children" (p. 7).

Differences Between Educational and Mental Health Approaches

Such nuances would not matter much if they did not produce differences in perceptions of individuals, purposes for offering assistance, methods used, and expected outcomes as a result of communications between school psychologists and others. With the advent of behavioral, especially cognitive behavioral, means of dealing with human learning, the lines between education/training and therapy/treatment have blurred even more. It is possible that, for a wide spectrum of school and child clinical psychologists, the behaviors in which they engage are educative more than therapeutic. Whether one seeks to engage in primary prevention or organizational change, secondary prevention or education and training may well differentiate the purpose to remedy and prevent maladaptation or to enhance human cognitive, social, and affective learning. These differences in purpose alter methods used in identification and assessment of problems, language used to describe behavior and events, and recommendations made for actions to be taken. The view of people as disturbed, maladjusted, or in danger of becoming so lead to prevention, cure, amelioration, and treatment. The view of people as educable and trainable leads to concern for how competence, achievement, and mastery are reached and to how efforts are best made to reach these goals.

There is concern that the public has not responded well to programs dealing with primary prevention, and reasons for resistance are sought (Broskowski & Baker, 1974). It is conceivable that the same or similar programs might be acceptable and implemented if they are reshaped as programs for specified educational purposes that are compatible with the goals and interest of those who will benefit from having them carried out.

Time and increased knowledge have led us to a point in our own professional development in which the distinctions between health/treatment/clinic or hospital and education/schooling/schools can usefully be made. In schools, it may be necessary and desirable for school psychologists more clearly to determine when a problem is an educational one and when it involves pathology and to adjust methodology and language to better fit the nature of the concern. Even more desirable may be the further development of the specialty so that its practitioners are seen as experts in the application of psychology to the solution of educational problems who also can assist with problems involving maladaptation and emotional disturbance through their efforts to help others educate (teach and learn) more efficiently. At present, school psychologists tend, instead, to be seen more as mental health specialists (read: child clinical psychologists) who know something about schools, especially that portion of schools that is concerned with special education.

Both the educational and mental health views are useful orientations to human services. One, the educational view, may prove to be a better way to decrease dissonance between school psychologists and educators by providing compatible communications and improved perception of usefulness.

CONCLUDING COMMENTS

This chapter has tried to make the point that the process of daily professional activity has an important bearing on whether school psychologists achieve their purposes; i.e., actually do what they intend to do when carrying out their various responsibilities. Although such a statement seems patently obvious, it must not be so because so little has been written about it in the literature on school psychology; yet, the literature on school psychology does suggest that school psychology is not always successfully practiced and its goals are not always reached. In this chapter I have sought to cover aspects of process that may not be given explicit attention elsewhere in this book. Some ways in which these processes occur and selected theories and issues related to them have been presented briefly.

The intricacies of interrelationships, whether professional or personal, are not the domain of school psychologists alone. But there is something special about these interrelationships because the school psychologist is given assignments in or about a particular setting called school. The interaction of that setting, the professional psychologist, and the client and or consultee provides a unique set of circumstances that are not exactly duplicated in other psychological service settings. In addition, school psychologists are in a position to be involved in a central way in schooling as defined in this chapter. School psychologists may choose to ignore or minimize that schooling is part of their work and, instead, concentrate on those aspects of help giving that stress other possible variables involved. One of the major alternative ways in which one can view the needs of those who seek assistance and their clients is from a mental health point of view. Within either of these two broad frameworks, differences may exist in how school psychologists further conceptualize what is taking place. Behavioral and ecological approaches, for instance, can be used in either a mental health or an education mode, but the overarching framework will take school psychologists in somewhat different directions. They will lead school psychologists to ask different questions, to look for and emphasize different behaviors, perhaps to use different assessment tools (Ysseldyke & Algozzine, 1983), and ultimately to use or suggest different interventions. Adopting a framework for psychologist service that fits the language and goals of educators may serve to improve communication and may also serve to make psychological services even more useful.

As the field of school psychology continues to gain in sophistication through advances in knowledge and techniques applicable to schooling and through achieving higher levels of education for practitioners, it is hoped that parallel attention will be given to how psychologists can influence the settings which they work and the people who work and learn in those settings. Doing so involves study of the processes through which psychological services are offered in educational environments and the personal and professional characteristics of the practitioners who engage in these processes. An especially good start has been made by analysis of decision-making processes in special education team work (Maher & Pfeiffer, 1983; Ysseldyke, Algozzine, & Mitchell, 1982). But, as always, much remains to be done before we know enough to use ourselves well as instruments to directly help educators benefit from that body of knowledge called psychology.

REFERENCES

Albee, G. W. (1982). Preventing psychopathology and promoting human potential. *American Psychologist, 37*, 1043–1050.

American Board of Professional Psychology (1976). *Report of the president* (April 15), Rochester, NY.

Antaki, C. (1982). A brief introduction to attribution and attributional themes. In C. Antaki & C. Brewin (Eds.), *Attributions and psychological change* (pp. 3–22). New York: Academic Press.

Argyris, C. (1976). Theories of action that inhibit individual learning. *American Psychologist, 31*, 638–654.

Bailey, S. (1976). *The purposes of education.* Bloomington, IN: Phi Delta Kappa.

Bandura, A. (1974). Behavior theory and the models of man. *American Psychologist, 29*, 859–869.

Bandura, A. (1977). Self-efficacy: Toward a unifying theory of behavioral change. *Psychological Review, 84*, 191–215.

Bandura, A. (1978). The self system in reciprocal determinism. *American Psychologist, 33*, 344–358.

Bandura, A. (1982). Self-efficacy mechanism in human agency. *American Psychologist, 37*, 122–147.

Bannister, D., & Salmon, P. (1975). A personal construct view of education. *New York University Education Quarterly, 4,* 29–31.
Barclay, J. R. (1981). *The missing link in education.* Unpublished manuscript, University of Kentucky, based on an invited address, April 1981, Division E. American Educational Research Association.
Bardon, J. I. (1976). The state of the art (and science) of school psychology. *American Psychologist, 31,* 8–18.
Bardon, J. I. (1982). The psychology of school psychology. In C. R. Reynolds & T. B. Gutkin (Eds.), *The handbook of school psychology* (pp. 3–13). New York: Wiley.
Bardon, J. I. (1983a). Psychology applied to education: A specialty in search of an identity. *American Psychologist, 38,* 185–196
Bardon, J. I. (1983b). Viewpoints on multidisciplinary teams in schools. *School Psychology Review, 12,* 186–189.
Bardon, J. I., & Bennett, V. C. (1974). *School psychology.* Englewood Cliffs, NJ: Prentice-Hall.
Bronfenbrenner, V. (1979). *The ecology of human development: Experiments by nature and design.* Cambridge, MA: Harvard University Press.
Broskowski, A., & Baker, F. (1974). Professional, organizational, and social barriers to primary prevention. *American Journal of Orthopsychiatry, 44,* 707–719.
Burke, J. P., Haworth, C. C., & Brantley, J. C. (1980). Scientific problem solving model: A resolution for professional controversies in school psychology. *Professional Psychology, 11,* 823–832.
Carroll, J. L., Harris, J. D., & Bretzing, B. H. (1979). A survey of psychologists serving secondary schools. *Professional Psychology, 10,* 766–770.
Chin, J. L. (1976). Cognitive tutoring as a mental health service for children with learning problems. *Professional Psychology, 7,* 518–523.
Cohen, R. (1975). Co-professional collaborative school consultation model. In C. A. Parker (Ed.), *Psychological consultation: Helping teachers meet special needs* (pp. 211–224). Minneapolis, MN: Council for Exceptional Children.
Coleman, J. S. (1972, February). The children have outgrown the schools. *Psychology Today,* pp. 72–75.
Conyne, R. K. (1983). Two critical issues in primary prevention: What it is and how to do it. *Personnel and Guidance Journal, 61,* 331–333.
Cotterell, J. L. (1982). Matching teaching to learners: A review of a decade of research. *Psychology in the Schools, 19,* 106–112.
Cremin, L. A. (1980). *American education: The national experience, 1783–1836.* New York: Harper & Row.
Cronbach, L. J. (1975). Beyond the two disciplines of scientific psychology. *American Psychologist, 30,* 116–125.
Cronbach, L. J., & Snow, R. E. (1977). *Aptitude and instructional methods: A handbook for research on interactions.* New York: Irvington.
Dappen, L. (Ed.). (1979). *Nine lives of a school psychologist in Nebraska.* (Available from Public Information Committee, Nebraska School Psychologists Association, Box 31020, Omaha, NB 68131.)
de Charm, R. (1972). Personal causation training in the schools. *Journal of Applied Social Psychology, 2,* 95–113.
Edinger, J. A. & Patterson, M. (1983). Nonverbal involvement and social control. *Psychological Bulletin, 93,* 30–56.
Eliott, S. N., Piersel, W. C., & Galvin, G. A. (1983). Psychological re-evaluations: A survey of practices and perceptions of school psychologists. *Journal of School Psychology, 21,* 99–105.
Estes, W. K. (1972). Reinforcement in human behavior. *American Scientist, 60,* 723–729.

Fullan, M., Miles, M. B., & Taylor, G. (1980). Organizational development in schools: The state of the art. *Review of Educational Research, 50*, 121–183.

Goldstein, A. P. (1980). Relationship-enhancement methods. In F. H. Kanfer & A. P. Goldstein (Eds.), *Helping people change.* (2nd ed., pp. 18–57). New York: Pergamon Press.

Goodlad, J. I. (1977, March). What goes on in our schools? *Educational Researcher*, pp. 3–6.

Grimley, L. K. (1978). Identity crisis in school psychology. *Journal of School Health, 48*, 538–540.

Gutkin, T. B., Singer, J. H., & Brown, R. (1980). Teacher reactions to school-based consultation services: A multivariate analysis. *Journal of School Psychology, 18*, 126–134.

Hare, A. P. (1976). *Handbook of small group research.* New York: Free Press.

Harŕe, R., & Secord, P. (1972). *The explanation of social behavior.* Oxford, England: Basil Blackwell.

Heider, F. (1958). *The psychology of interpersonal relations.* New York: Wiley.

Henry, S. A. (1981). Current dimensions of parent training. *School Psychology Review, 10*, 4–14.

Hessler, G. L., & Sosnowsky, W. P. (1979). A review of aptitude-treatment interaction studies with the handicapped. *Psychology in the Schools, 16*, 388–394.

Howell, K. (1983). *Inside special education.* Columbus, OH: Merrill.

Hunt, D. E. (1975). Person-environment interaction: A challenge found wanting before it was tried. *Review of Educational Research, 45*, 209–230.

Kuhn, A., & Beam, R. D. (1982). *The logic of organization.* San Francisco: Jossey-Bass.

Lacayo, N., & Sherwood, G. (1981). Daily activity of school psychologists: A national survey. *Psychology in the Schools, 18*, 184–190.

Lambert, N. M. (1964). Introduction. In N. M. Lambert (Ed.), *The protection and promotion of mental health in schools.* Bethesda, MD: U. S. Department of Health, Education, and Welfare.

Macdonald, J. B. (1975). The quality of everyday life in school. In J. B. Macdonald & E. Zaret (Eds.), *Schools in search of meaning* (pp. 78–94). Washington, DC: Association for Supervision and Curriculum.

Maher, C. A., & Pfeiffer, S. I. (Eds.). (1983). Multidisciplinary teams in the schools: Perspectives, practices, possibilities. (Special issue). *School Psychology Review, 12*(2).

Martin, R. (1978). Expert and referent power: A framework for understanding and maximizing consultation effectiveness. *Journal of School Psychology, 16*, 50–55.

Miller, A. (1981). Conceptual matching models and interactional research in education. *Review of Educational Research, 51*, 33–84.

Mischel, W. (1973). Toward a cognitive social learning reconceptualization of personality. *Psychological Review, 80*, 252–283.

New, P. K. (1968). An analysis of the concept of teamwork. *Community Mental Health Journal, 4*, 326–333.

Nichols, J. G. (1979). Quality and equality in intellectual development: The role of motivation in education. *American Psychologist, 34*, 1071–1084.

Nisbett, R. C., & Valins, S. (1971). *Perceiving the causes of one's own behavior.* Morristown, NJ: General Learning Press.

Palmer, D. J. (1979). Regular classroom teachers' attributions and instructional prescriptions for handicapped and nonhandicapped pupils. *Journal of Special Education, 13*, 325–337.

Peterson, D. R., & Bry, B. H. (1980). Dimensions of perceived competence in professional psychology. *Professional Psychology, 11*, 965–971.

Phillips, B. N. (1982). Reading and evaluating research in school psychology. In C. R. Reynolds & T. B. Gutkin (Eds.), *The handbook of school psychology* (pp. 24–47). New York: Wiley.

Ramage, J. C. (1979). National survey of school psychologists. Update. *School Psychology Digest, 10*, 153–162.

Raven, J. (1983). The relationship between educational institutions and society with particular reference to the role of assessment. *International Review of Applied Psychology, 32*, 249–274.

Reschly, D. J., & Lamprecht, M. J. (1979). Expectancy effects of labels: Fact or artifact? *Exceptional Children, 46*, 55–58.

Rogers, C. (1982). *A social psychology of schooling: The expectancy process.* London: Routledge & Kegan Paul.

Rogers, E. M., & Rogers, R. A. (1976). *Communication in organizations.* New York: Free Press.

Rosenthal, R., & Jacobson, L. (1968). *Pygmalion in the classroom: Teacher expectation and pupils' intellectual development.* New York: Holt, Rinehart & Winston.

Ross, A. O. (1981). *Child behavior therapy: Principles, procedures and empirical bases.* New York: Wiley.

Sarason, S. B. (1983). *Schooling in America: Scapegoat and salvation.* New York: Free Press.

Schowengerdt, R. V., Fine, M. J., & Poggio, J. P. (1976). An examination of some bases of teacher satisfaction with school psychological services. *Psychology in the Schools, 13*, 269–275.

Senft, L. B., & Snider, B. (1980). Elementary school principals assess services of school psychologists nationwide. *Journal of School Psychology, 18*, 276–282.

Smith, K. K. (1982). Philosophical problems in thinking about organizational change. In P. S. Goodman & Associates, *Change in organizations* (pp. 316–374). San Francisco: Jossey-Bass.

Stephens, J. M. (1967). *The process of education: A psychological examination.* New York: Holt, Rinehart & Winston.

Truax, C. B., & Carkhuff, R. R. (1967). *Toward effective counseling and psychotherapy: Training and practice.* Chicago: Aldine.

Weick, K. E. (1982). Management of organizational change among loosely coupled elements. In P. S. Goodman & Associates, *Change in organizations* (pp. 375–408). San Francisco: Jossey-Bass.

Weiner, B., Graham, S., Taylor, S. E., & Meyer, W. V. (1983). Social cognition in the classroom. *Educational Psychologist, 18*, 109–124.

Weiner, B., (1980). The role of affect in rational (attributional) approaches to human motivation. *Educational Researcher*, July–August, 4–11.

Weiner, B. (1972). *Theories of motivation: From mechanism to cognition.* Chicago: Markham.

Weiner, B. (1976). Attribution theory, achievement motivation, and the educational process. *Review of Educational Research, 42*, 201–215.

Welfel, E. R. (1982). The development of reflective judgment: Implications for career counseling of college students. *Personnel and Guidance Journal, 61*, 17–21.

White, B. L. (1980). Primary prevention: Beginning at the beginning. *Personnel and Guidance Journal, 58*, 338–343.

White, M. A., & Duker, J. (1973). *Education: A conceptual and empirical approach.* New York: Holt, Rinehart & Winston.

Ysseldyke, J. E., & Algozzine, B. (1982). *Critical issues in special education.* Boston: Houghton Mifflin.

Ysseldyke, J. E., Algozzine, B., & Mitchell, J. (1982). Special education team decision making: An analysis of current practice. *Personnel and Guidance Journal, 60*, 308–313.

Ysseldyke, J. E., & Foster, G. G. (1978). Bias in teachers' observations of emotional disturbed and learning disabled children. *Exceptional Children, 45*, 613–615.

Ysseldyke, J. E., & Algozzine, B. (1983). On making psychoeducational decisions. *Journal of Psychoeducational Assessment, 1*, 187–195.

Zander, A. (1982). *Making groups effective.* San Francisco: Jossey-Bass.

4 Disentangling the Complexities of Clientage

Krista J. Stewart
Tulane University

The question of clientage is an issue that has long been raised in school psychology circles and has been a topic of much debate. At the Thayer Conference the point was made that the "school psychologist must often decide whether or not his first obligation is to an individual child or to the school as an organization" (Cutts, 1955, p. 87). Twenty-five years later, Trachtman (1981), in a presentation at the Springhill Symposium on the Future of Psychology in the Schools, acknowledged that still "our profession never has satisfactorily defined its client" (p. 145).

Perhaps the word *client* itself contributes to the lack of consensus about clientage in school psychology. *Webster's New Collegiate Dictionary* (1975) defines "client" either as "a person under protection of another . . . a person who engages the professional advice or services of another . . . [or] a person served by or utilizing the services of a social agency" (p. 208). Even if consideration of clientage were to be centered around just these simple dictionary definitions, one can readily see how much confusion might arise.

Traditionally, when the issue of clientage has been considered in school psychology, the question has had emotional overtones due to the legal, ethical, and advocacy components tied to the topic. This chapter attempts, however, to address the question of clientage from a broader perspective. Initial portions of the chapter consider the question of clientage from a pragmatic viewpoint, evaluating the impact of model of human behavior adopted by a psychologist, focus of intervention, service delivery role, caseload, training, and structure of the system within which a psychologist works. Later portions of the chapter then address and review legal and ethical questions that have been raised relating to the clientage issue.

The discussion in this chapter is geared primarily to the question of clientage as it exists for those individuals practicing as school psychologists in school settings, by far the most common employment site for the school psychologist (Ramage, 1979). The reason for focusing on this setting is, as is seen later, that the organizational structure has specific impact on clientage. As Fagan (1980) has suggested, "it is impractical to have clientage specified outside the context of the problem and the setting" (p. 1).

The intent of this chapter is not to provide a definitive answer to the question of "Who is the school psychologist's client?" Many individuals in the past have addressed this question with no clear consensus being reached. Rather, the goal is to delineate various issues that need to be considered when the question of clientage is being addressed.

CLIENTAGE FROM A PRAGMATIC VIEWPOINT

One way to conceptualize clientage is to consider the client to be the individual or individuals receiving or benefiting from the services of the school psychologist. In the literature on clientage, those most typically considered clients of the school psychologist are the child or groups of children, parents, and the school (i.e., teachers, administrators, or the school organization). These groups constitute various "levels" of clientage. In any given case, the service efforts of the psychologist may be focused at one particular level (e.g., on the teacher), but a client at another level (e.g., the child) may benefit collaterally. Thus, the school psychologist might be thought of as simultaneously serving clients at more than one level, with the individual on whom the service is most directly focused being the primary client and the less direct recipient of the service being the secondary client. The ensuing discussion of factors influencing clientage adopts this general conceptualization.

Client as Determined by the Psychologist's Model of Human Behavior

In the first chapter in this book, Elliott and Witt have described four models of human behavior used by psychologists: the medical model, the behavioral model, the ecological model, and the reciprocal determinism model. How a school psychologist views human behavior in general and children's school problems more specifically will depend upon the model of behavior the psychologist primarily employs. In turn, the model of behavior adopted will at least in part determine who the school psychologist considers the client.

As is noted in previous chapters, the medical model assumes that a negative deviation in behavior is a reflection of some type of disorder within the individual and that the deviation can only be changed through some type of curative process

(Reger, 1972). The clientage of the school psychologist operating under this model is likely to be limited to children referred for specific problems by teachers, parents, or administrators. The psychologist's task then becomes one of "examining" the child in order to determine what internal disorder is causing the problem (e.g., a learning disability, a behavioral disorder, mental retardation) and in turn to determine some way to cure the problem. Environmental variables are essentially disregarded in this model. Because teachers, other children in the class, or parents are not seen as involved in or contributing to the problem, to that extent they would also not be considered clients under this model.

The behavioral and ecological models, however, take into consideration the influence factors outside the child have on behavior. The psychologist operating under either of these models does not assume that a child's problems are a result of some "illness" within the child but rather that the behavior is a function of the interaction between the child and the environment (Baker, 1965; Skinner, 1953). The reciprocal determinism model (Bandura, 1977) in addition takes into consideration an individual's cognitions and other internal events. Under this model, behavior is considered a function of the reciprocal interaction between these internal events, behavior, and the environment.

For psychologists who consider human behavior at least partially a function of environment, as would be the case for those employing these last three models, clientage would be conceptualized more broadly than under the medical model. Even if a particular child were referred by the teacher as having a problem, the psychologist would not assume that the evaluation of the problem would involve only the individual child. Rather the assessment would also take into account potentially influential factors in the child's environment, for example, the classroom setting, other students in the class, parents, and even the referring teacher. To the extent other individuals in the child's environment are involved in the behavior of concern, they too might appropriately be considered clients of the psychologist.

In some cases, the concern to the teacher is not an individual child but rather a situation in the classroom. Psychologists operating under behavioral, ecological, or reciprocal determinism models might in these instances be interested in evaluating the behavior of the various individuals in the classroom and other factors in the environment as well as the complex interactions occurring among the individuals and the environment. In such a case, the "classroom" might be considered to be the client of the psychologist.

Client as Determined by Focus of Intervention

Another important factor in determining the school psychologist's client is the focus of the intervention. Public Law 94–142 (Education for All Handicapped Children Act, 1975) mandates that certain services be provided for children having various handicapping conditions. No equivalent federal legislation exists, however, requiring comparable services for children who might have problems but who are not specifically classified as handicapped. Emphasis on the handicapped as opposed to other groups is further reflected by the fact that there is no federal requirement of services to the gifted; rather, determination to offer services to that group is made by each state.

Whether or not nonhandicapped children receive services from the school psychologist is left up to the discretion of the school. When caseloads are high, chances are that the greatest attention will be given to children with the most severe problems. In a national survey of school psychologists, the majority of respondents indicated that as a result of PL 94-142, they were spending increased time with the handicapped and decreased time with the nonhandicapped for all professional activities (Goldwasser, Meyers, Christenson, & Graden, 1983).

If the recipient of services is considered the client, then to some extent the law dictates that the handicapped are the school psychologist's primary clients. A more expanded conceptualization of clientage as a function of level of intervention, however, has been proposed by Clarizio (1979). He has suggested that in order for a mental health program to be comprehensive, three levels of intervention are necessary: primary, secondary, and tertiary prevention. This view of intervention is based on approaches to "prevention" that have been described by Cowen and Zax (1967). Although these discussions of intervention and prevention focus primarily on mental health services, academic interventions might be conceptualized in a similar manner.

Primary prevention targets the population in general, with the goal being to improve the functioning of the entire population. Such a stance aims at giving individuals a means of dealing with problems they are likely to encounter before the problem occurs. Examples of primary prevention intervention that might be provided by a school psychologist include teaching communication skills, furnishing information on the effects of drug and alcohol abuse, and helping teachers in knowing how to teach their students more effective study strategies.

In secondary prevention, the focus is on early identification of those children who are already having problems, but for whom the problems have not yet become seriously debilitating. The goal is to provide intervention aimed at reducing the problem before it becomes more severe, the assumption being the problem is highly amenable to change. Examples of secondary prevention interventions that might be offered by the school psychologist include short-term counseling for a child experiencing an emotional crisis or assisting a regular education teacher in setting up an individualized program for a child having a reading problem.

The focus of tertiary prevention is on providing services to children who have moderate to severe learning or emotional problems. The goal of this type of intervention is to remediate the problem so the child will be able to function at his or her optimal level. The school psychologist's role in tertiary prevention could include participating in the assessment process to identify a child's need for special education, consulting with special or regular education teachers, or providing counseling or direct treatment to the child.

The preventive level at which a school psychologist functions will determine the scope of his or her clientage. For the school psychologist operating at the level of primary prevention, all children would be considered the psychologist's client. If the psychologist functions at a level of secondary prevention, clients would be limited to those children already having at least some problems. Tertiary prevention would further constrain clientage to only those children with more serious problems. The level at which the psychologist functions, however, may not be self-determined but rather dictated by the constraints of the system in which the psychologist is employed. Moreover, PL 94–142, in particular, would seemingly serve to perpetuate tertiary prevention as the primary role for the school psychologist.

Client as Determined by Service Delivery Roles

Another factor that might be considered to have implications for the question of clientage is the service delivery role assumed by school psychologists. Monroe (1979) has outlined five primary roles for the school psychologist on a continuum of directness of service to the child from most to least: (a) counseling/therapy, (b) psychoeducational assessment, (c) consultative child study, (d) inservice, and (e) research. If the recipient of the service is presumed to have implications for clientage, then directness of influence would be an important consideration.

Therapy and Assessment

The most direct forms of service are counseling/therapy and psychoeducational assessment. Counseling services are at the furthest extreme on the directness continuum and are those provided by the psychologist directly to the child or to a small group of children. The assessment role, on the other hand, would be considered somewhat less direct. Although the psychologist may work directly with the child during assessment, activities also would typically involve gathering information from various sources in the environment. Nonetheless, because counseling and assessment services are the services delivered most directly to the child, considering the child as the primary client when the psychologist is functioning in either of these roles would seem logical.

Other services described by Monroe and commonly provided by school psychologists are less direct with respect to the child. Thus, whether or not the child should be considered the client, or at least the primary client, is more debatable for the service roles of consultation, inservice, and research.

Consultation

A role that has become increasingly popular with school psychologists over the years is that of consultation (Ramage, 1979). Consultation is an indirect service in that it is assumed ultimately to benefit the client (usually the child) but is delivered directly to the consultee (usually the teacher or parent). Consultation is a collaborative relationship that focuses on improving the ability of the consultee (i.e., the agent of change) to work with the client.

Several theoretical models of consultation have emerged, each having its own implications for clientage. Because consultation models are described in detail elsewhere in the book, the focus here is limited to addressing how each model relates to the question of clientage. The models that are discussed include (a) mental health consultation, (b) behavioral consultation, (c) process consultation, and (d) advocacy consultation.

Mental Health Consultation. Mental health consultation was first described by Caplan (1970) and has been made more applicable to the school setting by Meyers (1973). The component unique to this model of consultation is what Caplan (1970) has termed "consultee-centered case consultation" and Meyers (1973) has called "Level III" or "direct service to the teacher." Although the focus in consultee-centered case consultation is primarily on the teacher, the ultimate goal is to provide better service to the child. In this type of consultation, the psychologist would use an interview procedure with the teacher to assess whether or not the referral problem is related to any of the following: lack of understanding, lack of skill, lack of self-confidence, or lack of objectivity (Caplan, 1970). The consultant would then intervene directly with the teacher using an intervention appropriate to the problem. Based strictly on theory, the child in this case is the client; but in light of the direct service being provided to the teacher, one might argue for conceptualizing two levels of clientage as being involved.

Behavioral Consultation. As has been described by Bergan (1977) and others (Bergan & Tombari, 1975; Keller, 1981), behavioral consultation typically involves the psychologist-consultant consulting with a teacher-consultee regarding a child-client about whom the teacher has concerns. The focus of the consultation process is to identify and analyze the problem, to intervene, and subsequently to evaluate the problem to see if change has occurred. This process involves a collaborative effort between the teacher and the psychologist. The ultimate beneficiary of the service is again considered to be the child, even though as a result of the consultation the teacher may show, for example, improved classroom management skills.

One contradiction emerges, however, when the child is conceptualized as the client of behavioral consultation: The child may have little or no input into the process. Typically, the teacher is the one to decide when a problem exists, to define the problem, to select the intervention to be employed, and to decide when the problem situation has improved to the extent that it no longer needs special attention. In some cases, however, change in the child's behavior may not even occur; rather, the only change may be in the teacher's attitudes and perceptions.

The question that arises is whether success in behavioral consultation is best defined as when the child's behavior actually changes to the desired level or when the teacher no longer perceives a problem. The answer to this question would seem, in turn, to have implications for clientage. If, in fact, actual changes in the child's behavior are of secondary importance compared to the teacher's attitudes and perceptions, the teacher might more appropriately be considered the primary client.

In addition, because consultation is in theory a voluntary process, the teacher has the prerogative to withdraw from the process at any point, regardless of whether or not an improvement has occurred. Such a response is not to be unexpected of teachers who may find the consultation process more time consuming than they had suspected it would be (Abidin, 1975). Thus in this case, the legitimacy of considering the child the primary client becomes even more questionable.

Another point to consider when thinking about clientage in behavioral consultation is that teachers sometimes may be unrealistic in defining what would be considered desirable behaviors for the child-client. Conoley and Conoley (1982) have warned the behavioral consultant to beware of "dead man targets" (e.g., sitting still, being quiet, and stopping disruption) that the teacher may see as desirable but that would be unrealistic to expect of the child-client.

The matter, moreover, becomes an ethical dilemma when a teacher's stated behavior goal is not in the child's best interest (Fanibanda, 1976). Consider the following example: A teacher, known for being non-nurturant, feels a particular child seeks too much attention. The child, in fact, comes from an environment in which neglect except for punishment is the norm. The teacher's goal is to eliminate the child's need for attention. This situation is particularly sensitive, because the teacher might withdraw from consultation if he or she feels the expected service is not being provided. The approach to be taken with the child-client would then be totally left up to the discretion of the disappointed teacher. A case such as the one described would require skill and diplomacy on the part of the psychologist and possibly a shift from a behavioral consultation to a consultee-centered mental health consultation approach in order to deal with the teacher's apparent lack of objectivity.

On the other hand, a psychologist, frustrated because of a difference in philosophy with a teacher, may also wish to withdraw from the consultation relationship. Fanibanda (1975) maintains that "a consultant who knowingly withdraws his services because of a conflict of philosophies with the consultee is abdicating his responsibility to the [client] society" (p. 549).

Finally, the question might be raised as to how the parents fit into the question of clientage as it relates to behavioral consultation. Simpson and Poplin (1981), for example, have discussed the benefit of including parents in behavioral management programs and have stressed the importance of coordination of intervention efforts. Presumably, if parents are considered clients of the school psychologist, they would be included in the behavioral intervention efforts. The parents' rights and their role in their child's educational program is discussed in detail in a later section of this chapter.

Process Consultation. A third model of consultation is that of process consultation. As described by Schmuck (1976), "process consultation aims at improving the interpersonal and group procedures used by administrators, teachers, students, and parents to reach their educational objectives" (p. 626). The focus is primarily on group and interpersonal interactions, particularly as might be related to the planning or decision-making process. As is true of the other consultation models, the ultimate client in process consultation is assumed to be the child, even though the focus might be on factors such as communication among staff members.

Process consultation is not commonly used by psychologists working in schools (Lennox, Flanagan, & Meyers, 1979). Moreover, just what impact process consultation actually has on the behavior of the child is unclear and is in need of empirical investigation. Again, the primary client in this type of consultation might most appropriately be considered the most direct recipient of the service, that is, the teachers and educational staff rather than the child.

Advocacy Consultation. The last model of consultation to be addressed is that of advocacy consultation as described by Conoley and Conoley (1982). There has been debate whether or not advocacy should indeed be considered a form of consultation. Because of the political nature of advocacy, the advocate consultant would typically ally himself or herself with one group, usually the underpowered group, in fighting another group. Thus, while working to aid one faction, the consultant would necessarily be putting himself or herself at odds with the opposing group.

Conoley and Conoley (1982) believe all consultants are advocate consultants in that they act to facilitate consultees' goals. A problem arises, however, when the goals of the school psychologist's client at various levels are at odds. An example given by Conoley and Conoley is one of a school system that systematically withholds information on due process procedures from the parents of handicapped children. The school system (i.e, the direct employer of the psychologist) and the parents are indeed both clients of the school psychologist. In such situations school psychologists face the question of to whom they owe their primary allegiance. Again, the difficult clientage question emerges.

A number of individuals have attempted to address the issue of the consultant as an advocate. Chesler, Bryant, and Crowfoot's (1976) conception of school consultation impels the consultant to attend to patterns of conflict both in schools and in society and to make positive use of this conflict for change. They maintain that the school consultant has the responsibility of making hidden injustices visible in order to keep from contributing to social injustice. Gallessich (1974) has proposed that the client for the advocate consultant is the "community," not the established institution. According to Gallessich, consultants acting in such a role would provide direct services to their clients as educators and catalysts and would serve their clients indirectly by acting as their advocates with representatives from the school. Mearig (1974) has suggested that support of the parents, in particular, is an important responsibility of school psychologists functioning in an advocacy role and follows naturally when the psychologist has a clear primary allegiance to the child rather than to the school as an institution. She warns, however, that a psychologist acting as a consultant must be prepared to function without full sanction of the school organization and to deal with any resulting repercussions. Later in this chapter discussion focuses more specifically on the various allegiances of the school psychologist.

Inservice

Another role for school psychologists (Monroe, 1979) is that of inservice training. Schools are required by law (Education for All Handicapped Children Act, 1975) to provide inservice training for teachers. Often a school psychologist is called upon to provide inservice training on topics such as behavior management in the classroom, children's learning problems, and child development. As inservice trainers, school psychologists typically take on more of an expert and less of a collaborative role, thus differentiating this process from consultation. Like consultation, however, the assumption is that improvement of a teacher's skills will ultimately benefit the child. Again two levels of clientage might be assumed, with the teacher being the primary and the child being the secondary client. If, however, clientage is in part considered a function of who desires the service, in the case of inservice training, the client might more accurately be considered the school administrators who organize inservice programs. Two studies (Ford & Migles, 1979; Stewart-Lester, 1981b) have indicated that teachers place less value on the inservice training role for school psychologists than on other roles.

Research

The last role described by Monroe (1979) is that of researcher. Survey data suggest that more school psychologists would like to engage in research than actually do (Ramage, 1979). For school psychologists in applied settings, time demands in the form of assessment, counseling, consultation, and inservice training often result in research taking a low priority. A further obstacle is that those who evaluate the school psychologist (i.e., administrators and teachers) in terms of the number of client contacts made may not see the relevance of research (Stewart, 1984). In other words, school personnel may not see research as providing a service to the client, a perception that may in part be a function of the indirectness of the service. In order for the school psychologist to convince school personnel of the value of systematic research in the school, a creative approach to carrying out research projects is likely to be necessary (Stewart, 1984). Once the schools are able, however, to see the usefulness of research information (i.e., how the clients of the school psychologist are actually benefiting), then such a role is more likely to be accepted and even encouraged.

As can be seen from this discussion, the role in which a psychologist functions and in turn the type of service offered will at least to some extent determine clientage. In general, as the directness of service decreases, the scope of the psychologist's clientage expands. As a result of the dictates of his or her particular job, however, the school psychologist may have little choice in what roles are actually assumed.

Client as Determined by Caseload

One factor closely tied to the focus of intervention and the service delivery role in determining the school psychologist's client is that of caseload. The types of services the school psychologist might provide and in turn who the school psychologist's client would be depend at least in part on the psychologist's caseload. Psychologist to pupil ratios have been reported to range from 1:500 or less (7% of those reporting) to 1:9000 or more (5% of those reporting) with a majority reporting a ratio between 1:2000 to 1:4000 (Ramage, 1979). However, 90% of the psychologists believed the ratio should be no more than 1:2000, the same ratio that is recommended in the "Specialty Guidelines for the Delivery of Services by School Psychologists" (American Psychological Association, 1981). From her 1976 survey, Ramage (1979) concluded that the "role and function a school psychologist is trained for and is expected to carry out is made more difficult due to high ratios of students to school psychologists" (p. 160).

When the school psychologist has a large caseload, services rendered may necessarily be restricted to those required by law (cf. Education for All Handicapped Children Act, 1975). Under such circumstances, clientage would be confined primarily to those children suspected of having handicapping conditions, interventions would be mainly at a tertiary level, and the services provided would be limited largely to assessment. When faced with large caseloads, the psychologist who wants to expand his or her clientage must be prepared either to engage in some tough negotiations with school administrators for smaller caseloads or to employ creative strategies for expanding services (Stewart & Medway, 1978). One general strategy that has been suggested is to attempt to reduce the amount of what might be considered unnecessary assessment (i.e., those assessments not leading to special class placements) through the use of some type of pre-assessment screening (Grubb, Petty, & Flynn, 1976; Lambert, Sandoval, & Corder, 1975; Stewart-Lester, 1981a). Only when the psychologist is able to find a means for reducing time spent in testing for special education placement can expanded services be provided to a wider range of clients.

Clientage as Determined by Training

Another important factor in determining clientage is the psychologist's training and expertise in various areas of service. This matter is addressed in the "National Association of School Psychologists Principles for Professional Ethics" (National Association of School Psychologists [NASP], 1979), the "Ethical Principles of Psychologists" (American Psychological Association, 1981), and the "Specialty Guidelines for the Delivery of Services by School Psychologists" (APA, 1981).

According to the NASP Principles, "the most basic ethical principle is that of the responsibility of a professional person to perform only those services for which that person has acquired a recognized level of competency" (p. 90). Similarly, the APA Ethical Principles indicate that psychologists "only provide services and only use techniques for which they are qualified by training and experience" (p. 634). Finally, the APA Specialty Guidelines state that "school psychologists limit their practice to their demonstrated areas of professional competence" (p. 674). In cases where psychologists find it necessary to extend services beyond their usual range of practice, they are expected to "obtain pertinent training or appropriate professional supervision" (p. 674). A need for such additional training might be a function of a change in the psychologist's theoretical orientation, techniques used, client's age group, or types of problems addressed.

In a previous section, various types of services that might be offered by the school psychologist and their implications for clientage were discussed. The NASP Principles, APA Ethical Principles, and APA Specialty Guidelines, however, would serve to restrict services provided only to those areas for which the school psychologist has had specific training. Accordingly, clientage would be defined by the type of service the psychologist is competent to provide.

Client as Determined by Organizational Factors

In order to understand clientage in school psychology, consideration must also be given to the structure of the organization in which the psychologist is working and the impact that structure has on the relationships of the client to the professionals within that organization. A model to describe how certain structural variables in an organization affect the professional-client relationship has been developed by May (1976).

May's Model of Clientage

Structural Variables May has identified three structural variables relevant to the professional-client relationship. The first of these is whether professionals are *salaried* or *receive a fee* for their services. An example of a salaried professional would be a professional employed full-time by an agency to deliver services. A private practitioner would be an example of a professional working for a fee. The second structural variable is whether services are provided for clients who are *employers* or *consumers*. An example of an employer client is a patient of a private physician. In the case of a consumer client, an administrative agency, not the client, employs the professional. The other structural variable identified by May is whether clients are *organized* (e.g., a private organization hiring a professional to perform a service), or *unorganized* (e.g., a single client contracting with an independent professional).

Professional-Client Relationship Variables. May has also identified three properties of the professional-client relationship that are important in influencing the nature of that relationship. The first of these is the *extent to which colleagues supervise a professional's performance*. May proposes that "professionals who interact frequently with colleagues usually prefer their favor to the favor of their clients with the consequence that they reduce their responsiveness to clients" (p. 11).

The second property identified is the *extent to which clients exercise market controls over the professional*. According to May's model, "clients have more control over professionals who perform services for a fee than over salaried professionals" (p. 12); "employer clients have more control over salaried professionals than consumer clients do" (p. 13); "employer clients exercise less market control over professionals when the supply of professionals is smaller than the demand for their services" (p. 14); and "even when they do not pay for services directly, consuming clients may exercise market control over professionals if the supervising agency gives them a say about whom is hired and how their work is evaluated" (p. 14).

The third property identified is the *extent to which an agency exercises administrative* (hierarchical) *control over the professional-client relationship*. May argues that "when professionals have autonomy, their responsiveness to clients is a function of the extent to which they share expectations with clients; and when they lack autonomy, it is a function of the extent to which bureaucrats share expectations with the clients" (p. 16).

May's Model Applied to Psychologists in Schools

Structural Variables. May's model focuses on organizational structure and professional-client relationships in general but can be applied specifically to schools and school psychologists (cf. Fagan, 1980). In a school setting, the typical structure as defined by May's model is that the school psychologist is a full-time employee in a salaried professional position as opposed to a professional working for a fee. An example of the latter might be a private consultant who is contracted by the school to provide specific services. Second, in the case of the school psychologist practicing in the schools, services are provided primarily to clients who are consumers (i.e., children, parents, and teachers) and only to a lesser extent to the direct employer (i.e., the school administration). A school psychologist in private practice would be an example, although less common, of a school psychologist who would provide services directly to an employer client. Finally, in the school setting, clients would most typically be considered unorganized (i.e., usually individual children, parents, or teachers) rather than organized groups.

Professional-Client Relationship Variables. In a situation where the structure is such that salaried professionals are employed by an agency (i.e., a school system) and provide services to unorganized consumer clients (i.e, parents, children, teachers), May's model predicts certain characteristics in the relationships to emerge. In school systems where several school psychologists are employed, collegial control would be expected to be high resulting in a tendency for professionals to prefer the favor of their colleagues. In turn, the professionals' responsiveness to their clients would be expected to be reduced. May notes, however, that some professionals, even though they are placed in bureaucratic settings, maintain their professional preference for the respect of their clients. Presumably, such would typically be the case for school psychologists in schools, individuals often having at least some orientation toward advocacy. In a school system where only one school psychologist is employed, the professional would be expected to prefer the favor of his or her clients over more distant colleagues.

May's model also predicts the extent to which clients exercise market controls over professionals. Within the structure of the school organization, market control by the unorganized consumer would be expected to be low in that the decision to purchase the services of the school psychologist and the particular professional to be selected is not made by the consumer client. The consumer client can exercise indirect control by deciding whether or not to make use of the services of the professional within the system. In the case of the school psychologist, however, only if consumers (i.e., parents or teachers) were to make an organized effort to boycott the school psychologist would the dissatisfaction of the consumer be noticeable. Dissatisfaction of individual consumer clients with the services of the psychologist is likely to have little impact unless formal charges are made against the psychologist on legal or ethical grounds.

According to the model, client control over the professional is greatest in the case where the client is the employer. Because the typical school psychologist is employed (i.e., hired, paid, and fired) by the school administration, he or she would be expected to feel pressure to meet the employer's demands, possibly ignoring the consequences his or her actions might have on consumer clients. A common example of such pressure might be the school administrator who requires the school psychologist to perform an inordinant number of evaluations per week even though the consumer client might best be served by an increase in consultation or intervention services.

Finally, May's model predicts the extent to which the agency (i.e., the school) exercises control over the professional-client relationship based on the amount of autonomy given to the professional by the agency. The school psychologist who is given a fair degree of autonomy and who operates from an advocacy stance would be expected to place greater priority on meeting the client's needs. If, on the other hand, the system allows the psychologist little autonomy and dictates to the psychologist how he or she will function, then whether or not the psychologist will provide services that best meet the needs of the client would be expected to depend upon whether the goals for service held by the school administrators are similar to those held by the client. Differences in expectations resulting in a seeming insensitivity to clients might occur in a situation where a school administration would insist upon the provision of a certain amount of assessment services when parents would prefer family counseling or counseling for their children.

May's model is useful in helping to provide some understanding of how the structural variables within the organization interact with properties of the professional-client relationship resulting in certain characteristic patterns. What has not been mentioned to this point is that even though the clients of the school psychologist are not typically the direct employer of the school psychologist, they are indeed an indirect employer; at least, that is true for parents who pay taxes, which in turn support the schools and pay the salaries of the psychologists. As one can see, however, as a result of various factors mentioned, parent clients may at best have only very little indirect control over the psychologists' services.

Clients as Consumers

The issue of providing services that best meet the needs of the clients is a practical as well as an ethical one. Humes (1974) has reported finding consumers more interested in outcomes, whereas the school psychologists were more process-oriented. He emphasized that to increase the acceptance of service goals, broad participation of the consumer of the psychological services in the formulation of the goals is essential. Fishman and Neigher (1982) have warned that if the profession of psychology is not proactive in addressing the question of what the public is receiving for their investment, then others less knowledgeable about psychology and less sympathetic to its goals will do so.

LEGAL AND ETHICAL ISSUES RELATING TO CLIENTAGE

Client as Determined by Legal Mandates

According to Overcast and Sales (1982), "it would be fair to assert that 50 years ago students in public schools were recognized as having few, if any, legal rights" (p. 1075). Even parents' power over their children's education historically has been limited. Although the original English concept of *in loco parentis* assumed parental power given to tutors could be taken away by parents (Hyman, 1983), schools in the first part of this century standing *in loco parentis* in relationship with the child were given almost total control over the education and socialization of the child (Overcast & Sales, 1982). Legal mandates of the past decade, however, have served to shift some of this power away from the schools. In turn, these laws have implications for how school psychologists relate to their clients.

In California in 1959, the right of parents to inspect school records became a formal issue (Trachtman, 1972). In subsequent years numerous states dealt with this matter. A few leaders in the area of school psychology began to advocate parents' access to their children's school records (Hyman & Schreiber, 1975; Trachtman, 1972). Finally in 1976, major federal legislation regulating access to educational records was passed. The Family Educational Rights and Privacy Act (FERPA, 1976), more commonly referred to as the Buckley Amendment, gave parents access to their children's educational records, enabled them to challenge records they felt might be inaccurate, and required their written consent before the records could be given to a third party. Included as part of the child's educational records open to parents' inspection were clearly psychological reports and potentially individual test protocols (Reynolds, Gutkin, Elliott, & Witt, 1984).

Kicklighter (1983) has suggested that "school psychologists were the major beneficiaries of the era of secrecy when their reports were treated as if their contents were unquestionable and their conclusions unassailable" (p. 119). He goes on to say that as a result of the Buckley amendment, however, everyone has benefited: "children were guaranteed more comprehensive consideration, parents more meaningful participation in their children's educational programs, schools more stringent and objective decision-making processes, and school psychologists more thoughtful and realistic considerations of their work and judgment" (pp. 119–120). In essence, the Buckley Amendment has resulted in school psychologists becoming more accountable to their clients, particularly parents, for the quality and types of services provided.

Another law that has had implications for the question of clientage is PL 94–142, the Education for All Handicapped Children Act of 1975. Of particular relevance to the matter of clientage for the school psychologist is the portion of the law describing procedural safeguards that must be provided. The "Implementation of Part B of the Education of the Handicapped Act" (1977) requires that parental consent be obtained before an evaluation can be conducted and before initial placement can be made in a program providing special education and related services. If the parent refuses to give consent for evaluation, the public agency (i.e., the school) may take the case to a due process hearing or follow state-defined procedures in order to determine if the child can be evaluated or placed without the parental consent. As Pryzwansky and Bersoff (1978) point out:

> By requiring consent, allowing the school to challenge the refusal to consent, and developing a forum in which both sides will be heard by a neutral adjudicator, the regulations serve the interests at stake of all parties—parents, whose constitutional rights to direct their child's upbringing is protected; the school, which is carrying out its statutory duty to provide an appropriate education for handicapped children; and most importantly, the children whose very future may be imperiled or enhanced by the actions of the adults around them. (p. 277)

Perhaps the greatest significance of the consent requirement, however, is for the parents who traditionally had been given little control over their children's education. In terms of how the consent requirement impacts the school psychologist's clientage, the psychologist is put in a position in which he or she must take into consideration the parent-client's concerns.

Not only does PL 94–142 (Education of Handicapped Children, 1977) require that consent be sought from parents but that "the parent has been fully informed of all information relevant to the activity for which consent is sought, in his or her native language, or other mode of communication" (p. 42494) and that "the parent understands and agrees in writing to the carrying out of the activity for which his or her consent is sought" (p. 42494). Thus, not only must permission be sought from the parent, but also the school has the responsibility for making sure that the parent understands what it is for which consent is being given. In addition, the law requires that parents be invited to the meeting of the placement team where decisions are made about eligibility and placement for their handicapped child.

The stipulations of the law are quite clear. Just how well they are put into practice, however, may be another matter. Hoff, Fenton, Yoshida, and Kaufman (1978) interviewed parents to assess their understanding of four components of the special education decision: eligibility, placement, program goals, and review data. Their results indicated that no more than 50% of the time did parents have a clear and accurate understanding of any of the four components, even though they were present at the team meeting where the decisions were made. Just how well the parent-client is being served under such circumstances is certainly open to debate.

One further provision of PL 94–142 is the right of the parent to examine all records relating to the identification and placement of their child in special education. This provision is based on the Family Educational Rights and Privacy Act (FERPA, 1976) and especially gives the parent access to special education records. The impact of open records on the matter of clientage has already been discussed.

Both the Buckley Amendment and PL 94–142 have served to increase parents' control and involvement in the educational programs of their children. With this increased emphasis on parents' rights in their children's education, the parents' role as client of the school psychologist takes on a more central focus. Addressing this matter, Pantaleno (1983) posed the question, "in the face of this increased legalization and mandated parental involvement, is it not clear that the underlying theme present is one which suggests the parent as primary client?" (p. 110).

Client as Determined by Ethical Standards

Attention must finally be given to the implications that ethical codes might have when the question of clientage is considered. Principle II of the "National Association of School Psychologists Principles for Professional Ethics" (NASP, 1979) states that "the school psychologist is committed to the application of professional expertise for promoting improvement in the quality of life available to each person" (p. 90). More specifically, Principle IIa asserts that "the school psychologist defines the direction and the nature of personal loyalties, objectives, and competencies, and advises and informs all persons concerned of these commitments" (p. 91). Part d of Principle II further stresses that "where a situation occurs in which there are divided or conflicting interests (as parent—school—student), the psychologist is responsible for working out a pattern of action which assures mutual benefit and protection of rights for all concerned" (p. 91).

These standards place a great demand on the school psychologist who attempts to function in an ethical manner. The implication of these principles for clientage is that the client is "each person" or "all concerned." The psychologist's responsibility is to serve all of these clients, to keep them informed, and to work to protect the rights of each one. Of course, meeting these standards is no small task and at best would seem to be an idealistic goal.

In a similar vein, Principle 6 of the "Ethical Principles of Psychologists" of the American Psychologist Association (1981) requires that "psychologists respect the integrity and protect the welfare of the people and groups with whom they work. When conflicts of interest arise between clients and psychologists' employing institutions, psychologists clarify the nature and direction of their loyalties and responsibilities and keep all parties informed of their commitments" (p. 636). As Martin (1983) has aptly pointed out in commenting about this principle, "this kind of situation is almost inevitable given the nature of the job description of the school psychologist and the fact that the school psychologist is hired by the school district in which he/she works" (p. 6). As has already been shown from May's model (1976), the emergence of such conflict can be explained at least in part by the structural variables within the organization and the nature of the professional-client relationship.

An ethical dilemma emerges for the school psychologist when the wishes of one client are at odds with those of another client or with the psychologist's own ethical and professional standards. For example, school psychologist Muriel Forrest (*Forrest v. Ambach*, 1980) attempted to defend the right of parents and their handicapped children for services. She was prohibited, however, by her Westchester County, New York, school district from conducting full evaluations and from writing comprehensive reports discussing the results of these evaluations, from stating in her reports recommendations for appropriate services to handicapped children, from discussing with parents recommendations for special education and related services, and from attending a meeting where she had been asked to discuss her experiences in planning for handicapped children. In addition, she was chastised for criticizing the school's policy of recommending for the handicapped only those services available rather than the services needed (Bersoff, 1980).

Even though Ms. Forrest had an excellent record of service for 13 years and was attempting to function in what she perceived as an ethical, legal, and professional manner, she was fired from her job. Ms. Forrest took the case to the Commissioner of Education claiming that the school district was acting illegally with regard to special education placements and that her firing was based on having criticized the school board's policy, a move that violated her freedom of speech. The decision handed down by the courts after a series of appeals, however, was that Ms. Forrest's exercise of her first amendment right was not the motivating factor in her firing and that sufficient other fault with Forrest's service existed to justify her dismissal.

Although the courts upheld Ms. Forrest's right to speak out and to be guided by the ethical standards of her profession, they never ordered that she be reinstated in her job. The outcome of this case yields at least one undeniable lesson: School systems' policies, unless clearly illegal, will be upheld despite the school psychologist's invocation of ethical and professional standards. Clearly, school psycholgists take significant risks when they advocate on behalf of parents and children when that advocacy places them in conflict with the interest of their employer.

Not in all cases, however, will school psychologists be at odds with their employer with regard to ethical questions; at times their positions may be in conflict with parents. Cases exist in which parents have made demands for residential private school placements costing from $20,000 or more annually per child. With the aid of their legal advisors they have argued that the treatment facility "best" met the need of their handicapped child as required under PL 94–142 (Franzoni & Jones, 1981). Such residential placements, as well as other specialized educational services, put a tremendous financial strain on school systems and potentially limit resources available to other students. In cases in which parents demand costly services, the school psychologist must make a decision whether to support the financially limited school system that is able to provide "appropriate" but not "ideal" placement or services for the child or to advocate ideal placement or services as desired by the parents.

In this struggle, the Supreme Court has clearly sided with the school system, as evidenced by a precedent-setting decision rendered in 1982. In *Hendrick Hudson District Board of Education v. Rowley* (1982), the Court ruled that "the requirement that a State provide specialized educational services to handicapped children generated no additional requirement that the services so provided be sufficient to maximize each child's potential 'commensurate with the opportunity provided to other children' " (p. 198). Amy Rowley's educational program was found to be adequate and therefore appropriate because she was able to move from grade to grade thus not necessitating the sign-language interpreter insisted upon by her parents. The results of this case suggest that even if a school psychologist supports parents' requests for ideal placements or services, the courts are unlikely to uphold such requests.

Based on their professional ethics, school psychologists may choose in some situations to support parents and children and in others, their employer. As can be seen from the examples cited, in making such decisions, the ethical questions become intricately intertwined with legal considerations.

In some instances the school psychologist's reliance on professional codes of ethics may actually lead to unanticipated legal consequences. In his classic article "Professional Ethics and Legal Responsibilities: On the Horns of a Dilemma," Bersoff (1975) has described a day in the life of a hypothetical school psychologist "Ethy Kal." The description focuses on the unexpected problems encountered by Dr. Kal, who is attempting to function in a highly ethical manner. Bersoff points out that "some of these consequences may be the result of ignorance of the law and some the failure to predict courts' decisions as judges face conflicts never before litigated" (p. 364). In other cases, however, codes of ethics and the law may actually present competing demands for the psychologist.

Adolescents, for example, frequently seek the services of the school psychologist on their own, asking that their parents not be informed. Seeing a client in need, the psychologist may be tempted to offer services respecting the adolescent's requested restrictions. The right of adolescents to seek help without parental consent, however, is currently limited to "certain modes of intervention by certain classes of practitioners" (Bersoff, 1975, p. 371). Those psychologists who decide to offer services without parental permission, thinking they are acting ethically and in the best interest of their adolescent client, may in fact be making themselves vulnerable to civil law suits.

Another area in which some discrepancy may exist between the law and ethical standards has to do with "privileged confidential communication." The principle of privileged communication is based on a citizen's right to privacy and is legislated at a state level. According to Prasse (1979), "The doctrine of privileged communication prevents, where expressly stated by State Statute, certain professionals from sharing information about their clients gathered within the context of the professional relationship . . . it is a privilege which is granted to the client of the professional (psychologist), not to the professional" (p. 3). Confidentiality, on the other hand, is embodied in ethical standards, not State Statutes, and is a promise made by the psychologist to the client to keep communication confidential unless there is legal cause to do otherwise.

Whether a school psychologist's services are covered under privileged communication will depend upon the laws of the particular state. If not, the school psychologist may be forced by parents via legal channels to break their promise of confidentiality given to the child (Panteleno, 1983). Consequently, the ethical standard of confidentiality will not be able to be upheld unless there is the related legal protection given to the client. The psychologist who gives the ethical promise of confidentiality to the child may be considering the child as the primary client, but in essence the law may make the psychologist directly accountable to the parent.

Bersoff (1975) has suggested several factors that may be responsible for the discrepancy between ethical codes and the law. Two of these seem to be of particular relevance when considering the question of clientage. First, ethical codes are rarely developed with help from consumers or clients who receive the services and mainly reflect the professional group's viewpoint, one that may not necessarily be the same as that of the consumer. Second, ethical standards are typically written on such an abstract level that practitioners may not know how to apply them in specific situations when dealing with clients. Particularly in cases in which desires of various clients are at odds (e.g., the parent client and the child client) and the question of allegiance arises, ethical codes may not be very helpful. The answers may in fact be more clear-cut when based on legal considerations.

THE DEBATE OVER CLIENTAGE

As should be apparent from the previous discussions in this chapter, school psychologists are continually faced with mixed allegiances primarily among the school, the parent, and the child. To this point an attempt has been made to demonstrate objectively how various factors influence clientage. Little attention, however, has been given to the specific arguments that have been given for making one specific group the primary client over another. However, several of these positions from the literature deserve mention.

A recent issue of the *Journal of School Psychology* included three articles which to date have been probably the most in depth statements on clientage. Included were an article by Anthony Pantaleno and responses to it by Irwin Hyman and Richard Kicklighter. Pantaleno (1983) has proposed that the parent should be considered the primary client of the school psychologist. According to Pantaleno, "school psychologists are in the schools to serve children, teachers, and administrators, but all of these groups are best served when the parents are viewed as primary clients" (p. 112). Pantaleno bases his position on the idea that if parents criticize or even do not support school psychological services, then the future of the profession is in jeopardy. According to Pantaleno, in times when financial crunches are occurring, school psychologists, if seen as dispensable by parents, may be the first to go. He goes on to say that "if parents were perceived and treated by school psychologists as primary clients, with all of the mutual concern and trust that such a relationship implies, they [parents] would not be likely to stand back and watch the decimation of such valuable school-based service providers" (p. 109).

A second reason that Pantaleno gives for his parent-as-client stance is the legalization and mandated parent involvement in special education. Finally, Pantaleno argues that even if the school psychologist wishes to function as a child advocate, this role might best be integrated within a parent-as-client framework. He notes that even in cases of child abuse, children are rarely taken out of the home; thus, the road ultimately leads back to gaining the trust of and working with the parent. He points out that when psychologists attempt to take on a child-as-client orientation when dealing with child abuse, the child may actually suffer more if cases are closed for lack of evidence and if the child fears reporting additional instances of abuse.

Hyman (1983), on the other hand, has argued that "we should not cite the system's malfunctioning as a rationale for a parent as client rather than a child as client focus" (p. 116). Hyman goes on to raise the following points in questioning the parent as primary client stance:

> Should we then encourage teachers to hit children in class when parents insist? Should we ignore children who come to school unkempt, ill fed, or reeking of body odor? Should we change classification of children in order to assuage parents' guilt or denial? In divorce cases, should we present evidence favoring custody of the parent who happens to be on the school board or who has political influence capable of increasing "school psychological services much in the same way that parents of exceptional children have done in the past"? (p. 116–117)

Hyman suggests that in cases such as these, parents are likely to be alienated when the psychologist considers the child the primary client.

Hyman does support the schools' attempts to become more responsive to parents' wishes. However, he notes that if given the choice between supporting the parents and the child, he will "opt for the rights of the child over the parent . . . not because as a school psychologist I am onmiscient, but because society has provided me with the training, knowledge, experiences, and skill to focus all of my efforts toward parental, governmental, educational, and clinical resources to aid children" (p. 117). Hyman maintains the successful school psychologist can in fact serve the child as primary client and still earn the respect of parents.

In addressing the debate of child versus parent as client, Kicklighter (1983) has suggested that "in the majority of cases, the child's interests are identical and compatible with those of their parents. When we serve one, we serve the other" (p. 120). He feels, however, that unless there is clear evidence parental concern is lacking, the parents' interest in the child is presumed superior to that of all others. According to Kicklighter, the parent is the primary client in the sense that even though we are serving the child, the parent is presumed to be the primary guardian of the child's rights.

Kicklighter argues, nonetheless, that the question of "Who is the client?" is one on which school psychologists would do well not to expend all of their energies. He voices his agreement with Bersoff's (1975) position that in reality our clients are everyone whose lives we touch and suggests that we use our best skills to serve parents, children, and teachers.

Another person who has specifically addressed the clientage question is Trachtman. In his address at the Spring Hill Symposium on the Future of Psychology in the Schools, Trachtman (1981) noted that over the years his own child-as-client philosophy has evolved into one of parent-as-client. His rationale is as follows:

> Whereas the school-as-client reflects a pragmatic employer-employee relation, the child-as-client reflects a much more satisfying moral commitment for most of us, but the two definitions are frequently irreconcilable although the parent-as-client may offer a slightly more workable perspective. Here one can see parents as both ultimate employer and ultimately responsible for children's welfare. The working premise, therefore, is that our employer is the parents, collectively, and our client, the individual parent. (p. 145)

Goldman (1972) has also argued for the parent-as-client stance. According to Goldman, the assumption that the school staff knows better than do parents what is best for the child is ridiculous. He emphasizes that the parents are the ones who actually have to live with the outcomes and should therefore be involved in our intervention efforts.

With the exception of Hyman (1983), support appears generally to be in the direction of parent-as-client. The reasons given for supporting this stance are generally, first, that parents are in fact the ultimate employer of the school psychologist and thus must be served to their satisfaction and second, that parents hold ultimate legal responsibility for their children. Although some consistency in opinions would appear to exist, this discussion of the clientage question cannot be considered complete without considering it specifically from a child advocacy perspective.

THE SCHOOL PSYCHOLOGIST AS A CHILD ADVOCATE

In an earlier part of this chapter, advocacy as a type of "consultation" with its resulting implications for clientage was discussed. In this section, however, attention is given more specifically to the rationale behind child advocacy, a position that would hold the child as the ultimate client.

Biklen (1976) has defined advocacy as "an independent movement of consumers (e.g., parents, people with disabilities, and children) and their allies to monitor and change human service agencies" (p. 310). In order to promote quality services, the advocate attempts to understand the feelings of the person and the conditions that make that person dependent; does not feel pity for the individual but rather is committed to changing dehumanizing conditions; treats the person as a strong capable individual; and accepts the fact that he or she may be criticized by those agencies or persons who are being questioned.

Of relevance here is seeing how such a definition relates to advocacy for children. However, considerations must first be given to how the advocate conceptualizes children's rights. Generally, the attitudes of advocates fall between two broad dimensions (Melton, 1983). The first of these is a position of "nurturance" in which the rights advocated for children "involve protection and provision of goods and services necessary for self-actualization and quality of life" (Melton, 1983, p. 9). Such a stance is based on ideas of paternalistic responsibility. At the other extreme is a position of "self-determinism" in which the rights advocated for children would involve "determination of one's own fate and freedom from coercion and government intervention" (Melton, 1983, p. 9). This stance is based on the idea that children are due the same civil liberties that are extended to adults. Stated more succinctly, advocacy for children might be in the direction either of supporting the rights of the child to be protected from others or, on the other hand, of supporting the rights of the child to make his or her own choices.

According to Bersoff (1982), the greatest advances in the child advocacy movement have fallen into the protective dimension. As he points out, however, those who act "in behalf of" children are "under no obligation to consult with their beneficiaries or abide by their wishes" (p. 1072). Such an approach is to be differentiated from acting "on behalf of" the child or acting as the one being represented might act. Bersoff stresses that if the advocate is committed to expanding the rights of the child, then such advocacy must include the right of children to full participation in the making of decisions that will affect their lives.

By and large, however, the courts have not supported the rights of children in the decision-making process. The assumption has been that children lack sufficient maturity and stability to competently make important decisions in their lives. Bersoff argues, however, that insufficient data have been gathered in the situations in which children live (i.e., opposed to laboratory situations) to provide persuasive evidence in either direction. Bersoff (1982) suggests the following:

> Rather than assume that children are too young emotionally, experientially, and cognitively to make appropriate decisions, we can alternatively presume that children are capable of making those decisions no less disastrously than adults. Only if there is a significant risk of irreversible damage or clear and convincing evidence that at a particular age children do not have sufficiently developed skills to exercise discretion should parents and the state have the right to make unilateral decisions that affect children. (p. 1074)

With this orientation the burden of proof would fall on those wishing to deny children the rights of choice rather than on those advocating children's freedom of choice. Such a position is consistent with legal doctrine that an individual's rights can be deprived only after incompetence has been shown (Bersoff, 1982).

Thus, the child advocate who supports a position of "self-determinism" for the child is in essence taking on the purest form of the child-as-client stance. As has been noted, the data with respect to the appropriateness of this orientation are at best limited and indirect. Those choosing to take this stance can do so only based on personal opinion or philosophy until data more directly addressing children's abilities to make decisions can be gathered.

SUMMARY

This chapter has examined the question of clientage from perhaps a somewhat broader perspective than it has been to this point in the literature. As has been noted, the question is a multidimensional one with determining factors ranging from such pragmatic matters as the psychologist's model of human behavior, the focus of intervention, the service delivery role adopted by the psychologist, the psychologist's caseload, the psychologist's training, and the structure of the system, to less clear-cut dimensions including legal, ethical, and philosophical aspects of the question. No one factor alone determines the psychologist's answer to "Who is the school psychologist's client?" Rather, all of the various interacting dimensions must be considered.

As promised, no definitive answer to the question has been formulated here. The goal, rather, has been to provide the reader with a fuller appreciation of the complexity of what on the surface appears to be a rather simple question.

REFERENCES

Abidin, R. R., Jr. (1975). Negative effects of behavioral consultation: "I know I ought to, but it hurts too much." *Journal of School Psychology, 13,* 51–57.

American Psychological Association. (1981). Ethical principles of psychologists. *American Psychologist, 36,* 633–638.

American Psychological Association. (1981). Specialty guidelines for the delivery of services by school psychologists. *American Psychologist, 36,* 670–681.
Baker, R. G. (1965). Explorations in ecological psychology. *American Psychologist, 20,* 1–14.
Bandura, A. (1977). *Social learning theory.* Englewood Cliffs, NJ: Prentice-Hall.
Bergan, J. R. (1977). *Behavioral consultation.* Columbus, OH: Charles E. Merrill.
Bergan, J. R., & Tombari, M. L. (1975). The analysis of verbal interactions occurring during consultation. *Journal of School Psychology, 13,* 209–225.
Bersoff, D. N. (1975). Professional ethics and legal responsibilities: On the horns of a dilemma. *Journal of School Psychology, 13,* 359–376.
Bersoff, D. N. (1980, September). *In the matter of Muriel Forrest v. Gordon M. Ambach, Commissioner: Brief for amici curiae.* American Psychological Association.
Bersoff, D. N. (1982). The legal regulation of school psychology. In C. R. Reynolds & T. B. Gutkin (Eds.), *The handbook of school psychology* (pp. 1043–1074). New York: Wiley.
Biklen, D. (1976). Advocacy comes of age. *Exceptional Children, 43,* 308–313.
Caplan, G. (1970). *The theory and practice of mental health consultation.* New York: Basic Books.
Chesler, M. A., Bryant, B. I., & Crowfoot, J. E. (1976). Consultation in schools: Inevitable conflict, partisanship, and advocacy. *Professional Psychology, 7,* 637–645.
Clarizio, H. F. (1979). School psychologists and the mental health needs of students. In G. D. Phye & D. J. Reschly (Eds.), *School psychology: Perspectives and issues.* (pp. 309–341). New York: Academic Press.
Conoley, J. C., & Conoley, C. W. (1982). *School consultation: A guide to practice and training.* New York: Pergamon Press.
Cowen, E. L., & Zax, M. (1967). The mental health fields today: Issues and problems. In E. L. Cowen, E. A. Gardner, & M. Zax (Eds.), *Emergent approaches to mental health problems* (pp. 3–29). New York: Appleton-Century-Crofts.
Cutts, N. E. (Ed.). (1955). *School psychology at mid-century.* Washington, DC: American Psychological Association.
Education of handicapped children: Implementation of Part B of the Education of the Handicapped Act. (1977, August 23). *Federal Register,* Part II.
Fagan, T. (1980, November). The dilemma of clientage. *NASP Communique,* p. 1.
Family Educational Rights and Privacy Act. (1976, June 17). *Federal Register.*
Fanibanda, D. K. (1976). Ethical issues of mental health consultation. *Professional Psychology, 7,* 547–552.
Fishman, D. B., & Neigher, W. D. (1982). American psychology in the eighties: Who will buy? *American Psychologist, 37,* 533–546.
Ford, J. D., & Migles, M. (1979). The role of the school psychologist; Teachers' preferences as a function of personal and professional characteristics. *Journal of School Psychology, 17,* 372–378.
Forrest v. Ambach, N. 7715-80 (N.Y. Sup. Ct. Dec. 11, 1980).
Franzoni, J. B., & Jones, R. W. (1981). Implications for school psychologists: The challenge of Public Law 94-192. *Professional Psychology, 12,* 356–362.
Gallessich, J. (1974). Training the school psychologist for consultation. *Journal of School Psychology, 12,* 138–149.
Goldman, L. (1972). Psychological secrecy and openness in the public schools. *Professional Psychology, 3,* 370–374.
Goldwasser, E., Meyers, J., Christenson, S., & Graden, J. (1983). The impact of PL 94–142 on the practice of school psychology: A national survey. *Psychology in the Schools, 20,* 153–165.
Grubb, R. D., Petty, S. Z., & Flynn, D. L. (1976). A strategy for the delivery of accountable school psychological services. *Psychology in the Schools, 13,* 39–44.
Hendrick Hudson District Board of Education v. Rowley; 458 U.S. 176 (1982).

Hoff, M. K., Fenton, K. S., Yoshida, R. K., & Kaufman, M. J. (1978). Notice and consent: The school's responsibility to inform parents. *Journal of School Psychology, 16,* 265–273.

Humes, C. W., II. (1974). School psychologist accountability via PPBS. *Journal of School Psychology, 12,* 40–45.

Hyman, I. (1983). We are here for the kids: A reply to Pantaleno. *Journal of School Psychology, 21,* 115–117.

Hyman, I., & Schreiber, K. (1975). Selected concepts and practices of child advocacy in school psychology. *Psychology in the Schools, 12,* 50–57.

Keller, H. R. (1981). Behavioral consultation. In J. C. Conoley (Ed.), *Consultation in the schools: Theory, research, procedures* (pp. 59–99). New York: Academic Press.

Kicklighter, R. H. (1983). Clients all. *Journal of School Psychology, 21,* 119–121.

Lambert, N. M., Sandoval, J., & Corder, R. (1975). Teacher perceptions of school-based consultants. *Professional Psychology, 6,* 204–215.

Lennox, N., Flanagan, D., & Meyers, J. (1979). Organizational consultation to facilitate communication within a school staff. *Psychology in the Schools, 16,* 520–526.

Martin, R. P. (1983, February). Ethics column. *The School Psychologist,* p. 6.

May, J. V. (1976). *Professionals and clients: A constitutional struggle.* Beverly Hills, CA: Sage Publications.

Mearig, J. S. (1974). On becoming a child advocate in school psychology. *Journal of School Psychology, 12,* 121–129.

Melton, G. B. (1983). *Child advocacy: Psychological issues and interventions.* New York: Plenum Press.

Meyers, J. (1973). A consultation model for school psychological services. *Journal of School Psychology, 11,* 5–15.

Monroe, V. (1979). Roles and status of school psychology. In G. D. Phye & D. J. Reschly (Eds.), *School psychology: Perspectives and issues* (pp. 25–47). New York: Academic Press.

National Association of School Psychologists. (1979). National Association of School Psychologists principles for professional ethics. *National Association of School Psychologists membership directory* (pp. 90–96).

Overcast, T. D., & Sales, B. D. (1982). The legal rights of students in the elementary and secondary public schools. In C. R. Reynolds & T. B. Gutkin (Eds.), *The handbook of school psychology* (pp. 1075–1100). New York: Wiley.

Pantaleno, A. P. (1983). Parents as primary clients of the school psychologist or why is it we are here? *Journal of School Psychology, 21,* 107–113.

Prasse, D. (1979, March). Privileged confidential communication: Who is protected? *NASP Communique,* pp. 3,5.

Pryzwansky, W. B., & Bersoff, D. N. (1978). Parental consent for psychological evaluations: Legal, ethical and practical considerations. *Journal of School Psychology, 16,* 274–281.

Public Law 94–142. Education for All Handicapped Children Act of 1975. (1975, November 29).

Ramage, J. C. (1979). National survey of school psychologists: Update. *School Psychology Digest, 8,* 153–161.

Reger, R. (1972). The medical model in special education. *Psychology in the Schools, 9,* 8–12.

Reynolds, C. R., Gutkin, T. B., Elliott, S. N., & Witt, J. C. (1984). *School psychology: Essentials of theory and practice.* New York: Wiley.

Schmuck, R. A. (1976). Process consultation and organizational development. *Professional Psychology, 7,* 626–631.

Simpson, R. L., & Poplin, M. S. (1981). Parents as agents of change. *School Psychology Review, 10,* 15–25.

Skinner, B. F. (1953). *Science and human behavior.* New York: Free Press.

Stewart, K. J. (1984). School psychologists as researchers: An approach for initiating training and practice. *Psychology in the Schools, 21,* 211–214.

Stewart, K. J., & Medway, F. J. (1978). School psychologists as consultants: Issues in training, practice, and accountability. *Professional Psychology, 9,* 711–718.

Stewart-Lester, K. J. (1981a). Increased consultation opportunities for school psychologists: A service delivery model. *Psychology in the Schools, 19,* 86–91.

Stewart-Lester, K. J. (1981b, April). *Is consultation the service teachers really want?* Paper presented at the meeting of the National Association of School Psychologists, Houston.

Trachtman, G. M. (1972). Pupils, parents, privacy, & the school psychologist. *American Psychologist, 27,* 37–45.

Trachtman, G. M. (1981). On such a full sea. *School Psychology Review, 10,* 138–181.

Webster's new collegiate dictionary. (1975). Springfield, MA: G. & S. Merriam.

5 The Organization and Structuring of Psychological Services within Educational Settings

Michael J. Curtis
Joseph E. Zins
University of Cincinnati

The quality of education afforded children is influenced to a significant degree by the extent to which educational services are organized in an efficient and effective manner. As an integral part of the educational system, school psychological services similarly require close scrutiny of their organization and structure.

Although a somewhat greater level of consistency in the organization of school psychological services seems to have evolved over the last 10 to 15 years, the approaches to organization for the most part tend to vary markedly. Diversity results from and is often necessitated by a variety of idiosyncratic factors within each setting such as the specific needs of the organization, its size and financial resource base, the background and training of the staff, its educational philosophy, and so forth.

The range of such factors to be considered in a discussion about the organization of services is compounded by the variety of educational settings within which school psychologists are employed. Among them are public and private schools, vocational schools, residential facilities, special schools for the handicapped, and adult learning centers. Consequently, there is no single organizational structure which would be equally applicable to all settings. A number of primary forces, however, frequently serve as determinants of the organization and structuring of services. It is the purpose of this chapter to discuss factors both internal and external to the organization, as well as to examine some of the ways in which they may influence the organization of services.

THE APPLICATION OF SYSTEMS THEORY

In view of the number of factors that must be considered and the multitude of possible interactional combinations among them, it may be helpful to examine the topic from a "systems" perspective. In this section, we introduce some of the fundamental systems concepts that may be helpful in clarifying and understanding the various interrelationships that bear upon the organization of school psychological services within any given setting.

Systems applications to business and industry began shortly after World War II, but applications to the behavioral sciences did not emerge until the mid 1950s (Miller, 1955). A system can be defined as the orderly combination of a set of component parts (subsystems) that serves to produce a definable outcome or product. Furthermore, any system must always be viewed as a subsystem itself within a larger system (suprasystem). In other words, the focus of attention will always represent the *system*, those components of which it is comprised are the *subsystems*, and that larger context within which it exists is the *suprasystem*.

Basic to systems theory and of central importance to our discussion of the organization of school psychological services is the concept of *reciprocal interaction*. Operationally, this concept refers to the tendency for a change in any system component to affect other components within the system, as well as the output of the system as a whole. Similarly, any change in the suprasystem within which the system operates is likely to result in a change in the system itself.

However, unlike a mechanical system that is inert and will always respond to the same forces in exactly the same way (as long as the system remains unchanged) a *living system* (in this case one involving people) is more flexible and has more degrees of freedom in terms of how it will respond. Curtis and Yager (1981) illustrate this contrast through a comparison of a stereo system (inert) with a person (living system) who has burned a hand. The stereo will either project very loud auditory output or break when the amplifier (a subsystem) is turned to maximum capacity. Actually, it is the speaker (another subsystem) that would break, but it would thereby preclude the stereo system as a whole from producing the desired output. In contrast, a person, upon placing a hand in very hot water, would very likely select the alternative of immediately removing the hand from the pain-causing liquid. At that point, the individual could scream, curse, cry, silently bear the pain, or engage in some other behavior. In addition, the person is very likely to learn from the event in terms of trying to avoid similar situations in the future. On the other hand, the stereo system will continue to respond in exactly the same way every time as long as the system remains unchanged.

A system with the capacity to respond to external forces is called an *open system*. All living systems are open systems. The school is a good example of an open system. Because it includes people, it is a living system and includes numerous subsystems (e.g., different grade levels, administrators, special service personnel including the school psychologist, custodial services, cafeteria services). Each of the subsystems is interrelated with the others in efforts to attain the goal of the school, to educate its students.

Change in any one subsystem will affect the others and will influence the efforts of the school to reach its defined goal. As an illustration, consider the case of a school in which there is a significant decline in the quality of custodial services. It is easy to imagine the impact on the educational process over time as classrooms are left unclean, blackboards go for days without being washed, burned-out lightbulbs are not replaced, supplies go unpacked, and so forth. The effectiveness with which functions assigned to custodial personnel are carried out will affect each of the other components through the lack of supplies and materials needed to carry out their functions, poor lighting and generally uncomfortable working conditions, declining morale, and even physical health problems. As the effectiveness of each subsystem declines, the ability of the school to attain its goals also declines.

As an open system, the school also must be able to respond to the influence of forces from the external environment, the suprasystem (e.g., community norms and values, funding, legislation, state regulations for education). The failure of the school to respond appropriately to such forces obviously would result in problems for the organization. As any of those external forces changed, it would affect the functioning of the school. The school, as a system, commonly experiences changes in its component parts, as well as in the environment within which it exists.

One concept to consider in terms of open systems is that of *boundary permeability*. If we view systems as being more or less separated by imaginary "boundaries," then the "permeability" of each boundary becomes critical in determining the functioning of each component. The permeability determines the extent to which the system selectively allows itself to be impacted by external forces, and the extent to which it responds to such forces.

A brief discussion of three different levels of boundary permeability may help to clarify this concept. The first case would be the system with an *impermeable boundary*. All external forces, regardless of magnitude or significance, are rejected. Data from the environment are ignored. Such systems tend to be inflexible and stagnant. An example of this type of system would be the school that ignores all outside information and attempts at input, including the frequent expressions of concern by numerous parents throughout the community.

The second case would be a system from the extreme opposite end of the "openness" continuum. This would be a system with a *dysfuunctional boundary*, i.e., the boundary is practically nonexistent. The system almost becomes fused with its environment. It accepts all input from the outside, regardless of significance. Furthermore, it responds with the same level of intensity to every external force. Because this type of system responds to everything, it tends to be overwhelmed and functions in a chaotic manner. An example of this type of system would be the school that seems to overreact to every outside stimulus. The school has no identity of its own and is run by parents in the sense that every complaint results in a change in the school's operation.

The third case is the system midway between the first two, which are extreme opposites. This type of system is able to accept selectively certain external forces and reject others. Each force that is accepted is responded to in a manner commensurate with its perceived importance. The system is able to maintain its own identity while remaining open to outside information and new learning experiences. A system like this is referred to as being in a state of *dynamic equilibrium*. When input is received, the system uses it constructively and responds in a way that allows it to maintain stability. This is the most desirable state and represents the goal of systems change efforts.

Systems that have attained dynamic equilibrium are said to be *self-renewing*. They reflect a capacity for understanding the external environment, anticipating change, and solving problems effectively when they arise.

Systems theory offers a framework for understanding the complex interactions that influence an organization. However, it is important to remember that a living system is always in a state of dynamic change. There are changes in both internal forces and external forces which affect one another and the system as a whole. Consequently, systems analysis should be viewed as an ongoing process during which the interactive components of the system are assessed on a continual basis.

In the preceding section, we have examined some of the fundamental concepts from systems theory. It now may be helpful to consider the application of systems theory specifically to the organization of school psychological services.

Systems Theory and School Psychological Services

System. School psychological services will represent the system for purposes of our discussion. As a unit, it represents the focus of our attention and it meets the definition of a system. The system is composed of subsystem component parts, and it functions within the context of a larger suprasystem. Although psychological services, as a system, has desired outcomes, it is a subsystem for the larger system which also seeks desired outcomes, an effort to which school psychological services contributes.

Subsystems. With some variance, school psychological services may consist of one or more administrators, clerical support ranging from one part-time to several full-time personnel, psychological services personnel who also could range from one part-time to a large number of professionals, and so forth.

Suprasystem. School psychological services always exist within the context of a larger system whether it is a school district, a particular private school, or a special setting.

Open system. Unquestionably, psychological services would be an open, "living" system. It is composed of people and is significantly influenced by forces beyond its own boundaries. A clear example would be the legislative and judicial actions that have had a major impact on all of school psychology in recent years. At the same time, the flexibility of response that is characteristic of living systems is evident by the fact that the same laws and court decisions have had widely different effects on the delivery of school psychological services in settings that in every other way would be remarkably similar. Each "system" chooses how to respond from among a range of alternatives.

Reciprocal Interaction. Change within any subsystem will have an effect on school psychological services as a whole, as well as on other subsystems. For example, a change in the secretarial services staff can affect services. Even on a large staff, if one highly efficient and effective secretary leaves and is replaced by a less skilled individual, the impact can be seen on the unit administrator, the psychological services personnel, and on the other secretaries. Of course, it is probable that the effect on school psychological services will have some effect on the larger system as well. A change in one school psychologist position to a better or less adequately trained individual would very likely have an effect on services as a whole. Equally significant effects can result from changes in the larger suprasystem, including such factors as demographic changes within the local community.

Permeability of Boundaries. There is no doubt that different school psychological service systems respond differentially in terms of the effectiveness of their anticipation of and response to change. The passage of Public Law 94–142 (The Education For All Handicapped Children Act of 1975) and its impact represent an excellent example. Some service systems monitored the developments leading up to the passage of the federal legislation as well as those that followed at the state level. They were able to anticipate the eventual implications of the law for practice and began to prepare for its implementation. Those systems experienced relatively less stress and discomfort in making the necessary adjustments. In some cases, all necessary changes were fully implemented before the requirements of the law became effective. In contrast, some service systems experienced extreme stress and a serious disruption of services when the federal law and/or related state statutes became effective. Their capacity for anticipating change and responding appropriately was very limited. From a systems perspective, such units suffer from "impermeable" boundaries; they are unable to interact effectively and constructively with their environments.

A very different service system, but equally ineffective, is one that seems to lack functional boundaries. In this case, the system seems to respond to *every* environmental stimulus and is unable to differentiate between those that merit response and those that do not. This type of system typically is overwhelmed by the demands it faces and is unable to prioritize the investment of its resources. Everything is a crisis!

DETERMINANT FACTORS IN THE ORGANIZATION AND STRUCTURING OF SCHOOL PSYCHOLOGICAL SERVICES

Within the context of what has been presented thus far, it should be apparent that we believe school psychological services cannot be viewed as isolated and autonomous units. Rather, they must be considered in terms of the various components that comprise them, as well as in terms of the larger environments within which they exist. Consequently, it will be essential to examine some of the forces that can influence school psychological services. Corresponding to the concepts of subsystems and suprasystems, the discussion of those influences will be organized according to external and internal forces.

External Forces

As noted earlier, the focus of our attention is on school psychological services as an organizational entity. Therefore, from a systems perspective, school psychological services will represent the system during the remainder of our discussion. However, it should be noted that the individual psychologist who typically is responsible for the delivery of services at the building level could also represent the "system" level if our purpose was to examine the delivery of services in a particular building. In that case, school psychological services as an organizational unit would represent part of the suprasystem to the individual, i.e., a part of the environment within which the individual functioned. This point illustrates that the "system" is determined by the focus of attention.

There is no doubt whatsoever that the delivery of school psychological services is influenced by forces beyond the organizational unit itself. Some of the more significant external forces are discussed in the following sections.

Legislation and Court Decisions. At both the federal and state levels, legislators have enacted statutes that incorporate a wide range of requirements pertaining to education. Although some of these legislative mandates are directed at education in general, they still influence the delivery of psychological services because they determine to some degree the educational context within which the psychologist must work. Other legislation is much more direct in its impact. The most significant example is P.L. 94–142. This federal law guarantees a free and appropriate public education for *all* children and requires that handicapped students be educated within the environment that is least restrictive for each child. Rules and regulations following from P.L. 94–142 were enacted at the

TABLE 5.1
Forces Affecting the Organization
and Structuring of School
Psychological Services

External Forces
    Legislation and Court Decisions
    Funding
    Standards of Professional Organizations
    Societal and Community Norms
    Recipients of Services
    Technology
    Research
    Training and Continuing Education
Internal Forces
    Educational Philosophy
    Political Forces
    Gatekeepers
    Other Organizational Units
    Role Expectations
    Capabilities of Personnel
    Funding
    Uniqueness of System

state level mandating a range of services including school psychological services. In addition to legislative mandates, a number of court decisions in the past two decades have had significant impact upon the delivery of educational services, particularly for handicapped students. These court decisions also have had major influence on the practice of school psychology, especially concerning assessment (e.g., *P. v. Riles,* 1972, 1974, 1979) and intervention (*Parham v. J.L.,* 1979). A discussion of the regulatory impact of major laws and court cases on school psychology is presented by Bersoff (1982). Because of the potential vulnerability of school districts with regard to services for the handicapped and psychological services, some districts have added additional levels of bureaucracy and developed specific procedures that provide directives regarding how these services are to be delivered.

Funding. Local school districts in most states receive funds from governmental agencies to provide special services for handicapped children. To receive such financial support, schools in almost every state are required to identify and label children as handicapped (Gutkin & Tieger, 1979). School psychological services frequently are funded through the revenue associated with assessment-related activities. As a result, a close alliance between special education and school psychology is frequently found, with the two commonly housed together administratively and often directed by a special educator.

With funding closely linked to the labeling process, school psychologists frequently experience substantial pressure to restrict their services to assessment activities, rather than also providing consultation and intervention efforts. An emphasis on direct service (primarily individual assessment) may result in a need for more psychologists since an *exclusive* reliance on this type of service tends to be not as efficient as with indirect services. Nevertheless, it is not an uncommon practice for school districts to resist adding psychologists and to mechanically require that those available simply work faster and complete more child study evaluations. Such approaches overlook or ignore the reality that even the completion of a comprehensive evaluation is in itself a very time-consuming effort when the objective is to develop appropriate and effective services for children. Conversely, if the goal simply is to compile a set of numbers regarding the caseload of each psychologist or the total number of children served by the district, regardless of the quality of services, an assembly line procedure is understandable (but not justifiable).

In addition, there generally is no reimbursement to schools for primary and secondary prevention and mental health promotion services despite the empirical evidence that generally indicates the success of such interventions (Cowen et al., 1975; Goldstein, Sprafkin, Gershaw, & Klein, 1980; Jason, 1980; Zins, Wagner, & Maher, 1985). School psychological service units therefore often receive little support to provide prevention services and are not organized to do so.

Major changes in school psychological services are often initiated by changes in funding patterns. Regrettably, funding sometimes outweighs the needs of children in determining the nature, extent, and patterns for the delivery of school psychological services. The profession faces the challenge of "marketing" health promotion and prevention services to consumers and administrators in order to enhance the adjustment of *all* children.

Professional Standards. Standards and guidelines developed by professional organizations have had some influence on how psychological services are organized within educational settings. In some cases, state agencies have used these documents as guides in developing their own state-wide requirements and guidelines (e.g., the Kentucky Department of Education's handbook, *Comprehensive School Psychological Services*, 1984). At the local level, psychologists themselves are sometimes able to use professional standards to influence service delivery decisions within their districts. On the other hand, there will continue to be educational settings in which only *specifically* mandated services will be provided, and then in the "easiest" and most inexpensive manner possible (with little apparent concern for quality).

Professional standards and guidelines address such matters as the administrative organization of services, requirements for preparation of personnel, appropriate types and levels of supervision, and so forth. On a national level, both the National Association of School Psychologists (NASP) and the American Psychological Association (APA) have developed relevant standards and guidelines. The NASP *Standards for the Provision of School Psychological Services* (1984a) indicates that the goals, objectives, and procedural guidelines of school psychological services should be available in written form. In addition, the *Standards* suggests that a school psychologist direct the school psychology unit and that sufficient support services be available to enable the staff to achieve its goals and objectives. Moreover, the school psychology unit should establish and maintain relationships with other professionals both within and outside of the educational setting.

The APA *Specialty Guidelines for the Delivery of Services by School Psychologists* (1981) provides similar recommendations. For example, it describes the types of services that should be provided by school psychologists (e.g., assessment, consultation, program development) and suggests school psychologists conduct periodic and systematic evaluations of services. Furthermore, the *Guidelines* specifies that school psychological services should be responsive to needs of the school population served in terms of its organizational structure and the procedures utilized. Both NASP and APA also provide specific recommendations regarding supervision, which is described in a later section of the chapter.

Societal and Community Norms. Sociological characteristics of the community and the school may be additional influences on psychological services. Community standards may encourage or discourage the use of mental health resources. Attention to student mental health issues is sometimes interpreted as being separate from basic educational programs. Consequently, communities that hold such views and find themselves participating in the "back to basics" movement may dictate a narrowing of the scope of psychological services so that only mandated services are provided. The reverse might also be true wherein a community believes that a broad range of services should be available to all students.

Community norms might suggest some of the functions that could be provided by psychologists, such as counseling, should more properly be provided by parents. Aside from the financial support a community is *able* to provide to the schools, there, of course, is the issue of what it is willing to support and what it is actually willing to provide.

Recipients of Services. The potential recipients of services are an additional determining factor regarding service organization. The developmental and educational levels of students should influence the types of services provided (Reynolds, Gutkin, Elliott, & Witt, 1984) and thus the organization of services. In Michigan, for example, school psychologists have been directed to serve only handicapped children. Primary and secondary prevention services have not been emphasized or supported. If the clients of school psychologists are exclusively handicapped children, it follows that school psychological services should be organized to facilitate communication and interaction with special educators.

Evidence also suggests that school psychologists tend to focus their services on elementary rather than secondary students (Kramer & Nagle, 1980; Nagle & Medway, 1982). A survey of 40 school psychologists providing services to high schools found that 70% of them spent the majority of their time *outside* of the high school, with the result that the equivalent psychologist-to-student ratio was over 1:6000 (Carroll, Bretzing, & Harris, 1981). The point is that very few school psychologists work full-time in secondary schools. Consequently, psychological services are usually organized to emphasize elementary rather than secondary services. Furthermore, different services are usually required for these two age groups. For example, screening for potential handicaps may be appropriate for kindergarten students. At a secondary level, the psychologist is more likely to engage in activities such as assisting in the development of chemical abuse prevention programs, or more typically, providing direct services such as counseling. Obviously, the needs of clients should be a principal factor in developing an appropriate structure for the delivery of services.

Technology. Technological advances show promise of dramatically affecting education. Significant applications already are evident. For example, computer-assisted instruction (CAI) has become commonplace in many schools. Computers are becoming more widely used in record keeping and data management, and in the instruction of students.

In recent years many new tests have been developed and revisions completed on others. These instruments frequently are based on complex theories with which many practitioners may not be familiar. Furthermore, the use of those tests requires additional training. In both instances, there may be implications for the organization and structuring of psychological services.

Numerous intervention programs for dealing with problems in the schools are aggressively marketed by their developers. Consequently, many districts adopt intervention programs despite the absence of adequate research and evaluation data regarding the effectiveness of the approach. School psychologists can help to evaluate such new "technology" and to introduce it in an appropriate manner.

These examples serve to highlight the need for school psychologists to be cautious in their desire to incorporate new technology into practice, while remaining aware of emerging approaches and open to new ideas. Supervisors of school psychological services in particular need to exert leadership in this respect. Service units might find it helpful to establish committees to investigate new developments and make recommendations to other staff members.

Research. Although there has been no notable research effort regarding how school psychological services should be organized to be most efficient, there is a significant body of data indicating the types of services that consumers of services prefer (e.g., Gutkin, 1980; Hughes, 1979; Manley & Manley, 1978; Waters, 1973; Zins & Curtis, 1981). In addition, there is considerable evidence indicating the effectiveness of selected forms of service such as consultation (Meyers, 1981). On the other hand, few supportive accountability data exist for many of the more traditional direct service functions (Zins & Curtis, 1984).

Research need not be considered only from the perspective of the literature at large. Situation-specific research would provide a strong basis from which to organize services for any given educational setting. For example, research on the effectiveness of special education classes would generate critical information. Data specific to any system regarding many of the influential forces discussed in this chapter would be important considerations in deciding which organizational structure would be most effective and most efficient under existing conditions.

Training and Continuing Education. In thinking about school psychology training as a potential influence in the organization of services, our first tendency is to examine the issue from the perspective of the capabilities of the school psychology personnel within any given district. From that perspective, training would more appopriately be considered as a force *internal* to the system. From a very different perspective, however, training might well be viewed as an *external* force.

Both the availability and the quality of school psychology training programs tend to vary considerably by state, and even by region within the same state. In some states, effective school psychology training is in its infancy and lags far behind that of other states in terms of the comprehensiveness and quality of the preparation afforded trainees. In other states, regardless of the quality, there simply are not enough training programs to meet the demands of the field. Unless educational agencies have the special capability of attracting school psychologists from states where programs are sufficient in number and of high quality, they will continue to face limitations in terms of the personnel available to them. Some of the same limitations can even be found within states in which the numbers and quality of programs are adequate overall. For example, there may be a great deal of difficulty in getting school psychologists to accept employment in very rural areas. The problem typically is compounded by the fact that many rural educational systems do not have the financial resources to offer salaries comparable to those available in urban or suburban areas. However, even when attractive salaries are offered, often it continues to be difficult to hire well-qualified personnel, particularly if the training institutions are not located in the rural areas. A related issue is that if qualified individuals are not available, states may "lower" practice standards as well as the necessary qualifications of practitioners (e.g., Mason & Remer, 1979).

Internal Forces

In addition to external forces such as those discussed above, other factors internal to the educational setting may influence the organization and structuring of psychological services. Some of the major forces to be considered are discussed in the following section.

Educational Philosophy. Just as the values and norms of the community can serve as an external influence, the educational philosophy of the educational system itself will act as a determining factor in how psychological services are organized. Philosophy will play an important part in determining the "atmosphere" or organizational climate within any given setting. In turn, the climate will influence organizational characteristics such as the formal and informal norms, staff morale, trust, values, lines and effectiveness of communication, relationships among staff, students and parents, and cohesiveness and cooperation among the staff. For example, Kuehnel (1975) studied elementary schools and found a significant relationship between organizational climate and the use of mental health resources.

At the same time, the values that are reflected in the educational philosophy of the system often will bear directly upon the types of services offered by school psychologists. The relationship between the norms and values of the community and the philosophy of the system is highly significant. In an earlier example, the community that strongly advocated a "back to basics" philosophy was used as an illustration. Given the influence that community values typically have on school systems, it is exceedingly likely the system itself would reflect that same philosophy (or would at least move in that direction starting with the next election for members of the board of education). In a setting that reflected "back to basics" values, it might be expected that school psychologists would invest most of their time and energy in addressing academic achievement issues. It is doubtful that mental health promotion activities would receive much emphasis. Consequently, psychological services would reflect the priorities of the educational system as a whole, which in turn reflect the priorities of the community. As Sarason (1971) has noted, it is important to recognize that "the school culture reflects and is a part of larger society" (p. 1).

Political Forces. Recent years have witnessed the growing influence of various political forces within the educational setting. Schools have been politicized from top to bottom. Boards of education, once commonly consisting of citizens whose primary motivation seemed to be contributing to the betterment of the local schools, now often represent political stepping stones for individuals whose personal motivations look beyond the schools they purport to serve.

Besides the politically sensitive members of the boards of education, schools also must face the realities of unionized employees, including administrators, teachers, special services personnel, clerical workers, and custodial staffs. Each group attempts to influence not just its own economic well-being, but the philosophy and operation of the educational system itself. There is little doubt that strong employee unions frequently influence decisions that may involve school psychologists and the services they perform.

Of late, an additional problem has emerged for school psychologists. Some states have enacted legislation that legalizes collective bargaining and varying related activities for public employees. One implication of such legislation for school psychologists is that they subsequently find themselves officially aligned with either the administrators or the teachers, sometimes without any input regarding the decision. There also are cases in which the school psychologists are in a separate bargaining unit or are aligned with personnel other than the administrators and teachers. Regardless of the specific arrangement, the fact that school psychologists are aligned with any group is likely to have a significant bearing on how they are perceived, where they are housed, what they are expected to do, and how they carry out their responsibilities.

Gatekeepers. Those who have significant control over access and influence are often referred to as "gatekeepers." Although we tend most often to think of administrators as the gatekeepers, in reality, people with this level of influence can be found in many different roles. For example, within any given office or building, one particular secretary may have far more power in terms of central functions than does the administrator in charge. Psychologists who do not identify the gatekeeper(s) correctly will likely experience considerable frustration in trying to operate within the area of influence. This point takes on special significance in light of the problems discussed above regarding the alignment of school psychologists with any given group. Since gatekeepers tend to vary by role across different buildings and settings, it is probable that school psychologists would not be aligned with the gatekeepers in some of the settings within which they work. An even worse situation would be one in which at the system level school psychological services were perceived by influential gatekeepers as being aligned with competitive or even adversarial groups or individuals.

Other Organizational Units. As is discussed more fully in a later section of the chapter, other organizational units can have a significant influence on psychological services. A collaborative relationship can be developed that will enhance the delivery of services; or on the other hand, there might be only minimal cooperation among the various units. The types of services offered can also be affected. For example, it is highly unlikely that services at an organizational level could be provided unless a good relationship had been established with the administrative units.

Role Expectations. Role expectations essentially are determined by history, title, and behavior. *History* refers to the norms established by the behaviors of earlier persons within the same role. Based on what they did, others within the same role are expected to do the same. For example, administrators and other consumers of psychological services may have preconceived ideas about what types of services should be provided based upon previous experiences. Their expectations would obviously be in large part determined by the capabilities of the preceding psychologists. Of course, the behaviors of those persons might have been defined by what they were *allowed* to do, as well as by their own capabilities. However, the point is that the behaviors of previous psychologists might be very poor indicators of the capabilities of current personnel. Consequently, potential consumers might not be familiar with the range of services that could be available and may misconstrue them as being quite limited (Zins & Curtis, 1984). Conversely, services provided by earlier personnel might lead to the expectation that similar services should continue to be available, regardless of the capabilities of the current staff. However, it is quite common that their misconceptions may be a reflection of *expectations* rather than *desires* (Zins & Curtis, 1981). That is, they may expect the psychologists to provide only a limited range of services even though they want comprehensive services. Thus, services can be influenced by administrators' (and others') understanding of what services are available (whether accurate or not), as well as by their personal views regarding how important those services are.

In addition to history (the behavior of preceding psychologists), role expectations also are influenced by *title* itself. Even if an individual or a group has never worked with a school psychologist, there are certain expectations instilled by the title "school psychologist." The expectations are likely to be determined by "what a school psychologist does" as understood by the other person. That information tends to be general and of course may or may not be accurate in terms of current personnel.

Finally, the *actual behaviors* of current psychologists will influence role expectations. Regardless of history and regardless of the expectations associated with title, the actual behaviors eventually will determine role expectations. That is why the responsibility for establishing a clear understanding of potential services rests ultimately with the school psychological services unit and individual personnel. It is absolutely essential that others have an accurate understanding of what the school psychologists *can* do in deciding what it is that they *will* do.

Expectations regarding what school psychologists have to offer, combined with other factors such as educational philosophy, will play a major part in determining who will be the recipients of school psychological services. The identification of the recipients of services will be especially important in deciding the organization of services. For example, if *all* children are viewed as potential clients, it would probably be more appropriate to place school psychologists in a separate unit or within Pupil Personnel Services rather than in a Special Education unit (Reynolds et al., 1984). Additional discussion of the administrative location of school psychological services is included later in the chapter.

Capabilities of Personnel. There is a great deal of variation in the training of school psychologists. Much of this is because school psychology is a relatively young field. Many practitioners who have been in the field for an extended period of time did not complete a school psychology training program, but rather were originally trained in clinical psychology, guidance and counseling, special education, or other related fields. A study by Keough, Kukic, Becker, McLoughlin, and Kukic (1975) found that only 21% of their sample held a degree in school psychology. The degree of similarity often seems minimal between the preparation of those trained primarily in areas other than school psychology and that provided through many of today's programs.

For the most part, those originally trained in other areas became credentialed as school psychologists through the completion of a relatively small number of courses that led to certification by the state education agency. Their preparation for entry level practice typically was far less than the 60 semester hour minimum advocated today the the National Association of School Psychologists (1984b). Furthermore, training focused almost exclusively on the testing function, and even that was from a rather narrow perspective. Training in areas such as consultation, organization development, group counseling, parent conferencing, inservice education, applied behavior analysis, and low-incidence and multifactored assessment techniques typically was not included in their programs.

Recent years have witnessed notable progress in the preparation of school psychologists. Although the preparation of master's level psychologists has remained relatively constant between 1978 and 1982, there have been marked increases in the number of doctoral (62%) and specialist (24%) graduates (Brown & Minke, 1984). It is highly likely that there will continue to be significant changes in the preparation of school psychologists overall in the years ahead.

Funding. School districts make decisions about how they will appropriate available funds. Teacher salaries can be raised, buildings improved, computers purchased, or school psychologists hired, to note only a few of the options. Although some of these decisions are not entirely in the hands of the district (e.g., state mandates for specific student:teacher ratios), there is a certain amount of discretion involved in how they spend their money. A survey by Eberst (1983) found that school psychologists were employed through local funds in 27 of the 34 states responding. Many of the factors noted above will bear upon how well school psychological services fare in the division of resources. Those decisions are amplified in importance when the district faces particular funding problems overall.

Uniqueness of the System. The fact remains that school districts and even individual schools within each district are unique. The possible interrelationships among those factors discussed earlier, as well as numerous others, result in system characteristics and needs that can vary markedly. As noted earlier, a firm grasp of systems theory and its application will be of tremendous benefit to those who bear the responsibility for the organization and structure of school psychological services.

ORGANIZATION OF SCHOOL PSYCHOLOGICAL SERVICES

In this section, we examine a variety of options from which school psychological services might be organized. It is the *structure* and *organization* of a unit that "provides a foundation for functioning and helps determine its effectiveness and efficiency" (Maher, Illback, & Zins, 1984, p. 10). Alternatives are discussed along several dimensions according to which organizational decisions must be made, including orientation/philosophy, staffing, structure, supervision, administrative location, and coordination.

Orientation/Philosophy

Although it may or may not be explicitly stated, school psychologists have an *orientation* or *philosophy* that greatly influences the manner in which services are organized and delivered. The philosophy consists of those ideals valued by the staff, and, as a result, become intentions toward which the organization aspires (Maher et al., 1984). For example, the psychological services unit may emphasize a preventive or a clinical/remedial approach, and may direct its services to individuals, groups, and/or the entire organization. Although direct services (e.g., assessment) most likely will have to be provided to individual students as a significant function within any school psychological services unit, there usually is also the possibility to offer other types of services as well. For example, the psychologist may also develop a primary prevention program at an organizational level in addition to individual services. If the practitioner is able to offer such services, he or she may then be able to operate on a more proactive rather than strictly reactive basis (e.g., dealing only with referrals for special education placement).

The orientation that is adopted has a number of implications for the organization and structuring of psychological services. For example, an emphasis on remedial services to individual students may result in a need for a larger staff since there is a need to spend considerable time working with more serious types of problems. Cases will often be dealt with on a reactive basis, and a more structured approach to day-to-day service will be taken (e.g., formal appointments to see the psychologist, large blocks of time set aside for assessment or

TABLE 5.2
Decision Points in the Organization
of School Psychological Services

Orientation/Philosophy
Staffing
Structure
    Single versus multiple staff
    Centralized versus decentralized services
    Districts versus educational cooperatives
    Staff versus contractual services
Supervision
    Professional guidelines
    Self-supervision and peer review
    Program evaluation and accountability
Administrative Location
    Pupil personnel services
    Special education
    Psychological services
    Other locations
Coordination of Services
    Program planning
    Multidisciplinary teams

---

counseling). Individual children will be the primary focus of the services rather than groups or organizational level interventions.

On the other hand, if an organizational level approach is utilized, it is likely that the person providing such services will be able to serve a relatively large population. Assignment to a large number of buildings may therefore be possible. Of course, it is probable that a "mixture" in approaches will be taken rather than a complete emphasis on one approach to the exclusion of others.

What is critical, however, is that a carefully thought through and conscious decision be made regarding the orientation/philosophy of the school psychological services unit. That decision, of course, will need to be made within the context of the many factors discussed earlier in this chapter. Organizational *policies* should be derived from the unit's philosophy. Policies are written statements that inform others—staff, pupils, and parents—about what the unit is intended to do and how it will accomplish its purpose (Maher et al., 1984). All of the other decisions regarding the organization of services must begin at this level and reflect the philosophy of the unit.

Staffing

Staffing decisions must address several issues such as the number of personnel and their backgrounds and capabilities. Those decisions themselves will be influenced largely by factors such as the orientation/philosophy of the service unit as noted above and the resources allocated to the unit. With respect to the number of staff needed, several guidelines have been developed by professional organizations and state education agencies. Recommended figures range from one psychologist per 1000 students (NASP, 1984a) to one per 2000 (APA, 1981), although individual states tend to vary widely. Georgia, for example, has established a goal of 1:3500 (Georgia Department of Education, 1982), Kansas recommends 1:1500 (Kansas Department of Education, 1982), and Kentucky and Illinois (as well as a number of other states) have no suggested number. The survey noted earlier by Eberst (1983) found that the actual ratios varied even more widely. Wyoming had approximately one school psychologist for every 750 pupils, whereas Kentucky had one for every 12,000 students. The national average was 1:4300. Of course, in any case, the number will be influenced by the population served. For example, a ratio of 1:1000 may be ideal in most settings, but in a school for the severely and profoundly handicapped, that number would be inappropriate.

Another approach includes defining the number of individual case studies a psychologist should perform each year. Ohio specifies that the annual caseload shall include a minimum of 75 and a maximum of 125 intensive psychoeducational evaluations per year (Ohio Department of Education, 1982).

North Carolina, in contrast, notes that the number of *schools* per psychologist appears to be an important consideration in determining the number of staff needed to provide comprehensive services (North Carolina Department of Public Instruction, 1983). They suggest that three schools per psychologist appear to be the maximum number possible in providing adequate services, whereas NASP recommends a maximum of four schools (NASP, 1984a).

Travel time between schools is a major concern in rural areas where distances between schools may be excessive. In these settings, psychologists may invest a great deal of time in travel, thereby restricting the time available for actual service activities. In order to provide the same level of services to such settings, a greater number of personnel would be required (i.e., a lower psychologist:student ratio) than would be true in settings that did not involve as much travel time.

In addition to the number of staff needed, a related issue concerns the level and types of training of these individuals. Most school psychologists have been trained as "generalists" and are prepared to work with the majority of the children from kindergarten through high school. On the other hand, they may not have had training appropriate for working with certain populations such as the severely and profoundly handicapped. It is much more likely that school psychologists prepared at the doctoral level will have received training in specialty areas such as organization development, early childhood, vocational education, group counseling, consultation, supervision, and/or low incidence assessment and programming, although such training might be offered in some cases at the non-doctoral level. Decisions must be made regarding the manner in which these individuals are employed and their services used.

Many practitioners are employed in relatively small districts as the only psychologist on staff. In such instances, it generally is necessary for them to provide a broad range of services to district students, their families, and staff. Being a competent "generalist" in school psychology would be advantageous in such settings. As noted above, a problem with this model is that the practitioner may be faced with cases in which he or she has little or no expertise and minimal opportunity to develop it through experience. For example, where there may be one or two visually handicapped children in a district, the school psychologist will most likely not have the opportunity to adequately develop his/her skills with such children because they are so few in number. Contact with these children may occur only once every year during their annual review of placement and for their reevaluations every third year. As a result, the psychologist's skills in working with this population may remain marginal.

In contrast, a large school district might have an entire school or several special classes for the visually handicapped. In this case, one or more psychologists with special training and/or experience could be assigned to serve those children on a regular basis. Consequently, those psychologists would be in a better position to develop and/or maintain their special expertise with this group of children.

The decision that must be made is how to assign staff. What role should specialization play in determining assignments? Obviously there are benefits to having one psychologist assigned to one building on a regular basis rather than having a different one assigned for each case depending on the presenting problem. Although having a specialist in areas such as the assessment of low incidence handicaps has beneficial aspects, it also has the disadvantage of that person not being as familiar with the organizational climate, philosophy, and personnel of each school.

Structure

As noted at the beginning of the chapter, there is no one agreed-upon manner of organizing and structuring school psychological services. However, several relatively common patterns are found in the field. They can be considered in the following way: single psychologist versus multiple staff; centralized versus decentralized services; districts versus educational cooperatives; and staff versus contractual services.

Single Psychologist Versus Multiple Staff. The issues involved in single psychologist versus multiple staffing structures were discussed briefly under "Staffing." The organization of services is much less complex with one versus many staff members in terms of lines of responsibility and authority, and relations with other units within the organization. There is only one person with whom to deal. Yet, that fact reflects one of the problems referred to earlier, i.e., that person is a generalist who has to do "everything." The multiple psychologist situation allows for the implementation of a differentiated staffing structure whereby specific types of problems are referred to particular staff members based upon their areas of expertise. This type of system provides for a broader range of services by psychologists with a greater level of expertise in each area. However, one drawback relates to the difficulty of several people each becoming familiar with the various settings in which they must function, as well as with the many people with whom they must work. Those factors can be as essential to problem resolution as is expertise pertaining to the particular problem. Of course, there also are likely to be many more problems regarding lines of authority, communication, responsibility, and interpersonal relationships.

Centralized Versus Decentralized Services. Some service units operate rather autonomously whereas others receive a great deal of direction and control from the central administration. Both forms of management have strengths and limitations. Centralized services allow for greater coordination of overall services, encourage and facilitate consultation with peers and the sharing of knowledge, and promote a great deal of direction and control. On the other hand, a psychologist operating within a decentralized service plan tends to be reasonably autonomous in that he or she largely decides how the job will be done on a day-to-day basis. There is a minimum of administrative control and direction (and less administrative overhead in terms of time, energy, and resources). A major advantage is that the individual practitioner is more knowledgeable about the specific needs of the schools being served than is the central office, and thus may be better able to address the schools' needs. Visits and reporting to the central office tend to be much less frequent, as might be collaboration with school psychology colleagues.

Districts Versus Educational Cooperatives. In many areas, particularly those that are more rural, school districts are not large enough to hire a full-time school psychologist or other special services providers. As a result, several districts may join together to establish "educational cooperatives" for providing such services. Even in urban areas, several districts might develop cooperative arrangements to provide specialized services personnel (e.g., family counseling, low incidence assessments) that none of them could afford to employ on their own. For fiscal reasons, however, the psychologist is considered a regular employee of one of the districts and therefore is entitled to the usual employee benefits (retirement, sick leave, etc.). Furthermore, the psychologist typically is expected to provide a full range of services consistent with the position. For example, a psychologist hired to provide related services to the low incidence handicapped would not just conduct evaluations, but also would engage in teacher consultation, serve on multidisciplinary teams, hold parent conferences, and engage in ongoing follow-up activities.

Staff Versus Contractual Services. A current, but very controversial, arrangement involves the use of contractual services. This refers to the practice in which school districts "contract" with an individual private practitioner to provide psychological services from outside the district rather than hiring district employees. In essence, the psychologist is not an employee of the district and receives neither a standard employee contract nor benefits (from the district). Rather, an agreement is established that indicates specific services or amounts of time that will be provided and the payment for such services. As more and more school psychologists have gained the right to engage in private practice (particularly at the non-doctoral level), there has been a corresponding increase in the number who wish to provide services to school districts on a contractual basis.

On the surface, there does not appear to be much difference between this type of arrangement and that involving educational cooperatives. If these individuals contract to provide "comprehensive psychological services" (NASP, 1984a), there may in fact be little distinction. However, in practice, contractual service arrangements are often entered into merely as a means of saving money for the school district at the expense of providing fewer services to children and their families, or at the expense of the individual psychologist. Districts may contract for "testing" services on a per case basis with no provision for follow-up, parent and teacher conferences, and so forth. At other times some districts have contracted for services in order to avoid paying legitimate employee benefits such as sick leave, retirement, and insurance (again, as a means of cutting expenses).

The underlying assumption in the last two cases seems to be that psychological services consist of testing only and that they are of little importance to children and families. The controversy surrounding contractual services arises from these types of arrangements. As implied earlier, contractual services are not inherently "bad"; the specifics of the contract and characteristics of the individual practitioner determine their quality. Such arrangements will most likely increase as more school psychologists attain private practice eligibility. However, the commissioner of education in at least one state (Gordon M. Ambaugh, New York) has ruled against school districts' being able to contract for psychological services (in the matter of *Friedman v. Ballston Spa Central School District,* April 2, 1980). Empirical research that identifies the characteristics of effective service units clearly is needed.

Supervision

Professional Guidelines. Although most states do not have specific rules and regulations regarding professional supervision of school psychologists employed by educational agencies, the major school psychology organizations have adopted practice guidelines specifying the need for and manner in which supervision should be carried out. The American Psychological Association indicates that all *non-doctoral* school psychologists should have their professional practice supervised by a doctoral-level psychologist (APA, 1981). Face-to-face supervision should be provided for a minimum of one hour per week per staff member. According to these guidelines, supervision for non-doctoral psychologists should continue throughout the professional's career. The National Association of Psychologists also recommends supervision, but for *all* school psychologists (NASP, 1984a). For the first 3 years of practice, supervision should consist of at least one hour of face-to-face interaction each week (similar to APA). Thereafter, school psychologists should continue to engage in supervision and/or peer review activities on a regular basis in addition to continuing their professional development through participation in continuing education programs (NASP, 1984a).

Supervision as recommended by these organizations, although providing guidance for good professional practice, can be difficult to implement. This is particularly true in rural settings where there are not likely to be adequate numbers of supervising school psychologists (whether doctoral or nondoctoral). Furthermore, excessive distances between some districts would require inordinate amounts of time for travel, even where a small number of appropriate potential supervisors do exist. Of course, there also is the issue of a district's being willing to hire a psychologist to perform this function when there is a shortage of school psychologists to provide services in general.

A related issue, which can have significant impact upon the organization of services, is that of professional supervision of school psychologists by non-school psychologists (frequently special educators). The practice standards adopted by NASP (1984a) clearly state that professional supervision should be provided by school psychologists. However, many practitioners continue to work under the supervision of non-school psychologists. In such instances, school psychologists may be administratively housed within a special education unit (see later section of chapter) and their needs may not be adequately represented. Furthermore, they may not be able to discuss technical issues and professional problems with a supervisor who has an adequate knowledge of the field. In such instances, the school psychologist may be in a severely restricted role (e.g., can only conduct assessments) or have unreasonable expectations placed upon him/her (e.g., conduct two assessments every day). We know one school psychologist who was supervised by the special education director of her district, an individual with no background in school psychology. The psychologist was reprimanded because she could not conduct psychological evaluations in one to two hours as the director expected. Furthermore, she was discouraged from attending IEP conferences for children she had evaluated. Such situations create ethical dilemmas for the practitioner and are not in the best interests of children.

Self-Supervision and Peer Review *Supervision*, broadly defined, also can be provided in different ways such as through *self-supervision* and/or *peer review*. Self-supervision is a self-directed, systematic, formal process of personal development designed to assure the delivery of quality services (Fleming, Fleming, Oksman, & Roach, 1984). A major goal of the activities is to monitor professional functioning in order to maintain or improve one's skills. It assists the professional in becoming aware of his/her service delivery activities and in designing strategies for making needed changes in job performance.

Peer review consists of formal, systematic consultation with colleagues regarding professional issues and concerns. The goal is to assist with problem solving, decision making, and appropriate practice (NASP, 1984a). It may involve discussions of cases, observation of professional functioning, and/or sharing of professional approaches to problems and techniques.

Regardless of the specific way in which supervision is conceptualized or provided for, it remains an important element in the provision of school psychological services. The integration of supervision into the organization of services deserves major attention and consideration.

Program Evaluation and Accountability. There is a great need today to engage in systematic evaluations of services to aid in decision making and program planning. The organization of services will require that information be obtained regarding the effectiveness of the psychological services delivery program. Such information can aid in (a) clarifying program strengths and needs, and suggesting areas of modification, (b) charting program progress toward goals, (c) determining patterns in the use of services, (d) indicating possible changes in staff assignments, and (e) aiding in professional development (Zins & Curtis, 1984). The type of evaluation conducted and the information collected will depend upon the needs of the organization as well as those of the individual psychologist. Relevant information should be shared with administrative units, as well as with consumers of psychological services. It can also be used in supervisory sessions to aid in professional development and to determine whether duties outlined in a job description are met.

Administrative Location

The delivery of effective and efficient school psychological services is dependent largely upon the relationships established with other professionals within the educational organization. An increased emphasis upon a "team approach" in recent years has put additional emphasis on collaboration. To a certain extent, interprofessional relationships will be influenced by the administrative organization of the school district. In general, school psychologists usually occupy staff positions rather than line positions within organizations, and this arrangement facilitates their functioning as consultants. Several common organizational structures are reviewed in this section. As with the other decisions regarding the organization of school psychological services, administrative location is similarly influenced by a variety of factors such as the size of the district, funding, and so forth.

Cutts (1955) identified four types of staff organizations in which school psychologists typically work. Three of these units (departments of pupil personnel services, special education, and psychology) continue to be common today. The fourth, in which psychological services are a function of the state departments of mental health or education, is employed less frequently.

Pupil Personnel Services. One of the more common locations for school psychological services is within a pupil personnel services unit or an instructional support unit. These units usually include a number of special services professionals such as school nurses and/or health educators, guidance counselors, instructors of the home-bound, and school social workers, as well as school psychologists. In most instances there is a director or administrator of the pupil personnel services team, who is responsible for developing a systematic approach to the organization of services and for ensuring coordination among the various staff members. Although there undoubtedly is a definite need for this coordination, it also is important that each component within the team have its own identifiable goals and objectives.

In some states, the director must acquire a special professional certificate in order to occupy such a position, in addition to being a member of one of the pupil personnel services disciplines. Some states require a teaching credential for a person to acquire the administrative certification necessary to direct these units. However, other experiences may not be acceptable in lieu of teaching. As of October, 1982, only 8 states out of 43 responding to a national survey indicated that school psychologists could obtain administrative certification based solely on their certification as school psychologists (Sebso, 1982). Since many states are restrictive in this regard, the pool of school psychologists available as candidates for the director role is rather limited. Consequently, it might be more likely that such units would be directed by persons who are not school psychologists.

There are a number of advantages to working within a pupil personnel services unit. Most obvious is that professionals from different disciplines often work with the same children. Consequently, the opportunities for collaboration are enhanced. There is some overlap in the types of skills they posses, and without a coordination of efforts, there could easily be unnecessary duplication in services. However, with a systematic approach to the direction of services, this potential duplication can be avoided. An effective communication network can lead to coordinated, high quality services. It will encourage the discussion of mutual concerns and can lead to more systematic planning, coordination, and service delivery. Gaps in services can be eliminated, duplication avoided, and the competencies of those who provide the services maximized.

An advantage that is not as evident is the opportunity for professional consultation with other colleagues on the pupil personnel services team. Each of the professions included has a somewhat different perspective from which to view a child or situation, and each can benefit from the perspective of the others. Too often, these specialists work in isolation and do not have adequate opportunity to consult with colleagues. By being administratively housed within the same unit, the possibility of collaboration is enhanced.

Special Education. Another administrative location for school psychological services is within a special education unit, usually under the leadership of a director of special education. A number of professionals might be included within this unit including special education teachers, speech and language therapists, occupational and physical therapists, interpreters, special education aides, audiologists, and adaptive physical educators, in addition to school psychologists.

This type of structure is logical in view of the fact that special education and school psychology have a great deal in common in terms of goals and clients. One of the reasons for this arrangement is that school psychologists traditionally have spent much or most of their time and effort working with special education students. Thus, housing school psychologists with special education professionals may facilitate communication among them and thereby facilitate services for special education students. The advantages of coordinating school psychological and special education services are similar to those described above for the pupil personnel services arrangement. In addition, much of the funding for school psychological services comes through special education monies.

There are, however, more obvious disadvantages to this arrangement. Most apparent is that it tends to restrict school psychological services to *only* special education students, despite the fact that these services are needed by non-handicapped students and by regular education teachers. There is a growing concern among some consumers of educational services that the large group of non-handicapped students and those with special needs who do not qualify for special education are being ignored in contrast to the emphasis given to services for the handicapped, gifted, and disadvantaged. Parents want services available for their children who commonly experience the "problems" associated with normal development. If psychological services are to be housed within a special education unit, specific efforts must be taken to ensure coordination with other programs.

By emphasizing the delivery of services to handicapped students, little thought may be given to the provision of preventive and health promotion services. Thus, students may have developed more severe problems by the time they finally receive services, with the chances for overcoming these difficulties being significantly reduced. In recent years many professionals within psychology and education have recognized the need for more preventive and health promotion activities to increase the life-long opportunities of all children.

Psychological Services. Although less common, psychological services may be organized into a separate unit, most commonly in large urban or suburban districts or within educational cooperatives. In these settings, the typically large number of school psychologists (and possibly psychometrists and psychological aides) on the staff necessitates a separate organizational unit. With a large staff, it is frequently possible to organize the psychologists according to areas of interest or "specialization." For example, some staff members might work exclusively with children with low incidence handicaps. Others could serve students at the secondary level and provide counseling and vocational programming services. A third group might work only at the elementary level rather than from K through 12. As a result of these "individualized" assignments which are based upon interest, need, and expertise, psychologists might more readily be able to develop their skills in specific areas and thus deliver more effective and efficient services. Case consultation among members of the unit might also be more common and thereby contribute to better services. Finally, since such a unit would be directed by a school psychologist, assignments and expectations would tend to be more realistic and professionally sound based upon the director's knowledge of the field. Furthermore, in discussions with district-level administrators, the director of psychological services would be able competently to articulate the needs of this unit and not be responsible for other, less familiar service providers.

The major disadvantage of this type of organizational structure is that communication with other units may be limited. Unless the planning and delivery of different services are provided in accordance with a systematic framework, there can easily be duplication of services and areas of unmet need. There may be a tendency to overlook the need for coordinating efforts with other units in delivering services, that is, less emphasis on a team approach.

Other Locations. There are a number of possible administrative locations for school psychological services within a school organization. Small districts, in particular, might tend to assign school psychologists to locations different from those described above. For example, the psychologist might report directly to the superintendent or to a principal. In reality, the psychologist might function in a relatively autonomous manner, setting his/her own goals, priorities, procedures, schedule, and so forth. The administrator typically does not possess sufficient knowledge of school psychological services to direct the psychologist. Although this type of arrangement has some advantages, the psychologist can also be quite vulnerable if conflict arises.

Cutts (1955) noted that when psychologists are assigned to a single school, they usually are considered to be part of the principal's staff. This type of structure is not commonly found in public schools, but some private schools may be organized in this manner if they individually contract for services from a regional board of education. The psychologists would be employees of the board of education, but responsible to the nonpublic school regarding day-to-day services.

Coordination of Services

Program Planning. As has been emphasized in the previous section of this chapter, it is crucial that a systematic approach be adopted in organizing the school psychology program to enhance coordination of efforts with other administrative units. Since many of the pupil personnel specialists with whom school psychologists must frequently work operate relatively independently of one another, it is necessary that a concerted effort be undertaken to ensure that these professionals coordinate their services. In making such an effort, communication among them must be a primary focus of concern. As a result, "professional territoriality issues" (i.e., one profession believing that it has certain "rights" to provide specific services even though another group also has the training and background to engage in these activities) may be minimized.

The development of a formal plan for delivering psychological services (as described above under "Pupil Personnel Services") should include steps for coordination with other units including special education, guidance counseling, social work, and health. Leaving such interactions to chance is a rather haphazard method of organization that is doomed to failure.

In addition to coordinating efforts with units internal to the school, similar linkages should be established with community and social service agencies and professionals (e.g., probation officers, community mental health centers, welfare departments, child protective agencies). They are frequent collaborators in the delivery of services, and therefore are important contributors to the development of the plan to ensure a coordinated and comprehensive approach to service delivery. By including them, a broader and more comprehensive range of services potentially is available to students, parents, and school personnel. They can help to supplement, complement, and expand the continuum of services provided by the educational agency.

Multidisciplinary Teams. School psychologists frequently operate as members of multidisciplinary teams (MDT). As a result, they must coordinate their efforts with those of the other professionals and the parents who also are on the team. Participation on these teams may serve as an enhancer of interdisciplinary collaboration. Although there have been many difficulties and problems associated with MDTs, they also can be significant forces in terms of improving services. Regardless of the manner in which school psychological services are organized, it is crucial that there be cooperative efforts among the various professionals who serve children. "Good communication, collaborative problem solving, and mutual knowledge and respect for other disciplines . . . are critical factors in multidisciplinary services" (Reynolds et al., 1984, p. 55).

CONCLUDING REMARKS

It is clear that there is no single organizational structure for school psychological services which is common across settings. It also is obvious that there are a variety of interactive factors that influence the type of structure most appropriate for any particular setting. However, we continue to have little clear guidance for determining the most effective and efficient structure.

This chapter was intended to highlight some of the critical issues that influence the organization and structuring, and therefore the delivery, of psychological services in educational settings. The professional literature contains little examination of these issues. Furthermore, there has been virtually no research published regarding the effectiveness of differing organizational structures. For example, there are no data to indicate whether more children are actually served appropriately by housing school psychologists within a pupil personnel services unit rather than in a special education unit. Are some approaches to organizing services more cost-effective than others? Data-based comparisons of contractual and school-based services are not available. Is it realistic to expect many services to be provided by "specialists" or is "generalist" training still the most appropriate model? Are there other models for organizing services that should be explored?

Answers to these types of questions have significant implications for training programs, as well as for practicing school psychologists. Research and further discussion clearly are needed. A more thorough understanding of these issues is essential if efforts to provide effective and efficient services for children are to be successful.

REFERENCES

American Psychological Association. (1981). Specialty guidelines for the delivery of services by school psychologists. *American Psychologist, 36,* 670–681.

Bersoff, D. N. (1982). The legal regulation of school psychology. In C. R. Reynolds & T. B. Gutkin (Eds.), *The handbook of school psychology* (pp. 1043–1074). New York: Wiley.

Brown, D. T., & Minke, K. M. (1984). *Directory of school psychology training programs.* Washington, DC: National Association of School Psychologists.

Carroll, J. L., Bretzing, B. H., & Harris, J. D. (1981). Psychologists in secondary schools: Training and present patterns of service. *Journal of School Psychology, 19,* 267–273.

Cowen, E. L., Trost, M. A., Lorion, R. P., Dorr, D., Izzo, L. D., & Isaacson, R. (1975). *New ways in school mental health: Early detection and prevention of school maladaptation.* New York: Human Sciences Press.

Curtis, M. J., & Yager, G. G. (1981). A systems model for the supervision of school psychological services. *School Psychology Review, 10,* 425–433.

Curtis, M. J., & Zins, J. E. (Eds.). (1981). *The theory and practice of school consultation.* Springfield, IL: Charles C Thomas.

Cutts, N. E. (Ed.). (1955). *School psychologists at mid-century.* Washington, DC: American Psychological Association.

Eberst, N. D. (1983). *Sources of funding of school psychologists.* Washington, DC: National Association of School Psychologists.

Fleming, D. D., Fleming, E. R., Oksman, P. F., & Roach, K. S. (1984). An approach to self-supervision for school practitioners. In C. A. Maher, R. J. Illback, & J. E. Zins (Eds.), *Organizational psychology in the schools: A handbook for practitioners* (pp. 323–344). Springfield, IL: Charles C Thomas.

Georgia Department of Education. (1982). *School psychological services handbook.* Atlanta: Author.

Goldstein, A. P., Sprafkin, R. P., Gershaw, N. J., & Klein, P. (1980). Social skills training through structured learning. In G. Cartledge & J. F. Milburn (Eds.), *Teaching social skills to children* (pp. 249–279). New York: Pergamon Press.

Gutkin, T. B. (1980). Teacher perceptions of consultative services provided by school psychologists. *Professional Psychology, 11,* 637–642.

Gutkin, T. B., & Tieger, A. G. (1979). Funding patterns for exceptional children: Current approaches and suggested alternatives. *Professional Psychology, 10,* 670–680.

Hughes, J. N. (1979). Consistency of administrators' and psychologists' actual and ideal perceptions of school psychologists' activities. *Psychology in the Schools, 16,* 234–239.

Jason, L. D. (1980). Prevention in the schools: Behavioral approaches. In R. H. Price, R. F. Ketterer, B. C. Bader, & J. Monahan (Eds.), *Prevention in mental health* (pp. 109–134). Beverly Hills, CA: Sage.

Kansas Department of Education. (1982). *Kansas state plan for special education.* Topeka, KS: Author.

Kentucky Department of Education. (1984). *Comprehensive school psychological services.* Frankfort, KY: Author.

Keough, B. K., Kukic, S. J., Becker, L. D., McLoughlin, R. J., & Kukic, M. B. (1975). School psychologists' services in special education programs. *Journal of School Psychology, 13,* 142–148.

Kramer, J. J., & Nagle, R. J. (1980). Suggestions for the delivery of psychological services in secondary schools. *Psychology in the Schools, 17,* 53–59.

Kuehnel, J. (1975). Faculty, school and organizational characteristics, and schools' openness to mental health resources. *Dissertation Abstracts International, 36,* 2716-A.

Maher, C. A., Illback, R. J., & Zins, J. E. (1984). Applying organizational psychology in schools: Perspectives and framework. In C. A. Maher, R. J. Illback, & J. E. Zins (Eds.), *Organizational psychology in the schools: A handbook for practitioners* (pp. 5–20). Springfield, IL: Charles C Thomas.

Manley, T. R., & Manley, E. T. (1978). A comparison of the personal values and operative goals of school psychologists and school superintendents. *Journal of School Psychology, 16,* 99–109.

Mason, E. J., & Remer, R. (1979). Politics and school psychology: A case study. *Journal of School Psychology, 17,* 74–81.

Meyers, J. (1981). Mental health consultation. In T. R. Kratochwill (Ed.), *Advances in school psychology* (Vol. 1, pp. 133–168). Hillsdale, NJ: Lawrence Erlbaum Associates.

Miller, J. G. (1955). Toward a general theory for the behavioral sciences. *American Psychologist, 10,* 513–553.

Nagle, R. J., & Medway, F. J. (1982). Issues in providing psychological services at the high school level. *School Psychology Review, 11*, 359–369.

National Association of School Psychologists. (1984a). *Standards for the provision of school psychological services.* Washington, DC: Author.

National Association of School Psychologists. (1984b). *Standards for training and field placement programs in school psychology.* Washington, DC: Author.

North Carolina Department of Public Instruction. (1983). *Comprehensive school psychology programs.* Raleigh, NC: Author.

Ohio Department of Education. (1982). *Rules for the education of handicapped children.* Columbus: Author.

P. v. Riles, 343 F. Supp. 1306 (N.D. Cal. 1972).

P. v. Riles, 502 F. 2d 963 (9th Cir. 1974).

P. v. Riles, 495 F. Supp. 926 (N.D., Cal. 1979).

Parham v. J.L., 422 U.S. 584 (1979).

Reynolds, C. R., Gutkin, T. B., Elliott, S. N., & Witt, J. C. (1984). *School psychology: Essentials of theory and practice.* New York: Wiley.

Sarason, S. B. (1971). *The culture of the school and the problem of change.* Boston, MA: Allyn & Bacon.

Sebso, M. (1982). *Administrative certification for school psychologists.* Washington, DC: National Association of School Psychologists.

Waters, L. G. (1973). School psychologists as perceived by school personnel: Support for a consultant model. *Journal of School Psychology, 11*, 40–46.

Zins, J. E., & Curtis, M. J. (1981). Teacher preferences for differing consultation models. In M. J. Curtis & J. E. Zins (Eds.), *The theory and practice of school consultation* (pp. 184–189). Springfield, IL: Charles C Thomas.

Zins, J. E., & Curtis, M. J. (1984). Building consultation into the educational service delivery system. In C. A. Maher, R. J. Illback, & J. E. Zins (Eds.), *Organizational psychology in the schools: A handbook for practitioners* (pp. 213–242). Springfield, IL: Charles C Thomas.

Zins, J. E., Wagner, D. I., & Maher, C. A. (Eds.). (1985). *Health promotion in the schools: Innovative approaches to facilitating physical and emotional well-being.* New York: Haworth Press.

6 Models of School Psychological Service Delivery

Jonathan Sandoval
University of California, Davis

A model of how school psychologists go about delivering services in educational settings, like any other model of a professional's activity, is an idealized notion of how an individual should behave in a work setting. Such a model is an abstraction and often represents internal thoughts that govern external behaviors in the workplace. Because it is an abstraction, a model should explain behavior over a variety of activities. That is, it should dictate how the school psychologist goes about the various roles of assessment, consultation, counseling, intervention, program evaluation, research, and so on.

Any model of how people behave is doomed to failure for many reasons. People are inconsistent and alter their behavior to meet the demands of an environment that is constantly shifting and evolving. People who create models do so to highlight a particular behavior or to implement a particular theoretical position and are not concerned with mapping reality. Nevertheless, models can be used as roadmaps that professionals consult from time to time to adjust the ways they are behaving in serving clients. Although a model may not be complete and may fail to give direction in performing certain duties, it can make some statements about what is important among the duties and where the emphasis should be placed in the day-to-day activities of the school psychologist.

In this chapter I discuss six models of school psychological services delivery. All six of the models have appeared in the literature in one form or another although new versions and extensions are discussed in this volume. A decade ago Reilly (1973) identified six models as well, and there is some congruence between his scheme and mine. A trichotomy of models was proposed by Granowsky and Davis (1974) but one of their models, the community-based school psychologist, is not discussed (see also Brantley, 1971). Only models relating to service in the school have been considered. There is nothing sacred about the number six; no doubt others exist.

I evaluate the models on the basis of a number of criteria important to consider in the delivery of services. Most of these are theoretical and may have little to do with day-to-day realities in a school district. One strategy for evaluating the models would be to see how completely they match the day-to-day activities of school psychologists. There have been a number of attempts to learn the common duties of school psychologists (Carroll, Harris, & Bretzing, 1979; Cook & Patterson, 1977; Flax & Anderson, 1966; Lacayo, Sherwood, & Morris, 1981). Typically, this research is done through a survey of the way school psychologists spend their time. Unfortunately, knowing how a school psychologist spends his or her time does not indicate how important are the various aspects of the duties. Because an activity takes a lot of time does not mean that it leads to effective impact on clients. The time spent in testing and writing reports, the most commonly reported activity (Keogh, Kukic, Becker, McLoughlin, & Kukic, 1975), may not represent the overall importance of these activities in helping children to become appropriately educated.

Another shortcoming of surveys on what school psychologists do is that they represent averages across a number of school psychologists. We do not know from the surveys if there are subpopulations among school psychologists who allocate their time and function quite differently than others.

Yet another problem in using data about what school psychologists do is that forces other than models and training influence school psychologists' behavior (Ysseldyke, 1978). An obvious one is economics. School psychologists are often compensated out of funds earmarked for services to special education populations. Following the notion that the one who pays the piper calls the tune, many districts require school psychologists to justify their time on the basis of service to special education populations, Title I populations (i.e., economically depressed populations), or others for whom psychological services seem particularly relevant. Although a proactive role has been espoused for school psychologists by many who have created models, the schools have not been in a position to fund such preventative activities for school psychologists.

A further limitation on school psychologist's behavior that obscures the behavioral implementation of a model is lack of skill. It is an inescapable fact that the basic skills of assessment are easier to learn and practice than those of consultation, counseling, research, and evaluation. As a result, assessment activities often dominate a school psychologist's role because they are overlearned and easy to do. Actually the skills in assessment are difficult to learn at an advanced level, but it is certainly true that one can learn the rudiments of administering a test and scoring it in a short period of time (Meacham & Peckham, 1978). When faced with difficult problems, who among us has failed to fall back on the safe and comfortable role of tester, if only to gain some time to think about the problem. My assumption is that people do what they are most able to do and shy away from activities they have not gained competence in performing.

Another barrier to the implementation of a model is expectation. As social animals, school psychologists, like anyone else, are influenced by what others in the school or their social environment think they should be doing. The social system that has assigned a particular role to a psychologist is very slow in accepting behavior that departs from expectation. A school psychologist with a model that is inconsistent with the kinds of behaviors sanctioned has a very tough task in addressing and changing expectations. Since school psychologists are a mobile group, many psychologists find themselves in new settings where their predecessors have created a professional straightjacket for them.

It is interesting to note the congruence between the school psychologist's perception of his or her role and the perceptions of others. A number of studies of this issue of congruences appear in the literature (Culbertson, 1975; Ford & Migles, 1979; Gilmore & Chandy, 1973; Hughes, 1979; Kahl & Fine, 1978; Kaplan, Clancy, & Chrin, 1977; Landau & Gerkin, 1979; Manley & Manley, 1978; Miller, 1974; Waters, 1973). In general, school administrators agree that consultation is a valued activity but also emphasize case study and assessment, particularly when there is follow-up by the school psychologist.

Although it may be difficult to infer from behavior, and although it may not be consciously acknowledged, all school psychologists are following a model when they deliver services in the school. For the most part, I speculate that models of service delivery originate in the education and training the school psychologist receives. Much of this training takes place at the graduate level, where a program of preparation may feature one or another of the theoretical positions to be elucidated in the next section. Sometimes models are established through the school psychologist's undergraduate preparation in psychology. No doubt other forces are at play in determining the model a psychologist follows. Certainly the political and ethical values and assumptions that an individual holds make one or another model more attractive. Besides values, one might assume that personality, too, plays a role in the model embraced. Although I have no empirical basis on which to do so, I have supplied a sublabel to each of the models described, from which may be inferred my speculations about both personality and values that may go into the adoption of a model by a school psychologist.

Dimensions for Evaluating Models of School Psychological Services Delivery

In addition to presenting models of school psychological service delivery, the purpose of this chapter is to evaluate each model so that the reader may recognize a model being followed by a school psychologist, may choose a model to follow, or may create a model that represents a fusion or combination of those presented. To this end, I discuss each of the models using the following dimensions:

Who is the Client? For each model, it is important to ask the question "Who is the client?" The client can be designated as the school, a child's parent, or the child. Within the school, the client may be the regular education teacher, the school administration, the special education teacher, a school site, or a central administration administrator. Later in this volume there is an extensive discussion of the issue of clientage (see Stewart, Chapter 4).

Theories Used. On what theoretical position does the model draw? According to the American Psychological Association (1981), a school psychologist should be educated

> in such substantive areas as the biological basis of behavior, the cognitive and the affective basis of behavior, the social cultural ethnic and sex role basis of behavior, and individual differences. Coursework includes social and philosophical basis of education, curriculum theory and practice, etiology of learning and behavior disorders, exceptional children and special education. Organizational theory and administrative practice should also be included in the program.

If we follow this dictate, the psychologist should be familiar with a large number of psychological theories. Nevertheless, each model draws particularly upon certain of those psychological theories and downplays others.

Assumptions and Values. What are the values inherent in the model? Each model of service delivery has implicit in it a number of values about children's, parents', and teachers' rights. Also inherent in many models are ideas about what is ethically correct behavior, and how people are able to lead the most fulfilling and rewarding life within the confines of society. Assumptions about how people change are also featured. In choosing a model, one would hope that the values inherent in the model were consistent with the values subscribed to by the adherent.

Goals. What are the goals of school psychological services? Different models see the role and duties of school psychologists differently. The models vary on what they believe to be "the bottom line" as far as psychological services are concerned.

Methods. What are the special methods used? Just as psychologists receive exposure to a wide variety of theories and yet emphasize a relatively small number in adhering to a model, so it is with methods. Most psychologists are familiar with a number of methods: assessment, counseling, consultation, group work, research, teaching, and so forth. Usually a model features particular psychological methods, however, to the exclusion of others.

Problem Solving. What are the direct and indirect problem-solving activities? The emphasis in most models is on problem solving, and almost all incorporate the concept of school psychologists as scientific problem solvers (Burke, Hapworth, & Brantley, 1980; Sloves, Docherty, & Schneider, 1979). Scientific problem-solving steps are Problem Clarification, Planning, Development, Implementation, and Outcome Determination. Nevertheless, there are differences in how one approaches each step or places emphasis.

Specific Criticisms of the Model. Each of the models by virtue of taking a position on the client, theories, assumptions, methods, and so on may be criticized on the basis of sins of omission and commission. No model is adequate to prescribe all of the behavior of the school psychologist; what is missing is also quite important. In addition there are sins of commission. Some aspects of each of the models are difficult to justify in light of either research evidence or other important considerations. These "sins" must be brought out and made explicit in each of the models. Other criticisms of models may be based on problems due to a lack of internal consistency and in application to all of the settings in which school psychologists work.

In the next six sections I present models of school psychological services. In each section I comment on each of the evaluation criteria. To some extent I set up an overly strict representation of the model being discussed. Advocates of a model may accuse me of setting up a strawperson. I hope I am not using straw weapons to attack strawpersons, but rather illuminate the choices made in embracing a model. Most of the statements I make probably should be modified to make them softer, but in the interest of clarity I speak directly.

THE DIAGNOSTIC MODEL: THE WHITE-COATED GATE KEEPER

The diagnostic model is one that I equate with the "traditional" model of school psychological services. The diagnostic model is one that puts the school psychologist in the position of bringing to bear psychological theories and understandings in diagnosing children's problems as they emerge in the process of schooling. Following a diagnosis, a particular intervention will be attempted with the child, typically in the form of special education. I have applied the phrase "White Coated" to capture the medical model aspect (Reger, 1972) and "gate keeper" to acknowledge the important role the psychologist has in deciding which children will receive which extra services in the school. The central concept in this model is diagnosis. Intervention, although important, is secondary and follows from the diagnosis.

A number of texts in school psychology implicitly incorporate this model (e.g., Fein, 1974; Gottsegen, 1960; White & Harris, 1961), and the description seems most applicable when the school psychologist is defined as a clinical psychologist in the schools (Bardon, 1964). Although I can attribute the model to no author in particular, many have sought to contrast newer models with it (e.g., Bardon, 1963; Fairchild, 1976; Granowsky & Davis, 1974). The latest incarnation of this paradigm is in the writings on neuropsychology in the schools (e.g., Obrzut, 1981).

In most descriptions of this model, the client is the child. That is, the school psychologist is working for the child in an attempt to determine what difficulties the child is having. Although it is not often acknowledged, an important secondary client (and some would argue primary client) of the diagnostician is the school. The school psychologist is intimately involved in the operation of the special education system of the school and, as implied in the label, serves as a gate keeper. The school inadvertently becomes the client when the diagnostician works to keep the special education system functioning smoothly by finding clients for it and dismissing clients who are making progress.

The diagnostic model draws primarily on the psychology of individual differences and on psychometric theory. The diagnostician must be knowledgeable about the etiology of various psychological disturbances and be able to identify either psychological processes that are not operating properly or that are inappropriately developed for a child's age. The diagnostic psychologist must know developmental theories, learning theory, and personality theory, but the emphasis is on usually pathology rather than on normal learning and development. Part of the theoretical package is differential psychology; notions about children differ with respect to various cognitive, affective, and psychomotor characteristics. Lately psychologists have been turning to neuroanatomy and neuropsychology (e.g., Das, Kirby, & Jarman, 1979; Hynd & Obrzut, 1981; Luria, 1966) for notions of why children have difficulty in school.

A number of assumptions are inherent in this model. First, in order to make an appropriate decision about a child, it is necessary to make a diagnosis, that is, to understand the cause of the child's difficulty and the complete extent of that difficulty (Honigfeld, 1971). The assumption is that deficits in basic psychological processes make it difficult to learn in school. Another value is that tests or other procedures can yield important decisions about where children's difficulties lie (French, 1979). Although not a prominent value, another set of assumptions is that the problems a child encounters spring from deficits within the child. As Reger (1972) stated, "Two basic assumptions are . . . 1. Behavior that deviates in a negative direction from normative standards is a reflection of a personal disease (or illness, disturbance, disorder, dysfunction). 2. Behavior that has been classified as deviant must be changed within the individual by a curative process" (p. 9). It is not necessarily true that a child is responsible for the problem, but it is true that either biology or environment has left a child who is not functioning in school with a particular scar that must be detected and categorized. Other values are that labeling is more beneficial than hurtful to the child and that knowledge of deficits can be translated into ways of assisting a child (Honigfeld, 1971).

According to the diagnostic model, the goals of school psychological services are to create accurate diagnoses of children and prescriptions based on those diagnoses. Following this model, a school psychologist would serve the school best if he or she is able to render a diagnosis and prescription for each child who is encountering difficulty. The diagnostic psychologist aims to respond to referrals quickly and competently, and to leave a report outlining what might be done on the basis of the difficulties in the child that have been uncovered.

The psychological method emphasized by the diagnostician is assessment. A diagnostician needs to know about individual assessment devices, needs to be able to collect information through interviewing the child, teachers, parents, and others about the child, and to be able to serve the child by creating relevant educational contexts for him or her. The counseling interview, when used, is a diagnostic interview aimed at elucidating the child's problems, and evaluation is used to be sure a diagnosis is correct.

Problem-solving activities besides assessment have to do with translating behavior from a variety of sources into a careful and correct characterization of the psychological make-up of the child. Once the child has been accurately pigeon-holed, the next step is to assign the child to a particular program, either one already operating in the school, or one specially designed to allow a teacher to cope with the child's difficulties in the classroom. Given a correct diagnosis, interventions naturally follow. The diagnostician worries chiefly about the accuracy of the diagnosis, not about what should be done for a child once a particular diagnosis has been created.

The psychological literature is replete with criticism of the diagnostic model and the process of diagnosis. One important focus for opposition has to do with the overreliance on psychological assessment, particularly on cognitive assessment (Brooks, 1979). Criticisms of testing have often been considered to be simultaneous criticisms of this model of school psychological services (Cleveland, 1976). Critics of tests point out that tests often reveal information that is not relevant to interventions in the schools (Reschly, 1980). Information from tests does not have educational validity, goes the argument. IQ tests have been most roundly criticized in this regard. (See Hebb, 1978, for rebuttal to these criticisms.) Cleveland (1976), observing the decline of psychodiagnosis, attributes it to the poisoning of the public's mind about tests, overly high expectations for tests, and poor instruments. Defenders of the model point out that the criticisms are levied against tests, whereas a proper assessment uses multiple methods of deriving a diagnosis.

Others have attacked the diagnostic model on grounds there is an inherent bias in this model in perceiving the problem to lie within the child (Reger, 1972). These critics believe that often problems come either from the child's environment or in the match between the child and the environment (Grieger & Abidin, 1972).

More telling for the partisans of this model is the criticism that it is too narrowly conceived. Simply assuming the role of the diagnostician and making this the major activity of the school psychologist ignores both the problems inherent in the school and the vast array of psychological theory that can be brought to bear on problems in the educational environment. The assumption that the child's failure in school comes solely from a deficit in the child ignores the fact that causality is mutual and reciprocal. Children and their characteristics interact with an environment that may or may not be flexible enough to cope with them (Mischel, 1977).

In addition, Fairchild (1976) has pointed out that special educators have not supported this model because of their doubts about the efficacy of self-contained classes and the use of categorical programming. Although agreeing, Bersoff (1971) goes further and charges that the labeling done as a result of diagnosis is in itself *destructive* because of changes in social expectations placed on the child.

THE PREVENTION-PROMOTION MODEL: THE SMOOTH TALKER

Many authors have attempted to put forward as an alternative to the diagnostic model a model of the psychologist as a preventative mental health worker (Bardon, 1963; Bower, 1955; Cowen & Lorion, 1976). This model is offered particularly as a solution to the presumed inefficiency of assessment and remediation (Alpert, 1976; Fairchild, 1976; Meyers, 1973). The origins of the preventionist approach are closely identified with the early work in prevention done by public health specialists, particularly with the efforts by Lindeman and Caplan at Harvard (Alpert, 1976; Gilmore, 1974). As a result, adherents to this model usually adopt the strategy of mental health consultation, as outlined by Gerald Caplan (1970), although other methods are also consistent with this approach (Bower, 1955). The label "smooth talker" is used to reflect the use of consultation and other techniques to bring about individual change. The preventionist follows the dictate that a school psychologist is the representative in the schools of psychological theory and practice. As the knowledgeable expert on psychology, the preventionist must find ways to change the schools to make them responsive to children's needs. If successful, all children will be educated to their potential (primary prevention), children at risk will not fail (secondary prevention), and those failing will be helped to recover from their difficulties (tertiary prevention)

(Bower, 1964). The preventionist works to prevent mental and emotional disorders and to promote mental health.

In the prevention model the client varies depending on the activity. In most school settings the client is the child, although in consultation, where the consultee is a school administrator, the client may be a teacher or a parent. Because indirect services are featured, in some sense teachers and administrators are secondary clients because work is done with them to make them more sophisticated in the use of psychology to benefit children. In the prevention model, all children attending school are clients, not just those experiencing difficulty.

The prevention model draws on a number of psychological theories, but there is a tendency for adherents, particularly those doing mental health consultation, to draw on psychodynamic principles more often than the adherents of other models of school psychological services. Theories dealing with the origin of conflicts play an integral part in consultation. In addition, consultation is particularly congruent with various developmental theories as the emphasis in this model is on facilitating the development of both the client and the consultee. Understanding normal development and acquisition of skills helps one promote the normal acquisition of skills in the school setting.

The assumptions underlying the prevention model include the idea that an early intervention, or better yet, steps taken before a problem manifests itself, are more efficient approaches than remediation. Another assumption or value is that it is best for a psychologist not to intervene directly. As Bardon states "we do not teach people to change or understand; rather we provide the information, or better still, the conditions which make it possible to do these things for himself [sic]" (1963, p. 20). According to Alpert (1976), important assumptions in consultation are that the consultant can alter perceptions in a consultee, altered perceptions can affect behavior, and generalization will occur in the consultee from one client to another. Other values are on the importance of the relationship established between the school psychologist and others in the school. It is assumed that any change must be to the environment of the school, because problems do not simply arise in the child.

The goal of school psychological services under the prevention model is to improve the functioning of the school staff in meeting the needs of all children. Functioning is improved by making better teachers and administrators through the use of application of psychological theory. Another way of stating the goal is to make a school more psychologically minded.

Consultation is one method emphasized by the preventative school psychologist. Usually the approach followed is mental health consultation, but behavioral consultation or organizational consultation techniques may also be used (Meyers, 1973). The process of consultation can be defined as a talking relationship between a psychologist and the consultee, where the focus is on a client of the consultee and on solving problems related to the client's functioning, at the same time making the consultee better able to function in his or her role. The consulting school psychologist takes time to meet with the consultee and conduct much of the important work through the use of the consultation interview. Other important methods are screening, psychological education, crisis counseling, anticipatory guidance, research, and parent education (Bower, 1965).

The direct and indirect problem-solving activities in consultation revolve around work with the consultee. Following Caplan, the preventionist decides, after careful listening, whether the difficulty is caused by lack of knowledge, lack of skill, lack of objectivity, or lack of self-confidence on the part of the consultee. The problem-solving activities depend on which of these "lacks" is operating. If it is lack of knowledge or skill, the psychologist either supplies the needed information or encourages the consultee to seek appropriate additional training. If the difficulty is judged to be lack of objectivity or lack of self-confidence, the psychologist works with the consultee to alter the consultee's perceptions of the situation and to supply psychological support for any new undertakings the consultee may attempt.

The prevention model is most vulnerable to criticisms that point out that consultation and prevention activities are not what the school wants from the school psychologist, or at least they are not high priorities (Broskowski & Baker, 1974; Starkman, 1966). Because the duties of the psychologist often involve assessment of children, and because this model deemphasizes testing as tertiary prevention, it does not take into account the expectation that school psychologists do special education assessment. Reger (1965) also points out that the emphasis in the prevention model is often on negative events and on vague, hard-to-evaluate activities.

Although the goal of the prevention model is to make better teachers, there is a danger that the individual child may be overlooked in the process since the focus is on teacher change. In most schools, at the end of the year the child is promoted to another grade and teacher, and the efforts of the school psychologist have been lost to the child unless the problem has been resolved right away and does not reoccur the next year.

Another criticism is that this model depends much more directly on the openness of teachers and others to seek consultation or preventive activities. Experience has shown that those teachers least in need of help from the school psychologist are those who come for consultation. Teachers who are having the most difficulty in school often avoid school psychologists in an effort to minimize any feelings of failure or incompetence that might be implied if one seeks help from a school psychologist.

A parallel criticism is that in this model the difficulty rests in the school's failure to adapt to the child. There is a danger that the child will be excused from any responsibility for the problems in question and that unrealistic expectations may be generated for educational personnel to cope with exceedingly difficult children who truly cannot be educated in the public sector. In addition, as Reschly (1976) pointed out, the assumption that efforts made in consultation to help one client will transfer to other clients has not been demonstrated. There is little evidence that consultees improve their functioning with new clients.

This model may be the furthest removed from the day-to-day duties of the school psychologist. Particularly at the secondary level, the model may have limited applicability. Adherents claim, however, the fact that psychologists are overwhelmingly involved in tertiary prevention means that a great deal of reform is necessary. In addition, effective arguments can be made for the cost effectiveness of the model, (Harper & Balch, 1975).

THE SOCIAL LEARNING MODEL: THE NO-NONSENSE GURU

Few theoretical positions have been as far-reaching in psychology as behaviorism. It was natural that behavioral notions, particularly social learning theory, would soon be taken up by school psychologists. For example, White and Harris (1961) had a chapter in their early book on school psychology devoted to behavior modification. Although preventionists might use social learning theory ideas as a part of their efforts, behaviorists in school psychology have usually approached the field differently. Woody (1976) has traced the evolution of this model over the years showing the movement from therapist to consultant. I have included in the label "No Nonsense" to capture the operationalism and present orientation of the behaviorist, and "Guru" to denote the notion of the school psychologist as teacher and expert in behavioral technology that pervades this model.

In this model the child is the client, although the teacher is often the focus of efforts, and as a result, becomes a secondary client. A danger in this model, consequently, is that the client is forgotten in the process and the teacher becomes the one who gains from the efforts of the psychologist. A teacher's improved control over a child's behavior may not necessarily be in the child's best interest.

The psychological theory most often drawn on by the behavioral consultant is social learning theory, particularly as outlined by Albert Bandura (Bandura, 1969; Bandura & Walters, 1963). In brief, social learning theory emphasizes that all behaviors have both antecedents and consequences, and in order to change behaviors, attention must be paid to both of these factors. Behavior is changed through the careful application of reinforcements to create new response repertoires. Kazdin (1982a) and Kratochwill (1982) provide a comprehensive review of behavioral methods and the relevant research.

The values inherent in this model are the values that go along with social learning theory. That is, that behavior is neither good nor bad but is simply the outcome of past learning (Whitman & Whitman, 1971). Any behavior can be changed given sufficient control over the situation. The child's problem does not necessarily reside in any deficit in the child but rather comes from behaviors that the environment reinforces (Grieger & Abidin, 1972).

The goal of the social learning theorist is first to teach consultees to use behavioral strategies and principles, particularly behavior modification. A second goal is to reduce pupils' behavioral problems that are defined in terms of behaviors that are deemed inappropriate by others, particularly teachers.

The special methods used by the behavioral consultant are those of comprehensive behavior modification techniques and the teaching of those techniques. Basic principles are reinforcement of correct responses, immediate feedback, minimization of incorrect responses, enlistment of the learner's active participation, and allowance for individual differences in learning (Whitman & Whitman, 1971, p. 180). Other methods used are observation (Alessi, 1980), cognitive restructuring or behavioral self-control (Mahoney & Thoreson, 1974) and interview (Bersoff & Grieger, 1971; Breyer, Calchera, & Cann, 1971) in order to determine various response contingencies and reinforcers. Not all behavioral approaches, however, are applicable to the school setting (Woody, 1976).

The problem-solving activities are centered around observing the behavior of the child and the reaction of the teacher. It is particularly important to define baseline behavior. Next comes the process of identifying the problem inherent in the behavior that has been observed. The next step is to set objectives and begin shaping behavior toward identified goals. Other activities are modeling, stimulus control, and the evaluation of behaviors once the program is underway. Goodwin and Coates (1976) offer an excellent paradigm for problem-solving activities.

The social learning model for school psychologists' activities has been criticized on a number of grounds. A major criticism is that the problems identified and the changes made by the school psychologist may not be in the best interests of the child (Abidin, 1972; Grieger & Abidin, 1972). Since behaviors are defined by the teacher as inappropriate, there is always the danger that the child may be led to "be still, be quiet and be docile" (Winett & Winkler, 1972), which are not behaviors necessarily conducive to learning and good mental health. Many critics feel behavioral technology is too easy to learn (Abidin, 1972; Whitman & Whitman, 1971). Without humanistic values, many believe that it is irresponsible to teach behavioral techniques to teachers and parents who may use them in ways not appropriate in a democratic society.

Abidin (1972), for one, has questioned the adequacy of this theoretical orientation for work with humans. Because the research base came from work with animals, he believes there are difficulties in the direct application of many principles, particularly if the subject's beliefs and expectations are dealt with. Behavioral techniques will not be successful unless the affective state of the subject is properly addressed (Abidin, 1975).

Another old issue that continues to be debated is that of symptom substitution (Kazdin, 1982b; Whitman & Whitman, 1971). The argument goes that efforts directed at changing a symptomatic behavior, which ignore the underlying cause of the symptom, are doomed to failure. The untreated cause will ultimately lead to the emergence of more symptomatic behaviors.

Research has not borne out this contention (Whitman & Whitman, 1971). In addition, social learning theorists claim that if new behaviors turn up, much of the time they will be more appropriate than the symptoms suppressed.

A final criticism has to do with the narrowness of focus of social learning theory. Although there are virtues in a methodical approach to problems, the behaviors examined are often so discrete as to be relatively meaningless. It takes great skill on the part of practitioners to keep the focus in behavioral consultation on broad and meaningful behavior change. Criticisms aside, research has demonstrated the effectiveness of behavioral approaches (Medway, 1979).

THE ORGANIZATIONAL DEVELOPMENT MODEL: THE POLITICIAN

In reading articles describing the organizational development model (e.g., Schmuck & Miles, 1971), it is unclear to me whether this is a model for all of the school psychologists services in the schools or one particular role that a psychologist might assume in addition to others (Gallessich, 1973; Hannafin & Witt, 1983). Nevertheless, the writers are so clear in delineating important aspects of this model, it is included here as a separate model for organizing all psychological services in the school.

The notion that school psychologists should work with the entire school organization has been with us for some time (Gray, 1963). Like the other models, it has developed as a reaction to the ineffectiveness and time-consuming nature of testing and the need to make greater headway with school staff as the representatives of the discipline of psychology (Lee, 1974).

Briefly stated, the organizational development model proposes a school psychologist's work should be aimed at making the social system of the school operate efficiently in the best interest of its clients, the children. The school psychologist serves as a politician or diplomat who mediates and facilitates communication between relevant subgroups and applies organizational psychology in making the institution humanistic, effective, and democratic. Meyers, Martin, and Hyman (1977) describe two types of organizational development: (a) that designed to facilitate the resolution of specific organizational problems such as racial tension, and (b) that designed to focus on general interpersonal and communication problems.

In this model it is much more clear than in other models that the school system is the client of the school psychologist (Gallessich, 1972; Lennox, Flanagan, & Meyers, 1979). Making the organization a more relevant and effective system has the benefit of serving the children. The child and parents, then, are secondary clients.

The central psychological theories on which this model is based originate in the work of Kurt Lewin (1947) and others interested in field theory, group processes, and ecological psychology. It also draws from Gestalt psychology as well as humanistic approaches to psychology (Argyris, 1970) which focus on human nature and the importance of relationships between individuals in a social system. Another concept from humanistic psychology is the importance of allowing a client to take an active role in problem solving that influences the client's destiny.

The important values and assumptions in this model have to do with the notion that it is difficult or impossible to help a child if the social system in which the child functions is not addressed and influenced. Also important are those democratic values that stress the importance of change using open and public decision making. Conoley (1980) identified two additional assumptions. "We need to understand the context of the organization in order to understand the individual because organizational variables often override personality variables. The school system is not a self serving system, but rather one established for children; therefore systematic change and modification is a rational, and often preferred strategy" (p. 84).

The goals of school psychological services are to assist the organization of the school to be more efficient in serving children and to make the school more sensitive to children's needs (Reschly, 1976). Important subgoals are to improve communication (Lennox et al., 1979) and to facilitate the overall growth of the organization (Gallessich, 1973). Schmuck (1976) includes the establishment of collective goals, uncovering of confict, improvement of group processes, solving of organizational problems, collective decision making, and assessment of change.

The methods used in organizational development include interviewing and observation as well as the use of surveys in assessing the functioning of an organization, consultation with key personnel in helping them open up the organization to democratic decision-making, and feedback sessions aimed at increasing dialogue between important members of the organization. Group meetings and training also are important methods used by the organizational development psychologists. Of these methods, Conoley (1980) identified the primary one as "Organizational Assessment." The three components are to (a) understand the organization according to important systemic variables like power, competition, production nurturance; (b) understand the impact of these variables on the behaviors of the organization members; and (c) design and implement systems level change strategies that facilitate the learning and mental health coping skills of children in schools. Her article discusses the system variables and questions that should form the basis of organizational assessment.

Problem-solving activities consist of interviewing, observing, and analyzing an institution's functioning. Next comes describing the goals, norms, resources, and modes of interaction taking place within the system. Finally the school psychologist selects procedures for encouraging better communication and better use of resources by the organization. The psychologist may also moderate group activities and serve as a facilitator in order to bring about needed changes within the organization. Problem definition, assessment, intervention and evaluation can all take place on the systems level (Maher, 1981).

The model may be criticized on several grounds. Many of the activities and roles prescribed by this model overlap and come in conflict with those roles assigned to the school principal or the school superintendent. In addition, very few of the activities in this model are consistent with the traditional duties that occupy the time of school psychologists. The assumption that making a school more democratic and functioning better as an organization leads to an appropriate and complete education for all children has not been validated (Reschly, 1976). In addition, leadership styles other than the democratic one may also be effective within the school setting and it may not be reasonable to expect that methods derived from industry are applicable to the school (Levinson, 1972). The model, in addition, assumes that people are willing to change and that resistance to change can easily be overcome (Lennox et al., 1979). Naturally there is a great deal of evidence indicating this is not the case. Although arguments may be developed for how cost-effective organizational development can be, one might wonder whether or not school districts are financially willing or able to support this kind of activity. For a lively debate over the merits of organizational development see Sashkin, Burke, and Levinson (1973).

THE PRESCRIPTIVE INTERVENTION MODEL: THE DIAGNOSTIC EDUCATOR

This model of school psychological services is one that brings the psychologist's duties closest to those of the educator (Gilmore, 1974). Unlike the diagnostic model, the focus of this model is on gathering information of educational and classroom relevance (Forness, 1970) and delivering this information to multi-disciplinary teams creating prescriptions and individual educational plans.

Reger (1965) used the term *educational programmer* in an early description of this model. Pielstick (1963) declared a need for a learning-oriented model in distinction to the clinical diagnostic model. In this model, the school psychologist studies "the pupil's learning situation and how he responds to it, an analysis of the particular learning abilities and disabilities of the child, the history of his learning patterns in and out of the school situation and culminates in hypotheses or predictions (recommendations, if you wish) about what changes would be most likely to further the pupil's learning efficiency" (p. 16). Diagnoses in this model are not of underlying conditions but of skills the pupils lack; particularly skills that can be taught in the context of the school.

The difference between the prescriptive intervention model and the diagnostic model is that criterion-referenced assessment is preferred over norm-referenced assessment, and the stress is on responsibility for remediation, even to the extent of directly supervising tutorial personnel (Osguthorpe, 1979).

In this model, the client is primarily the child, who benefits from accurate prescriptions in educational settings, and secondarily the teacher, although the teacher is the main focus of the prescriptive interventions. The theories this model draws on are primarily the learning theories, particular classroom learning theories like those of Robert Gagne (1977) which allow the prescriptive educator to specify a learning hierarchy. Other theories that have come from the notion of learning modalities and perceptual deficits have occasionally been used (e.g., Valett, 1969).

The major assumption in this model is that information about a child's skills, particularly curricular skills, will lead to better decisions about the individualization of instruction for the child. Children's difficulties can be assessed and knowledge of the child's status can be transformed into educational prescriptions (Peter, 1965; Valett, 1963, 1968). The addition of information into the system will make it function better for the child. Another value is that the educational competence of children is of critical importance to the child's mental health and that by focusing on educational attainment, the child's functioning as a mentally healthy individual will be facilitated (Morrow, 1975). Another important assumption is that it is irresponsible to do diagnosis and not follow through with personal involvement in remediation or psychoeducational therapy (Jackson, 1970; Jackson & Bernauer, 1975).

The goal of the prescriptive interventionist is to prevent problems from becoming worse in the school setting by the accurate educational assessment of the child's educational needs and the design of educational programs to improve academic and social functioning. The special methods used by the prescriptive interventionist are those within the area of assessment. A prescriptive interventionist relies much more heavily on criterion-referenced tests and measures, makes observations, examines work samples, and orients most of the assessment toward the child's achievement of curriculum goals (Dickinson, 1980). A recent revived method used most by psychologists following this model is trial teaching as a means of assessment (Forness, 1970). The most radical proponent of this technique is Reuven Feuerstein (1979) with his system of instrumental enrichment.

The problem-solving strategies unique to the model are the analysis and description in educational terms of the child's skills and abilities. Problem solving is done through very detailed task analysis and specification of learning hierarchies.

This model has been criticized because the skills and methods are most removed from psychology (Gilmore, 1974). It is possible for skilled educators to perform most of the duties associated with the prescriptive model. In additon, the prescriptive interventionist ignores the importance of factors such as intelligence in the learning process. The importance of emotional status is also dismissed and underemphasized (Brooks, 1979). Many of the methods, procedures, and theories underpinning this model have not been validated in the research literature (Lidz, 1979). The modality theory coming from the ITPA embraced by many prescriptive interventionists, for example, has not held up well to research scrutiny (Arter & Jenkins, 1977). The use of criterion-referenced testing has also been criticized. Lidz (1979), for example, points out that the *how* and *why* of failure are not documented as well as the *what*. She also notes that there is a great deal of difficulty reaching consensus on the criteria to be used in assessment and that the psychometric procedures for analyzing these tests are different and not as completely worked out as those for norm-referenced tests.

THE CHILD ADVOCACY MODEL: THE CRUSADER

The child advocacy model places the school psychologist in the position of working on behalf of the child in a system that is seen as essentially antagonistic to children's needs and best interests. Child advocacy takes two forms (Mearig, 1974). The first is social advocacy or working for children's rights in the public arena and attempting to establish programs that are focused on primary prevention. In addition to social advocacy, child advocate school psychologists are interested in individual advocacy. They see themselves as standing up for children and children's rights against all comers, be they teachers, parents, administrators, or others.

Another distinction in the literature on this model is between change agent or activist, ombudsman or mediator, and child advocate (Catterall & Hinds, 1972; Chesler, Bryant, & Crowfoot, 1976). The first does social advocacy, the second protects the child from the school but also represents the institution (Trachtman, 1971b), and the third actively fights for the child alone.

I have used the term *crusader* to capture the willingness of the adherents of this model to do battle with a wide variety of forces on the child's behalf. Often these battles are against formidable odds.

For the child advocate, the child is the only client. Hyman and Schreiber (1974) pointed out how this position is consonant with the APA Code of Ethics. Others in the child's world are seen as potential antagonists and the subject of the school psychologist advocacy, including parents (Catterall & Hinds, 1972). In the ombudsman role, however, Trachtman (1971b) suggests that parents may be the client.

The psychological theories that the child advocate draws upon are those that prescribe the optimal environment in which a child functions. As a result, a child advocate must be familiar with both developmental theory and learning theory. Some special theoretical points of view may come from the notions of how environments can be destructive to children so that theories of learned helplessness and others are of great interest to the child advocate. The theoretical points of view of the organizational developer and the preventionist are more similar to those of the advocate than the diagnostician's.

The child advocate assumes that children are helpless and vulnerable and that they need protection in a society where all other interests groups but children are represented. The child has a basic "right to learn," both intellectually and emotionally (Catterall & Hinds, 1972), and the psychologist is in an excellent position to be of help. The advocate assumes that conflict, especially between democratic values and free enterprise values, is a given in this society (Chesler et al., 1976). The child advocate assumes that there is no difficulty within the child but only within an environment that is unable to cope with that child's special needs.

The goals of the school psychologists' activities are to create a situation in which children may flourish by opposing forces that stifle children's development and by working to create environments that are healthy for them.

The special methods used by child advocates are those focused on representing the child. Lobbying, the legal system, and use of the courts, are all part of social advocacy. Individual advocacy draws on methods for being persuasive in fighting for children's rights including conflict resolution techniques. Learning how to argue, how to use the system on the child's behalf, and fighting for children's rights are all special skills that must be developed for the child advocate. Mearig (1974) listed activities ranging from supporting parents who question the school's assessment results to helping adolescents on parole readjust to public school.

In addition, Hyman and Schreiber (1974, 1975) suggested that the school psychologist (a) always inform parents of their legal rights, (b) inform them of groups and agencies outside of the school (such as the American Civil Liberties Union) that may help them, (c) give them copies of reports that have gone into school records, (d) destroy out-of-date data on children, (e) try to avoid direct confrontation in favor of cooperation if possible, (f) use media to blow the whistle on detrimental school actions, (g) work for institutional change, (h) identify battered children, report them to authorities and sensitize school personnel to child abuse, and (i) bodily prevent corporal punishment.

The problem-solving activities in advocacy involve learning about what the child's special needs are, determining how the system may be encouraged to respond to the child's needs, diagnosing impediments to the delivery of appropriate programs to the children, and marshaling evidence and resources to see to it the child receives the best educational program possible.

The child advocacy model is usually criticized on the basis of its assumption that adults other than the school psychologist are basically antagonistic toward the child. This assumption and/or belief seems difficult to justify. In addition, the advocacy position seems to imply that the psychologist knows what is best for the child. Surely there needs to be a system of checks and balances to guard against the possibility that a given school psychologist may lose objectivity or may encounter countertransference problems which may interfere wtih effective advocacy. Although Trachtman (1981) is basically sympathetic to the child advocacy positions, he argues persuasively that parents, too, need to be considered clients of school psychologists and parents' rights should not be abrogated in the pursuit of child's rights.

Perhaps the major problem with the child advocates model is that it puts the psychologist in the basic position of antagonist (or adversary according to Hyman & Schreiber, 1974) in the school system. The psychologist may lose effectiveness in situations where the school staff is basically sympathetic to the child's needs, but resists the school psychologist's efforts because they are used to taking a combative stance with respect to anything the school psychologist proposes.

A SUMMARY COMPARISON AND EVALUATION OF THE SIX MODELS

The features of the six models presented have been outlined in Table 6.1. The six models are listed across the top and the major evaluative dimensions are listed down the side of the chart. The contents of the top half of the chart and the last row summarize the forgoing discussion. The lower section attempts to fit each model to the concept of the school psychologist as scientific problem solver, at the same time indicating the steps in the delivery of school psychology services in the schools.

Gilmore (1974) compared models of school psychological services on five bipolar dimensions: two operations dimensions and three source dimensions. The two operations dimensions are direct versus indirect services and service versus science. The three source dimensions are education versus psychology, adopted versus developed, and theory versus practice. He positioned each model along each dimension. Table 6.2 contains a chart using Gilmore's system. The prevention-promotion model is the most indirect service oriented and the prescriptive intervention model is the most direct service oriented. The advocate model is in the middle because it encompasses both individual advocacy and social advocacy.

Although all models are practitioner oriented rather than scientist oriented, the emphasis on careful data collection and evaluation in the social learning model makes these practitioners most like the scientist. The advocacy model is most service oriented.

In looking at the sources of the model, the prescriptive interventionist is tied most closely to education whereas the social learning model and the clinical diagnostician draw more heavily from psychology. The sources of the advocacy model are neither education nor psychology, whereas organizational development comes from industrial psychology and prevention promotion from public health so they are represented in mid-positions.

TABLE 6.1
Comparison of Six Models on Major Evaluative Dimensions

Model	Clinical Diagnostic	Prevention-Promotion	Social Learning Theory	Organizational Development	Prescriptive Intervention	Advocacy
Client	Child, school	Child, school, family	Child, school	School system	Child, school	Child (parents)
Theory	Abnormal Psychology Personality Theory	Learning Theory, Developmental Theory	Social learning theory	Organizational change	Classroom learning	Democratic Advocacy
Major Assumption	Psychological diagnosis useful to educators	Early intervention and use of psychology can prevent school failure	Behavior can be changed by careful analysis of antecedent, behaviors, and consequences	Behavior is a function of organization	Psychologists must be involved in direct remediation	Children are powerless and psychologists must represent them
Goals	Improve child's functioning	Prevent failure and promote mental health	Reduce behavioral excesses, develop stimulus control	Facilitate communication Facilitate systems growth and change	Mastery of academic and social skills	Secure child's rights including the child's right to learn
Special Methods	Testing to match program, talking therapy	Consultation Education Crisis counseling	Referral of child for behavioral difficulties	Systems analysis and intervention group work	Criterion referenced assessment, psychoeducational therapy	Confrontation mediation

6. MODELS   159

Problem Clarification	Referral of children with possible handicaps	Psychologist initiates may come from referral	Referral of child for behavioral difficulties	Invitation from system head or psychologist initiated	Referral of failing child	Psychologist initiates or receives referral
Planning	Normative testing interviewing	Observation interview	Observation interview	Organizational assessment	Devise individual plan including subgoals, methods	Identification of child's rights and how being denied
Development	Classification	Problem definition often in consultation (Mental Health)	Description of base rates Consultation (Behavioral)	Organizational assessment	Devise individual plan including subgoals, methods	Identification of child's rights and how being denied
Implementation	Program placement Brief therapy	Intervention often generated from consultation	Select behavioral principles, taught to teacher or others	Select methods for improving system efficiency and facilitate	Teachers implement plan or psychoeducational therapy	Advocacy Mediation
Outcome Determination	Reevaluation	Followup interview	Continuous behavioral monitoring	Measure organizational efficiency	Continuous monitoring and periodic evaluation of IEP	Evaluation of child's freedom to learn
Major Criticism	Assessment is not efficient use of time	Difficult to evaluate if prevention successful	Mechanistic and narrow view of children	Activities not sanctioned by school	Poor theoretical base	Subjectivity of school psychologist

Note: This chart was developed with the assistance of J. Harris, Arizona State University.

TABLE 6.2
A Further Comparison of Six Models for Service Delivery Using Gilmore's (1974) Five Bipolar Dimensions

	Operations		Source		
Direct	Service	Education	Adopted		Theory
Prescriptive Intervention Clinical-Diagnostic Social learning theory	Advocacy Prescriptive Intervention Clinical-Diagnostic Organizational Development Prevention-Promotion Social learning theory	Prescriptive Intervention	Clinical-Diagnostic Organizational Development Prevention-Promotion		Social learning Organizational development Prevention-Promotion
Advocacy		Advocacy Prevention-Promotion Organizational Development Clinical-Diagnostic Social learning theory	Advocacy		
Organizational development Prevention-Promotion			Social learning theory Educational Prescriptive		Prescriptive Intervention Clinical-Diagnostic Advocacy
Indirect	Science	Psychology	Developed		Practice

Note: This five dimensional model for comparing service delivery models was developed by Gilmore (1974).

6. MODELS   161

Most of the models have been adopted to some extent. The diagnostic model was adopted from clinical psychology, although there is evidence that the diagnostic model is a common ancestor of both school and clinical psychology. Organizational development came from industrial psychology and prevention from public health, as mentioned previously. Other models have developed within the school psychology literature but have been influenced by other professional endeavors such as behavioral counseling and social work.

Among the models, the social learning model is most tied to theory. Other models drawing heavily on theory rather than practice are the organizational development model and the prevention-promotion model.

Another way of looking at the models and evaluating them is to consider how completely they cover the basic duties of the school psychologist and whether or not they contribute to an integration of the activities. A chart of this kind appears in Table 6.3. In addition to the major duties, a list of emphasis by level of schooling is included. One might ask, how does each of these models adapt

TABLE 6.3
Emphasis Placed on Duties of School Psychologists by Six Models

	Clinical Diagnostic	Prevention Promotion	Social Learning	Organizational Development	Prescriptive Intervention	Advocacy
Child study (testing)	+ +	0	+	−	+ +	0
Consultation	0	+ +	+	+ +	+	0
Intervention	+	+	+ +	+	+ +	+ +
Parent Education	−	+	0	−	−	+
Therapeutic Counseling	+	0	0	−		0
Crisis Counseling	0	+	−	−	0	+
Inservice Education	−	+	+	−	0	
Program Evaluation	−	0	−	+ +	0	+
Research	0	0	0	+	0	0
Preschool Level	0	+	+	+	0	0
Elementary	+	+	+	+	+	+
Secondary	0	+	0	+	0	+
Higher Education	−	+	−	+	−	−

or change depending on the age of the students involved? From the chart it is apparent that no particular model encompasses all of the duties and activities and levels that characterize the duties of the school psychologist. Depending on the duties involved, a practitioner might assume a different model. For example, in the secondary schools, the child advocacy model may make more sense than the diagnostic model or the behavioral consultant model. Some individuals may find themselves shifting their model depending on their assignment or the sanctions operating within the school system.

I find myself attracted most to the prevention-promotion model. Along with the social learning model it incorporates more of the roles and activities of the school psychologist than the other models. In addition, it suggests activities at all of the levels as does the organizational development model. I see the model as the most comprehensive one for school psychology. In the descriptions of prevention-promotion model the activities of child study, therapeutic counseling, program evaluation, and research have not been emphasized. Nevertheless, the model can easily incorporate these activities and make some statements about how these activities might be approached and why one would undertake them. The direct service activities of this model should be spelled out more fully, however.

Many of the powerful concepts of the social learning position, the organizational development approach, and advocacy can be subsumed under prevention-promotion but many cannot. The prevention promotion approach revolves around the democratic value of involving individuals in their own destiny and keeping decision making participatory. For this reason preventionist approaches to testing, consultation, and counseling do not emphasize strong, set roles and activities because these activities must serve a particular purpose and be negotiated with a consultee or client before proceeding. More work needs to be done in explicating this model but perhaps effort would be more appropriately devoted to creation of fusions or other hybrids of models.

There is good reason for keeping all of the models active in school psychology. In a paper entitled "Doing Your Thing in School Psychology, Trachtman (1971a) pointed out that over the years school psychologists have adopted a number of roles and duties, and that it may be difficult for one person to do all of them. One solution suggested by Trachtman is that school psychologists specialize. A school district staff might consist of a number of psychologists each embracing a different model and, as a result, providing different services to the school district as a whole. It may be unrealistic or unfair to try and create one model of school psychological services delivery that will cover all of the contingencies or possibilities for school psychological services. Reilly (1974) suggested that those following indirect service models be employed at different organizational levels such as district or county-wide. Others have tried to use the models to differentiate MA versus PhD level training (Bardon, 1963).

THE FUSION OF MODELS—LOOKING TO NEW MODELS

I am certain that most school psychologists, if asked which model they follow, would reply they are eclectic. The reaction of many to the claim of eclecticism is that the term is a sign that the person has taken no firm position on any one way of behaving. To be eclectic one must draw from different sources to form a unique new system. This is an exceedingly difficult process because of the interrelationship between goals, methods, values, and psychological theories.

In the search for a new model or a fusion of models one would first turn to the research literature to see if effectiveness research has pointed to the superiority of certain features of models. Unfortunately, the body of research evaluating these models is somewhat inconclusive (Medway, 1979; Waters, 1973).

Another approach to creating new models is to address each of the roles of the school psychologist and to look for a theory that unifies them. From Table 6.3, it is evident that no current model incorporates them all.

In the creation of a model it is necessary to make some decisions and to be explicit about what the school psychologist's goal is, who his or her client is, what values and assumptions about human nature and human interactions are important, and to avoid many of the criticisms that have been attached to the competing models. Meyers (1973) has attempted to bring together levels of service to create an overall consultation model bringing together many features of the traditional, the preventative, and the organizational development model. The model, however, is incomplete with respect to all of the roles, theories, and values.

The first decision to make in creating a new model is to decide who is the client. In most models the client is clearly the child, although acknowledgment of the parents' rights is an important point. Focusing on the child's rights to the exclusion of the parents' rights is intolerable. Because we are dealing with indirect service as well as direct services we must acknowledge that there are secondary clients who are teachers, administrators, and others who come into contact with the child.

One would hope to draw on as many of the psychological theories as possible. One cannot ignore learning theory and the contributions that it has made, particularly the exciting new advances being made in cognitive psychology and information processing theory. Another important body of theory is social psychology as well as developmental psychology. Finding a way to draw from as many theories as possible is a goal for any complete model.

Given the nature of our society it is important for us to adopt and embrace the democratic values on which it is based. Our model must not contain features that violate codes of ethics developed to acknowledge these fundamental democratic values and human rights.

Any new model must embrace all of the features of the goals of the various models thus far discussed. It must focus on academic, social, and affective functioning of children and must also aim at creating an appropriate school climate for children. The goal must be to encourage the functioning and development both of individuals and of the systems that have been designed to accommodate their needs.

Whatever special methods are adapted for the model, they must be ones that are possible to learn and that can be learned in the amount of time prospective school psychologists have available in training programs. The method must be demonstrated to have effectiveness and be tied to the values and goals that have been adopted.

Finally, the model must adopt and acknowledge the complex problem solving that characterizes school psychology. Eliott and Witt (this volume) discuss a service model by Grimes and Reschly that encompasses most of the activities of a school psychologist. The problem-solving processes and decisions to be made must be consistent with a coherent model.

Other chapters in this book attempt to imply new models of psychological services delivery. The reader may use these imperatives to evaluate what lies ahead.

CONCLUSION

A model helps a school psychologist to the extent that it organizes and prescribes activities that are ordinarily perceived to be random. Models may guide training and the curriculum for school psychologists, but they may be more important for helping school psychologists in the field avoid burnout, resist attempts of others in the schools to dictate the school psychologist's role, and fight for the individuality and uniqueness of school psychological services.

One may wonder whether or not there will be new models of school psychological services in the future. Will there be new breakthroughs that will produce new methods, new psychological theories that will change the base of school psychology? I for one do not believe that radical new models will come into existence. Instead, the existing models will be refined and combined, and compete in the market place for adherents. I agree with Trachtman that at present, there is room for a number of psychologists following different models in providing a total network of services to a school district.

I personally believe the preventative model has the most promise for development into a comprehensive approach to school psychology in the future. Although many of the activities encompassed by this model are not in the repertoire of school psychologists, it does point to exciting possibilities for the future development of our field.

ACKNOWLEDGMENTS

I would like to thank Gay Bourguigon, Susan Craig, Lisa Jordan, Connie Muschietty, Peter Newton, Cindy Orrett, and Doris Takayama for their stimulation during the writing of this chapter.

REFERENCES

Abidin, R. R. (1972). A psychosocial look at consultation and behavior modification. *Psychology in the Schools, 9,* 358–363.
Abidin, R. R. (1975). Negative effects of behavioral consultation: I know I ought to, but it hurts too much. *Journal of School Psychology, 13,* 51–57.
Alessi, G. J. (1980). Behavioral observation for the school psychologist. Responsive-discrepancy model. *School Psychology Review, 9,* 31–45.
Alpert, J. L. (1976). Conceptual bases of mental health consultation in the schools. *Professional Psychology, 7,* 619–625.
American Psychological Association (1981). Specialty guidelines for the delivery of services by school psychologists. *American Psychologist, 36,* 670–681.
Argyris, C. (1970). *Intervention theory and method: A behavioral science view.* Reading, MA: Addison-Wesley.
Arter, J. A., & Jenkins, J. R. (1977). Examining the benefits and prevalence of modality considerations in special education. *The Journal of Special Education, 11,* 281–298.
Bandura, A. (1969). *Principles of behavior modification.* New York: Holt, Rinehart & Winston.
Bandura, A., & Walters, R. W. (1963). *Social learning and personality development.* New York: Holt, Rinehart & Winston.
Bardon, J. I. (1963). Mental health education: A framework for psychological services in the schools. *Journal of School Psychology,* 1(1), 20–27.
Bardon, J. F. (1964). Summary of views presented to the conference. *Journal of School Psychology,* 3(2), 6–14.
Bersoff, D. N. (1971). School psychology as "institutional psychiatry." *Professional Psychology, 2,* 266–269.
Bersoff, D. N., & Greiger, R. M. (1971). An interview model for the psychosituational assessment of children's behavior. *American Journal of Orthopsychiatry, 41,* 483–493.
Bower, E. M. (1955). The school psychologist. *Bulletin of the California State Department of Education, 24,*(12).
Bower, E. M. (1964). Psychology in the schools: Concepts, processes and territories. *Psychology in the Schools, 1,* 3–11.
Bower, E. M. (1965). Primary prevention of mental and emotional disorders: A frame of reference. In N. M. Lambert (Ed.), *The protection and promotion of mental health in schools* (pp. 1–9). Mental Health Monograph 5. Washington, DC: U.S. Department of Health, Education and Welfare.
Brantley, J. C. (1971). Psycho-educational centers and the school psychologist. *Psychology in the Schools, 8,* 313–318.
Breyer, N. L., Calchera, D. J., & Cann, C. (1971). Behavioral consulting from a distance. *Psychology in the Schools, 8,* 172–176.
Brooks, R. (1979). Psychoeducational assessment: A broader perspective. *Professional Psychology, 10,* 708–722.

Broskowski, A., & Baker, F. (1974). Professional, organizational, and social barriers to primary prevention. *School Psychology Digest, 3*(4), 19–23.

Burke, J. P., Hapworth, C. E., & Brantley, J. C. (1980). Scientific problem solver model: A resolution for professional controversies in school psychology. *Professional Psychology, 11*, 823–832.

Caplan, G. (1970). *Theory and practice of mental health consultation.* New York: Basic Books.

Carroll, J. L., Harris, J. D., & Bretzing, B. H. (1979). A survey of psychologists serving secondary schools. *Professional Psychology, 10*, 766–770.

Catterall, C. D., & Hinds, R. (1972). Child advocate—emerging role for the school psychologist. *School Psychology Digest, 1*, 14–22.

Chesler, M. A., Bryant, B. I., & Crowfoot, J. E. (1976). Consultation in schools: Inevitable conflict, partisanship, and advocacy. *Professional Psychology, 7*, 637–645.

Cleveland, S. E. (1976). Reflections on the rise and fall of psychodiagnosis. *Professional Psychology, 7*, 309–318.

Conoley, J. C. (1980). Organizational assessment. *School Psychology Review, 9*, 83–89.

Cook, V. J., & Patterson, J. G. (1977). Psychologists in the schools of Nebraska: Professional functions. *Psychology in the Schools, 14*, 371–376.

Cowen, E. L., & Lorion, R. P. (1976). Changing roles for the school mental health professional. *Journal of School Psychology, 14*, 131–138.

Culbertson, F. M. (1975). Average students' needs and perceptions of school psychologists. *Psychology in the Schools, 12*, 191–196.

Das, J. P., Kirby, J. R., & Jarman, R. F. (1979). *Simultaneous and successive cognitive processes.* New York: Academic Press.

Dickinson, D. J. (1980), The direct assessment: An alternative to psychometric testing. *Journal of Learning Disabilities, 13*, 472–476.

Fairchild, T. N. (1976). School psychological services: An empirical comparison of two models. *Psychology in the Schools, 13*, 156–162.

Fein, L. G. (1974). *The changing school scene: Challenge to psychology.* New York: Wiley.

Feuerstein, R. (1979). *The dynamic assessment of retarded performers.* Baltimore: University Park Press.

Flax, M., & Anderson, D. (1966). A survey of school psychologists in Colorado. *Psychology in the Schools, 3*, 52–54.

Ford, J. D., & Migles, M. (1979). The role of the school psychologist: Teachers' preferences as a function of personal and professional characteristics. *Journal of School Psychology, 17*, 372–378.

Forness, S. R. (1970). Educational prescription for the school psychologist. *Journal of School Psychology, 8*, 96–98.

French, J. L. (1979). Intelligence: Its measurement and relevance for education. *Professional Psychology, 10*, 753–759.

Gagne, R. M. (1977). *The conditions of learning (3rd ed.)* New York: Holt, Rinehart & Winston.

Gallessich, J. (1972). A Systems model of mental health consultation. *Psychology in the Schools, 9*, 13–15.

Gallessich, J. (1973). Organizational factors influencing consultation in schools. *Journal of School Psychology, 11*, 57–65.

Gilmore, G. E. (1974). Models for school psychology: Dimensions, barriers and implications. *Journal of School Psychology, 12*, 95–101.

Gilmore, G. E., & Chandy, J. (1973). Teachers' perceptions of school psychological services. *Journal of School Psychology, 11*, 139–148.

Goodwin, D. L., & Coates, T. J. (1976). *Helping students help themselves.* Englewood Cliffs, NJ: Prentice-Hall.

Gottsegen, M. G. (1960). The role of the school psychologist. In M. G. Gottsegen (Ed.), *Professional school psychology* (pp. 2–17). New York: Grune & Stratton.

Granowsky, S., & Davis, L. T. (1974). Three alternative roles for the school psychologist. *Psychology in the Schools, 11,* 415–421.

Gray, S. W. (1963). *The psychologist in the schools.* New York: Holt, Rinehart & Winston.

Grieger, R. M., & Abidin, R. R. (1972). Psychosocial assessment: A model for the school community psychologist. *Psychology in the Schools, 9,* 112–119.

Hannafin, M. J., & Witt, J. C. (1983). System intervention and the school psychologist: Maximizing interplay among roles and functions. *Professional Psychology, 14,* 128–136.

Harper, R., & Balch, P. (1975). Some economic arguments in favor of primary prevention. *Professional Psychology, 6,* 17–25.

Hebb, D. (1978). Comment: Open letter to a friend who thinks IQ is a social evil. *American Psychologist, 33,* 1143–1144.

Honigfeld, G. (1971). In defense of diagnosis. *Professional Psychology, 2,* 289–291.

Hughes, J. N. (1979). Consistency of administrators' and psychologists' actual and ideal perceptions of school psychologists' activities. *Psychology in the Schools, 16,* 234–239.

Hyman, I., & Schreiber, K. (1974). The school psychologist as child advocate. *Children Today,* 21–23, 36.

Hyman, I., & Schreiber, K. (1975). Selected concepts and practices of child advocacy in school psychology. *Psychology in the Schools, 2,* 50–57.

Hyman, I., & Schreiber, K. (1977). Some personal reflections on the changing role of the school psychologist as child advocate. *School Psychology Digest, 6,* 6–10.

Hynd, G. W., & Obrzut, J. E. (1981). *Neuropsychological assessment and the school-age child: issues and procedures.* New York: Grune & Stratton.

Jackson, J. H. (1970). Psychoeducational therapy as the primary activity of school psychologists. *Journal of School Psychology, 8,* 186–190.

Jackson, J. H., & Bernauer, M. (1975). A responsibility model for the practice of professional school psychology: Psychoeducational therapy. *Journal of School Psychology, 13,* 76–81.

Kahl, L. J., & Fine, M. J. (1978). Teachers' perceptions of the school psychologist as a function of teaching experience, amount of contact, and socioeconomic status of the school. *Psychology in the Schools, 15,* 577–582.

Kaplan, M. S., Clancy, B., & Chrin (1977). Priority roles for school psychologists as seen by superintendents. *Journal of School Psychology, 15,* 75–80.

Kazdin, A. E. (1982a). Applying behavioral principles in the schools. In C. R. Reynolds & T. B. Gutkin, *The handbook of school psychology* (pp. 501–529). New York: Wiley.

Kazdin, A. E. (1982b). Symptom substitution, generalization, and response covariation: Implications for psychotherapy outcome. *Psychological Bulletin, 91,* 349–365.

Keogh, B. K., Kukic, S. J., Becker, L. D., McLoughlin, R. J., & Kukic, M. B. (1975). School psychologists' services in special education programs. *Journal of School Psychology, 13,* 142–148.

Kratochwill, T. (1982). Advances in behavioral assessment. In C. R. Reynolds & T. B. Gutkin (Eds.), *The handbook of school psychology* (pp. 314–350). New York: Wiley.

Lacayo, N., Sherwood, G., & Morris, J. (1981). Daily activities of school psychologists: A national survey. *Psychology in the schools, 18,* 184–190.

Landau, S. E., & Gerken, K. C. (1979). Requiem for the testing role? The perceptions of administrators vs. teachers. *School Psychology Digest, 8,* 202–206.

Lee, W. S. (1974). A new model for psychological services in educational systems. *School Psychology Digest, 3*(4), 50–55.

Lennox, N., Flanagan, D., & Meyers, J. (1979). Organizational consultation to facilitate communication within a school staff. *Psychology in the Schools, 16,* 520–526.

Lewin, K. (1947). Group decision and social change. In T. Newcomb & E. Hartley (Eds.), *Readings in social psychology* (pp. 330–344). New York: Holt, Rinehart & Winston.

Levinson, H. (1972). The clinical psychologist as organizational diagnostician. *Professional Psychology, 3,* 34–40.

Litz (1979). Criteria referenced assessment: The new bandwagon. *Exceptional Children, 46,* 131–132.

Luria, A. R. (1966). *Higher cortical functions in man.* New York: Basic Books.

Maher, C. A. (1981). Intervention with school social systems: A behavioral-systems approach. *School Psychology Review, 10,* 499–508.

Mahoney, M. J., & Thoresen, C. E. (1974). Self control: Power to the person. Monterey, CA: Brooks/Cole.

Manley, T. R., & Manley, E. T. (1978). A comparison of the personal values and operative goals of school psychologists and school superintendents. *Journal of School Psychology, 16,* 99–109.

Meacham, M. L., & Peckham, P. D. (1978). School psychologists at three-quarters century: Congruence between training, practice, preferred role and competence. *Journal of School Psychology, 16,* 195–206.

Mearig, J. S. (1974). On becoming a child advocate in school psychology. *Journal of School Psychology, 12,* 121–129.

Medway, F. J. (1979). How effective is school consultation: A review of recent research. *Journal of School Psychology, 17,* 275–282.

Meyers, J. (1973). A consultation model for school psychological services. *Journal of School Psychology, 11,* 5–15.

Meyers, J., Martin, R., & Hyman, I. (Eds.). (1977). *School Consultation.* Springfield, IL: Charles C Thomas.

Miller, J. N. (1974). Consumer response to theoretical role models in school psychology. *Journal of School Psychology, 12,* 310–317.

Mischel, W. (1977). On the future of personality measurement. *American Psychologist, 32,* 246–254.

Morrow, L. (1975). An alternative approach to the delivery of school psychological services. *Psychology in the Schools, 12,* 274–278.

Obrzut, J. E. (1981). Neuropsychological assessment in the schools. *School Psychology Review, 10,* 331–340.

Osguthorpe, R. T. (1979). The school psychologist as a tutorial systems supervisor. *Psychology in the Schools, 16,* 88–92.

Peter, L. J. (1965). *Prescriptive teaching.* New York: McGraw-Hill.

Pielstick, N. L. (1963). School psychology, a focus on learning. *Journal of School Psychology, 1*(1), 14–19.

Reger, R. (1965). *School psychology.* Springfield, IL. Charles C Thomas.

Reger, R. (1972). The medical model in special education. *Psychology in the Schools, 9,* 8–12.

Reilly, D. H. (1973). School psychology: View from the second generation. *Psychology in the Schools, 10,* 151–155.

Reilly, D. H. (1974). A conceptual model for school psychology. *Psychology in the Schools, 11,* 165–169.

Reschly, D. J. (1976). School Psychology Consultation: "Frenzied, faddish, or fundamental?" *Journal of School Psychology, 14,* 105–113.

Reschly, D. J. (1980). School Psychologists and assessment in the future. *Professional Psychology, 11,* 841–848.

Sashkin, M., Burke, W. W., & Levinson, H. H. (1973). Organizational development pro and con (a dialogue). *Professional Psychology, 4,* 187–208.

Schmuck, R. (1976). Process consultation and organizational development. *Professional Psychology, 7,* 626–631.

Schmuck, R., & Miles, M. (1971). *Organization development in schools.* Palo Alto, CA: National Press Books.

Sloves, R. E., Docherty, E. M., & Schneider, K. C. (1979). A scientific problem-solving model of psychological assessment. *Professional Psychology, 10,* 28–35.

Starkman, S. (1966). The professional model: Paradox in school psychology. *American Psychologist, 21,* 807–808.

Trachtman, G. M. (1971a). Doing your thing in school psychology. *Professional Psychology, 2,* 377–382.

Trachtman, G. M. (1971b). From the editor. *Journal of School Psychology, 9,* 98.

Valett, R. E. (1963). *The practice of school psychology.* New York: Wiley.

Trachtman, G. M. (1981). On such a full sea. *School Psychology Review, 10,* 138–181.

Valett, R. E. (1968). The evaluation and programming of basic learning abilities. *Journal of School Psychology, 6,* 227–236.

Valett, R. E. (1969). *Programming learning disabilities.* Palo Alto, CA: Fearon.

Waters, L. G. (1973). School psychologists as perceived by school personnel: Support for a consultant model. *Journal of School Psychology, 11,* 40–45.

White, M. A., & Harris, M. W. (1961). *The school psychologist.* New York: Harper & Brothers.

Whitman, M., & Whitman, J. (1971). Behavior modification in the classroom. *Psychology in the Schools, 8,* 176–186.

Winett, R. A., & Winkler, R. C. (1972). Current behavior modification in the classroom: Be still, be quiet, be docile. *Journal of Applied Behavior Analysis, 5,* 499–504.

Woody, R. H. (1976). The school psychologist as a behavior therapist: Past and future. *Psychology in the Schools, 13,* 266–268.

Ysseldyke, J. E. (1978). Who's calling the plays in school psychology? *Psychology in the Schools, 15,* 373–378.

7 Conceptual and Logistical Hurdles: Service Delivery to Urban Schools

John H. Jackson
Board of School Directors
Milwaukee, Wisconsin

This chapter initially presents relevant definitional clarifications and informational background against which we may consider conceptual and logistical hurdles to the delivery of psychological services in urban schools. It is the opinion of this author that conceptual and logistical hurdles to service delivery arise from a variety of sources, from both within and outside the schools. Finally, some consideration is devoted to future service delivery and potential conceptual and logistical hurdles.

DEFINITIONS

What are "Schools?" What are "Urban Schools?" What is service delivery? What are conceptual hurdles? What are logistical hurdles?

Urban schools, within this chapter, are defined as the schools within the 28 "Great Cities" of the United States (Bins & Walker, 1980). They are the public school systems or districts within these cities. Urban schools also include public schools or districts in smaller cities and in large metropolitan areas and counties that possess characteristics similar to those of the "Great Cities." The term urban schools, as used here, does not include non-public schools, suburban schools, exurban schools, or rural schools. Nor is it likely to refer to most service board districts that often are found in suburban or country areas.

Within an urban school system, the term *school* does not necessarily refer to the traditional school building and what takes place within. It is much broader, and may refer to any of an array of teaching-learning arrangements under the aegis of the urban public schools, including classes held in business and industrial settings, in downtown law offices, at hospitals, or on city streets (White & Duker, 1973). All such classes presumably have access to whatever psychological services are available within the school system or district. This definition should not be interpreted as identifying all settings where school psychology is practiced; these other settings include clinics, community agencies, residential treatment centers, and correctional institutions.

Service delivery refers to the rather complicated, multistage process of providing services to those who have been referred for them. It is multistaged because it involves at a minimum conceptualization of services, development of services, staffing of services, and the actual delivery of services. Psychological services delivered include, but are not limited to, assessment/diagnosis, consultation, and interventions—including therapy—for students; consultation and counseling for school staffs and parents; and inservice training of school personnel.

Conceptual hurdles are created by ideas, policies, standards, and guidelines. Such policies, guidelines, and so forth usually are those that establish the nature of the schools. They define what the schools are, state or imply what the schools offer, and may withhold, retard, or dilute psychological services needed by students within the school community.

Logistical hurdles are practices, procedures, and staff deployment models that prevent timely delivery of psychological services. In some instances, services are delayed but ultimately delivered. In other instances, service delivery is not effected at all.

MAJOR CHARACTERISTICS OF URBAN SCHOOLS

Urban schools, for the most part, are distinguished by a large number of characteristic features (Jackson, 1977); some of the most important among these for service delivery are the following: large organized districts, large number and variety of students, relatively large size of the psychological services staff, broad diversity of co-professionals, requirements for implementation of legal mandates, volume of record-keeping, involvement of labor unions, outside contracting for service delivery, and funding burden for supportive services. These major features provide a context that affects psychological services delivery. This context of characteristic features creates the complexity of the urban school scene and, thereby, erects many of the hurdles to service delivery.

Characteristics to be considered are widely diverse. Some are related to the populations to be served, both type and size, and to the staffs that provide the service. Some are associated with legal mandates or requirements placed upon the school or school system. A number have to do with the overall economy.

Others pertain to the mechanics of providing services or to the structure of the school or school system.

Large Organizational Structures

In the largest urban school systems, students to be served are assigned to any of several hundred schools and/or programs. To deploy staff for service delivery throughout a large organizational structure requires major strategic planning. Such planning becomes especially complicated because it has to be adjusted fairly frequently, not merely between semesters or at the end of the school year, but in response to lay-offs and recalls, resignations, and professional leaves, where often there are union requirements that staff seniority must be considered and where sometimes there is a court order that requires maintenance of staff racial balance.

In delivering services to each school and program in the large urban school system, there is the varying accessibility to students from school to school, and to programs off campus. Uniformity of accessibility cannot be programmed; accessibility is in the hands of each administrator and school staff across the entire system.

The large size of many urban school systems makes it extremely difficult to assess the needs of the overall student body. A reliable needs assessment would require a research effort that is not easily mounted, certainly not on an annual or even biennial basis. Without an overall needs assessment or fairly stable needs indicators, each building administrator seems to strive to put forth the picture of greatest need for his or her building or program by constantly grinding out referrals so as to claim all the services possible. Thus, peak needs mushroom here and there across the schools of the system like brush fires needing to be controlled. Given this scenario, emergency redeployment becomes the *modus operandi*.

Communication across large systems about available services, modes of service delivery, schedules of school visitations, changes in procedures, and so on, is maintained only through much effort, and then may be spotty and tardy because of the inefficiency of communication channels. Communication may be less than desirable in urban systems where it has to be effected from a central office through area offices to the field or schools and programs.

Implications for service delivery in large organizational structures such as urban schools and school systems relate primarily to several aspects of the structures. These include plans for strategic deployment and redeployment of the psychological services staff across many, sometimes hundreds of, schools and programs geographically spread out across many miles; equity in services received by each school or program in the system; and other important aspects of administration such as overall program coordination and quality control of services delivery.

Number and Type of Students to be Served

In large urban schools the size of the potential student population to be served constitutes a major hurdle to service delivery. Size becomes especially challenging when the multiplicity of types of students is given consideration.

The great sizes of student populations in urban centers that potentially must be served give rise to large numbers of students who have actual needs for services. See Table 7.1 for representative figures on students who received psychological services during 1978–1979 in the urban school systems that responded to a survey conducted by Jackson (1979).

It has been estimated that at any given time 10% to 15% or more of the student population will be found seriously in need of help on the basis of their problems and disabilities. If this is true, the percentages reported in Table 7.1 indicate that many needy students are not being seen in most of the largest urban school systems.

Large numbers of potential and actual students in need of services have implications primarily for the size of the professional psychological staff that will be needed, and for the breadth and quality of services to be provided. The cities and metropolitan areas of the country include many types of people—people of all ethnic identities: all of the European nationalities plus Afro-Americans, native Americans, Asian-Americans, and Hispanics. The schools in these urban areas are intended to educate all children. They are not schools for students from single ethnic groups, or similar ethnic groups. The ethnic groups represented by students in urban schools are greatly dissimilar in many ways. These students come to school bearing different sets of cultural and personal values, interests, aspirations, politics, religions, and languages. The great variations in learning styles within ethnic groups are generalized across all groups. There are significant differences in their manifestations of personal problems. Barriers that stand between the schools and their families vary.

A primary implication of ethnic and cultural variations among the students of urban schools is that of the nature of the staffing composition required for effective service delivery. Urban schools have the concern of recruiting, hiring, and retaining an ethnically varied staff of psychological services providers, and it has not been easy to achieve this goal given the relatively few minority students in professional psychological practice and training. Russo, Olmedo, Stapp, and Fulcher (1981) estimated that of the total United States resident membership of the American Psychological Association (APA), only 1.2% were black, 0.7% Hispanic, 1.0% Asian, and 0.2% American Indian. They also estimated that only 3.6% of APA United States resident doctoral members were minorities,

TABLE 7.1
Number and Percentage of Students Receiving Psychological
Services In Urban School Systems, 1978–1979

Urban Location	Total School District Student Enrollment	Total Number of Students in District Who Rec'd Services	Percent of Total System Enrollment Receiving Services
Atlanta, GA	73.000	3,750	5
Buffalo, NY	51,206	3,251	6
Chicago, IL	489,274	17,670	4
Cleveland, OH	103,000	5,000	5
Dade County, FL	227,281	12,000	5
Dallas, TX	132,000	2,500	2
Denver, CO	64,497	4,000	6
Los Angeles, CA	545,000	38,000	7
Memphis, TN	113,000	2,700	2
Milwaukee, WI	98,000	8,260	8
Minneapolis, MN	45,623	1,237	3
Nashville, TN	71,662	3,040	4
New Orleans, LA	89,000	3,950	4
Norfolk, VA	43,000	1,800	4
Philadelphia, PA	237,000	28,011	12
Pittsburgh, PA	51,734	4,600	9
Portland, OR	53,670	3,700	7
Seattle, WA	50,000	2,700	5
St. Louis, MO	67,800	10,000	15
Toledo, OH	45,000	2,000	4

Note. Data from unpublished survey conducted by Jackson, 1979.

and that the percentage of minority doctorate recipients in psychology increased slowly from 6.7% in 1977 to 8.0% in 1980.

Large Size of the Psychological Services Staff

The psychological services staff in some urban school systems easily comprises the single largest concentration of psychologists within the respective state boundaries. Such large staffs mean that a multiplicity of theoretical approaches to the practice of psychology are brought to the psychological services unit, and must be accommodated. Communication between the administrator or supervisor and such large staffs is a complex operation requiring time and effort. Evaluation requires visitations to the field routinely, and clinical-level supervision. Supervision requires broad knowledge across many extant theoretical approaches represented, and the techniques subsumed by each. With the relatively large staffs in urban schools, field visits are continuing events and clinical-level supervision is a daily requirement if all staff are to be covered.

The large size of staffs required by urban schools has direct implications for both administrators and supervisors, who must organize a staff, deploy it most appropriately as needed across the schools in the system or district, and remain in effective control of it to ensure actual service delivery appropriate to needs. Recruitment, hiring, orientation, and monitoring, in addition to direct, ongoing field supervision and evaluation, are all complicated by the larger size of staff in urban schools.

Diversity of Co-Professionals Delivering Services in Urban Schools

Urban schools, unlike other types of schools, employ a relatively large number of different supportive professionals and specialists whose employment has implications for service delivery. Urban schools may have, in addition to psychologists, school social workers, guidance counselors, speech pathologists, special education testing personnel, school physicians, school nurses, and consulting psychiatrists. More often than not several of these professionals may be involved in the examination, staffing, and follow-up intervention. This means that the individual student is being perceived from a number of different perspectives—psychological, social, educational, and medical, at least. Simultaneous and multiple perceptions by a number of professionals from different specialties often appear to be at variance with each other or contradictory. Each professional must report data and concomitant perceptions only from within his or her own specialty or run the risk of being accused of performing outside his or her field of specialization and of not respecting other team specialists. Team thinking is required to articulate each set of perceptions with the others and to develop the consistent, clinical picture necessary to truly understand the student. Since the enactment of P.L. 94-142 in 1975, the multiplicity of professionals required to team in-service delivery to children has also enjoyed legal backing. Thus, it is required both professionally and legally.

The primary implication of the professional diversity of staff for the delivery of services is the necessity for the various involved professionals to reach agreed-upon diagnoses and prescriptions for programming and treatment. This, unfortunately, is not accomplished easily.

Legal Mandates and Service Delivery

In the last 20 years, some of the major legal mandates have come from court-ordered desegregation of the schools, including both students and staffs, and P.L. 94–142, which has required such actions as team evaluations, non-discriminatory testing, preparation of the student's individual education program, and appropriate interventions as recommended by the evaluation teams. Additional mandates originating from state legislatures and state departments of public instruction or education have related to a variety of concerns such as services to regular education students and student attendance. Local boards of education have added other mandates appropriate to local needs. All these legal and legislative requirements must be implemented in a system in which communication and change are difficult to achieve efficiently.

Legal mandates, per se, may be no different in urban schools from those in other types of schools. However, the exacted commitment to, and observance of, legal mandates within urban schools frequently seems to be greater. Reasons for this apparently greater commitment and observance are several. They include:

1. The existence of a multiplicity of ethnic minority groups to be served;
2. The perceived intransigence of the large urban schools;
3. The presence of larger numbers of sophisticated, determined parents; and
4. The likely presence of experienced citizen advocates.

More ethnic minority groups than others are often included in the categories of students directly affected by legal mandates; for example, more black and Hispanic students than white students were identified as handicapped prior to the enactment of P.L. 94–142. Sometimes the high visibility of the plight of minority children in urban schools has been the direct motivation for the legal mandates; the blatant segregation of students and the quality of their segregated education have led to court-ordered desegregation of students and staff in a number of urban schools, e.g., Los Angeles, Milwaukee, Boston, and Columbus.

Urban schools have been perceived as intransigent in the face of demands from ethnic minorities to redress their grievances, some of which, ultimately, are addressed by legal mandates. Especially during the 1960s and early 1970s was this confrontation of ethnic minorities and urban schools over segregation dramatized and vividly communicated via television to the nation and the world. In the South, black parents petitioned school authorities in urban areas to admit their children. Outside the South, all-black schools were boycotted. Generally, it was only through court orders that these urban schools were desegregated. Presumably, had the urban schools been more responsive to expressed ethnic minority concerns, court orders would not have been necessary.

Within large urban centers are significant numbers of parents with determination to make their schools work for them, parents who also possess considerable sophistication in terms of dealing with the urban school system. In this regard, parents of handicapped children from the majority group have been particularly effective; however, these parents have no monopoly in this respect, as many ethnic minority parents also have been effective. These parents have the know-how, and the persistence, to pursue their goals and objectives through the labyrinth of large and complicated urban school organizations. They have persisted sometimes in the face of hostility and/or indifference from urban school personnel. In some schools parents have worked through formal structures; for example, in the Milwaukee Public Schools, parents of handicapped children have worked with community agency personnel, union representatives, and mid-to-upper-level school administrators as members in a Broadly Based Parents Task Force, an organization recognized by the Board of School Directors, to advise, confront, and, when necessary, actively oppose the system. The Milwaukee approach has been very effective for parents.

Under the aegis of P.L. 94–142, the concept of "citizen advocate" has been developed. These are especially designated persons who represent the interests of the parent and child in a given case. They are knowledgeable of the federal and state statutes, and the due process and other prerogatives provided therein, for handicapped children and their families. They may be well practiced because of the sizable number of clients they have represented, and they know process and procedures to achieve their ends. The schools recognize the legal standing of advocates and the role they assume. Advocates have proved to be tenacious in the discharge of their responsibilities to the people they represent and the demands they place upon urban schools.

The intensity of commitment to legal mandates has important implications for service delivery. The extent of service delivery demanded by parents and others depends largely upon the adaptable capacity of the urban schools to remain in compliance with relevant statutes and administrative rules and regulations. The effort at adaptation may be extremely problematic and result in unprofessional and inadequate services to students, as apparently occurred in New York City in 1981. New York City schools combined their clinical and school-based supportive psychological services in an adaptive reorganization, which apparently resulted in the following: (a) the loss of professional supervision and leadership; (b) mass screening procedures that meet rigid quotas; and (c) educational evaluators being asked to perform certain psychological functions for which they had not been trained (Screening in New York State, 1980; APA, 1982a, 1982b).

Voluminous Record-Keeping

There are important reasons why good records need to be created and maintained. General accountability for the discharge of responsibility is one such reason. Second, the psychology profession requires practitioners in the several specialty areas to have appropriate record-keeping. These reasons for keeping records occur wherever psychology is practiced, and need not require voluminous record-keeping. The concern with record-keeping in urban schools is that it can be overdone all too easily, for any of several causes.

The large size of the student population to be served, and its complex make-up, alone may lead to a heavy volume of record-keeping. This can be simply an effort to keep track of service needs identified and services delivered or not delivered.

Another reason for a large variety and number of records is the necessity to document the needs served versus service needs in the schools, in order to maintain or increase funding. This type of documentation is especially desired by school boards and others who control funding. With the large number of students in urban schools referred, staff size becomes a real concern. Documentation of needs and services delivered can help provide a sound basis for adequate staff size.

Under such conditions, consideration of electronic data processing that allows for ease of recording and rapid and accurate retrieval of information is appropriate. Encouragement of staff acceptance of these techniques may be a major consideration; they may view the electronic devices as threats to their jobs or as a threat of "Big Brother."

Labor Unions As a Factor in Service Delivery

Labor unions for supportive service professional groups, e.g., psychologists, are more frequently found in urban schools than in other types of schools. In rural areas and suburbs, as well as in some urban areas, psychologists are represented by teachers' unions, which, more often than not, devote their energies to teacher or administrator issues primarily (Agin, 1979). Relatively little is included that is especially responsive to psychologists' needs. For example, in the Madison, Wisconsin, schools, psychologists are represented by the teachers' union, and the bargaining contract identifies the school principals as their evaluators (L. Zuberbier, personal communication, September 8, 1980). In the larger urban school systems, school psychologists have begun to form, or to consider forming, their own unions, which will address only their issues.

The formation of psychologists' unions may prove a major asset to psychologists in terms of wages, hours, and working conditions. However, there may be important implications in the resultant bargaining agreements in the areas of deploying staff and defining the work task, as well as in other areas of management prerogatives. To the extent that encroachments are made upon management rights, the administrators and supervisors of the psychological services unit will be hampered in their responsibility for the flexible planning and implementation of the overall program of services.

Outside Contracting for Service Delivery

Contracting with outside agencies for student services has become a major concern in urban schools over the last decade, especially since the passage of P.L. 94–142. In order to provide free, appropriate education and services required for handicapped students, the schools must provide a continuum of special education training and related services. Contracting has been employed to assist in making the training and related services continuum available. The magnitude and nature of contracting varies from one urban school system to another, depending upon a number of factors, e.g., programming, staffing, funding, and philosophy.

Contracting involves signed agreements with non-profit agencies, proprietary agencies, and paid individuals. For any referred student, the full range of school psychological services may be provided under contract, or, depending on the particular case, any part of the range may be provided.

Specific implications of contracting for service delivery are potentially numerous. However, basically, implications have to do with the relationship that contracting has with the overall program of service delivery in an urban school or school system. This relationship may suggest both positive and negative aspects of outside contracting.

Contracting generally has been seen by school psychologists as a negative factor in terms of perceived threat to security of jobs, contractor ignorance of individual school conditions and the subjecting of students to inappropriate recommendations and services, lack of direct supervision of practitioners who report to the contractor, and absence of practitioner accountability within the schools.

Contracting may be positive when it is a relatively small and perhaps a temporary, tactical approach of the psychological services unit itself. This may be necessary to ensure the delivery of a full range of services, when services needed are not available from staff inside the schools and can be obtained only from outside (e.g., a specific bilingual-bicultural psychological services delivery for Hispanic youth). It also may be necessary when the psychological services unit intends to hire part-time, hourly, peak-time, or seasonal staff that can be employed very flexibly to assist the regular staff with specified activities. Limited contracting also may be necessary under other conditions, such as for supervision when states require board certified/licensed psychologists for supervision of non-doctoral psychologists. In all instances, however, administrative guidance and professional supervision must be provided from the psychological services unit within the system, and accountability is to the unit.

Funding the Delivery of Services in Urban Schools

Funding appropriate to the needs for service delivery within urban schools is a matter of chronic concern. Urban schools have the problem of an "overburden" of students from the lower socioeconomic classes. Substantial funds are needed for this overburden of students from financially poor families with its attendant personal, behavioral, and learning problems. Much of this funding must come from tax levy on families and households in the same lower socioeconomic classes (Ornstein, 1982).

Hodge (1981) noted that in 37 of the large city systems, minorities comprised over half of the students in the school population in 1976; he added that a detailed study of the distribution of children from minority groups indicated that 65% of Colorado's black children attended Denver schools, and that 70% of Florida's Hispanic students attended the Dade County (Miami) schools. Hodge also made the point that handicapped children are concentrated in large city systems and often require special education.

Hoover, Kirschner-Stone, Detmer, and Nantume (1982) reported a survey of the responses of State Superintendents of Education to current federal funding. Ten of the 19 superintendents who said that state and local authorities would not be able to manage schools better with less federal assistance also indicated the greatest shortcoming in reduced federal assistance to be less money for programs for students with special needs. Wise (1981) commented that the current system of school finance often has the specific effect of distributing funds in proportion to wealth (or inversely to poverty).

Implications of funding for service delivery revolve around the ability of the urban schools to find sufficient dollars to match the identified service needs. This may involve identifying new funding sources, increasing the yield from established sources such as taxation, or effecting some combination of remedies.

RANGE OF PSYCHOLOGICAL SERVICE COMPONENTS IN URBAN SCHOOL SETTING

It is important to review briefly the range of psychological services components that may be delivered in urban schools, to see more clearly the conceptual and logistical hurdles. This view makes the assumptions that services reviewed will illustrate the full range of potential school psychological services, that they may be offered in all urban settings subsumed under the concept of school as defined earlier in this chapter, and that they are offered for the age range of the recipients of services identified earlier.

In the more advanced, modern urban school setting, the range of psychological services is broad. In these schools the usual primary components include psychodiagnosis; psychoeducational evaluation and assessment; psychological consultation to individuals, groups, and systems; and a variety of therapeutic and educational interventions for students (Jackson & Bernauer, 1975). Other major components include group testing and screening, inservice training of school personnel, school staff and parent counseling, specialized assessment and evaluation services, program development services, and supervision and administration of psychological service delivery to students, parents, and school staffs (APA, 1977). Also included here are affective education, and services directly related to attendance, discipline, and dropout. Research has proved to be a relatively minimal service in urban school settings.

In most, if not in all, urban school settings, school psychologists deliver both psychodiagnostic and psychoeducational evaluation/assessment/diagnosis. Psychodiagnostic service is provided where the presenting problem appears to be more mental health related than education related. Psychoeducational service is provided in cases that seem to be presenting both educational and psychological problems, usually intertwined.

Psychological consultation provided by school psychologists in urban schools may be a wide-ranging type of service delivery. In some of these urban school settings it may be even defined as a direct form of intervention. In these instances, consultation is delivered not only to parents, school staffs, agency personnel, or practitioners in the community, but also directly to referred students. It also may be provided to individuals, groups, or systems in the resolution of problems at these different levels.

Direct intervention for school psychologists has become a relatively active area of service delivery over the past two decades (Pryzwansky, Fishbein, & Jackson, 1984). A variety of approaches have been practiced. Primary interventions by school psychologists in urban schools may include therapy and counseling on an individual or a group basis. Therapy in this context refers to behavioral-cognitive approaches, behavior modification techniques, psychotherapy, or psychoeducational therapy (Jackson, 1970; Jackson & Bernauer, 1968; Jackson & Bernauer, 1975), depending upon the needs of the case and the orientation of the psychological services staff. As indicated by the *Specialty Guidelines for the Delivery of Services by School Psychologists* (APA, 1977), these are "interventions to facilitate the functioning of individuals or groups, with concern for how schooling influences and is influenced by their cognitive, conative, affective, and social development" (p. 35). It is interesting to note that school psychologists today are involved significantly more in ongoing therapy than at the time Frances Mullen (1967) wrote about the role of the school psychologist in the urban schools. She stated that only a few school systems even mentioned that continuing therapy or counseling were part of their treatment services. Other major interventions possible are those that "facilitate the educational services and child care functions of school personnel, parents, and community agencies" (APA, 1977, p. 35). These include therapy or counseling with school staffs or parents and families, parent education programs, and school staff inservice training.

Specialized assessment and evaluation services in urban schools are for determination of competency, superior ability grouping, early admissions to school, severely disabled, and academically and otherwise gifted and talented. The particular group or groups within a school or school system may depend upon the programming availabilities therein and the professional freedom exercised by the psychologist to reach diagnostic conclusions in cases for which there are no currently available programs within the system. The groups may depend upon freedom to communicate findings and recommendations to relevant parties. Unfortunately, these professional freedoms have to be fought for in some school systems, and sometimes at a heavy price; Muriel Forrest paid this price in her struggles with Westchester County, New York, schools ("APA Backs," 1983).

Therapeutic intervention with school staff members theoretically is limited to the examination or resolution of problems involved in the interaction of staff member(s) and student(s) in the school setting, where such problems inhibit the teaching-learning situation. For example, presenting problems may include negative teacher attitudes toward the ethnic or racial identity of the student, or vice versa; it may relate to student resentment of the teacher's exercise of authority; or it may involve the student's opposition to the subject matter as presented by the teacher.

Therapeutic intervention with the parents or the family of a student is limited essentially in the same manner as is the intervention with school personnel. It is limited to the interactions with the student that have a deleterious effect upon learning and behavior in the school setting.

Psychological service delivery for the improvement of attendance and discipline and for the prevention of dropouts ordinarily comprises a combination of techniques. The emphasis, however, usually is on therapy and counseling of the student. Additionally, consultation with school staffs, parents, or agency personnel may be conducted.

Inservice training of school staff entails the development and leadership of courses, seminars, and workshops for teachers, administrators, and school ancillary personnel (e.g., school social workers). Such inservice training relates to any of a large array of school-related topics. For example, such offerings as the following are available: management of teacher stress in the classroom, behavioral classroom management techniques, use of psychological findings in the classroom, and rational behavior therapy techniques for educators.

The foregoing does not exhaust the list of services that are needed and may be provided by school psychologists in modern urban school settings. They do, however, suggest the type of services provided in the more advanced urban school settings and what may be offered by many schools.

PROBLEMATIC IMPLICATIONS OF URBAN SCHOOL CHARACTERISTICS FOR PSYCHOLOGICAL SERVICE DELIVERY

Inherent within urban schools are serious problems for the delivery of psychological services to students, staffs, parents, and community agencies. These problems have the potential for delaying or denying the delivery of needed services. If, however, the problems are faced and managed, there is much potential within them for innovative and creative solutions. This section considers the conceptual and logistical hurdles for service delivery.

Conceptual hurdles are considered first, and apart from logistical hurdles. These are the hurdles in the realm of policy decisions by school boards and top administrative personnel in the schools. The policy referred to here defines which services are to be provided, to what extent, and to whom.

Although logistical hurdles may reside within policy decisions by school boards or top administrators, they also exist within administrative procedures. They determine the staff deployment model to be used and decide how services will be delivered.

CONCEPTUAL HURDLES

Services Within the Schools or Community Services

Many school board members, activist citizens, private practitioners, and some school superintendents, for numerous reasons, take the position that the school should be narrowly defined. Therefore, they maintain that its only task is to teach students the basic academic subjects or maybe applied skills by means of which students will be able to earn their living. These are the decision makers that Heaston (1982) has identified as being most difficult to communicate with successfully, and who have little comprehension of the role of the school psychologist other than that of test giver.

These individuals maintain that personal difficulties students might have should be dealt with by private practitioners or by community agencies. Needed services, it is postulated, could be made available to those students who need them after school hours or on weekends. It is maintained that to offer psychological services in the schools is to be in competition with the private sector, and that schools were never intended to enter into this type of competition. Some school psychology training programs take essentially the same position in that they teach few skills other than testing to their students, for whatever reason. The combination of school and university professionals with this conceptualization of school psychology is a powerful hurdle to broad service delivery to students.

Other school board members, citizen activists, private practitioners, and school superintendents conceptualize the schools diametrically opposite to the foregoing. They conceptualize the schools far more broadly; they view the schools as special settings for the intellectual, affective, physical, and ethical development of children and youth. Within this concept, schools provide academic and physical instruction and opportunities for affective and ethical development. Schools also provide supportive services, one of which is psychological services, to help students remove emotional and other personal blocks to their learning and development, as well as to assist them in the increment of positive personal functioning as citizens. This is not viewed as competition with the private sector.

The decline in financial resources available to the schools in recent years and the accompanying staff layoffs have intensified the debate between the forces aligned on each side of the issue of whether or not psychological services, other than minimal testing, should be provided within the schools. The adequacy of service delivery for the individual urban school or school system depends upon who is in control at the moment. Adequate service delivery, represented in terms of sufficient staff, may be delayed seriously in the face of debate or foot-dragging on the issue. In the end it may be denied altogether.

The decline in financial resources for schools that occurred in the late 1970s and early 1980s gave support to opponents of school-based service delivery. It was with relative ease that they were able to effect reductions in service staffs. Where staffs were reduced, service opponents were able to rationalize their actions largely on the basis of the concomitant drop in the student population that had occurred across the country.

The hurdles of ignorance among decision makers of what school psychology is all about and the opposition of opponents of school-based service delivery, at least with regard to some types of services described earlier in this chapter, are actively operational throughout the country. In practically all "Great Cities" schools and many other sizable urban systems, the ratio of school psychologists to students is far too large to satisfy the APA standard of 1 to 1500 (APA, 1977). Thus, only some of the basic functions of school psychologists can be carried out, meaning that there is a severe restriction on service delivery in many of the nation's urban schools. This bias is explicated later in this chapter.

The hurdle resulting from the efforts of opponents to school-based service delivery is very basic. Several other hurdles that are discussed are a limited variation of this more basic hurdle.

Diagnostic Testing and Consultation or Full-Range Service Delivery

In most urban schools or school systems the primary conceptual allegiance is to diagnostic case study rather than to therapeutic intervention. The assumption is that it is appropriate to provide school-based assessment in order to identify for referral to community services students with personal problems that might interfere with learning. This will enable the school to proceed with its attention and resources focused upon academic learning, while the students receive needed help from outside the school.

In the past, this model of service delivery has not led to adequate provision of service for students in these schools, and learning continued to be frustrated. Over the years, outside agencies to which the students have been referred have not had the resources to serve these students; therefore, they have placed the students on long waiting lists. Further, when some of the agencies have provided students with intervention services, the schools have complained that no progress has been made, at best, and that the students have decompensated, at worst. As students' negative behaviors become more intense, there often is increased interference with the learning of the students and classroom peers.

The commitment to this model of service delivery has been so great that some urban schools or systems have apparently violated federal law, and possibly the companion state law. Public Law 94–142 mandates a free, appropriate education and related services (which includes school psychology). Related services recommended by the interdisciplinary team must be provided by the school or system. Yet, even with this type of legal requirement therapeutic interventions are not being provided in all systems. Given professional assessment and diagnosis under P.L. 94–142, one would expect many conditions to be uncovered that would require therapeutic intervention directly by the school psychologist. This seems not to be the case in some systems.

As discussed earlier, in some urban schools and systems psychologists have been given to understand by the administration that recommendations made by the interdisciplinary team are to fit existing programs and services, which was implicit in the case of Armstrong v. Kline (Prasse, 1981), or as in the case of Forrest v. Ambach, that no recommendations be made (Prasse, 1983). In some urban schools, this precludes recommendations for therapy and counseling altogether; this was at issue in the case of T. G. v. Board of Education (1983). Even in schools and systems committed to the delivery of a full range of services, there is the recurrent request to reduce therapy services temporarily in order to catch up with required assessment and diagnostic testing.

Health Service Delivery Within Psychology or Services for Special Education Placement

Health services delivery has been defined by the Council for the National Register of Health Service Providers in Psychology as "the delivery of direct, preventive, assessment and therapeutic intervention services to individuals whose growth, adjustment or functioning is actually impaired or is demonstrably at high risk of impairment" (1983, p. xiii).

School psychology as a specialty within the profession of psychology was begun to assess and evaluate students for placement in special education classes. In more recent years, school psychology has evolved beyond this original mission to the provision of psychoeducational and health services to students, school staff, and parents/families (Bernauer & Jackson, 1974).

Services for special education placement is the assessment of students to determine if they satisfy entry criteria for programs in special education, e.g., language pathology and a range of low-incidence disabilities. However, criteria for special education programs in certain urban schools may not be consistent with criteria for a given syndrome that is acceptable generally to the psychological profession at large. In those situations, the school psychologist has the task of clearly differentiating between the relatively narrow criteria of the special education program and the broader criteria of the psychological profession. This theme also has been pursued by Slenkovich (1983). Further, the school psychologist helps school educators to understand the differences between the narrower and broader interpretations of the same syndromes or disabilities. The narrower definition of the usual special education program is for teaching purposes—for teaching reading, arithmetic, and so forth to students who happen to be emotionally disturbed, learning disabled, mentally retarded, or otherwise disabled. The broader definition of the school psychologist is not only for the purpose of facilitating learning, but also for the psychological welfare of the student as a learner and the psychological management of the disability by the student.

With the passage of P.L. 94–142, there has generally been a serious erosion of health services delivery by psychologists in the schools, dramatized by the layoff of school psychologists and other providers. This has come about for at least two reasons. First of all, there is partial federal/state reimbursement to school districts for salaries of school psychologists who assess or evaluate students for special education placement. At the same time, there is little or no federal/state government reimbursement for the delivery of health treatment services to students, which has contributed to the layoffs indicated above and in other urban areas. In fact, there is little or no federal/state reimbursement for the delivery of assessment or evaluation services to regular education students. Thus, in most, if not in all, urban schools, available assessment service delivery has been made under P.L. 94–142 (Poll, 1982) because the money was readily available for it. Second, even where state reimbursement has been promised for health treatment service delivery to students (both regular education students and special education students) preference in service delivery has been made under P.L. 94–142 instead of under the health services treatment reimbursement statute. School psychologists continue to devote an inordinate amount of time to P.L. 94–142 services and have not evidenced consistent efforts within their schools to effect fewer P.L. 94–142 referrals and more health treatment referrals. This is true in schools where over 50% of the P.L. 94–142 referrals ultimately are found not to have special education needs. Primary reasons for this situation are that school psychologists in urban schools and school systems are keenly aware that P.L. 94–142 *mandates* service delivery pursuant to the referral of a student suspected of having a special education need, and that state departments of education or public instruction constantly monitor local compliance with the provisions of P.L. 94–142, with sanctions for those schools that are out of compliance. Where reimbursement is promised for health treatment services, they are not likely mandated by the State; rather, they are permissive. Also, under health treatment services funding, there may be a lack of constant and intense monitoring. Some school psychologists also hold the opinion that P.L. 94–142 funds are more predictable than health treatment funding, and thus under the former their jobs are more secure.

The net result of the erosion of health services is that the practice of school psychology is definitely threatened with being reduced or returned to the level of a psychometric service, and only for special education students. All services, other than assessment services for the placement of students, will be reduced drastically, and service for regular education students will not exist.

Another conceptual hurdle relative to P.L. 94–142 is the perception of many educators that services are provided primarily, if not exclusively, to special education students. The students they refer as regular education students fail to receive help, at least on a timely basis. The conclusion is reached, therefore, that the way to guarantee service delivery to regular education students is to refer them as suspected of possessing special education needs; they must then be seen by the interdisciplinary team (including the school psychologist), and within a limited period of time. The implication for service delivery of this idea, and procedures leading therefrom, is that it takes an unnecessary, prolonged space of time, part of which otherwise could be devoted to services for several regular education students. That is to say, the time could be used for regular education students if school psychologists and the schools could be encouraged routinely to devote it to them. It is not a small number of students who are referred inappropriately in this manner to school psychologists and other members of the interdisciplinary team. Responsible school system administrators have indicated that over half of the students referred from some schools suspected of having special education needs have been found not to have such needs when assessed. It has been reported by S. Grant (personal communication, July 19, 1984) that the total average percentage of "inappropriate" initial referrals (cases found not to have special education needs) made under P.L. 94–142 in her large, urban school system during the 1983–84 school year was 40%. The average percentage of such cases for high schools during the same period of time was 45%, for middle schools 45%, and for elementary schools 38%. For regular high schools, the range of inappropriate initial referrals was 26% to 67%, and for both middle schools and elementary schools 0% to 80%. The time lost by referring large numbers of students to multidisciplinary teams, which proceeds through many formal, lengthy, and meticulous steps, instead of working flexibly with students as regular education referrals, is enormous. Within schools where this is happening some of the motivation is known; it does not result primarily from mistakenly referring students as suspected of having special education needs. Of course, some of the referrals occur through honest error.

The number of referrals generated in response to P.L. 94–142 and state special education mandates generally is huge. It ranged up to 6 or 7 out of 8 in one of the more "progressive" urban systems for 1983–84 (S. Grant, personal communication, September, 1984). These proportions indicate that a conceptual hurdle to service delivery resides in the fact that some urban school systems have not developed mechanisms that allow an equitable distribution of staff time for regular and special education students.

Even if the foregoing hurdles could be overcome, the attitudes and role perception of some school psychologists must also be viewed as a major hurdle. Cameron, Asbury, Cameron, and Gettone (1982) surveyed a random sample of the members of the National Association of School Psychologists (NASP) and the Association of Black Psychologists (AB Psy). They found that these psychologists saw the responsibility of providing psychotherapy and the assumption of a mental health role as outside their purview *as pupil personnel specialists.* Thus, professional self-image within the school system can be a hurdle to service delivery.

In-District Service Delivery or Out-of-District Contracting

Out-of-district contracting is the purchase of services for students by schools from community agencies or private practitioners. Services purchased are those not offered or offered on a limited basis by the schools, those a school wishes to replace with the contracted services, or those offered by a school but not to the extent necessary to meet the requested demands.

Given the large numbers of students served by urban schools, their socioeconomic condition, and the associated overburden of special psychological and other needs they have, service delivery in response to the full spectrum of presenting problems will require either comprehensive services within the schools or out-of-district contracting.

Out-of-district contracting has been of major concern since the passage of P.L. 94-142 with its requirement that handicapped students be provided *free,* appropriate education, even if the schools do not have the program in place. Thus, if the schools do not have the program the student needs, they must provide such a program. Contracting is one means for acquiring the needed services.

Contracting is perceived as a major threat to jobs by many school psychologists, especially where their schools have given consideration to large-scale contracting or where school psychologist positions are disappearing as more cases are put out for contract. Psychologists are resisting some contracting through their unions, and professional associations (APA, 1983; NASP, 1984) have drafted guidelines on contracting.

Hurdles to psychological services delivery under out-of-district contracting reside in the fact that most community agencies and institutions in an area do not employ school psychologists on their staffs. Therefore, when the service contract with one or more of these agencies is for a special education student and the student's individual educational plan (IEP) requires services from a school psychologist, the agency often is technically unable to deliver the required services.

An additional hurdle to service delivery under out-of-district contracting is that professional supervision and monitoring of services delivery are not usually available. Under P.L. 94–142 contracting, the students contracted into agencies and institutions remain the responsibilities of the schools; however, even where a school psychologist may be in the agency, the school psychological services supervisor from the schools is not on-site for supervision and monitoring. There is no ready way of affecting quality control of service delivery, beyond what the provider school psychologist reports. Annual updating of IEPs provides some monitoring and opportunity for direct observation of the student, but this is minimal.

Perhaps the greatest hurdle to psychological service delivery under out-of-district contracting is that agency personnel may not understand specific schools or what is needed by students to function well in specific schools. Therefore, in some instances, services provided by them are not the services that are needed.

Non-Discriminatory Testing or "Standards"

Non-discriminatory testing concerns of recent years have been, to a large extent, in response to P.L. 94–142 requirements. Specific instruments of concern have included the Mercer and Lewis System of Multicultural Pluralistic Assessment (SOMPA), (Mercer & Lewis, 1977), the Kaufman Assessment Battery for Children (K-ABC), (Kaufman & Kaufman, 1983), and the assessment approaches developed by the National School Psychology Inservice Training Network at the University of Minnesota (Oakland, 1980; Tucker, 1981). Both special educators and regular educators in urban schools have exhibited varying degrees of skepticism regarding tests and methods especially developed as means of non-discriminatory testing. As a result of this skepticism, these educators may engage in tactics that delay or frustrate the use of non-discriminatory testing instruments, e.g., refusing to accept diagnostic conclusions and recommendations based upon the instruments, insisting upon long and drawn-out inservice on the instruments for themselves to the point where their doubts are dispelled or until controls to the level of their comfort are placed upon the use of the instruments, or requiring time-consuming special reports documenting the results of the use of the instruments.

As for the testing approaches that have come out of the National School Psychology Inservice Training Network, non-test based assessment does not always fit into the placement/diagnostic formulas of special education programs criteria. Special education personnel want psychometric results in the areas of intelligence and achievement, an observation that also seems to have been made by Ysseldyke, Algozzine, Regan, and McGue (1981). These researchers indicated an agreement with Matuszek and Oakland (1979) that school decision-makers reported heavy reliance upon *scores* that students obtain on intelligence and achievement measures.

In essence, non-discriminatory testing instruments do not fare well unless they fit into the various criteria of special education programs. Yet, P.L. 94–142 requires non-discriminatory testing instruments. Adjusting these instruments to a special education program criteria is proving difficult; the active opposition to their use is a major hurdle.

In some urban schools, e.g., Chicago and San Francisco, psychologists are denied the use of intelligence tests in the examination of students for special education. Consequently, they are denied the non-discriminatory use of "standardized" tests with students, which potentially could be achieved through clinical interpretations of the test data presented as hypotheses or clinical judgment on the part of psychologists who have acquired background knowledge and experience in one or more of the ethnic minority cultures. This is practical, particularly when these tests are part of larger batteries from which some degree of validity may be discerned.

LOGISTICAL HURDLES

Centralized, Decentralized, or Location Budgeted Services Delivery

Historically, staff deployment for service delivery has been on a centralized or decentralized or centralized/decentralized combination basis. With a centralized organization, staff psychologists are assigned to quarters at the central administration building or some other building in an urban school system, or to one or more clinics within the system; in any case, the school psychologists are assigned to one or two sites in the system, where parents bring their child for services. With decentralized deployment, psychologists are assigned to area offices, and/or each is assigned to a small group of two or three schools, among which they rotate in order to work with students. With centralized/decentralized deployment, psychologists are assigned to a central site, but also visit assigned schools to which they deliver services; some services may be provided at the central site.

A fourth approach to deployment of staff is that of location budgeting. Here a certain percentage of a school psychologist's professional on-the-job time is budgeted to each of a given number of schools. For example, a psychologist may have 45% of his or her time budgeted to School A, 25% to School B, and 30% to School C.

Troubling logistical hurdles exist in both centralized and decentralized staff deployment schemes. Logistical hurdles associated with location budgeting potentially can rigidify service delivery. Centralized services eliminate the opportunity to make important observations of students in the natural setting of their respective schools. Thus, quality of service delivery may be affected negatively by centralized service delivery. Decentralized service delivery requires the school psychologist to travel between two schools or among several. Important time that could be devoted to working with a student or students may be spent in traveling. In location budgeting, each school administrator potentially may claim all of the psychologist's time budgeted to his or her school, whether the school actually needs it or not; this would prevent the psychologist's supervisor from redeploying the psychologist temporarily to other schools where there might be a large and demanding backlog. It would also prevent the psychologist from adjusting his or her time among the schools regularly served when work at one school is significantly more demanding than is that of another. Flexibility of staff redeployment during the school year could be lost with location budgeting.

Specialized Staffing or General Service Staffing

In order to serve small, difficult, or complicated student populations, it sometimes becomes necessary to provide specialized staffing. For example, one school psychologist may be assigned to the program for autistic children, or one to the classes for deaf and hard-of-hearing, or two to the orthopedic programs. For the most part, specialized staffing is effected in special education programs. However, a degree of specialization is effected in regular schools by assigning school psychologists exclusively to elementary, middle, or high schools.

Service delivery to large student population groups such as regular education students is ordinarily effected through general services staffing. That is to say, one school psychologist will deliver psychological services to all students referred in his or her schools, meaning that one school psychologist delivers services to students representing many syndromes.

Specialized staffing is a procedure for improving quality of services that are delivered. At the same time, specialization makes those who become specialized less accessible for flexible redeployment to help with service needs outside the area of specialization. Due to lack of practice in broader skills, the specialized psychologists are reluctant to take on assignments outside their specialty.

Direct Control of Field Staff or Indirect Control of Field Staff

The degree of control that the professional psychological services unit exercises over field staff is controversial as a hurdle to be overcome. Both direct control and indirect control are viewed as hurdles to be negotiated, depending upon who is doing the viewing. Professional psychologists more often than not see indirect control as delaying service delivery. Special educational services administrators frequently see direct professional control as less than desirable in service delivery.

With direct professional control of staff, the psychologist-administrator or psychologist-supervisor is in immediate charge of not only the professional activities of staff psychologists, but also of the psychologist's non-professional activities, e.g., scheduling of students for examination. With indirect professional control of the psychological services staff, the psychologist-administrator or psychologist-supervisor has immediate responsibility for the professional activities of the psychologists, and the educational administrator in, for example, a special education program has responsibility for the psychologist's non-professional, administrative-type activities (e.g., being on time and having reports prepared on time).

The hurdle perceived in direct professional control is that of the difficulty of coordination of psychological services delivery with the delivery of other services to a student client, e.g., speech pathology and social work. The educational program administrator tends to feel that he or she has no authority to utilize the clinical staff assigned to his or her program to insure service delivery or to utilize the clinical staff flexibly. The educational administrator may have an idea of which services are needed, but he or she cannot do much about effective delivery, since complete control resides in the hands of professional administrators and supervisors at the "central office."

Indirect control hurdles as seen by the professional psychological services administrator involve the difficulty of gaining access to field staff for inservice training, special assignments, and staff meetings. The educational program administrator may refuse to allow field staff to attend the meetings called by the professional administrator. Major problems can develop in a power struggle for control of the field psychologists, sometimes with the psychologists not really knowing in which direction to move. In these instances, and they can be many, services to students may be seriously delayed.

Importance of the Cultural Background Match Between Psychologists and Student Clients

Students from ethnic minorities frequently exhibit the need, and not infrequently the demand, for school psychologists who share the culture of their own ethnic group or who share their language. Hispanic students and their families frequently demand Hispanic psychologists because of the common language, as well as cultural background. Black students and their families frequently demand black psychologists for the expected greater understanding that comes from psychologists having had the black experience (Vontress, 1970; Warren, Jackson, Nugaris, Farley, 1973). Other students who may exhibit needs for psychologists who share their own backgrounds include native Americans and those from Appalachia.

In selected instances, and in some instances on a temporary basis, the psychological services unit administrator may choose to effect assignments so that a psychologist with a certain cultural background may be able to work with given students of similar backgrounds. These psychologists may be of the same ethnic background as the student or may have special experience with the culture of the student.

Several factors serve as hurdles to the matching of psychologists with students. There is the practical impossibility of recruiting and hiring American Indian psychologists, because they are so few and in such great demand. The Hispanic and black recruiting and hiring picture is hardly any better in most parts of the country. Those minority school psychologists who are hired are difficult to keep during layoffs that are frequent in periods of economic recessions. Seniority rules written into contracts between the urban schools and unions that represent psychologists serve effectively to interfere with the flexible assignment and reassignment of staff to the schools and programs where the best psychologist-student cultural match can be effected. These union contracts establish seniority over competency as the basis for staff assignments. The failure of some urban schools to fund appropriate numbers of school psychologists is also a hurdle to effecting psychologist-student match.

The need to effect the psychologist-student match is fairly peculiar to the urban schools where many different nationality and ethnic groups are represented. For a more detailed discussion of this issue, the reader is referred to Argulewicz's chapter (this volume) on the delivery of psychological services in bicultural settings.

Psychology has developed tools that are appropriate to its practice. It has also developed uses within the profession for tools and instruments developed outside the profession. Delivery of psychological services usually involves the employment of selected tools and instruments. Particular ones employed depend upon the needs of, and service to, the individual client or situation.

Evaluation, assessment, and diagnosis traditionally have involved the employment of objective and projective tests, and a variety of related measures. These are expensive, with at least one commonly used test—the Leiter—costing over $600. Materials for therapy, especially play or activity therapy, and other types of therapeutic intervention are varied and expensive. Nevertheless, testing equipment and treatment materials are necessary to adequate service delivery.

Delivery of psychological services involves access not only to a wide range of materials but to other types of resources. These resources include any assistance that helps to ensure appropriate service to students. Examples of other resources include neuropsychological, psychiatric, and medical consultants. Consultation may be required for individual cases, groups, or systems. In addition to access to consultation, and access to professional books and journals, opportunity to attend conventions and other professional meetings is also important to the delivery of psychological services; they are means of staying current with the status of the profession and of receiving critical reactions and feedback from colleagues in other geographical areas to one's own reported professional activities in the areas of service delivery.

Serious hurdles are faced in providing needed materials and other resources.

These include inadequate funding, unsecured storage, lack of time to work with consultants, insufficient professional supervision, and lack of professional leave policies that encourage or allow staff participation in the activities of their professional associations.

Cooperative Team Procedures in Service Delivery

As indicated earlier in this chapter, the majority of services currently delivered by school psychologists have been significantly influenced by P.L. 94–142. Within the context of this federal statute, psychological services are delivered as part of the services of an interdisciplinary team, and herein lie hurdles to services delivery. Cooperating as a member of the team is a time-consuming process. Referral review, articulated scheduling for testing, staffings, reaching consensus, filing disagreement reports, contesting with educational program testing and placement officers—whatever the specific procedures in a given urban school or system—comprise a rigid, formal system of service delivery that consumes time that school psychologists maintain could be devoted to services for additional students. Little fault has been found with the team concept; the problem for service delivery has been with the rigid, formal, time-consuming process through which the team functions, and on stressful and time-consuming hassles with teachers who perform educational testing as members of the team and with those who have the final word on placement of students. Fleming and Fleming (1983) have attested to some of these problems in their discussion of challenges facing teams.

In recent years, absolutely the heaviest burden of P.L. 94–142 testing and required cooperative functioning of the school psychologist with other team members is in the area of the 3-year reevaluation. Each year this becomes more burdensome as additional students are placed in special education classes. Serious questions are beginning to be raised about the efficacy of the 3-year reevaluation, which takes time that could be devoted to other and more useful services for students (Elliott, Piersel, & Galvin, 1983; Galvin & Elliott, 1985). Some efforts are already underway to make routine reevaluations more economical of time.

Employment of the Optimum Sized Staff for Service Delivery

Urban school systems ordinarily make no attempt to achieve optimum staff size. The American Psychological Association's Specialty Guidelines for Services Delivery by School Psychologists (APA, 1977) suggest a school psychologist to student ratio of 1 to 1,500. Wisconsin was the only state in an unpublished survey conducted by Jackson to have a state-recommended ratio. Wisconsin encourages a 1 to 1,000 ratio. More students per psychologist than indicated by these ratios are expected to be less than what is required to do the job adequately. Most urban schools are chronically far off the optimum set by the American

196 JACKSON

Psychological Association. An unpublished mail survey in 1979 and a telephone survey in 1982, both by Jackson, provide psychologist-to-student ratios for several urban districts across the United States (See Table 7.2).

Accountability Through Recordkeeping

Extensive recordkeeping has been instituted in schools as a means of achieving accountability. All too often, this requires a school psychologist to spend considerable time filling out forms for each student who is provided services. In

TABLE 7.2
Comparative Staffing Analysis for School Psychologists In Selected Urban School Systems

Urban School Systems	School Psychologists to Student Ratios 1978–1979	1981–82
Atlanta, GA	1: 4,292	—
Buffalo, NY	1: 2,438	—
Chicago, IL	1: 3,000	—
Cleveland, OH	1: 3,000	—
Dallas, TX	1: 4,256	—
Denver, CO	1: 2,081	1: 1,714
Detroit, MI	1: 4,231	1:3,786
Indianapolis, IN	1: 4,603	1: 2,640
Memphis, TN	1: 24,000	1: 2,545
Milwaukee, WI	1: 1,225	1: 1,165
Minneapolis, MN	1: 3,800	1: 3,289
Nashville-Davidson County, TN	1: 2, 866	—
Norfolk, VA	1: 4,300	—
Oakland, CA	1: 2,207	—
Philadelphia, PA	1: 2,324	—
Pittsburgh, PA	1: 2,587	1: 2,100
Portland, OR	1: 3,834	—
Seattle, WA	1: 1,634	—
Toledo, OH	1: 3,000	—

Note. Data obtained from surveys conducted in 1979 and 1982 by Jackson.

addition to case reports and IEP's, the school psychologist completes data forms of a wide description documenting what has happened to the student. Completing large numbers of forms is time-consuming (although required) and takes the school psychologist away from the business of providing services directly to the student.

Serious consideration to ways of eliminating large amounts of paper work could include several approaches. In large school systems a forms-control position might be helpful in curtailing a proliferation of new forms. At the same time, a review of forms in use might prove a useful process for weeding out those not essential. The substitution of brief forms, where such will suffice, could require reduced time to complete. The telephone, and electronic means of transmitting data to computers for management information systems, may be *the* approach to the future.

FUTURE SERVICE DELIVERY AND ITS POTENTIAL CONCEPTUAL AND LOGISTICAL HURDLES

Future service delivery will depend, to a large extent, upon the state of education in the urban setting and the relationship of school services providers, e.g., school psychologists, to the educational enterprise. It is, therefore, important to conjecture the shape of the urban schools or school systems through the 1980s.

Educational Trends

Much has been happening in the schools within the last 3 or 4 years that is quite relevant to school psychological services. One such cluster of events is known as mastery learning (Block, 1979) and effective schools (Cuban, 1983; Eubanks & Levine, 1983; Ralph & Fennessey, 1983). Both the mastery learning and effective schools focus on high achievement in academic skills across all students and all classrooms, not on humane classroom environments, may be the wave of the future. Numbers of regular education teachers are of the opinion that what is needed is responsible, dedicated, energetic, and repetitive instruction. In the literature and in discussions there appears to be no consideration given to the supportive help of school psychologists and other ancillary staff. It is as if they are not needed.

In recent years, psychologists and other supportive staff have reinforced teacher attitudes that their services may not be needed by virtue of the fact that they have been, in many or most schools and systems, almost exclusively involved with special education students or those suspected of needing this type of programming. Psychologists, indeed, have acted as if their services were not relevant to regular education students. If they are to become reinvolved in the overall school and educational enterprise, as they were before the advent of P.L. 94–142, they will need to view carefully where regular, as well as special, education is going. Passow (1982) has summarized part of a report that was prepared by the 3-year Urban Education Studies project 1977–1980, which was directed by Francis Chase. Chase and associates found 10 factors and three trends in all of the 16 urban school systems studied, which may provide realistic insight as to where schools really are or are going. As summarized by Passow (1982), the 10 factors included:

- the formation of partnerships or other collaborative relationships between schools and other community agencies and organizations;
- active involvement of parents and other citizens in educational planning, curriculum development, and instruction;
- the establishment of new types of schools that offer alternatives to neighborhood elementary schools, middle schools, and comprehensive high schools;
- extended provisions for early childhood education;
- new emphases on the teaching of basic skills;
- the introduction of bilingual and multicultural programs;
- the initiation of new programs for the handicapped;
- broadened roles for the creative and performing arts;
- the installation of instructional management systems; and
- the initiation of approaches to systemwide planning, management, and evaluation.

Three trends were found in all 16 cities: (a) participation in educational decision making by significantly larger numbers of minority groups and the poor, (b) increased attention by school boards and administrators to advice from individuals and groups outside the profession, and (c) unprecedented collaboration between schools and nonschool agencies. (p. 521)

Service Delivery

Assuming the reliability of the 10 identified factors and the validity of the three reported trends, one can anticipate considerable change in the schools during the remainder of the 1980s. To adjust to these trends and the anticipated changes, school psychology will need to be broadened rather dramatically in its scope and reach. At least three thrusts must be given serious consideration:

1. Renewed emphasis upon consulting with regular educators to help remediate children's learning;
2. Continued focus upon serving through a variety of interventions, including therapy, the mental health needs of students in support of improved learning, personality functioning, and overt behavior; and
3. First-time concentration and advisement upon a variety of school/community problems that impact students.

Example of school/community problems might include psychological aspects of programming for, and services to, latchkey children; child and parental education in protective and safety measures against sexual abuse; nuclear fears of children and adolescents; school staff-community relationship difficulties, especially where the difficulties involve sub-cultures within the community; gang activity diffusion and control; and a host of other problems emergent out of the future sociocultural context of the immediate and distant future.

Means of service delivery, in view of the foregoing, will need to be reevaluated. My evaluation of future service delivery systems suggests at least three changes.

1. Increased use of the new electronic technology and its hardware and software:
   a. Computer-based test interpretation (especially when improved to the point where it can provide integrated interpretations of batteries of tests and there are acceptable industry-wide guidelines for its operation).
   b. Word processing for removing the drudgery and reducing time for writing and proofing reports.
   c. Electronic mail and bulletin board networks for continued contact among urban school systems.
   d. Management information systems for tracking and monitoring delivery of services in the field.

2. Revisions in the usual procedures for providing services to students under P.L. 94–142, especially in the nature of the reevaluation and the reevaluation report.

3. Collaboration and cooperation, through new type arrangements, with community professionals (agencies or individuals) in providing services to students and their families.

Associated Conceptual and Logistical Hurdles to Service Delivery

Potential hurdles in this future projection of service delivery to students are several, and they include as possibilities:

1. Continued lack of clear understanding by school personnel of the role and functions of school psychologists and failure to facilitate the best possible services delivery.

2. Lack of clear understanding by community professionals of the role and functions of school psychologists and difficulties or clashes in efforts to collaborate.

3. Lags in data reporting or processing so that management information system printouts do not match reality on a *timely basis*, causing needless efforts by psychologists to account for the missing data, with a resulting waste of time that otherwise might be employed for service delivery.

4. Lag in readiness of the school psychologist to function broadly across the spectrum of the school psychologist's expanded role and function.

5. Lack of sufficiently broad education and training by university school psychology programs for school psychologists to have the attitudes and skills needed for services subsumed by their expanded role and function and that the urban schools require.

Another view of educational trends that differs from that cited above might require different service delivery and associated hurdles. Regardless, the challenges to school psychologists working in urban settings will remain significant; it is hoped that school psychology will continue to meet these challenges through improved service delivery to children, educators, and their communities.

REFERENCES

Agin, T. C. (1979). The school psychologist and collective bargaining: The brokerage of influence and professional concerns. *School Psychology Digest, 8,* 187–192.

American Psychological Association. (1977). *Specialty guidelines for the delivery of services.* Washington, DC: Author.

American Psychological Association. (1982a). Committee on Professional Standards *Agenda book 1,* March 12–15.

American Psychological Association. (1982b). Committee on Professional Standards *Agenda book 1,* October 24–26.

American Psychological Association. (1983). Contracting for school psychological services. A report of the executive council of the division of school psychology. Washington, DC: Author.

APA Backs Forrest. (1983, February). *APA Monitor,* p. 2.

Bernauer, M., & Jackson, J. H. (1974). Review of school psychology for 1973. *Professional Psychology, 5,* 155–165.

Block, J. H. (1979). Mastery learning. The current state of the craft. *Educational Leadership, 36,* 114–117.

Bins, M., & Walker, J. (1980). *Great city schools directory 1980–81.* Washington, DC: The Council of the Great City Schools.

Cameron, H. K., Asbury, C. A., Cameron, W. F., & Gettone, V. G. (1982). *Perceived professional roles of urban school psychologists.* Washington, DC: Howard University.

Council for the National Register of Health Service Providers in Psychology. (1983). *National register of health service providers in psychology.* Washington, DC: Author.

Cuban, L. (1983). Effective schools: A friendly but cautionary note. *Phi Delta Kappan, 64,* 695–696.

Elliott, S. N., Piersel, W. C., & Galvin, G. A. (1983). Psychological re-evaluations: A survey of practices and perceptions of school psychologists. *Journal of School Psychology, 21,* 99–105.

Eubanks, E. E., & Levine, D. U. (1983). A first look at effective school projects in New York City and Milwaukee. *Phi Delta Kappan, 64,* 697–702.

Fleming, D. C., & Fleming, E. R. (1983). Problems in implementation of the team approach: A practitioner's perspective. *School Psychology Review, 12,* 144–149.

Galvin, G. A., & Elliott, S. N. (1985). Psychological reevaluation of handicapped children: A survey of practitioners and policy makers. *Professional Psychology: Research and Practice, 16,* 64–75.

Heaston, P. (1982, August). *Urban school psychology: Current perspectives.* Paper presented at the annual meeting of the American Psychological Association, Washington, DC.

Hodge, M. V. (1981). Improving finance and governance of education for special populations. In K. F. Jordan & N. H. Cambron-McCabe (Eds.), *Perspectives in state school support programs* (pp. 3–38). Cambridge, MA: Ballinger.

Hoover, T., Kirschner-Stone, M., Detmer, M., & Nantume, G. (1982). State superintendents respond to Reaganomics. *Phi Delta Kappan, 64,* 124–125.

Jackson, J. H. (1970). Psychoeducational therapy as the primary activity of school psychologists. *Journal of School Psychologists, 8,* 183–190.

Jackson, J. H. (Chairman). (1977). *Records of corresponding committee of administrators of psychological services in large urban school districts.* Washington, DC: Division of School Psychology (Division 16), American Psychological Association.

Jackson, J. H. (1979). [Survey of school psychology staffing patterns in selected urban school systems.] Unpublished raw data.

Jackson, J. H., & Bernauer, M. (Eds.). (1968). *The school psychologist as a therapist.* Milwaukee, WI: Milwaukee Public Schools.

Jackson, J. H., & Bernauer, M. (1975). *Skills for comprehensive and effective psychological services in large urban school districts.* Summary Report of the Division of School Psychology, Division 16. American Psychological Association, Pre-Convention Workshop. Washington, DC: American Psychological Association.

Kaufman, A. S., & Kaufman, N. L. (1983). *Kaufman assessment battery for children.* Circle Pines, MN: American Guidance Service.

Matuszek, P., & Oakland, T. (1979). Factors influencing teachers' and psychologists' recommendations regarding special class placement, *Journal of School Psychology, 17,* 116–125.

Mercer, J. R., & Lewis, J. F. *System of multicultural pluralistic assessment.* New York: Psychological Corp.

Mullen, F. A. (1967). The role of the school psychologist in the urban school system. In J. F. Magary (Ed.), *School Psychological Services* (pp. 30–67). Englewood Cliffs, NJ: Prentice-Hall.

National Association of School Psychologists (1984). *Policy statement on contractual services,* draft copy.

Oakland, T. (1979). Research on the Adaptive Behavior Inventory for Children and the Estimated Learning Potential. *School Psychology Digest, 8,* 63–70.

Oakland, T. (1980). Nonbiased assessment. In T. Oakland (Ed.), *Nonbiased assessment.* Minneapolis, MN: National School Psychology Inservice Training Network.

Ornstein, A. C. (1982). The urban setting: frostbelt/sunbelt differences. *Phi Delta Kappan, 64,* 102–107.

Passow, A. H. (1982). Urban education for the 1980's: Trends and issues. *Phi Delta Kappan, 63,* 519–522.

Poll, B. G. (1982, August). *Urban school psychology: Current perspectives.* Paper presented at the annual meeting of the American Psychological Association, Washington, DC.

Prasse, D. (1981). Armstrong v. Kline: Defining appropriate programming. *Communique,* p. 3.

Prasse, D. (1983, December). The matter of Forrest v. Ambach. *Communique,* p. 3.

Pryzwansky, W., Fishbein, J., & Jackson, J. H. (1984). Therapy/counseling practices of urban school psychologists. *Professional psychology: Research and Practice, 15,* 396–404.

Ralph, J. H., & Fennessey, J. (1983). Science or reform: Some questions about the effective schools model. *Phi Delta Kappan, 64,* 689–694.

Russo, N., Olmedo, E., Stapp, J., & Fulcher, R. (1981). Women and minorities in psychology. *American Psychologist, 36,* 1315–1363.

Screening in New York State. (1980). The University of the State of New York, The State Education Department, Office for Education of Children with Handicapping Conditions, Albany, NY.

Slenkovich, J. E. (1983). *P.L. 94-142 as applied to DSM III diagnoses; an analysis of DSM III diagnoses vis-à-vis special education law.* Cupertino, CA: Kinghorn Press.

T.G. v. Board of Education, *576 F. Supp.* 420 (Piscataway, NJ, 1983).

Tucker, J. A. (1981). Non-test based assessment. In T. Oakland (Ed.), *Nonbiased assessment*. Minneapolis, MN: National School Psychology Inservice Training Network.

Vontress, C. E. (1970). Counseling blacks. *Personnel and Guidance Journal, 48,* 713–719.

Warren, R. C., Jackson, A. M., Nugaris, J., & Farley, G. K. (1973). Differential attitudes of black and white patients toward treatment in a child guidance clinic. *American Journal of Orthopsychiatry, 43,* 384–393.

White, M. A., & Duker, J. (1973). *Education: A conceptual and empirical approach.* New York: Holt, Rinehart & Winston.

Wise, A. E. (1981). Educational needs—Accounting for school finance. In K. F. Jordan & N. H. Cambron-McCabe (Eds.), *Perspectives in state school support programs.* (pp. 281–314). Cambridge, MA: Ballinger.

Ysseldyke, J., Algozzine, B., Regan, R., & McGue, M. (1981). The influence of test scores and naturally occurring pupil characteristic on psychoeducational decision making with children. *Journal of School Psychology, 19,* 167–177.

8 Service Delivery to Rural Schools: Conceptual and Logistical Hurdles

Jack J. Kramer
University of Nebraska-Lincoln

Glenda J. Peters
University of Oklahoma

Psychology has discovered rural America. Efforts to uncover and understand the unique features of this setting are in progress all across the nation. Although it would be a mistake to claim that previous generations had ignored the behavioral effects of the rural environment (e.g., Cameron, 1948; Ebaugh & Lloyd, 1927), it is apparent that over the last 10–15 years the mental health community has witnessed a dramatic increase in the study of "ruralness" (Bagarozzi, 1982; Melton, 1983). Most previous and many recent efforts have examined the problems involved with the delivery of psychological services in rural community and/or clinical settings (Buxton, 1973; Daniels, 1967; Flax, Wagenfeld, Ivans, & Weiss, 1979; Huessy, 1972). Rural school psychological services have received little attention in the professional literature. This problem continues to some extent as evidenced by a new text examining rural psychology (Childs & Melton, 1983) in which the impact of psychology on rural schools was virtually ignored.

It is true, nonetheless, that just as interest in a generic rural psychology has grown, there has been increased concern with the problems related to the delivery of psychological services in rural schools. This surge does not come as a total surprise in light of the fact that school psychological services did not exist in any systematic fashion in most rural areas prior to the last decade. Legislative action requiring the development of programs and the attempt to implement that mandate have led to efforts to draw attention to the nature of the problems endemic to rural special education (Helge, 1981; Heller, 1975; Illback & Ellis, 1981) and rural school psychology (Benson, 1985; Gerken, 1981; Goetz & Doerksen, 1978; Hamblin, 1981; Hughes & Clark, 1981; Kramer & Peters, 1985). Special interest groups have formed (e.g., American Council on Rural

Special Education, Handicapped Children's Early Education Rural Network, National Rural Preservice Training Consortium, National Association of School Psychologists Special Interest Group), and resources have been allocated for the examination of rural special education and rural school psychology (e.g., National Rural Research Project).

In this chapter we focus on the process of delivering psychological services to rural schools. We have attempted to provide a thorough examination of the structure that has evolved and the manner in which services have been delivered. In order to accomplish these goals we briefly review the historical and logistical factors that have influenced service delivery in rural areas, examine practitioners' perceptions of rural problems and rural practice, evaluate the apparent strengths and weaknesses of the service delivery models currently in place, and provide suggestions for rural service providers. We have used three major conceptual dimensions of service, centralized-decentralized, direct-indirect, and proactive-reactive models presented in the opening chapter of this volume to provide a framework within which we examine rural school psychological services.

RURAL SCHOOL PSYCHOLOGY: DEFINING CHARACTERISTICS AND EARLY HISTORY

Although a variety of authors have written about some aspect of ruralness in America, several common elements about the concept appear. These elements typically include variables related to population, geography, occupation, economics, and personal characteristics. Researchers may discuss rurality as an objective concept, whereby a United States Census Bureau Standard may apply, or rurality may reflect the author's individual concept of what country living or country people must be like. Throughout this chapter, ruralness will be considered from both objective and subjective perspectives to provide a comprehensive treatment of the concept as it applies to the organization and administration of school psychology. Hence, the "rural" client referred to in this chapter may be living in a more or less densely populated community, may be near or far in proximity to a Standard Metropolitan Statistical Area, may attend a small, single-class or large consolidated school. The rural client's psychological service need may to some degree reflect the conditions of his/her surroundings, though to date there have been no findings to suggest a "rural-syndrome," wherein the school psychologist would expect students, parents, and/or school personnel to behave in a predetermined "rural" pattern. An urban child might be characterized as street-smart, which implies that a certain kind of knowledge about the local neighborhood has been acquired through experience in a perplexing environment. Is the rural environment any less perplexing? Does the rural child rely any less on his/her wit? Answers to such questions are problematic, for as Childs and Melton (1983) report, there are no clearly defined models of ruralness to date.

They note the ambivalence of existing definitions and point to the inadequacy in the unidimensional approach to creating such definitions. We find no reason to differ with this interpretation, except to state clearly that taken together, the intuitive and quantifiable definitions provide a meaningful framework for the analysis of issues inherent in the delivery of psychological services to rural clients.

Objective Definitions

Statistically based definitions of rurality include the United States Census Bureau's Standards (communities with less than 2500 inhabitants) as well as Helge's (1980a) modification of those standards:

> A district is considered rural when the number of inhabitants is fewer than 150 per square mile or when located in counties with 60% or more of the population living in communities no larger than 5,000 inhabitants. [School] Districts with more than 10,000 students and those within a Standard Metropolitan Statistical Area (SMSA), as determined by the U.S. Census Bureau, are not considered rural. (p. 3)

Other school-related definitions are based on straightforward enrollment or attendance counts, commonly referring to a rural school district as one with less than 3,000 students (Hughes & Clark, 1981).

Subjective Definitions

Aside from the population variables described above, many notions about ruralness derive from one's concept of who is to be found in rural America and answers to questions such as what does the rural American do for a living, how much money does he or she earn, and how important is the family to a rural individual? Although we tend to speculate about stereotypic answers to such inquiries, there is very little evidence to permit us to create a unified profile of the rural American. Photiadis and Simoni (1983) present a cogent summary of recent literature pertaining to the demographics as well as the social variables associated with rural living, in which they make the following observations about contemporary rurality:

1. The economic development in rural areas, spurred by dramatic growth in agriculture, forestry, and rural industry, has been a boon to many rural residents, while inflicting burdens on others.

2. Equality of educational opportunity for children attending rural schools differs substantially from district to district. Where school consolidation exists, empirical evidence to suggest its positive benefits does not.

3. The "new-rural" population, i.e., inhabitants of non-isolated rural regions, are likely to be acquiring "attributes described for urban families a few decades earlier" (p. 27). Examples of changes in rural family life include modifications in women's roles, increased tolerance for premarital and extramarital relationships, and a decrease in tolerance of the double standard. As social and economic institutions change face, the inhabitants of rural regions may no longer fit the mold traditionally associated with "country folk."

Thus, we see the need for a broader, modified subjective definition of rural America and Americans, which leaves the task of tailoring a psychological practice in rural schools to each practitioner. We believe rural practice may in some instances reflect previously held expectations, while emphasizing that there seem to be fewer and fewer predictable conditions/qualities associated with rural inhabitants, schools, and communities.

With this "conceptual hurdle" in mind, we call the reader's attention to the work of Huessy (1972) who, in an attempt to distinguish rural from urban psychological practice, has described variables that set one apart from the other. Those variables include the underestimation by the rural community of its potential mental health or handicapping problems, the difficulty in obtaining qualified personnel, excessive social visibility of the mental health professional, federal imposition of urban needs on rural districts (mandated legislation), and low tax bases yielding inadequate financial support. Furthermore, Huessy indicates that rural areas have a higher prevalence of high school dropouts, students with learning disabilities or neonatal or fetal neurological damage. These findings appear to be substantiated in government documents citing higher incidences of inadequate or no prenatal care in rural counties, higher numbers of live births to teen-age mothers, and comparatively more infant deaths in rural counties (Oklahoma State Department of Health, 1982). Clearly, if such conditions exist in certain communities across this country, a thorough examination of the issues that impact on rural psychology is, in fact, warranted. School psychologists who find themselves in the midst of those conditions have distinctive questions and solutions to consider in examining the environment from which the student is likely to have emerged.

To what extent does rurality affect the school psychologist's practice? Fagan (1981) reports that one third of the 16,000 American school psychologists are employed in school districts with student populations below 5,000; that one fifth work alone, and that one half are in environments with fewer than five colleagues. Helge (1981) reports that 67% of all school districts are classified on the basis of population density or geographic isolation as either rural, remote, or isolated. As many as 1.8 million of the nation's 15 million rural school children have been assessed as handicapped (Sher, 1978), thus ensuring the potential need for psychological services. Obviously, the impact of rurality, whether empirically or subjectively defined, is a concept that forces critical issues to the forefront. The remainder of this chapter examines those issues.

The Evolution of Rural School Psychology

The evolution of psychology in the schools has been traced to earlier centuries when Greek philosophers debated the nature of man and universal laws of behavior (Tindall, 1979). Others suggest that its creation coincided with the child-study movement and the formal association of psychology and the public schools that occurred at the turn of the century (Slater, 1980). Arnold Gesell was the first to be labeled a school psychologist, in Connecticut in 1915, as noted by Bardon and Bennett (1974) who also proposed that the development of the specialty was still occuring, and that although early pioneers "pointed the way" toward sound psychological practice in the school, it has only recently become possible (timely) for the profession to mature. Regardless of the century, decade, or year of its "creation," the merger of psychology and American schools has evolved in an interesting and somewhat controversial fashion. The following sections of this chapter outline three stages in the evolution of the delivery of psychological services to rural school children.

Early History: The Itinerant Model. Bardon (1981) refers to the early period (prior to 1944) as school psychology's "prehistory," since there was no formal professional organization to define issues or conduct discussions pertaining to practitioners' and researchers' interests in providing positive benefits to children in schools. Bardon states that "Although there were school psychological services in some urban and suburban school districts prior to 1944, the practice of psychology in the schools until about the end of World War II tended to reflect developments that were not closely related to a particular field of psychology or of education" (p. 199). This perception seems slightly awry, as others (Slater, 1980) might argue, indeed as early psychologists in schools might have argued. Experimental and physiological psychologists sought to work in Chicago schools as early as 1899, in attempts to practice those branches of the discipline in a setting as abundant in subjects as the public schools. In the same year, the Chicago Bureau of Child Study was established as the first psychoeducational clinic serving a public school district and offering formal training in school psychology, and by 1920, school districts in 18 major cities were delivering services to pupils (Guydish, Zelhart, Jackson, & Markley, 1982; Tindall, 1979). Meanwhile, in rural districts where financial constraints and distance from urban and university clinics were factors, efforts to provide psychological services were hindered, though occasionally reported. Itinerant psychologists such as Arnold Gesell, T. Ernest Newland, Marie Skodak, and George Kelly "rode the circuits" in rural areas of the country, conducting psychological evaluations, academic assessments, preschool screenings and consulting with parents and school personnel. The emergence of field and extension clinics appeared during the 1930s, thus providing rural schools with centralized, yet available services. From the educational arena entered Dr. O. Latham Hatcher, a pioneer in providing rural students with inspiration and guidance. Her first efforts directed toward the vocational guidance of southern rural females gradually expanded to include all rural students, and led to the 1938 organization of the Alliance for Guidance of Rural Youth. That organization, under the leadership of Dr. Hatcher, a former Associate Professor of English at Bryn Mawr College (1903–1915), sponsored regional institutes for teachers (Warburton, 1964). During these training institutes, child development, curriculum, instructional techniques and counseling were considered and examined as integral components in the students' education.

Clearly, the early history of the practice of school psychology in rural schools was limited in scope and in significance; however, itinerant services reported to have been established prior to World War II are on record, and to some extent serve as original models for the effective delivery of services to contemporary rural students.

Post World War II: Toward Specialization. Prior to World War II, psychology was being practiced in the schools, albeit infrequently. However, there was not a distinct school psychology. Others (e.g., Bardon & Bennett, 1974) have described some of the events within American psychology that have helped to provide school psychology with an identity, including the creation of the first school psychology training programs, the establishment of Division 16 of the American Psychological Association, and the Thayer Conference. Within American society this was a time of social emphasis on achievement and emotional well-being. These factors, as well as surging economic development and opportunity, gave rise to the demand for more psychological services to children. There were, after all, *more* children in the schools, which exacerbated the already problematic educational climate. As the demand for services rose, and more psychologists were hired by schools, tighter controls on quality and accountability began to surface. Although quite important to the practice of school psychology in general, these events had less immediate impact on rural service delivery, where programs remained very much a "one-person operation" (Herron, Green, Guild, Smith, & Kantor, 1970). It is true, however, that school psychology was beginning to gain an identity as a specialty area within psychology and was positioning itself for future contributions to public education.

Multidisciplinary Services: The Impact of Judicial and Legislative Involvement. During the past two decades the future of the practice of psychology in the schools has been irrevocably shaped. The judicial decisions pertaining to the constitutionality of testing, the protection of individual and parental rights, and bias toward minority students have altered the very essence of rural school psychology in particular. As Jackson (1985) notes in the previous chapter on urban school psychology, the impact of judicial decisions and the subsequent landmark legislation, Public Law 94–142, The Education for All Handicapped Children Act of 1975, is immeasureable. As a result, service delivery to rural students has changed in both quantitative and qualitative aspects. Where little or no psychological assistance to rural school children was required prior to 1975, services have expanded to become comprehensive and multidisciplinary in nature. Since the introduction of P.L. 94–142, *every* handicapped student from ages 3 through 21 has become entitled to a "free, appropriate" education, which therefore increases the number of students requiring services and certainly ensures a focus on the handicapped population and special education. These students cannot be placed or appropriately educated unless comprehensive evaluations, requiring the participation of numerous school personnel and the child's parents, have been conducted. These mandates, while providing for the legal rights of handicapped students, include provisions (Blankenship & Lilly, 1981) that directly impact and potentially hinder the rural school psychologist because the greatest number of underserved and unserved children reside in rural areas (Helge, 1980a).

1. Right to an Education. This proviso of the law makes it incumbent on each school district to provide an educational program for any child diagnosed as handicapped. The distance between children similarly aged and afflicted may be prohibitive in some instances, resulting in either inappropriate placement or non-compliance with the law.

2. Placement Procedures. Distance between schools (travel time), caseload, facilitating placement committee meetings, and so on, may be difficult in settings where personnel are scarce or where less camaraderie exists. If unaccepted, the psychologist in the rural district may be less effective and is apt to experience alienation.

3. Due Process. Reese (1970) has reported the potential for loss of confidentiality in small, less populated schools where families maintain a high degree of familiarity with one another, thereby diminishing the prospect of legal privacy for either the system or the individual. On the contrary, in districts where psychologists serve several schools separated by large distances, maintaining a sufficient level of communication with other professionals and with parents becomes an issue.

4. Non-Discriminatory Assessment. Although there has been some evidence to suggest that this mandate has not altered the nature of the school psychologist's practice insofar as the use of specific "non-biased" instruments is concerned (Goldwasser, Meyers, Christenson, & Graden, 1983), we believe it has brought about a heightened awareness of the principle underlying the law; i.e., every student is entitled to an evaluation that is most likely to reflect in an unbiased fashion his/her greatest potential for performance. In the rural setting the interaction and understanding between client and psychologist is extremely important if certain pitfalls are to be avoided, e.g., over-reliance on "environmental deprivation" as cause for child's problem, parental mistrust of the professional or evaluation procedures, and so forth.

5. Least Restrictive Environment. It may be difficult for the rural school psychologist to arrange for the least restricting educational setting for a child if local support services and institutions are few or narrow in focus. Here the school district's location, tax base, and level of sophistication impact on its ability to serve the handicapped in least restrictive settings.

As we have already seen, the nature and extent of psychological services in rural schools changed dramatically following the implementation of P.L. 94–142. States and rural school districts were required to develop plans detailing how remote areas with very little in the way of special education services would, in a relatively short period of time, provide "free, appropriate" education for all handicapped children. It is clear that no other event prior or subsequent to the passage of P.L. 94–142 has done as much as has this legislation in guaranteeing the existence of psychological services in rural schools. This mandate has also inexorably intertwined school psychological and special education services in the schools of rural America. Neither existed at current levels prior to P.L. 94–142, and it is unlikely that states and local districts would be able to fund these services is the law were repealed.

PSYCHOLOGICAL SERVICES IN RURAL SCHOOLS: CURRENT STATUS

State Level Planning: Impact on Local Services

It appears that state agencies responsible for developing school psychological services in rural schools have generally implemented plans that fall in one of two broad categories. These approaches for organizing and administering psychological services can be characterized as either state-controlled agencies developed for the expressed purpose of delivering psychoeducational services to handicapped children, or local/regional departments typically organized and administered by the local school district(s) involved.

Conceptualization of rural service delivery models in this fashion is not a new idea (Herron et al., 1970) and although most systems appear to fit within one of the general categories listed above, there is a great deal of variability within each model. For example, some state-controlled "psychoeducational service centers" are designed to be diagnostic facilities, whereas others are more broadly defined as assessment and remediation centers. Sometimes the chief administrative officer (at both the state and service center level) has a special education background, sometimes a school psychological background, and sometimes a regular education background. In contrast to state-organized and -administered operations, many states have provided general guidelines for local administrators to follow, but have allowed for local autonomy in designing the nature of school psychological and special education services. In rural settings one (or more) of the following types of arrangements have typically emerged: cooperative agreements, interlocal agreements, and contractual agreements. Cooperative agreements, sometimes referred to as "sponsoring district special education cooperatives" (Kansas Department of Education, 1983), call for two or more school districts to enter into an agreement to provide special education services on a shared cost basis. In many instances the district designated as the sponsoring district becomes the legal body of the cooperative. Interlocal agreements, on the other hand, call for the establishment of a coadjuvant legal entity, composed of members from each of the participating school districts, with responsibility for the organization and administration of services (e.g., psychoeducational, vocational). As suggested by the title, contractual agreements allow school districts to contract with other schools, agencies, or individuals in order to provide for the needs of handicapped (or other) students.

It is not at all clear how state versus local control differentially affects service delivery; in fact, the two models often look a great deal like one another. Regardless of where administrative control resides, rural agencies/cooperatives are usually responsible for providing services to a scattered populace in several school districts. School psychologists working in these settings are usually assigned to specific schools or school districts and appear to be involved in 10 general types of activities including:

1. Early screening and identification of preschool/unserved children,
2. Reviewing referrals for possible testing and evaluation,
3. Providing notice of rights and proposed actions to parents,
4. Completing psychoeducational evaluations,
5. Reporting evaluation information to school personnel and parents,
6. Determining program eligibility,
7. Planning the educational program,
8. Implementing the IEP,
9. Monitoring the effectiveness of the IEP, and
10. Re-evaluating the student's program and progress.

We are aware that not all school psychologists/psychometrists are able to be involved in each of the duties listed above and that many practitioners are engaged in other activities as well. There is ample evidence, however, that rural practitioners are involved in at least these types of activities (Hughes & Clark, 1981; Meacham & Peckham, 1978). It is also clear that state policy regarding the nature of school psychological services has a profound impact on which of these functions is likely to be part of a particular school psychologist's job. There is a simple and direct relationship between state policy and the role of the psychological provider in the local school district. Where states have defined the role of the school practitioner in a narrow fashion (e.g., Oklahoma and Arkansas) practitioners typically function as testers. In contrast, where states provide for a broader role definition (e.g., Kansas and Iowa) there is greater role diversity.

Furthermore, we find little evidence to indicate that the existence of a particular model (state vs. local/regional control) has anything to do with the rural/urban nature of the state. It may be that the most critical variable influencing the adoption of a particular service delivery model is the belief system of the individual(s) responsible for designing the model.

Finally, we believe that it is important to attend to the influence of state training and certification standards on the delivery of psychological services in rural schools. Although there has been a push to improve training and credentialing standards by professional organizations (e.g., American Psychological Assocation and the National Association of School Psychologists) and accrediting bodies (e.g., the National Council for Accreditation of Teacher Education), many states fall far short of the standards proposed by these groups. Our own data, presented later in the chapter, provide some evidence indicating that rural practitioners are more likely to be certified at lower levels and to have less experience. Some have suggested that in order to alleviate the shortage of school psychologists available to rural schools rural states should consider preparing "educational examiners" (Helge, 1983b). We believe this to be a short-sighted approach potentially fraught with danger for children and for the profession. Although the urban/suburban setting may continue to be more attractive to the well-trained, experienced school psychologist, we do not recommend that rural (or for that matter any other) settings be staffed primarily by minimally trained individuals.

We are not asserting that individuals trained as school psychometrists or educational evaluators are unlikely to provide appropriate services, rather that most practitioners working at this level have not had the training that would allow them to provide a broad range of services. Our experience in Oklahoma demonstrates that when the state decrees that it will only recognize and pay individuals at the lowest certificate level, individuals have less incentive to seek additional training. It is our belief that the reliance on individuals trained in this fashion perpetuates the notion of the practitioner "as a tester, a number-getter, whose sole usefulness is his or her authority to remove a deviant youngster from a classroom" (Ysseldyke, 1978, p. 374). Although it appears true that P.L. 94-142 has established the general framework under which school psychological services have been organized, states must take the responsibility for ensuring appropriate training and certification standards. Failure to address that responsibility increases the likelihood of inferior services.

Local Options/Initiatives in Rural Settings

In the previous section the organizational and administrative structure of school psychological services at the state department level was reviewed. It is clear that P.L. 94-142 served as the primary consideration when states planned for the delivery and evaluation of psychological services in rural schools. It is just as obvious that local districts have strived to implement services that comply with the states' directives (i.e., the state plan). Regardless of whether school psychologists find themselves in rural or urban districts, state-run agencies, or district-sponsored cooperatives, they have been asked to fulfill essentially the same roles, and these roles correspond to the requirements of P.L. 94-142.

This is not to imply, however, that there are no reasons for studying the rural environment and the effects of this setting on rural practice. Indeed, the perception of many individuals has been that rural practitioners are likely to have fewer professional contacts (Gelinas & Gelinas, 1968); have fewer referral options (Eiserer, 1963); function with a greater deal of autonomy (Herron et al., 1970); move to an urban setting if the opportunity presents itself (Helge, 1983a); have difficulty keeping one's private and professional lives separate (Reese, 1970); and experience difficulty getting to know and understand minority children (Gerken, 1981). The list goes on and on (Helge, 1980b; Hamblin, 1981) and it is characterized by much speculation about the difficulties and unique problems confronting rural practitioners. Unfortunately, little data exist that would confirm or refute these assertions. The available research (Benson, Bischoff, & Boland, 1983; Hamblin, 1981; Hughes & Clark, 1981; Meachem & Peckham, 1978; Trenary, 1980) provides a few answers but fails to provide a clear picture of the rural practitioner or the manner in which psychological services have been provided in rural schools. These studies have concentrated on role and function issues to a much greater extent than organizational and administrative issues. There remain many unanswered questions.

In order to answer some of these questions and to compare current practice with conventional wisdom we surveyed practitioners. Although we attempted to learn about the role of the rural psychologist in the schools, we also asked for practitioners' perceptions of the manner in which local services have been organized and delivered in their respective work settings. In following this approach we have tried to provide additional information on the role and function of the rural school psychologist as well as the factors that impinge on service delivery at the local level.

Rural Survey: Subjects and Methodology

Surveys were mailed to 500 individuals identified as members of the National Association of School Psychologists (NASP). Names were culled at random from the NASP Membership Directory (NASP, 1983) and included 50 individuals from each of the following 10 states: California, Georgia, Illinois, Indiana, Michigan, New York, North Carolina, Ohio, Pennsylvania, and Texas. These states were identified as having large concentrations of rural residents based on data from the 1980 United States Census.

Over 200 individuals responded to the survey. The data reported here include only those individuals ($n = 158$) who identified themselves as either school psychometrists or school psychologists. Of this total, 69 indicated that they were working in a rural setting, 30 in an urban setting, and 59 in a suburban setting. As a result of the similarity of the data from the urban and suburban samples, these groups were collapsed for all subsequent analyses, which resulted in a total of 89 individuals in the urban/suburban group.

Data describing the sample are presented in Table 8.1. Although the rural and urban/suburban samples appear similar in many regards (Hamblin, 1981), there are differences worth noting. The rural sample is slightly younger (36.1 yrs. vs. 40.5 yrs.) and composed of a higher percentage of school psychometrists. They are not as experienced, have not been in their present position as long, and have spent less time in the classroom as teachers.

Our sample suggests that regardless of the location of the work setting, there tends to be a ratio of approximately two female psychologists to every male psychologist. Most practitioners are trained in school psychology, have had more than one year of graduate training, and work full time out of a central office. In contrast to the findings of earlier investigations (e.g., Hamblin, 1981) there is little difference between the rural and urban/suburban groups in the amount of time spent traveling between schools/work sites (although the difference is in the expected direction, rural > urban). However, rural school practitioners do tend to visit more sites per week than do their urban/suburban counterparts (5.38 vs. 4.00). The finding of no difference in the extent to which the rural and urban/suburban samples have attended workshops or had the opportunity to consult with other professionals is consistent with previous research (Hamblin, 1981).

Our results reveal a striking difference between the groups in the percentage of individuals trained at the doctoral level. The percentages reported (4.3% vs. 23.6%) are very similar to those obtained by Hamblin (7% vs. 30%). Given that a higher percentage of rural practitioners are school psychometrists, this finding tends to confirm the suspicion that rural schools are likely to employ individuals with less training and/or less experience.

Rural Survey: Results and Discussion

Individuals were asked to rate a series of problems/issues according to the effects of the particular issue on their functioning as psychological providers. The items were presented on a 5-point Likert-type scale (1-not a problem, 2-mild problem, 3-moderate problem, 4-serious problem, 5-severe problem). The ratings of the survey respondents are presented in Table 8.2. The degree to which the rural

TABLE 8.1
Rural Survey: Sample Identification

	Rural (n = 69)		Urban/Suburban (n = 89)	
Job Title: Psychologist		87.0%		97.8%
School Psychometrist		13.0%		2.2%
Age	36.1	(8.75)	40.5	(8.98)
Sex: Males		38.2%		33.0%
Females		61.8%		67.0%
Graduate major: School Psychology		75.4%		75.3%
Educational Psychology		8.7%		10.1%
Clinical Psychology		4.3%		7.9%
Counseling Psychology		2.9%		3.4%
Guidance and Counseling		5.8%		2.2%
Special Education		1.4%		1.1%
Other		1.4%		0.0%
Educational Training:				
One year masters		11.6%		5.6%
Two years master		68.1%		56.2%
Educational Specialist		13.0%		14.6%
Non-degree certificate		2.9%		0.0%
Doctoral		4.3%		23.6%
Years of experience	5.34	(4.01)	7.27	(4.69)
Years in present position	4.97	(4.00)	6.89	(5.30)
Years of teaching experience	2.59	(4.71)	3.52	(4.58)
Employment status: Full-time		89.9%		86.5%
Part-time		10.1%		13.5%
Primary office: Central Office		52.2%		58.4%
School		31.9%		31.5%
Private		4.3%		5.6%
Other		11.6%		4.5%
Average number of sites visited per week	5.38	(4.94)	4.00	(2.24)
Average number of hours of travel time per week	3.45	(2.66)	3.20	(2.55)
Average number of workshops attended per year	4.07	(5.04)	3.88	(5.61)
Average number of hours of consultation with other psychologists per week	2.01	(2.03)	2.17	(2.09)

Note: All data not reported as percentages (%) are presented as means (standard deviations).

and urban/suburban samples overlap in their perceptions of the relative importance of the issues is extensive. The reactions of the survey respondents also correspond to that obtained by previous researchers (Hamblin, 1981; Gerken, 1981; Trenary, 1980).

According to both rural and urban/suburban school psychologists and psychometrists, the biggest problem facing them is the lack of understanding that

TABLE 8.2
Rural Survey: Issues

Issue	Mean Rating	Rural	Rank Urban/Suburban
The degree to which the school board understands exceptional children	3.56(3.23)	1	1
The degree to which administrators understand exceptional children	3.23(2.94)	2	4
The degree to which teachers understand exceptional children	3.19(3.01)	3	3
The degree to which parents understand exceptional children	3.08(2.76)	4	5
The degree to which administrators understand the role of the school psychologists	3.00(2.48)	5	7
Caseload wthin school(s)	2.97(3.06)	6	2
The degree to which parents understand the role of the school psychologist	2.93(2.47)	7	8
Distance from universities	2.77(1.98)	8	18
The degree to which teachers understand the role of the school psychologist	2.73(2.46)	9	9
Office space	2.70(2.50)	10	6
Number of outside referral agencies	2.60(2.21)	11	14
Comprehensiveness of special education services, including assessment, remediation, diversity of placement possibilities, services for low incidence handicaps, etc.	2.51(2.34)	12	11
Opportunity for contact with other psychologists	2.49(2.25)	13	13
Inservice opportunities	2.45(2.37)	14	10
Diversity of the school psychologist's job	2.38(2.28)	15	12
Job satisfaction	2.22(2.17)	16	15
Travel time	2.15(1.89)	17	19
Level of training of school psychometrists	2.00(1.72)	18	21
Culturally biased tests used in assessment of children	1.99(2.01)	19	17
The extent to which the school psychologist is accepted by other school personnel	1.94(1.75)	20	20
Retaining professionals to work as school psychologists/psychometrists	1.89(2.07)	21	16
Recruiting professionals to work as school psychologists/psychometrists	1.72(1.57)	22	22
Level of training of school psychologists	1.70(1.53)	23	23

Note: Issues are rank ordered based on the mean ratings of the rural sample. The mean ratings of the urban/suburban respondents are presented in parentheses.

school boards, administrators, teachers, and parents have regarding exceptional children and the role of psychological providers in the schools. Also ranked as a significant problem by both groups were the heavy case-loads encountered by practitioners. In light of previous research and the beliefs of most individuals who have worked as practitioners, these findings are not at all surprising. Relatively speaking, the respondents were less concerned with their own level of training, their acceptance by other school personnel, the tests they use, or the problem of recruiting and retaining trained professional staff. As might be expected, rural respondents were much more concerned about the impact of distance from university centers on their practice than were the urban/suburban respondents.

Centralized/Decentralized Services. Since the inception of psychological service delivery in rural schools, the trend has been toward centralization of services. Our data (see Table 8.1) indicate that over 50% of the rural practitioners surveyed are housed in central offices (approximately 10% of our sample indicated that they had central office space as well as school offices). There are numerous reasons for this trend and Elkin (1963) has provided a cogent analysis of the benefits of centralized services. More recently, states have provided school districts the option of entering into various types of agreements that would allow the cooperating districts to meet the psychoeducational needs of handicapped children. These agreements often allow rural schools to provide a full range of diagnostic and remedial services and for the delivery of psychological services out of a central office location. It is clear that over the last half century, rural school psychological services have changed from an infrequent luxury provided by an urban-based clinically trained psychologist to a regularly occurring phenomenon typically delivered by a centrally located trained school psychologist.

This shift toward centralization of services has tended to move rural school psychological services out of the realm of the "lone ranger" and, combined with the need for multidisciplinary input, has made it much more likely that numerous individuals will be involved in the psychoeducational assessment/remediation process. Although this is undeniably true, most rural practitioners still work in what has been described as an "itinerant-interval" manner (Georgia Department of Education, 1982). That is, most school psychologists working in rural settings continue to serve several student attendance centers one day a week or one day bi-weekly. For many parents, teachers, and administrators the school psychologist provides the only contact with the professional *psychological* community. Today the opportunity for these types of contacts exist, they occur in the rural setting with individuals who typically live and work in the rural environment, and there is a much greater probability now than there was only a decade ago that a variety of professionals will be working together to develop appropriate psychoeducational programming for rural school children.

Proactive/Reactive Services. The perception of our sample is that they spend less than one quarter of their time in proactive services (see Table 8.3). Both

TABLE 8.3
Rural Survey: Conceptual Dimensions of Service

Direct/Indirect	Rural	Urban/Suburban
Average percentage (%) of *actual* time in direct/indirect services	65/35	63/37
Average percentage (%) of *desired* time in direct/indirect services	55/45	57/43
Proactive/Reactive		
Average percentage (%) of *actual* time in proactive/reactive services	16/83	19/81
Average percentage (%) of *desired* time in proactive/reactive services	43/56	43/58

rural and urban/suburban practitioners indicated that they would like to be able to strike a more even balance between proactive and reactive services. Although this reaction seems quite natural, we wonder whether most practitioners have the training and experience to function effectively in a preventative/proactive fashion? We doubt it, especially in rural settings, and furthermore, we hypothesize that many school psychologists were attracted to this professional because of a desire to help people with problems rather than to be involved in preventative psychoeducational or mental health services. The attraction to and potential for immediate reinforcement in direct service delivery is intuitively more appealing than the thought of developing a program that may reduce the incidence of learning disabilities or adolescent pregnancies at some future data. It is certainly not that one set of goals is less desirable or admirable, only less feasible.

Direct/Indirect Services. These results indicate that respondents believe they spend almost two thirds of their time in direct services (see Table 8.3). There is not a great discrepancy between the amount of time they see themselves devoting to direct or indirect services and the amount of time they desire to spend in each of those areas, nor is there any difference between urban and rural respondents on this issue. It is interesting to note the amount of time that school psychologists spend in direct or indirect services: however, we agree with others (Elliott & Witt, 1985, this volume) who suggest that the more important question is whether or not a school psychologist possesses a variety of skills, both direct and indirect. Chances are there will be ample opportunity to exercise them all.

Rural Survey: Summary and Conclusions

We have concluded that rural school psychologists are increasingly being organized out of central locations, that they see themselves as functioning in a reactive capacity and being involved primarily in direct services. They are slightly younger, less well trained and less experienced than their urban/surburban counterparts. They believe that parents, teachers, and administrators fail to understand their role in the schools.

Our analysis suggests that although some differences exist, the rural sample is very similar to other school psychologists. Regardless of whether we examine conceptual dimensions of service or practitioners' views of significant issues, substantial overlap across groups is found. Logistical hurdles do exist in the rural environment and they are perceived to have a negative impact on the quality of services. The rural population is by definition more widely dispersed and the rural environment is generally less desirable. We have described some of the steps that states and local districts have taken to alleviate the problems associated with the first problem; however, there are fewer options for dealing with the second.

One area not yet addressed is the importance of effective collaboration among health care and educational professionals in the rural community. Whether or not this type of collaboration is any more important in the rural environment is debatable; however, there are usually fewer individuals (or agencies) with whom school psychologists can consult. Scarcity of opportunities is only one of the problems confronting school practitioners desiring this type of professional interaction. An examination of the mental health literature reveals a "consensus of speculation" (Schellenberg, personal communication) indicating that rural professionals are likely to be viewed as outsiders and pressured to conform to the values and behavioral patterns of the rural inhabitants. If rural school psychologists want to have the cooperation of agencies/groups, they must be willing to meet with visible, significant members of the community who are willing to facilitate that interaction (Henggeler, 1983). This type of "preliminary spadework" (Solomon & Hiesberger, 1980) may be a critical component of effective practice in the rural setting.

EVALUATING SERVICE DELIVERY IN RURAL SETTINGS

The importance of needs assessment and program evaluation activities in the rural setting is obvious. An excellent starting point for individuals interested in developing and/or evaluating rural delivery systems is an understanding of the ecological model (Hobbs, 1966). the relevance of this model for school psychologists has been detailed elsewhere (Elliott & Witt, this volume), and the basic propositions of the model are well understood by most. Proponents focus on the interaction and interrelationship of systems within an environment as evidenced by the straightforward description of Anderson (1983): "Conceptualizing development as progressive mutual accommodation between individual and environment, the ecological approach assumes that development occurs in the context of several related systems" (p. 181); and the more complex pronouncement of Barker (1968): "The ecological environment of human molar behavior and its inhabitants are not independent; rather the environment is a set of homeostatically governed ecobehavioral entities consisting of nonhuman components, human components and control circuits that modify the components in predictable ways to maintain the environmental entities in their characteristic states" (p. 17).

Attention to the interaction of the diverse systems that impact on delivery of psychological services in schools is important in any setting. In rural settings it seems essential, in that there are limited amounts of professional expertise, which increases the need for school psychologists to be involved in the social, behavioral, familial, and economic problems of their clients. As indicated earlier, one mechanism for fostering involvement in the systems that impact on rural inhabitants is for rural school practitioners to become associated with significant personnel/organizations/agencies. Henggeler (1983) has provided a succinct analysis of the potential benefits of this approach as it relates to needs assessment. Regardless of the type of needs assessment or program evaluation activity to be undertaken, we believe that the work of the school psychologist will be facilitated by involvement in the rural community and by an attempt to understand the multitude of factors that comprise "ruralness" in a particular location.

Evaluation Models

It has often been alleged that one of the major problems with the delivery of social and educational services in rural areas has been the application of urban models to rural settings (Helge, 1983b; Huessy, 1972). To the extent that this is true, it seems a forgivable sin. Many urban school districts were providing for the mental health and psychoeducational needs of urban inhabitants long before any systematic attempt was made to establish similar services in rural settings. It seems only natural that early attempts to provide for these services would mimic many of the strategies that had been successful in other locations. Our analysis suggests, in fact, that rural and urban delivery systems are similar and that many strategies that are effective in one setting are effective in others. We expect that the best strategies for assessing and evaluating these systems are also similar across very diverse settings. Numerous authors have discussed general evaluation models (Howard, 1980), guidelines for evaluating school psychological services (Maher, 1979), and approaches more appropriate for the rural setting (Beare & Lynch, 1983; Illback & Ellis, 1981). There is no need to repeat the specific components, but only to say that the models have generally focused on the importance of needs assessment, compliance with federal and state laws, consumer satisfaction, intervention effectiveness, and program efficiency.

Finally, we wish to point out that in our study of rural school psychological services we have reviewed the state plans for special education of more than 20 states. Almost without exception, program evaluation activities are described in terms of whether local school districts or cooperatives are in compliance with state and federal laws. We understand that states are required to make this type of declaration in the state plan; however, program evaluation activities must not stop with an assessment of compliance. There is a dearth of research that would allow us to make informed decisions about the types of psychoeducational programs that result in the best services to schools and children. We have demonstrated that rural schools are capable of developing diverse approaches that satisfy the mandates of state and federal law; however, we believe that it is ultimately more important for schools to attend to the unique needs of each rural area and to go about the business of assessing the extent to which those needs are being met.

SUMMARY AND CONCLUSIONS

The delivery of school psychology services in rural areas has received an increased amount of attention during the last 10 to 15 years. Due, in large part, to the implementation of P.L. 94-142, services exist in most rural communities in a much more comprehensive fashion than was true only a quarter century ago. The specific provisions of this federal law and the manner in which states have operationalized its directives have had a significant effect on the delivery of services at the local level. Although states have chosen to organize and adminster school psychological services in different fashions, we have concluded that regardless of whether control resides at the state, regional, or local level, school psychologists continue to perform similar roles. We have found, however, that states do differ markedly in the manner in which school psychological services are defined, and we have suggested that training and credentialing standards within a state do have the potential to profoundly impact on the nature of services to rural schools and rural inhabitants. The available evidence reveals that rural school psychologists are being organized out of central locations and that they function primarily in a direct, reactive capacity. They have less training and are less experienced than their urban/suburban counterparts.

We cannot escape the feeling, however, that rural school psychological practice has significantly more in common with urban/suburban practice than has generally been thought. Others have suggested urban and rural differences and emphasized the importance of a generalist type of training for rural psychologists (e.g., Hargrove, 1982). This may be a legitimate need. However, the available data indicate that practice and perceptions of urban and rural school psychologists are very similar to each other. Our examination of the conceptual dimensions of service (centralized-decentralized, proactive-reactive, direct-indirect) found little difference across groups of psychologists working in rural, urban, or suburban districts. We have pointed out some of the logistical hurdles to effective service delivery in rural settings and the manner in which they alter the nature of services in rural areas. These differences are minor, however, and we believe that they contribute little to the variance accounted for in good/bad psychological practice or effective/ineffective models of service delivery. We have discussed some of the factors that we believe to have the greatest impact on the delivery of psychological services in rural schools; however, our list is far from exhaustive. Goldwasser et al. (1983) have shown that the ratio of pupils to school psychologists had more to do with effective practice (number of evaluations, number of IEP meetings, opportunities to consult with other professionals and parents, etc.) than did the rural/suburban/urban nature of the job setting. This finding serves to substantiate our contention that by paying too much attention to rurality, we may neglect to study, teach, or learn about the factors that do contribute to effective practice in *any* setting.

We offer three suggestions for individuals who desire to or who already work in rural settings.

1. Get the best school psychology training possible. We realize the simplistic nature of this statement, but are quite serious in advancing it. We suspect that programs that train the best school psychologists will be able to place their graduates in urban settings, rural settings, schools, clinics, or wherever school psychologists are needed. In fact, good graduates, regardless of the training program, will be viewed as competent because they have mastered skills related to effective practice.

2. Be active in state politics and state organizations related to school psychology. This is where the practice of school psychology, for the most part, will be operationally defined. School psychologists must become active in lobbying and influencing public policy. Training standards, certification standards, licensure standards, pupil to school psychologist ratio, and so forth, have all been shown to have an impact on service delivery and the roles filled by the rural psychologist in the schools. Regarding the organization and administration of psychological services in rural schools, we must take a proactive stance in support of a service delivery model that allows for school psychologists to apply psychology in the schools. Although the school psychology community recognizes that school psychological practice involves more than the generation of numbers with standardized tests, many states do not. We cannot assume that states will necessarily develop good plans or release the funds needed for effective services. We must take an active role in seeing that these things happen.

3. Develop an awareness of rural issues and the impact of the rural environment on behavior. There is a need for school psychologists to learn about the differential impact of rural, urban, and suburban environments. This awareness should come about as a result of every school psychologist's training, just as we teach students about the influence of different cultural heritages, different developmental stages, and so forth, on behavior.

We expect that future researchers will provide better answers to questions about the specific effects of the rural environment and about the types of organizational structures that result in effective programming for rural schools. The psychologist practicing in such settings in the 1980s is presented the unique challenge of minimizing the conceptual and logistical hurdles reviewed herein, in a way most apt to benefit the rural school child. The challenge is an individual one, best faced by the careful study, not of a rural psychology, but rather, of children, of child development, of theories of learning, of intervention techniques, and of educational policy. It is in this manner that the rural school psychologist will be best able to serve.

REFERENCES

Anderson, C. (1983). An ecological developmental model for a family orientation in school psychology. *Journal of School Psychology, 21,* 179–189.

Bagarozzi, D. A. (1982). The family therapist's role in treating families in rural communities: A general systems approach. *Journal of Marital and Family Therapy, 8,* 51–57.

Bardon, J. I. (1981). A personalized account of the development and status of school psychology. *Journal of School Psychology, 19,* 199–210.

Bardon, J. I., & Bennett, V. C. (1974). *School psychology.* Englewood Cliffs, NJ: Prentice-Hall.

Barker, R. G. (1968). *Ecological psychology: Concepts and methods for studying the environment of human behavior.* Stanford, CA: Stanford University Press.

Beare, P. L., & Lynch, E. C. (1983). Rural area emotional disturbance service delivery: Problems and future directions. *Behavioral Disorders, 8,* 113–119.

Benson, A. J. (1985). Best practices in rural school psychology. In A. Thomas & J. Grimes (Eds.), *Best practices in school psychology* (pp. 17–29). Kent, OH: National Association of School Psychologists.

Benson, A. J., Bischoff, H. G., & Boland, P. A. (1983). *Issues in rural school psychology: Survey report.* Washington, DC: National Association of School Psychologists.

Blankenship, C., & Lilly, M. (1981). *Mainstreaming students with learning and behavior problems.* New York: Holt, Rinehart, & Winston.

Buxton, E. B. (1973). Delivering social services in rural areas. *Public Welfare, 31,* 15–20.

Cameron, E. (1948). Child guidance services in semi-rural and neglected areas. *American Journal of Orthopsychiatry, 18,* 536–540.

Childs, A. W., & Melton, G. B. (1983). *Rural psychology.* New York: Plenum.

Daniels, D. N. (1967). The community mental health center in the rural area: Is the present model apropriate? *American Journal of Psychiatry, 124,* 32–37.

Ebaugh, F. S., & Lloyd, R. (1927). The role of a mobile clinic in the educational program of a state psychopathic hospital. *Mental Hygiene, 2,* 346–356.

Eiserer, P. E. (1963). *The school psychologist.* Washington, DC: The Center for Applied Research in Education.

Elkin, V. B. (1963). Structuring school psychological services: Internal and interdisciplinary considerations. In M. G. Gottsegen & G. B. Gottsegen (Eds.), *Professional school psychology* Vol. II (pp. 200–226). New York: Grune & Stratton.

Fagan, T. K. (1981). Special educational services and the school psychologist. *Journal of Learning Disabilities, 14,* 383–384.

Flax, J. E., Wagenfeld, M. O., Ivens, R. E., & Weiss, R. J. (1979). *Mental health in rural America.* Rockville, MD: National Institute of Mental Health.

Gelinas, R. P., & Gelinas, P. J. (1968). *Your future in school psychology.* New York: Rosen Press.

Georgia Department of Education. (1982). *School psychological services handbook.* Atlanta: Georgia Department of Education.

Gerken, K. C. (1981). *Serving minority children in rural settings: A personal perspective.* Paper presented at the annual meeting of the American Psychological Association, Los Angeles, CA.

Goetz, E., & Doerksen, H. (1978). Rural school psychological services and practical graduate training: A cooperative project. *Canadian Counselor, 12,* 99–105.

Goldwasser, E., Meyers, I., Christenson, S., & Graden, J. (1983). The impact of P.L. 94–142 on the practice of school psychology: A national survey. *Psychology in the Schools, 20,* 153–165.

Guydish, J., Zelhart, P. F., Jackson, T. T., & Markley, R. P. (1982). George A. Kelly's contribution to early rural school psychology. *University Forum, 28,* 4–7.

Hamblin, A. (1981). *School psychology in rural areas: A needs assessment.* Unpublished doctoral dissertation, Rutgers University.

Hargrove, D. S. (1982). The rural school psychologist as generalist: A challenge for professional identity. *Professional Psychology, 13*(2), 302–308.

Helge, D. I. (1980a). *A national comparative study regarding rural special education delivery systems before and after passage of PL 94–142.* Murray, KY: National Rural Research and Personnel Preparation Project, Center for Innovation and Development, Murray State University.

Helge, D. I. (1980b). *Effective service delivery strategies appropriate for specific rural subcultures.* Murray, KY: National Rural Research and Personnel Preparation Project, Center for Innovation and Development, Murray State University.

Helge, D. I. (1981). Problems in implementing comprehensive special education in rural areas. *Exceptional Children, 47,* 514–520.

Helge, D. (1983a). *The state of the art of rural special education.* Murray, KY: National Rural Research and Personnel Preparation Project, Center for Innovation and Development, Murray State University.

Helge, D. (1983b). *Models for serving rural children with low-incidence handicapping conditions.* Murray, KY: National Rural Research and Preparation Project, Center for Innovation and Development, Murray State University.

Heller, H. (1975). Rural special education: A dilemma. *Theory Into Practice, 14,* 137–142.

Henggeler, S. W. (1983). Needs assessment in rural areas: Isues and problems. In A. W. Childs & G. B. Melton (Eds.), *Rural psychology* (pp. 217–231). New York: Plenum.

Herron, W. G., Green, G., Guild, M., Smith, A., & Kantor, R. E. (1970). *Contemporary school psychology.* Scranton, PA: Intext Education Publishers.

Hobbs, N. (1966). Helping disturbed children: Psychological and ecological strategies. *American Psychologist, 21,* 1105–1115.

Howard, J. S. (1980). *Systems intervention and school psychology.* Paper presented at the International Colloquium in School Psychology, Jerusalem, Israel.

Huessy, H. R. (1972). Tactics and targets in the rural setting. In S. E. Golann & C. Eisdorfer (Eds.), *Handbook of community and mental health* (pp. 699–710). New York: Appleton-Century-Crofts.

Hughes, J. N., & Clark, R. D. (1981). Differences between urban and rural school psychology: Training implications. *Psychology in the Schools, 18,* 191–196.

Illback, R. J., & Ellis, J. L. (1981). *Evaluation of special education in rural settings.* Paper presented at the annual meeting of the American Psychological Association, Los Angeles, CA.

Kansas Department of Education. (1983). *State plan for special education.* Topeka: Kansas Department of Education.

Kramer, J. J., & Peters, G. J. (1985). What we know about rural school psychology: A brief review and analysis. *School Psychology Review, 14*, 452–456.

Maher, C. A. (1979). Guidelines for planning and evaluating school psychology service delivery systems. *Journal of School Psychology, 17*, 203–212.

Meacham, M. L., & Peckham, P. (1978). School psychologists at three-quarters century: Congruence between training, practice, preferred role and competence. *Journal of School Psychology, 16*, 195–206.

Melton, G. B. (1983). Ruralness as a psychological construct. In A. W. Childs & G. B. Melton (Eds.), *Rural psychology* (pp. 1–13). New York: Plenum.

National Association of School Psychologists. (1983). *Membership directory.* Washington, DC: National Association of School Psychologists.

Oklahoma State Department of Health. (1982). *Oklahoma Department of Health statistics.* Oklahoma City: State Printing Office.

Photiadis, J. D, & Simoni, J. J. (1983). Characteristics of rural America. In A. W. Childs & G. B. Melton (Eds.), *Rural psychology* (pp. 15–32). New York: Plenum.

Reese, T. A. (1970). *Public relations and the role of the rural school psychologist.* Paper presented at the annual meeting of the American Personnel and Guidance Association, New Orleans, LA.

Sher, J. P. (1978). A proposal to end federal neglect of rural schools. *Phi Delta Kappan, 60*, 280–282.

Slater, R. (1980). The organizational origins of public school psychology. *Educational Studies, 11*, 1–11.

Solomon, G., & Hiesberger, J. (1980). Community mental health in rural schools: A demonstration project. *Journal of Community Psychology, 8*, 353–356.

Tindall, R. H. (1979). School psychology: The development of a profession. In G. D. Phye & D. J. Reschly (Eds.), *School psychology* (pp. 3–24). New York: Academic Press.

Trenary, D. S. (1980). The unique problems of school psychologists. *The School Psychologist, 23*, 13.

Warburton, A. A. (1964). *Stimulating guidance in rural schools.* Washington, DC: American Personnel and Guidance Association.

Ysseldyke, J. E. (1978). Who's calling the plays in school psychology? *Psychology in the Schools, 15*(3), 373–378.

9
School Psychology in Bicultural Settings: Implications for Service Delivery

Ed N. Argulewicz*
Arizona State University

The need for greater sensitivity, responsibility, and skills in providing psychological services to culturally different children and their families has been acknowledged by a number of sources. Endorsement of a greater responsiveness on the part of mental-health service providers has taken place on professional (Korman, 1974; Olmedo, 1981), political (President's Commission on Mental Health, 1978), and legal levels (Bersoff, 1981, 1982). A repeated issue on the professional level has been the underrepresentation of ethnic minorities in professional psychology. The United States Census Bureau (1981) reported that more than 19% of the population residing in the United States are identified as minority status. Yet the American Psychological Association (APA) estimates that only 3.1% of its members consider themselves minorities, with a fairly similar percentage of members in each of the divisions of clinical (3.6%), counseling (2.8%), and school psychology (3.6%) (Russo, Olmedo, Stapp, & Fulcher, 1981).

While the need for greater minority representation in professional psychology should improve psychological services to ethnic minorities, it is still within nonminority psychologists' capability to provide responsible and competent services to culturally different children and their families. Certainly, the emergence in the past decade of terminology such as *multicultural counseling, nonbiased assessment,* and *pluralistic norms* is evidence of the recognition of, and responsiveness to, the influence of variations in cultural background.

---

*This chapter is posthumous and appears in the author's final written form. It is testimony to Ed Argulewicz's respect for the influence of cultural differences on the practice of school psychology.

The purpose of this chapter is to review the cultural characteristics, values, and attitudes that are most salient to the delivery of school psychology services to culturally diverse populations. Since the issues surrounding service delivery to blacks has been dealt with to some extent in the chapter on urban school psychology (see Jackson, this volume), the focus of the present chapter is on Hispanic and American Indian populations. Particular attention is given to Hispanics[1] because they are currently the largest ethnic minority (U.S. Census Bureau, 1981) and are predicted to be the largest racial/ethnic minority by the year 2000. Also, the extreme heterogeneity within the Hispanic population makes it an excellent model for demonstrating the diversity of values school psychologists must consider when working in bicultural or multicultural settings. An underlying premise of this chapter is that culture has a powerful influence on an individual's behavior, in that it "consists of standards for deciding what is . . . what can be, . . . how one feels about it, . . . what to do about it, . . . and how to go about doing it" (Goodenough, 1963, p. 259). With this definition in mind, it should be recognized that an understanding of cultural differences is essential in psychological service delivery systems.

ATTITUDES TOWARD PSYCHOLOGICAL SERVICES

The underutilization of mental health services by Hispanics and American Indians has been documented in a number of studies (Keefe, Padilla, & Carlos, 1978; Padilla & Ruiz, 1973; Slaughter, 1976; Torrey, 1972). Other authors, however, have reported utilization of mental health services by Mexican Americans to be in proportion to their distributions in local populations (Moll, Rueda, Reza, Herrera, & Vasquez, 1976). An important variable in explaining these different findings may be the professional staffs' orientation and sensitivity to delivering services specifically for bicultural clients.

In public schools, the issue of utilization or representation of culturally different students in special programs is concerned more with *over*representation than *under*representation. The primary concern has been overrepresentation in special education classes, particularly those for educable mentally handicapped students. Controversies have revolved around the questions of test bias, labeling effects, and the effectiveness of special education classes. These issues have been reviewed elsewhere (Reschly, 1981; Reynolds, 1982), and further elaboration is outside the scope of the present chapter's goals. However, it is important

---

[1]For purposes of this chapter, Hispanic refers to people of Mexican, Puerto Rican, Cuban, and other Latin American or Spanish descent. American Indian refers to those tribes recognized as Native American by the Bureau of Indian Affairs. Whenever subgroup distinctions are made in the literature, they are so described in the text.

to note that discussion and debate over these issues have reached beyond the arenas of professional psychology and education to social and legal areas. This attention has in all likelihood resulted in caution, if not suspicion, on the part of minority parents when they are approached regarding intervention, evaluation, or special programs for their children. For this reason, establishing trust between client and professional helper is essential for working with both Mexican Americans and American Indians (Buchanan & Choca, 1979; La Fromboise, Dauphinais, & Rowe, 1980).

Achieving trust between parties is thus a critical first step in developing a constructive relationship in which effective service delivery can proceed. However, given the currently unresolved state of affairs regarding testing and special education placement of ethnic minorities, the establishment of trust is likely to require additional skills and take longer than with majority group students and families. Cultural distrust may even have to be dealt with at some point during service delivery (Lockhart, 1981). Also, by demonstrating knowledge and experience with the cultural standards from which a student comes, school psychologists will greatly improve the likelihood that they will be accepted and even appreciated by their clients.

In many ways, the feeling of ethnic minorities that they are perceived differently by school personnel is supported by research. A number of studies have examined teacher-student interactions, and found significant differences between teachers' responses to Mexican-American and Anglo-American students. In a well-designed study by Buriel (1983), which controlled for student socioeconomic status, English proficiency and academic achievement, teachers were found to provide more affirmation following correct responses by Anglo students than by Mexican-American students. Laosa (1977) found that teachers and classroom aides engaged in disapproving behavior most frequently for Mexican-American children who had limited English proficiency than for Anglo or English-dominant Mexican-American children. Regarding teachers' perceptions of ethnic minority children, Elliott and Argulewicz (1983) found that teachers rated Mexican-American students significantly lower than Anglo-American students on the comprehension, creative initiative, and closeness to the teacher factors of the Devereaux Elementary School Behavior Rating Scale. Differences in ratings persist even among groups of culturally different gifted students. Argulewicz, Elliott, and Hall (1982) reported that teachers rated gifted Mexican-American students significantly lower than their Anglo-American counterparts on the Learning and Motivation subscales of the Scales for Rating the Behavioral Characteristics of Superior Students.

Knowledge of teachers' perceptions of culturally different students is important for two reasons. First, their perceptions of students' abilities and classroom behaviors has a significant influence in deciding whether or not a child's problem warrants psychological intervention or evaluation. In fact, teacher referral has been found to be the most important first step in eventual special education placement (Algozinne, Christenson, & Ysseldyke, 1982). Thus, a disproportionate referral rate may be a major factor in explaining minority overrepresentation in special education. Supporting this notion, Argulewicz and Sanchez (1983) found that in a large suburban school district in the Southwest, low SES Mexican-American students from Spanish-speaking homes were referred for special education at almost twice the rate that they existed in the district population. Further evidence of bias in educational decisions was reported by Zucker and Prieto (1977). Using a case study format, the authors found that special education placement was recommended as being more appropriate for Mexican-American children than for white children.

A second reason for being aware of and understanding teachers' interactions with and expectations for culturally different students lies in designing and recommending classroom intervention strategies. Witt and Elliott (1985) have reviewed the growing body of research regarding the degree of severity that teachers ascribe to various problems and the major factors that influence teacher acceptance of treatment programs. However, to date, no investigations have been conducted that examine student, teacher, and parent ethnicity as variables in intervention acceptability. The results of such studies will ultimately provide information about the personological and sociocultural elements involved in treatment acceptability. This knowledge can then be used by school psychologists to maximize the probability that effective treatment programs will be accepted and implemented. In the meantime, school psychologists working in bicultural settings can begin to document for themselves the factors that appear to influence intervention acceptability as function of student and teacher ethnicity. By modifying intervention recommendations accordingly, they can benefit the student as well as improve the attitudes that many bicultural clients have toward psychological services.

ALTERNATIVE AVENUES TO SOLVING PSYCHOLOGICAL AND EDUCATIONAL PROBLEMS

Hispanics, particularly Mexican Americans, as well as American Indians have been characterized as having extended family support networks (Everett, Proctor, & Cartwell, 1983; Jaco, 1957; Locklear, 1972). This phenomenon is considered to be one reason for lower use of psychological services by these ethnic groups than by Anglo Americans. If one examines the literature, however, it is apparent that this characterization is largely impressionistic, based upon general observations in various mental health settings. Little current empirical evidence exists comparing ethnic groups' reliance on kin as a resource for psychological problems.

One study that did address this issue of differences in use of kin for emotional support was conducted by Keefe et al. (1978). The authors found that Mexican

Americans did, in fact, consult a family member for emotional support more frequently than Anglo Americans did in the year preceding the study. However, further data suggested that this was the result of Mexican Americans' having a greater number of kin in the immediate geographical area, and the fact that Anglos rely on both friends *and* relatives for emotional support. Keefe et al. conclude that during times of emotional problems Anglos do not distinguish between friends and family as much as Mexican Americans.

In view of the limited research in this area, generalizations regarding the role and function of the extended family among bicultural populations should be made with caution. Like other questions involving culturally diverse groups, socioeconomic, acculturation, and regional differences are likely to have a significant impact on the nature of extended family relationships. As is discussed later in this chapter, a great deal of diversity in these variables exists even within ethnic groups. It behooves the school psychologist to recognize this variability, and when applicable, rather than perceive reliance on the extended family as an obstacle, utilize it in designing intervention programs.

Use of Folk Medicine

Many Hispanics and American Indians subscribe to folk systems to explain physical illness and psychological problems (Jilek-Aall, 1976; Martinez & Martin, 1966; Torrey, 1972). However, there is evidence, based on large samples of Mexican Americans, to suggest that the tendency to use folk healers is minimal in urban areas of the United States (Edgerton, Karno, & Fernandez, 1970; Farge, 1977; Keefe et al., 1978). Nonetheless, school psychologists in bicultural settings must be prepared to encounter convictions such as the American Indians' belief in the medicine man, Mexican Americans in *curandismo,* Puerto Ricans in *esperitismo,* and Cubans in *santeria*.

Folk healers, like many mental health care professionals, recognize the relationships between physical and psychological pathologies. The major differences between folk healers and mental health professionals are in the causes of the pathology and the method of treatment. In the folk systems, symptoms may be caused by natural *or* supernatural events, such as spiritual possession, witchcraft, or witnessing a traumatic event. Treatment consists of a set of rituals and practices that reflect the historical, religious, and social backgrounds of the particular ethnic group (see Crapanzano & Garrison, 1977; Harwood, 1977; Sandoval, 1975, for a description of some of these beliefs and practices).

When a school psychologist is confronted with a family that subscribes to folk beliefs, it is important to remember that such beliefs are not necessarily an impediment to traditional psychological intervention. It has been the author's experience that families who seek advice from *curanderos* are also receptive to diagnosis and interventions by school personnel. Arenas, Cross, and Willard (1980) report that *curanderos* themselves are open to cooperating with mental health professionals on many of their cases. Reciprocal cooperation can demonstrate a school psychologist's cultural sensitivity and responsiveness. It can also be an enlightening experience that results in positive treatment outcomes for the school psychologist's client.

UNDERSTANDING OTHER LINGUISTIC SYSTEMS

Language reflects culture. A culture's linguistic system is an expression of how that culture perceives and interprets reality. Understanding the characteristics of a language thus helps us know more about how persons from culturally different backgrounds experience the world. A basic example of this is: in English, we say *I forgot the books,* with no indication of whether the event was intentional or not; in Spanish, one says, *Se me olvidó el libro* (the book forget itself somehow to me), making it clear that the act was not purposeful. There is an enormous number of these types of language system differences.

School psychologists who understand the features of the linguistic system of the cultural group with whom they work will also be better equipped to assess and diagnose the nature of bilingual students' spoken and written communication difficulties. Certainly, the most desirable situation is one where the school psychologist is proficient in the language(s) of the population(s) he or she serves. Even then, proficiency in a language does not necessarily mean that a person is fluent in the particular dialect of a region. The Spanish-speaking population especially is characterized by considerable heterogeneity in phonological expression, regional dialects, and incidence and type of codeswitching (combining two or more linguistic and/or grammatical systems during speech). While these first two phenomena are relatively easily acquired speech acts, the third, codeswitching, represents a complex aspect of bilingual development. The meaning attached to the codeswitching occurrence varies, depending on such factors as the developmental age of the speaker, level of second language proficiency, social situation, and ethnic identity of the speakers (Garcia, Maez, & Gonzalez, 1983; Gumperz, 1976; Lindholm & Padilla, 1977).

Even though not proficient in the child's language, a psychologist can be knowledgeable about the stages of first language (L_1) acquisition, the processes of second language (L_2) acquisition, and the variables that influence them. Although monolingual and bilingual acquisition (the simultaneous learning of two languages) generally follow the same developmental patterns, the processes involved in successive acquisition of two languages is more individualistic in nature. Variables such as level of proficiency in L_1, sociocultural exposure to L_2, motivation, and type of instruction are influential in determining the level of attained proficiency in L_2 (Cummins, 1979; Gardner & Lambert, 1972; McLaughlin, 1977). Research regarding the complex interplay of these factors has only recently begun. Definitive answers pinpointing the relative impact of these variables awaits future investigation. Meanwhile, the school psychologists should be aware of these potentially influential factors in order to identify those which may be contributing to an acquisition difficulty, and thus be subject to intervention.

In addition to providing more competent service delivery, school psychologists who make it a point of acquiring even minimal functional-level proficiency in L_2 will be helping create an educational environment that facilitates the social and emotional development of children from culturally diverse backgrounds. Supportive of this premise is a study by Goebes and Shore (1978) in which self-image, peer-group organization, acdeptance of cultural differences, and role-taking ability were compared for groups of Anglos and Latinos in monocultural and bicultural schools. Students in the bicultural school showed stronger self-image, greater heterogeneity in forming peer groups, and greater acceptance of cultural differences. The investigators attribute these differences to the school staff's fostering of a bilingual/bicultural atmosphere.

ACCULTURATION AND CULTURAL IDENTITY

Intertwined with the bilingual characteristic of culturally diverse children and families are the issues of cultural identity and acculturation. In fact, some theorists consider language usage to be a measure of acculturation (Ramirez & Castaneda, 1974), the thinking being that the maintenance of one's native language reflects a desire to preserve cultural identity. On a more global level, cultural identification is the process by which individuals define themselves by language, values, attitudes, and standards that are shared with other members of the cultural group. The need for cultural identity is readily apparent in the large numbers of individuals who choose to live in the *barrio* or *colonia* with other members of their culture.

Though the study of acculturation as been subject to definitional and measurement difficulties (Olmedo, 1979; Szapocnik, Scopetta, Kurtines, & Arnalde, 1978; Teske & Nelson, 1974), the need of many individuals to live and adjust to two cultural systems is a very real phenomenon. Many do not achieve adjustment, the result being the "marginal" person, who is unable to identify successfully with either culture.

Ambiguous or mixed cultural orientations are associated with personal stress and maladjustment; the greater the press for acculturation, the greater the potential for distress. Difficulty in integrating the values of the majority culture with one's home may be particularly evident during adolescence and may compound the psychosocial demands of that developmental period (Allen, 1973). An investigation of the adjustment processes of Mexican-American adolescents found that Mexican-American students who rejected their traditional cultural values experienced more psychosomatic symptoms, self-derogation, and guilt than those who accepted their ethnic heritage (Ramirez, 1969). The increase in substance abuse among Mexican-American and Indian adolescents in recent years may be caused, in part, by their confusion in trying to establish a cultural identity (Gilbert, 1977; President's Commission on Mental Health, 1978).

The struggle for cultural identity exists even within ethnic groups. The word Hispanic incorporates peoples of all Latin-American descent, and Native-American encompasses 16 Indian tribes. These general terms are useful in unifying the various groups to promote their social and political interests, but many individuals do not want to be mixed under one name. They would rather be identified with a more specific appelation such as Navaho, Papago, and Yaqui, or Cuban, Puerto Rican, and Mexican. Americans of Mexican descent seem to be especially concerned with a self-identifying name, choosing between Chicano, Mexican American, and Hispanic. Since ethnic or racial appellations can affect the way the group in question perceives itself (Lessing & Zagorin, 1972; Longshore, 1979), as well as the perceptions of the majority culture (Fairchild & Cozens, 1981; Longshore, 1979), the choice of an ethnic label has important implications for crosscultural attitudes and relations.

In their work with persons from culturally diverse backgrounds, school psychologists should make an effort to determine their client's cultural background and acknowledge that identity. Superficial indications, such as Spanish surnames, may be misleading. In the Southwest particularly, a large number of Yaquis and Papagos, as well as Mexican Americans, have Spanish surnames. Yet each of these groups has very unique cultural values and standards for interpersonal relationships. It would also be a mistake to assume that someone with a Spanish surname speaks Spanish. Third generation Mexican Americans or children from an interethnic marriage may speak little or no Spanish.

Given these issues, it is crucial that the school psychologist make efforts to acknowledge and accommodate the child's and the parents' cultural expectations. This is particularly important during the first interaction. By establishing such a psychological environment, all parties involved can work together in operationalizing problems and establishing mutually acceptable goals.

Variations in Bicultural Identity

It is an error to believe that in their search for cultural identity, all ethnic minority group members are bound to be racked by emotional turmoil. Many decide to become completely assimilated by the majority culture. Others live unacculturated lives completely within the confines of the *barrio* or reservation. Still others are able to live biculturally, enjoying meaningful interactions with people from both cultural groups.

Like bilingualism, the level of acculturation or biculturalism varies tremendously within ethnic groups. Simply categorizing individuals into gross ethnic categories provides only minimal information about a person's sociocultural background. Yet this information is essential to interpreting individual psychological assessment results and crosscultural research findings.

Accordingly, recent efforts have been made to define quantitatively acculturation based on the degree to which one has acquired the values, standards, and characteristics of the majority culture (Cuellar, Harris, & Jasso, 1980; Mercer & Lewis, 1978; Olmedo, Martinez, & Martinez, 1978; Szapocznik et al., 1978). Olmedo (1979) points out that the process of acculturation is multidimensional, and quantitative measures will vary depending on whether emphasis has been placed on linguistic, psychological, or sociocultural items, *and* on the procedures of item selection, criterion measures, and validation methods. Each of these models contributes to attaining a more comprehensive view of within-ethnic-group differences. Use of acculturation measures is encouraged in order to understand better the nature of the acculturation process itself, and the psychological functioning of culturally diverse groups.

ASSESSMENT PRACTICES

The past two decades have witnessed intense professional, social, and judicial debate over the issue of assessment of minority groups. This controversy has had far-reaching consequences. Legislation has been enacted to safeguard the rights of minority children during assessment (PL 94–142). In recognition of the need for school psychologists who work with limited-English-proficient children, states are developing additional credentialing competencies (Figueroa, Sandoval, & Merino, 1984). And, in response to questions regarding test bias, an abundance of research has been conducted on the reliability, validity, and meaningfulness of aptitude testing of children from minority groups (Jensen, 1980; Reynolds, 1982).

In this section, I outline the major factors that should be considered when evaluating children from culturally diverse backgrounds. These factors are testwiseness, bilingualism, and test selection.

Testwiseness

Testwiseness refers to the examinees' familiarity with the test format, understanding of the language used in the test instructions, and comprehension of the achievement aspect of the testing situation. Deficiencies in any of these test-taking prerequisites can seriously handicap a child's test performance and thereby jeopardize the validity of the assessment results. It has been suggested that limited test-taking skills may be one reason for the relatively low aptitude test performance by ethnic minority children (Dreisbach & Keogh, 1982; Sattler, 1982).

The importance of testwiseness has been demonstrated in research designed to evaluate the effectiveness of training in test-taking skills. A number of studies have shown that by familiarizing students with test format and procedures and encouraging them in attending and on-task behaviors, test performance can be improved (Callenbach, 1973; Moore, Schutz, & Baker, 1966; Oakland, 1972; Wahlstrom & Boersma, 1968). Most of these studies, however, dealt with low SES Anglos or subjects comprised of several racial/ethnic combinations. Dreisback and Keogh (1982) examined the effects of training Mexican-American children in test-taking skills on a school readiness test. To control for language competence in English, the authors tested all subjects in English and Spanish. Results indicated that the children who received the training performed better than an untrained control group regardless of language of the test. Dreisback and Keogh conclude that testwiseness is an important influence on test performance of young children from minority backgrounds. They suggest that this factor be considered when administering readiness tests and interpreting their results.

Obviously, children's lack of test-taking skills is related to variables much larger in scope, such as level of parental education and socioeconomic status. However, it remains the responsibility of the school psychologist to take the necessary steps to insure that test results are a valid indication of a child's competence on the ability being assessed. Even after this assurance has been made, the psychologist's interaction with and observations of a student may lead to the identification of behaviors and skills that are independent from the domain being assessed, yet impede optimal performance in that area. In such cases, the behaviors can often be remediated by a short-term intervention rather than an inappropriate special education placement.

Bilingualism and Language Assessment

Since the vast majority of the assessment instruments used to assess cognitive abilities and academic skills are verbal in nature, it seems clear that language proficiency would be one of the first considerations before any further evaluation proceeded. Yet the flagrant absence of this practice was a major impetus in class action suits concerning overrepresentation in special education (Diana v. California State Board of Education, 1970; Guadalupe v. Tempe Elementary School District, 1972). Perhaps this neglect for language assessment was related to the once prevalent thinking that bilingualism is a handicap to cognitive and linguistic development (see the review by Darcy, 1953). However, the literature responsible for this popular myth was poorly designed, with such flaws as absence of control groups, failure to control for socioeconomic and acculturation differences, and use of tests standardized in other cultures (Cummins, 1979; Peal & Lambert, 1962). More recent research has reported no negative effects of bilingualism on cognitive functioning (Jones, 1966), and occasionally it has been found that bilinguals demonstrate more flexible thinking and problem-solving abilities than monolinguals (Barik & Swain, 1976; Oren, 1981).

In addition to the aforementioned methodological difficulties, the level of language proficiency in one or both languages may be the most important variable in explaining the conflicting results in research on the topic of bilingualism and cognitive functioning. Cummins (1979) has proposed that there are threshold levels of linguistic competence a bilingual child must reach in order to avoid negative cognitive effects and facilitate general cognitive and academic progress. Thus, in addition to being necessary for determining the appropriateness of administering tests in a child's L_2, language assessment provides a source of data that has implications for a child's general cognitive and academic development. This information can then be used in diagnosing reading problems (Argulewicz & Sanchez, 1982) and in planning instructional programming (Cummins, 1979).

The task of accurately assessing the language development of bilingual children is a challenging one. One reason for this is the complexity of interrelated factors associated with second language acquisition alluded to earlier in this chapter. Matluck and Mace (1973) describe how Mexican-American children's English speech deviations are characterized by a diversity of patterns, most of which are the result of normal developmental and acquisitional processes. The phenomenon of codeswitching alone has distinguishing developmental, regional, and contextual norms (Garcia et al., 1983). The intricate interplay between linguistic and sociocultural factors has implications for school psychologists in that they must be aware of these factors and exercise caution against diagnosing normal developmental features of acquiring L_2 as a weakness in language proficiency or, worse, a communicative disorder.

Language assessment is typically accomplished by using a standardized language test. A number of measures are available to assess language dominance, language proficiency, or both. Language dominance refers to the primary language a child uses most often at home and in which the child is more competent. Language dominance measures are generally quick screening devices composed of one or more of the following: (a) self-report measures in which students respond to questions about their language usage; (b) questionnaires to parents regarding a child's early language acquisition and present usage in the family; (c) oral vocabulary measures in which the child is asked to identify or describe pictorial stimuli; (d) verbal comprehension measures in which the child responds verbally or motorically to a series of questions and/or commands. On the basis of responses to these items in each language, a child's dominant language is determined.

Language proficiency is a more comprehensive indicator of language status, in that the *level* of competence in each language is assessed. Measures of language proficiency assess the linguistic components of phonology, syntax/morphology, and semantics. These areas are assessed primarily for oral language skills, but reading and writing tests are also available. One's language proficiency score is based on one's performance relative to that of a normative sample.

Some bilingual children score at low, or moderately low, proficiency levels in both languages. In these cases, supplementary assessment techniques can be used to gain additional information about a child's language ability in order to determine the most appropriate instructional programming. One supplementary technique, "pragmatics," entails observing children across a variety of settings and recording their verbalizations and responses to those of other children. A great deal of information can be obtained by using pragmatic methods, but they require a trained observer and are time consuming (see Erikson & Omark, 1981, for details on pragmatic techniques).

Another supplementary technique is a structured interview. Examiners who use structured interviews are often interested in seeing how children uses their overall communicative resources rather than in evaluating proficiency in each language per se (Garcia, 1980). Language proficiency is viewed as one skill with components from both languages, and children are thus allowed to demonstrate their linguistic competence without the constraint of responding entirely in one language. Codeswitching is not considered interference from one language to another, unless the usage is inappropriate. A structured interview naturally requires a bilingual examiner, preferably one familiar with the sociolinguistic nuances of the area.

School psychologists can perform a valuable service to school districts that must assess language on a regular basis. Even though they may not have second language skills, the psychologists are likely to be the staff members most highly trained in psychometrics. They are thereby in the responsible position of counseling others as to whether a certain language proficiency test meets acceptable reliability and validity criteria and was standardized on a comparable norm group. These skills, coupled with a knowledge of the dynamics of second language acquisition, can contribute greatly to the overall assessment of bilingual children. That assessment, in turn, will lead to more positive cognitive and affective treatment outcomes.

Selection and Use of Assessment Instruments

Psychoeducational assessments are conducted for the purpose of making diagnostic and placement decisions. Fortunately, school psychologists have a number of well-constructed psychological and educational instruments at their disposal to help them achieve this goal. From this pool of instruments, the psychologist must select, administer, and interpret appropriate formal and informal measures. These findings must then be synthesized in a way that leads to meaningful treatment recommendations. When done conscientiously, this process is a complex, yet rewarding, task.

The task becomes more complex and hence presents a greater challenge when the child being evaluated is from a minority culture background. Several solutions have been proposed in response to the issue of conducting nonbiased assessments.

These proposals include: (a) issuing a moratorium on testing, (b) using culture fair tests, (c) developing pluralistic norms, (d) translating existing measures, and (e) conducting multifactored assessments. The first four of these proposals are reviewed here briefly. The last, multifactored assessment, is discussed in greater detail, as it is currently the proposed practice that holds the most promise, although it is still marked by shortcomings and potential abuses.

Moratorium on Testing. This extreme recommendation, first made by black psychologist Robert Williams (1970), is based on the belief that current assessment measures are culturally biased against minorities. Tests thus prevent minorities from being chosen in employment selection and are also responsible for the misidentification and overrepresentation of minorities in classes for the educable mentally retarded.

It has been argued that if educational programming were left to more subjective decision-making procedures, such as teacher referral, it would result in even greater overrepresentation of minorities (Reschly, 1981). Argulewicz and Sanchez (1983) found that in both low- and mid-SES schools, the psychoeducational evaluation process did, in fact, moderate the number of children placed in special education from the number referred for placement by teachers, and/or counselors.

Culture-Fair or Culture-Reduced Tests. A number of attempts have been made to construct tests which limit the use of language, cultural content and specific skills, and emphasize, instead, various problem-solving abilities. To date, however, culture-fair tests have been characterized by psychometric shortcomings, such as small, nonrepresentative population samples and inadequate validity and reliability (Jensen, 1980; Salvia & Ysseldyke, 1978).

Pluralistic Norms for Conventional Tests. Stimulated primarily by the work of Mercer (1978, Mercer & Lewis, 1979), many psychologists, educators, and sociologists endorsed the use of separate racial and ethnic norms for use with existing tests. With pluralistic norms, the same raw scores would result in different standard scores, depending on the examinee's sociocultural background. This score would represent one's deviation from the mean of one's sociocultural group.

Advocates of pluralistic norms claim that their use allow a more accurate assessment of children's intellectual ability in that inferences about their potential are based on their performance relative to others with similar sociocultural backgrounds and experiences. Hence children are not penalized because they do not belong to the same cultural group (primarily Anglo) on which a test was standardized.

Adversaries to the use of pluralistic norms point out that when one's purpose is to predict academic success, scores obtained from pluralistic norms are less valid than scores from the existing norms (Oakland, 1979). A second criticism is that information from using pluralistic norms does not lead to improved educational programming for the student. Finally, the heterogeneous nature of various cultural groups would require the development of a number of regional norms that must be frequently updated.

Translating Existing Measures. In an attempt to reduce the influence language has on assessment results, many tests have been translated into other languages, most notably Spanish. However, this practice is beset with several problems. First, depending on the country, or even the region, an individual is from, different words are used for the same meaning. Similarly, the same word may have a different meaning from region to region. Another problem is that the level of item difficulty may change in the translation of verbal tests. This essentially changes the test's psychometric properties. The translated version of the test is then without normative or validity data. In any case, language variations among examinees, along with the nature of the translation, are likely to be the primary reasons for the conflicting research results regarding test translations (cf., Bergan & Parra, 1979; Holland, 1960; Oplesch & Genshaft, 1981; Palmer & Gaffney, 1972; Sattler, Avila, Houston, & Toney, 1980; Shellenberger, 1977; Swanson & DeBlassie, 1979).

Multifactored Assessment. A nonbiased assessment practice that has received wide professional endorsement (Lutey & Copeland, 1982; Reschly, 1979; Tucker, 1977) and appears to meet the requirement of PL 94–142, which calls for assessment data's being drawn from a broad variety of areas, is multifactored assessment. Multifactored assessment is comprehensive in nature, utilizing a variety of measures and sources in evaluating sensory, cognitive, affective, social, and perceptual domains. This information is integrated into a comprehensive description of the child, which is then used in making educational decisions and planning appropriate interventions.

In order for multifactored assessment practices to truly serve the needs of culturally different children, however, the assessment instruments must, according to PL 94–142 (and APA Ethical Principles), be validated for the specific purpose for which they are used. This process of test selection, as Padilla and Garza (1975) suggest, may be the activity subject to the most abuse. Supporting this notion, research on the measures used by school personnel in making special education decisions shows that technically inadequate tests were frequently included in the decision-making test battery (Thurlow & Ysseldyke, 1979; Ysseldyke, Algozinne, Regan, & Potter, 1980). Further, even though a test may be technically adequate for members of the majority culture, it still may be biased against minority cultures.

Because individual intelligence tests are the primary instrument used in making special education classification decisions, and because of the high value people place on the meaning of intelligence, the issue of bias in tests of mental ability has been the focus of a profusion of empirical investigations. A description of the methods used to evaluate bias and a review of the findings have been elucidated elsewhere in the literature (see Berk, 1982; Jensen, 1980; Reynolds, 1982). Let it suffice to say here that the vast majority of studies (most which have been conducted on blacks, fewer on Hispanics, and even fewer on American Indians and Asian-Americans) show an absence of internal or external evidence of bias. However, before the research conducted with the last three ethnic groups mentioned is unequivocally accepted as indicators that these tests can be used as nonbiased measures, several factors must be considered.

Research on the cognitive abilities of culturally different groups has typically not controlled for contaminating variables such as language dominance or proficiency, testwiseness, acculturation, socioeconomic status, or parental level of education. These are all variables that could potentially influence research findings (DeBlassie, 1980; Valencia, Henderson, & Rankin, 1981). The few studies assessing or controlling for language status have found that screening measures and cognitive ability tests have lower validity coefficients for groups with primary language other than English than for the groups of Anglo children (Gandara, Keogh, & Yoshioka-Maxwell, 1980; Valencia, 1982).

Associated with language status is level of acculturation. As mentioned earlier in this chapter, there is consierable heterogeneity in acculturation among culturally different populations. Since test norms are developed as a basis for interpreting a child's performance, relative to his or her peers, it makes sense that a child's cultural and educational experience be similar to those on whom the test is standardized. When a child's level of acculturation departs significantly from a test's norm, the test results evade meaningful interpretation. It is for this reason that simply using nonverbal measures for bilingual students does not remedy the problem. The issue of similar experiential backgrounds still exists.

Research supporting the predictive validity of cognitive ability tests with scholastic achievement for culturally different children should thus be viewed tentatively as the criterion measures suffer from the same normative inadequacy as the predictors. What is needed to truly validate these measures is long-term prediction studies to help uncover the real significance of test scores for individuals from culturally diverse backgrounds. As Anastasi (1976) pointed out:

> The most frequent misgivings regarding the use of tests with minority group members stem from misinterpretations of scores. If a minority examinee obtains a low score on an aptitude test or a deviant score on a personality test, it is essential to investigate why he did so. . . . Tests are designed to show what an individual can do at a given point in time. They cannot tell us why he performs as he does. To answer that question, we need to investigate his background, motivations, and other pertinent circumstances. (pp. 59–60)

Although tests normed on children from the mainstream predict how well a child will do in the mainstream educational environment, they do not tell us how well an ethnic minority child is doing, given his or her unique sociocultural and linguistic background. Certainly, both types of information are important in planning educational programs and designing intervention strategies. The need for multiple data sources in achieving this goal is apparent. This practice involves collecting information in the cognitive, affective, social, and perceptual domains from test and non-test data sources. In addition to using traditional psychometric measures, data is acquired through behavioral assessment techniques, interviews with parents and teachers, examining work samples, and autobiographic and narrative self-reports. In this way, school psychologists can obtain a picture of how a child is performing in the various areas, as well as identify the variables and conditions that are influencing that performance. Within this framework, the focus of assesment shifts from *what* test scores a child receives to *how* and *why* the child is performing the way he or she is. Attention can then be given to the frequently discussed, but less often implemented undertaking of developing and evaluating educational environments that are meaningful for children from all cultures.

CONCLUSION

The impact of culture on the psychological makeup of an individual is significant enough to warrant serious consideration in the delivery of psychological services. In this chapter, I have attempted to delineate those variables which exercise the most influence on the behavior of cultural minorities currently living in the United States. Underscored was the fact that considerable heterogeneity in characteristics exists within various ethnic groups. It is high time that crosscultural research went beyond simple between-groups comparisons to investigate variables affecting within-group differences. However, even when such group data becomes available, practicing school psychologists serving culturally different populations will have to be sensitive to diversity in standards, attitudes, language, and acculturation as they exist in various combinations among different students.

Given the variability within cultural minority populations, a few global recommendations for service delivery can be made:

1. Acquire a knowledge and understanding of the cultural background(s) of the population(s) with whom you are working. This entails recognizing the differences among cultural groups and subgroups as well as within group variation. Particularly, get to know the values of the local cultural community. This can be accomplished by conducting surveys and making contact with a community leader.

2. Become aware of and sensitive to cultural differences in the perception of psychological problems and attitudes toward ameliorating them. Different cultural groups have different perceptions regarding the causes, implications and methods of treating various handicapping conditions. Sensitivity to these differences will help establish trust between psychologists and their clients.

3. Be receptive to working cooperatively with family relatives or spiritual healers in implementing interventions. Cooperative efforts not only increase trust, but also may lead to effective intervention strategies.

4. Understand the stresses and anxieties associated with acculturation. For many children, their first long-term experience outside their cultural community is their entry to school. It is important that signs of cultural adjustment not be interpreted as maladaptive behavior. Be prepared to discuss the problems associated with acculturation, respecting the individual's attempt at achieving a meaningful cultural identity.

5. Understand the developmental processes involved in second language learning. This information should be applied in the assessment of reading progress and other cognitive abilities. Bilingualism appears to have cognitive advantages and maintenance of one's native language should be encouraged.

6. Conduct multifactored assessments drawing from multiple data sources. Findings from test and non-test data sources should be cross validated. When discrepancies exist, reasons should be sought, including but not limited to test-wiseness, language, acculturation, and biased data sources.

7. Carefully evaluate the technical adequacy and appropriateness of existing and newly developed assessment instruments. In reviewing test bias studies, be aware that these are usually short-term predictions and that the underlying value judgment is that the criterion measures are relevant to every child's personal growth and development. Consider the possibility of modifying instructional goals and procedures rather than changing the child.

Delivering school psychology services in bicultural and multicultural settings is a challenging and exciting venture. It calls for applying the best of the skills in which we were trained and developing new ones. In so doing, it affords a tremendous opportunity for personal and professional growth. Everywhere in this country, culturally diverse people are making efforts to grow economically, socially, and politically. School psychologists can contribute to those efforts by working and learning with these people, and in turn, can grow with them.

REFERENCES

Allen, J. R. (1973). The Indian adolescent: Psychosocial tasks of the Plains Indian of Western Oklahoma. *American Journal of Orthopsychiatry, 43,* 368–375.

Algozinne, B., Christenson, S., & Ysseldyke, J. E. (1982). Probabilities associated with the referral to placement process. *Teacher Education and Special Education, 5,* 19–23.

Anastasi, A. (1976). *Psychological testing* (4th ed.). New York: Macmillan.

Arenas, S., Cross, H., & Willard, W. (1980). Curanderos and mental health professionals: A comparative study on perceptions of psychopathology. *Hispanic Journal of Behavioral Sciences, 4,* 407–421.

Argulewicz, E. N., Eliott, S. N., & Hall, R. (1982). Comparison of behavioral ratings of Anglo-American and Mexican-American gifted students. *Psychology in the Schools, 14,* 469–472.

Argulewicz, E. N., & Sanchez, D. T. (1982). Considerations in the assessment of reading difficulties in bilingual children. *School Psychology Review, 11,* 281–289.

Argulewicz, E. N., & Sanchez, D. T. (1983). The special education evaluation process as a moderator of false positives. *Exceptional Children, 49,* 452–454.

Barik, H. C., & Swain, M. A. (1976). A longitudinal study of bilingual and cognitive development. *International Journal of Psychology, 11,* 251–263.

Bergan, J. R., & Parra, E. B. (1979). Variations in IQ testing and instruction and the letter learning and achievement of Anglo and bilingual Mexican-American children. *Journal of Educational Psychology, 71,* 819–826.

Berk, R. A. (Ed.). (1982). *Handbook of methods for detecting test bias.* Baltimore: Johns Hopkins University Press.

Bersoff, D. N. (1981). Testing and the law. *American Psychologist, 36,* 1047–1056.

Bersoff, D. N. (1982). The legal regulation of school psychology. In C. R. Reynolds & T. B. Gutkin (Eds.), *The handbook of school psychology* (pp. 1043–1074). New York: Wiley.

Buchanan, B., & Choca, P. R. (1979). Mutuality of expectations and cultural etiquette: Some considerations and a proposal. In P. R. Martin (Ed.), *La Frontera perspective: Providing mental health services to Mexican Americans.* Tucson: La Frontera Center.

Buriel, R. (1983). Teacher-student interactions and their relationship to student achievement: A comparison of Mexican-American and Anglo-American children. *Journal of Educational Psychology, 75,* 889–897.

Callenbach, C. (1973). The effects of instructions and practice in content-independent test-taking techniques upon the standardized reading test scores of select second-grade students. *Journal of Educational Measurement, 10*(1), 24–30.

Crapanzano, V., & Garrison, V. (1977). *Case studies in spirit possession.* New York: Wiley.

Cuellar, I., Harris, L. C., & Jasso, R. (1980). An acculturation scale for Mexican American normal and clinical populations. *Hispanic Journal of Behavioral Sciences, 2,* 199–217.

Cummins, J. (1979). Linguistic interdependence and the educational development of bilingual children. *Review of Educational Research, 49,* 222–251.

Darcy, N. T. (1963). A review of the literature on the effects of bilingualism on the measurement of intelligence. *Journal of Genetic Psychology, 82,* 21–57.

DeBlassie, R. R. (1980). *Testing Mexican American youth.* Hingham, MS: Teaching Resources.

Diana v. State Board of Education. C-70 37 70 RFP. District court for Northern California. (February 1970).

Dreisbach, M., & Keogh, B. K. (1982). Testwiseness as a factor in readiness test performance of young Mexican-American children. *Journal of Educational Psychology, 74,* 224–229.

Edgerton, R. B., Karno, M., & Fernandez, I. (1970). *Curanderismo* in the metropolis: The diminishing role of folk-psychiatry among Los Angeles Mexican-Americans. *American Journal of Psychotherapy, 24*(1), 124–234.

Elliott, S. N., & Argulewicz, E. N. (1983). The influence of student ethnicity on teacher's behavior ratings of normal and learning disabled students. *Hispanic Journal of Behavioral Sciences, 5,* 337–345.

Erikson, J. G., & Omark, D. R. (Eds.). (1981). *Communication assessment of bilingual children: Issues and guidelines.* Baltimore: University Park Press.

Everett, F., Proctor, N., & Cartwell, B. (1983). Providing psychological services to American Indian children and families. *Professional Psychology: Research and Practice, 14,* 588–603.

Fairchild, H. H., & Cozens, J. A. (1981). Chicano, Hispanic, or Mexican American? What's in a name? *Hispanic Journal of Behavioral Sciences, 3,* 191–198.

Farge, E. J. (1977). A review of findings from 'three generations' of Chicano health care behavior. *Social Science Quarterly, 58,* 407–411.

Figueroa, R. A., Sandoval, J., & Merino, B. (1984). School psychology and limited-English-proficient (LEP) children: New competencies. *Journal of School Psychology, 22,* 131–143.

Franco, J. N. (1983). An acculturation scale for Mexican-American children. *The Journal of General Psychology, 108,* 175–181.

Gandara, P., Keogh, B. K., & Yoshioka-Maxwell, B. (1980). Predicting academic performance of Anglo and Mexican-American kindergarten children. *Psychology in the Schools, 17,* 174–177.

Garcia, E. E., Maez, L., & Gonzalez, G. (1983). The incidence of language switching in Spanish/English bilingual children in the United States. In E. E. Garcia (Ed.), *The Mexican-American child: Language, cognition and social development* (pp. 19–42). Tempe, AZ: Center for Bilingual Educaton, Arizona State University.

Garcia, M. (1980). *Linguistic proficiency: How bilingual discourse can show that a child has it.* Paper presented at the Forum on Ethnoperspectives in Bilingual Education Research, Ypsilanti.

Gardner, R. C., & Lambert, W. E. (1972). *Attitudes and motivation in second language learning.* Rowley, MA: Newbury House.

Gilbert, M. J. (1977). *Qualitative analysis of the drinking practices and alcohol-related problems of the Spanish speaking in three California locales.* Alhambra, CA: Technical Systems Institute.

Goebes, D. D., & Shore, M. F. (1978). Some effects of bicultural and monocultural school environments on personality development. *American Journal of Orthopsychiatry, 48,* 398–407.

Goodenough, W. H. (1963). *Cooperation in change.* New York: Russell Sage Foundation.

Guadalupe v. Tempe Elementary School District, 71–435 (D. C. of Arizona, January, 1972).

Gumperz, J. J. (1976). The sociolinguistic significance of conversational codeswitching. *Papers in language and context.* Berkeley: University of California Language Behavior Research Laboratory.

Harwood, A. (1977). *Rx: Spiritist as needed.* New York: Wiley.

Holland, W. R. (1960). Language barrier as an educational problem of Spanish-speaking children. *Exceptional Children, 27,* 42–50.

Jaco, E. G. (1957). Social factors in mental disorders in Texas. *Social Problems, 4,* 322–328.

Jensen, A. R. (1980). *Bias in mental testing.* New York: The Free Press.

Jilek-Aall, L. (1976). The western psychiatrist and his nonwestern clientele. *Canadian Psychiatric Association Journal, 21*(6), 353–359.

Jones, W. R. (1966). *Bilingualism in Welsh education.* Cardiff, Wales: University of Wales Press.

Keefe, S. E., Padilla, A. M., & Carlos, M. L. (1978). *Emotional support systems in two cultures: A comparison of Mexican Americans and Anglo Americans* (Occasional Paper No. 7). Los Angeles: Spanish Speaking Mental Health Research Center, UCLA.

Korman, M. (1974). National conference on levels and patterns of professional training in psychology: The major themes. *American Psychologist, 29,* 441–449.

La Fromboise, T., Dauphinais, P., & Rowe, W. (1980). Indian students' perception of positive helper attributes. *Journal of American Indian Education, 19,* 13–16.

Laosa, L. M. (1977). Inequality in the classroom: Observational research on teacher-student interactions. *Aztlan: International Journal of Chicano Studies Research, 8,* 51–67.

Lessing, E. E., & Zagorin, S. W. (1972). Black power ideology and college students' attitudes toward their own and other racial groups. *Journal of Personality and Social Psychology, 21,* 61–73.

Lindholm, K. J., & Padilla, A. M. (1977). Language mixing in bilingual children. *Journal of Child Language, 5,* 327–335.

Lockhart, B. (1981). Historic distrust and the counseling of American Indians and Alaska Natives. *White Cloud Journal, 2*(3), 31–34.

Locklear, H. H. (1972). American Indian myths. *Social Work, 17,* 72–80.

Longshore, D. (1979). Color connotations and racial attitudes. *Journal of Black Studies, 10,* 183–197.
Lutey, C., & Copeland, E. (1982). Cognitive assessments of the school age child. In C. R. Reynolds & T. B. Gutkin (Eds.), *The handbook of school psychology* (pp. 121–155). New York: Wiley.
Martinez, C., & Martin, H. W. (1966). Folk diseases among urban Mexican-Americans. *Journal of the American Medical Association, 196,* 161–164.
Matluck, J. H., & Mace, B. J. (1973). Language characteristics of Mexican American children: Implications for assessment. *Journal of School Psychology, 11,* 365–386.
McLaughlin, B. (1977). Second-language learning in children. *Psychological Bulletin, 84,* 438–459.
Mercer, J. R. (1979). In defense of racially and culturally nondiscriminatory assessment. *School Psychology Digest, 8,* 89–115.
Mercer, J. R., & Lewis, J. F. (1978). *System of Multicultural Pluralistic Assessment.* New York: The Psychological Corporation.
Moll, L. C., Rueda, R. S., Reza, R., Herrera, J., & Vasquez, L. P. (1976). Mental health services in east Los Angeles: An urban community case study. In M. Miranda (Ed.), *Psychotherapy for the Spanish-speaking* (pp.). Los Angeles: Spanish Speaking Mental Health Center.
Moore, J. C., Schutz, R. E., Baker, R. L. (1966). The application of a self-instructional technique to develop a test-taking strategy. *American Educational Research Journal, 3,* 13–17.
Oakland, T. (1972). The effects of test-wiseness materials on standardized test performance of preschool disadvantaged children. *Journal of School Psychology, 10,* 355–360.
Oakland, T. (1979). Research on the Adaptive Behavior Inventory for Children and the Estimated Learning Potential. *School Psychology Digest, 8,* 63–70.
Olmedo, E. L. (1979). Acculturation: A psychometric perspective. *American Psychologist, 34,* 1061–1070.
Olmedo, E. L. (1981). Testing linguistic minorities. *American Psychologist, 36,* 1078–1085.
Olmedo, E. L., Martinez, J. L., & Martinez, S. R. (1978). Measure of acculturation for Chicano adolescents. *Psychological Reports, 42,* 159–170.
Oplesch, M., & Genshaft, J. (1981). Comparison of bilingual children on the WISC-R and the Escalade Inteligencia Wechsler Para Niños. *Psychology in the Schools, 18,* 159–163.
Oren, D. L. (1981). Cognitive advantages of bilingual children related to labeling ability. *Journal of Educational Research, 74,* 163–169.
Padilla, A. M., & Garza, B. M. (1975). Six cases of cultural myopia. *The National Elementary Principal, 54*(4), 53–58.
Padilla, A. M., & Ruiz, R. A. (1973). *Latino mental health: A review of the literature* (DHEW Publication No. HSM 73–9143). Washington, DC: U.S. Government Printing Office.
Palmer, M., & Gaffney, P. D. (1972). Effects of administration of the WISC in Spanish and English and relationship of social class to performance. *Psychology in the Schools, 9,* 61–64.
Peal, E., & Lambert, W. E. (1962). The relation of bilingualism to intelligence. *Psychological Monographs: General and Applied, 76*(27).
President's Commission on Mental Health, Special Populations Subpanel. (1978). *Mental health of American Indians and Alaskan Natives.* Washington, DC: U.S. Government Printing Office.
Ramirez, M. (1969). Identification with Mexican-American values and psychological adjustment in Mexican-American adolescents. *International Journal of Social Psychiatry, 15,* 151–156.
Ramirez, M. III, & Castaneda, A. (1974). *Cultural democracy, bicognitive development, and education.* New York: Academic Press.
Reschly, D. J. (1979). Nonbiased assessment. In G. D. Phye & D. T. Reschly (Eds.), *School psychology: Perspectives and issues* (pp. 215–253). New York: Academic Press.
Reschly, D. J. (1981). Psychological testing in educational classification and placement. *American Psychologist, 36,* 1094–1102.
Reynolds, C. R. (1982). The problem of bias in psychological assessment. In C. R. Reynolds & T. B. Gutkin (Eds.), *The handbook of school psychology* (pp. 178–208). New York: Wiley.

Russo, N. F., Olmedo, E. L., Stapp, J., & Fulcher, R. (1981). Women and minorities in psychology. *American Psychologist, 36,* 1315–1363.

Salvia, J., & Ysseldyke, J. E. (1978). *Assessment in special and remedial education.* Boston: Houghton Mifflin.

Sandoval, M. C. (1975). *La religion Afrocuban.* Madrid, Spain: Playor.

Sattler, J. M. (1982). *Assessment of children's intelligence and special abilities.* Boston: Allyn & Bacon.

Sattler, J. M., Avila, V., Houston, W. B., & Toney, D. H. (1980). Performance of bilingual Mexican American children on Spanish and English versions of the Peabody Picture Vocabulary Test. *Journal of Consulting and Clinical Psychology, 46,* 782–784.

Shellenberger, S. (1977). *A cross-cultural investigation of the Spanish version of the McCarthy Scales of Children's Abilities for Puerto Rican children.* Unpublished doctoral dissertation, University of Georgia, Athens.

Slaughter, E. L. (1976). *Indian child welfare: A review of the literature.* Denver: Center for Social Research and Development, Denver Research Institute.

Swanson, E. N., & DeBlassie, R. R. (1979). Interpreter and Spanish administration effects on the WISC performance of Mexican-American children. *Journal of School Psychology, 17,* 231–236.

Szapocznik, J., Scopeta, M. H., Kurtines, W., & Arnalde, M. A. (1978). A theory and measurement of acculturation. *Interamerican Journal of Psychology, 12,* 113–130.

Teske, R. H. C., & Nelson, B. H. (1974). Acculturation and assimilation: A clarification. *American Ethnologist, 1,* 351–367.

Thomas, P. J. (1977). Administration of a dialectical Spanish version and standard English version of the Peabody Picture Vocabulary Test. *Psychological Reports, 40,* 747–750.

Thurlow, M., & Ysseldyke, J. E. (1979). Current assessment and decision making practices in model programs for learning disabled students. *Learning Disability Quarterly, 2,* 15–24.

Torrey, E. F. (1972). *The mind game: Witch doctors and psychiatrists.* New York: Emerson Hall.

Tucker, J. A. (1977). Operationalizing the diagnostic-intervention process. In T. Oakland (Ed.), *Psychological and educational assessment of minority children* (pp. 91–111). New York: Brunner/Mazel.

U.S. Census Bureau. (1981). *General population characteristics* (Vol. 1). Washington, DC: U.S. Government Printing Office.

Valencia, R. R. (1982). Predicting academic achievement of Mexican American children: Preliminary analysis of the McCarthy Scales. *Educational and Psychological Measurement, 42,* 1269–1278.

Valencia, R. R., Henderson, R. W., & Rankin, R. J. (1981). Relationship of family constellation and schooling to intellectual performance of Mexican-American children. *Journal of School Psychology, 73,* 524–532.

Wahlstrom, M., & Boersma, F. (1968). The influence of test-wiseness upon achievement. *Educational and Psychological Measurement, 28,* 413–420.

Williams, R. L. (1970). Danger: Testing and dehumanizing Black children. *Clinical Child Psychology Newsletter, 9,* 5–6.

Witt, J. C., & Elliott, S. N. (1985). Acceptability of classroom management strategies. In T. R. Kratchowill (Ed.), *Advances in School Psychology* (pp. 251–288). New York: Lawrence Erlbaum Associates.

Ysseldyke, J. E., Algozinne, B., Regan, R. R., & Potter, M. (1980). Technical adequacy of tests used by professionals in simulated decision making. *Psychology in the Schools, 17,* 202–209.

Zigler, E., & Butterfield, E. C. (1968). Motivational aspects of changes in IQ test performance of culturally deprived nursery school children. *Child Development, 39,* 1–14.

Zucker, S. H., & Prieto, A. G. (1977). Ethnicity and teacher bias in educational decisions. *Journal of Instructional Psychology, 4,* 2–5.

10 The Effectiveness of School Psychological Services

Thomas R. Kratochwill
University of Wisconsin-Madison

Jason K. Feld
University of Arizona

Kurt R. Van Someren
University of Wisconsin-Madison

The effectiveness of school psychological services continues to be a major concern in the field of psychology and education. Determining which types of services and which service delivery models are most effective in our schools should be a major focus of future research for several reasons. For example, it has been estimated that 20% to 30% of children enter elementary school with some behavior problems that are moderate to severe, and that of this group approximately half have severe problems that require professional intervention (Weiner, 1982). Figures such as these suggest that many children are in need of psychological services and that demonstrably effective services would be of great benefit to the children, parents, and the schools. Second, extensive research has focused on the efficacy of various types of school-based interventions and service delivery models. In some cases research has produced treatments that are effective and should be incorporated into school psychology practice. Third, there is, and will continue to be, great interest in the cost associated with school psychology services. Issues surrounding the cost of psychological services become especially salient during difficult economic times and when there have been pleas to shift resources into regular education and teacher salaries. Fourth, another possible impetus is the general trend in society toward accountability.

Each of these issues has helped to focus attention on the need to evaluate the effectiveness of school psychological services. Of course, there has been a great increase in research and reviews of research on various aspects of school psychological services. However, there is hardly unanimity concerning the effectiveness of these services from professionals in the field. The lack of consensus is due to several conceptual and methodological factors. First of all, there is the problem of the wide scope of services available that need to be evaluated. Virtually every therapeutic procedure or technique for academic and social problems has been implemented in schools at one time or another. For example, the numerous intervention strategies discussed in *The Handbook of School Psychology* (Reynolds & Gutkin, 1982), although extensive, just scratch the surface of available technologies, therapeutic procedures, and psychotherapy models that might be implemented in the schools.

A second and related issue surrounds the manner in which psychological service efficacy questions are posed. Using the question "Are school psychological services effective?" may retard the development of our understanding of the broad range of services available. The answer to the question should be guided by Paul's (1967) question: "What treatment, by whom, is most effective with the individual with that specific problem under which set of circumstances?" (p. 111). This conceptualization, like that in the psychotherapy field (e.g., Garfield, 1983a), means that our research questions must be more focused and specific with respect to the type of services being evaluated.

Third, the type and scope of measurement strategies used to determine the effectiveness of services is subject to considerable debate and reflects the perennial and more general controversy over the use of various measures in psychotherapy research (e.g., Kazdin & Wilson, 1978; Strupp & Hadley, 1977). The list of measures seems infinite and could include such strategies as standardized tests of academic skills and personality, interviews, checklists and rating scales, self-report measures, self-monitoring, analogue strategies, and direct observational measures (Kratochwill, 1982). Debate has centered on the types of measures (e.g., self-report vs. direct observation) and the scope of measures to be included in the evaluation (e.g., social validation, cost-effectiveness). Moreover, each school or model of intervention has tended to embrace somewhat different measurement strategies. It is unlikely that there will be agreement on specific outcome measures in the near future.

Fourth, many different design and evaluation strategies can be used to determine the effectiveness of various intervention or program services. The methodologies include historical procedures, passive observational, quasi-experimental and experimental methodologies including single-case and group designs. The degree to which various research questions can be answered by these procedures varies greatly across the methodologies employed.

Fifth, there is growing debate over the most useful methods to evaluate the literature to draw conclusions regarding the effectiveness of areas of investigation (e.g., Garfield, 1983b; Smith, Glass, & Miller, 1980). For example, an investigator might conduct a traditional literature review of an area of investigation (e.g., consultation, grade retention) or employ meta-analysis to draw conclusions from existing research.

Another concern that has yet to emerge as a major issue in the school psychology literature relates to the nature of research and its relevance to the practice of school psychology. In the clinical psychology literature research has sometimes been referred to as *analogue.* Analogue research has been characterized as that type of investigation which has low or little relevance to applied settings such as the schools. For example, research conducted in a clinic with students on hypothetical subjects or only mildly disturbed children would be regarded as an analogue to the usual conditions of therapeutic practice in schools. At issue is whether results from analogue research generalize to applied settings (Bernstein & Paul, 1971; Kazdin, 1978).

A final issue surrounds the degree to which research strategies can be incorporated in actual school psychology practice. The issue encompasses two prominent concerns. The first relates to whether or not school psychologists should be involved in research/program evaluation as a part of their practice; the second refers to the issue of how applied programs are to be evaluated as a part of regular clinical practice. Both issues have an important bearing on the involvement of school psychologists in research and the ultimate quality and dissemination of research findings (Barlow, Hayes, & Nelson, 1984).[1]

Each of the aforementioned concerns has an important bearing on the effectiveness of school psychological services. In this chapter, we provide an overview of several dimensions of research and program evaluation in school psychology. Specifically, we review various evaluation models that can be employed in school service evaluation and discuss some types of research and program evaluation strategies that have been employed in school settings. In the latter case, consultation is used as an example of how various research strategies are used to answer questions regarding the knowledge-base in an area of investigation. Consultation research was selected because (a) it represents a prominent role function in school psychology (Gutkin & Curtis, 1982), (b) research has been conducted on various models or approaches to consultation, and (c) fundamental disagreement exists regarding the appropriate methodologies that should be used to evaluate consultation (e.g., Alpert & Yammer, 1983; Medway, 1979, 1982; Van Someren & Kratochwill, 1983). The chapter concludes with a review of some methodological and conceptual issues that have relevance to future research and practice in school psychology.

EVALUATION MODELS

Broadly conceived, evaluation services are composed of systematic applications of diversified assessment strategies, research methods, and data analytic procedures to assess and enhance the development, monitoring, and effectiveness of human service programs (Maher & Kratochwill, 1980). Evaluation services in school settings involve developing, monitoring, and assessing the effects of

---

[1]The interested reader is referred to Barlow, Hayes, and Nelson (1984), chapter 1, for an excellent historical overview of the scientist practitioner model in psychology.

psychological and educational services/programs for facilitating decision-making activities. Decision-making activities are important within the context of the school system to the extent that they have a direct impact on program management activities (Bergan, Feld, & Stone, 1984). Program management may be viewed as a process by which educators, administrators, school psychologists, and school-related personnel integrate their expertise and resources toward the goals of providing programs and services to students or other clients.

This section provides a description of some of the types of evaluation models that may be considered for implementation in evaluating psychological and related educational services/programs. These models serve the purposes of evaluation in that they provide a mechanism for linking evaluation to decision-making and program management activities. Evaluation is viewed as "the process of delineating, obtaining, and providing useful information for judging decision alternatives (Stufflebeam et al., 1971, p. 40). In this regard, the evaluation of psychological and related educational services/programs necessarily involves development evaluation, process evaluation, and outcome evaluation (Maher & Kratochwill, 1980). These types of evaluation are articulated to different, yet interrelated goals for program management.

These types of evaluation are incorporated to a greater or lesser degree in models that have been proposed to guide and focus inquiry during the evaluation process. The type of model selected to guide the evaluation process will depend on the orientation of the evaluator and the need of the individuals and decision makers to be served through the process of evaluation. Nevertheless, the effectiveness of a particular model in guiding evaluation depends as much on the utility of its assumption as it does on the manner in which it is applied. As Carter (1975) points out, models must be efficient, heuristic, internally logical, and complete. They must be capable of being extended by empirical study and capable of providing the evaluator with information for decision making.

The evaluation literature contains an abundance of models for use in evaluating the effectiveness of psychological and related educational programs/services (Carter, 1975). The models presented in this chapter represent a cross-section of some of the more widely used and potentially effective models for evaluation. These models include two relatively new approaches to evaluation: The Causal Modeling Approach (Cooley, Bond, & Mao, 1981) and the Path-referenced Approach (Bergan, 1981). Also presented are the Synoptic Evaluation Framework (Maher, 1978) and the Consultation Model (Bergan, 1977; Bergan & Kratochwill, in press).

The Causal Modeling Approach

Evaluating program or service effectiveness necessarily implies an evaluation of the most important components or all of that program or service. The components of a program or service may be categorized into separate but related units. These units are composed of input variables, process variables, and outcome variables (Maher, 1978). Input variables include type of client to be served, client needs, client goals, program resources, and program technology. Process variables include program operations and program side effects. Outcome variables include progress toward goals, maintenance of program change, adaption and adoption by others. These variables may be related to one another through causal modeling techniques (Cooley et al., 1981).

Causal modeling allows for the investigation of causal influences on student outcomes that are not manipulated experimentally (Bergan, Feld, & Stone, 1984). This approach involves the modeling of causal relations between explanatory and dependent variables through the application of structural equation techniques (see Bentler, 1980; Goodman, 1973; Joreskog & Sorbom, 1979). Explanatory variables may include those subject to experimental manipulation as well as those not subject to such manipulation. For example, a causal analysis might include an assessment of the effects of student background variables (e.g., socioeconomic status) on student performance on achievement tests.

Cooley et al. (1981) developed a multilevel approach to causal modeling that may be applied to the evaluation of the effects of educational services/programs. They note that causal influences may occur at different levels within the school setting. For example, operations that occur at the administrative level of the school, such as budget and resource allocations, generally do not affect student performance directly, but they do affect such classroom variables as class size, teacher qualifications, and instructional content. What goes on at the administrative level in terms of decisions concerning resource input variables may affect process variables. Process variables, in turn, influence outcomes. The availability of teacher aides, for example, may influence the proportion of skills that are targeted for instruction and that have been taught.

The causal modeling approach has been shown to be a useful tool for evaluating the effects of educational programs on student outcomes and the relative influence of various factors that are assumed to influence these outcomes. For example, the causal modeling approach has successfully been applied to assess program effects in the Head Start Organization (Bergan et al., 1984). There is an abundance of evidence that the Head Start instructional program has positive effects on children's general cognitive and social development (Collins, 1983). Examination of program effects involving the *Head Start Measures Battery* affords the opportunity to examine the relation between various aspects of instruction and specific areas of competence targeted for instruction in Head Start. Information about program effects on specific competency areas provides a useful program management tool, making it possible to link instructional planning to the specific developmental achievements of children. In addition to providing useful information about instructional influences on achievement, the analysis of program effects provides the basis for determining instructional influences on achievement on a continuous basis, guiding the management of instruction.

The causal modeling approach applied to the evaluation of educational services has two attractive features. First, the fact that causal modeling does not require experimental manipulation makes it possible for the program evaluator to investigate variables that either cannot or may not be convenient to manipulate experimentally. For example, in evaluating a remedial reading program, it would most likely not be practical or advisable to systematically vary the proportion of skills taught across resource classrooms. Yet, it may well be of interest to have some indication of the effects of this variable on student performance. Second, the multilevel character of this approach encourages evaluation that interrelates effects occurring at different levels in the educational system. Such interrelationships are essential to effective decision-making and program management activities.

Systematically evaluating the causal relation between explanatory and dependent variables may provide the program evaluator with a major source of information concerning the effects of educational programs and services. Moreover, this approach can facilitate efficient data collection procedures during the input, process, and outcome stages of educational programs. Finally, this approach is useful in identifying variables that may facilitate the effectiveness of educational programs in enhancing student progress.

The Path-Referenced Approach to Program Evaluation

As mentioned above, a major goal of evaluation services is to provide educational and psychological professionals with information that is useful in decision-making activities and in the management of learning environments. Effective learning requires effective instructional management. School administrators are often regarded as being most directly involved in management activities, but it is important to note that teachers may also be thought of as instructional managers (Berliner, 1983). The heart of management is decision making, and teachers are constantly engaged in decision-making activities (Salmon-Cox, 1980). Moreover, the nature of teacher decisions may have a profound effect on learning.

The effectiveness of instructional management is necessarily limited by the types of information provided by assessment and evaluation procedures used by the teacher in making instructional decisions. School personnel have sought three kinds of information from assessment to determine student needs for program development activities: Information on the relative standing of students in norm groups, information about the specific instructional objectives that students have mastered, and information about the progress that students have made as a result of instructional and service programs. Traditionally, norm-referenced assessment has provided the schools with information about relative standing. Criterion-referenced assessment has traditionally afforded information about the mastery of objectives (Cancelli & Kratochwill, 1981). However, until recently there has been no adequate procedure for assessing student progress. Progress assessment is essential to effective decision making and management activities for existing educational programs and services and for new programs and services. In this sense, one of the most fundamental questions involved in evaluating school psychological and educational services is that of determining the effects of these services on student progress.

What is required then is a data-based assessment system that is perceived by teachers as providing *useful* information on students' skills so that decision making can occur. Moreover, a set of procedures is required that *relate* assessment information to the instructional decision-making process.

Path-referenced techniques (Bergan, 1981) were established to provide an effective way to determine progress along empirically validated learning paths reflecting development. The path-referenced approach to assessment is particularly well-suited for use in the evaluation of educational programs. A fundamental issue in evaluating the effects of educational programs is that of determining changes that can be attributed to those programs. In this sense, assessment focusing on the kinds of skill possessed by children may be particularly useful in instructional decision making. The teacher who has an in-depth knowledge of children's skills is in a better position to guide instruction and forestall future problems than one who does not. Consequently, decisions regarding the instructional needs of students ought to include a consideration of objective data on children's learning and achievements. Moreover, the incorporation of path-referenced technology into consultation services may be used as an effective means for bringing assessment information to bear on instructional decision making (Feld, Bergan, & Stone, in press).

Path-referenced technology is intended to serve as a tool for the development and management of educational services. Path-referenced technology provides a perspective that links educational decisions to information about the organization of learning environments and change in student knowledge. In the path-referenced approach information about current student status is tied both to possible future achievement and to past accomplishment in order to facilitate the assessment of change. This dynamic view relates educational program development and decision making to the fundamental goal of enhancing student progress (Feld et al., in press).

Recent applications of path-referenced assessment in consultation serve to demonstrate how path-referenced technology can provide an innovative way of evaluating psychological and educational services in the schools. The following example illustrates this point.

The Center for Educational Evaluation and Measurement in the College of Education at the University of Arizona has completed a project for the Head Start organization that illustrates the use of assessment in instructional management and the role that consultation may play in relating assessment to instructional decision making (Bergan et al., 1984). The project called for the construction of developmental measures for use in instructional management in Head Start. Consultation technology was used to apply the measures in instructional management. The measures project eventuated in the production of the *Head Start Measures Battery,* which is composed of six scales (Language, Math, Nature & Science, Perception, Reading, and Social Development) designed to assess children's cognitive and social competencies.

These measures are based on a path-referenced approach to assessment (Bergan, 1981; Bergan, Stone, & Feld, in press) in which child performance is referenced to positions in empirically validated developmental sequences. Path-referencing is particularly useful for evaluating educational services and facilitating instructional management because the information provided by path-referenced assessment indicates what a child or a group of children has accomplished and what new learning challenges lie ahead. This tie relates instructional decisions to what the child has accomplished and to the direction to be taken by the teacher to promote further growth.

Path-referenced assessment instruments such as the *Head Start Measures Battery* and recording devices such as the planning guides provide the tools by which evaluation services such as consultation may achieve the goals of instructional management. Path-referenced instruments afford a means for placing teaching level, planning level, and developmental level on the same scale. Consequently, the consultant and consultee are in a position to make a *direct* comparison between each of these vital components as they relate to the management of instruction.

The teaching and planning information obtained from planning guides can be used with the assessment information obtained from path-referenced instruments to guide the consultation process. This information is used during the identification of learning needs for determining whether there is an incongruence between the child's developmental level, the teaching level, and the planning level for instruction.

Path-referenced instruments provide information about a child's developmental level by way of path scores and path profiles. Path scores and path profiles can be used in consultation for identifying needs, planning instructional content, and evaluating the extent to which the goals of instructional management have been achieved. A path score represents the child's position in a developmental path. It describes the child's overall level of performance in each content area that is being assessed with path-referenced devices and, in addition, generates a profile of the child's level of competence (i.e., the level of mastery for specific skills in terms of the percentage of time that a child will accurately perform a specified set of tasks representing a skill). The profile provides the teacher with an indication of what types of learning activities should be challenging for the child, at his/her current level of development, and what activities are probably still too difficult for the child.

Path scores are designed to provide the teacher with information about developmental levels that can be combined with information provided by behavioral assessment strategies to arrive at an appropriate level of classroom planning and opportunities to learn new skills. For example, the teacher using path scores may decide to provide instruction at the current developmental level of the child or slightly above it in order to challenge the child. On the other hand, there may be instances in which it seems advisable to provide the child with immediate success by focusing on skills somewhat below the current level of functioning.

When a child is having difficulty mastering a particular skill, path score information may be used to identify subordinate skills that the child may not possess and that may affect mastery of the skill in question. Characteristics of instruction may then be directed toward the mastery of these subordinate skills.

Developmental level, planning level, and teaching level are not only useful in needs identification and instructional analysis and planning; they can also be used in instructional evaluation. A major goal in instructional evaluation is the determination of the level of goal attainment. This can be achieved through a comparison between planning level and teaching level and a comparison between teaching level and developmental level.

Planning level and teaching level should be approximately the same. If planning level is much higher than teaching level, then many skills have been planned for instruction but have not been taught. If planning level is substantially lower than teaching level, skills have been taught that were not targeted for instruction. These discrepancies signal the need to go back to the instructional analysis phase of consultation to determine the source of the discrepancy. The analysis will indicate one of two possible courses of action. One is to revise what is planned for instruction during the next needs identification phase of consultation. The other is to engage in an effort to make planning level and teaching level more congruent.

The second comparison that is made in evaluating the level of goal attainment is the congruence between teaching level and developmental level. Teaching level should be approximately the same as developmental level. When teaching level is substantially higher than developmental level, large numbers of skills are being taught that children are not learning. This suggests either that the skills are too difficult for the children or that the instructional procedures are not effective in promoting skill acquisition.

When teaching level is well below developmental level, the children are not being challenged in the content area under consideration. This suggests a need to examine the goals of instruction reflected in teacher plans. For example, it may be that a teacher would underestimate the learning capabilities of the children in the class. Under these circumstances, the teacher would probably want to revise instructional plans to increase planning and teaching level.

The Synoptic Evaluation Framework

Maher (1978) developed the Synoptic Evaluation Framework (SEF) as a model that can be applied to design school evaluation studies. The model conceptualizes evaluation as an information gathering and reporting process to assist in decision making relative to a range of school programmatic units (Maher, 1978). Maher points out that this framework has been successfully applied in evaluation efforts for group counseling programs, supplemental instructional programs, the design of alternative school programs for socially maladjusted adolescents, the needs and goals of a pupil personnel delivery system, and the management performance of school districts. The SEF consists of an *Evaluation Unit, Evaluation Purpose,* and an *Evaluation Service.*

The Evaluation Unit. The Evaluation Unit provides a means for identifying the program or service and for specifying input processes and outcome variables. The Evaluation Unit consists of three levels on which evaluation can focus: the individual level, the group level, and the organizational level. At each of these levels evaluation may focus on program or services. At the individual level, evaluation may focus on programs designed in response to individual needs or on a service delivered by a service provider to clients (e.g., an individual therapy program). At the group level, evaluation may focus on programs for groups of clients (e.g., group counseling) or on services delivered by a group service provider (e.g., a psychoeducational clinic). At the organizational level evaluation may focus on programs within organizational structures (e.g., vocational training programs) or on service delivery systems (e.g., guidance departments in a school district).

The Evaluation Purpose. The Evaluation Purpose involves three types of evaluation strategies that allow the evaluator to design studies based on the needs of decision makers. The three types of evaluation strategies are development evaluation, implementation evaluation, and outcome evaluation.

Development evaluation occurs when a program or service is in an initial planning stage. The focus in this type of evaluation is on programmatic input. Program development or formative evaluation (Scriven, 1967) may be conducted through a needs assessment (Maher & Kratochwill, 1980), which is implemented to identify the needs of a client or group of clients and to prioritize those needs. A needs assessment involves several questions that the psychologist must ask: What is the extent of need for the development of a new program or service; where do the needs of the client(s) exist; is the program or service an appropriate approach for addressing the identified needs of the client(s); are the goals of the program or service appropriate given the identified needs; are the methods and materials suggested for use in the program or service appropriate; what kind of staffing is required to implement the program or service; what type of funding will be necessary; are there other programs or services already being provided to the client(s); can the development of the program be justified in terms of its cost-effectiveness and cost benefit (Maher & Kratochwill, 1980)?

A needs assessment can be conducted on individuals or groups for the purpose of individual, group, or organizational program or service development. Needs can be measured by objective means such as standardized tests (e.g., achievement tests or psychological batteries), observational techniques, school records, and by subjective means such as asking clients (e.g., teachers or administrators) where a need exists. Whatever the measurement strategy, however, a value judgment is necessary, an acceptable level of performance must be established, and a rating of the degree of need that exists must be established (Maher & Kratochwill, 1980).

Implementation evaluation is carried out for the purpose of deciding whether or not to modify a psychological or educational program or service. The evaluative concern in implementation evaluation is with program process variables (Maher, 1978). Here, the program evaluator may assist the decision maker by obtaining information that addresses evaluation issues in the service of program modification (Maher, 1978; Maher & Kratochwill, 1980). The evaluator should address several questions in helping the decision maker to modify a program or service. The questions to be addressed include the following: Has instructional staff been able to apply the components of the program in a manner consistent with the principles outlined in the procedures for implementing the program; have the students been active in the program or service on a regular basis; are the individuals concerned with the program or service satisfied with the procedures that are being implemented; are concerned individuals being provided with feedback about the progress of the students involved in the program or service? Implementation evaluation, also known as process evaluation (Stufflebeam et al., 1971) is implemented to answer these questions.

In conducting an implementation or process evaluation, several factors must be considered by the evaluator. First, evaluation activities must focus on program or service processes, and not on the progress of clients toward specified goals. Second, the essential defining properties of the program or service must be determined, including knowledge of how they operate, so that a degree of reliability can be obtained on their operations. Four major benefits can be derived from this form of evaluation (Maher & Kratochwill, 1980). First, information on whether the program or service was actually implemented as planned would be important to policy makers, program or service managers, and funding agencies. This is especially important with regard to program validation and in decisions about program dissemination and generalizability. Second, evaluation information can be useful in explaining why a program has failed to reach its goals. Third, this form of evaluation allows the evaluator to examine the interrelationships between program outcomes and program processes. Fourth, implementation evaluation can provide information about possible side effects of the service or program that can lead to program modification procedures.

Implementation or process evaluation can also be used to assess the variables of program or service operation, personnel, and context (Freeman, 1977). Several questions can be asked to assess these variables (Maher & Kratochwill, 1980). When assessing operations the evaluator may ask, Are the proposed materials being applied by program staff in the appropriate manner? Are clients (e.g., students) actively participating in the program? What negative side effects seem to occur as a result of the program? When assessing personnel the evaluator may ask, Are staff and consultants engaging in the activities prescribed by the service or program? Are clients responding to staff and activities as expected? What negative side effects are related to the staff? When assessing context the evaluator may ask, If any structural changes occurred in the program or service, do these changes suggest a need to implement modification of the program or service?

Outcome or summative evaluation (Scriven, 1967) allows judgments to be made about program validity, including experimental validity, social validity, and program goal attainment. Experimental and social validity are important in outcome evaluation since each provides the evaluator, decision maker, and program or service manager with a different perspective about the program or service (Abt, 1977). Goal attainment systems provide a systematic measurement approach for determining the extent to which goals have been attained. (For a complete description of various goal attainment systems, see Lloyd, 1983.) Outcome evaluation provides information for use in determining the degree to which program or service goals have been attained, the effectiveness of the program or service relative to other programs and services targeted at the same goals, and how well the program or service maintains the desired change after termination. Outcome evaluation information may be used to assist in making decisions regarding program revision or termination as well as decisions regarding program dissemination. To the extent that goals and indicators of those goals are made explicit and that data are collected on progress toward those goals, the following questions can be answered: To what degree have the program or service goals been attained; how confident are we that change has resulted from implementation of the program or service? The first question is answered if program or service goals have been clearly operationalized and if data have been collected throughout implementation. The second question requires the use of experimental controls that are not always possible in program or service environments. Thus, evaluation methods not necessarily contingent upon these controls need to be implemented. Time series designs (see Kratochwill, 1978; Kratochwill & Bergan, 1978), to be discussed later in this chapter, may be applied for estimating the extent to which the program or service has produced change.

Evaluation Service. Evaluation Service involves the types of studies that are provided for evaluation recipients (Maher, 1978). An evaluation effort responsive to the concerns of recipients must include studies about the design of the evaluation, the conduct of the evaluation, and the dissemination of the evaluation results.

The design of the evaluation is a cooperative effort between the evaluator and decision maker designed to clarify the purpose of the evaluation and design activities to respond to the purpose (Maher, 1978). This component involves specifying the evaluation purpose and evaluation unit, delineating the evaluation questions, and agreeing upon an evaluation design for collecting and reporting evaluation information. The conduct of the evaluation is concerned with devising a well-designed study through the implementation of evaluation activities established in the evaluation design. This component involves identifying operational considerations, ensuring adequate data collection procedures, and analyzing and interpreting data. Dissemination of evaluation results involves reporting the results of the evaluative effort. This component involves drawing appropriate conclusions, determining reporting formats, and reporting the information in a timely manner to decision makers and program and service managers.

The Consultation Model

Consultation can be used as a conceptual format for the conduct of program evaluation/research (Kratochwill & Bergan, 1978). Program evaluation should focus on two general issues: Have the goals of the program been achieved, and have the plans implemented to achieve these goals been effective (Bergan, 1977)? Evaluation information regarding the first question guides decision making for purposes of immediate program/service modification and management. Evaluation information regarding the second question guides future planning including the development of new programs or services. In this sense, program or service evaluation may be conceived as a problem-solving process through which psychologists, along with educators and administrators engaged in program evaluation activities, make decisions that guide the direction of psychological and related educational services.

The problem-solving approach applied to program evaluation may occur at both the classroom level and the administrative level in educational settings. Effective programming eventuating in desired outcomes for students involves coordinated activites among administrators, teachers, and support personnel in the school. For example, some evidence indicates that the way in which school principals work with teachers has a significant effect on learning (Fullan, 1981). The problem-solving model to be presented here is an adaptation of the four-stage Consultation Model developed by Bergan (1977) and expanded by Bergan and Kratochwill (in press). The four stages include problem identification, problem analysis, treatment implementation, and treatment evaluation. Each of these components may be applied to a greater or lesser extent to the several types of program management decisions that are served by program evaluation. These decisions include program development decisions, program modification decisions, and program outcome decisions (Maher & Kratochwill, 1980). The problem-solving approach provides a comprehensive system for the development and evaluation of programs and services while facilitating the types of decisions specified above.

Problem Identification. The first phase in the problem-solving process is problem identification and involves the specification of goals and objectives of a psychological or educational program/service and the assessment of the performance of clients (e.g., individuals, classes, districts) in the program/service with respect to established goals and objectives. For example, in providing educational services the fundamental problem is to find ways to assist students to move from their current level of performance to a level reflecting mastery of instructional content. The articulation of planning, goals, and objectives achieved through problem identification needs assessment (Maher & Kratochwill, 1980) and path-referenced technology (Bergan, 1981) will enhance the probability that program development decisions result in producing the outcome effect for which the program was designed. Evaluation for program/service development is composed of a series of steps to produce several outcomes. In designing an educational program, the first outcome is the formulation of goals and objectives articulated to plans specifying the content of instruction in a way that reflects the structure of knowledge in the subject matter under consideration and the needs of clients. The second is the collection of data related to the goals and objectives of the program to be developed or the program to be evaluated in terms of its present effects. The third is the determination of the difference between current and desired performance level of the students. These steps may be applied to the planning or evaluation of any psychological program/service in the same manner as provided by this example.

Problem Analysis. Problem analysis for the purpose of evaluating psychological and related educational service/programs is composed of two kinds of activities. Continuing to use an educational program as an example, the first involves analyzing the instructional content and student and environmental characteristics to determine factors believed to influence social and educational progress. The second consists of formulating plans utilizing hypothesized influential factors to promote learning. Problem analysis for evaluation and decision-making activities begins with the planning of specific activities articulated to the long-range planning carried out at the beginning of the school year. Environmental factors considered in the generation of activity plans include available materials, personnel, available time and funding, and instructional methods. These factors are among those used in constructing activities in a way intended to ensure that the program will operate in an orderly fashion and that the general outcomes specified in problem identification will be achieved. A major benefit of the data-based approach (Bergan et al., 1984) to program development and program evaluation is that it provides increased opportunities for school personnel to use information about the skills of individual students in program planning. For example, path-referenced assessment information on the sequencing of skills affords information on the position of each student in learning sequences that have been targeted for instruction as part of a program. This information can be related to data on the skill level being taught. If instruction is well in advance of the level at which the student is functioning, or if it is well below the student's current level, plans may be made to make appropriate adjustments in program content. It will also be necessary to conduct a detailed functional analysis of the instructional environment or of student and teacher behavior as a basis for the generation of treatment outcomes. It will also be beneficial to examine environmental and/or instructional characteristics to determine new ways to promote learning.

Problem analysis is also made up of an examination of resources that may affect the implementation of psychological or educational programs/services. This examination should be a joint effort of the program evaluator, teacher, and administrator. This analysis is followed by the formulation of plans to make needed resources available to promote the achievement of program goals.

Time is an important variable to consider with respect to ensuring that an adequate proportion of goal-related skills are planned and actually implemented. A number of time variables may be considered in problem analysis (Bergan et al., 1984). Among the more important is the amount of time allocated for implementation of the program or service. If allocated time is too low, the proportion of skills to be taught or the proportion of services to be rendered will necessarily be too low. The time that students actually engage in tasks appropriate to program or service is a second variable that may be important in program analysis. For example, research has indicated strong relations between allocated and engaged time and achievement outcomes (Fisher et al., 1980). Another variable of importance in problem analysis is the amount of time that an individual student participated in the instructional program. For example, some school systems are faced with extremely high student turnover. As a result, students may be available for psychological or educational services for only a short period of time.

Personnel is another type of resource that may be considered in problem analysis. Personnel issues that may be considered include the training of personnel, and the numbers and types of personnel available to pursue program goals.

Treatment Implementation. During treatment implementation, the plans formulated in problem analysis are put into effect and monitored. Two major types of activities occur during the process of plan implementation. The first of these is preparation for implementation. The initial preparation activity is that of assigning implementation roles. Decisions must be made as to who will direct the implementation, who will execute it, and who will collect the necessary data to ensure adequate monitoring of the operation of the plan. The second major activity is that of operating the implementation plan. Operation includes not only putting the program into effect, but also monitoring the implementation and revising it when required. The role of the program evaluator in this phase comes about when departures from expectations about the program trigger the need for reflective decision making that involves one or more revisions of the plan (Shavelson & Stern, 1981). At this point, program modification decisions may be made.

Treatment Evaluation. Treatment evaluation is initiated to determine the extent of goal attainment and plan effectiveness. Problem evaluation for program or service evaluation focuses on two questions: Have the goals of the program been achieved, and have the plans implemented been effective? If the goals of the program have been attained, then the problem-solving process is complete. In this case, the evaluator may suggest termination of the program as well as suggest that the program be applied to other similar clients. For example, if the service provided has been a remedial reading program, a decision may be made to implement this program with a group of students that have similar reading problems. If the goals of the program have not been achieved, then the problem-solving process may move back to problem analysis so that the original plan may be revised or a new plan considered. In some cases even after one or more programs have been implemented, there may still be no progress toward goal attainment. Under these conditions the program may be terminated or the program evaluator along with teachers and administrators may go back to problem identification.

The evaluation of plan effectiveness is implemented to establish the utility of the program for future use. The central tasks to be accomplished in carrying out an evaluation of effectiveness are to select and implement appropriate evaluation designs. Time series designs are often useful in establishing plan effectiveness for individual student programs. The designs that can be used in the determination of plan effectiveness have been described by Kratochwill (1978) and are reviewed later in this chapter.

TYPES OF RESEARCH/PROGRAM EVALUATION STRATEGIES

Several different types of research strategies can be employed in the evaluation of school psychological services. Sometimes program evaluators will be able to conduct well-controlled experimental investigations to evaluate a program. However, in applied settings this is usually difficult and often compromises must be made. The choice of a particular methodology depends on the level of program services being evaluated, resources available, and questions of interest to the investigator, among other features. In this section of the chapter, we provide a framework for consideration of various research/program evaluation strategies including research review/analysis procedures and historical, descriptive, passive observational, and experimentally oriented investigations.

Each of these types of methodologies is discussed within the context of research in consultation. Currently, in the school psychology literature four models or approaches to consultation have developed including mental health consultation (e.g., Caplan, 1970; Meyers, Parsons, & Martin, 1979), organization development (e.g., Schmuck, 1982), problem-centered consultation (Gutkin & Curtis, 1982), and behavioral consultation (Bergan, 1977; Bergan & Kratochwill, in press). Although we illustrate several methodological approaches through examples across various consultation approaches, the specific limitations of a certain study should not be perceived as a limitation of a particular consultation model generally. Readers interested in specific reviews of the consultation outcome research literature should examine the various articles available (e.g., Alpert & Yammer, 1983; Gutkin & Curtis, 1982; Medway, 1979; Van Someren & Kratochwill, 1983).

Literature Reviews

A research method that has an important, but often overlooked, contribution to make to our understanding of the knowledge base in school psychology is the literature review. Most of the journals in the school psychology field publish literature reviews in which individual empirical studies are reviewed and conclusions are drawn regarding what is known in the area and what directions might be pursued for research and practice. A major problem with the traditional literature review is the reliability of conclusions that are reached from the articles reviewed. Basically, different individuals reach different conclusions after reviewing the same literature. However, the problem with traditional literature reviews extends beyond this concern and includes potential problems of imprecision, subjectivity and bias, and omission of important information from the studies being researched (Glass, 1976).

A number of strategies have been proposed to overcome some of the problems associated with traditional literature reviews. For example, scientific guidelines have been proposed for conducting integrative research reviews (e.g., Cooper, 1982). A major contribution to conducting a literature review, however, is the development of meta-analysis (e.g., Glass, 1976, 1977; Glass, McGaw, & Smith, 1981). Meta-analysis is a quantitatively based procedure that actually consists of a variety of techniques for combining probabilities across studies, estimating average effect size across individual studies, determining the stability of results, and locating factors that moderate outcomes of separate studies (Strube & Hartmann, 1983).

Meta-analytic procedures are gaining wide appeal in psychology and education. In the area of school consultation it has been argued (Medway, 1982) that meta-analysis would be a desirable tool for the conduct of further literature reviews on consultation effectiveness. As an example study in one area, Carlberg and Kavale (1980) studied the efficiency of special versus regular class placement for exceptional children using meta-analysis strategies. The authors identified 50 primary research studies of special versus regular class placement for use in their study. The authors argued that "no confident conclusion about the relative superiority of special versus regular class placement can be drawn from simple inspection of empirical findings" (p. 297). To answer the question of whether special versus regular class placement was effective, an effect size (ES) was calculated. The ES was defined as the posttreatment difference between special and regular placement means expressed in standard deviation units. The ES was used as a dependent variable in order to assess the effects of independent variables including placement, type of outcome measure, internal validity, and several other variables.

Based on their meta-analysis, the authors found special classes significantly inferior to regular class placement for students with below average IQs, and significantly superior to regular classes for behaviorally disordered, emotionally disturbed, and learning-disabled children. Moreover, other independent variables had a significant relationship to ES. The authors suggest that the recent trend toward mainstreaming by placing/keeping children in regular classrooms may not be appropriate for certain children.

As their study illustrates, meta-analysis can make an important contribution in drawing conclusions from a body of literature. However, meta-analysis raises special concerns that must be considered in use of the technique (Cook & Leviton, 1980; Kazdin & Wilson, 1978; Leviton & Cook, 1981; Rachman & Wilson, 1980; Strube & Hartmann, 1982, 1983). A recent series of articles in the *Journal of Consulting and Clinical Psychology* also provides an overview of the issues surrounding the application of meta-analysis in psychotherapy research (Fiske, 1983; Glass & Kliegl, 1983; Mintz, 1983; Rosenthal, 1983; Shapiro & Shapiro, 1983; Strube & Hartmann, 1983; Wilson & Rachman, 1983). Although these issues are not discussed in any detail here, a list of the most salient considerations is noteworthy. First, there is the potential bias resulting in the studies chosen to be included in a meta-analysis. Thus, a researcher might regard some studies as meeting criteria for inclusion whereas others might not consider the studies as relevant. Second, and related to the first issue, is that some meta-analytic techniques rule out certain forms of methodology such as single-case research designs. Third, the results from individual studies are aggregated and may not represent individual studies where the usual statistical assumptions are met. Fourth, the reporting of results from individual studies may be selective in that positive results supporting a hypothesis might be emphasized. Related to this concern is the potential problem that occurs when dependent outcome variables are used that vary widely in quality. For example, some outcome measures that have been gathered by observers may have no controls for bias, drift, reliability, and a host of factors known to influence their quality. Sixth, conditions being compared in the meta-analysis (i.e., experimental and control groups) are sometimes not well-specified, and therefore, it is unclear what is being compared. For example, in the Carlberg and Kavale (1980) study, special versus regular class placement was being compared. However, in individual studies, it is very likely that "special" services varied widely and therefore such services were not uniform across individual subjects. Finally, a large number of methodological and statistical criteria must be used in the meta-analysis. For example, meta-analysis involves statistical procedures that fall under two general domains (Strube & Hartmann, 1983): (a) combination of significance levels, and (b) combination of effect sizes.

Meta-analysis will continue to be a popular method of conducting a literature/research review. However, it is apparent that a growing number of methodological, conceptual, and statistical issues must be considered in use of the procedure. Although we believe that meta-analysis represents an important advance in research reviews, the limitations of the procedures have not been completely disseminated or elucidated for application in applied fields.

Historical Research/Evaluation

Sometimes the research/program evaluator is interested in analyzing past events or drawing inferences from data that already exist. In this type of investigation, called historical research, the primary focus is on drawing implications from data that exist as part of an institution or agency (e.g., school, clinic) or among members who are part of the system. An example of a historical evaluation is a project reported by Ritter (1978) in which the effects of a school consultation program were reviewed through an analysis of referral patterns of teachers over a 7-year period. A school consultation program was established in 1969 with the focus of service being on eight elementary schools (grades K through 6). The approach involved direct consultation with the teacher to improve the school functioning of the children referred for learning and behavior problems. The effectiveness of the consultation program was examined through an analysis of referral patterns over the years 1969 to 1975. Ritter (1978) hypothesized that if consultation services were effective, the number of children referred by teachers would decrease.

Data were presented demonstrating that the referrals decreased over the time period examined, possibly suggesting that consultation benefited the teachers in developing their own skills in dealing with the children's problems. However, Ritter (1978) appropriately noted that several alternative hypotheses might account for the decreasing referral patterns, including the possibility of decreasing enrollment, reduced class size, and increased availability of alternative resources. Although these possiblities were eliminated, this historical research project provides relatively weak inference for the effect of consultation services. Only more well-controlled historical research would allow the research hypothesis to be tested adequately.

This example of historical research shows how program evaluators can obtain data related to the past activities in a public school setting. Obviously the data could be obtained in other ways. For example, historical data could be obtained by examining children's academic performance or evaluations of teacher performance ratings. Nevertheless, none of these data provide strong inference for the effects of consultation services.

Descriptive Survey Investigation

Descriptive investigation involves an evaluation of the current status of some activity or event. In this type of research/program evaluation, the investigator might use techniques such as interviews, questionnaires, checklists, or direct observation to obtain data. One of the more common forms of descriptive investigation involves the survey. Surveys can often be conducted within a school psychologist's district to evaluate various perspectives, such as degree of satisfaction individuals might have of the services rendered. For example, Ford and Migles (1979) surveyed 150 teachers from five schools in the De La Warr School District in New Castle, Delaware, concerning the importance of 12 potential roles for school psychologists (e.g., screening students, counseling, case or program consultation, community liaison, psychodiagnostics). An existing questionnaire (i.e., Sandoval & Lambert, 1977) was modified and consisted of 12 paragraph-long descriptions of school psychologist's roles (e.g., "the school psychologist conducts personal and professional development workshops for teachers and serves as a resource person and facilitator at teacher staff meetings" [p. 373]). The respondents were asked how valuable the services were to them as teachers from *unimportant* to *very important* (on a 5-point scale). Results of this evaluation indicated direct and remedial services that did not require school psychologists to intrude on a teacher's prerogative were the most valuable. Remedial case consultation (i.e., collaboration with the teacher on program remedial procedures for pupils) received a mean teacher rating of 3.75. Teachers who reported using "open education" methods were more likely to value indirect, preventative, and collaborative school psychology services than their colleagues. The authors also found that grade level taught, gender, experience, and teaching speciality had virtually no effect on the respondents' ratings of the school psychologist's role.

This survey shows how an investigator might evaluate the current status of a particular issue or concern. However, a number of factors play a role in drawing valid inferences from this type of evaluation. A first consideration is sampling characteristics. In this type of investigation, the researcher is drawing inferences concerning the population within the school district being sampled. Generally, no attempt is made to make inferences beyond the characteristics of the population involved since the investigation focused specifically on an individual district. Another issue related to this is how representative the sample is of the individuals in the district. Here the researcher must be concerned about the return rate or the number of people participating. Another concern is the instrument that was used, because it has a bearing on the quality of data that are produced. In this case the investigator modified an already existing instrument to conduct the program evaluation. Finally, there might be bias in the data in terms of the way it is interpreted or the way the individuals sent out the survey. Attempts must still be made to reduce various sources of artifact and bias in survey methods (Rossi, Freeman, & Wright, 1979).

Passive Observational Investigation

In many instances a researcher must employ a passive observational methodology (sometimes referred to as correlational or ex post facto investigation). In this type of investigation, evaluation occurs on variables that are not directly manipulated by the researcher. Thus, there is no direct manipulation of an independent variable as might occur in experimental research. Typically, passive-observational strategies can be used to investigate hypothesis that can later be confirmed through direct experimental manipulation (Cook & Campbell, 1979).

Passive-observational strategies actually can include a number of different types of investigations. The most common form involves a study in which an investigator is trying to determine relations among variables, such as intelligence and achievement, or personality characteristics and intelligence. In another form of investigation a researcher may explore differences among existing groups such as learning-disabled and behavior-disordered students and children in regular classrooms. In both types of investigations the variables already exist and there is an attempt to describe the characteristics or relations among the variables.

An example of the passive observational strategy in research on consultation occurs in a study by Bergan and Tombari (1976) who investigated behavioral consultation services rendered by school psychologists to teachers. The study examined the predictive power of measures of consultant efficiency (i.e., average time from referral to the initial interview and psychologist case load), skill in applying psychological principles (e.g., modeling, prompting), and interviewing skill (i.e., message content, message process, and message control). Results of the study indicated that the predictor variables exerted maximum impact on the initial problem identification phase of the consultation process. Consultants who lacked skills failed to identify consultee problems and, consequently, never reached treatment development and implementation. Moreover, consultants successful in problem identification generally solved the referred problem through consultation with the teacher.

It is important to emphasize that causal interpretations cannot be made from passive observational research. Passive observational research does not allow the investigator to have the usual controls that characterize more well controlled experimental research (e.g., random assignment of subjects to treatment conditions, manipulations of a variable, etc.). Nevertheless, passive observational methods present the researcher with an option to investigate variables that cannot be manipulated directly. They also allow investigators to draw relations between variables that already exist, as was the case in the Bergan and Tombari (1976) study.

Preexperimental Case Studies

Although a number of research strategies are used to evaluate the effectiveness of school psychological services, case study investigation continues to occupy a prominent role in school psychology (Kratochwill, 1985). In the consultation research area, case studies have been employed across the various models of consultation (Albert & Yammer, 1983; Van Someren & Kratochwill, 1983). Case study research is sometimes subsumed under the rubric of single-case research design or time-series investigation (discussed in more detail below). However, case studies can be distinguished from more well controlled single-case time-series investigation on both methodological and conceptual grounds (Kazdin, 1981; Kratochwill, 1979). Generally, case study investigation is characterized by the absence of most, if not all, experimental controls considered essential to drawing valid inferences in experimental research. Case study investigation takes many forms, such as anecdotal descriptions of client characteristics and narrative accounts of treatment and treatment outcome. Some case studies employ preexperimental designs (e.g., A/B), but the common element across these investigations is the rather low level of experimental control (i.e., the inability to rule out threats to internal validity).

An example of a case study investigation in the consultation field will help elucidate the contributions this method makes to scientific knowledge. Gresham and Nagle (1981) reported the treatment of a case of school phobia using a behavioral consultation format. A problem identification and analysis interview (Bergan, 1977) was conducted to (a) establish a precise description of a "school phobic" girl's behavior of concern to the teacher, (b) obtain a description of antecedent, consequent, and sequential conditions of the behaviors, and (c) determine the severity of the problem. The teacher reported that the child's behavior consisted of crying, screaming, whining, and running out of the room.

The treatment procedure consisted of a mild time-out procedure that involved placing the child in a corner of the classroom, contingent upon crying and whining. The child could leave the time-out area whenever she stopped crying and whining. When she returned to the classroom group a differential reinforcement of other behavior (DRO) procedure was employed (i.e., positive behaviors were reinforced). Thus, the intervention contained two active components.

Results reported in Fig. 10.1 demonstrate that crying and whining behavior were reduced to zero levels during the intervention phase. Moreover, the follow-up suggested maintenance of the treatment outcome.

Case study investigations, such as the one described above in the consultation field, have been important to the development of knowledge in school psychology for several reasons. First, case study research allows for some degree of evaluation of the case by researchers in applied or clinical settings. Second, clinicians/researchers often encounter relatively rare clinical cases that could not be investigated through other more well controlled methods of investigation such as single-case time-series studies or group research strategies. Third, case study investigations also provide an alternative to group research designs because of the ethical and legal barriers that the investigator faces with these strategies. Finally, case study methods have provided an option for practitioners to be involved in research. Generally, case studies do not necessitate the usual kinds of restrictions that other forms of investigation involve in practice (Kazdin, 1981).

Although the usual case study does not allow the same degree of inference in drawing conclusions from the data that a more well controlled experiment would provide, methods have been recommended to improve the usual intervention

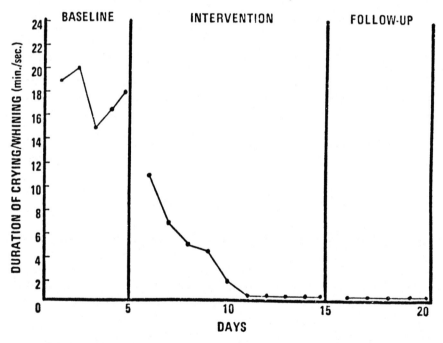

FIG. 10.1 The duration of crying/whining behavior in minutes and seconds as a function of design phase. From "Treating school phobia using behavioral consultation: A case study" by F. M. Gresham & R. J. Nagle, 1981, *School Psychology Review, 10,* 104–107. Reprinted by permission.

case study (Kazdin, 1981, 1982a; Kratochwill, 1985). Among the more important factors that can improve case studies are (a) the use of objective assessment strategies, (b) frequent and repeated measurement, (c) establishment of the stability of the problem/disorder and previous treatment over extended time periods, (d) application of treatments that have an immediate and large impact, and (e) replication of results across heterogeneous subjects (Kazdin, 1981). For example, the Gresham and Nagle (1981) study generally met these criteria, with the exception of replication of the intervention. Moreover, the case employed reliability assessment and follow-up, two factors that can further increase valid inferences in a case study investigation (Kratochwill, 1985).

Quasi-Experimental Research/Evaluation

Quasi-experimental research designs have been used relatively often in evaluation of school psychological services. These procedures usually involve many of the characteristics of true experiments, such as manipulation of an independent variable and measurement of various dependent variables. Nevertheless, one essential aspect of these research procedures that relegates them to a quasi-experimental status is that randomization is not used to form the groups or conditions being compared (Cook & Campbell, 1979). Although randomization is not used to improve inferences, the researcher can employ criteria similar to those used to improve case study research described above.

Within the general rubric of quasi-experimental procedures the investigator can employ time-series designs or non-equivalent group designs. Each of these domains of research designs is discussed within the context of examples from the consultation research literature.

Time-Series Designs. In the most basic form of time-series design, inferences for an intervention effect are made by comparing repeated measures of the dependent variable prior to and following the intervention. This basic design, sometimes labeled the A/B design or case study, was the type used by Gresham and Nagle (1981) and described in the previous section. However, this design, as noted in that previous context, does not allow strong inference for an intervention effect. Experimental time-series designs include characteristics of the preexperimental case study described above (e.g., repeated measurement, monitoring variability in the series), but one essential element is lacking, that is, *replication* of the independent variable, through one of several design options. Nevertheless, what separates most time-series investigation from the experimental research is that randomization is not used.[2]

---

[2]In some forms of time-series investigations, random assignment and/or random sequencing can be employed to increase experimental validity. In such instances, the study rivals the more conventional randomized group design in drawing valid experimental inferences.

Three basic design options are available in time-series research. These options include the within series, between-series, and combined series. The interested reader is referred to some primary sources where these design options are discussed in more detail (e.g., Barlow et al., 1984; Hayes, 1981). In the within-series design, changes in level and trend for the dependent variable(s) are examined across phases of the investigation. The A/B component forms a basic structure that is replicated across phases (e.g., A/B/A, A/B/A/B, A/B/A/B/A/B . . . A/B). Options available for use of the design type include those used for comparing one treatment to baseline (A/B/A/B, changing criterion) and more complex "interaction designs" that can be used to examine multiple intervention components (e.g., A/B + C/A/B + C).

Between-series designs allow an investigator to compare two or more data series across time. Comparisons are made between the series, taking into account level and trend differences for the same dependent variable(s) as the subject is assessed across phases. Replication is scheduled in either a counter-balanced or a random fashion. The alternating treatments or simultaneous treatments designs represent the class of procedures used in this domain.

Finally, in combined-series designs, comparisons of the independent variable are made both within and between the time-series. Thus, the basic within-series component (A/B) could be replicated across various between-series components consisting of either subjects, settings, behaviors/dependent variables, or experimenters. The multiple baseline and its variations represent an example of this strategy.

In the consultation literature a number of investigations have used single-case time-series designs. As an illustration of this methodology, Piersel and Kratochwill (1981) used a behavioral consultation framework in the treatment of two selectively mute children. Initially, a combined series design (i.e., multiple baseline across two subjects) was employed. A contingency management package including extinction and positive reinforcement was implemented by the classroom teachers. Results reported in Fig. 10.2 show that the treatment package was effective with only one child and had to be revised with the second subject. In this case, it was necessary to implement a negative reinforcement contingency by requiring the child to speak in order to leave a particular situation. When this component was added to the contingency management package, a multiple baseline analysis across three settings was formed. This added design feature indicated that the procedure resulted in successful treatment of the child.

Several advantages of time-series designs are evident in evaluation of school psychological services. Some of these advantages are shared with case study investigation noted above. For example, time-series designs provide an option to group designs, are appropriate for the evaluation of the single case, especially rare disorders or cases, and allow investigation in applied and clinical settings. However, the main advantage of these procedures is that they improve upon the

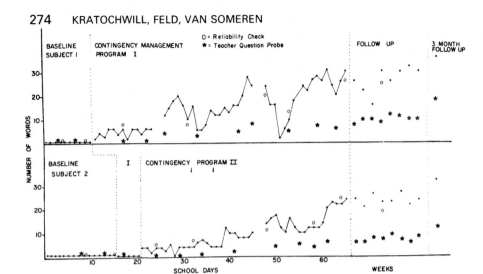

FIG. 10.2 The number of words spoken by Shannon (Subject 1) and Patrick (Subject 2) during baseline and treatment phases across all settings where behavior was observed. Open circles represent reliability checks. Stars indicate teacher probes in the generalization settings. Missing data refer to those days when the subjects were absent from school. Follow-up data were gathered in the classroom and generalization setting over eight weeks and upon return to school the following fall. From "A teacher-implemented contingency management package to assess and treat selective mutism" by W. C. Piersel & T. R. Kratochwill, 1981, *Behavioral Assessment, 3*, 371–382. Reprinted by permission.

typical case study investigation. Thus, in the well-controlled time-series study, the researcher can generally obtain results that are more interpretable.

Nonequivalent Group Designs. Several different types of nonequivalent group designs can be employed to evaluate school psychological services. Some of the more common designs include the One Group Posttest Only Design, Posttest Only Design with Nonequivalent Groups, and the One Group Pretest-Posttest Design. In the Posttest Only Design, the researcher usually tries to match subjects on certain characteristics so as to make them as equivalent as possible. However, all the designs share the characteristic that results in their being quasi-experimental: Randomization is not used to develop inference for treatment-related changes.

In one of the most frequently cited studies that compared different models or approaches to consultation, Jason, Ferone, and Anderegg (1979) evaluated the effectiveness of ecological, behavioral, and process consultation. A no-treatment control condition was also included. The measures used to assess differences among the three treatments included (a) behavioral, process, and ecological observational measures, (b) teacher perceptions of target children and the classroom environments, (c) achievement scores and grades, and (d) teacher's perception of program usefulness. Four schools were selected for the investigation.

Each was randomly assigned to one of the four conditions. In each school first- and third-grade teachers were involved. Each teacher selected the four or five children who were the most disruptive within a particular classroom. The respective consultation programs were implemented weekly for 50-minute sessions for 2 months, and the children were monitored through baseline, treatment, and follow-up phases.

Results suggested significant reductions in observed and rated behavioral problems only in classes provided behavioral consultation. Also, significant increases in achievement scores were noted for the children exposed to process consultation. Less consistent changes were noted for the ecological and control classes. Finally, the teachers rated the behavioral and process consultation approaches as most helpful and beneficial.

Although this investigation is often cited as support of the behavioral consultation approach, various features of the study limit conclusions that can be drawn from the data. To begin with, the study must be regarded as quasi-experimental because schools were nested under treatment conditions. Thus, although schools were randomly assigned, students (subjects) were not, and therefore the effects could be due to certain idiosyncratic characteristics of schools rather than the treatments. In this study, classrooms should be the unit of analysis, but this would require more than four classrooms. Other aspects of the study that limit conclusions that can be drawn were discussed by the authors and included the lack of equivalence of the baseline measures, small sample size, unequal sex and race proportions, unreliability of some process measures, short observational periods, and lack of long-term follow-up measures. Despite these limitations, the study represents one of the best large-scale attempts to evaluate different consultation approaches.

Quasi-experimental group designs allow some degree of inference for evaluation of psychological services, but represent the less desirable option to more well controlled randomized experiments. Typically, quasi-experiments can be improved by rationally trying to reduce as many plausible threats to validity as possible. In addition, various tactics such as matching subjects so as to make groups more equivalent should be employed. Generally these designs have been employed under conditions where random assignment and other strong inference procedures cannot easily be adopted, such as in large-scale program evaluation efforts (Maher & Kratochwill, 1980).

Randomized Group Designs

Randomized experiments use random assignment or some randomization scheme to increase inference for treatment-related change. Randomized group designs are usually of two general types: Between-groups designs and within-subjects designs. In the between-groups design subjects are assigned to experimental and control conditions. The most basic form of the design includes an experimental and control condition, but this can be extended to any number, given practical and statistical considerations. The within-subjects design involves having each subject receive each of the different treatments or conditions. All groups receive all treatments, but in different order.

Goodwin, Garvey, and Barclay (1971) evaluated a training procedure, called microconsultation, for transmitting a set of interview skills for using behavior modification with teachers in a between-groups design. In the study, a pool of 112 school psychologists applying for an 8-week institute were assigned to the experimental conditions, 30 to a video-tape control, and 30 to an inactive control (an additional 20 subjects were retained as alternates). Each group of 30 was a stratified random sample based on geographical location and size of the school district. The active treatment consisted of a number of components including televised experience, didactic instruction, group critiquing, and microconsultation (microconsultation consists of five steps including an interview, videotape feedback, discussion and roleplay, a second interview, and further video feedback). Outcome variables consisted of behavioral measures to determine whether microconsultation training resulted in specific changes in interview style or the presence or absence of specific behavioral responses. Results of the study indicated that posttest measures of interview techniques at the end of the training program and after a 2-month follow-up in the psychologists' home school districts were significantly better than the two control conditions.

Randomized group designs have typically represented the mainstay of experimental research in psychology and education. These designs are regarded as strong inference because randomization helps to reduce various threats to internal validity. However, random assignment to conditions does not ensure that various threats to validity will always be controlled (Cook & Campbell, 1979). For example, in cases where the researcher tests subjects in intact groups some extraneous event that occurs simultaneously with the testing can introduce a systematic bias. Different experimenters or therapists may cause confounding of treatments and if they are not balanced across conditions, systematic bias may occur. Especially in therapy research, differential group status may systematically bias one group over another.

In within-subjects designs, special considerations relate to the complexity of the design as the number of conditions are increased. Consider the case in which three treatments are employed. The counterbalancing in this instance requires that for each group to receive the treatments in a different order, six possible variations in the order of conditions is necessary. Ceiling and floor effects can also be problematic in within-subject designs. In this situation the dependent variable could permit an artificial ceiling or floor because change that occurred under the first condition does not permit the extent of change (ceiling or floor) when subjects are exposed to the next condition. Thus, the dependent variable may not have a sufficient range to allow change to be detected across various conditions. Within-subjects designs also present the problem of sequence effects.

That is, the order of appearance of treatments may influence outcomes (i.e., subjects receiving treatment 2 after treatment 1 may not be the same as subjects receiving treatment 1 after treatment 2). Finally, aside from potential sequence effects, certain treatments that the researcher may want to compare may not lend themselves to having all subjects experience each treatment option. For example, it would be difficult to have a subject receive behavioral consultation followed by mental health consultation, unless "preference" was being evaluated. The interested reader is referred elsewhere for further information and detailed discussions of group designs in research and program evaluation (Cook & Campbell, 1979; Kazdin, 1980).

FURTHER METHODOLOGICAL, CONCEPTUAL, AND ASSESSMENT ISSUES IN THE EVALUATION OF PSYCHOLOGICAL SERVICES

Once the researcher has considered the evaluation model and the design of the investigation, attention should then focus on the variety of methodological, conceptual, and assessment considerations that have emerged in the applied research literature. A number of these issues are discussed within the context of the consultation literature in school psychology.

Assessment Considerations

One of the major considerations in conducting an effective research/program evaluation is the dependent measure(s) selected. Ideally, assessment methods used would serve multiple roles. That is, they would be used to help select problems experienced by the clients, design an intervention program, and assist in monitoring the program and its outcomes. Within this context, different assessment methods would be useful at different stages or phases of assessment.

Cone and his associates (Cone, 1977, 1978; Cone & Hawkins, 1977) provided a conceptual framework to help organize the diverse procedures used in behavioral assessment that is also useful in research/program evaluation of psychological services. The taxonomy is based on the simultaneous consideration of three components, including (a) the contents of functioning assessed, (b) the methods used to assess them, and (c) the types of generalizability (reliability and validity) established for scores on the measure being classified. This conceptual framework, called the Behavioral Assessment Grid (BAG), is presented in Fig. 10.3.

Contents. The contents involved in assessment can be organized into three content areas (Cone, 1977; Cone & Hawkins, 1977), systems (Lang, 1971) or channels (Paul & Bernstein, 1973). Based on Lang's (1971) view that three

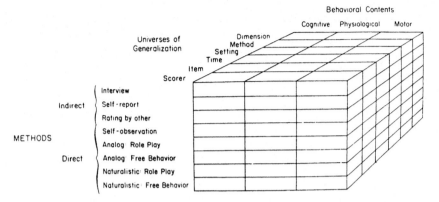

FIG. 10.3 The Behavioral Assessment Grid (BAG), a taxonomy of behavioral assessment integrating contents, methods, and universes of generalization. From "The behavioral assessment grid (BAG): A conceptual framework and a taxonomy," by J. D. Cone, 1978, *Behavior Therapy, 9,* 822–828. Copyright 1978 by the Association for Advancement of Behavior Therapy. Reprinted by permission.

different systems may be involved in the expression of emotion, many behavioral researchers have focused on cognitive, motor, and physiological systems. Study of this "triple response mode assessment" has increased in recent years (Bellack & Hersen, 1978; Cone, 1979; Hersen & Barlow, 1976; Morris & Kratochwill, 1983). Each content refers to different domains of performance. Motor content includes activities of the striate musculature usually observable without instrumentation. Such responses as walking, talking, jumping, academic responding, and so forth are included within this category. Physiological contents include activities of the muscles and glands autonomically innervated, and tonic muscle activity. Examples include muscle tension, heart rate, respiration, and galvanic skin response. Cognitive contents are defined within the context of the specific referents used. For example, verbal behavior (self-report) is categorized as motoric when one is referring to the speech act, but the referents may include motor, cognitive, or physiological components. Verbal behavior may refer to private events (e.g., images, feelings) and therefore referents are cognitive. When it refers to a publiclly verifiable behavior, the referent may be either motoric or physiological.

Although the assessment framework is useful, there are some conceptual and methodological problems with the triple response mode conceptualization (Cone, 1979). First, there has been little consensus as to what is meant by each of the modes (e.g., Hersen & Barlow, 1976; Morris & Kratochwill, 1983). Varying interpretations of the cognitive-verbal-self-report modes have been especially problematic because these areas refer to different variables across different studies, making comparisons difficult. For example, Paul and Bernstein (1973) refer to the self-report channel as a response system under direct voluntary control used to report behaviors, but Lang (1977) employs a language system conceptualization in which the primary function of language is to differentiate expression, perception, and control of emotion.

Second, a conceptual problem with the three-mode assessment format relates to its utility in organizing responses. Presumably, use of the system may add construct measurement into assessment, something that may be of questionable utility. For example, anxiety, as a construct, can be defined in terms of the three-response systems. But, there is likely to be disagreement among researchers about the numbers and type of measures used to establish that anxiety has been assessed (Morris & Kratochwill, 1983). Thus, is the researcher measuring anxiety when a self-report and motor content procedure are used? Some individuals might argue that physiological measures must also be used to establish construct validity.

A third problem has been methodological, in that many research efforts have varied both method of assessment and content. When examining the relations among the content areas, for example, a confounding occurs when self-reports of cognitive content are correlated with overt observations of motor and physiological contents. To help deal with this concern, Cone (1979) proposed a multitrait-multimethod format to assist researchers in identifying method variance in behavioral assessment. In contrast to the traditional trait conceptualizations that multitrait-multimethod procedures were designed to identify (cf. Campbell & Fiske, 1959), the use of this methodology in behavioral assessment is premised on situation-specificity of responding. Thus, in behavioral assessment the analysis of settings or situations in which responding occurs should be the primary focus.

This tactic of directly observing behavior appears promising in advancing psychological knowledge in many fields. Fiske (1979) noted that validity problems are reduced in research focused on overt behaviors:

> Investigators interested in understanding behaviors can directly observe their phenomena: These investigators are trying to understand the rapidly changing events they see before them. In contrast, those studying characteristics of people cannot observe these characteristics directly, but only as reported by some observer. These investigators postulate that persons possess various characteristics in some degree and then try to assess the degree. Since they assume their data are indications of the unobserved characteristics, they must confront the problems of estimating the characteristics from undependable data that are affected by the individual observer and by the various aspects of the method used to elicit the observer's report. The poor reliability of such data imposes a low ceiling on their maximum possible validity. (p. 37)

Of course, the focus on observable behavior rather than constructs, and the use of direct observation to study these phenomena, begs the question of whether certain channels are necessary. At this point it does appear that any statement about response system independence is an empirical issue (Cone, 1979).

Method. A number of different assessment procedures have been used in program evaluation and research. Cone (1977, 1978) ordered various assessment methods along a continuum of "directness" representing the extent to which they

1. *Measure the target behavior of clinical relevance,* and
2. *Measure the target behavior at the time and place of its natural occurrence.*

Based on this framework various assessment procedures are organized into indirect and direct dimensions (see Fig. 10.3). Interviews, self-reports, and rating scales are indirect measures. Both interview responses and self-report data are a verbal representation of relevant behavior occurring at some other time and place. Ratings by others usually involve retrospective descriptions of behavior in that the rating occurs subsequent to the actual occurrence of the behavior.

Direct assessment methods are organized according to *who* does the observing, the *instructions* provided the observer, and *where* the observation occurs. Self-monitoring involves the client/subject observing and recording his/her own behavior at the time of its occurrence. Analogue measures involve assessment of behavior in situations that are analogous to, but removed from, the environment in which the target behavior occurs. For example, assessment can be ordered along a continuum of how representative the measures reflect actual performance in the natural environment. In naturalistic observational assessment, the subject is observed under either role play or naturalistic conditions.

Each of the three assessment methods has advantages and disadvantages in program evaluation and research. Direct assessment methods are usually preferred in research, especially on program outcome measures. Thus, direct observational methods are discussed in more detail later in the chapter.

Universes of Generalization. Cone (1977, 1978) employed generalizability theory as a model for indexing the different ways in which various scores resulting from assessment can be generalized. The six major universes include (a) scorer, (b) item, (c) time, (d) setting, (e) method, and (f) dimension (see Fig. 10.1).

Scorer generalization refers to the extent to which data obtained by the observer are comparable to the mean of the observations of all scorers that were observing the target response. Agreement must be established among the observers, and when agreement is demonstrated, scores are said to generalize across scorers. Typically, a measure of interobserver agreement is used to assess whether observers have been reliable. *Item generalization* refers to the extent to which response(s) is/are representative of a larger universe of similar responses. For example, item generalization could be established on direct observational measures by comparing odd-even scores over various phases of a within-subject experiment. The scores would be derived from the various baseline and treatment phases. *Time generality* measures the extent to which data collected at one point in time are representative of those that might have been collected at another time. Consistency would be a primary focus of this generalization dimension. *Setting generality* refers to the extent to which data obtained in one setting are representative of those obtained in other situations. For example, the program evaluator will usually be interested in knowing the degree to which scores generalize from the home to the school. *Method generality* provides information on the extent to which data from different assessment methodologies produce consistency. The extent to which direct obtrusive and unobtrusive measures produce consistency on a target behavior would be a question of method generality. Finally, *dimension generality* refers to the comparability of data on two or more different behaviors. Behaviors that form the same response class or domain would be measuring the same dimension.

These universes, conceptualized within the context of generalizability theory (Cronbach, Gleser, Nada, & Rajaratman, 1972), are applied to the techniques of behavioral assessment with the recognition that there are different assumptions between behavioral assessment and traditional assessment procedures. Nelson and Hayes (1979) noted that demonstrations of generalizability (or lack of generalizability) cannot be used as the sole criterion of the quality of behavioral assessment for two reasons: (a) inconsistencies in measurement may be produced by actual changes in behavior and not by an imprecise behavioral assessment technique; (b) the quality of behavioral assessment must be determined by the functional value of increasing scientific understanding of behavior and the success of therapeutic interventions (p. 496).

Although generalizability theory (G-theory) has made a number of conceptual contributions to assessment (e.g., Coates & Thoresen, 1978; Cone, 1977; Jones, Reid, & Patterson, 1974; Kazdin, 1977a; Nelson, Rudin-Hay, & Hay, 1977), some controversy has occurred in its use in single-subject time-series research. For example, Jones (1977) noted that the statistical assumptions and mathematical developments of reliability theory and G-theory are not appropriate for single-subject designs in which data are collected over ordered time samples. In contrast, Strossen, Coates, and Thoresen (1979) noted that G-theory provides two approaches for assessing the generalizability of data from single-subject designs. First, estimates are computed for a population of subjects expected to include the target subject. Second, given the interest in generalizing from the group to the individual, the single subject is considered a fixed factor. Thus, only the target person is considered and results are not generalized to all people.

Direct Assessment Methods. We believe that direct behavioral assessment strategies are the preferred means of measuring program outcomes over various phases of a research project. Although self-monitoring and analogue measures are usually included within this direct assessment category, observation of a target response in some naturalistic setting is the most common method used in research. A naturalistic observational system includes "recording of behavioral events in their natural settings at the time they occur, not retrospectively, the use of trained impartial observer-coders, and descriptions of behavior which require little if any inference by observers to code the events" (Jones et al., 1974, p. 46).

The use of direct observational assessment strategies has had wide appeal in psychology and education. There have also been recent pleas for the use of direct observational assessment in school psychology research and practice (e.g., Alessi, 1980; Hunter, 1977; Keller, 1980; Kratochwill, 1980a, 1980b; Lynch, 1977). Since various conceptual and methodological issues in the use of direct observational assessment have been discussed quite extensively in the behavioral literature (e.g., Ciminero, Calhoun, & Adams, 1977; Cone & Hawkins, 1977; Hartmann & Wood, 1982; Haynes, 1978; Haynes & Wilson, 1979; Hersen & Bellack, 1976), we present only a brief overview of some of the highlights of this assessment strategy.

Considerations. The researcher who employs direct observation of behavior in his/her evaluation of school psychology services must attend to numerous methodological issues (Hartmann, 1982). Of primary concern is the ability to select and implement objective, valid, and reliable measurements of behavior. The specific procedures used by the researcher must carefully balance these criteria with the idiosyncracies of the subject and target behavior, and with practical considerations such as cost and the availability of staff and equipment.

One of the first considerations in using observational procedures is development of a code specific to the problem identified. There are relatively few codes and those that exist focus on a rather specific range of behaviors. Codes have been developed for institutional program evaluation (Alevizos, DeRissi, Liberman, Eckman, & Callahan, 1978), home (Patterson, Reid, Jones, & Conger, 1975), school (O'Leary, Romanczyk, Kass, Dietz, & Santogrossi, 1979), and home and school settings (Wahler, House, & Stambaugh, 1976). Usually a code will have to be developed for the particular research problem.

Given that the researcher is developing a specific code, a second issue will be with the target definitions of the behaviors. Maintaining the objectivity of behavioral measures begins with well-operationalized definitions of the specific behaviors to be assessed. Asking individuals to record "aggressive behaviors," for example, leaves room for much interpretation. Personal value systems, past experience, and temporary emotional states are likely to contribute significantly to variability in the data with such measures. On the other hand, behaviors such as hitting, approach threat behaviors, physical contact, and shouting are much more easily determined by the observer and less subject to interpretation and distortion.

Typically, the researcher must emphasize topography or function (Johnston & Pennypacker, 1980). A topographically based definition emphasizes the movements comprising the response (e.g., aggression refers to physical contact of the child's fist with any part of another child's body). Functionally based definitions emphasize the consequence of the behavior (e.g., aggression could be defined as behavior intended to cause injury to another child or object). A third consideration is the relation between the specific measures chosen and the experimental hypothesis. The experimental hypothesis makes some statement about behavior, and the researcher must demonstrate clearly that the measures taken by the observers are, in fact, representative of that behavior; that is, they must be *valid* measures of the behavior of interest. The data must not give a distorted picture of the subject's behavior, and therefore validity depends heavily on objectivity. Thus, the specific measures must be truly representative of the subject's behavior. Response dimensions usually involve consideration of frequency, duration, and quality. Measures employed should be those widely used and considered acceptable by other researchers, or those measures that bear a logical or obvious relation to the behavior in question (e.g., academic output measured through amount of work completed, or the duration of smiling as a measure of pleasure).

A fourth consideration relates to problems inherent in the actual recording methods used in assessment. Basically, five observational procedures can be used in direct observational assessment. These include real-time observations, event recording, duration recording, scan sampling, and interval recording (Hartmann, 1984). Although it is beyond the scope of the present chapter to discuss each of those measures in detail, Table 10.1 provides a brief overview of the advantages and disadvantages associated with each measure.

Fifth, observers should be well-trained. The researcher or program evaluator can further promote good observational assessment by training observers under conditions as similar to the experimental conditions as possible, and reinstating training sessions or providing feedback throughout the experiment to guard against observer "drift" away from the standards originally imposed.

Sixth, two or more observers should be involved in assessment so that a measure of interobserver agreement can be established. Observers should be trained together and their scores compared with a single formal criterion. Training should also be long enough to ensure that there is agreement to a specified criterion on each code. Again, precise, operational definitions on all measures are crucial. The observers and the instructions provided to them must be guided by a well-defined standard in order to yield consistent data. The type of recording system used and its appropriateness to the target behavior are factors contributing to reliability. Event recording in the case of extremely high frequency behavior (e.g., eye blinking) or very short intervals (e.g., less than 2 seconds) strain the human capabilities of the observers and therefore could lead to unreliable data. Moreover, researchers or program evaluators should arrange for the observer to record simultaneously as few measures as possible without sacrificing the experimental questions. Mechanical devices can often be used to increase the accuracy of duration recording, and cueing devices such as timed lights and recorded signals more precisely define the limits of intervals for the observers. Various counting gadgets such as miniature calculators or an abacus also facilitate accuracy in event recording. Notifying the observers that they will be assessed both

TABLE 10.1
Factors to Consider in Selecting an Appropriate Recording Technique

Method	Advantages and Disadvantages
Real-Time Recording	Advantages: —Provides unbiased estimates of frequency and duration. —Data capable of complex analyses such as conditional probability analysis. —Data susceptible to sophisticated reliability analysis. Disadvantages: —Demanding task for observers. —May require costly equipment. —Requires responses to have clearly distinguishable beginnings and ends.
Event or Duration Recording	Advantages: —Measures are of a fundamental response characteristic (i.e., frequency or duration). —Can be used by participant–observers (e.g., parents or teachers) with low rate responses. Disadvantages: —Requires responses to have clearly distinguishable beginnings and ends. Unless responses are located in real time (e.g., by dividing a session into brief recording intervals), some forms of reliability assessment may be impossible. —May be difficult with multiple behaviors unless mechanical aids are available.
Momentary Time Samples	Advantages: —Response duration of primary interest. —Time-saving and convenient. —Useful with multiple behaviors and/or children. —Applicable to responses without clear beginnings or ends. Disadvantages: —Unless samples are taken frequently, continuity of behavior may be lost. —May miss most occurrences of brief, rare responses.
Interval Recording	Advantages: —Sensitive to both response frequency and duration. —Applicable to wide range of responses. —Facilitates observer training and reliability assessment. —Applicable to responses without clearly distinguishable beginnings and ends. Disadvantages: —Confounds frequency and duration. —May under- or overestimate response and frequency and duration.

Note. From "Assessment Strategies," by D. P. Hartmann. In D. H. Barlow and M. Hersen (Eds.). *Single case experimental design*, 1984. Elmsford, NY: Pergamon Press. Reprinted by permission.

overtly and covertly on a random basis should also increase their reliability (Reid, 1970; Romanczyk, Kent, Diament, & O'Leary, 1973; Taplin & Reid, 1973). Finally, methods of calculating observer reliability may also contribute to the quality of the reliability score. It is beyond the scope of this presentation to review various methods of calculating observer agreement estimates. However, this is an important methodological issue and the reader should consult one of several sources that present information on this topic (e.g., Cone & Foster, 1982; Hartmann, 1982, 1984; Haynes, 1978; Haynes & Wilson, 1979; Kazdin, 1982a).

A seventh issue that must be considered in gathering observational data is observer effect. Much research has been done to determine whether expectations regarding experimental outcome affect the observer (see Kent & Foster, 1977). Although the results of various studies have been somewhat inconsistent, it is generally accepted that the less the observer is told regarding the expected experimental outcomes, the better, or at least, the more objective the data will be. Such knowledge could lead to the observers' trying to "please" the experimenter, thus being predisposed to score the behavior in certain ways, or being more sensitive to types of behavior. A much more subtle but equally troublesome problem is a general predisposition on the part of the observer to consistently choose one category over another, or record behavior earlier or later than other observers. Any such predisposition, if detected early, can be minimized through careful training, a change in the recording methods, or as a last resort, by replacing the observer(s). A further precaution against observer bias is to discourage personal contact between the observer and the subject(s) or between the observer and anyone knowledgeable about the experimental hypothesis (e.g., experimenter, research assistant, teaching staff, etc.).

Another consideration in the use of direct observational assessment relates to the obtrusiveness of the measures (Kazdin, 1979). Obrusiveness in this case refers to the fact that subjects may be aware that assessment is being conducted. Sometimes obtrusive data may be reactive, i.e., promote a change in the dependent variable. For example, when observers enter a classroom to observe a particular child, the child may become aware that his/her behavior is being recorded and begin to attend to an academic task, or stop being disruptive, among other possibilities. A variety of procedures have been recommended to reduce reactivity (Kazdin, 1979), including the use of unobtrusive assessment procedures, scheduling an adaptation phase prior to formal assessment, using observers who are a part of the natural setting (e.g., teachers, parents), disguising observers, and employing data that are obtained from multiple sources, including indirect assessment techniques.

Analogue Research

Research investigating the effectiveness of school psychological services is sometimes regarded as analogue in that it is conducted under conditions analogous to those in the actual school setting. An example of analogue research in the consultation area is a study reported by Bergan, Byrnes, and Kratochwill (1979). Sixty first- and second-grade teachers were assigned to one of four conditions representing different consultation approaches in which they were required to teach a hypothetical child to add (the fact that a hypothetical child was used is a definite indication that this study had analogue characteristics). The first condition involved face-to-face behavioral consultation in which a consultant used a teacher to verbalize various antecedent and consequent conditions that could influence learning and prompted the teacher to specify the kinds of capabilities that the child would need in order to master the academic task (learning to add). In the second behavioral consultation condition, face-to-face consultation was supplemented by a task analysis report that specified prerequisite skills needed to successfully complete the task. In the third condition, medical model consultation involved face-to-face interaction focusing on temporally remote environmental circumstances accompanied by a traditional psychological report specifying that the child was of low ability. In the control condition, teachers were asked general questions about the school.

Results of the study suggested that behavioral consultation with the task analysis was associated with significantly more teaching success than was the control, medical model, and behavioral consultation without task analysis condition was better than the medical model consultation condition.

It is evident that this study, although providing well-controlled data on different consultation outcomes, cannot easily be generalized to clinical settings. The point is that certain characteristics of the study limit generalization; however, research should not be characterized as either analogue or nonanalogue because generalization to clinical or applied settings can be obscured in at least two ways (Kazdin, 1980). To begin with, the distinction obscures the analogue nature of many different types of research studies in school psychology, including those conducted in the actual school setting. Thus, all research in applied settings has some characteristics (e.g., assessment strategies, experimenters) that will influence the generalization of the results to other applied settings. Many of the research studies discussed in this chapter contain certain characteristics that are an analogue to the school setting. For example, well-controlled case studies include such components as an experimenter/therapist who gathers data in a systematic manner. These conditions may vary from those of more typical cases seen in the daily practice of the school psychologist.

Second, the usual dichotomy between analogue versus nonanalogue research does not provide researchers with guidelines for distinguishing among various studies on what could be relevant analogue dimensions. In order to assist researchers in this process of analyzing studies on analogue dimensions, Kazdin (1980) proposed a continuum for this process. The dimensions include the target problem (e.g., severity of the problem), clients (e.g., real versus hypothetical), manner of recruitment (e.g., referred versus non-referred), therapist (trained versus untrained), set, selection, and setting of treatment (e.g., clinic versus school), variation of treatment (controlled versus noncontrolled) and assessment methods (self-report versus direct observational measures). Thus, although the Bergan et al. (1979) study can be regarded as more analogue (and more well controlled) than the Jason et al. (1979) study, both have analogue characteristics that have an important bearing on generalizing the results to actual school psychology practice.

Strength and Integrity of Psychological Services

Psychological services usually involve one or several specific treatment activities that are implemented in an applied setting. Important in this service delivery are the strength and integrity of treatment (Sechrest, West, Phillips, Redner, & Yeaton, 1979; Yeaton & Sechrest, 1981). The strength of treatment refers to its intensity and frequency of administration. For example, using consultation as an illustration of the importance of strength of treatment, the researcher or program evaluator would need to ensure that consultation contacts occurred with sufficient intensity (e.g., length of consultation contact) and frequency (e.g., number of contacts with the teacher) to test its effectiveness. However, since consultation involves a consultant-consultee relationship with the consultee usually designated as responsible for treatment implementation, the strength construct must be considered at this level as well. For example, the consultee must implement a classroom treatment (e.g., contingency management program) with sufficient intensity and frequency to increase the chances that it will be effective. This strength of treatment is a very important variable in the delivery of psychological treatments in school settings, and in certain forms for service delivery models, such as consultation, must be addressed at multiple levels.

In addition to the strength of treatment, the researcher must also address treatment or intervention integrity. Simply stated, treatment integrity is the degree to which the treatment is delivered as intended. In research on consultation, treatment integrity refers to the degree to which the consultant follows or adheres to the consultation model or procedures being tested. For example, in behavioral consultation, the researcher would need to ensure that problem identification, problem analysis, and plan evaluation interviews were carried out according to the model. Moreover, during the treatment plan implementation phase of consultation, the consultant must determine if the treatment was implemented by the consultee as intended.

The integrity of consultation is very important because researchers must document that consultation is, in fact, being practiced. Unfortunately, much of the research on school psychological services in general (e.g., Peterson, Homer, & Wonderlich, 1982), and in consultation in particular (Van Someren & Kratochwill, 1983), has not included measures of strength and integrity of treatment. Of course, practitioners should also attempt to implement procedures as designed in research. Strength and integrity of treatment must be demonstrated so that the researcher/practitioner can conclude that the services (independent variables) were responsible for client change (dependent variables). Failure to gather measures on strength and integrity can therefore threaten the reliability and validity of research and program evaluation.

Checking on the integrity of treatments can usually be determined in the same manner as assessment of the dependent variable. A wide variety of assessment strategies are available, including interviews, checklists and rating scales. self-report, self-monitoring, and direct observation. Some studies in the consultation research literature included measures on the integrity of treatment. In the Jason and Ferone (1978) consultation project, the authors noted that all consultation sessions were taped and coded. Workman, Kindall, and Williams (1980) had observers record both teacher and student behavior, thereby providing a check on the reliability of both the independent and the dependent variable. In the future, researchers/program evaluators should include these strategies and demonstrate that both the strength and the integrity of services have been assessed.

Standardization of Psychological Services

Related to the strength and integrity of services is the standardization of treatment. Standardized treatment refers to the use of a specific format for implementation of services including, for example, a treatment manual, criteria for training, specific strategies for treatment delivery, among other features (Kazdin, 1982b). Unfortunately, few standardized formats have been developed for delivery of psychological services in the schools. Recently, Kratochwill and Bergan (in press) developed a standardized format for consultation service delivery through consultant-consultee interactions, but virtually no standardized consultee treatment implemented packages have been developed. Nevertheless, there are various treatment packages that are relatively standardized and that might be implemented through a psychologist-consultant. For example, in the social skills area several packages have appeared, including Stephens' (1978) social skills curriculum, Jackson, Jackson, and Monroe's (1984) social effectiveness training procedures, Goldstein, Sprafkin, Gershaw, and Klein's (1978) adolescent skill-training materials, the Asset program by Hazel, Schumaker, Sherman, and Sheldon-Wildgren (1981), and Hops et al.'s (1978) relationship materials called PEERS.

Several advantages to a standardized approach to research on school psychological treatment services can be noted (see Kazdin, 1982b, for a discussion of these positive features in the psychotherapy literature). First, standardization will help the researcher address the strength and integrity of treatment procedures across research investigations and practice. That is, a standardized treatment package will likely be more easily assessed on dimensions of strength and integrity.

Second, standardization of treatment would allow training clinicians in the treatment approach to some level of mastery or competency. A major problem with many treatment services in the schools is that individuals have not been trained in their use to specified criterion levels. In school psychology training programs students are taught to administer standardized tests to criterion levels of performance, but less often have treatment procedures received the same emphasis in training. Yet, a number of psychotherapeutic skills have been taught in a systematic manner in the psychotherapy field (cf. Garfield, 1977; Matarazzo, 1978) and many of these could be extended into school psychology training programs.

In school psychology standardized approaches to consultation service delivery models have been taught using competency-based criteria (e.g., Bergan, Kratochwill, & Luiten, 1978; Brown, Kratochwill, & Bergan, 1982). For example, in the Brown et al. (1982) study, students were taught problem identification interview skills on analogue problems. The training approach has been extended to motivational analyses interview skills (Duley, Cancelli, Kratochwill, Bergan, & Meredith, 1983) and work is currently underway to extend the procedures to the full range of consultation interviews.

A third reason for a standardized approach to treatment services is that once standardized approaches are tested in research and found to be effective, they may have a higher probability of being implemented in practice. Ultimately, the purpose of applied or clinical research is to influence practice. The standardized approach will likely influence practice because it is packaged and available as a package and, therefore, is more likely to be disseminated. Thus, the packaged treatment approach would bear similarity to package assessment strategies or tests that have been so pervasive in school psychology practice.

Criteria for Evaluation of Psychological Services

In recent years, important developments have occurred in the criteria for evaluation of school psychological services, especially in the methods used to measure program outcomes. The range and type of outcome measures have expanded considerably and include experimental and therapeutic criteria, and client-related criteria (Kazdin & Wilson, 1978; Rachman & Wilson, 1980).

Experimental and Therapeutic Outcome Criteria. Formal criteria have been proposed for data analysis in therapy research, namely, experimental and therapeutic (cf. Kazdin, 1977a; Wolf, 1978). An experimental criterion involves comparison of the dependent variable before and after the introduction of the independent variable. Essentially, experimental criteria are met through the use of credible design and sometimes inferential statistical tests. Such criteria would be applied in both quasi-experimental time-series and group designs and randomized-group designs. Some debate has occurred over the use of statistical tests in single-case time-series therapy research and the interested reader is referred to some sources where these issues are discussed in more detail (see Kazdin, 1982a, and Kazdin & Wilson, 1978).

Clinical or therapeutic criteria have been proposed as a method to increase the practical significance of therapeutic achievement. To the degree that such procedures promote large therapeutic changes on outcome measures, they lend support to program success. Researchers have increasingly been concerned with determining the clinical importance of change in client behavior. This has most commonly been referred to as *social validation* (Kazdin, 1977b) and according to Wolf (1978) can be assessed on three dimensions, including (a) the social significance of the *goals* (i.e., Are the specific behavioral goals really what society wants?), (b) the social appropriateness of the *procedures* (i.e., Do the ends justify the means? That is, do the participants, caregivers, and other consumers consider the treatment procedures acceptable?), (c) the social importance of the *effects* (i.e., Are consumers satisfied with *all* the results, including any unpredicted ones?) (p. 207).

Two social validation procedures have been outlined by Kazdin (1977b). First, behavior of a client is compared with that of individuals who have not been defined as experiencing problems. Second, evaluations of the client's performance are solicited by individuals in the natural setting such as in the school and home. Behavior change is viewed as clinically important when the intervention program brings the client's performance within socially acceptable levels as determined from social judgments of significant others such as teachers and parents. When this clinical level of significance is established, a more formal criterion is available for evaluating the intervention than would occur without this dimension.

Social validation procedures can be readily adapted to a variety of research designs, involving between-group and quasi-experimental procedures. In all cases therapeutic criteria are added to design and statistical criteria for an overall evaluation of the therapeutic program. Several studies evaluating the effectiveness of consultation services have employed social validation procedures (e.g., Jason & Ferone, 1978; Jason et al., 1979; Piersel & Kratochwill, 1981).

Conceptually related to, or even growing out of, the social validation area is the consumer satisfaction focus in evaluation of psychological services. The focus is considered a "Type II" evaluation[3] by Miller and Dyer (1980) in which the views of professionals other than school psychologists are taken into consideration. For example, studies have been conducted on superintendents' knowledge of and attitude toward school psychologists, principals' attitudes toward school psychologists, and teachers' perceptions of school psychological services.

---

[3]Type II evaluations are distinguished from Type I evaluations with the latter referring to internal evaluations of psychological services, usually conducted by school psychologists. For example, school psychologists might evaluate how much time they spend in various professional roles (e.g., testing, intervention, research).

The assessment of consumer satisfaction has been a relatively new focus in behavior therapy (e.g., Bornstein & Rychtarik, 1983; Kiesler, 1983; McMahon & Forehand, 1983) and is the subject of controversy and debate (e.g., Garfield, 1983c; Parloff, 1983). Consumer satisfaction generally involves three domains underlying satisfaction with treatment outcome: satisfaction with the therapist, with aspects of the treatment procedures, and with the teaching format used in the treatment program (McMahon & Forehand, 1983). Based on work in this area, McMahon and Forehand (1983) advanced the following recommendations for the future (pp. 222–223):

1. Consumer satisfaction measures should be used in behavior therapy and assessment.
2. More psychometrically sound instruments must be developed for use in this area.
3. Research should focus these efforts on comparative assessments of satisfaction as well as absolute levels.
4. Children's satisfaction with services should be assessed as well as adults'.
5. Measures of consumer satisfaction must be compared to other outcome measures used in behavior therapy.

Client-Related Criteria. Four client-related criteria can be examined in program evaluation or research on school psychological services (Kazdin & Wilson, 1978). Of primary concern is the importance of change or improvement in the client(s). To begin with, the researcher needs to determine if the problem or focus on intervention has been addressed as a function of the psychological service program. Change can be examined on the social validation dimensions described in the previous section.

Another issue relates to the proportion of clients who improve in a group investigation. In a group experiment (experimental or quasi-experimental) it is advisable for the researcher to present data on individual subjects so that it is possible to examine possible failures of the program. Reporting the proportion of clients who improve is particularly important in consultation research in view of recent recommendations to use large sample sizes in the future (Medway, 1979, 1982). Although this strategy may promote the external validity of results, it could present interpretation problems. To begin with, group outcomes are usually reported as a mean across subjects in a particular treatment condition. Yet, such reporting could cause the researcher to lose sight of clients who actually become worse or do not improve as a function of services. This is an especially important concern when the proportion of client improvement differs across groups (i.e., one condition may have clients who actually became worse, even though it, on the average, was significantly better than another condition where fewer clients became worse). In the consultation literature where groups were compared, some researchers reported information on the proportion of clients who improved. For example, Tyler (1981) reported improvement in 34 of 44 subjects. Unfortunately, no data were presented on how many actually deteriorated.

Another consideration in evaluation of psychological services concerns the breadth of changes in the client. The efficacy of a treatment is usually evaluated on the basis of how well the original problem has been ameliorated. But, treatment effects may extend beyond the original problem and could be positive or negative for the client (Petrie et al., 1980). In consultation research, investigations have reported academic improvement when disruptive behavior was reduced (e.g., Farber & Mayer, 1972; Moracco & Kazandkian, 1977) and an increase in desirable behavior when undesirable target behaviors were decreased or eliminated (e.g., Jason et al., 1979; Hops, 1971; Zwald & Gresham, 1982). At the consultee level, teachers have reported an improvement in their ability to manage their classrooms in an effective manner after participation in consultation focused on individual client change (Ritter, 1978).

A final client-related criterion involves assessment of the durability of improvements. In evaluation of psychological services, the researcher should be concerned with a careful follow-up to determine if the effects that occurred during treatment have maintained. Conversely, a comparison of two treatments at the end of the program may yield different results when these two treatments are compared again at several months or years. Various assessment procedures will need to be used to determine if treatment effects have been durable. Usually the same assessment procedures that were employed during the program should be employed to assess the durability of the program effects.

Efficiency and Cost-Related Criteria. In addition to the aforementioned assessment of client outcomes, efficiency and cost-related criteria should be employed in an evaluation of school psychological services (Kazdin & Wilson, 1978). First, the efficiency in duration of the program must be determined inasmuch as one program demonstrating the same effect as an alternative program should be preferred if it takes considerably less time to implement. For example, if mental health and process consultation are being evaluated in the school setting, it is possible that the same outcome may occur on the dependent measures in the program. However, the program that was the most efficient to implement would generally be preferred, given the time needed for services.

Another issue involves efficiency in the manner of administering the program. An important question that can be asked is whether the program can be implemented in groups or only with individuals. For example, a consultant may find that consultation services that involve procedures to facilitate generalization are much more efficient than services that do not include this component. Presumably, services that contain the generalization component would assist the teacher in treating other similar problems without the same amount of consultant assistance. Some treatment programs can be administered through various media formats (e.g., video-tapes, films, reading, etc.). Such materials can be disseminated widely, thereby reducing therapeutic time and expense. For example, various classroom management programs can be presented to large groups through reading materials and films, thereby involving a large savings in consultant time over individual work with each teacher.

A third criterion involves the costs of professional expertise. For example, a school psychologist involved in direct treatment services has usually had extensive and costly training (e.g., from 2 to 5 years). However, many therapeutic programs can be implemented by teachers (or paraprofessionals), thereby reducing the cost of school-based professional services. Consultation is frequently cited as a form of professional services that is cost-efficient, as in behavioral consultation, where the psychologist works with a teacher-consultee to implement services to a client (Bergan, 1977; Tombari & Davis, 1979). Unfortunately, little information is available to document the cost of these professional school psychological services.

A fourth issue relates to client costs. In private settings, the cost of service is a major consideration in evaluation of treatment. Clients receiving services in public school settings do not pay directly for these services because a psychologist is employed by the school district. Nevertheless, certain service programs may cost the district a great deal of money that could be used for other alternatives, and so the cost issue will still be salient in program evaluation. Costs also extend beyond monetary considerations. Client costs involve the client's physical well-being and general mental health. For example, in a program comparing two alternative treatments for adolescent depression, an investigator must be concerned about the effects of treatment in the least effective program. The emotional costs to the client may be too high to use a program that may be ineffective with some students.

A fifth consideration relates to the cost-effectiveness of treatments. This issue refers to how costly the treatment is and whether the cost for the desired outcome is justified. Certain problems (e.g., mild social withdrawal) may not justify the spending of vast amounts of time and effort and money to effect some change. This is a major issue with transient problems or those that appear to be developmental (e.g., certain fears) with few negative consequences with nonintervention.

Generalization and Follow-up

Many procedures have been developed to measure and program generalization (Drabman, Hammer, & Rosenbaum, 1979; Stokes & Baer, 1977). Demonstration of generalization and maintenance is both a practical and an ethical concern (Drabman et al., 1979). From a practical perspective, treatment should demonstrate positive effects on the person's life beyond the specific target behavior chosen for the client (Kazdin, 1985). From an ethical perspective it is important to know that the program effects do not disappear when the treatment is withdrawn or discontinued.

Stokes and Baer (1977) defined generalization as "the occurrence of relevant behavior under different, non-training conditions (e.g., across subjects, settings, people, behaviors and/or time) without the scheduling of the same events in those conditions as had been scheduled in the training conditions" (p. 350). This view is based on conceptualizing generalization according to the processes associated with generalized effects (Stokes & Baer, 1977); generalization can also be conceptualized according to the methods used and data recorded (Drabman et al., 1979).

Programming Generalization. Stokes and Baer (1977) conceptualized generalization as an active process and technology. Based upon their review of the literature, seven general categories of generalization were identified. The categories and associated definition/operation are presented in Table 10.2. Various research studies continue to be published that build on this technology.

TABLE 10.2
A Technology of Generalization

Category	*Definition/Operation*
Natural maintaining contingencies	Generalization is programmed by suitable trapping manipulations wherein responses are introduced to natural reinforcement communities that refine and maintain those skills without further treatment.
Training sufficient exemplars	Generalization to untrained stimulus conditions and to untrained responses is programmed by the training of sufficient exemplars to those stimulus conditions or responses.
Train loosely	Training is implemented with relatively little control over the stimuli and responses involved, thereby enhancing generalization.
Indiscrimable Contingencies	In this procedure reinforcement or punishment contingencies, or the setting events marking the presence or absence of those contingencies, are deliberately made less predictable, so that it becomes difficult to discriminate reinforcement occasions from nonreinforcement occasions.
Common Stimulus	This generalization programming strategy involves incorporating into training those settings and physical stimuli that are salient in generalization settings and that can be made to assume functional or obvious roles in the training setting.
Mediated Generalization	This procedure requires establishing a response as part of new learning that is likely to be utilized in other problems, also, and therefore to result in generalization.
Train "to generalize"	The procedure invovles reinforcing generalization itself as if it were an explicit behavior.

Note. From "An implicit technology of generalization" by T. F. Stokes and D. M. Baer, 1977, *Journal of Applied Behavior Analysis, 10,* 349–368. Adopted by permission.

10. SCHOOL PSYCHOLOGICAL SERVICES 295

Assessment of Generalization. Drabman and his associates (1979) presented a conceptual framework for various classes of generalization called the "Generalization Map" (see Fig. 10.4). It provides an assessment guideline that encompasses 16 classes of generalization. Within this framework there are four general categories of generalization. In the first type, typically labeled generalization across time, response maintenance, or follow-up, program change is assessed in the treatment setting following the withdrawal of the program. In this form of generalization assessment one must note whether the treatment continues or whether it was discontinued. An issue that emerges in follow-up assessment is how long and how frequent the assessment should be. Although this will depend on the type of problem involved as well as practical considerations, a general rule is that measures be taken at 6 months and 12 months, and even longer if possible. Also, the longer and more frequently these measures are taken, the more that can be said about the effects of the program.

A second type of generalization involves measurement across settings and refers to change in behavior in settings separate from the specific environment in which treatment was programmed. Drabman et al. (1979) note that the criterion for a new environment can be established by the presence or absence of salient discriminative stimuli present in the treatment environment. For example, a more obvious change in environment would occur if the researcher assessed behavior across school and home environments.

Generalization across behaviors involves a change in a behavior not specifically programmed during treatment. This type of generalization would be assessed by determining if the behavior said to be generalized can be defined independently of the definition of the target behavior conceptualized at the beginning of the program. For example, if the researcher has implemented a consultation program

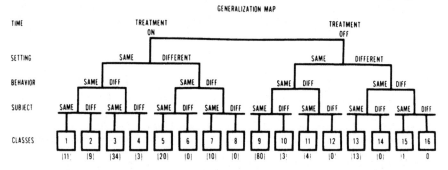

FIG. 10.4 The generalization map depicting the 16 different classes of generalized treatment effects. The numbers in parentheses indicate the number of studies found which illustrated a particular class of generalization.

Note: From "Assessing generalization in behavior modification with children: The generalization map" by R. S. Drabman, D. Hammer, & M. S. Rosenbaum, 1979, *Behavior Assessment, 1,* 203–219. Copyright, 1979 by the Association for Advancement of Behavior Therapy. Reproduced by permission.

to increase compliance with teacher rules, generalization would be said to occur on improved academic performance (not part of the original target problem).

The final category of generalization is assessed by measuring the change in behavior of nonprogram subjects. In this procedure, generalization to a different subject is recorded when a nontarget subject (to whom no services are applied) demonstrates a change following implementation of the treatment program. An example of this generalization phenomenon occurs when the researcher finds that a teacher demonstrates positive change when the intervention is applied to a child in the classroom.

SUMMARY

In this chapter we discussed a number of issues involved in the evaluation of school psychological services. School-based psychological services have been evaluated in various research and program evaluation activities over many years. Research and program evaluation activities are important to the field of school psychology because the incidence of school psychological and educational problems is quite high, and determining effective services is a high priority. Also, questions regarding the efficacy of school psychological services continue to be asked by those who support such services through taxes and related modes.

ACKNOWLEDGMENT

The authors express appreciation to Ms. Karen Kraemer and Ms. Sue Baker for their assistance in word processing this manuscript.

REFERENCES

Abt, C. C. (1977). *The evaluation of social programs.* Beverly Hills: Sage Publications.
Alessi, G. J. (1980). Behavioral observation for the school psychologist: Responsive-discrepancy model. *School Psychology Review, 9,* 31–45.
Alevizos, P., DeRisi, W., Liberman, R., Eckman, T., & Callahan, E. (1978). The behavior observation instrument: A method of direct observation for program evaluation. *Journal of Applied Behavior Analysis, 11,* 243–257.
Alpert, J. L., & Yammer, M. D. (1983). Research in school consultation: A content analysis of selected journals. *Professional Psychology: Research and Practice, 14,* 604–612.
Barlow, D. H., Hayes, S. C., & Nelson, R. O. (1984). *The scientist practitioner: Research and accountability in clinical and educational settings.* New York: Pergamon Press.
Bellack, A. A., & Hersen, M. (1978). Assessment and single-case research. In M. Hersen & A. S. Bellack (Eds.), *Behavior therapy in the psychiatric setting* (pp. 3–39). Baltimore: Williams & Wilkins.

Bentler, P. M. (1980). Multivariate analysis with latent variables. In M. R. Rozenweig & L. W. Porter (Eds.), *Annual review of psychology* (Vol. 31, pp. 419–456). Palo Alto, CA: Annual Reviews.

Bergan, J. R. (1977). *Behavioral consultation*. Columbus, OH: Merrill.

Bergan, J. R. (1981). Path-referenced assessment in school psychology. In T. R. Kratochwill (Ed.), *Advances in school psychology* (Vol. 1, pp. 255–280). Hillsdale, NJ: Lawrence Erlbaum Associates.

Bergan, J. R., Anderson, D. O., Feld, J. K., Henderson, R., Johnson, D. M., Lane, S., Mott, S. E., Parra, E., Robinson, L., Schnaps, A., Stone, C. A., & Swarner, J. C. (1984). *Head Start Measures Project Final Report*. (Contract number HHS-105-081-C-008). Tucson: University of Arizona. Center for Educational Evaluation and Measurement.

Bergan, J. R., Byrnes, I. M., & Kratochwill, T. R. (1979). Effects of behavioral and medical models of consultation on teacher expectancies and instruction of a hypothetical child. *Journal of School Psychology, 17,* 307–316.

Bergan, J. R., Feld, J. K., & Stone, C. A. (1984). *Consultation and data-based instructional management*. Unpublished manuscript, University of Arizona.

Bergan, J. R., & Kratochwill, T. R. (in press). *Behavioral consultation in applied settings*. New York: Plenum.

Bergan, J. R., Kratochwill, T. R., & Luiten, J. (1978). Competency-based training in behavioral consultation. *Journal of School Psychology, 18,* 91–97.

Bergan, J. R., Stone, C. A., & Feld, J. C. (in press). Path-referenced assessment of individual differences. In C. R. Reynolds & V. L. Willson (Eds.), *Methodological and statistical advances in the study of individual differences*. New York: Plenum.

Bergan, J. R., & Tombari, M. L. (1976). Consultant skill and efficiency and the implementation and outcomes of consultation. *Journal of School Psychology, 14,* 3–14.

Berliner, D. C. (1983, September). Executive functions of teaching. *Instructor, 93,* 28–40.

Bernstein, D. A., & Paul, G. L. (1971). Some comments on therapy analogue research with small animal "phobias." *Journal of Behavior Therapy and Experimental Psychiatry, 2,* 225–237.

Bornstein, P. H., & Rychtarik, R. C. (1983). Consumer satisfaction in adult behavior therapy: Procedures, problems, and future perspectives. *Behavior Therapy, 14,* 191–208.

Brown, D. K., Kratochwill, T. R., & Bergan, J. R. (1982). Teaching interview skills for problem identification: An analogue study. *Behavioral Assessment, 4,* 63–73.

Campbell, D. T., & Fiske, D. (1959). Convergent and discriminant validation by the multitrait-multimethod matrix. *Psychological Bulletin, 56,* 81–105.

Cancelli, A. A., & Kratochwill, T. R. (1981). Advances in criterion-referenced assessment. In T. R. Kratochwill (Ed.), *Advances in school psychology* (Vol. 1, pp. 154–217). Hillsdale, NJ: Lawrence Erlbaum Associates.

Caplan, G. (1970). *The theory and practice of mental health consultation*. New York: Basic Books.

Carlberg, C., & Kavale, K. (1980). The efficacy of special versus regular class placement for exceptional children. *The Journal of Special Education, 14,* 295–309.

Carter, W. E. (1975, April). *A taxonomy of evaluation models: Use of evaluation models in program evaluation*. A paper presented at the annual meeting of the American Educational Research Association, Washington, DC.

Ciminero, A. R., Calhoun, K. S., & Adams, H. E. (Eds.). (1977). *Handbook of behavioral assessment*. New York: Wiley.

Coates, T. J., & Thoresen, C. E. (1978). Using generalizability theory in behavioral observations. *Behavior Therapy, 9,* 605–613.

Collins, R. C. (1983). *Head Start: An update on program effects*. Society for Research in Child Development, Inc., Summer Newsletter (pp. 1–2).

Cone, J. D. (1977). The relevance of reliability and validity for behavioral assessment. *Behavior Therapy, 8,* 411–426.

Cone, J. D. (1978). The behavioral assessment grid (BAG): A conceptual framework and a taxonomy. *Behavior Therapy, 9,* 882–888.

Cone, J. D. (1979). Confounded comparisons in triple response mode assessment research. *Behavioral Assessment, 1,* 85–95.

Cone, J. D., & Foster, S. L. (1982). Direct observation in clinical psychology. In P. C. Kendall, & J. N. Butcher (Eds.), *Handbook of research methods in clinical psychology* (pp. 311–354). New York: Wiley.

Cone, J. D., & Hawkins, R. P. (Eds.). (1977). *Behavioral assessment.* New York: Brunner/Mazel.

Cook, T. D., & Campbell, D. T. (Eds.). (1979). *Quasi-experimentation: Design and analysis issues for field settings.* Chicago: Rand McNally.

Cook, T., & Leviton, L. (1980). Reviewing the literature: A comparison of traditional methods with meta-analysis. *Journal of Personality, 48,* 449–471.

Cooley, W. W., Bond, L., & Mao, B. J. (1981). Analyzing multilevel data. In R. A. Berk (Ed.), *Educational evaluation methodology: The state of the art* (pp. 64–73). Baltimore: Johns Hopkins University Press.

Cooper, H. M. (1982). Scientific guidelines for conducting intergrative research reviews. *Review of Educational Research, 52,* 291–302.

Cronbach, J., Glaser, G. C., Nada, H., & Rajaratman, N. (1972). *The dependability of behavioral measures.* New York: Wiley.

Drabman, R. S., Hammer, D. C., & Rosenbaum, M. S. (1979). Assessing generalization in behavior modification with children: The generalization map. *Behavioral Assessment, 1,* 203–219.

Duley, S. M., Cancelli, A. A., Kratochwill, T. R., Bergan, J. R., & Meredith, K. E. (1983). Training and generalization of motivational analysis interview assessment skills. *Behavioral Assessment, 5,* 281–293.

Farber, H., & Mayer, G. R. (1972). Behavior consultation in a barrio high school. *Personnel and Guidance Journal, 51,* 273–279.

Feld, J. K., Bergan, J. R., & Stone, C. A. (in press). Behavioral approaches to school-based consultation: Current status and future directions. In C. A. Maher & S. G. Forman (Eds.), *Providing educational services in the schools: A behavioral approach.* Hillsdale, NJ: Lawrence Erlbaum Associates.

Fisher, C. W., Berliner, D. C., Filby, W. W., Marliave, R. S., Cahen, L. S., & Dishaw, M. M. (1980). Teaching behaviors, academic learning time and student achievement: An overview. In C. Denham & A. Lieberman (Eds.), *Time to learn* (pp. 7–32). Washington, DC: Department of Education, National Institute of Education.

Fiske, D. W. (1979). Two worlds of psychological phenomena. *American Psychologist, 34,* 733–739.

Fiske, D. W. (1983). The meta-analytic revolution in outcome research. *Journal of Consulting and Clinical Psychology, 51,* 65–70.

Ford, J. D., & Migles, M. (1979). The role of the school psychologist: Teachers' preferences as a function of personal and professional characteristics. *Journal of School Psychology, 17,* 372–378.

Freeman, H. E. (1977). The present status of evaluation research. In M. Guttentag (Ed.), *Evaluation studies review-Annual* (Vol. 2, pp. 17–51). Beverly Hills, CA: Sage Publications.

Fullan, M. (1981). *The role of human agents in knowledge utilization.* Unpublished paper prepared for the National Institute of Education.

Garfield, S. L. (1977). Research on the training of professional psychotherapists. In A. S. Garman & A. M. Razin (Eds.), *Effective psychotherapy: A handbook of research* (pp. 63–83). Oxford: Pergamon Press.

Garfield, S. L. (1983a). Effectiveness of psychotherapy: The perennial controversy. *Professional Psychology, 14,* 35–43.

Garfield, S. L. (1983b). Special section: Meta-analysis and psychotherapy. *Journal of Consulting and Clinical Psychology, 51,* 3.

Garfield, S. L. (1983c). Some comments on consumer satisfaction in behavior therapy. *Behavior Therapy, 14,* 237–241.

Glass, G. V. (1976). Primary, secondary, and meta-analysis research. *Educational Researcher, 5,* 3–8.

Glass, G. V. (1977). Integrating findings: The meta-analysis of research. *Review of Research in Education, 5,* 351–379.

Glass, G. V., & Kliegl, R. M. (1983). An apology for research integration in the study of psychotherapy. *Journal of Consulting and Clinical Psychology, 51,* 28–41.

Glass, G. V., McGaw, B., & Smith, M. L. (1981). *Meta-analysis in social research.* Beverly Hills, CA: Sage Publications.

Goldstein, A. P., Sprafkin, R. P., Gershaw, N. J., & Klein, P. (1978). *Skillstreaming the adolescent: A structured learning approach to teaching prosocial behavior.* Champaign: IL: Research Press.

Goodman, L. A. (1973). The analysis of multidimensional contingency tables when some variables are posterior to others: A modified path analysis approach. *Biometrika, 60,* 215–231.

Goodwin, D. L., Garvey, W. P., & Barclay, J. R. (1971). Microconsultation and behavior analysis: A method of training psychologists as behavioral consultants. *Journal of Consulting and Clinical Psychology, 37,* 355–363.

Gresham, F. M., & Nagle, R. J. (1981). Treating school phobia using behavioral consultation: A case study. *School Psychology Review, 10,* 104–107.

Gutkin, T. B., & Curtis, M. J. (1982). School-based consultation: Theory and techniques. In C. R. Reynolds & T. B. Gutkin (Eds.), *The handbook of school psychology* (pp. 797–828). New York: Wiley.

Hartmann, D. P. (Ed.). (1982). *Using observers to study behavior: New directions for methodology of social and behavioral science.* San Francisco: Jossey-Bass.

Hartmann, D. P. (1984). Assessment Strategies. In D. H. Barlow & M. Hensen (Eds.), *single case experimental designs: Strategies for studying behavior change* (2nd ed., pp. 107–139). Elmsford, NY: Pergamon Press.

Hartmann, D. P., & Wood, D. D. (1982). Observational methods. In A. S. Bellack, M. Hersen, & A. E. Kazdin (Eds.), *International handbook of behavior modification and therapy* (pp. 109–138). New York: Plenum.

Hayes, S. C. (1981). Single-case experimental design and empirical clinical practice. *Journal of Consulting and Clinical Psychology, 49,* 193–211.

Haynes, S. N. (1978). *Principles of behavioral assessment.* New York: Gardner Press.

Haynes, S. N., & Wilson, C. C. (1979). *Recent advances in behavioral assessment.* San Francisco: Jossey-Bass.

Hazel, J. S., Schumaker, J. B., Sherman, J. A., & Sheldon-Wildgren, J. (1981). *Asset: A social skills program for adolescents.* Champaign, IL: Research Press.

Hersen, M., & Barlow, D. H. (1976). *Single-case experimental designs: Strategies for studying behavior change.* New York: Pergamon Press.

Hersen, M., & Bellack, A. S. (Eds.). (1976). *Behavioral assessment: A practical handbook.* New York: Pergamon Press.

Hops, H. (1971). The school psychologist as a behavior management consultant in a special class setting. *Journal of School Psychology, 9,* 473–483.

Hops, H., Fleischman, D., Guild, J., Paine, S., Street, A., Walker, H. M., & Greenwood, C. (1978). *Procedures for establishing effective relationship skills (PEERS): Consultant manual.* Eugene: University of Oregon, Center at Oregon for Research in the Behavioral Education of the Handicapped.

Hunter, C. P. (1977). Classroom observation instruments and teacher inservice training by school psychologists. *School Psychology Monograph, 3,* 45–88.

Jackson, N. F., Jackson, D. A., & Monroe, C. (1984). *Teaching social effectiveness to children.* Champaign, IL: Research Press.

Jason, L. A., & Ferone, L. (1978). Behavioral versus process consultation interventions in school settings. *American Journal of Community Psychology, 6,* 531–543.

Jason, L. A., Ferone, L., & Anderegg, T. (1979). Evaluating ecological behavioral, and process consultation interventions. *Journal of School Psychology, 17,* 103–115.

Johnston, J., & Pennypacker, H. S. (1980). *Strategies and tactics of human behavioral research.* Hillsdale, NJ: Lawrence Erlbaum Associates.

Jones, R. R. (1977). Conceptual vs. analytic uses of generalizability theory in behavioral assessment. In J. D. Cone & R. P. Hawkins (Eds.), *Behavioral assessment: New directions in clinical psychology* (pp. 330–343). New York: Brunner/Mazel.

Jones, R. R., Reid, J. B., & Patterson, G. R. (1974). Naturalistic observation in clinical assessment. In P. McReynolds (Ed.), *Advances in psychological assessment* (Vol. 3, pp. 42–95). San Francisco: Jossey-Bass.

Joreskog, K. G., & Sorbom, D. (1979). *Advances in factor analysis and structural equation models.* Cambridge, MA: Abt.

Kazdin, A. E. (1977a). Methodology of applied behavior analysis. In A. C. Catania & T. A. Brigham (Eds.), *Social and instructional processes: Foundations and applications of a behavior analysis* (pp. 61–104). New York: Irvington/Narbury-Wiley.

Kazdin, A. E. (1977b). *The token economy: A review and evaluation.* New York: Plenum.

Kazdin, A. E. (1978). *History of behavior modification: Experimental foundations of contemporary research.* Baltimore: University Park Press.

Kazdin, A. E. (1979). Fictions, factions, and function of behavior therapy. *Behavior Therapy, 10,* 629–654.

Kazdin, A. E. (1980). *Research design in clinical psychology.* New York: Harper & Row.

Kazdin, A. E. (1981). Drawing valid inferences from case studies. *Journal of Consulting and Clinical Psychology, 49,* 183–192.

Kazdin, A. E. (1982a). *Single-case research designs: Methods for clinical and applied settings.* New York: Oxford University Press.

Kazdin, A. E. (1982b). Methodology of psychotherapy outcome research: Recent developments and remaining limitations. In J. H. Harvey & M. M. Parker (Eds.), *Psychotherapy research and behavior change: The Master Lecture Series* (Vol. 1, pp. 155–193). Washington, DC: American Psychological Association.

Kazdin, A. E. (1985). Selection of target behaviors: The relationship of the treatment focus to clinical dysfunction. *Behavioral Assessment, 1,* 33–47.

Kazdin, A. E., & Wilson, G. T. (1978). *Evaluation of behavior therapy: Issues, evidence and research strategies.* Cambridge, MA: Ballinger.

Keller, H. R. (1980). Issues in the use of observational assessment. *School Psychology Review, 9,* 21–30.

Kent, R. N., & Foster, S. L. (1977). Direct observational procedures: Methodological issues in naturalistic settings. In A. R. Ciminero, K. S. Calhoun, & H. E. Adams (Eds.), *Handbook of behavioral assessment* (pp. 279–328). New York: Wiley.

Kiesler, C. A. (1983). Social psychological issues in studying consumer satisfaction with behavior therapy. *Behavior Therapy, 14,* 226–236.

Kratochwill, T. R. (Ed.). (1978). *Single subject research: Strategies for evaluating change.* New York: Academic Press.

Kratochwill, T. R. (1979). Intensive research: A review of methodological issues in clinical, school, and counseling psychology. In D. C. Berliner (Ed.), *Review of research in education* (pp. 46–91). Itasca, IL: F. E. Peacock.

Kratochwill, T. R. (Ed.). (1980a). *Advances in school psychology* (Vol. 1, pp.). Hillsdale, NJ: Lawrence Erlbaum Associates.

Kratochwill, T. R. (1980b). Behavioral assessment of academic and social problems: Implications for the individual education program. *School Psychology Review, 9,* 199–206.

Kratochwill, T. R. (1982). Advances in behavioral assessment. In C. R. Reynolds & T. B. Gutkin (Eds.), *Handbook of school psychology* (pp. 314–350). New York: Wiley.
Kratochwill, T. R. (1985). Case study research in school psychology. *School Psychology Review, 14*, 204–215.
Kratochwill, T. R., & Bergan, J. R. (1978). Evaluating programs in applied settings through behavioral consultation. *Journal of School Psychology, 16*, 375–386.
Kratochwill, T. R., & Bergan, J. R. (in press). *Behavioral consultation in applied settings: An individual guide.* New York: Plenum.
Lang, P. J. (1971). The application of psychophysiological methods to the study of psychotherapy and behavior modification. In A. E. Bergin & S. L. Garfield (Eds.), *Handbook of psychotherapy and behavior change* (pp. 75–125). New York: Wiley.
Lang, P. J. (1977). The psychophysiology of anxiety. In J. Akiskal (Ed.), *Psychiatric diagnosis: Exploration of biological criteria.* New York: Spectrum.
Leviton, L. C., & Cook, T. D. (1981). What differentiates meta-analysis from other forms of review. *Journal of Personality, 49*, 231–236.
Lloyd, M. E. (1983). Selecting systems to measure client outcome in human service agencies. *Behavioral Assessment, 5*, 55–70.
Lynch, W. W. (1977). Guidelines to the use of classroom observation instruments by school psychologists. *School Psychology Monographs, 3*, 1–22.
Maher, C. A. (1978). A synoptic framework for school program evaluation. *Journal of School Psychology, 16*, 322–333.
Maher, C. A., & Kratochwill, T. R. (1980). Principles and procedures of program evaluation: An overview. *School Psychology Monographs, 4*, 1–24.
Matarazzo, R. G. (1978). Research on the teaching and learning of psychotherapeutic skills. In S. L. Garfield & A. E. Bergin (Eds.), *Handbook of psychotherapy and behavior change* (2nd ed., pp. 941–966). New York: Wiley.
McMahon, R. J., & Forehand, R. L. (1983). Consumer satisfaction in behavioral treatment of children: Types, issues, and recommendations. *Behavior Therapy, 14*, 209–225.
Medway, F. J. (1979). How effective is school consultation? A review of recent research. *Journal of School Psychology, 17*, 275–282.
Medway, F. J. (1982). School consultation research: Past trends and future directions. *Professional Psychology, 13*, 422–430.
Meyers, J., Parsons, R. D., & Martin, R. (1979). *Mental health consultation in the schools.* San Francisco: Jossey-Bass.
Miller, T. L., & Dyer, C. O. (1980). Role-model implements of school psychology with special education. In L. Mann & D. A. Sabatino (Eds.), *The fourth review of special education* (pp. 391–428). New York: Grune & Stratton.
Mintz, J. (1983). Integrating research evidence: A commentary on metaanalysis. *Journal of Consulting and Clinical Psychology, 51*, 71–75.
Moracco, J., & Kazandkian, A. (1977). Effectiveness of behavior counseling and consulting with non-Western elementary school children. *Elementary School Guidance and Counseling, 11*, 244–251.
Morris, R. J., & Kratochwill, T. R. (1983). *Treating children's fears and phobias: A behavioral approach.* New York: Pergamon Press.
Nelson, R. O., & Hayes, S. C. (1979). Some current dimensions of behavioral assessment. *Behavioral Assessment, 1*, 1–16.
Nelson, R. O., Rudin-Hay, L., & Hay, W. D. (1977). Comments on Cone's "relevance of reliability and validity for behavioral assessment." *Behavior Therapy, 8*, 427–430.
O'Leary, K. D., Romancyzk, R. G., Kass, R. E., Dietz, A. T., & Santogrossi, D. (1979). *Procedures for classroom observations of teachers and children* (2nd ed.). Unpublished manuscript, State University of New York at Stony Brook.
Parloff, M. B. (1983). Who will be satisfied by "consumer satisfaction" evidence? *Behavior Therapy, 14*, 242–246.

Patterson, G. R., Reid, J. B., Jones, R. R., & Conger, R. E. (1975). *A social learning approach to family intervention, Vol. 1: Families with aggressive children.* Eugene, OR: Castalia.

Paul, G. P. (1967). Outcome research in psychotherapy. *Journal of Consulting Psychology, 31,* 109–118.

Paul, G. P., & Bernstein, D. A. (1973). *Anxiety and clinical problems: Systematic desensitization and related techniques.* Morristown, NJ: General Learning Press.

Peterson, L., Homer, A. L., & Wonderlich, S. A. (1982). The integrity of independent variables in behavior analysis. *Journal of Applied Behavior Analysis, 15,* 477–492.

Petrie, P., Brown, D. K., Piersel, W. C., Frinfrock, S. R., Schelble, M., LeBlanc, C. P., & Kratochwill, T. R. (1980). The school psychologist as behavioral ecologist. *Journal of School Psychology, 18,* 222–223.

Piersel, W. C., & Kratochwill, T. R. (1981). A teacher-implemented contingency management package to assess and treat selective mutism. *Behavioral Assessment, 3,* 371–382.

Rachman, S. J., & Wilson, G. T. (1980). *The effects of psychological therapy* (2nd ed.) New York: Pergamon Press.

Reid, J. B. (1970). Reliability assessment of observation data: A possible methodological problem. *Child Development, 41,* 1143–1150.

Reynolds, C. R., & Gutkin, T. B. (Eds.). (1982). *Handbook of school psychology.* New York: Wiley.

Ritter, D. R. (1978). Effects of a school consultation program upon referral patterns of teachers. *Psychology in the Schools, 15,* 239–243.

Romanczyk, R. G., Kent, R. N., Diament, C., & O'Leary, K. D. (1973). Measuring the reliability of observational data: A reactive process. *Journal of Applied Behavior Analysis, 6,* 175–184.

Rosenthal, R. (1983). Assessing the statistical and social importance of the effects of psychotherapy. *Journal of Consulting and Clinical Psychology, 51,* 4–13.

Rossi, P. H., Freeman, H. E., & Wright, S. R. (1979). *Evaluation: A systematic approach.* Beverly Hills: Sage Publications.

Salmon-Cox, L. (1980). *Teachers and tests: What's really happening.* Paper presented at the annual meeting of the American Research Association, Washington, DC.

Sandoval, J., & Lambert, N. (1977). Instruments for evaluating school psychologists' functioning and service. *Psychology in the Schools, 14,* 172–179.

Schmuck, R. (1982). Organization development in the schools. In C. R. Reynolds & T. B. Gutkin (Eds.), *The handbook of school psychology* (pp. 829–857). New York: Wiley.

Scriven, M. S. (1967). The methodology of evaluation. In R. Tyler, R. Gagne, & M. Scriven (Eds.), *Perspectives of curriculum evaluation,* (pp.   ). (AERA Monograph Series on Curriculum Evaluation). Chicago: Rand McNally.

Sechrest, L., West, S. G., Phillips, M. A., Redner, R., & Yeaton, W. (1979). *Some neglected problems in evaluation research: Strength and integrity of treatments.* In L. Sechrest, S. G West, M. A. Phillips, R. Redner, & W. Yeaton (Eds.), *Evaluation studies: Review annual* (Vol. 4, pp.   ). Beverly Hills: Sage Publications.

Shapiro, D. A., & Shapiro, D. (1983). Comparative therapy outcome research: Methodological implications of meta-analysis. *Journal of Consulting and Clinical Psychology, 51,* 42–53.

Shavelson, R. J., & Stern, P. (1981). Research on teachers pedagogical thoughts, judgments, decisions, and behavior. *Review of Educational Research, 51,* 455–498.

Smith, M. L., Glass, G. V., & Miller, T. I. (1980). *Benefits of psychotherapy.* Baltimore, MD: Johns Hopkins University Press.

Stephens, T. M. (1978). *Social skills in the classroom.* Columbus, OH: Cedars Press.

Stokes, T. F., & Baer, D. M. (1977). An implicit technology of generalization. *Journal of Applied Behavior Analysis, 10,* 349–368.

Strossen, R. J., Coates, T. J., & Thoresen, C. E. (1979). Extending generalizability theory to single subject designs. *Behavior Therapy, 10,* 606–614.

Strube, M. J., & Hartmann, D. P. (1982). A critical appraisal of meta-analysis. *British Journal of Clinical Psychology, 21,* 129–139.
Strube, M. J., & Hartmann, D. P. (1983). Meta-analysis: Techniques, applications, and functions. *Journal of Consulting and Clinical Psychology, 51,* 14–27.
Strupp, H. H., & Hadley, S. W. (1977). A triparite model of mental health and therapeutic outcomes. *American Psychologist, 32,* 187–196.
Stufflebeam, D. J., Foley, W. J., Gephart, W. J., Guba, E. G., Hammond, R. L., Merriman, H. O., & Provus, M. M. (1971). *Educational evaluation and decision making.* Itasca, IL: F. E. Peacock.
Taplin, P. S., & Reid, J. B. (1973). Effects of instructional set and experimenter influence on observer reliability. *Child Development, 44,* 547–554.
Tombari, M. L., & Davis, R. A. (1979). Behavioral consultation. In G. D. Phye & D. J. Reschly (Eds.), *School psychology: Perspectives and issues* (pp. 281–307). New York: Academic press.
Tyler, V. O. (1981). Aggressive consultation in the schools with mini-consultants, college credits- and a show of power. *Psychology in the Schools, 18,* 341–348.
Van Someren, K. R., & Kratochwill, T. R. (1983). *A review of the empirical literature in behavioral consultation.* Unpublished manuscript.
Wahler, R. G., House, A. E., & Stambaugh, E. E. (1976). *Ecological assessment of child problem behavior: A clinical package for home, school, and institutional settings.* New York: Pergamon Press.
Weiner, I. B. (1982). *Child and adolescent psychopathology.* New York: Wiley.
Wilson, G. T., & Rachman, S. J. (1983). Meta-analysis and the evaluation of psychotherapy outcome: Limitations and liabilities. *Journal of Consulting and Clinical Psychology, 51,* 54–64.
Wolf, M. M. (1978). Social validity. The case for subjective measurement or how applied behavior analysis is finding its heart. *Journal of Applied Behavior Analysis, 11,* 203–214.
Workman, E. A., Kindall, L. M., & Williams, R. L. (1980). The consultative merits of praise-ignore versus praise-reprimand instruction. *Journal of School Psychology, 18,* 373–380.
Yeaton, W. H., & Sechrest, L. (1981). Critical dimensions in the choice and maintenance of successful treatments: Strength, integrity and effectiveness. *Journal of Consulting and Clinical Psychology, 49,* 156–167.
Zwald, L., & Gresham, F. M. (1982). Behavioral consultation in a secondary class: Using DRL to decrease negative verbal interactions. *School Psychology Review, 11,* 428–432.

11 The Connections Among Educational and Psychological Research and the Practice of School Psychology

Maurine A. Fry
Arizona State University

Unanimity is rare in a relatively new profession and especially so among professionals as diverse in background and function as school psychologists. Yet, there seems to be nearly unanimous agreement that research has had little impact on the practice of school psychology (cf. Phillips, 1982). In this respect the profession is true to its heritage; i.e., most educators believe research has had little effect on educational practice (cf. Biddle & Ellena, 1964; Bolster, 1983), and clinical psychologists believe clinical research has had little influence on clinical practice (cf. Barlow, 1981).

Why then write this chapter? Perhaps because pessimists about past impact are often optimistic about the future (cf. Glaser, 1978), and I, along with others, continue to believe that research should inform practice and perhaps even does.

I have organized the first quarter of this chapter around two questions that plague those who start from the premise that research should inform practice: (a) Why hasn't research had greater impact on education in general, and the practice of school psychology in particular? and (b) How might research have greater impact on the practice of school psychology? In the remainder of the chapter, I play the "devil's advocate" and discuss (c) What research has influenced practice and why?

WHY HAS RESEARCH NOT HAD GREATER IMPACT?

This problem has not suffered from lack of analysis (cf. Farley, 1982; Phillips, 1982; Tuthill & Ashton, 1983). These analyses begin typically with the assertion that educational research has had little impact on educational practice, and then proceed to present evidence that leads to the conclusion that the fault lies with the quantity and quality of the research base in education.

Quantity

A discussion of the quantity of educational research often leads to two opposite conclusions, i.e., (a) there is too little and (b) there is too much. Until recently, it was often said that there was just too little research in education due to lack of money, lack of trained people, and lack of time (research being a part-time activity of trained people). Now, when an argument is made for too little educational research, it is typically research of a particular type. That is, this view of quantity interacts with the particular author's view of quality or importance; e.g., there is not enough educational research that asks important questions, systematically, over the long term.

On the other hand, if all social science research is viewed as having potential impact on education, there is too much to be aware of, to integrate, and to assimilate. Empirical inquiry in the social and behavioral sciences is vast, and articles, theses, and dissertations are strewn over hundreds of journals and libraries. As Glass, McGaw, and Smith (1981) point out, "Determining what knowledge this enterprise has produced on some questions is, itself, a genuinely important scholarly endeavor" (p. 12). Gage (1982) and others see it as a hopeful sign that research integration and the publication of meta-analyses seem to be increasing (cf. Walberg & Haertel, 1980). For a less optimistic view of this activity, see Tuthill and Ashton (1983, p. 10).

Quality

It is commonplace to bemoan the generally poor quality of educational research and to indict such factors as underfunding, part-time involvement of personnel, poor training of research personnel, trivial and constantly changing problem selection, inadequate designs (cf. Phillips, 1982). Since no one wants trivial, inaccurate, or unreliable findings applied to practice, the answer to why educational research has not had greater impact on practice is obvious to those who believe this characterization is an accurate picture of educational research. A majority of practitioners in education and practitioners in training are told repeatedly that the research base is abysmal. Why then would we expect practitioners to want to know what educational research says or how it might be applied?

If educational research is generally of poor quality, it does not necessarily follow that there is no good, or even exemplary, research in education. Nor does it follow that this research has had no impact on practice or that we cannot take steps to ensure greater impact on practice in the future.

HOW MIGHT RESEARCH HAVE GREATER IMPACT ON THE PRACTICE OF SCHOOL PSYCHOLOGY?

Recent reports, e.g., the presidential commission's *A Nation at Risk* and Boyer (1983), augur well for a national resurgence of concern for quality education. If research is to impact practice, educational researchers must help to direct this concern toward eradicating old problems and criticisms of educational research, e.g., research funding, personnel selection, and training. The nation must continue to look at our investment in educational research and development in relation to our investment in research and development in other professions. In relation to personnel selection, a career in education must be made more attractive so that we can succeed in stemming the "brain-drain" and become competitive with other professions in obtaining our fair share of the best minds to train (Feistritzer, 1983). Even without additional funding, we can improve the training of educational researchers, school psychologists, and teachers. As a first step, I would get the existing research base and the value of disciplined inquiry back in their programs.

To increase the impact of educational research on practice, we must also continue to improve the quality of educational research. Perhaps the foremost suggestion to date to improve research quality has been the call for more interaction research (Cronbach & Snow, 1977; Phillips, 1982). A suggestion that may have greater impact on practice is gaining momentum in the eighties. This is the suggestion that we build in the "extension mechanism" or somehow forge the "missing link" between the educational researchers and the educational practitioners.

The "Missing Link"

Several researchers who have attempted to implement their theories in the classroom have called attention to the "missing link" (Kohlberg, 1980; Lovitt, 1981; Resnick, 1981). Barlow (1981) has pointed to a similar problem in relating clinical research to practice in clinical psychology.

Because it is common to read that education, when compared to other professions (e.g., engineering, law, medicine, and so on) is least affected by research, I found an article by Johnson (1981) on misconceptions about the early land-grant colleges relevant and interesting. It is, after all, to these early land-grant colleges that those of us in academe owe the emphasis on research and service, in addition to instruction. In rebellion against purely classical instruction, the early land-grant colleges put science at the center. Around this central core, they developed an unusually strong research orientation with an emphasis on application and problem solving. Although we often speak as if agriculture, engineering, and so forth, have long been influenced by this focus, Johnson makes the point that the direct developmental impact of these colleges has been primarily a phenomenon of the 20th century—*after* the agricultural experiment stations were established, *after* research knowledge was given an extension mechanism, and *after* there were thousands of practicing professionals. In this context, it is well to remember that the training of teachers generally took place in normal schools prior to World War II, and only in the latter half of this century did the training of educational practitioners (including school psychologists) and educational researchers become common in the universities. (Peak production of educational researchers probably occurred in the 1960s and the number of training programs in school psychology increased by 500% in the 1960s [Goh, 1977].)

In a sense, we now have our equivalent of agricultural experiment stations established in major universities and in the national laboratories, and there are certainly thousands of practicing professionals. What we don't yet have in education is the "extension mechanism." The call for such a mechanism has been made by others (cf. Orlich, 1979, who actually suggested that each land-grant college might link with a public school). Was the time not right earlier because the other parts of the equation were not yet in place or are there other impediments to establishing this link?

After extensive on-site examination of graduate schools of education in the United States, H. Judge (1982) concluded that by deliberate choice these schools have tended to distance themselves from the task of training teachers and from addressing the problems and needs of elementary and secondary schools. If one accepts Judge's conclusion (and I do), the reasons for this deliberate choice not to establish "links" are undoubtedly complex, but at least three possibilities come to mind. The importance of the first will be questioned by some readers, the second reason should be generally accepted, and the third reason is a matter of current debate.

Differing Orientations. The orientations of educational researchers and educational practitioners are more in opposition than is true of other professional fields. No aura of femininity hangs over the medical researcher or the medical practitioner, the engineer in academe or the engineer in practice—all are clearly masculine and can talk man to man. (I'll grant there is some tension in the system because the one is almost always telling the other how to improve, i.e., research does impact practice).

The same conditions do not prevail in education. The aura of femininity hangs over the entire educational enterprise—especially so for the first 8 years. Thus, we have a logical, objective, reasonable, masculine educational researcher (typically in academe where he is striving with limited success to be considered equal to his colleagues), being asked to communicate and cooperate with the illogical, emotional, subjective, feminine educational practitioner. It is difficult, if not impossible, to reconcile these differing orientations. (For the reader who believes I have overstated the case, I recommend Keller, 1983, and reflection upon some of our conscious and not so conscious beliefs.)

We Don't Know Enough. Often the best educational researchers have protested, with justification, that their findings under controlled conditions were not sufficiently reliable or generalizable to apply in the real classroom. This is still true in many areas, but I agree with Schutz (1979) that in regard to elementary schooling we do know enough to be of real-time help. (Some evidence for this statement is presented in the next section.)

A variation on this theme is "once my theory is solidly research-based, good educational practice can be deduced from it." Hence, we have believed the educational researcher's role was to develop the data-based theory of learning, or of teaching, and the practitioner's role was to deduce from theory the appropriate classroom practices. Kohlberg (1983) now views this way of relating theory to practice, as the "psychologist's fallacy." The "psychologist's fallacy" assumes that the variables seen by the psychologist as important to his/her research are also the important variables for teachers to use in thinking about educational practice. After working in the schools with teachers, Kohlberg now believes that to be a valid foundation for practice, a theory must be genuinely accepted by teachers within their own autonomous thinking and blend reasonably well with their own common sense and observation. Such statements coming from a psychologist, especially one of Kohlberg's stature, have to be read several times to be believed. Views are changing!

The Goal of Educational Research. Tuthill and Ashton (1983) discussed the division among educational researchers regarding the goal of educational science. The view that the goal of science in education was to develop theory has been most powerful since the 1950s. One now hears a diverse group of psychoeducational researchers (Cooley, 1983; Kohlberg, 1983), educational philosophers (Scriven, 1980), and university presidents (*Education Week,* August 24, 1983, p. 17) calling on educational researchers to improve practice and insisting upon the need for educational scientists and practitioners to work together. Some of these efforts to encourage researchers to let practitioners tell them what the problems are that need to be solved and the epistemological shift they imply may result in forging that "missing-link" to the classroom. Researchers may come to work with teachers, counselors, school social workers, and school psychologists in attempting to solve problems so as to ensure the influence of research on practice.

WHAT RESEARCH HAS INFLUENCED THE PRACTICE OF SCHOOL PSYCHOLOGY?

In preparing to write this chapter and in talking to teachers and colleagues about it, my own views on this topic have changed. First, I came to the same conclusion that I found Gage (1982) had expressed in reaction to the general skepticism and devaluing of educational research: "This skepticism concerning what we have achieved, or can ever achieve, seems to me to be a kind of 'weltschmerz chic'. There are important and consistently found main effects in educational research" (p. 11).

Sadly, it seems that in most educational circles, it has become a sign of intellect and erudition to disparage educational research—regardless of whether or not one is personally engaged in it. In the remainder of this chapter I accentuate the positive and discuss important educational or psychoeducational research I believe has influenced the practice of school psychology. The discussion is not intended to be exhaustive and other examples will undoubtedly occur to the reader. The reader will have to judge for herself/himself whether the evidence presented for importance or influence is convincing.

Second, the research that I eventually included is more varied than originally intended, but I believe the focus is consistent with the changing role of the school psychologist (Goh, 1977; Meacham & Peckham, 1978). I tried to be guided by the question; Did (or perhaps would) this research influence the practice of a school-based consultant and problem solver? One could argue that a piece of research could have been included under several headings or that other headings entirely would have been more appropriate; however, I chose to organize the discussion under the following subheads: (a) Developmental/Clinical research, (b) Assessment research, (c) Research on learning and teaching, and (d) Research on schooling.

Developmental/Clinical Research

Developmental/clinical research that has influenced the practice of school psychology stems from two quite distinct directions. One line comes from research that interacted with or followed from social policy decisions. The other line comes from basic research and theory originally developed in an academic setting.

Social Policy. Research played some part in a court decision (i.e., Brown v. Board of Education) having monumental impact on public schooling in the United States and, consequently, on the practice of school psychology. As one of the psychologists (Clark, 1965) involved acknowledges, the research apparently was not considered important prior to being cited by the court.

> It is interesting to speculate on the significance of the fact that during the ten years after the U.S. Supreme Court school desegregation decision, an increasing number of social scientists have raised questions concerning the "scientific validity," of the psychological and sociological data cited by the Court as evidence of the damage which segregation inflicts upon personality. Not one of these critics had questioned these data and their interpretations prior to the Court's decision, although the studies

on which they were based had been published and available for critical reactions for many years prior to their use in the historic decision. (p. 76)

Obviously, the effect of this research was not directly on the schools, but on a court decision that impacted the schools and much federal legislation since that time—including P.L. 94–142. Would the ruling in Brown v. the Board of Education, which concluded that segregated education was inherently unequal education have been the same in the absence of this research? No one knows. What is perhaps more important is that you never hear this research mentioned in the context of a discussion questioning the effects of research on education, nor do I believe that many present educators—including many educational researchers—remember that research was cited.

Thirty years later, research at Johns Hopkins and in other settings continues to have impact as questions are asked regarding the long-range effects of desegregated schooling. The pattern of effects shows that desegregated schooling is helping to create a less racially isolated adult society. A study of 25 central cities showed that in city school districts that attained high levels of school desegregation from 1967 to 1976, higher levels of housing desegregation occurred between 1970 and 1980 (Pearce & Crain, 1983). Desegregated high schools promoted more positive perceptions and social contacts among blacks and whites in racially heterogeneous work groups, contributed to desegregation in higher education, and to desegregation in adult work environments—especially in the North (Braddock & McPartland, 1982).

The civil rights movement of the sixties led to other legislation. Head Start programs were established under the Economic Opportunity Act of 1964. Head Start programs and Follow Through programs have had a significant impact on increasing employment opportunities for school psychologists, and many school psychologists became involved in preschool education for the first time.

Research conclusions regarding the benefits of Head Start have changed several times in the past 20 years. First, the government released a study in 1969 conducted by Westinghouse Learning Corporation and Ohio University. The report found the effects of Head Start in the first years to be slight to negligible. Since its release, this report has received its share of criticism from other educational researchers for failing to consider when a child entered the program and for defining improvement as change in intellectual functioning as measured by intelligence tests.

In 1975, 14 Head Start studies were pooled to become the Consortium for Longitudinal Studies (CLS) under the direction of Irving Lazar and Richard Darlington of Cornell University. The positive findings of these studies have done much to eliminate the negative perceptions of the benefits of Head Start among educators, social-policy analysts, and the public as a whole.

One of the 14 studies included in the CLS is the Perry Preschool Project in Ypsilanti, Michigan. Data obtained at age 19 for the first wave of children accepted in this project in 1962 were recently released (*Education Week*, September 7, 1983). Results indicated children who attended the Preschool in the Fall of 1962 were far more likely to have graduated from high school (67% vs. 49% of the controls), and to have become economically self-sufficient (50% employed vs. 32% of the controls; 27% receiving welfare benefits vs. 37% of the controls). These children were less likely to have been enrolled in special education programs and more likely to have avoided breaking the law by the time they reached age 19 than were other students from the same south-side Ypsilanti neighborhood who did not attend the school. School personnel and school boards will be especially interested in the indication that benefits to school systems from reduced special education costs are close to being sufficient by themselves to justify the original outlay of funds.

Follow-through projects followed from Head Start, and perhaps the best known evaluation was conducted by Cooley and Lohnes (1976). Cooley and Lohnes found the vast variability in effectiveness among sites implementing the same instructional model more impressive than differences between models. (For a discussion of what factors seem responsible for differences in implementation, see the section on effective schools.)

Basic Research. No one can talk about research in developmental psychology without mentioning Piaget. No one presents a better example among researchers of a research program that dealt with an important problem, i.e., "What does intelligence look like and how does it develop?" in a thorough and systematic manner over the long term (50 years). His impact on American psychology is indisputable, and in that sense, Piaget has had an impact on the training of school psychologists. However, I have my doubts about his influence on the practice of school psychology. Certainly there is some indirect influence through Kohlberg and his research program, through the inclusion of different types of assessment, e.g., the Goldschmid-Bentler Concept Assessment Kit, which may now be included among the school psychologists' assessment techniques. What appears to be missing again is the "link" between basic research, theory, and practice. Piaget was quite clear about his disinterest in it. Piaget was concerned with answering questions about shared regularities rather than attempting to measure systematic differences or attempting interventions to effect these differences. If these "links" are to be forged, it is now up to the Neo-Piagetians, such as Robbie Case (1978), to do it. Case's research and that of other Neo-Piagetians, certainly, are known to some school psychologists and teachers, but it is perhaps too soon to attempt to assess impact.

Lawrence Kohlberg, like Jean Piaget, is one of those relatively rare social scientists who has essentially devoted his entire professional life to the study of one important topic, i.e., morality and its development over the human life span. As Kohlberg's cognitive-developmental theory of moral development has evolved, he has consistently acknowledged his debt to Piaget and to John Dewey (Kohlberg, 1980). Kohlberg's theory and research program are discussed in some detail as it may be one of our best examples of the reasoned application of research knowledge and scholarly thought to public education.

Beginning in 1955, Kohlberg started to define and validate stages in moral development through the use of structured interviews. Three basic levels of moral development (Preconventional, Conventional, and Postconventional, Autonomous, or Principled) with two stages per level were defined. Briefly, summarized from Kohlberg (1980, pp. 22–23), the six stages are as follows:

Stage 1: The punishment-and-obedience orientation. (Physical consequences of action determine its goodness or badness regardless of the human meaning or value of these consequences.)

Stage 2: The instrumental-relativist orientation. (Right action consists of that which instrumentally satisfies one's own needs and occasionally the needs of others. Reciprocity is a matter of "you scratch my back and I'll scratch yours," not of loyalty, gratitude or justice.)

Stage 3: The interpersonal concordance or "good boy-nice girl" orientation. (Good behavior in that which pleases or helps others and is approved by them. There is much conformity to stereotypical images of what is majority or "natural" behavior.)

Stage 4: The "law and order" orientation. (Right behavior consists of doing one's duty, following fixed rules, showing respect for authority and maintaining the given social order for its own sake.)

Stage 5: The social-contract legalistic orientation, generally with utilitarian overtones. (Aside from what is constitutionally and democratically agreed upon, the right is a matter of personal "values" and "opinion." The result is an emphasis upon the "legal point of view," but with an emphasis upon the possibility of changing law in terms of rational considerations of social utility.)

Stage 6: The universal-ethical-principle orientation. (Right is defined by the decision of conscience in accord with self-chosen *ethical principles* appealing to logical comprehensiveness, universality, and consistency. At heart, these are universal principles of justice, of the reciprocity and *equality* of human *rights,* and of respect for the dignity of human beings as *individual persons.*)

Kohlberg and his colleagues claim to have validated these stages through longitudinal and cross-sectional study (Colby, Kohlberg, Gibbs, & Lieberman, 1983). Piaget and Kohlberg used the term *stage* to imply the following empirical characteristics: (a) Stages are "structured wholes," or organized systems of thought. Individuals are consistent in level of moral judgment. (b) Stages form an invariant sequence; under all conditions except extreme trauma, movement is always forward, never backward. Individuals never skip stages; movement is always to the next stage up. (c) Stages are "hierarchical integrations." Thinking at a higher stage includes or comprehends within it lower stage thinking, and there is also a tendency to prefer the highest stage of thinking available.

In the early 1970s, Kohlberg and colleagues were themselves the prime movers behind the influence of Kohlberg's theory on education as they began to work directly in correctional institutions and public schools. Kohlberg's theory of the development of moral reasoning offered a unique view of moral education. His theory suggested that rather than emphasizing socialization or indoctrination in social norms, moral education should seek to stimulate that level of social reasoning that is natural to the child's stage of development. Kohlberg also argued originally that teachers should focus more upon the process of the child's reasoning than upon content (Scharf, 1978). Continuing work in the schools, however, has led Kohlberg to a view closer to that of many of his critics; i.e., moral education must deal directly with action and not just with reasoning. This change in view led him to focus on the "hidden curriculum" and to the formation of a participatory democracy or "just community" school.

Kohlberg's attempts to intervene in the classroom to effect moral development began with Blatt's dissertation (Blatt & Kohlberg, 1975). Blatt led classroom discussions of hypothetical moral dilemmas. His instructional method involved arousing controversy about choice and Socratic questioning about reasons to justify conclusions about dilemmas on which students disagreed. Blatt's research-based premise was that students would comprehend and assimilate reasoning by peers at the next higher stage while discarding reasoning by peers at the stage below. Blatt found that one fourth to one half of the students moved up (partially or totally) to the next stage in one semester. This change was not found in control groups.

The "Blatt effect" was replicated in the Stone Foundation project. This project engaged over 20 high school social studies teachers in the Boston and Pittsburgh areas in developmental moral discussion of hypothetical dilemmas. (These dilemmas were later incorporated into Fenton's Carnegie-Mellon social studies curriculum in ninth-grade civics.) The Stone Foundation project indicated that the following three elements had to be present if any changes were to occur: (a) controversial, moral dilemmas in areas that would arouse disagreement among students or "cognitive conflict" in choice, (b) a mixture of students functioning at two or three different stages in the classroom, and (c) a teacher who used extensive Socratic probes to challenge students' reasoning.

During the last half of the 1970s, Kohlberg's research and thought were experimentally introduced in public schools through several projects, e.g., the Danforth-Brookline Moral Education Project, the Cambridge Project, and the Pittsburgh-Carnegie Mellon projects. These efforts were all essentially demonstration projects in teacher training and curriculum writing in moral education at the high school level—although they explored similar objectives at the middle school level (grades 6–8), developed courses for parents in the psychology of the child's moral development and the parents' role in moral education, and helped to support and research two different democratic mini-school projects in the Boston area.

Results of these projects are discussed in detail in Mosher (1980), Reimer, Paolitto, and Hersh (1983), and Scharf (1978). These projects were among the first to test and act upon the idea that we can add both to our conceptualizing in educational research and to practice in education by validating one against the other. This test seems to have met with some success. From a research point of view, questions were answered and new questions raised. Social role taking, moral dialogue, exposure to higher stage thinking, and a "just community" all seem related to change in moral reasoning. The comparative effectiveness of these strategies in the classroom and a better understanding of the relation between moral reasoning and moral action are questions for further investigation (Sperber & Miron, 1980). From a practical standpoint, "just community" school settings seemed to lead to greater responsibility and trust among students, virtually no stealing or vandalism, and lower absenteeism (Sperber & Miron, 1980). These practical gains, however, do not come easily. Application of Kohlberg's cognitive-developmental theory in the classroom demands a great deal from teachers. The theory is too complex to be used by teachers who lack philosophical or psychological training, and the support of the highest levels of the school administration is essential to successful implementation in the classroom (Mosher, 1980; Scharf, 1978).

Research on Assessment

Psychometrics has as firm a scientific knowledge base as any subfield in the social sciences. Yet, this knowledge base has had less than optimal impact both on assessment practices in the schools and on court decisions affecting these practices.

Assessment of any particular aspect of a child's functioning is an extremely complex matter—at any particular time or in assessing change over time. But, we do have knowledge of the complex issues in child assessment and of the trade-offs inherent in any assessment situation (cf. Messick, 1983). What we do not seem to be doing is transmitting our knowledge adequately to the public at large or, worse yet, to many of our teachers, counselors, and school psychologists in training.

Since the 1960s, social movements with legitimate concern for equality of opportunity have translated their concerns into litigation against the public schools. Two areas of particular concern have been (a) the admittance and treatment of handicapped children, and (b) the over-representation of minority-group students in classes for the mildly retarded. This litigation and ensuing legislation have impacted assessment practice in at least two related areas which have come to be known as (a) nonbiased assessment, and (b) competency-based assessment.

Nonbiased Assessment. Once again, this is not a simple solution, but rather, a multifaceted area of concern involving context, persons, instruments, processes, and goals. The litigation and legislation leading to the concern for nonbiased assessment, as well as many of the issues raised (e.g., content bias in tests, atmosphere bias, and bias in use), have been reviewed by Reschly (1979). There is no need to cover the same ground in this chapter. Instead, I would like to alert the reader to Messick's discussion of the System of Multicultural Pluralistic Assessment (SOMPA) and expand slightly on one of Reschly's (1979) conclusions.

Messick (1983) in his chapter on assessment of children discusses the SOMPA at some length. Messick chose the SOMPA as "an example of a comprehensive assessment procedure that systematically utilizes physical, personal/social, and cultural information in the assessment of child characteristics" (p. 495). Although Messick is positive about the SOMPA's comprehensive assessment of intrapersonal and environmental context, he also discusses serious problems of measurement and interpretation in "the unsupported utilization of statistically adjusted WISC-R scores to estimate 'learning potential,' a construct reminiscent of the notion of 'capacity' " (pp. 495–496). Sattler (1982) has also expressed concern regarding the lack of either empirical or construct validity for the "learning potential" construct at this time. If research does not precede practice, research and caution must accompany it! The press of the public call for "nonbiased assessment" does not make basic psychometric concepts, e.g., reliability and various types of validity, less important. As we all know, these concepts are essential to nonbiased assessment.

The importance of basic measurement concepts brings me to my second point. Reschly (1979) concluded his chapter with the suggestion that "we view nonbiased assessment as a *process* rather than as a set of instruments" (p. 250). I am in total agreement with that statement. However, this is an issue for training programs because that process must be inside the head of the practicing school psychologist. A competently trained school psychologist will be aware that the "process" involves many concepts, including multifactored assessment, interpretation of assessment results in context, and the knowledge that "issues of validity and values are inherently intertwined and that the ethics of assessment is a fundamental and continuing concern in all test interpretation and use" (Messick, 1983, p. 478).

Competency-Based Assessment. Related to the concern for nonbiased assessment has been a growing dissatisfaction in recent years with norm-referenced measurement. Initially, there was the legitimate concern that certain normative samples did not include appropriate minority group representation, geographic distribution, and so forth. Concerns for equality of opportunity raised serious questions in certain contexts whether an individual's performance need be compared to the performance of others at all or was simply indicating a level of performance "competence" sufficient? In addition, public concern regarding the level of reading, writing, and arithmetic skill of elementary and high school graduates has led to a powerful minimum competency-testing movement in many states. "Minimum-competency" examinations are now required in 37 states (Boyer, 1983). The topic is a subject of almost daily debate in newspapers and on television, and it is an area where research might impact practice. As yet, there are primarily questions. Will competency-based assessment lead to early detection and appropriate intervention? (Detection without intervention will not solve the problem.) Will the "minimum" tend to become the "maximum" and thus lower standards? Will we be able to adequately assess higher levels of cognitive competence (e.g., critical thinking), problem solving, and judgment skills? (This is a crucial question in the use of competency testing for teacher certification.)

Research On Learning and Teaching

Research on learning and research on teaching are not the same, although, as Gage (1963) pointed out, we have often acted as if they were. The effects of research on learning are discussed first, followed by a discussion of the effects of research on teaching.

Learning Research. Certainly many people believe that B. F. Skinner's theories about, and studies on, operant conditioning have had a substantial impact on education—as well as psychology (cf. Suppes, 1978; Walton, 1983). Skinner's theory has been a force behind the adoption in the schools of a variety of techniques and strategies to facilitate learning.

One of these techniques was the "teaching machine" advocated by Skinner in the 1960s. Although the "teaching machine" movement was short lived, the movement did lead to research on computer-assisted instruction (CAI). CAI was often effective in the schools (cf. Gagné & Dick's, 1983, discussion of the Ontario project), but the medium of instruction was too expensive for massive implementation in the public schools. With the development of the microcomputer, cost effectiveness is being reconsidered. Microcomputers are moving into the public schools, and instruction for use in these microprocessors, as well as the evaluation of program effectiveness, will likely be extensively investigated in the decade ahead.

Skinner's work has played a part also in the debate over individualized instruction (considered to some extent in the section on research on schooling) and in the development of mastery learning techniques. (For a recent review of mastery learning, see Gagné and Dick, 1983.)

Skinner's most central effect on public education, however, undoubtedly stems from a variety of methodologies that have taken the critical features of operant conditioning and adapted them to the study of instructional problems at all levels of education. The methodology most familiar to school psychologists is behavior modification, and the application of behavior modification in the schools has changed considerably since the 1960s (cf. Bijou & Ruiz, 1981).

Early applications of behavior modification targeted individual atypical students (i.e., severe deficits or maladaptive behaviors) and atypical classroom consequences (i.e., food, electric shock). Recent trends have emphasized (a) adaptations to groups as well as individuals, teachers, and aides as well as students, (b) antecedents as well as consequences, (c) targeting adaptive academic, social, and personal skills, and (d) more "natural" classroom consequences such as attention, praise, privileges, and preferred activities. More efforts are also beginning to be directed toward the prevention of problem behaviors by identifying and managing ecological conditions in the classroom, e.g., scheduling quiet activities prior to academic work periods.

With the paradigm swing from a behavioral to a cognitive emphasis in psychology, the variables of interest in learning research have changed also. Comprehension of text, and factors that affect it, has been the primary research topic of the 1970s. Since comprehension of written material is now, and is likely to remain, an important aspect of schooling, this research would seem to have great potential for application. With one exception, however, the effects of this research may be more evident in the construction of new textbooks than in changes in school psychological services.

The exception is research in metacognition. Research in metacognition stems from Flavell's original concern with metamemory (Flavell & Wellman, 1977). More recently, Flavell (1979) has described a domain of intellectual functioning, i.e., metacognition, which includes a wide range of cognitive phenomena. These phenomena include (a) situation variables (knowing what situations call for intentional cognitive activity), (b) person variables (knowledge of those human attributes that influence learning and memory), (c) task variables (characteristics of the task that influence performance), and (d) strategies (procedures for successful performance). Brown (1978) has written a comprehensive review of metacognitive effects, particularly as they relate to classroom activities, which provides the school psychologist with many ideas to effect interventions with children and consultation with teachers.

Research on Teaching. A special issue of a recent *Educational Psychologist* was devoted to the topic of research on teaching, and in many respects, to the utility of this research for classroom practice. As Berliner (1983) pointed out in the introduction, much of this research since the early 1960s has been conducted in classrooms, and thus, represents another area where a link between researchers and practitioners is being forged.

We now know considerably more about classroom teaching than we did a decade ago. Good (1983) attributes this stronger knowledge base to (a) improvements in both quality of conceptualization and research methodology,

(b) the publication of excellent reviews of research on teaching, (c) more systematic research, and (d) the funding of large field studies by the National Institute of Education.

Recent research findings indicate that teachers vary widely in (a) how they use time in the classroom, (b) how they manage classroom activities and select and design classroom learning tasks, (c) how actively they teach and communicate with students about classroom learning tasks, and (d) the expectations and academic standards they hold for themselves, peers, their classes, and individual students (Good, 1983). Teachers not only vary across these four dimensions; these variables are related to student achievement—albeit mediated by student and task factors.

Time spent on instruction varies among classrooms in accord with such factors as grouping practices, instructional techniques, class size, student ability, interruptions, and teacher skill in classroom management. Basically, studies indicate that about 50%–60% of the school day is used for instruction. A more refined measure, e.g., time-on-task, may equal about 70%–75% of the time used for instruction (Good, 1983). When effects of ability are controlled, low to moderate correlations (.09–.43) between time-on-task and learning are found. Logically, time-on-task is not strongly associated with learning if the time is not spent on appropriate and relevant tasks. Indications that a student is on-task can be misleading and the data are correlational so a causative inference is inappropriate. Nonetheless, it makes a great deal of sense that the amount of time engaged in appropriate learning activities relates to amount learned. Consultation that helps a teacher to better organize the school day to maximize each student's time-on-task should be viewed as helpful.

Good classroom managers and poor classroom managers react to student misbehavior in much the same way. Good classroom managers are distinguished by the techniques they use to prevent misbehavior and elicit student cooperation and involvement in assigned work. Effective classroom managers express clear expectations in the first days of the school year, teach classroom routines, and systematically follow through on adherence to these routines. These teacher behaviors save time spent on classroom management because they allow students to continuously monitor their own behavior more effectively. Effectiveness, however, of these management skills interacts with the teacher's knowledge of learning and development, e.g., developmental changes in attention span, interests, and cognitive capabilities and how to adapt learning tasks to these changes to ensure a high probability that the student will succeed.

Recent research on teacher effectiveness indicates clearly that individual teachers do make a difference in student learning (Brophy, 1979; Good, 1983; Rosenshine, 1983). Further, teachers have been taught principles derived from this research, and student performance has improved (Good, 1983). Teachers whose students make good achievement gains are active teachers; i.e., they actively present concepts, provide appropriate practice activities, and monitor student understanding. In Good's (1983) view, active teaching is a way of looking at teaching and not a set of behavioral prescriptions.

Much research in the 1970s investigated what teachers do in their interactons with high- and low-achieving students. One outcome was the evidence that teachers do differ in their interactions with individual students and undoubtedly should. Teachers make instructional mistakes by treating students alike, as well as by treating them differently. Teacher expectations is a complex topic, but more has been learned in the eighties regarding the communication of expectations on classroom thought and action (cf. Good, 1983).

Research on effective teaching has increased greatly in quantity and quality. The tremendous complexity of the enterprise is better revealed, if not yet totally understood. School psychologists will be hard pressed to stay informed, but the potential utility of this knowledge base in consultation is clear.

Research on Schooling

As in so many areas of educational research, research on the effects of schooling appears at first glance to be totally contradictory. There are two lines of research, each leading to a different conclusion. In all of educational research, some of these reports on the effects of schooling clearly stand out because of the importance and breadth of the question asked (Does schooling make any difference?), and because of the public attention these reports have received. As often is the case in education, the negative reports have received far more public attention than the positive, and reanalyses and criticisms of negative reports never seem to attract attention comparable to the publication of the original.

Schooling Has No Effect. Since the late 1960s, laymen and social scientists alike have raised serious questions about the effectiveness of schooling in America. Some questions are based on the failure of the schools to cure real or perceived-to-be-real social problems. Other questions are based on the research that follows. The research that follows and the recent report of a National Commission ("A Nation at Risk") have made many of us defensive; i.e., why worry about what research has impact on services provided by the school psychologist if schooling itself has no impact or effect on students?

Coleman et al. (1966) and the Plowden Report (1967) both concluded that schools bring little influence to bear on children's achievement that is independent of their family background and social environment. That is, input variables (primarily social status of parents) predict output. These negative findings were further supported in this country by the results of many evaluations undertaken under the auspices of the Elementary and Secondary Education Act (Austin, 1981).

More recently, Coleman, Hoffer, and Kilgore (1982) reported that private schools have a more positive impact on achievement than public schools. There have been almost as many reanalyses of this report as of the original Coleman Report, but only one reanalysis of Coleman et al. (1982) is discussed here. (All reanalyses have similar criticisms and reach similar conclusions.)

After removing those students with missing data on outcome measures, Walberg and Shanahan (1983) reanalyzed the 12th-grade data ($N = 24,159$). Walberg and Shanahan's reanalysis (a) employed a more comprehensive set of covariates than Coleman et al. (1982) used in the original analysis, (b) used students rather than schools as units of analysis, and (c) related the design of the analysis and interpretation of findings to quantitative syntheses of prior research on factors productive of in-school and out-of-school learning. Variables were divided into two categories: (a) those that seemed fixed, or beyond the power of educators to alter directly, except by selecting students (e.g., parental social class); and (b) those that seemed alterable by educators (i.e., facilities and curriculum). The achievement regressions were computed on the educationally alterable and relatively fixed variable sets and all independent variables together to determine the variance added by each set. (The regressions were also run using vocabulary as a covariate.) The fixed factors accounted for about four times as much variance as the alterable factors. Nevertheless, alterable factors accounted for about 13% of the total variance without vocabulary as a covariate and about 6% with vocabulary as a covariate. In either case, the effects of the alterable factors are highly significant ($p < .001$). The educationally alterable variable that emerges as a relatively strong correlate of output is the quantity of instruction—indexed by the number of academic year-long courses taken in English, mathematics, French, German, Spanish, history, and science (which averages about five). The partial correlations for various types of private schools were very close to zero.

School Has an Effect. The "effective schools" research was singled out by the new director of NIE (Justiz, 1983) as an example of research that prepared us to do something about the situation in American education. According to Justiz, "Many schools and school districts around the country are trying out the tenets of this research. Some are having little success, others report encouraging improvement" (p. 11).

Once again, an entire issue of a recent journal, the *Educational Researcher* in this case, was devoted to this topic. The topic of effective schools has generated a wealth of literature and many of the sources are included in Bickel (1983). Since these research findings are being implemented in the schools, it is important that school psychologists are aware of these findings, questions regarding them, and the directions of future research on effective schools.

The effective schools movement grew out of a number of related concerns: (a) concerns about the early discouraging results on the effects of Head Start and other compensatory education programs (Austin, 1981), (b) concerns about the negative impression left by such studies as Coleman et al. (1966), and (c) concerns among educators that the public was not getting the whole story, which led them to be receptive to effective schools researchers.

Some reviews of the effective schools literature include the literature previously reviewed in this chapter under teacher research (cf. Mackenzie, 1983). In this section, I concentrate on the effective schools literature at the school level.

We have always known that there were schools with very similar demographic characteristics that produced quite different levels of student achievement. From 1965 until 1972, a variety of investigators compared effective and ineffective schools to identify specific school characteristics that led to higher levels of student achievement (cf. Edmonds, 1979).

In general, these studies have found that the following characteristics associate with higher achievement in the basic skills: (a) a school leader (often, but not exclusively, the principal) who is seen as a strong programmatic leader (dynamic, resourceful, competent) who sets high standards, frequently observes classrooms, and creates incentives for learning, (b) a school-wide emphasis on traditional subject matter (reading, writing, arithmetic, etc.) and an unusually high degree of concern for articulation between one grade level and another, (c) a school climate conducive to learning, i.e., relatively free of disciplinary problems, and high expectations for performance supported by both school personnel and parents, (d) a learning environment that tends to be highly structured, with a system of clear instructional objectives for assessing and monitoring performance (Austin, 1981; Rowan, Bossart, & Dwyer, 1983).

First, we should be mindful that these characteristics have been found to associate with, not necessarily cause, higher levels of achievement. Most states have one or more projects that attempt to implement the tenets of this literature (Bickel, 1983; Justiz, 1983). Thus, present research that is attempting to manipulate these variables may shed some light on presumed causation. Other questions regarding this literature focus on the choice of a single dimension of school effectiveness (basic skills, the research designs, and other methodological and conceptual problems) (cf. Rowan et al., 1983).

Effects of Instructional Setting. A discussion of research on schooling would not be complete without considering the effects of placing children in special classes. This topic also provides a fitting conclusion to this chapter since much of the research discussed previously is related to and involved in this issue.

The question of special versus regular classes (mainstreaming) has been one of the most controversial issues of the decade. The controversy was sparked by questions of equity, i.e., why should boys and black children be disproportionately represented in classes for the educable mentally retarded (EMR)? The most immediate answer to this question was that these children were being stigmatized for life by a label that resulted from biased assessment (intelligence tests and consequent placement in ineffective special classes).

The question here and potential solutions are as complex as the nature of schooling. Fortunately, some light has been shed on the problem and many more research questions have been raised by the report recently released by a panel appointed by the National Research Council (Heller, Holtzman, & Messick, 1982). The major findings and implications of this report were discussed at a symposium organized by Jeremy Finn and presented at the 1983 Annual Meeting of the American Educational Research Association. Articles resulting from this symposium were published in the March 1984 *Educational Researcher*. (The reader should consult the full report and these reaction papers, as only three brief points are covered here.)

The panel addressed the queston of, "Why is disproportional representation in special classes a problem?" The conclusion they reached was that disproportionate placement is not a problem in and of itself, but a symptom of a deeper educational problem. The real key issues are the validity of referral and assessment procedures and of the quality of instruction received—in whatever setting. Inequity results if students (a) are unduly at risk of EMR placement because of poor instruction in the regular classroom, (b) are subjected to invalid assessments for special programs, and (c) are subjected to poor instruction in special programs, which blocks their chances of return to a regular classroom.

For assessment, the panel recommended two phases. The first phase would require a systematic examination of the student's present learning environment and the nature and quality of the instruction received there. Phase One assessment would place the emphasis on learning processes rather than learning outcomes. Questions to be asked in the assessment would include, (a) Are the school's programs and curricula generally effective for the students served? (b) Has the student in question received adequate exposure to these programs? (c) Is there objective evidence that the student has *not* learned what was taught? (d) Is there objective evidence that attempts were made to diagnose the student's learning difficulty and that alternative approaches/materials were tried and failed? All of these questions must be answered in the affirmative before moving to Phase Two, i.e., assessment of the student's functional needs. Although these recommendations are in line with prevailing best practice, both the panel and Reschly's (1984) review indicate the need for additional research and additional analysis of policy questions. For example, research is needed (a) to improve the design and psychometric properties of procedures for classroom observation and criterion-referenced tests for slow learners, (b) to resolve controversies surrounding adaptive behavior measures, and (c) to better tie assessment devices to educational programming. From a policy viewpoint, what changes in the special education classification system are needed and how can resources be allocated most efficiently?

The placement question must focus on the quality of instruction received rather than the setting in which it occurs. The panel reviewed a number of summaries of the research contrasting settings—regular classroom (mainstreaming), resource room, or self-contained special classroom. The conclusion reached was that the preoccupation with setting is probably misplaced and that this type of research has led, and likely will continue to lead, to inconclusive and contradictory results. Rather than setting, the focus should be on identifying the most effective instructional process for these children. As a beginning, the research reviewed previously in this chapter on teaching and "effective schools" was suggested for implementation. These techniques (e.g., direct instruction) appear to improve learning across a variety of learners. However, when we talk about the most effective instructional process for a specific group or groups, we inevitably are talking about aptitude-instructional treatment interactions (ATIs). Much ATI research could be done here, but to a large extent, this research depends on the outcomes of needed assessment research and research to develop measurement systems that describe the major dimensions of learning environments.

It occurs to me that although the NAS panel was charged with the study of selection and placement of students in programs for the mentally retarded, their review and conclusions have broad applicability to most special programs in education. Wouldn't our conclusions and recommendation today be much the same for bilingual programs?

SUMMARY AND CONCLUSIONS

There are some definite consistencies in the research reviewed even though they stem from diverse interests and settings. Such consistency is likely to point to some truth and many of these consistent findings have intuitive appeal.

There may not be as much psychoeducational research as we would like and certainly not enough of the best research that we are capable of doing. It is, however, impossible to review the history of American education since World War II (cf. Ravitch, 1983) and not believe that research has had an impact on schooling and the practice of school psychology. Fads and movements receive more attention, but possibly cautious change, inspired by educational science, will be the more effective and lasting. The school psychologist of the eighties is uniquely suited to contribute to this effort.

ACKNOWLEDGMENT

I thank Maureen Stanley and Pat Suciu for help with the library research, and Jim Caroll for many helpful comments on the manuscript.

REFERENCES

Austin, G. R. (1981). Exemplary schools and their identification. *New Directions for Testing and Measurement, 10,* 31–48.
Barlow, D. H. (1981). On the relation of clinical research to clinical practice: Current issues, new directions. *Journal of Consulting and Clinical Psychology, 49,* 147–155.
Berliner, D. C. (1983). Introduction to special issue on research on teaching. *Educational Psychologist, 18*(3), 125–126.
Bickel, W. E. (1983). Effective schools: Knowledge, dissemination, inquiry. *Educational Researcher, 12*(4), 3–5.
Biddle, B. J., & Ellena, W. J. (1964). *Contemporary research on teacher effectiveness.* New York: Holt, Rinehart, & Winston.
Bijou, S. W., & Ruiz, R. (1981). *Behavior modification: Contributions to education.* Hillsdale, NJ: Lawrence Erlbaum Associates.
Blatt, M., & Kohlberg, L. (1975). Effects of classroom moral discussions upon children's levels of moral judgment. *Journal of Moral Education, 4,* 129–162.
Bolster, A. S. (1983). Toward a more effective model of research on teaching. *Harvard Educational Review, 53,* 294–308.
Boyer, E. L. (1983). *High school: A report on secondary education in America.* New York: Harper & Row.
Braddock, J. H., II, & McPartland, J. M. (1982). Assessing school desegregation effects: New directions in research. In A. C. Kerckhoff & R. C. Corwin (Eds.), *Research in sociology of education and socialization* (Vol. 3, pp. 259–282). Greenwich, CT: JAI Press.
Brophy, J. (1979). Teacher behavior and its effects. *Journal of Educational Psychology, 71,* 733–750.
Brown, A. L. (1978). Knowing when, where, and how to remember: A problem of metacognition. In R. Glaser (Ed.), *Advances in instructional psychology* (Vol. 1, pp. 77–165). Hillsdale, NJ: Lawrence Erlbaum Associates.
Case, R. (1978). A developmentally based theory and technology of instruction. *Review of Educational Research, 48,* 439–463.
Clark, K. B. (1965). *Dark ghetto: Dilemmas of social power.* New York: Harper & Row.
Colby, A., Kohlberg, L., Gibbs, J., & Lieberman, M. (1983). A longitudinal study of moral judgment. *Monographs for the Society for Research in Child Development, 48*(1–2, Serial No. 200).
Coleman, J. S., Campbell, E. Q., Hobson, C. J., McPartland, J., Mood, A. M., Weinfeld, F. D., & York, R. L. (1966). *Equality of educational opportunity.* Washington, DC: U.S. Government Printing Office.
Coleman, J. S., Hoffer, T., & Kilgore, S. (1982). *High school achievement: Public, Catholic and private schools compared.* New York: Basic Books.
Cooley, W. W. (1983). Improving the performance of an educational system. *Educational Researcher, 12*(6), 4–12.
Cooley, W. W., & Lohnes, P. (1976). *Evaluation research in education.* New York: Irvington.
Cronbach, L. J., & Snow, R. E. (1977). *Aptitudes and instructional methods: A handbook for research on interactions.* New York: Irvington.
Edmonds, R. R. (1979). Some schools work and more can. *Social Policy, 9,* 28–32.
Farley, F. H. (Ed.). (1982). The future of educational research. *Educational Researcher, 11*(8), 11–19.
Feistritzer, C. E. (1983). *The conditions of teaching: A state by state analysis.* Princeton, NJ: The Carnegie Foundation for the Advancement of Teaching.
Flavell, J. H. (1979). Metacognition and cognitive monitoring: A new area of cognitive-developmental inquiry. *American Psychologist, 34*(10), 906–911.

Flavell, J. H., & Wellman, H. M. (1977). Metamemory. In R. V. Kail & J. W. Hagen (Eds.), *Perspectives on the development of memory and cognition* (pp. 437–481). Hillsdale, NJ: Lawrence Erlbaum Associates.

Gage, N. L. (1963). Paradigms for research on teaching. In N. L. Gage (Ed.), *Handbook of research on teaching* (pp. 94–141). Chicago: Rand McNally.

Gage, N. L. (1982). The future of educational research. *Educational Researcher, 11*(8), 11–12.

Gagné, R. M., & Dick, W. (1983). Instructional psychology. In M. R. Rosenzweig & L. W. Porter (Eds.), *Annual review of psychology* (Vol. 34, pp. 223–260). Palo Alto, CA: Annual Reviews.

Glass, G. V., McGaw, B., & Smith, M. L. (1981). *Meta-analysis in social research*. Beverly Hills, CA: Sage Publications.

Goh, D. S. (1977). Graduate training in school psychology. *Journal of School Psychology, 15*, 207–218.

Good, T. L. (1983). Classroom research: A decade of progress. *Educational Psychologist, 18*(3), 127–144.

Heller, K. A., Holtzman, W. H., & Messick, S. (Eds.). (1982). *Placing children in special educaton: A strategy for equity*. Washington, DC: National Academy Press.

Johnson, E. L. (1981). Misconceptions about the early land-grant colleges. *Journal of Higher Education, 52*(4), 333–351.

Judge, H. (1982). *American graduate schools of education: A view from abroad*. New York: Ford Foundation.

Justiz, M. J. (1983). Emerging themes and new partnerships for the '80s. *Educational Researcher, 12*(7), 10–12.

Keller, E. F. (1983). Feminism as an analytic tool for the study of science. *Academe, 69*(5), 15–21.

Kohlberg, L. (1980). High school democracy and educating for a just society. In R. L. Mosher (Ed.), *Moral education: A first generation of research and development* (pp. 20–57). New York: Praeger.

Kohlberg, L. (1983). Foreward. In J. Reimer, D. P. Paolitto, & R. H. Hersh (Eds.), *Promoting moral growth: From Piaget to Kohlberg* (2nd ed., pp. ix–xviii). New York: Longman.

Lovitt, T. C. (1981). Graphing academic performances of mildly handicapped children. In S. W. Bijou & R. Ruiz (Eds.), *Behavior modification: Contributions to education* (pp. 111–143). Hillsdale, NJ: Lawrence Erlbaum Associates.

MacKenzie, D. E. (1983). Research for school improvement: An appraisal of some recent trends. *Eeucational Researcher, 12*(4), 5–17.

Meacham, M. L., & Peckham, P. D. (1978). School psychologists at three-quarters century: Congruence between training, practice, preferred role and competence. *Journal of School Psychology, 16*, 195–206.

Messick, S. (1983). Assessment of children. In E. M. Hetherington (Ed.), *Social development* (Vol. 4, pp. 477–526). In P. Mussen (Ed.), *Handbook of child psychology*. New York: Wiley.

Mosher, R. L. (Ed.). (1980). *Moral education: A first generation of research and development*. New York: Praeger.

Orlich, D. C. (1979). Federal educational policy: The paradox of innovation and centralization. *Educational Researcher, 8*(7), 4–9.

Pearce, D., & Crain, R. (1983). *School desegregation and housing desegregation in central cities* (Report No. 350). Baltimore, MD: Johns Hopkins University, Center for Social Organization of Schools.

Phillips, B. N. (1982). Reading and evaluating research in school psychology. In C. Reynolds & T. Gutkin (Eds.), *The handbook of school psychology* (pp. 24–47). New York: Wiley.

Plowden Report. (1967). *Children and their primary schools* (Vols. 1 and 2). London: Central Advisory Council for Education, Her Majesty's Stationery Office.

Ravitch, D. (1983). *The troubled crusade: American education 1945–1980*. New York: Basic Books.
Reimer, J., Paolitto, D. P., & Hersh, R. H. (1983). *Promoting moral growth: From Piaget to Kohlberg* (2nd ed.). New York: Longman.
Reschly, D. J. (1979). Nonbiased assessment. In G. D. Phye & D. J. Reschly (Eds.), *School psychology: Perspectives and issues* (pp. 215–253). New York: Academic Press.
Reschly, D. J. (1984). Beyond IQ test bias: The national academy panel's analysis of minority EMR overrepresentation. *Educational Researcher, 13*(3), 15–19.
Resnick, L. B. (1981). Instructional psychology. In M. R. Rosenzweig & L. W. Porter (Eds.), *Annual review of psychology* (Vol. 32, pp. 659–704). Palo Alto: Annual Reviews.
Rosenshine, B. (1983). Teaching functions in instructional programs. *Elementary School Journal, 83*, 335–351.
Rowan, B., Bossert, S. T., & Dwyer, D. C. (1983). Research on effective schools: A cautionary note. *Educational Researcher, 12*(4), 24–31.
Sattler, J. M. (1982). *Assessment of children's intelligence and special abilities* (2nd ed.). Boston: Allyn & Bacon.
Scharf, P. (1978). *Moral education*. Davis, CA: Responsible Action.
Schutz, R. E. (1979). Where we've been, where we are, and where we're going in educational research and development. *Educational Researcher, 24*, 6–8.
Scriven, M. (1980). Self-referent research. *Educational Researcher, 9*(6), 11–18; 30.
Sperber, R., & Miron, D. (1980). Organizing a school system for ethics education. In R. L. Mosher (Ed.), *Moral education: A first generation of research and development* (pp. 58–82). New York: Praeger.
Suppes, P. (Ed.). (1978). *Impact of research on education: Some case studies*. Washington, DC: National Academy of Education.
Tuthill, D., & Ashton, P. (1983). Improving educational research through the development of educational paradigms. *Educational Researcher, 12*(10), 6–14.
Walberg, H., & Haertel, E. (Eds.). (1980). Research integration: The state of the art. *Evaluation of Education: International Progress, 4*, 1–142.
Walberg, H. J., & Shanahan, T. (1983). High school effects on individual students. *Educational Researcher, 12*(7), 4–9.
Walton, S. (1983, August 31). There has been a conspiracy of silence about teaching. *Education Week*, p. 5.

12 The Impact of Education and Training on School Psychological Services

Beeman N. Phillips
The University of Texas at Austin

The study of education and training (E & T) and their impact on services has had a short and infertile history. Few studies have been sparked by all the attention E & T has regularly received in the professional literature. Thus, neither the construct of impact nor the construct of education and training is well defined. One of the purposes of this chapter, therefore, is to attempt to reformulate definitions, giving the constructs more pervasive meaning and extending their scope.

From this touchstone, the chapter tackles methodological issues, recognizing that there are important problems in explicating relationships between E & T and services. The central thesis is that causal analysis cannot be reduced to a set of experimental procedures, and there is at least room for a full partnership for naturalistic methods.

Beyond these issues, more practical questions are examined. The contexts in which E & T and practice occur are discussed, and the chapter reaches for an integration of ideas in terms of the use of this knowledge of E & T and its relationship to practice in shaping policy.

E & T Models

Education and training in school psychology can draw upon two models, the scientist-practitioner or Boulder model adopted at the Boulder Conference (Rainey, 1950), and the professional model legitimized by the Vail Conference (Korman, 1974). To some extent the professional model was a response to alleged deficiencies of the scientist-practitioner model. But much more was involved.

In the resolutions endorsed by the conference[1] there was a major emphasis on individual and cultural diversity, and societal needs and goals. Some conference themes may even be seen as antiprofessional and antiscientific, denigrating psychological knowledge and subordinating professonal values to societal values (Phillips, 1985).

Although the Vail Conference gave impetus to the professional school movement, whether the professional model is well represented by what is happening in these schools is conjectural. For example, Perry (1979) has expressed considerable concern that the isolation from the depth and breadth of the unviersity environment and dependence on student tuition and fees undermines the quality of E & T that is offered. Dependence on part-time faculty and a high student-faculty ratio are other common problems in such schools. But the most compelling concern is the implicit assumption that research and practice are incompatible, so that professional schools need to trade scientific for more practical training to fulfill their mission (Phillips, 1985).

E & T shaped by the Boulder model also has been criticized on various grounds. One such criticism is that professional training is tacked onto the end of other requirements for the Ph.D. degree, or is farmed out to agencies, with the department doing little beyond coordination (Perry, 1979). Another is that research and scholarship take precedence over professional training and competence.

One might argue, however, that criticisms like this are not intrinsic to the models themselves, since in such cases the model is not being fully implemented. That is, a model may be thought of as an ideal that provides the conceptual underpinning for programs. Although shaped to the conception represented by the ideal, programs vary widely in terms of their specific operational emphases. Some E & T programs patterned after the professional model may actually give more emphasis to research than others based on the scientist-practitioner model (Phillips, 1985).

Distinction Between "Education" and "Training"

Over the next decade, considerable interest is likely to develop in the distinction between education and training. Not usually applied with the rigor that is required, this distinction provides a grounding on which the professional versus the scientist-practitioner model of E & T can be more adequately analyzed. However, it is an interesting professional development that distinctions between education and training are not usually made in professional psychology. E & T programs are

---

[1] *Conference Follow-Up Committee, National Conference on Levels and Patterns of Training in Professional Psychology*, September, 1973.

typically referred to as "training" programs, and the terms *education* and *training* are often used interchangeably.

The distinction is potentially complicated. But for the purpose of this chapter, and following the logic developed by Phillips (1985), which is summarized in Fig. 12.1, education may be considered as a source of generalizations. These allow professionals to construct the technological foundations of practice and are useful for the interpretation and understanding of practice. In contrast, training yields the rules of practice, and is the source of prescriptions to apply in practice. In principle, therefore, education is a prerequisite or corollary of training in professional programs.

However, in an era characterized by the speed and extent of changes in professional practice, a point that is especially pertinent to school psychological practice, one can argue that E & T programs need to devote the bulk of their energies to two endeavors. The first is retraining in terms of the changing and increasingly sophisticated skills demanded in the school setting. Second, training needs to become more salient in preservice programs, with efforts increasingly shifted toward the technological, vocational, and career needs of students.

But to move in these directions prompts two other kinds of concerns. One is that programs that make such shifts will not deal sufficiently with the principles

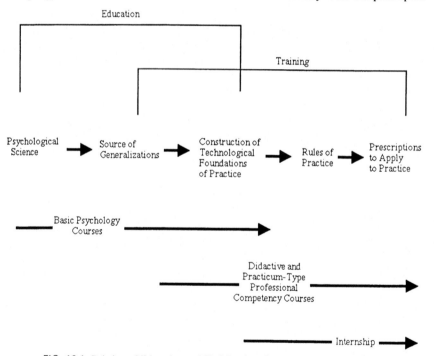

FIG. 12.1 Relation of Education and Training in a Program.

that serve as the generative source of practice. Second, there is the concern that such E & T efforts will not be sufficiently broad in scope to minimize the danger that the technology, rules of practice, and prescriptions acquired will be made quickly obsolete by those rapidly changing conditions and times alluded to.

NATURE OF A PROGRAM

E & T has benefited, more than often is recognized, by symbiotic interactions between E & T and practice. To provide a perspective on such interactions, the nature of an E & T program needs to be reviewed. Various conceptual frameworks might be applied. But one that is widely shared among professionals is that which undergirds APA accreditation criteria, policies, and procedures (APA, 1980). The rationale for these standards also represents, to a lesser extent, the accreditation system developed by NCATE/NASP (1978). This rationale is not only intrinsic to the objectives of psychology as a profession, but it also follows from and reflects the distillation of expert professional opinion. It has, in effect, evolved over the years in conjunction with ongoing professional experience rather than as a product of research.

Nevertheless, these standards represent truly important assumptions about the nature of E & T programs, and the elaboration of the specific elements of an E & T program, as shown in Fig. 12.2, makes it possible to study the impact of E & T on services with greater precision. By providing a "second window" into the relationship, data can be collected that will be more helpful in teasing apart effects related to resource inputs, processes and program outputs.

The value of such a model is that it is more comprehensive, permitting analysis of a large set of factors. It also recognizes that E & T programs are complex interventions that not only vary from site to site, but also develop and change

Input	Process	Output
Students and their characteristics, including social and cultural diversity	Curriculum, including sequence and structure	Student attrition
	Field experiences, including supervision	Student knowledge, skills and attitudes
Academic resources	Interpersonal relations	Job placement and career success of graduates
Program leadership and faculty	Extracurricular experiences	Stability of program and its future
Clinical facilities on campus	Interrelationship of academic and professional resources	Cost-effectiveness of program
Field setting resources	Orientation to the field, education and training model	Reputation of the program and its impact on the field
Student support systems		Involvement in continued professional development of graduates

FIG. 12.2 A conceptual model of education and training in school psychology. (From "Education and Training" by B. N. Phillips. In *School Psychology in Contemporary Society.* Columbus, OH: Charles Merrill. Copyright 1985. Reprinted by permission.)

over time. Moreover, it has heuristic value in sorting through the complicated issues in evaluating a program's outcomes and impact.

The basic assumption underlying this paradigm is that a program can be described multidimensionally, and the results ultimately used to infer which programmatic characteristics may be most important for professional competence and job performance. Obviously no such programmatic capability as this has yet been accomplished. We need first to confirm the reality of program dimensions, and the empirical connections between these dimensions and those of professional competence and job performance. It is equally obvious that there are thorny issues that stand in the way of fully realizing this goal. Some of the most important are (1) proper sampling of the *total* program, using a paradigm such as that in Fig. 12.2 as a starting point; (2) appropriate criteria for determining program dimensions, and methods for measuring the identified dimensions accurately; and (3) a meaningful link of input and process variables with output variables. After these issues have received attention, and significant headway has been made, we then can look at similarities/differences between programs, and examine relationships between program characteristics and professional competence, job performance, and the quality of school psychological services.

"Equivalence" of Specialist and Doctoral E & T

A multidimensional framework provides an almost inexorable logic that can be used to address an important issue embedded in assessment of E & T outcomes and impact. This is the equivalence issue, and given the controversy that surrounds Specialist versus Doctoral E & T, it seems clear that a critique of the "levels of E & T" approach to equivalence would be useful.

The evaluation of E & T programs is a difficult and time-consuming activity. For these reasons, among others, the *level* of E & T is sometimes the foundation of efforts to evaluate outcomes and impact. But those who have most frequently applied the concept of levels have done so inconsistently, seeing differences in outcome and impact between the Master's and specialist levels of E & T, but advocating that there are no meaningful differences between the specialist and doctoral levels of E & T. This justification of important differences in the former situation but not in the latter seems a bit strained, to say the least, and it only confuses the real issues in evaluation of E & T program outcomes and impact.

In order to see equivalence for what it is, we must recognize that to say things are equivalent is first to have an assumption or theory of the features or properties in respect to which the equivalence relation is to be judged. Equivalence is thus more a property of judgment than of the things judged, and it is in the nature of "equivalence" that at some level of description any two levels of E & T can be shown to be equivalent. Hence, to say that specialist and doctoral E & T are equivalent is actually to say very little about them. One might even argue that to state that they are equivalent represents failure in more accurate description of or sensitivity to differences among levels of E & T; and insisting that specialist and doctoral E & T are fundamentally equivalent because they are similar in some features hinders fuller understanding of their real differences.

Student Characteristics and E & T Programs

E & T programs are expected to have lasting effects on the professional capabilities and dispositions of students. But some student characteristics may be viewed as unalterable by means of E & T. Others are more or less stable, and their alterability through E & T is questionable, or at least not firmly established. Still other personal qualities can demonstrably be changed by E & T, and thus become positive influences on professional achievement.

For E & T programs, there would appear to be three main courses of possible action with regard to the use of relationships between student characteristics and desirable E & T outcomes. First, students can be selected by E & T programs on the basis of traits correlated with such outcome results. In this case, it cannot be expected that predictions of outcomes, based on the use of many of the student characteristics that have been investigated, can be raised significantly beyond predictions provided by measures of general ability and prior achievement.

A second possibility is to give attention to student characteristics that are alterable by E & T programs. Characteristics of this sort are usually not viewed as traits, but as cognitive strategies, verbal knowledge, attitudes, and so forth. E & T programs can select students on the basis of *prior* learning of these capabilities, or they can be systematically designed to develop those learned capabilities that are important in E & T program outcomes. However, such a remedial emphasis raises important questions about professional E & T generally, including its cost-effectiveness.

A third possibility is to consider the effect of student characteristics on outcomes in developing matches between aptitudes and E & T. Adaptation *within* and *between* E & T programs has the potential of bringing about a general increase in desirable E & T outcomes. To some extent this is done now, with student self-selection and programmatic selectivity; but it might be done more systematically through subspecialization within programs and by putting more emphasis in recruitment of students on compatibility with program demands, opportunities, and mission.

Student Aptitudes versus E & T in Professional Performance: An Analytic Issue

If one believes that E & T is the sole determinant of professional performance, then there would be no reason to test, interview, or collect information on prospective students; it is only necessary to structure E & T properly. Similarly, if aptitudes solely determined professional performance then there would be no point in E & T. In point of fact, however, aptitudes and E & T both influence professional performance, and some of the influence is probably the result of Aptitude × E & T interactions.

There is, then, the important question of which (aptitudes, E & T, or interactions) accounts for the most variance in professional performance. Such studies are likely, however, to be inconclusive because the variance ratios will be large or small, depending on the variance for aptitudes and E & T. If the variance for aptitudes is small, as when there is highly selective student admission, then the variance for E & T may be larger. In contrast, if the variance for E & T is large, where poor and good E & T programs are included, then the variance for aptitudes may be equally large. To some extent, one can control for this bias by adequately sampling aptitudes and E & T programs, although this does not completely solve the problem. It is difficult, therefore, to determine whether aptitudes, E & T, or interactions account for more of the variance in professional performance.

It is even possible for aptitudes and E & T to simultaneously have a highly predictable effect on professional performance. Though the professional performance of school psychologists who have attended different E & T programs may vary systematically, their rank order on different aptitudes may remain constant within their group. Professional performance in this case is equally predictable from aptitudes or E & T program attended.

Student Differences and Later Job Performance and Productivity

Despite general cognitive ability and other differences between nondoctoral and doctoral students, one might theorize that such differences do not have much impact on the performance and productivity of the resultant school psychologist work force. From this, it would follow that procedures for admitting students to E & T programs can be manipulated to achieve other professionally related objectives. However, basic equations for determining the impact of selection on later performance and productivity are available, although they require that a critical parameter be estimated. This is the standard deviation (SD) of measures of the job performance of school psychologists that indexes individual differences in the yearly output, in dollars, of the services of school psychologists. The larger this SD is, the greater is the payoff in improved productivity from selecting potentially high-performing students.

Methods have been devised for estimating this SD value in industry, business, and government (Schmidt, Hunter, McKenzie, & Muldrow, 1979). For example, for computer programmers this SD was $10,413, so that a computer programmer at the 85th percentile in job performance is worth $20,800 more per year to the organization than a programmer at the 15th percentile. Use of valid tests to select computer programmers, therefore, would substantially increase the average level of job performance of the resultant computer programmer workforce, and thus would improve productivity.

The theory that student selection is not important to later professional performance is sometimes presented in another form. This holds that all that is important is that students be "qualified" and that only "minimum" standards be met with respect to the amount and quality of their E & T. Again, the impact of such an approach can be gauged from research that has been conducted in other fields. Schmidt, Hunter, and Pearlman (1981) report that if the U.S. Government, with 4,000,000 employees, were to move to such a minimum competency system, using a cutoff at the 20th percentile on employee selection instruments, the loss of productivity gains on an annual basis would be about 13 billion dollars.

The problem with this minimum qualifications approach is that there is no real dividing line between the qualified and the unqualified, and productivity of employees is on a continuum. The relation between scores on selection instruments and job performance also is usually linear. Thus a reduction in acceptable scores at any point results in lower productivity in the employees selected.

Applied to student selection, this means that upgrading the quality of the students admitted to E & T programs will increase the performance and productivity of the resultant school psychologist workforce. In contrast, utilizing less selective student admission criteria will yield reductions in subsequent job performance and productivity.

None of the advances in knowledge summarized in this section changes the fact that, in school psychology, the relation of student qualities to their later job performance has not been studied. But it is difficult to entertain the belief that the outcomes would not be similar, although the *possibility* should not be ruled out. However, it would be intellectually dishonest not to acknowledge these relevant empirical facts, or to put the *total* burden of proof on those who believe that they are applicable to school psychology.

THE QUALITY OF E & T PROGRAMS AND JOB PERFORMANCE

Concerns about the quality of E & T programs are not new. Educator/trainers, practitioners, and professional organizations (through accrediting and other activities) have attempted to write prescriptions for excellence for many years. What would be new is attempts at empirical study and theorizing about determinants and dimensions of accomplishment in E & T programs.

Quality can be conceptualized at different levels of analysis and aggregation. The emphasis can be upon the competencies of *students* within E & T programs or upon *programmatic* characteristics. The emphasis probably should not be exclusively on the student or the program. Rather, the student perspective is complemented by a programmatic approach to quality.

But some would argue that the construct of programmatic accomplishment is too global, too multidimensional, and too ideological to be subject to scientific inquiry. Certainly a considerable amount of construct clarification would be necessary. In either case, a close connection between theory, operational definitions, and research methods is needed, including longitudinal designs examining relevant factors over time.

With regard to student success in E & T programs, there are those that hold that success in E & T is related to later job performance. Unfortunately, there are no tests of the hypothesis in school psychology. However, there has been research on this question in other areas of employment. Until recently, such research has been plagued by small sample sizes and other methodological problems. Nevertheless, even this research has tended to show that measures of success in training have significant, although low, correlations with job performance measures. But such problems have been overcome in recent research. For example, in a massive study based on almost 370,000 subjects it was found that success in training was consistently related to job performance (Pearlman, Schmidt, & Hunter, 1980). Although this study focused on clerical positions, other studies across a wide range of occupations recently have been completed with similar results.

Given that there is a relation between success in E & T and job performance, there are two possible limits on this relationship. One would hold that the validity of E & T is situationally specific. That is, success in an E & T program that is a valid predictor of job performance as a school psychologist in one organization or school setting may be invalid *for the same job* in another organization or school setting. The empirical case for or against situational specificity has not been determined. But, indirectly, recent large-scale studies of employees argues against situational specificity (Schmidt, Gast-Rosenberg, & Hunter, 1980).

Another possibility is that job differences might moderate the predictive validity of success in a given E & T program. Success in a particular program might be useful in predicting performance in all jobs school psychologists perform, but be more predictive for certain types of jobs. Second, success in an E & T program might be valid for some jobs and not others. In this latter case it could be argued that E & T has job-specific validity. Again, there is no empirical evidence in school psychology directly testing either proposition.

Another aspect of E & T program quality concerns the initial job placement of graduates. In contrast to selection decisions by E & T programs in accepting students, when they graduate it is students who make initial job placement decisions. Given that they ultimately determine such decisions, the program influences the process only in subtle ways, and in exerting such influence probably treats its graduates on the basis of merit, and so on. For example, better qualified graduates are given preference over less qualified graduates in recommendations to employers. In general, E & T programs probably attempt to help place their graduates in a way that is optimal for the graduates involved, and for the mission of the program/institution. Such decisions of course occur within the context of the actual number and type of jobs available at the time.

Given this situation, there is the suggestion that there are significant differences between categories of E & T programs (e.g., doctoral versus nondoctoral) in the types of professional positions obtained by graduates from these programs. Further, if performance of graduates in different types of jobs were evaluated, one might find that the pattern of job success differs from one program to another, and between different categories of E & T programs. An understanding of the impact of E & T on job performance thus requires a consideration of interaction between E & T program characteristics, the types of jobs their graduates typically obtain, and their degree of success in different types of positions. To date, the accumulated research on differential outcomes of this kind is very limited, and the main burden for conclusionary statements is on impressionistic evidence. For example, it appears that some doctoral programs in school psychology have far more graduates in academic positions than other doctoral programs.

Quality of Services Provided, and Congruence Between E & T and Services, as Measures of Impact

Definitions of the impact of E & T on services are of necessity stipulative in nature. But among the conceptions of impact, one stems from a focus on defining impact in terms of the quality of the services provided. In this approach, psychological services can be viewed (a) as a set of psychological constructs, with quality being reflected in how well they are operationalized; (b) from a social systems perspective, where management and decision-making criteria are important indices of quality; and (c) as a set of psychological and educational activities, so that description, goal specification, and progress assessment are keys to the quality of the services provided.

Another approach to the definition of impact is to start with the premise that E & T should be related to practice. The extent to which prior E & T is congruent with future practice is, therefore, an indication of impact, although congruence obviously is a contingent relationship, depending on factors beyond the reach of E & T. Meacham and Peckham (1978) have conducted such a study, although their emphasis was on obtaining normative information rather than on differentiating E & T factors associated with congruence. It is significant, however, that only 35% of their sample received their E & T and degree from a school psychology program. This, and the lack of differences for level of E & T and job setting in their results, as well as the severe constraints that we know from other sources are imposed on school psychologists' roles in the schools, raises the question of the appropriateness and significance of congruence as a measure of E & T impact (Phillips, 1985). For example, if the jobs school psychologists are hired to do are very narrow, an emphasis on congruence between E & T and practice would mean that programs would be shaping their E & T to the roles that school psychologists are permitted to engage in, and thus set up a circular pattern which would further reinforce the status quo. It is possible of course that school psychologists basically do what they have been trained to do, and that E & T could therefore be a force for change. if it is guided by what *ought* to be rather than by what *is*. In this connection, perhaps the most important thing to remember is that success in E & T has been related to job performance in a number of research studies, which offers some support for the contention that personal and professional characteristics can change organizational pressures and job demands. That is, the professional psychologist/work environment *interaction* needs to be emphasized. There is an exchange process between the work organization and the professional which is active and ongoing, and going in two directions. In essence, it is a developmental process, one in which change is inherent, and good E & T leads to good performance that in turn leads to valued organizational outcomes. Thus, it is suggested that the work organization's expectancies will indeed reflect these job performance/organizational outcome relationships, especially where E & T prepares professionals whose job performance is a major source of organizational effectiveness.

E & T and Socialization into School Practice

The socialization process that faces newcomers entering school organizations is virtually unexplored, and the role of E & T in developing realistic expectations is an example of an important issue in this area. One hypothesis could be that school psychologists who enter work environments with realistic expectations might have better morale and performance, and lower turnover. E & T programs that provide realistic expectations through job previews, and so on, should lessen the reality shock, and create a more positive view of the school psychological services program, as well as of the organization as a whole.

The design of E & T programs that provide for continuing education and career needs beyond the entry level also is needed (Phillips, 1985). The rapid knowledge explosion, changing school needs, concerns about consumer protection, and so forth, have resulted in political, professional and institutional decisions that have greatly increased the need for continuing education. Models for continuing education should be developed that deal with work environment factors, as well as professional knowledge and skills. Career development programs for middle career school psychologists also need development. But unfortunately, theoretical and empirical efforts in all these areas are proceeding slowly. In spite of this, E & T programs must attend to the socialization tasks to be carried out, and to the personal characteristics of the individuals involved, if they are to be maximally effective in preparing their graduates for the work world. However, failure will still typically be the result when work environment factors have not been sufficiently considered, especially where there are system constraints that often reduce transfer to the job of the competencies acquired through E & T.

It is also important that such E & T efforts not be characterized by assumptions that the purpose of socialization into school psychological practice is to adapt to a middle-class white organizational structure. The degree of supportiveness of the school organizational climate for new minority and women school psychologists has special weight. In support of the importance of this issue, we need to know more about the personal costs of entry for these school psychologists, whether they have a higher level of job-related stress and distrust of the system, and what mental health services for professionals are available in school districts. If the barriers are to be overcome, other organizational variables such as the salary system, promotional opportunities, and type of job assignment also need to be taken into account in E & T efforts to socialize students into school psychological practice.

E & T and Underemployment in Schools

E & T programs may be judged to be less than fully successful because of organizational constraints. One example is school systems that do not utilize the professional competencies taught by E & T programs. Among other things, this leads to underemployment, which is a major issue in consideration of the impact of E & T on services. It is generally assumed that underemployment for psychologists in schools is widespread. Some would even argue that it is the inevitable by-product of working in an institutionalized bureaucratic setting. But this is a benign view of underemployment, and the problem of school psychologists' underemployment in schools is considerably more complex. For example, it is not entirely clear that doctoral school psychologists who work in schools are underemployed to a greater degree than those with nondoctoral E & T. It is also important to differentiate between the form and the substance of psychological roles. Two school psychologists can be engaging in the same amount of consultation *activity*, but differ dramatically in the *substance* of what they are doing.

Underemployment also does not just happen to individual school psychologists; it may be structurally induced. The structural and formal interdependencies that describe present-day school systems are the channels through which individuals are affected. Policies relevant to the problem of underemployment are constantly being formulated and implemented, and an explicit effort would need to be made to describe how they contribute to the context in which underemployment occurs. Regardless of the circumstances, one can assume that underemployment has implications for physical and mental health, although such consequences would be complex, and one cannot assume that underemployment inevitably impairs an individual's job performance or health (Phillips, 1981).

E & T and Supervisory and Management Functions

There is no extensive literature on the supervisory and management functions of school psychologists. The needs assessment literature does indicate that school psychologists do, or ought to, have such functions in schools (e.g., Hunter & Lambert, 1974), although similar emphases in E & T programs are harder to find. The sad state of E & T in this area is consistent with the lack of theory and knowledge development. An exception is the topic of leadership, although the research on leadership styles has occurred in other work organizations, and has not examined very systematically the consequences of E & T in leadership. A summary description of the situation, therefore, is that we need to know much more about how E & T programs can affect supervision and management skills. Concomitantly, it also is necessary to institutionalize, to a greater extent than is now the case, supervision and management as important job functions of (doctoral) school psychologists.

EVALUATING THE IMPACT OF E & T ON SERVICES: A METHODOLOGICAL PERSPECTIVE

The scientific evaluation of the impact of E & T on psychological services would be a difficult, time-consuming, and expensive activity under the best of circumstances. One aspect of such evaluation is methodological, and the need for unequivocal designs and guidelines is unimpeachable. Although randomized E & T experiments are usually impossible, strong quasi-experiments would be a feasible alternative in some very limited and special circumstances.

Internal validity, for example, is not of salient importance in an evaluation of the impact of E & T on services. What counts more in determining impact is external validity. "Tight" research designs often would compromise relevance, and impact is such a complex phenomenon that it is likely to always reach beyond the experimental data one might obtain.

There is also the issue of the extent to which evaluation of impact should rely on "qualitative" as opposed to "quantitative" modes of knowing. There is a tendency to denigrate qualitative methodology, but the quantitative paradigm that is dominant in psychological and educational research is inadequate for elucidating some aspects of the complex problem of determining impact. Quantitative methods would sometimes force the researcher to examine a limited, and probably biased, set of impact outcomes. Moreover, a strictly quantitative approach would be unrealistic and unworkable because there is not sufficient control over E & T programs, or over what happens to program graduates in job placement and activities. It is not necessary, however, to take an all or none position on this matter, and there are potential benefits to be gained from combining and using both methodologies as circumstances permit.

A Causal Modeling Approach to Evaluating the Impact of E & T on School Psychological Services

Although the ultimate scientific test of impact would be replicability of results in a series of longitudinal experimental studies, high costs, policy issues, and other considerations make the opportunity of doing such research rather unlikely. An alternative that might be advocated is causal modeling techniques (Bentler, 1980). In this section, we consider such approaches, commonly termed causal models or structural equation models, and their applicability to the problem of evaluating the impact of E & T on school psychological services.

As a first step, it is useful to distinguish between explanation and description. A descriptive statement addresses questions of how, and how much, whereas an explanatory statement addresses the question of why, and thus involves causal inference. For example, measurement of a child's intelligence is a description, whereas investigating the dependence of intelligence on family background is an example of explanation. However, no formal description of a causal effect is attempted here, except to note that one way to think of causality is to ask whether a change in one variable, i.e., the antecedent or causal variable, results in a change in an outcome variable.

In terms of the logic of causal models, a causal model is a quantitative statement of postulated causal links between the variables of interest. In its formulation the important variables must be identified, and the causal links specified. On psychological grounds, some variables can be said to influence others; in other instances a causal link may be assumed not to exist. However, these causal-modeling techniques cannot prove causality.

A special problem that illustrates the importance of careful interpretation of relationships between variables is spurious correlation where the relationship between two variables is due to a common (third) factor. Whether an association is spurious or true, from a causal standpoint, cannot be determined on the basis of correlations alone. Information about the causal ordering of the system of variables is required since correlation is a descriptive statistic that contains no information about the direction of association.

In the construction of a causal model it also is important to remember that we are dealing with an observational rather than an experimental technique. The importance of a theory, as symbolized by the path model, is therefore crucial. In causal modeling we are inferring causation from regression coefficients or correlations, and the only reason we can do this is because we have explicitly stated a theory that specifies the relationships to be expected. If the theory is substantially wrong, or the model is badly misspecified, the results cannot be meaningfully interpreted.

To illustrate how causal modeling might be applied to the problem of determining the impact of E & T on school psychological services, we now advance a statement on the interrelations among E & T program characteristics, student aptitudes, professional competence of graduates (at the end of E & T), organization factors (in the school psychologist's work environment), job performance, and school psychological services program characteristics. The model that is proposed is depicted in Fig. 12.3.

This path analysis model has six explicit variables, although the analysis is formulated into four stages, each being a three-variable model. In the first, we have the three variables of X_6, X_5 and X_4. For this path analysis we are willing to argue that Professional Competence is directly affected by E & T and Student Aptitude, and that E & T also influences Professional Competence indirectly through Student Aptitude (which is not, by the way, limited to general cognitive ability).

The second stage of the model involves X_5, X_4, and X_2. Here Student Aptitude and Professional Competence influence Job Performance directly. Student Aptitude also influences Job Performance indirectly through Professional Competence. The third stage involves X_4, X_3 and X_2, with Professional Competence and Organizational Factors influencing Job Performance directly. Professional Competence effects also are mediated by Organizational Factors and thus have an indirect influence. The last stage concerns X_3, X_2 and X_1. Job Performance and Organizational factors directly influence School Psychological Services, with the effects of Organizational factors also being mediated by Job Performance.

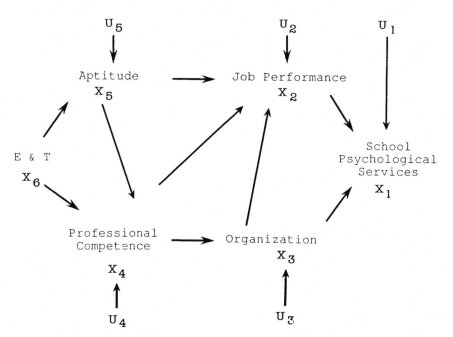

FIG. 12.3 Possible path diagram representing impact of E & T on school psychological services.

To assess the completeness of each of these three-variable subsystems, one would need to examine the path coefficients of the latent variables (i.e., the U's). For example, U_5 and U_4 represent all the residual causes of variation in Aptitude and Professional Competence, respectively. If these latent influences are large, then a substantial portion of variation in Student Aptitude and Professional Competence is unexplained by the causal relations explicitly included in the model. Similar statements can be made of course about other three-variable models.

At a technical level, one might have some misgivings about the model presented in Fig. 12.3. More specifically, one might argue that the model is misspecified in the placement of the aptitude variable. It would seem to be an input into an E & T program, and because of its prior time precedence should therefore come before E & T in the causal chain. In the model, however, variables that might have an impact on entry into an E & T program are not taken into account. Because of this, aptitude is considered only as a mediating variable in relation to the effects of E & T. Additional explanation of some of the variables in the model also might be helpful. This, however, would go beyond the purpose of this section, which is to suggest that path analysis might help answer some of the questions concerning the impact of E & T programs, questions that need to be answered.

Although a number of contributions have been made to the path analytic literature, there are still problems for which satisfactory answers are difficult to find. A good overview of the literature up to 1975 has been provided by Alwin and Hauser (1975). A more recent case for path analysis has been made by MacDonald (1979) and Cooley (1978), and suggestions for the use of path analysis have been offered by James (1980) and Billings and Wroten (1978).

Two special problems in the decomposition of effects, so that dependent variable variance may be attributed to antecedent variables, are whether the path model is fully recursive, and whether the antecedent variables are correlated. Nonrecursive structures which allow for reciprocal causation are more difficult to interpret causally, and decomposing variance among correlated antecedent variables has no completely satisfactory statistical solution (Bentler, 1980).

How Can Research on the Impact of E & T on School Psychological Services be Useful?

New understandings from research on the impact of E & T on school psychological services ought to inform both E & T activities and school psychological practice (Phillips, 1982). Even though it has this potential the evidence up to now indicates that we have not been very effective at evaluating the impact of E & T on practice. This is true, in part, because of the complexity and lack of theoretical analysis of the relationships. Professional behavior not only is influenced by forces *currently* acting on the practicing school psychologist, but by sequences of experiences and events leading to current performance. In principle, however, the problems can be solved and psychological science can provide a useful framework for descriptive study and thoughtful examination and analysis of the linkage between E & T and services. Such research could serve the vital function of encouraging more communication between educators/trainers and practitioners. It also can be a key catalyst in bridging gaps between the E & T and practice aspects of school psychology, and even lead to new forms of E & T and practice.

At a more concrete level, research may provide clear-cut, practical prescriptions for E & T that can be used in direct instrumental ways for making particular E & T decisions, or for justifying previously held positions about practice. Such research also is useful when it challenges the political status quo in E & T or practice settings. The raising of new issues is another highly important aspect of research on E & T and its impact on services; and still other uses are depicted in Fig. 12.4.

In summary, research on the impact of E & T on services could be useful directly and instrumentally by educators/trainers or decision makers in practice settings as solutions to particular problems. But this is only one of the many ways in which research evidence and ideas on E & T and its linkage to practice can contribute. However, some of these other important uses raise questions about the potential for misuse of such research and may create further dilemmas for educators/trainers and practitioners. But these complications are part of the larger issue of the dangers of the utilization of theory, research, and knowledge in school psychology generally (Phillips, 1982).

Professional Knowledge	Definition of Problems	Advocacy	Problem Solving
Helping to keep up with developments in E & T and practice	Framing or conceptualizing E & T or practice problems	Bringing new ideas to attention of decision makers	Providing clearcut, practical prescriptions for action by educator/trainers or practitioners
		Legitimizing budget allocations to E & T or services	
		Attacking established policies	
		Lobbying for new E & T or psychological service programs	

FIG. 12.4 Aspects of the "usefulness" of research on E & T and its impact on practice.

Pluralism in Evaluating the Impact of E & T on School Psychological Services

Evaluation of the impact of E & T on school psychological services is a large and complex task. The type of E & T program which is "best" may vary from student to student, institution to institution, and from one services situation to another. In addition, professional performance is a personal activity, with the hallmark of a professional being independence of performance, pride in the services rendered, allegiance to professional traditions, adherence to a code of ethics, and maintenance of competence through continuing education. This means that attempts to develop a general strategy for evaluating the impact of E & T may result in research that lacks insight, significance, and usefulness. Pluralistic and informal strategies for evaluating impact may, in fact, provide what systematic research may lack.

For example, there is a difference between a statement of fact that is generally accepted, and a statement of value that has only limited acceptance. If there are value differences among educators/trainers, practitioners, and decision makers in applied settings, then a general system for evaluating the impact of E & T that these groups agree upon might be a land of thin gruel, offensive to no one but lacking in nourishment. Consensus, therefore, may not be a realistic goal, and pluralistic evaluation efforts with different sets of constructs, variables, and criteria would be a necessity.

At the center of this contention is the documented fact that the information required to make decisions about E & T and its impact on practice will never be exactly the same as data collected in evaluation studies. There is always extrapolation; and understanding ultimately is more important to action than facts. In essence, evaluative efforts must draw appropriately on humanistic and pragmatic as well as scientific approaches (Cronbach, 1980, 1982). Evaluation is an art in which the facts produced by scientific methods are merged in the processes of planning, negotiating, accommodating, and choosing. Thus, in the shaping of policy, evaluators of E & T and its impact can only serve as advisors to the polity of educators/trainers and practitioners, using the knowledge gained to speak to the concerns of these and other constituencies. In addition, they should act as educators, attempting to communicate and lead others to understand how the results of evaluation can make their way into E & T and practice.

CONCLUDING COMMENT

The entire school psychology enterprise is undergoing a major full-scale re-evaluation. For example, Bardon (1982, 1983) has proposed a new doctoral psychology applied to education specialty; Phillips (1983) has made extrapolations of the future of school psychology that envision the field going through a series of transition stages; and developments in accreditation, certification and licensure, and other aspects of E & T and practice are reaching a critical impact state. In substance, school psychology appears to be entering a period where there will be more readiness to consider professionally responsible alternatives to traditional ways of viewing school psychology E & T and practice.

One of the important implications of such a Zeitgeist is that there perhaps will be a growing interest in the challenge of trying to understand the impact of E & T on school psychological services. Although this is an enormously complicated task, the complications are as much conceptual as methodological and statistical. What is needed to guide this endeavor is an overreaching plan that leads to cumulative and conclusively integratable results, rather than disparate conglomerations of results. Some of the steps toward such a broad perspective have been outlined in this chapter.

REFERENCES

Alwin, D. F., & Hauser, R. M. (1975). The decomposition of effects in path analysis. *American Social Review, 40,* 37–47.
American Psychological Association (1980). *Accreditation handbook.* Washington, DC: Author.
Bardon, J. I. (1982). School psychology's dilemma: A proposal for resolution. *Professional Psychology, 13,* 955–968.
Bardon, J. I. (1983). Psychology applied to education: A specialty in search of an identity. *American Psychologist, 38,* 185–196.
Bentler, P. M. (1980). Multivariate analysis with latent variables: Causal modeling. *Annual Review of Psychology, 31,* 419–456.
Billings, R. S., & Wroten, S. P. (1978). Use of path analysis in industrial/organizational psychology: Criticisms and suggestions. *Journal of Applied Psychology, 63,* 677–688.
Cooley, W. W. (1978). Explanatory observational studies. *Educational Research, 7,* 9–15.
Cronbach, L. J. (1980). *Toward reform of program evaluation.* San Francisco: Jossey-Bass.
Cronbach, L. J. (1982). *Designing evaluations of educational and social programs.* San Francisco: Jossey-Bass.
Hunter, C. P., & Lambert, N. M. (1974). Needs assessment activities in school psychology program development. *Journal of School Psychology, 12,* 130–137.
James, L. R. (1980). The unmeasured variables problem in path analysis. *Journal of Applied Psychology, 65,* 415–421.
Korman, M. (1974). National Conference on Levels and Patterns of Professional Training: The major themes. *American Psychologist, 29,* 441–449.
MacDonald, K. I. (1979). Interpretation of residual paths and decomposition of variance. *Social Methods Research, 7,* 289–304.
Meacham, M. L., & Peckham, P. D. (1978). School psychologists at three-quarters century: Congruence between training, practice, preferred role and competence. *Journal of School Psychology, 16,* 196–206.
National Association of School Psychologists (1978). *Standards for training programs in school psychology.* Washington, DC: Author.
Pearlman, K., Schmidt, F. L., & Hunter, J. E. (1980). Validity generalization results for tests to predict training success and job proficiency in clerical positions. *Journal of Applied Psychology, 65,* 373–406.

Perry, N. W., Jr. (1979). Why clinical psychology does not need alternative training models. *American Psychologist, 34,* 603–611.

Phillips, B. N. (1981). School psychology in the 1980's: Some critical issues related to practice. In T. R. Kratochwill (Ed.), *Advances in school psychology* Volume 1 (pp. 19–43). Hillsdale, NJ: Lawrence Erlbaum Associates.

Phillips, B. N. (1982). Reading and evaluating research in school psychology. In C. Reynolds & T. Gutkin (Eds.), *The handbook of school psychology,* (pp. 24–47). New York: Wiley.

Phillips, B. N. (1985). Education and training. In J. R. Bergan, (Ed.), *School psychology in contemporary society* (pp. 92–115). Columbus: OH: Merrill.

Phillips, B. N. (1983). *The future of school psychology.* Unpublished manuscript.

Rainey, V. C. (Ed.). (1950). *Training in clinical psychology.* Englewood Cliffs, NJ: Prentice-Hall.

Schmidt, F. L., Gast-Rosenberg, I., & Hunter, J. E. (1980). Validity generalization results for computer programmers. *Journal of Applied Psychology, 65,* 643–661.

Schmidt, F. L., Hunter, J. E., McKenzie, R., & Muldrow, T. (1979). The impact of valid selection procedures on workforce productivity. *Journal of Applied Research, 64,* 609–626.

Schmidt, F. L., Hunter, J. E., & Pearlman, K. (1981). Task difference and validity of aptitude tests in selection: A red herring. *Journal of Applied Psychology, 66,* 166–185.

13 An Alternative Model for the Delivery of Psychological Services in the School Community

Sandra Christenson
Brian Abery
Richard A. Weinberg
University of Minnesota

Even a perfunctory review of the contemporary school psychology literature results in the conclusion that the roles and functions of the school psychologist continue to be a primary target of discussion. Alternative directions for professional practice are often suggested and new laundry lists of skills are developed for the training programs. It seems to us, however, that the vigorous interest in new roles and functions is often tempered by a lack of reflection on the basic philosophical and theoretical underpinnings that underlie professional practice. It is an appreciation of this gap in thinking that has provided direction to this paper. This chapter examines the traditional perspective underlying school psychological services—a view based on a medical model and focusing on the diagnosis, treatment, and cure of a particular student's disorder. Employing diverse theoretical orientations (e.g., behavioral) or indirect modes of service (e.g., consultation) does not necessarily negate the dominant role of the medical model in mainstream professional practice. An alternative model for conceptualizing the nature of psychological services in the school community is presented. This model is based on a developmental perspective, rooted in ecological and transactional theories and affirming a proactive and preventive stance for the school psychologist. The chapter is organized into four sections:

1. A review and critique of the pervasive *traditional medical model* of school psychological service delivery;
2. A challenge of the major assumptions underlying the medical model;
3. An outline of the defining characteristics of an *alternative, developmental perspective* for providing school psychological services, highlights of some of

the major theoretical implications of a developmental model for practice in contemporary school psychology; and

4. A brief discussion of building the perspective into existing training structures within professional school psychology and charting a course of action for future policy and practices.

DEFINING A TRADITIONAL VIEW— THE MEDICAL MODEL

The primary function of a model is to render a complex set of events manageable and to allow one to view selected aspects of reality in order that it may be organized, evaluated, and better understood (Wine, 1981). Models or conceptual frameworks for delivery of services are essential to the growth and practice of professional psychology. A specialty such as school psychology progresses through a life cycle in much the same way as a family. At certain points in its development the system must effectively deal with particular developmental tasks or issues if it is to remain a viable entity. Certainly, the specific behaviors of individual family members cannot be adequately characterized solely through knowledge of the particular stage at which the system as a whole is functioning. However, by employing a broad perspective of the overarching tasks with which the family must deal, one can more easily identify issues within the functional system. Similarly, an overview and critical examination of the traditional conceptual model underlying school psychological services, although admittedly inaccurate in capturing the viewpoint of any individual practitioner, may sensitize us to certain developmental issues that school psychology faces today.

The Primary Level of Service Delivery: Testing, Diagnoses, and Labels

The evolution of psychological services for children in general, and school psychology in particular, cannot be separated from the parallel development of psychometric techniques to assess cognitive-intellectual, personality, and academic functioning. Psychometric assessment has been the one service desired by educational personnel. Rarely, if ever, have preventive programs been developed and implemented. The results of a recent nationwide survey of school psychologists (Goldwasser, Meyers, Christenson, & Graden, 1983) suggest that practitioners spend the majority of their time engaged in the individual assessment of children, especially testing, and that time spent involved in intervention is relatively small. Given these results, one is forced to accept Bardon's (1982) conclusion that the major reasons why school systems employ school psychologists have not changed over a period of 50 years.

At the most basic, primitive level of service delivery, each of us serves individuals directly. One consequence of employing an individually based, nonpreventive model in attempting to provide necessary human services is that there will always be those whose behavior is deviant enough from normative standards not to be tolerated within the system. In the mental health professions, including those dealing with children's school problems, such "difficulties" have long been handled through the use of a "defect" approach, which appears to have developed primarily as a result of the medical roots of both clinical and school psychology. "Children, whose academic or social behavior deviates from the cultural mores of the classroom or . . . school system, possess some deficit which has resulted in their failure to function successfully" (Minor, 1972, p. 227). Deviant behavior viewed through the lens of such a conceptual framework is attributed to stable states within the person (personal disease or disturbance), the cause of which lies deep within the individual's past. Adherents of such an approach assume that "pathological" behaviors, be they aggressive or acting-out, or an inability to keep up instructionally with one's classmates, are the most important elements to observe about an individual (Wine, 1981).

Placing the cause of deviance within the individual tends to discount the influences of social-environmental factors. The use of preventive interventions and strategies of a systems/organizational nature are also precluded by placing blame on the individual. The degree of impact a school psychologist can have upon the development and education of children is therefore limited to the very small percentage of those who need direct services.

The labeling of psychopathology is a vestige of the medical model. Traditionally, the detection and treatment of learning disorders was in the realm of medicine and neurology. The development and rapid proliferation of tests to assess academic and psychoeducational functioning in the first half of this century, however, led to significant changes in the personnel who filled this role. Cutts (1955) has documented the relationship between the introduction of individual "mental tests" and the development of special services for children who did not fit into the mainstream of education. The existence of trained individuals to administer such tests, and the association between test administration, diagnoses, and underlying pathology, led to the further demand for one service from school psychologists (Bardon, 1982). Although the term *diagnosis* is derived from the medical model, the labeling problem exists whether this term is used or one more often advocated by proponents of an educational model (i.e., "meets criteria for placement"). In recent years, school psychologists have certainly fought to divest themselves of this "defect" model, but the specialty's history and the passage of Public Law 94–142 appear to have firmly established in the minds of both teachers and administrative personnel that labeling children and determining whether they meet state and federal criteria for special education services is what school psychologists are supposed to do.

Many individuals (e.g., Garmezy, 1979) have expressed concern that the penchant of psychologists to label children has brought us one step closer to almost totally advocating a medical model; we continue to focus solely upon the individual and bring under medicine's wing educational problems and deficits that are not mental disorders. In addition, the first requirement of a classification system is that it be reliable. Labeling and diagnosis, in psychology in general and in school psychology in particular, have yet to demonstrate this characteristic. Despite the inherent dangers of classification, school psychologists continue to function primarily in the role of "labelers." Although, labeling alone does not constitute special education, many school psychologists continue to appear to view it as such.

The Diagnostic-Treatment-Cure Regimen

Consistent with the current role they fill, school psychologists often have little to no contact with a student until his/her behavior deviates from that of accepted social standards and is intolerable to educational personnel. At that time, the school psychologist typically receives a "patient" referral, which starts in motion a diagnosis-treatment-cure regimen. The "problem" child is often seen individually, an assessment undertaken, a diagnostic impression formed, and a treatment plan developed and implemented. Although ideally those supplying psychological services will conduct a reliable assessment and then work with other relevant educational personnel to formulate a "cure"—an individualized instructional program—this rarely appears to be the case. Special education programs continue to use psychologists primarily as testers and classifiers with few making substantive or continuing contributions to program development (Goldwasser et al., 1983). The analysis and assessment of a child's current state or performance could provide information helpful in improving the quality of his/her instruction, but too often this information is used solely to classify and label the individual for general educational assignment. Indeed, the preoccupation with classification, categorization, and labeling evidenced by the psychological community in this century has led to its losing sight of the goal of relating assessment to intervention (Meyers, Pfeffer, & Erlbaum, 1982).

If the work of Goldwasser et al. (1983) is accurate, most psychologists in public schools spend three out of four hours on the job pursuing the physical mechanics of assessment. Although we have no empirical evidence to support the hypothesis, past experience suggests that other educational specialists (e.g., speech and language clinicians, reading specialists) also spend much of their workday engaged in similar activities. A child's capacities are therefore assessed independently in a number of areas (e.g., cognitive, speech-language, affective, etc.) with performance in each of these interpreted through the use of a separate, independent theory of psychoeducational functioning. The result is that at child-study team meetings one is typically presented with a number of evaluations, each conducted by a separate individual who views the child through his/her own professional "lens." School psychology is still heavily influenced by the practice of psychology in general and as such our thinking remains imprisoned in an individual psychology (Sarason, 1980). Rarely viewing each aspect of the child's functioning as part of an integrated whole or system, school psychologists/ special educators continue to encounter difficulty when attempting to provide a program that will best fit the child's needs.

Since intervention is deemed appropriate only after a "problem" has been identified, school psychologists tend to initiate such efforts rather late in the diagnostic-treatment sequence after a teacher-initiated referral has been made (Wine, 1981). Because the site of any "defect" found is placed within the individual, little attention has been given by members of the profession to alternative contextual or ecological factors. Whether the intervention is physical or psychological in nature it is administered in an attempt to alter a defect, the site of which is thought to be internal or intrapsychic. In practice, intervention programs of this sort tend to be extremely expensive, in the long run relying upon highly educated personnel who are in short supply. Furthermore, research tends to indicate that such treatments are not particularly effective whether they are primarily physical, psychic, or educational in nature (Paul, 1981).

In the Testing Room

Sarason (1980) has stated that school psychology was born in the prison of a test and although the cell has been enlarged somewhat, it is still a prison. Sarason's comments on the practice of school psychology still aptly describe the provision of psychological services in the majority of school systems in this country. Based upon the philosophy of a defect-oriented model, school psychological services are primarily provided within a testing room much as a physician conducts a practice out of a hospital. As was true 20 years ago, a referral for psychological services typically results in a child being pulled out of his/her classroom and standardized tests administered in an individualized format. The student's performance is then compared to national norms, and determination is made as to eligibility for special education services. Little if any effort is given to the assessment of the possible contextual bases of a child's problems, nor are comparisons made between the functioning of the referred student and that of his/her classmates. In addition, the assessment techniques used are rarely if ever based upon the curriculum a referred student is receiving or has received in the past. Although the recent work of Kaufman (1979), Bersoff and Grieger (1971), and Meyers et al. (1982) has resulted in many school psychologists expanding their conceptions of assessment and intervention, the broader setting or context in which problems have become manifest and the child's interactions within these settings remain relatively ignored. When intervention strategies are based on a medical-defect model, if any treatment is applied, it is with the goal of changing the person with limited, if any interest given to the setting. For example, a physician would be ill advised to treat a case of lead poisoning without first determining that he would not be sending a patient back into the same environment that had led to the problem initially. This simple tenet of an interactionist approach is more often than not ignored by the psychologist dealing with a child's educational or behavioral problems within the schools.

The psychoeducational assessment of a child referred for learning or behavioral problems is one step in the diagnosis-treatment-cure regimen. Once this element of "problem solving" has been undertaken it is typical that an interdisciplinary team will meet as part of the decision-making process. At such meetings the psychologist will in all likelihood describe the results of his/her assessment, and a treatment program will be prescribed for the student. For all intents and purposes the role of the school psychologist ends here. Although he/she may occasionally "sit in" on annual or bi-annual IEP meetings (Goldwasser et al., 1983) it is unlikely that any further interaction of a substantive nature will occur with teachers, parents, or the child. The physician's often-used phrase, "call me in the morning," becomes "call me at the end of the year."

For those children deemed eligible for special education services the most important phase of assessment begins once an intervention is implemented. It is highly unlikely, however, that those responsible for the provision of psychological services will continue the assessment process to determine whether the prescriptions have been effective on either a short- or long-term basis. Continued assessment in the form of behavioral observation, screening, and so on would also seem of importance to many of those children who are declared eligible for services, given that on the basis of their behavior/performance such students are often at high risk. The most negative by-product of our current model of functioning is that unlike physicians, we rarely know when we "lose a patient." One might conclude that even when the medical model is the basis for delivering school psychological services, the proponents are often weak in implementing the "cure!"

The Behaviorist's Alternatives

Through the primary employment of a medical-defect model, school psychologists' attention has been primarily directed to the internal state of the student. At most we have paid lip service to the concept of behavior as a function of the interaction of the student with the classroom setting.

Among the theoretical frameworks from which one can choose in an attempt to better understand human functioning, the behavioral tradition, more than any other, has emphasized the importance of the setting in determining behavior. From the early work of Watson, James, and Skinner to more recent theorists such as Mischel, situational factors have been given attention. Behaviorists have rejected the medical model as well as all other defect approaches in favor of a position that emphasizes the environmental control of behavior (Rimm & Masters, 1979; Ullmann & Krasner, 1969). In fact, the early behavioral approaches have provided a powerful challenge to the medical model that has dominated both psychology in general and school psychology in particular.

The impact of a wide variety of behavioral approaches from behavior analysis and assessment to direct behavioral intervention upon education and school psychological services has been tremendous (Sulzer-Azaroff & Mayer, 1977). Yet, the behavioral model of human functioning currently used by many school psychologists and those in related professional disciplines is both limited and incomplete. Although behavioral approaches may be effective in what they do, one can legitimately argue that this is not enough. For example, behavioral consultants have often reported difficulties in implementing intervention programs due to changes that would have to be made at another level of the system, including the behavior of administration and staff. Baer and Bushell (1981) have pointed out that because of this, the overall impact of behavioral approaches in the schools has been limited. Kazdin (1979) noted that although attempts to change the behavior of individual parents, teachers, and children have been successful, most behavioral programs have yet to be proven effective on a larger scale. Often, behavioral approaches have done an excellent job in bringing deviant behavior in line with the expected norms of the reference group, but is this form of intervention any different than the traditional approach based upon a defect model (Trachtman, 1981)?

Behaviorists have spent much time and effort examining the environment or setting and its effects upon the observable actions of individuals by concentrating on rather narrow "slices of life." That individual differences do exist in response to specific behavioral settings (based upon more than mere differences in reinforcement history) has been pointed out (e.g., Taylor, 1979). Behavioral approaches may fall short when they provide one with a rather limited, oversimplified picture of schools and schooling and ignore the influences of cultural, community, family, and other variables on the educational process. Such an orientation, sharing an emphasis on linear causality with the medical model, does little to help one understand the importance of the influence of the many complex contextual/situational factors in the development of children and in their instruction and learning.

New Professional Collaborations

In recent years, school psychologists have cultivated new professional collaborations. What effect do these changes have on the service delivery model? The implementation of P.L. 94–142 mandated the use of a school-based, team approach to the identification and placement of children requiring special education services. Required by law, it is likely that multidisciplinary teams will be with us for some time. They represent what has been referred to as a trend toward increasing specialization of functions within the public schools (Bardon, 1983). Even prior to their being mandated there were a number of advocates of such an approach (e.g., Hogenson, 1973). Although the intention of legislation was to provide educational services to children with special needs, attainment of this goal has been slow, with the resistance of staff members to adopting new roles and functions one primary reason (Hyman, Carroll, Duffey, Manni, & Winikur, 1973). For the most part, school-based multidisciplinary teams have remained narrowly focused on their mandated responsibilities—eligibility determinations and program planning (Pryzwansky & Rzepski, 1983). Golin and Duncanis (1981) have found that in some instances multidisciplinary teams have had to define their roles so narrowly in order to remain in compliance with state legislation that they have primarily become child-centered decision-making teams based upon a traditional medical-defect model.

True professional collaboration has not been achieved. "Specialists" meet to discuss individual cases; actual teamwork is a rare occurrence. Rather than integrating data on a referred child with input from each discipline/specialty, looking for common threads and forming a set of conclusions, what is often produced is a series of "reports" detailing that child's performance in a number of discrete areas. In their search for pathology, team members have become technique-oriented, defining their responsibilities in specific, narrowly defined spheres and making little attempt to integrate information to form a coherent picture of the child and the environment within which he/she must function. It appears that there is often, across all team functions, the unstated assumption that all individuals will remain focused on the referred child as the identified patient and object of inquiry (Pfeiffer, 1981; Pfeiffer & Tittler, 1983). The result of such an orientation is that often the team remains isolated from many aspects of the educational arena and views the child out of context. A defect-oriented model remains at the heart of the team's activities as they search for factors internal to the child while ignoring important aspects of those systems within which the child functions. Through the use of such a model, parents, family, and community remain isolated from the school. Therefore, although a multidisciplinary team approach to the delivery of special education services may have its merits, one must question whether operating from a traditional perspective is the best way to introduce such a format in the schools.

New Work Settings

A recent trend in the delivery of psychological services to the schools has been the move of school psychologists into new settings, such as a community mental health center, a child guidance clinic, or a department of psychiatry in a major hospital. Within these settings school psychologists function as external consultants, operate from outside the educational system, and provide traditional services.

If adequate psychological services are to be offered to school-age children, professionals and staff in a variety of settings including schools and community service agencies must coordinate their efforts on an ongoing basis. Although it is a generally accepted fact that coordinated services are most effective and cost-efficient, evidence suggests that such collaboration is rare (Steinberg & Chandler, 1976). The findings of the Joint Commission on the Mental Health of Children (1973) over a decade ago remain quite accurate in that there is currently no "system" for the provision of mental health services to children. Typically what services are available are uncoordinated and seldom designed to provide intervention in light of total client needs (Mearig, 1982). Programs are developed and implemented in a piecemeal fashion, with much overlap and little collaboration. Children and families are often referred from one agency to another with efforts often duplicated and greater emphasis placed on finding "defects," labeling, and categorization than on preventive programming. In the past decade many attempts have been made to increase the coordination of school psychological services and those offered by other community services agencies. However, it seems that as a whole we have failed to recognize that integration is qualitatively different from calling in external consultants or referring children out of schools (Mearig, 1982). Using multidisciplinary teaming, changing the environment where one performs one's services, and coordinating delivery systems do not in themselves guarantee that a traditional perspective on offering school psychological services has been modified.

The Form versus Content Issue

In a cogent essay written for the Spring Hill Symposium, Trachtman (1981) has suggested that many of us in school psychology frequently tend to be more concerned with the appearance of things than with their substance. He refers to this as the "form versus content issue." As school psychology has developed through its infant stages and into adolescence, new theories, innovations, panaceas, and programs have been embraced by those in the field, and attempts have been made to assimilate them into the existing model. However, in many cases these theories and strategies have been so poorly conceived and hastily tested and implemented that they have resulted in nothing but the superficial adoption of new "forms," with there being little or no difference in the underlying rationale when compared to traditional approaches. At other times innovative approaches to the delivery of psychological services have been prostituted and changed in an attempt to fit them into the existing model such that they have had limited impact upon the profession. In recent years, for example, much interest has been expressed in school-based consultation. The role of the school psychologist as consultant has certainly not been ignored in the literature. As early as 1963, Gray presented the consultation model of Caplan (1961) as a viable framework. Since that time numerous articles and books have appeared (e.g., Berkowitz, 1973; Gutkin & Curtis, 1982; Meyers, Martin, & Hyman, 1977; Meyers, Parsons, & Martin, 1979) which have suggested that consultation become one of the major professional roles of the school psychologist. Surveys and position papers have indicated that practitioners view consultation as one of their most preferred job functions (Cook & Patterson, 1977; Meacham & Peckham, 1978). Similarly, educational personnel appear to consider consultation one of the most important aspects of service that psychologists bring to the schools (Bardon, 1979). Today, many in the profession view the psychologist-teacher relationship and consultation as pivotal for effective service. However, although the "consultation movement" developed in response to growing dissatisfaction with more traditional approaches to meeting the mental health needs of children and adults, the mode upon which school consultation is often based continues to be traditional. Most often the settings in which consultation develops have been those in which there has been a prior relationship based upon direct service involvement, predicated upon a medical perspective. The referred child often remains the primary "object of inquiry" and educational personnel under the guidance of a consultant search for internal states within the student that may be "causing" his/her difficulties or at best explore the immediate behavioral context of the "problem." The school psychologist, although having shifted from a direct to an indirect service mode, typically continues to employ a framework in which one searches for linear-causal relationships.

Dissatisfaction with the Medical Model

In our opinion, school psychology has yet to reach its true potential. Since the Thayer Conference (Cutts, 1955), school psychologists have voiced their dissatisfaction with the traditional medical perspective for offering school psychological services. This message was echoed at the more recent Spring Hill Symposium on *The Future of Psychology in the Schools* (Ysseldyke & Weinberg, 1981). Consensus exists that there are serious weaknesses in our current theoretical framework. Behavior analysis, multidimensional assessment, family counseling, and many other innovative approaches to dealing with students' educational difficulties, although important, have not moved us far enough away from a traditional perspective. The lack of any substantive conceptual changes in the theoretical framework from which specific practices emerge has weakened to varying extents the contributions that each of these new approaches might make to improving the services that school psychologists offer. Unfortunately, the traditional view of school psychology is quite contemporary. We have done no more than transfer old wine into new bottles.

A PRESS FOR AN ALTERNATIVE CONCEPTUALIZATION OF PSYCHOLOGICAL SERVICES FOR SCHOOLS: CHALLENGING THE ASSUMPTIONS OF THE TRADITIONAL MODEL

To eschew theory or a conceptual model altogether is to lack a roadmap for direction. Without such guidance, it would be difficult, if not impossible, to understand human behavior and to provide a rational, systematic program of psychological services. We believe progress in this area cannot be made piecemeal, but must result from what Kuhn (1962) refers to as a change or shift in paradigms. All paradigms or models contain a cluster of relevant assumptions that, ideally, should be related systematically to one another. These assumptions should help one to conceptualize and understand those empirical events with which the model is concerned and define both the field of observations and the methods to be used in research and practice (Hall & Lindzey, 1978). A paradigm is not right or wrong but must instead be judged with respect to its usefulness. When empirical events cannot be adequately understood based upon the assumptions underlying a model, both the model and its assumptions must be challenged and, if found wanting, discarded.

The nature of assumptions underlying a paradigm represents its distinctive qualities (Pervin, 1980). One either accepts them, and thus the model, or presses to construct an alternative viewpoint. The medical paradigm and the alternative we are proposing are distinctly different ways of conceptualizing the delivery of psychological services. They are predicated upon decidedly different assumptions, many of which relate directly to the provision of psychological services in the schools. Challenging the traditional manner in which such services are offered and proposing an alternative approach, one needs to compare and contrast the major assumptions of each approach. In the following section, we examine four major assumptions.

Static Versus Developmental View of the Individual

Traditionally, psychological services have been provided to individuals under the tacit assumption that one is dealing with a relatively static situation. The individual is thought of as a closed or semi-closed system with minimal or at best very slow exchange with the environment (Grinker, 1975). Cognitive and emotional changes in a child have been viewed as the result of the acquisition of a variety of discrete skills and abilities and "development" is conceived of as an additive, linear process. Consequently, psychological services for children have tended to consist of attempts to "capture" a given pupil's functioning at one point in time and space and then to develop an intervention program based upon a limited set of data. Programmatic decisions are based upon "historical" (some would say prehistoric) data from the child's past with few, if any, changes being made over time in the services offered a student. From this perspective, reassessment is typically undertaken solely to comply with state and federal regulations; few programmatic modifications are seen as warranted. (Exceptions include the formative evaluation used in precision teaching and the changing criterion designs used in applied behavior analysis.)

A contrasting view is that the child is a living system that is continually developing. Even in the absence of external stimuli, an individual or any other living organism is not a passive, but rather an extrinsically active, system, "an order of parts and processes standing in mutual interaction" (Bertalanffy, 1975, p. 1101). Complex feedback mechanisms operate to enable the organism to function effectively. Bertalanffy's (1968) general systems theory lends support to the notion that development is continuous and ongoing as opposed to a static quality that can be attained at a particular point in time or when the individual has mastered a set of specific skills.

Development as defined from this perspective involves progression through a series of stages in an orderly, coherent fashion. It is a complex process which involves the integration of many structures and functions. The human being is never static—from the moment of conception to the time of death he/she is changing and in a state of "becoming" (Garbarino, 1982). What exists at one particular stage becomes transformed into something related to, but also quite different from, what existed earlier (Breger, 1974). A dynamic, developmental perspective emphasizes that a child is a coherent person and that despite the changes that will occur over time, he/she remains, in important ways, the same individual (Sroufe, 1979). In this view children play an active role in seeking solutions to a series of developmental issues with which society confronts them. While behavior changes lawfully, the person remains the same (Erikson, 1963; Waters & Sroufe, 1985). The separation of cognitive and conative aspects of functioning/development, therefore, is purely artificial; each affects the other in a reciprocal manner.

Furthermore, development is not conceptualized to proceed in a linear, incremental fashion. As a child matures, both new capabilities are acquired and changes in the organization of behavior occur. As a result of such changes, an infant is transformed, being qualitatively different in the way it perceives and transacts with the world. Viewed through such a "lens," the nonlinear, interactive effects of genetic endowment, learning, and the psychosituational demands of the child's environment must be considered in any attempt to assess functioning. In addition, the notion of outcome must take into consideration both *distal* and *proximate* criteria. Distal criteria generally refer to health and adaptation in adulthood. Proximate criteria on the other hand may be conceptualized in terms of pivotal issues of specific developmental periods (Waters & Sroufe, 1983). In both assessment and intervention one must be cautious not to place too much emphasis on the latter. Specific skills a child learns are likely to be both situationally and age specific and therefore irrelevant to understanding and predicting the individual's adaptation in later years. The concept of competence, viewed developmentally, is broader than intelligence or any discrete set of skills that can be "measured" at one point in time in a testing room (Zigler & Trickett, 1978). Labeling and diagnosis thus become rather trivial endeavors that fail to capture important aspects of an individual's functioning.

Acontextual Versus Contextual Perspective

Viewing behavior in multiple contexts over time becomes an absolute necessity in light of changes in the individual's behavioral organization, perceptions, and exchanges with the world. The provision of school psychological services has, in the past, been primarily oriented toward the individual (closed system) with minimal or no consideration given to the context within which he/she functions. We have typically viewed children in isolation, assuming their performance/ behavior in one setting automatically generalizes to others. When a student's behavior in school does not conform to the normative expectations of those in that setting, we are quick to conclude that there is something "wrong" with the child and fail to consider whether such actions may indeed be functional within a different context. This orientation led to describing behavior within a particular setting and attempting to "cure" the behavior by changing the individual or the immediate environment within which the behavior occurs.

Such a model appears to ignore the multiple contexts in which an individual behaves and develops. If few or no interactions existed among a child's school, home, peer group, and community, it would be quite appropriate to view behavior as essentially acontextual or as only loosely tied to the context within which it occurs. However, this is not the case. Such a view fails to take into account the seminal work of Mischel (1973) and Bandura (1977), who have articulated the situational specificity of behavior and the concept of *reciprocal determinism*— the notion of an ongoing reciprocal interaction among behavior, internal states, and the external environment (Reynolds, Gutkin, Elliott, & Witt, 1984).

Children do, in fact, become members and participants in a number of systems and subsystems (*ecosystems*). As they develop, the original systems within which they function (e.g., the parent-child system of infancy) become subsystems of larger organizations of ever-increasing complexity (Grinker, 1975). As Hobbs (1966) has noted, "the child is an inseparable part of a small social system, of an ecological unit composed of the child himself, his family, his school, his neighborhood, and community" (p. 1108).

Bronfenbrenner's (1974) ecological approach assumes that human development and behavior are facilitated through the mutually influencing exchanges of persons in various roles at points where subsystems interface (Garbarino, 1982; Lewin, 1951). Perhaps the ecological model's most important and fundamental concept is that an individual is but one component of a comprehensive system of dynamic interdependencies (Rogers, 1962).

The environment within which one functions is at least in part the individual's creation (Bandura, 1978; Scarr & McCartney, 1983). Through the process of development and the subsequent reorganization of behavior, the "helpless" infant develops the capacity to voluntarily change his/her environment. Past transactions with the environment (i.e., experience) also change the individual, which may result in his/her having still different perceptions of the same settings. As children develop, of course, the network of systems and subsystems of which they are a part and the interactions and reciprocal influences among them become increasingly complex and difficult to understand (Anderson, 1983). An awareness of all of the settings/contexts within which a child functions is a prerequisite for the psychologist working with the schools.

An acontextual model is, therefore, an inadequate approach upon which to base the delivery of psychological services. It ignores the assumptions that (a) children function within an ever-increasing number of systems and subsystems as they develop; (b) the settings within which an individual functions are in a constant state of change; and (c) children themselves are not static, but continuously developing organisms with a capacity and proclivity to construct a different view of their settings and to create new environments.

The Client: Individual or System?

A question often asked by psychologists in the schools is, "Who is our client?" The issue of whether one's first obligation is to the individual child or to the school as an organization has been debated (Cutts, 1955). The range of clients defended in a literature spanning about 30 years has included the child (Cutts, 1955; Hyman, 1983), the parent (Pantaleno, 1983; Trachtman, 1981), the teacher (Meyers et al., 1977), and the total school organization (Cutts, 1955; Bardon, 1979).

A myriad of factors determine an individual practitioner's choice of exactly who the client is, however, the conceptual framework or lens through which one views service delivery is of considerable importance. Psychologists guided by the medical model will typically view the individual child or youth (as a closed system) as their primary client (Elliott & Witt, this volume; Reynolds et al., 1984). An alternative perspective is that the total set of ecosystems in which the child exists is the client. As a consequence, all forces that impinge upon and interact with the developing child come within the purview of the psychologist.

Viewing the individual as the client may at first glance seem to simplify matters, but we believe this view has several drawbacks. First, focusing on an individual child while ignoring his/her family, school, and community makes accurate identification and effective intervention difficult, if not impossible. Second, it leads school psychologists to limit their interaction with the child to "strange situations" (Bronfenbrenner, 1974) such as the testing room. Third, a perspective that conceptualizes problems as a result of categorical states or processes within the child fails to recognize the iatrogenic nature of many of the difficulties encountered in an educational setting. Fourth, an individual, defect-oriented viewpoint leads to a search for singular causes and gives only lip service to the concept of multiple causality.

There is considerable empirical evidence to support the premise that to provide effective psychological services, ecosystems must be perceived as the primary client. The importance of the family's influence on academic, behavioral, and emotional functioning (Hetherington & Martin, 1979; Kozloff, 1979), the adverse affect of home problems on school learning (Coleman, 1975; Esterson, Feldman, & Krigsman, 1975; Marjoribanks, 1981; 1979), the adverse effect of school difficulties on the family system (Rist & Harrell, 1982; Seligman, 1979), and the reciprocal influences between home and school problems (Ehrlich, 1983; Green & Fine, 1980; Smith, 1978; Tucker & Dyson, 1976) have all been studied. Conceptualizing the ecosystems of the child as the client provides one with the opportunity to change attitudes: Those who at one time would see themselves as victims of a problem can think of themselves instead as problem solvers. Finally, and most critically, such an orientation maximizes opportunities for growth and increased social competence in the child. Parenthetically, when the teacher, classroom, or school organization are targeted as clients, an ecosystems approach still provides a different framework than the medical model for dealing at these client levels.

Reactive Versus Proactive Intervention

Traditional approaches to service delivery focus on a "prescription" in an attempt to "cure" deviant behavior displayed by the individual. Intervention of this nature has been characterized as tertiary in that psychological services are offered primarily to children who display major learning and/or emotional/behavior problems (Caplan, 1961; Elliott & Witt, this volume; Reynolds et al., 1984). This approach can be characterized as reactive in that a major emphasis is placed on "putting out fires" that have been identified by socially sanctioned labelers (i.e., psychologists, members of child study teams, etc.). If for no other reason, such an approach is hopeless because, as Sarason (1976) has noted, "we can never train clinicians in other than miniscule numbers relative to defined needs" (p. 318).

The proposed approach to intervention derived from a developmental ecosystems model has a major defining characteristic: It is proactive and is aimed at primary prevention. The role of the school in developing preventive measures is not a new concept. Ringers (1976) has argued that schools are our mental health centers; Apter (1977) has developed the "total school" concept; and Hobbs (1975) has outlined a number of reasons for schools to accept responsibility for the coordinated delivery of a wide variety of services. A systematic coordination of resources is needed in order to facilitate such a proactive approach to providing services. Attitudinal changes must take place such that regular education teachers no longer feel their responsibility to the child ends with referral, nor that school psychologists believe their role terminates following assessment.

As advocates of a proactive approach to the delivery of psychological services within the school community, we agree with Rappaport (1977) that "the aim of our endeavor is not the prevention of illness, but rather the promotion and utilization of already existing strengths of a community" (pp. 526–27). Emphasis can be placed upon intervening prior to the development of problems in an attempt to ensure the maximum development of all members of the system. We concur with Waters and Sroufe's (1983) definition of the component individual as "one who is able to make use of environmental and personal resources to achieve a good developmental outcome" (p. 81) as well as Garbarino's (1982) definition as "one who can succeed in specific social contexts" (p. 2). Behavior is a means to create a desired outcome and in many cases may have adaptive value for the individual while not meeting societal standards of competence. Emphasis needs to be placed on the individual's ability to mobilize and coordinate personal resources within his/her ecosystems. It is through such a competence-focused approach that we have the best chance to enhance the adaptive functioning of an individual as he/she "transacts" with the environment.

AN ALTERNATIVE PARADIGM: THE DEVELOPMENTAL PERSPECTIVE

The alternative model we propose is a different way of viewing the delivery of psychological services in the *school community*, which we call the *developmental perspective* and which is grounded in the following assumptions:[1]

1. Psychology, as a behavioral science, has the capability to become a productive partner in broad-gauge educational programming. The range of school psychology's impact includes the application of theory and research in psychosocial development of *all* children, psychoeducational aspects of teaching and learning, social interaction processes, and systems change among other areas of critical impact.

2. A developmental perspective, in which learning functions cannot be dichotomized from personality development, will affect change in curriculum and instructional programs as the school psychologist brings knowledge of psychosocial development to bear on curricular decision making. The school psychologist is the person on the educational team responsible for recognizing that the child brings the totality of his/her life experience into the classroom and that,

---

[1]These assumptions are adapted from the conceptual model of the Psychology in the Schools Training Program at the University of Minnesota, presented in greater detail in the program brochure, "Psychology in the School-Community."

in turn, the classroom has a powerful, reciprocal shaping influence on the child's life.

3. Schools are critical determinants of the social competence of individuals and groups, a conclusion that has implications for the development of cognitive skills, socioemotional patterns, and mental health, not only for individual children but for society.

4. The home is viewed as an educative environment. School psychologists support and strengthen the family through parent education. They also help parents realize how they are effective educators of their children.

5. Responsiveness to community needs, awareness of the impact of subcultures, and concern for optimizing the total learning environment for all children are central in the professional practice of school psychology.

6. The interrelatedness of the health-education-welfare triad shapes the "optimal learning environment." Education cannot flourish where the personal development of children is severely limited by poverty and disease. The psychologist must, therefore, attend to the multiple contexts in which children develop.

7. Professional school psychologists need to be prepared for a wide range of roles within the educational enterprise—preparing practitioners and trainers of practitioners who are committed to translating data from developmental psychology, personality and learning theory, social psychology, and systems analysis into operational bases for collaborative problem solving, decision making, and program implementation in every phase of education and within various community settings.

8. The competencies needed by the school psychologist for problem solving include assessing individual/organization needs, generating and implementing a wide range of alternative intervention strategies, and evaluating and redesigning programs to meet the needs of individuals and the school community.

9. It becomes increasingly apparent that diverse problem-solving models designed to match methods of inquiry to the uniqueness of problem settings are needed. Using a broad data base and multiple assessment methods, the psychologist-educator team must seek to arrive at appropriate action programs.

10. Skill areas are not to be conceived as isolated, separate domains of expertise (assessment, intervention, consultation, research, and evaluation). In addition, professional competencies are part of a network that expands from a central focus on an individual's ecosystems, through family, small group and classroom applications, to system-wide problems and issues that involve the total community, including such supraordinate bodies as state and federal agencies.

11. Professional psychologists working within the educational arena must fill diverse roles, with varying degrees of specialization: consultative, administrative, educative, and evaluative.

Certainly, many of these assumptions alone or even in some combination are shared by those whose work is guided by the medical model. However, together they contribute an alternative framework, a different foundation, upon which one can build a program of services in the school community.

Depicting the Developmental Model

The proposed model has seven defining characteristics:

A developmental base: Development, an ongoing process throughout an individual's life span, results from complex interactions between the individual and his/her worlds. A developmental perspective focuses on the quality of a person's adaptation while confronting particular psychosocial tasks. Attaining social competence in one developmental phase provides a foundation for dealing with subsequent developmental issues. Genotype-environment relationships help account for individual differences in development.

An ecological view: Ecological psychology emphasizes the importance of interactions between internal organisms' characteristics and external, environmental factors. Individual behavior is better understood within the various environmental contexts in which it naturally occurs. Ecosystems at both immediate and distal levels must be considered in understanding and enhancing an individual's development.

A transactional view: Individuals do not simply react to environmental influences. Rather, individuals create and change their environments and in a reciprocal manner are also affected by those same environments. Thus, individuals are active participants in their own development, being shaped by factors that they in turn have influenced in a bidirectional manner.

A general systems theory orientation: As a complex living system, the individual encompasses a comprehensive set of intertwining social systems. A holistic view of an individual is dependent upon appreciating and understanding the interrelationships of these systems, their mutual influences, and reciprocal effects.

Multiple, non-linear explanations of behavior: The complex nature of behavior often cannot be accounted for by simple linear cause-and-effect relationships. The explanations are more likely dependent upon multiple causes that have nonlinear linkages with observed behavior.

A proactive, preventive focus: Emphasizing the facilitation of competency and social adaptation in all individuals is a basis for focusing on the prevention of problems and taking initiatives in providing school psychological services. Comprehensive, coordinated programs to meet the developmental needs of clients are a necessity.

A collaborative focus: Interprofessional collaboration within the health-education-welfare triad is essential to coordinate resources for the developing person. Creating optimal learning environments within the individual's complex ecosystems is dependent upon cooperation among the significant people within those settings. (See Table 13.1 for a comparison of descriptors of the traditional medical and alternative developmental models.)

Rather than conceptualizing the school as the "identifier" of and "treatment provider" for "troubled" individuals, the developmental model affirms the roles of the school, home, and community as primary socializing agents aimed at enhancing every child's development and providing opportunities to achieve competence.

TABLE 13.1
The Traditional and Alternative Models: Comparing their Descriptors

Medical Model	*Developmental Model*
a contextual	contextual-ecological
individual	individual/ecosystems
deficit bases	competence bases
static	dynamic, developmental
linear explanations	non-linear explanations (multiple)
interactional	transactional
reactive	proactive/preventive

Psychologists in the school community have been suggested as appropriate linkers, in "an unique position to understand, interrelate, and mobilize resources among the important settings of children" (Anderson, 1983, p. 188). The proposed model provides direction to such a professional commitment and is, in fact, congruent with the point of view represented earlier in the history of mental health services for children and youth (Levine & Levine, 1970).

Putting the Model to Practice

The developmental model for providing school psychological services draws upon a wide range of philosophical, theoretical, and empirical bases. We elaborate some of the major forces noted earlier in this paper that underlie this perspective and briefly explore implications of those ideas for school psychological services.

Contributions of Ecological Psychology: Lewin, Barker and Wright, and Bronfenbrenner

Kurt Lewin's work (1951) widened the scope of psychologist's thinking by observing that individuals function within social systems, each of which affects the nature of behavior. The family, peer group, church, school, and other formal and informal institutions and social groups in which the individual participates have unique influences on development. Lewin articulated the importance of understanding a child's "life space," particularly the child's interpretation of that space. The child's perception or interpretation of the environment varies as a function of the developmental levels and/or motivational states of the child.

Bronfenbrenner (1977; 1980) and Garbarino (1982) have extended the work of Lewin by describing a nested arrangement of four systems in which every individual develops (see Fig. 13.1). The *microsystem* is the immediate behavior

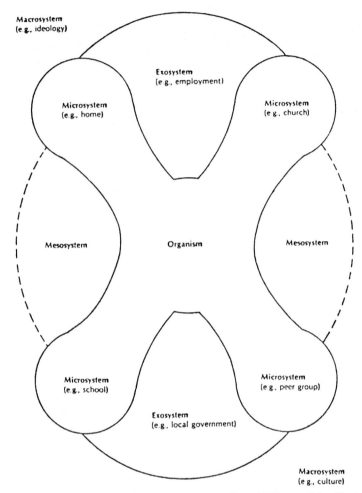

FIG. 13.1 The ecology of human development. From *Children and Families in the Social Environment* by J. Garbarino. New York: Aldine Press, Copyright 1982. Reprinted by permission.

setting of a child at any point in time, and the *mesosystem* comprises the interactions between the various settings, such as home and school, regular and special education classrooms, and school and community. The child directly participates and occupies roles within the micro- and mesosystems. Bronfenbrenner also proposes that children are affected by situations or settings in which they do not directly participate. Examples on the *exosystem* level include school board decisions, federal/state legislation, events in the parents' workplaces, and events in a teacher's family. Finally, *macrosystem* influences involve institutional and structural patterns of the culture, specifically economic, social, educational, legal, and political factors.

A child's development is influenced then by the immediate settings, such as school, home, peer group; by linkages among these settings; and by the institutional systems and social contexts in which the immediate settings are embedded—for example, shopping centers, educational operations, public transportation facilities, and political and economic policies. The environment is critical in understanding developmental outcomes. As a result, individual behavior has meaning only when viewed in the context of the interpersonal relationships in which it is embedded.

Implications for Practice

There are direct implications derived from the study of ecological psychology for professional practice in school psychology. Since the ecological perspective on development stresses the salience of understanding children's behavior within their natural contexts, there is a directive to observe and interact with children in their natural environments (rather than exclusively test) (Boehm & Weinberg, 1977). The child can continue to be a target of referral, but the goal is not to cure the child; rather, it is to understand the complex array of ecosystems that affect and are affected by the individual. The goal is to mobilize these systems to enhance the child's learning, adjustment, or social adaptation, albeit the subjectivity of the task. Since an individual's behavior is seen as conditional (i.e., it varies under different environmental conditions) school psychologists' perceptions may need to be altered. Operating from a medical model philosophy, the psychologist often uses behavioral descriptions or characteristics as sweeping generalizations. For example, the psychologist may write, "John sees no value in school learning; he is uninterested in academic work." In contrast, an ecologically oriented psychologist would specify the conditions under which this statement was true—"John appears uninterested in school work when he does not know what is expected of him. He becomes an active participant when the assignment is presented in a step-by-step manner." Furthermore, to adopt an ecological view, the psychologist must develop the skill of shifting to multiple lenses—from the microsystem to the meso-, exo-, and macrosystems. Approaching a problem, initiating a program, or targeting a need from such a perspective can result in quite different solutions or priorities.

Accepting a Transactional View of Development

In a transactional view of development, one acknowledges that there is a continual and progressive interplay between the organism and its environment. The characteristics of both the child and environment change each minute, month, or year. The cyclical nature of the individual's impact on the environment as well as the impact of the environment on the individual—this transaction—is the defining characteristic of the transactional view.

An empirical basis for a transactional view is provided by Sameroff and Chandler (1975) who compared a developmental view in which a child's outcome was related only to child characteristics with a developmental view in which both child and environment characteristics were included. The linear chain of cause and effect assumed to underlie the connection between earlier trauma (for example, reproductive causality) and later deviant outcomes was not empirically supported. Infants with reproductive complications (anoxia, prematurity) experienced differential outcomes due to multiple environmental factors such as family constellation or socioeconomic status. Children raised in affluent socioeconomic environments with an intact family and an educated mother showed few to no negative effects from earlier complications. However, children with identical complications raised in socioeconomically depressed environments with an unstable family situation and an uneducated mother often were labeled mentally retarded or described as having various personality problems. This research with "high-risk" populations suggests that if the child elicited or was provided nurturance from his/her caretakers, positive developmental outcomes resulted. To the extent that the child elicited negative responses from the environment, he/she was identified to be at "high risk" for developmental delays.

The potential socializing effect of the environment to allow the child to respond adaptively in spite of child characteristics led Sameroff and Chandler (1975) to support a transactional rather than an interactional model of development. In this view, the *constants* in development are not some set of traits but rather the *processes* by which these traits are maintained in the transactions between organisms and environment (p. 235).

Additional support for a transactional view of development comes from a review of the literature pertaining to the home environment of learning disabled students (Freund, Bradley, & Caldwell, 1979). In their summary of empirical studies, these researchers presented a unique typology representing the home environments of learning disabled students. Despite identifying several patterns of environmental characteristics common to learning disabled students, the authors clearly indicated that they do not naively assume that the home environment is always the causative agent in learning disabilities. Rather, "the home environment of learning disabled children is a reaction to, as well as a determinant, of the child's behavior" (p. 48). The mother-child relationship and use of rewards for learning disabled children provide a case in point. Despite a mother's carefully planned use of reinforcements, she may reward her learning disabled child inconsistently. Her poor sense of timing may be due in part to the child's sporadic, impulsive, and unpredictable behavior.

Implications for Practice

Transactional theory has implications for school psychologists' assessment-intervention practices. Children's deviant behavior is not perceived as a function of an inborn inability to respond appropriately but rather as a function of some maladaptation between the child and significant others (parents, teachers) in his/her environment. The discordance between the child and the environmental expectations prevents the child from organizing the world adaptively. The focus of assessment becomes the interactions between individuals. The characteristics of both the child and individuals with whom the child interacts—parents, teachers, peers, and neighbors—must be considered in order to help the child produce socially competent behavior. Thus, as a systems advocate, the school psychologist must acknowledge parent, teacher, and school community needs as well as the referred individual's needs throughout the assessment-intervention process.

It appears that developmental outcomes for children may be mediated, in part, by the attitudes of the child's caretakers. School psychologists must continuously be aware that, unfortunately, children often try to conform to the niches in which they have been placed. To the extent the student is seen as being emotionally disturbed, learning disabled, or different, educators' and parents' attitudes may lead to treating the child consistent with these labels.

School psychologists adopting the transactional view of child development are less attuned to observing and diagnosing pathology and more attuned to understanding individual differences. The individual's response repertoires, coping skills, and problem-solving abilities must be considered along with influences from the child's ecosystems—teacher's attitudes, parents' expectations, racial/ethnic identity, the cultural value system, and so forth—to develop a valid, comprehensive picture of the child's functioning. For example, an "inattentive" kindergartner begins to learn sound-symbol relationships in part due to his parents' involvement in drillwork at home. A fourth-grade boy attains mastery on his weekly spelling lists as a result of explicit parental expectations regarding studying and a teacher-directed review session with a classmate. Rather than assessing for a memory deficit, the psychologist adopting a transactional view observes the effect that changes in parental expectations and teacher's instructional patterns have on student performance. A second example involves a tenth-grade boy referred immediately to the child study team after his termination in a court-ordered residential treatment center. A child study team applying transactional theory would use the assessment process to get to know the student personally and to understand the student's needs within the mainstream suburban high school. This team would not assess the student in order to diagnose or label him/her emotionally disturbed; in fact, in this actual situation it was determined that this student no longer needed special education services.

The Nature and Nurture Problem Revisited

In our view, a developmental perspective demands a more careful account of *how* individuals' genotypes relate to environments and produce individual differences in development. Throughout intellectual history, although the social, political, and religious contexts have varied, the nature-nurture question has remained about the same: to what extent are genes *and* environments important variables in accounting for the development of human behavior.[2] The question basically has gone unanswered despite an expanded knowledge base in the fields of behavioral genetics and psychology, an increased repertoire of methodologies in research design and statistical analyses, and the availability of populations appropriate for studying the problem. Counterbalancing these advances is a plethora of value and moral issues rooted in the rich soil of the social-political and judicial arenas.

In the past decade or so, the writings of Jensen (1973), Lewontin (1970), Herrnstein (1973), and Kamin (1974) have generated an overheated emotional climate. Hereditarian arguments have been used both to defend notions of racial inferiority and supremacy in various domains of human behavior (e.g., intellectual ability) and to attack compensatory education programs such as Head Start and other intervention programs as naive, untenable exploitations of federal funds. "Pure" environmentalists have offered a rationale for developing specific intervention programs and general social policies that guarantee major changes in an individual's behavior presumed to be genetically determined by hereditarians. Environmentalism, run amok, has provided the basis for Pygmalion schemes that promise geniuses in every home and scholars in every classroom.

This "either-or" philosophy must create confusion for members of the school psychology community, whose primary interest is fostering an individual's development by creating optimal learning *environments*. If intellectual ability, cognitive skills, school achievement, personality characteristics, and other parameters of behavior are predetermined by genetic blueprints, then what role can educational environment contribute to the development of a child's behavior? Can the level of an individual's performance be altered as the result of classroom instruction and psychoeducational interventions? Are there no limits to the impact of such interventions? To help address these questions, it is important to explore some facts about the roles that genes and environments *together* play in affecting a person's development. Sophisticated research is not required to demonstrate that environments can have a major impact on one's development. Children reared in an abusive family situation will generally not be as well adjusted or "turn out" as well as children who grow up in a warm, supportive home. Furthermore, changes in one's environment can produce changes in behavior—a phenomenon called *malleability* (Scarr & Weinberg, 1976).

There is a myth that if a behavior or characteristic is genetic, it cannot be changed. Genes do not fix behavior; rather they establish a range of possible reactions to the range of *possible experiences* that environments can provide. How people behave, what their measured IQs turn out to be (if IQs warrant value or have meaning in our social world), or how quickly they learn depends

---

[2]This section relies heavily on a previously published article by R. A. Weinberg entitled, "A case of a misplaced conjunction: Nature or nurture?" *Journal of School Psychology*, 1983, 21, 9–12.

on the nature of their environments and on their genetic endowments bestowed at conception. Discussions of the impact of environments on development often rest on the unspoken assumption that the environment is something *out there*, something that happens *to* people and over which they have no control. It is important to distinguish between the environment to which people are exposed and the environment they actively experience (Scarr & McCartney, 1983). Clearly the meaning of events change with development. The child who has "caught on" that things have names, and who demands to know the names for everything, experiences a different verbal environment than the one experienced earlier. The child's parents and others have been talking to him/her since birth, but because he/she has changed, his/her world has changed.

Genotypes do not determine environments. Rather, individuals with certain genotypes are more likely to receive certain kinds of parenting, evoke certain responses from others, and seek out certain experiences. What feelings they evoke in others depend in part on those other people; what aspects of the environment they select for special attention depend on what is available. The key point is that genotypes and environments *combine* to produce human development, and that genetic and environmental differences *combine* to produce variations in development.

Implications for Practice

The conclusion that our genetic heritage contributes to the complex accounting of variation in our performance is not pessimistic and does not bode evil for social and educational policy. Scarr and Weinberg (1978) summarize this position:

> Social policy should be determined by political and ethical values . . . once social policy has been determined, however, research can be useful. Governments can do a better job of designing effective intervention programs if people know which variations in the environment make a difference and which do not. The average level of a culture's environment determines the average level of achievement: by providing good schools, nutrition, health care, and psychological services, a society can raise the overall level of health and attainment for the whole population. Resources spent in these areas should eliminate conditions that have definite deleterious effects on individual development.
>
> But governments will never turn their entire populations into geniuses, or altruists, or entrepreneurs, or whatever their philosophy is. Biological diversity is a fact of life, and respect for individual differences derives from the genetic perspective. (p. 36)

Those of us who devote our professional efforts to the educational enterprises can appreciate individual differences and accept the challenge to create those educational environments that effectively "match" a child's abilities and talents. We can attempt to provide the necessary full range of environments that will facilitate optimal learning outcomes for every child. We can become more enlightened about the varying impact of alternative types of planned educational environments on children with different learner characteristics. Although genetic endowment might set limits on development, as school psychologists we can be reassured that the environments created for children at school and at home can indeed make a difference.

Drawing upon General Systems Theory

Sameroff (1983) has made a critical distinction between systems approaches and general systems theory: "A systems approach is usually treated synonymously with an interactionist position in which one cannot examine the bits and pieces of behavior in isolation" (p. 261). For example, the importance of the family's influence in academic, behavioral, and emotional problems of children (e.g., Hetherington & Martin, 1979); the effects of home problems on school learning (e.g., Coleman, 1975); and the adverse effect of labeling a child as a handicapped learner on the family system (e.g., Turnbull & Turnbull, 1978) are research findings that can be interpreted from an interactionist position.

In contrast, general systems theory (Bertalanffy, 1968) provides a framework for organizing the reciprocal influences of the various ecosystems of the developing child. Emphasis is placed on understanding the individual as part of separate ecosystems (e.g., home or school) and in relation to the child's whole system. When a child is referred, a true systems thinker never debates whether the "cause" is at home or school or elsewhere. Each ecosystem is critical, and therefore, systems thinkers choose not to disengage home, school, and other context variables. Recent research has identified the *reciprocal* influence between home and school problems (Ehrlich, 1983; Green & Fine, 1980; Smith, 1978; Tucker & Dyson, 1976). Although systems thinkers observe and interact with individuals, such as a parent, a teacher, or a child, they never lose sight of the entire system in which the individual functions. Efforts are directed to the system as a whole with the goal of helping the system to work better for the individual (Hobbs, 1975).

According to general systems theory (Bertalanffy, 1968; Buckley, 1967) certain organizational principles govern interactions between subsystems (e.g., the developing child's ecosystems):

1. Circular causality. A system can be defined as a group of interrelated individuals; thus, a change in one individual affects other individuals and the group as a whole. Causality is circular rather than linear because every action is also a reaction. School difficulties affect a child's behavior within the family, and conversely family problems influence a student's achievement and/or behavior in school.

2. Nonsummativity. The system as a whole is greater than the sum of its parts; a whole adds the property of relationship to the parts (synergism). The coordination of efforts among home, school, and community resources achieves a synergistic relationship. The notion of synergism further underscores that school-home-community together can achieve more than any one alone.

3. Equifinality. According to this principle the same outcome may result from different antecedents. For example, two different sets of families whose interactional styles are quite diverse may both produce children who steal.

4. Multifinality. This principle suggests that similar initial conditions may lead to dissimilar end states; thus, identical twins may in adulthood function in different ways.

5. Communication. All behavior is regarded as communication—transmitting interpersonal messages. Kaplan (1971) has suggested that when the home and school operate as two separate worlds, the child becomes the burdened one, carrying messages between the two systems and "the role of message bearer may take a heavy toll on the child physically, emotionally, and/or academically" (p. 38).

6. Rules. Rules within schools and rules within families serve to organize the respective interactions and function to maintain a stable system by prescribing and limiting an individual's behavior. The rules provide expectations about roles, actions, and consequences that guide either school or family life. Difficulties emerge for children when the rules and values of each ecosystem are not shared. Parents may jump to conclusions about the teacher's disciplinary philosophy; teachers may stereotype parental attitudes. Since rules are essential to maintain the intactness of the whole system, a set of operating rules for the entire, overarching system of school *and* family is critical.

7. Morphostasis. Systems operate to maintain a steady, stable state of functioning. All members contribute to the homeostatic balance through a mutually reinforcing feedback loop. If an individual member (parent, student, teacher) deviates too far from the system norm, creating conflict or disruption, the negative feedback process occurs and generates pressure to restore system equilibrium.

8. Morphogenesis. In addition to homeostasis, flexibility is required for the system to adapt to internal and external change. Change is required in response to new developmental periods and the corresponding developmental tasks of its members that evolve over the life cycle. School changes come about not only in response to developmental demands but also from mandated laws and new educational knowledge and technology.

Implications for Practice

As a systems thinker, school psychologists need to adopt different attitudes regarding the delivery of services. Larson (1980) has articulated assumptions of a general systems vantage point that could alter significantly the nature of the school psychologist's professional work. She argues that individual dysfunction (academic, emotional, social) is a manifestation of total system disorganization (family, school, community, *and* child). The dysfunction develops as a patterned attempt by the individual to adapt to the demands of his/her environment; it may in fact serve an adaptive or positive function for the system. In this context, purposes of diagnosis are twofold: (a) to assess the function of a particular set of behaviors within the total system and between ecosystems (For example, does the child's problem behavior serve some function within the classroom or between family and school?) and (b) to assess points of discordance between the child's capabilities and demands or expectations of the environment. Targets for intervention are the interactions or relationships among people. Three potential areas of intervention include changing the child in context, changing the environments, and changing system attitudes and expectations.

On another level, if we accept that a child in school is faced with membership and participation in at the very minimum two ecosystems—the home and school setting—and that the child must maintain relationships with each ecosystem, then it is logical to conclude that the child forms a natural triangle between home and school (Mullen, Abnate, & Constanzo, 1982). Many handicapped children form a natural triangle between regular and special education teachers. As a child advocate, the school psychologist can be a natural link between the child's primary ecosystems—home and school—or between the special and regular education settings. The psychologist aligns with teachers *and* parents to understand their perception. In a sense, the psychologist joins their systems (Minuchin & Fishman, 1981), enabling him/her to work closely with them in a consultative role.

The daily activity of school psychologists concerned with creating linkages is different from that of those in traditional practice. For example, parent-teacher interviews would be employed to assess home-school perceptions of a referral problem. The psychologist would also attend regularly scheduled parent-teacher conferences in order to ensure coordination of goals (Turnbull & Leonard, 1981). Thus, effective home-school partnerships become essential in light of general systems theory analyses (Anderson, 1983; Loven, 1978; Pfeiffer & Tittler, 1983), and the school psychologist is an excellent candidate to stimulate the courtship.

An ecological systems perspective also offers support for the integration of school and community-based psychological services (Plas, 1981). Mearig (1982) reviewed the elements of providing integrated services, and Hall (1976) described comprehensive health care services based on a collaborative effort between medical and psychological personnel. Finally, various applications of ecological approaches involving clinical and community psychology are described in O'Connor and Labin's review (1984).

The principle of integration of services is not equivalent to hiring an external consultant for the school or to referring children and families to a mental health agency. It also is not equivalent to orchestrating consultation or referral services. It involves a multidisciplinary orientation based on sharing suggestions and ideas, joint planning and mutual decision making, and reciprocal teaching and learning (Armer & Thomas, 1978). The nature and composition of services is based on the needs of the child and his/her ecosystems rather than on diagnostic labels or the availability of existing services. Mearig (1982) has outlined four critical steps in attaining integrative services: (a) careful diagnostic study of the child's needs; (b) a reason for involving each service; (c) an ongoing relationship between the school and service providers; and (d) systematic follow-up.

For example, team members do not need to divvy up pieces of the child evaluation (e.g., family interview, observation) and perform these tasks in isolation. Rather, there can be a mutual understanding and agreement about the interrelationships of the various components; there can be a collaborative effort to integrate data into one statement of the child's needs; and a "service net" can be created to enable the *entire* system (teachers, parents, community professionals) to aid the child or be modified accordingly. Interprofessional collaboration substitutes "technique-thinking" (e.g., "I am responsible to do the classroom observation") with "systems-thinking" (e.g., "What are the effects of the assessment process on the various members of the system?").

Mearig (1982) concluded that "the school (is) the most logical clearinghouse for this integration, since it already serves almost all children, has legitimate contacts with families and established (or relatively easy to establish) links with community services, is a long-term influence in the child's life, and exists permanently" (p. 754). We believe the school psychologist is the most capable individual to assume the integrator and liaison role in light of training in child and adolescent development, flexibility in job description, skill at the group problem-solving process, knowledge of community mental health resources, and relative independence of functioning (Apter, 1982; Mearig, 1982). The leadership school psychologists might play in this effort is potentially great, but the lack of understanding of the philosophical orientations, content bases, and "grammars" of other psychoeducational specializations evidenced by academicians and practitioners alike prevents the early realization of such a goal (e.g., Christenson et al., 1981).

A simple schemata of the linker/liaison role is presented in Fig. 13.2. The school psychologist "links up" the school, family, and community resource ecosystems to provide comprehensive, coordinated services.

Psychologists adopting a medical or a developmental perspective can engage in similar activities or job functions—assessment, intervention, and consultation—but the meaning attached to these tasks is different. For example, individual

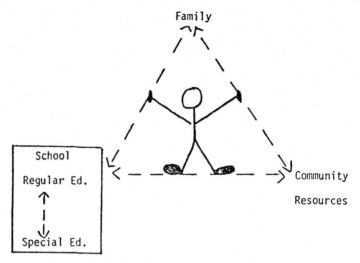

FIG. 13.2 Linkages provided by the school psychologist serving as liaison among ecosystems.

assessment is critical from either point of view; however, within a medical model, extensive child characteristic data are collected to confirm a "within-child" problem. In contrast, child characteristic data are essential in a developmental framework as one necessary step in assessing how multiple ecosystems can be mobilized to enhance the child's learning adaptation and general development. These differences between the models can be played out in other areas of the school psychologist's professional life.

THE ALTERNATIVE PERSPECTIVE AS A BASIS FOR POLICY AND PRACTICES

Comparison of Models Influencing Practice

Although we believe the developmental model is a viable alternative for providing psychological services in the school/community, the astute reader might ask, "Is this simply 'Ivory Tower' theorizing or a useful model for the delivery of school psychological services?" Recognizing that any attempt at comparing and contrasting daily job functions and attitudinal perspectives of psychologists' operating within two models invites criticism, we offer a comparison with, of course, several accompanying caveats: (a) the comparative activities are by no means exhaustive, (b) the developmental model requires a comprehensive commitment such that adoption of one or two listed activities does not qualify one as a "developmental" rather than a "traditional" psychologist, and (c) the elimination of traditional activities, such as "testing" students, is not proposed. Finally, the model needs to be "road-tested." We are ever hopeful that its use will increase our concrete understanding of how school psychologists' daily tasks differ as a result of the philosophical and theoretical stances adopted. Practical implications of the issues raised and summarized in the following chart should stimulate every school psychologist to identify ways in which a point of view affects one's professional agenda.

As a profession, collectively, we could do more to awaken the interest of our colleagues in the value of routinely and continually reassessing the philsophical and theoretical stances that guide professional practice in school psychology. Acceptance of the model that guides one's professional life is a personal endeavor heavily dependent upon the demonstrated usefulness of that particular model. We need to create training and practice environments that at least enable one to consider the alternative developmental model of service delivery.

Building the Perspective into University Training Programs and Continuing Education Opportunities

An overview of the description of extant training programs at the specialist and doctoral levels (*N.A.S.P. Directory of School Psychology Training Programs in the U.S. and Canada* and *APA Graduate Programs in Psychology*) will reveal that most programs claim to have a training model (e.g., scientist-practitioner, consultation, behavioral, generalist) but in fact, these labels do not communicate which philosophical bases underlie them. We believe that most programs are steered by an individual medical model, although there might be lip service to alternative views in specific courses or readings.

Assimilating the alternative model into the training enterprise requires at least three direct courses of action:

1. Systematically, take a hard look at one's core curriculum and adopt and assimilate new ideas and conceptualizations within the context of the current training setting. Assessment can be taught from a developmental ecological perspective; students can be taught naturalistic observation skills and still continue to acquire testing and interviewing competencies. One can focus on a preventive, ecosystems focus for intervention and still opt for a behavioral or humanistic lens. Making such changes can be dramatic but they do not require a total dismantling of one's training program.

2. Redefine relationships with other specialties of psychology, education, and the social sciences. Closer alignment with these groups is necessary in order to provide students with the range of coursework needed to acquire a broad developmental perspective. Family social science, child development, community psychology, and public health programs share interests with school psychology training programs and have faculty whose expertise is relevant to the alternative perspective.

TABLE 13.2
Practical Comparisons of Developmental and Traditional Models

	Developmental Model	Traditional Model
Premises	—While the student is the stimulus for referral, the psychologist looks for discordance between the student and the demands/expectations of his/her environment, focus is on transactional relationships between student-teacher, student-family, student-peers.	—Since the student is referred, it is assumed that there is something wrong with him/her; therefore, the psychologist looks for causes within the student; if student-teacher, student-parent, and/or student-peer relationships are analyzed, recommendations describe how the *student must change* to meet the external norm.
Differentiating Characteristics	—Causes are not debatable; one cannot disentangle home-school influences; circular causality, equifinality, and multifinality are the norm; thus the student is viewed as having an active role in creating the present environment as well as reacting to it.	—Causes may be debated (e.g., family or school); causal influences are seen as unidirectional.
	—While data collected describe the student, they are collected and used to achieve problem resolution, e.g., to teach the student missing information.	—Data are collected to describe the student's problem as a deficit; the focus of assessment is to confirm that something is wrong with the student.
	—Diagnostic labeling is not emphasized; ongoing intervention may explain the difference between a handicapped student and a student handicapped in current learning environment.	—Considerable resources directed toward diagnostic labeling; eligibility decisions are difficult and often inaccurate.
	—Assessment to Intervention Link	—Assessment to Placement Link
	—Problem Solving	—Problem Description
Referral Activities	—When a referral is received, the psychologist engages in a referral-sources interview with teachers, parents, and student present; the goal of interview is to reach consensus on specific behaviors of concern under various conditions; information obtained is reviewed by child study team.	—When referral is received, assumption is made that testing by the child study teams is necessary; less emphasis on information gathering prior to evaluation.

13. ALTERNATIVE MODEL

		—Vague, subjective referral statements, such as "poor math academic performance" are accepted, often resulting in administration of an extensive battery of tests.
		—Students are referred for a LD, ED, or language evaluation.
		—When testing occurs, a standard test battery is used.
		—Norm-referenced, standardized tests are primarily emphasized; the psychologist administers IQ measures routinely.
		—The goal of assessment is to make eligibility decisions. Therefore, once such a decision is made there is no longer any reason to continue assessment activities.
		—Inter-individual differences are emphasized during child study team evaluation; if the student is placed, the special education teacher emphasizes intra-individual differences to plan instruction.
		—Each discipline represented on child study assessment team administered his/her own tests and procedures; data organized into separate reports listing test scores and observations of student's behavior.
		—Assessment involves primarily child study team members, who are viewed as the expects in testing. There is limited parental and student involvement.
Assessment Activities		—Referral statements are changed into referral questions: rather than "Johnny never completes his math work," the question asked is "Does Johnny have the prerequisite knowledge in math to complete the current assignment?"
		—Student referred based upon specific, observable behaviors in the school-home environment.
		—Assessment devices are selected in order to collect data *relevant* to the referral questions.
		—While norm-referenced, standardized tests are administered to generate student characteristic data, observation, interviews, curricular diagnostic teaching and interventions are used to assess the demands of the environment and to identify resources to create change for the student, teacher, or parents.
		—Assessment is a continuous process that does not end eligibility decisions. The most important phase of the assessment process *begins* when an intervention is decided upon.
		—Both inter-individual differences (comparison to grade level peers) and intra-individual differences (comparison to self) are assessed during the child study evaluation.
		—Psychologist coordinates assessment of student by assuring that each discipline's evaluation results and hypothesis are continuously shared with other team members; all data collected are organized according to Hobb's profile analysis and ecomapping (Apter, 1982).
		—Assessment attempts to involve all significant others in data-gathering process; therefore, teachers, *parents*, and *students* may all collect data.

Table 13.2 (*Continued*)

Developmental Model	Traditional Model
—Asks *what* and *how* questions: Underlying reason for using circular questioning (what happens when, who contributes) is to identify student responses under difficult conditions. In what settings is the specific behavioral concern a problem? Not a problem? For whom does the behavior cause concern? Who contributes to the student's problem? How can parents, teachers, students bring about change in referred student's behavior? How does the student have to change to fit the current setting? How does the setting have to change to ensure a better "goodness-of-fit"? Is such change possible? What is expected of the student in each setting? How do the expectations vary and affect student behavior, for failures and successes? Where is student currently performing in math (i.e., actual level)? What is teacher's/parents' desired level of performance for the student? What interventions are reasonable to close discrepancy between the actual and desired levels of math performance? —Psychologist integrates data across disciplines; addresses unified concerns and goals; emphasis on interpretation of test scores, observations, and results of interventions. —Inferences about hypotheses from test data must be supported by corroborative evidence (e.g., scores on emotional tests supported by student's pattern of social-emotional adjustment).	—Asks *why* questions. How does student compare to age appropriate peers in IQ, mathachievement, etc.? Why is there a lag? What does the student do that concerns you? What causes he student to act this way? What are the student's strengths and limitations? Why does he/she have these? —A separate report is written by each child team member; reports added to "evaluation pile"; emphasis on reporting of test scores, which may reveal contradictions (e.g., WRAT reading, 4.8, PIAT word recognition, 3.2). —Inferences are often made about hypotheses from test data without providing supportive evidence: "child is withdrawn and insecure."

	—Feedback conferences have a structure: review of all data collected (student, teacher, classroom, parent, peer influences), needs of students, brainstorming about instructional interventions, identifications of who can deliver instruction (parent, teacher, special teacher), and finally eligibility for special services; parent, teachers, and students asked to validate accuracy of results; emphasis on *facilitating questions* and *discussion* about student.	—Feedback conferences often result in each child study member reporting his/her test scores and observations; use of formulas for student eligibility applied and decision is made; instructional interventions often not mentioned or extremely vague, unless in form of recommendations at end of report; emphasis on *reporting* data.
	—Psychologist avoids nonspecific recommendations; logical extension of the assessment process is ongoing consultation with teachers of referred student.	—Psychological recommendations often placement oriented; written at end of report.
Consultation Activities	—Psychologist uses group process skills to assist teachers, parents, students, and/or teams in generating interventions and needed modifications.	—Often solution-oriented, psychologist generates a list of ideas or recommendations for teachers or parents to try.
	—Psychologist initiates ongoing follow-up with teachers; psychologist monitors effectiveness of agreed-up interventions; thus, assessment data is collected on an ongoing basis not only at annual review.	—Less follow-up with teachers, perhaps only when teacher seeks out psychologist or when annual review occurs.
Intervention Activities	—Viewed as *working with* student and significant others in student's natural setting or total ecology.	—Viewed as placement of student in a program (special education, counseling, behavioral management).
	—There is an understanding that interventions can work because the environmental conditions are different, the teacher's or parents' attitude is different, and/or the student has changed; teachers understand the different coping styles of students.	—Statements like "I've tried that before, it doesn't work" are accepted.
	—Emphasis is placed on all targets of intervention: student, teacher, parents, peers, classroom, home environment; needs of all significant others are included in intervention plans.	—Emphasis on the student only; thus, outcome is "modify/change curriculum for the student" or the student him/herself.
	—Encourage school-home partnerships by explaining school process to parents.	—Parents often uninformed about the operations of schools, availability of programs, etc.

Table 13.2 (Continued)

	Developmental Model	Traditional Model
	—Train parents to be advocates for their own child; train parents to participate in IEP conferences; teach parents about child development and educational programs so they can become knowledgeable enough to make an informed decision and help solve the academic and behavioral concern (e.g., newsletter) (Turnbull & Leonard, 1981).	—Report child study team findings to parents; provide parents with written material about parental rights; recommend to parents what they should do.
	—Provide ongoing parental education/counseling; time contracts with school calendar events, e.g., before vacations, mid-marker, ecosystems within which child functions are viewed as primary sources of influence.	—Less contact with parents; parents used mostly as information-providers during assessment stage.
Community Involvement	—Psychologist increases his/her involvement in the community to include: 　Involvement on advisory boards. 　Strong liaison role between school and outside mental health facility. 　Ongoing contact with neurologists, pediatricians, psychiatrists, etc. in order to know them on first name basis and to use them as professional resource for critical cases.	—Community often ignored by psychologist unless to make a referral.
	—Psychologist proposes ongoing continuing education sessions based on *system* needs of district; emphasizes total ecology of student, e.g.: 　Discuss family systems issues with teachers. 　Train parents about the educational process.	—Psychologist used as resource for "one-shot" inservice training sessions; often in area of assessment (e.g., explain Kaufman ABC).
Research Activities	—Psychologist realizes value of conducting research for school district in program development and evaluation research for studies of program effectiveness.	—Psychologist's primary role is assessment; few are viewed as researchers by school professionals.

—Psychologist viewed as resource for child/adolescent development; thus psychologist spends time monthly in the library in order to interpret research findings for teachers/administrators and to help translate findings into applicable classroom interventions.

—Psychologist's goal is to understand the student's natural setting; thus, g eneration to local norms is an important activity, e.g., establishing local norms on behavioral checklist used by district to make ED placement decisions.

3. Provide collaborative training in some areas of practice—interviewing, systems analysis, consultation, and so on—for school psychology students as well as pre-service trainees in the related disciplines of special education, school administration, health care, and social work. Through shared cources, seminars, and practical experiences students are better able to role-take and understand the disciplinary perspectives of others with whom they will be working in the school community. Such efforts can "mow the turf" so cautiously guarded by professionals who do not appreciate the skills and training of their colleagues. The Career Growth Fellowship Program, established by the University of Minnesota's Center for Early Education and Development, is an example of an educational experience tailored for a multidisciplinary student group (Weinberg, Fishhaut, & Moore, 1983).

Continuing education through standing structures such as NASP, Division 16-APA, and the National School Psychology Inservice Training Network can also provide on-the-line practitioners with opportunities to explore the fit of a new philosophical model. Challenging one another's ideas in the supportive environment of a professional meeting might be a refreshing change from the usual "roles and functions" themes.

Charting a Course of Action for Professional School Psychology

Unfortunately, the field of school psychology has given priority to the survival and enhancement of the profession and less consideration to solutions of problems for which the specialty was created to solve (Hobbs, 1975). We believe that a developmental-proactive-preventive model can be the basis for a long-overdue national policy and action plan to provide for the educational and developmental needs of children and youth.

Over 10 years ago, Task Force I of the Joint Commission on Mental Health of Children (1973) set up guidelines for action in the service of children and youth that are congruent with the proposed model:

—Emphasis should be placed on prevention and early intervention rather than on later remediation.
—Emphasis should be placed on comprehensive, continuous, and coordinated service programs with the developmental needs of children in the forefront.
—Planning and intervention should have, as their basic context, the family as the primary child-rearing institution; the family's impact can be enhanced by appropriate, flexible, community-based resources.
—Deviance is viewed within a social context; therefore, solutions need to be sought in the matrix of social conditions that produce and maintain dysfunction in children.

—Emphasis should be placed on the changing characteristics of the developing individual—attributes of development that are salient, the most relevant environmental conditions, and opportunities for intervention differ across the life span.

–One should examine, observe, and anticipate ways to prevent potential problems.

School psychologists could play an active role in initiating and implementing such a plan if an appropriate model guides that implementation. We are suggesting that a developmental perspective might fill that bill.

REFERENCES

Anderson, C. (1983). An ecological developmental mode for a family orientation in school psychology. *Journal of School Psychology, 21,* 179–189.

Apter, S. J. (1977). Applications of ecological theory: Toward a community special education model. *Exceptional Children, 44,* 366–373.

Apter, S. J. (1982). *Troubled children, troubled systems.* New York: Pergamon Press.

Armer, B., & Thomas, B. K. (1978). Attitudes toward interdisciplinary collaboration in pupil personnel service teams. *Journal of School Psychology, 16*(2), 167–176.

Baer, D. M., & Bushell, J. D. (1981). The future of behavior analysis in the schools? Consider its recent past, and then ask a different question. *School Psychology Review, 10,* 259–270.

Bandura, A. (1977). *Social learning theory.* Englewood Cliffs, NJ: Prentice-Hall.

Bandura, A. (1978). The self-system in reciprocal determinism. *American Psychologist, 33,* 344–358.

Bardon, J. I. (1979). Educational development as school psychology. *Professional Psychology, 10,* 225–233.

Bardon, J. (1982). The psychology of school psychology. In C. R. Reynolds & T. B. Gutkin (Eds.), *The handbook of school psychology* (pp. 3–15). New York: Wiley.

Bardon, J. (1983). Viewpoints of multidisciplinary teams in schools. *School Psychology Review, 12*(2), 186–189.

Berkowitz, H. (1973). A collaborative approach to mental health consultation in school settings. In W. L. Claiborn & R. Cohen (Eds.), *School intervention* (Vol. 1, pp. 54–63). New York: Behavioral Publications.

Bersoff, D. N., & Grieger, R. N. (1971). An interview model for the psycho-situational assessment of children's behavior. *American Journal of Orthopsychiatry, 41,* 438–439.

Bertalanffy, L. (1968). *General systems theory: Foundation, developments, applications.* New York: Braziller.

Bertalanffy, L. (1975). General systems theory and psychiatry. In S. Arieti (Ed.), *American handbook of psychiatry* (2nd ed., Vol. 1, pp. 1095–1117). New York: Basic Books.

Boehm, A. E., & Weinberg, R. A. (1977). *The classroom observer: A guide for developing observation skills.* New York: Teachers College Press.

Breger, L. (1974). *From instinct to identity: The development of personality.* Englewood Cliffs, NJ:Prentice-Hall.

Bronfenbrenner, U. (1974). Is early intervention effective? In H. J. Leichter (Ed.), *The family as educator.* New York: Teachers College Press.

Bronfenbrenner, U. (1977). Toward an experimental ecology of human development. *American Psychologist, 32,* 513–531.
Bronfenbrenner, U. (1980). Ecology of childhood. *School Psychology Review, 9,* 294–297.
Buckley, W. (1967). *Sociology and modern systems theory.* Englewood Cliffs, NJ: Prentice-Hall.
Caplan, G. (Ed.). (1961). *Prevention of mental disorders in children.* New York: Basic Books.
Christenson, S., Graden, J., Potter, M., Taylor, J., Yanowitz, B., & Ysseldyke, J. (1981). *Current research on psychoeducational assessment and decision making: Implications for training and practice* (Monograph No. 16). Minneapolis: University of Minnesota, Institute for Research in Learning Disabilities.
Coleman, J. S. (1975). What is meant by "an equal educational opportunity"? *Oxford Review of Education, 1,* 27–29.
Cook, V. J., & Patterson, J. G. (1977). Psychologists in the schools in Nebraska: Professional functions. *Psychology in the Schools, 14,* 371–376.
Coopersmith, E. (1982). The place of family therapy in the homeostasis of larger systems. In R. Aronson & B. Wolberg (Eds.), *Group and family therapy.* New York: Brunner/Mazel.
Cutts, N. (Ed.). (1955). *School psychologists at midcentury.* Washington, DC: American Psychological Association.
Ehrlich, M. I. (1983). Psychofamilial correlates of school disorders. *Journal of School Psychology, 21,* 191–199.
Erikson, E. H. (1963). *Childhood and society* (2nd ed.). New York: Norton.
Esterson, H., Feldman, C., & Krigsman, S. W. (1975). Time-limited group counseling with parents of preadolescent underachievers: A pilot program. *Psychology in the Schools, 12,* 79–84.
Freund, J. H., Bradley, R. H., & Caldwell, B. M. (1979). The home environment in the assessment of learning disabilities. *Learning Disability Quarterly, 2,* 39–51.
Garbarino, J. (1982). *Children and families in the social environment.* New York: Aldine.
Garmezy, N. (1979). DSM III: Never mind the psychologists; is it good for the children? *Clinical Psychologist, 31*(3 & 4), 1, 4–6.
Goldwasser, E., Meyers, J., Christenson, S., & Graden, J. (1983). The impact of PL 94-142 on the practice of school psychology. *Psychology in the Schools, 20,* 153–165.
Golin, A. K., & Duncanis, A. J. (1981). *The interdisciplinary team.* Rockville, MD: Aspen Systems.
Gray, S. W. (1963). *The psychologist in the schools.* New York: Holt, Rinehart & Winston.
Green, K., & Fine, M. J. (1980). Family therapy: A case for training of school psychologists. *Psychology in the Schools, 17,* 241–248.
Grinker, R. R., Sr. (1975). The relevance of general systems theory and psychiatry. In S. Ariete (Ed.), *American handbook of psychiatry* (2nd ed., Vol. VI, pp. 215–272). New York: Basic Books.
Gutkin, T., & Curtis, M. (1982). School-based consultation: Theory, and techniques. In C. R. Reynolds & T. Gutkin (Eds.), *The handbook of school psychology* (pp. 796–828). New York: Wiley.
Hall, C. S., & Lindzey, G. (1978). *Theories of personality.* New York: Wiley.
Hall, M. D. (1976). The child psychologist in an ecologically oriented health care program. *Pediatric Psychology, 1*(4), 35–46.
Herrnstein, R. J. (1973). *IQ in the meritocracy.* Boston, MA: Little, Brown.
Hetherington, E. M., & Martin, B. (1979). Family interaction. In H. Quay & J. Werry (Eds.), *Psychopathological disorders of childhood* (pp. 247–303). New York: Wiley.
Hobbs, N. (1966). Helping disturbed children: Psychological and ecological strategies. *American Psychologist, 21,* 1105–1115.
Hobbs, N. (1975). *The futures of children.* San Francisco, CA: Jossey-Bass.
Hogenson, D. (1973). A multidisciplinary approach to the in-school management of acutely anxious and depressed students in a large urban senior high school setting. *Pupil Personnel Services Journal, 3,* 29–31.

Hyman, I. (1983). We are here for the kids: A reply to Pantaleno. *Journal of School Psychology, 21,* 115–117.
Hyman, I., Carroll, R., Duffey, J., Manni, J., & Winikur, D. (1973). Patterns of interprofessional conflict resolution on school child study teams. *Journal of School Psychology, 11,* 87–195.
Jensen, A. (1973). *Educability and group differences.* New York: Harper & Row.
Joint Commission on Mental Health of Children (1973). *Mental health: From infancy through adolescence.* New York: Harper & Row.
Kamin, L. J. (1974). *The science and politics of IQ.* Hillsdale, NJ: Lawrence Erlbaum Associates.
Kaplan, L. (1971). *Education and mental health.* New York: Harper & Row.
Kaufman, A. S. (1979). *Intelligent testing with the WISC-R.* New York: Wiley.
Kazdin, A. E. (1979). Situational specificity: The two edged sword of behavioral assessment. *Behavioral Assessment, 1,* 13–36.
Kozloff, M. A. (1979). *A program for families of children with learning and behavior problems.* New York: Wiley.
Kuhn, T. S. (1962). *The structure of scientific revolutions.* Chicago, IL: University of Chicago Press.
Larson, N. (1980). *An analysis of the effectiveness of a state sponsored training program in the treatment of family sexual abuse.* Unpublished doctoral dissertation, University of Minnesota, Minneapolis.
Levine, M., & Levine, A. (1970). *A social history of helping services: Clinic, court, school and community.* New York: Appleton-Century-Crofts.
Lewin, K. (1951). Psychological ecology. In D. Cartwright (Ed.), *Field theory in social science: Selected theoretical papers by Kurt Lewin* (pp. 170–187). New York: Harper & Row.
Lewontin, R. C. (1970). Race and intelligence. *Bulletin of the Atomic Scientists, 26*(3), 2–8.
Loven, M. D. (1978). Four alternative approaches to the family/school liaison role. *Psychology in the Schools, 10,* 296–301.
Marjoribanks, K. (1979). *Families and their learning environments.* London: Routledge & Kegan Paul.
Marjoribanks, K. (1981). School psychology and family environment research: A framework for analysis. *School Psychology International, 2*(1), 19–23.
Meacham, M. L., & Peckham, P. D. (1978). School psychologists at three-quarters century: Congruence between training, practice, preferred role, and competence. *Journal of School Psychology, 16,* 195–206.
Mearig, J. S. (1982). Integration of school and community services for children with special needs. In C. R. Reynolds & T. B. Gutkin (Eds.), *The handbook of school psychology.* New York: Wiley.
Meyers, J., Martin, R., & Hyman, I. (1977). *School consultation.* Springfield, IL: Charles C Thomas.
Meyers, J., Parsons, R. D., & Martin, R. (1979). *Mental health consultation in the schools.* San Francisco, CA: Jossey-Bass.
Meyers, J., Pfeffer, J., & Erlbaum, V. (1982, March). *Process assessment: A model for broadening the school psychologist's assessment role.* Paper presented at the annual meeting of the National Association of School Psychologists, Toronto, Canada.
Minor, M. W. (1972). Systems analysis and school psychology. *Journal of School Psychology, 10,* 227–232.
Minuchin, S., & Fishman, H. C. (1981). *Family therapy techniques.* Cambridge, MA: Harvard University Press.
Mischel, W. (1973). To a cognitive social learning reconceptualization of personality. *Psychological Review, 80,* 252–283.
Mullen, Y., Abnate, L., & Costanzo, J. P. (1982, March). *Family therapy and the school age child: The natural triangle.* Paper presented at the National Association of School Psychologists meeting, Toronto, Canada.

O'Connor, W. A., & Labin, B. (Eds.). (1984). *Ecological approaches to clinical and community psychology*. New York: Wiley.

Pantaleno, A. P. (1983). Parents as primary clients of the school psychologist or why is it we are here? *Journal of School Psychology, 21,* 107–113.

Paul, G. L. (1981). Social competence and the institutionalized mental patient. In J. D. Wine & M. D. Smye (Eds.), *Social competence* (pp. 232–257). New York: Guilford Press.

Pervin, L. A. (1980). *Personality: Theory, assessment, and research*. New York: Wiley.

Pfeiffer, S. I. (1981). The problems facing multidisciplinary teams: As perceived by team members. *Psychology in the Schools, 18,* 330–333.

Pfeiffer, S. I., & Tittler, B. I. (1983). Utilizing the multidisciplinary team to facilitate a school-family systems orientation. *School Psychology Review, 12,* 168–173.

Plas, J. M. (1981). The psychologist in the school community: A liaison role. *School Psychology Review, X,* 72–81.

Pryzwansky, W. B., & Rzepski, B. (1983). School-based teams: An untapped resource of consultation and technical assistance. *School Psychology Review, 12,* 174–179.

Rappaport, J. (1977). *Community psychology: Values, research and action*. New York: Holt, Rinehart, & Winston.

Reynolds, C. R., Gutkin, T. B., Elliott, S. N., & Witt, J. C. (1984). *School psychology: Essentials of theory and practice*. New York: Wiley.

Rimm, D. C., & Masters, J. C. (1979). *Behavior therapy: Techniques and findings*. New York: Academic Press.

Ringers, J., Jr. (1976). *Community schools and interagency programs: A guide*. Midland, MI: Pendell.

Rist, R. C., & Harrell, J. E. (1982). Labeling the learning disabled child: The social ecology of educational practice. *American Journal of Orthopsychiatry, 52*(1), 146–159.

Rogers, E. (1962). Man, ecology, and the control of disease. *Public Health Reports, 77,* 9.

Sameroff, A. J. (1983). Developmental systems: Contexts and evolution. In P. H. Mussen (Ed.), *Handbook of child psychology* (4th ed., pp. 237–293). New York: Wiley.

Sameroff, A. J., & Chandler, M. J. (1975). Reproductive risk and the continuum of caretaking casualty. In F. D. Horowitz, M. Hetherington, S. Scarr-Salapatek, & G. Siegel (Eds.), *Review of child development research* (Vol. 4, pp.   ). Chicago, IL: University of Chicago Press.

Sarason, S. B. (1976). Community psychology networks and Mr. Everyman. *American Psychologist, 31,* 317–328.

Sarason, S. B. (1980, September). *An asocial psychology and a misdirected clinical psychology*. Paper presented at the meetings of the American Psychological Association, Montreal, Canada.

Scarr, S., & McCartney, K. (1983). How people make their own environments: A theory of genotype→environmental effects. *Child Development, 54,* 424–435.

Scarr, S., & Weinberg, R. A. (1976). I.Q. test performance of black children adopted by white families. *American Psychologist, 31,* 726–739.

Scarr, S., & Weinberg, R. A. (1978). Attitudes, interests, and I.Q. *Human Nature, 1,* 29–36.

Seligman, M. (1979). *Strategies for helping parents of exceptional children: A guide for teachers*. New York: Free Press.

Shore, M. F., & Mannino, F. V. *Mental health services for children and youth: 1776–1976*. Unpublished and undated manuscript.

Smith, A. H. (1978). Encountering the family system in school-related behavior problems. *Psychology in the Schools, 15,* 379–386.

Sroufe, A. (1979). The coherence of individual development: Early care, attachment and subsequent developmental issues. *American Psychologist, 34,* 834–841.

Steinberg, M. A., & Chandler, G. E. (1976). Developing coordination of services between a mental health center and a public school system. *Journal of School Psychology, 14*(4), 355–361.

Sulzer-Azaroff, B., & Mayer, G. R. (1977). *Applying behavior analysis procedures with children and youth*. New York: Holt, Rinehart & Winston.

Taylor, R. B. (1979). Ecological psychology demystified: A review of A. W. Wicker, *An introduction to ecological psychology*. *Contemporary Psychology, 24,* 979–980.
Trachtman, G. (1981). On such a full sea. *School Psychology Review, 10,* 138–181.
Tucker, B. Z., & Dyson, E. (1976). The family and the school: Utilizing human resources to promote learning. *Family Process, 15,* 125–141.
Turnbull, A. P., & Leonard, J. (1981). Parent involvement in special education: Emerging advocacy roles. *School Psychology Review, 10,* 37–44.
Turnbull, A. P., & Turnbull, H. R., III (1978). *Parents speak out: Views from the other side of the two-way mirror.* Columbus, OH: Merrill.
Ullman, L. P., & Krasner, L. (1969). *A psychological approach to abnormal behavior.* Englewood Cliffs, NJ: Prentice-Hall.
Waters, E., & Sroufe, L. A. (1983). Social competence as a developmental construct. *Developmental Review, 3,* 79–97.
Weinberg, R. A. (1983). A case of a misplaced conjunction: Nature or nurture? *Journal of School Psychology, 21,* 9–12.
Weinberg, R. A., Fishhaut, E. H., & Moore, S. (1983). The Center for Early Education and Development: An innovation in higher education. *Young Children, 39,* 3–9.
Wine, J. D. (1981). From defect to competence models. In J. D. Wine & M. D. Smye (Eds.), *Social competence* (pp. 3–35). New York: Guilford Press.
Ysseldyke, J. E., & Weinberg, R. A. (Eds.). (1981). The future of psychology in the schools: Proceedings of the Spring Hill Symposium. *School Psychology Review, 10.*
Zigler, E., & Trickett, P. K. (1978). I.Q., social competence and evaluation of early childhood intervention programs. *American Psychologist, 33,* 789–798.

14 School Psychology: A Reconceptualization of Service Delivery Realities

Jane Close Conoley
Terry B. Gutkin
University of Nebraska-Lincoln

To date, the role and significance of service delivery has received only scant attention in the school psychology literature (Reynolds & Clark, 1984; Reynolds, Gutkin, Elliott, & Witt, 1984). This failure of school psychologists to come to grips with basic service delivery issues has been a major impediment to the field as it struggles to define and achieve a viable role for itself. Although psychology can make a multitude of significant contributions to schools, schooling, and school children (Takanishi, DeLeon, & Pallak, 1983), many, if not most, school psychologists find themselves in work situations that hinder their ability to apply the technical expertise they possess in ways that will improve the lives of the children they hope to serve. There is a sense of impotence and a belief that school psychologists are not in control of school psychology (Ysseldyke, 1978). This discomfort has persisted because service delivery has not received the serious empirical and theoretical attention it warrants. Most of the profession's scholarly and applied energies have gone into developing new and improved tests and, to a lesser extent, intervention techniques. These activities have not and will not meaningfully address the profession's problems, however, because service delivery difficulties are not the result of technological shortcomings. Although one always appreciates the development of a "better mousetrap," it is not the lack of effective assessment and treatment technologies that most hinders school psychologists from achieving their full professional potential. Much of the solution lies in a better understanding of the methods and models of service delivery that school psychologists use when working with consumers of school psychological services.

This chapter focuses on the concepts of direct and indirect service, a major dimension of service delivery models that is most relevant to school psychology.

After providing a brief definition of these terms, the chapter examines the implications of the direct-indirect service dimension for the field of school psychology.

DEFINITIONS OF DIRECT AND INDIRECT SERVICE DELIVERY

When school psychologists personally provide psychological services to clients, they are operating within a direct service delivery framework. Counseling and psychotherapy are good examples of direct services. When school psychologists work with third parties who implement psychological services for clients, they are functioning within an indirect service delivery mode. Consultation exemplifies this indirect method. Specifically, consulting psychologists (consultants) interact with teachers, parents, and administrators (consultees) to develop psychological and educational programs for children (clients) that will be carried out by the consultee(s) rather than the psychologists. These relationships are illustrated in Fig. 14.1.

CHARACTERIZING SCHOOL PSYCHOLOGY ON A DIRECT-INDIRECT SERVICE DELIVERY CONTINUUM

Over the past few decades, a variety of categorizations have been proposed to capture the real and ideal roles of school psychologists (e.g., American Psychological Association, 1981; Bardon, 1982; Cutts, 1955; Gilmore, 1974; Monroe, 1979; National Association of School Psychologists, 1978). The most

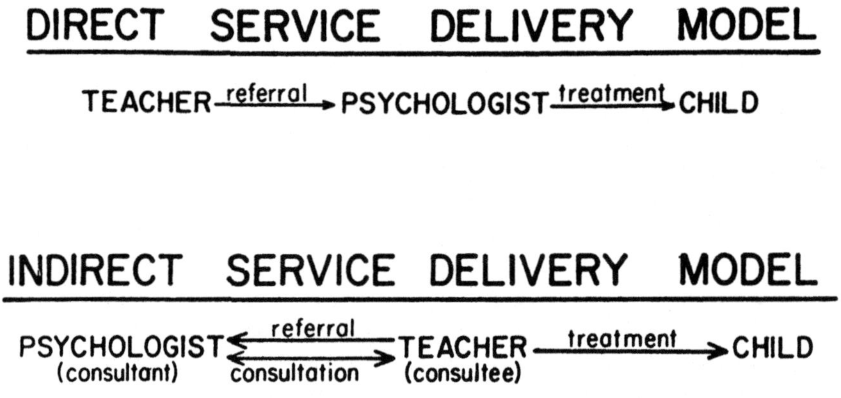

DIRECT SERVICE DELIVERY MODEL

TEACHER —referral→ PSYCHOLOGIST —treatment→ CHILD

INDIRECT SERVICE DELIVERY MODEL

PSYCHOLOGIST ⇄ referral / consultation ⇄ TEACHER —treatment→ CHILD
(consultant)   (consultee)

FIG. 14.1 Direct and indirect service delivery models. From "School-based consultation: Theory and techniques by T. B. Gutkin and M. J. Curtis. In C. R. Reynolds and T. B. Gutkin (Eds.). *The handbook of school psychology.* New York: Wiley. Reprinted by permission.

frequently cited activities have been assessment/diagnosis, consultation, inservice, remedial intervention, and program evaluation/research. There is a relatively high degree of agreement concerning the amount of time school psychologists spend performing each activity (Meacham & Peckham, 1978; Ramage, 1979). Typically, assessment/diagnosis functions take up the largest single chunk of a school psychologist's day. Although consultation also consistently appears as a major aspect of school psychologists' roles, it almost invariably absorbs less time than assessment/diagnosis. Inservice, remedial intervention (e.g., all forms of counseling and therapy) and program evaluation/research functions, on the other hand, appear to be relatively minor components of the typical school psychologist's job. Although few would find this division of activities to be ideal, it nonetheless reflects the current reality of the profession.

With the exception of the assessment/diagnosis role, each of the major job functions can be categorized easily as either direct or indirect service. Specifically, consultation, inservice, and program evaluation/research are clearly indirect services, whereas the provision of remedial intervention services is best viewed as a direct service.

Placing the assessment/diagnosis function on the direct-indirect dimension is a more difficult task. Because psychologists have a great deal of direct contact with referred children during testing and other assessment activities, these activities have been viewed traditionally as a direct service (cf. Monroe, 1979). When viewed from a service delivery perspective, however, the assessment/diagnosis function is best seen as a psychological activity rather than as either a direct or an indirect service. Assessment is a means to an end. Intellectual, behavioral, and personality assessments are activities prerequisite to problem solving and occur before appropriate interventions can be determined. Conducting assessments and making diagnoses *lead to* services but they are not services *in and of themselves*. As illustrated by the generic model of school psychological service delivery proposed by Reynolds et al. (1984), assessment and diagnosis are intermediate steps in a larger process that leads to service for children (see Fig. 14.2). The completion of assessment/diagnosis activities (step 10) should not be confused with the provision of services (steps 12–14). Thus, although assessment/diagnosis is a valuable and useful function that school psychologists perform, it is not a service to children per se. With this in mind, it is important to note that the great preponderance of services provided to children as a result of assessment/diagnosis activities are indirect, rather than direct. Special class placement and the implementation of school and/or home interventions, for example, are services typically carried out by teachers and parents rather than by psychologists.

Let us now state explicitly our central tenet. With the exception of remedial intervention services such as therapy and counseling, virtually all of the school psychologists' roles (i.e., assessment/diagnosis, consultation, inservice, program evaluation/research) are either indirect services or lead to indirect services. This conclusion has pervasive conceptual and practical implications for school

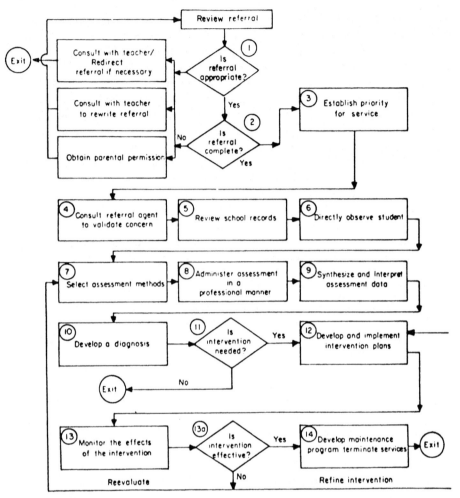

FIG. 14.2 Flowchart of consultation-assessment-intervention service system. From C. R. Reynolds, T. B. Gutkin, S. N. Elliott, & J. C. Witt (1984). *School psychology: Essentials of theory and practice.* New York: Wiley. Used with permission of the publisher.

psychologists who have historically viewed themselves and their roles in terms of direct service delivery.

The remainder of this chapter is devoted to analyzing the implications of school psychology as an indirect service profession. For the purposes of this discussion issues have been grouped into conceptual, practical, and research implications. Each of these topics is closely interrelated to the others. Most conceptual issues, for example, have direct and immediate implications for both practice and research. Likewise, topics classified under the practice and research categories often have important implications for each other and conceptual topics as well. The mutual and reciprocal interrelationships between conceptual, practical, and research issues reinforce the image of the school psychologist as a scientist-practitioner.

CONCEPTUAL IMPLICATIONS

Advantages and Disadvantages of Direct and Indirect Service Delivery Models

Indirect service delivery is the current situation for school psychology. Although direct service delivery has been the mainstay of applied psychology (primarily in the form of psychotherapy), it is important to consider the benefits derived from an indirect service delivery model. Miller (1969) made this point in his presidential address to the American Psychological Association (APA) when he stated, "Our responsibility is less to assume the role of experts and try to apply psychology ourselves than to give it away to people who really need it—and that includes everyone" (p. 1071). By working collaboratively with significant others in the lives of children, school psychologists are able to extend the scope of their services and overcome many of the disadvantages of the direct service delivery model.

The benefits of an indirect service delivery approach have long been recognized by physicians. The specialty of pediatrics provides a particularly good example. Although some portion of pediatricians' activities involve direct service such as surgery, the bulk of their time is spent using an indirect service approach. Specifically, pediatricians examine and diagnose children's illnesses but then typically depend on parents and medical "helpers" (e.g., nurses, paramedics, technicians) to carry out recommended treatments (e.g., injections, bed rest, dispensing drugs). If pediatricians personally had to administer more than a small minority of necessary medical treatments they would find themselves in a service delivery quagmire resulting in greatly curtailed availability of treatment for children. Inherent in the use of indirect service delivery by pediatricians and other physicians are several important points of direct relevance to psychologists, and school psychologists in particular.

First, there are too few professional personnel to provide direct treatment for all those in need of service. This point has been made repeatedly in regard to clinical psychology and psychiatry (Albee, 1968, 1982) and holds true for school psychology as well. It is estimated that 30% of the school-aged population suffer from moderate to severe school adjustment problems, one third of which are severe enough to require immediate professional help (Cowen & Gesten, 1978). Clearly, there are not enough school and clinical child psychologists to meet this need if every child is to be treated directly by a mental health specialist. In the 1980s, vast numbers of children in need of services are either ignored or given inadequate attention by the mental health establishment (Edelman, 1981).

Second, lesser trained individuals, available in abundant supply and at substantially lower costs, can make effective contributions to the well-being of children if they are given proper training and support by professionals. The common assumption that an advanced degree in psychology or psychiatry is a prerequisite to providing effective psychological treatment seems to be unwarranted. In the area of psychotherapy, for example, research has shown no differences between the effectiveness of psychologists and trained paraprofessionals (Durlak, 1973) and little if any clear relationship between years of experience as a therapist and the magnitude of therapeutic effects attained with patients (Parloff, Waskow, & Wolfe, 1978; Smith & Glass, 1977). Of even more direct significance for school psychology are projects that have demonstrated the therapeutic potential of paraprofessionals (e.g., teachers, parents, teacher-aides) trained to work with children (e.g., Cowen et al., 1975; Hobbs, 1966) and the studies showing that persons other than mental health professionals can be highly effective behavior modifers both in and out of school environments (O'Dell, 1974; Simpson & Poplin, 1981). It seems true that persons less well trained than psychologists and psychiatrists can be effective providers of psychological services if properly guided by appropriate professionals.

Above and beyond increasing the pool of resources immediately available for helping persons in need, indirect service leads to the real possibility of ripple effects, that may extend further the service impact of professionals. As nonprofessionals gain skills they are able to pass them on to other nonprofessionals. Turning again to medicine for examples, the large number of ordinary citizens who learned cardiopulmonary resuscitation (CPR) have successfully delivered services to thousands of people who might have died waiting for a physician or paramedic to arrive. The application of public health practices provide other examples. Water purification, garbage removal, draining of swamps, and widely available immunization programs have been most effective in reducing the prevalence of certain diseases (e.g., dysentery, malaria, smallpox). Almost none of these activities were/are carried out directly by physicians.

Another noteworthy ripple effect is that skills learned by nonprofessionals when they are treating client X may be applied in the future to client Y. Although too little research has been done to reach definitive conclusions, a number of studies support the concept that insights and skills learned as a result of indirect services from psychologists can be applied successfully by nonpsychologists to future problems and cases (Conoley & Conoley, 1982; Curtis & Watson, 1980; Gutkin, 1980; Gutkin, Singer, & Brown, 1980; Hinkle, Silverstein, & Walton, 1977; Jason & Ferone, 1978; Meyers, 1975; Ritter, 1978).

Indirect service delivery models also offer the advantage of providing psychological services for children in natural ecological contexts such as homes, schools, and communities rather than doctors' offices and therapy rooms. Indirect service provides psychologists with access to a greater diversity and number of problems than is possible under direct service models. As pointed out by Cowen (1982), "Only a small fraction of people's psychological problems reach the formal mental health establishment" (p. 385). Most child-related difficulties are, by necessity, routinely dealt with in the home, school, and community.

Beyond this, delivering psychological services outside of children's natural ecological contexts may lead to poor generalization of newly acquired skills, behaviors, and attitudes in school, home, and community settings. It is not unusual, for instance, to hear teachers complain that they are unimpressed by a child's gains in individual therapy because there has been little or no change of behavior in the classroom where teachers cope with this child and 25 to 30 others. In fact, there is a considerable body of research (Goldstein & Kanfer, 1979) highlighting the situationally specific nature of many gains resulting from psychological interventions. By focusing on significant others such as teachers, peers, parents, and community leaders, psychologists using indirect services are able to bring about significant changes within the natural environments of children, thus short-circuiting many of the stimulus generalization problems associated with direct services.

Despite all the potential advantages, indirect service delivery approaches do have some important limitations. The principal problem stems from the very nature of indirect service itself. Unlike direct service, where psychologists treat clients by themselves, those who use indirect services are dependent on third parties to execute treatment plans. This inclusion of one or more intermediaries between psychologists and their clients may substantially complicate service delivery. Among other possible difficulties, the individual responsible for carrying through on a treatment program may lack the motivation necessary to accomplish the task at hand. It is naive to assume that teachers, parents, or peers are always willing to expend the time and effort required for successful treatment programs. Second, some mental health paraprofessionals may lack the skill required to carry out various psychological interventions. Even though research cited previously indicated that uncredentialed persons can be as effective as those with advanced degrees in the mental health areas, unquestionably a number of paraprofessionals are unable to implement various treatment programs correctly (Repucci & Saunders, 1974). Finally, helpers in the natural environment may lack the necessary resources (e.g., time, funds, materials) to serve as useful third parties for psychologists. For example, many teachers may have the motivation and skill to carry out an intervention strategy but may be unable to find the necessary time during the school day.

In summary, indirect service delivery models place significant extra demands on psychologists. As with direct services, psychologists must determine which treatments are likely to succeed with their clients. Above this, however, those using an indirect approach have the additional burden of finding interventions that can and will be done by the nonpsychologists with whom they are working.

Depending on the circumstances, this latter task may be considerably more subtle and difficult than the former. In other words, getting third parties to implement treatment plans may be harder and more complex than determining what treatments are needed for a child. (See Haley, 1976, for a discussion of this issue in family therapy practice).

Models of Human Behavior and Their Relationship to Direct and Indirect Service Delivery Approaches

Service delivery decisions and the evolution of a service delivery model are affected by the theoretical bases of a field. School psychology has been influenced primarily by three theoretical models: medical (i.e., psychodynamic or ego psychology), behavioral (i.e., operant, respondent, and social learning theories), and the newly emerging ecological model that synthesizes previous models using a systems theory approach.

Medical Model. The medical model in psychology presumes that the source of psychological problems primarily lies within individuals. Specifically, psychopathology is conceptualized as a psychological disease entity that resides within the person, resulting from breakdowns of internal psychological processes such as defense mechanisms and incomplete development of psychological structures such as the ego and superego (Freud, 1949).

The impact of this model on the practice of school psychology is evident in the profession's heavy emphasis on personality and intellectual assessment. If what is preeminently important about a person is what is going on inside, then it follows that considerable energy must be spent by psychologists in discovering the nuances of this inner life. Ironically, it is especially clear from a medical model perspective how assessment/diagnosis is an *activity* performed by psychologists and not a direct *service* to a child. Although a patient (client) might be grateful for an insightful diagnosis made by a physician (psychologist), there is an expectation that something more will happen! The diagnosis serves the physician (psychologist) in treatment planning. Assessment done without subsequent direct or indirect service provision is obviously of little use to the patient (client).

Although the medical model is frequently credited (blamed) for the direct service mindset of most school psychologists, the services derived from this model are, in fact, quite diverse. Reflecting once again on the field of medicine, it is evident that both direct and indirect services can be easily accommodated. As previously discussed, some medical patients require direct service from a physician (e.g., surgery) whereas others are most efficiently treated indirectly (e.g., a parent enforcing bed rest). Likewise, clients being served by psychologists possessing a medical model view of student problems may rely on either direct (e.g., therapy) or indirect (e.g., treatment by special educators in special education programs) services. In fact, indirect service, such as home and special education intervention, is the predominant treatment mode among school psychologists. As discussed previously, research indicates that even those interventions traditionally restricted to direct service by psychologists can often be implemented effectively with indirect service methods (e.g., using paraprofessionals as lay therapists and counselors). The point is that contrary to prevailing beliefs, a medical model view of school psychological services is not at all incompatible with indirect service delivery approaches, although by focusing on internal psychological phenomena psychologists are encouraged to think primarily in terms of direct services to clients.

Behavioral Model. The behavioral model in psychology has grown from early experimental work by Pavlov (1927), Watson (1930), and Skinner (1938, 1953, 1957) to the more recent contributions by Bandura and Walters (1963), Bijou and Baer (1966), and Meichenbaum (1973). Instead of the medical model's emphasis on psychopathological internal processes, the behavioral perspective proposes that all behavior is a product of environmental contingencies interacting with the unique internal developmental stages of the individual. The internal conditions of interest are different in this model than in the medical model. In general, behavioral practitioners are interested in the conscious cognitions of clients and make no attempts to infer unconscious dynamic processes. The external environment is highlighted from this orientation, with special attention toward conditions antecedent and consequent to target behaviors. In addition, the reinforcement preferences and punishment sensitivities of a client are critical data to obtain to facilitate the success of behavioral treatment.

There is no doubt that interventions based on the behavioral model have been very successful in changing dysfunctional patterns of behavior in school-aged children (O'Leary & O'Leary, 1976). This is apparently psychology's most predictably successful intervention model in reducing specific symptomatic behaviors (Casey & Berman, 1985; Garfield & Bergin, 1978).

Like the medical model, the behavioral approach is also conceptually compatible with both direct (e.g., behavior therapy administered by psychologists in their offices) and indirect (e.g, behavior modification programs administered by teachers in classrooms) services. By focusing attention on the external environment, however, the behavioral model primes school psychologists to think of their work within an indirect service delivery framework. That is, although psychological expertise may be helpful when diagnosing behavioral problems and designing behavioral interventions, it is clear that training as a psychologist is not a prerequisite to implementing many behavioral programs. Rearranging environmental antecedents and consequences is well within the capabilities of most nonpsychologists, such as teachers and parents. It is logistically impossible for psychologists to directly implement each behavior therapy program, and theoretically, it would be folly to do so because of generalization, maintenance, and transfer concerns.

Ecological Model. The ecological model has grown from diverse theoretical streams. Lewin's (1935, 1948, 1951) early descriptions of force field analysis might be considered a cornerstone of the approach as would von Bertalanffy's (1966, 1967, 1968) general systems theory in theoretical biology. Hobb's (1966, 1982) well-known ReEd projects with children are examples of large-scale applications of the ecological model. From this perspective dysfunctional behavior patterns exhibited by individuals are seen as failures in matching environmental demands with individual skills, attitudes, or developmental stages. Problems exist not within people or environments per se, but rather within the interaction between individual and contextual complexity (Apter, 1982; Apter & Conoley, 1984).

Ecological or systems thinking is a recent addition to the theoretical bank of school psychology. It synthesizes some aspects of the medical and behavioral models. People are seen as complex, affected by their pasts, and by internal developmental events. Individuals are dynamically interrelated with their environments. They are not just targets for behavioral change interventions but active interpreters of such interventions and reciprocal actors as well. Several levels of environment are assessed—individuals, families, schools, communities, and government—and all are considered potential targets for intervention from the ecological perspective (Bronfenbrenner, 1979).

School psychology conceptualized as a primarily indirect service delivery profession fits nicely under the ecological umbrella. All the people who interact with a target child are potential consultees or therapists. Each of the child's environments deserves attention to discover which present compatible or incompatible matches with the individual characteristics of the child. Indirect service seems to be a natural consequence of the ecological model because it examines children's behavior within the context of their homes, schools, and communities populated by nonpsychologists and in which psychologists are not part of the daily reality. Although direct service within the ecological model is possible, it would occur as part of a coordinated treatment package.

Ecological thinking differs from the medical and behavioral models in two ways. First, it is a more *interactive* framework in contrast to the internal and environmental emphases of medical and behavioral thinking. Second, the "symptoms" exhibited by target individuals are seen as having adaptive systemic value. The symptoms are not due only to internal upset or poor learning histories but are actively developed accommodations to systemic realities.

Further specification of the ecological model is necessary so that its tenets are not so vague as to be difficult to translate into intervention. Existing intervention technologies are used within the ecological model but in a way that scans for targets and de-emphasizes the role of individual deficits in maintaining troubling circumstances.

Relevant Domains of Knowledge in Psychology

Conceptualizing school psychology as an indirect service delivery profession has important implications for school psychologists in specifying which domains of psychological knowledge are most relevant to practice. As with direct service, psychologists working within indirect service roles need a wide range of psychological expertise that helps them understand children and children's problems (e.g., child development; learning theory; educational psychology; cognitive psychology; personality theory; and, psychological assessment). To achieve successful indirect service, however, school psychologists must be expert in several additional areas of psychology. This need arises because indirect services are always implemented by mediating parties. As a result, school psychologists using indirect service approaches need expertise above and beyond those domains that address the psychology of children and children's problems. Specifically, school psychologists must be expert in the psychology of working with and influencing third-party adults.

Detailed knowledge of social, organizational, and community psychology is especially relevant to school psychologists providing indirect services. These areas are similar in that their theoretical and research bases see individual processes as embedded in larger interpersonal and social environments. Social psychology emphasizes interpersonal processes. Organizational theory points out the effects of norms and organizational cultures on individual behavior and provides a large number of interventions to change group behavior. Community psychology introduces political/advocacy elements into psychology, trying to grapple with the effects of, for example, social support, public policy, and minority status on individual and group behavior.

In summary, effective indirect service will depend to a large extent on psychologists' abilities to influence the behavior of third-party adults. To do so will require understanding the behavior of these persons within social/interpersonal, organizational, and community contexts.

Social Psychology. It is impossible to overestimate the importance of a command of the social psychological literature for school psychologists who intend to provide indirect services to children. Studies relating to group dynamics (Bales & Cohen, 1979; Deutsch & Krauss, 1962; Wahrman & Pugh, 1974), cooperation and competition (Aronson, Blaney, Stephan, Sikes, Snapp, 1978; Sherif, Harvey, White, Hood & Sherif, 1961; Thibaut & Kelley, 1959; Van Egeren, 1979), and attribution (Frieze & Snyder, 1980; Heider, 1958; Kelley, 1972; Rosenthal & Jacobson, 1968; Schachter & Singer, 1962; Wong & Weiner, 1981) all have relevant information for the practice of indirect service. The areas of attribution, group dynamics, and social influence (Asch, 1956; French & Raven, 1959; Milgram, 1974; Raven & Haley, 1980) may provide particularly important insights.

Attribution theory is the study of people's beliefs about why things happen. Attributions are made in order to predict and control events. There are many different kinds of attributions, but researchers typically have characterized them along the dimensions of internal/external and stable/unstable and global/specific.

Understanding the beliefs that caregivers hold about clients is very important. For example, a teacher who describes a student as "a bad child with serious learning disabilities" may be making an internal, stable, and global judgment and prediction about the child. Obviously, a psychologist would be interested in changing these particular attributions in ways that would promote intervention. For example, the psychologist might (a) highlight the external conditions that prompted the child's inappropriate behaviors to weaken the internal attribution of "badness", (b) model procedures for modifying the child's learning and behavioral difficulties to counter attributions of stability, and (c) identify and draw attention to the child's positive behaviors or academic strengths to confront the global attribution.

School psychologists should have a healthy respect for the attributions people use. They indicate the importance of subjective impressions. Over and over, the research literature has shown that "reality" exists uniquely for individuals (Asch, 1956; Milgram, 1974; Piaget, 1965; Zimbardo, 1969). Psychologists who behave as if clients or caregivers experience (or should experience) the world as the psychologist does frequently will be frustrated and ineffective in their work. In contrast, a framework that allows the psychologist to interpret caregivers' typical attributional styles can greatly enhance his or her individualized approaches to involving others in intervention plans (Hughes, 1983; Hughes & Falk, 1981).

Another application of attribution theory of interest to practicing psychologists was provided by Brickman et al. (1982). They described the behaviors people use and beliefs they hold when seeking or offering help as based on "distinctions between attributions of responsibility for a problem and attributions of responsibility for a solution" (p. 368). Each of the help-seeking and help-offering models seems to have different consequences. When people are held responsible for the solutions to their problems they are more likely to show an increase in competence (Chambliss & Murray, 1979; Davison & Valins, 1969; Liberman, 1978). When people believe their solutions or improvement are due to the action of others, their improvements tend to be short-lived and dependent on the continuing assistance of external helpers (deCharms, 1976; Deci, Nezlek, & Sheinman, 1981; Lepper & Greene, 1978). Helpers are also affected by their attributions. Burnout is associated with a decline in a sense of competence and self-esteem and affects therapists, social workers, nurses, and teachers who believe they are responsible for their clients' improvements (Freudenberger, 1974; Maslach, 1978).

Group dynamics or small-group behavior is another critical content area for psychologists. So much of the business of schooling is carried out by teams or through team decisions that school psychologists must be experts in leading groups and in facilitating team development. Children are better served educationally if teaching teams operate at high levels of cooperation and efficiency. In addition, they are better served if placement committees learn to use the diverse input available to them to plan truly individualized programs for children with special needs (Knoff & Smith, 1981). Psychologists who can mediate personality conflicts, model flexible problem-solving strategies and decision-making styles, teach about agenda setting, and make valid data available to the group for task activities are implementing high quality indirect service to children.

Understandings of interpersonal or social influence are directly relevant for indirect service providers. Viewing consultation as an interpersonal influence process, Martin (1978) examined consultative outcome in terms of referent and expert power theory. He relied upon French and Raven's (1959) theoretical framework that identifies five types of power providing leverage for one person to influence another. Reward and coercive power are based on a person's perception that the social agent (e.g., psychologist) has control over administration of rewards and punishers. Legitimate power is based on a person's perception that the social agent has the right to prescribe behavior. Referent power is based on a person's identification with the social agent, and expert power is based on a person's perception that the social agent has special knowledge or expertness.

Martin and Curtis (1981) found tentative support for the importance of expert power in providing indirect service to children by examining the effects of the relative age of psychologist and caregivers. They hypothesized that attempts to influence caregivers would be most successful when psychologists were relatively older than the caregivers. Cienki (1982) also found support for the importance of these dimensions in teachers' perceptions of psychologists.

Kinsala (1984) investigated factors thought to relate to expert and referent power: relative and absolute ages of psychologist and caregiver, sex of consultant, receptivity of caregiver to the psychologist, and the degree to which the psychologist and caregiver agreed on the severity of the presenting problem. She found strong support for the importance of the referent power factors. Receptivity toward the consultant and agreement on problem severity accounted for almost all the variance in the evaluation of consultation scores. The relative ages of the participants accounted for a very small amount of the variance, and were significant only in the cases when the psychologist was much younger than the caregiver. Younger caregivers were more positive about consultation. Gender of the psychologist was not significantly related to the evaluation score.

These relatively few attempts in the school psychology literature to investigate the importance of interpersonal influence can be augmented by a review of the counseling literature (Heppner & Dixon, 1981; LaCrosse, 1980; Strong, 1968;

Strong & Claiborn, 1982). Consistent support has been found pointing to the importance of counselor influence factors (e.g., credibility and attractiveness) in predicting counseling outcome.

This discussion illustrates the many forces operating in the relationships school psychologists establish with teachers, parents, and other caregivers. Given that school psychology is primarily an indirect service profession, such interactions must not be taken for granted but rather merit increased attention in the school psychology research literature and among practicing school psychologists. Because school psychologists' success in improving the lot of children will depend to a great extent on the degree to which they can influence relevant caregivers, it is imperative that they develop expertise regarding social psychology and its related theories.

Organizational Psychology. If school psychologists are to assist children effectively, they must be knowledgeable of organizational psychology, that is, the study of people in organizations and the internal and external forces that affect organizational viability. This is particularly true for the provision of indirect services dependent on communication and cooperation among individuals occupying different job roles (e.g., psychologist, teacher, special educator, speech pathologist, principal) within organizations. It is naive to believe, therefore, that organizational variables would not significantly affect practice. The impact of funding patterns, supervisory procedures, and group norms within multidisciplinary teams are but a few obvious examples of organizational effects on the practice of psychology in the schools. Psychologists insensitive to organizational variables and phenomena reflect the sense of an old Chinese proverb, "Only fish do not know of water." Students, teachers, and psychologists are dynamically dependent on the organizational climates in which they function, even though such climates are often difficult to discern.

In recent years, many concepts springing from general systems theory have been added to Lewin's (1948, 1951) force field analysis ideas as explanations of organizational dynamics. This systems orientation allows a psychologist to observe the organization as an example of an open system, that is, a living system with internal developmental processes that depend on interchange with a larger environment for continued viability. From this perspective certain processes emerge as critical to the dynamics of planned change (Cummings, 1980; Gallessich, 1973, 1982; Sarason, 1982). These include the prevalent administrative or leadership style, the social and emotional climate, levels of task accomplishment and role clarity, integration and interdependence of subsystems, adaptibility of the organization to changing environmental demands, and the history of change within the organization.

Each of these processes affects all persons who work within school organizations in a wide variety of ways. From an indirect service delivery perspective, it is useful to understand the psychology of organizations if one wishes to influence the behavior and attitudes of teachers, principals, and so forth, who are called upon to implement psychological treatments. The organizational literature provides a wealth of information regarding change strategies, assessment techniques, action research or program evaluation procedures, and role parameters of the organizational change agent. There are many studies reporting on organizational change efforts in schools (Alpert, 1982; Bassin & Gross, 1978; Gottfredson, Gottfredson, & Cook, 1983; Price & Politser, 1980; Schmuck & Miles, 1971), and of perhaps greater interest a few that point to the effects of organizational climate on the utilization of mental health services (e.g., Bossard & Gutkin, 1983; Gutkin & Bossard, 1984; Kuehnel, 1975).

Community Psychology. Psychological interest has grown from an emphasis on the individual to awareness of the individual in small and large groups. Community psychology continues along this dimension, investigating the relationships among organizations in communities, definitions of community, and strategies for enhancement of human skills and the prevention of psychological deficits (Heller, Price, Reinharz, Riger, & Wandersman, 1984; O'Neill & Trickett, 1982; Price & Politser, 1980). Community psychology embraces a wide array of change theories: from individual skill development to policy change through political action. In addition, community psychologists frequently use indirect service delivery methods such as consultation, program evaluation, facilitation of social support systems, training, and many preventive mental health activities in varied service settings.

Cowen and associates' (Cowen, 1973; Cowen, Pederson, Babigian, Izzo, Trost, 1973; Cowen et al., 1975) work in the Rochester public schools is a good example of community psychology in the schools. It is also a good example of the expert practice of school psychology: illustrating the power of the indirect service delivery methodology. Cowen conceptualizes the school psychologists' role as that of "quarterback." In the long history of the Primary Mental Health Project and those other programs inspired by this project, psychologists' roles have clustered around diagnostic screening, training of paraprofessionals to use play therapy with targeted children, teacher consultation, and the implementation of preventive programs aimed at children of divorce, children with a dead parent, and school-wide programs to teach social problem-solving skills to regular education children (Allen, Chinsky, Larcen, Loehman, & Selinger, 1976; Weissberg, Cowen, Lotyczewski, Gesten, 1983).

The willingness of community psychologists to participate in the political process or work within governmental bureaucracies is instructive to school psychologists interested in indirect service delivery (Goldenberg, 1973; Sarason, 1973, Lorion, 1978; Sarason, 1983). These activities are examples of service that occurs at great distances from the actual clients. Those school psychologists who believe their most potent contributions to children are through direct service should consider the effects of federal policy on their practice of psychology or on the well-being of children and families in general. Psychologists practicing in schools are well aware of the effects of busing, racial discrimination, poverty, unemployment, and economic recession on the psychological status of their clients. To influence these events, some psychologists must be willing to work at the federal level attempting to influence policy. An understanding of the community psychology literature provides an introduction to skills necessary to work in the macro-environment of children.

PRACTICAL IMPLICATIONS

The previous discussions of advantages and disadvantages of indirect service, models of human behavior, and relevant domains of psychological knowledge for conceptualizing school psychology within an indirect service delivery framework have many clear implications for practice. A conscious recognition of the indirect service nature of the profession would affect the way school psychologists spend their days and would greatly increase their sense of control over their professional destinies.

Current Traditional Work Roles

Recognizing that school psychology is an indirect service delivery profession leads to the conclusion that school psychologists must expend substantially more time and energy focusing their attention on the significant adults that populate the children's world. This conclusion holds true even if testing remains the dominant work role performed by school psychologist. Recommendations generated as a result of psychological testing that are not carried out by the teachers, parents, and school administrators for whom they were intended are of absolutely no benefit to the children school psychologists purport to serve. This statement seems so obvious that it hardly bears mentioning except that many school psychologists suspect (know) that many (most) of the treatment recommendations they make either are never implemented or are carried out incorrectly. The problem in these situations may not be the quality of the school psychologists' recommendations per se, but rather the psychologists' inability to get adult third parties to carry them out as intended. To cope successfully with this fact, school psychologists must understand the indirect service nature of psychological testing and work more intensively with school personnel and parents.

To some extent, school psychologists can be led astray by the example of their medical counterparts who work with children. Like school psychologists, pediatricians spend a large percentage of their time assessing children's problems, determining diagnoses, and making written and verbal recommendations for treatment. Traditionally, their recommendations were carried out properly and without any discernible resistance by parents and teachers. The analogy of the pediatrician and the school psychologist breaks down, however, on several important levels. First, many recommendations made by pediatricians are simple, quick, discrete acts that require little time or thought by teachers and parents (e.g., give the "hyperactive" child a pill every morning and evening). School psychologists' recommendations, on the other hand, most often are complex, time consuming, and difficult tasks in the eyes of teachers, who already feel overburdened with other children (e.g., individualize reading instruction for a child who is the slowest reader in the class). Second, physicians have very high status and prestige in our society. Nonphysicians, such as teachers and parents, attribute formidable and exclusive expertise to these persons and, thus, are often ready to follow their expert advice with little or no question. School psychologists, on the other hand, are not viewed with the same awe and respect. Their recommendations carry much less weight with many teachers and parents, who believe they themselves may have as much (or perhaps even more) expertise and insight into many aspects of children's psychoeducational problems. Third, health problems may be life threatening and so inspire more unquestioning and faithful compliance from parents than do the relatively less important questions of learning and psychological well being. Finally, medical problems seem to exist within the child, and intervention is most often directed at the child. The issue of responsibility for the symptom is secondary to the intervention. Psychoeducational problems, however, although apparently located within the child, tend to be assigned to someone for blame. Teachers cannot teach, or parents do not provide appropriate home stimulation and support, or the child is disabled. The scapegoating (labeling?) process absorbs more attention than the intervention process. This necessarily reduces the expert power attributed to the psychologist, because often no action or positive change follows the diagnostic sequence.

The end result is that significant adults in children's lives often do not willingly accept and implement school psychologists' treatment recommendations. When psychologists' recommendations are not consistent with the beliefs, wishes, and biases of teachers and parents, rather than labeling the consultees as "resistant," psychologists must explore avenues of influence instead. Parenthetically, with the growth of the consumer movement and our society's increasing sense of distrust in experts of all kinds, it should come as no surprise that physicians are beginning also to experience some resistance when their treatment recommendations are not consistent with the biases of their patients (e.g., Haire, 1982; Schneider, 1982; Weitz, 1983).

An examination of current practice reveals many instances of inadequate attention to third party adults, resulting in poor services for children. Two examples may be informative. First, there is too much emphasis on written reports and brief team meetings with teachers as vehicles for communicating treatment recommendations. The unexamined assumption behind these methods is that teachers will passively accept and adopt treatment recommendations put forth by psychologists if the recommendations derive from competent psychological evaluations. The social psychology literature tells us, however, that influencing people is a difficult and complex task. One-way communication methods such as written reports and brief interactions within the context of team meetings with 5 to 10 other persons are not particularly effective for changing the attitudes and behaviors of teachers. The result is that many excellent ideas and suggestions put forth in reports and team meetings may go unnoticed, or misunderstood, and unimplemented. More intensive, on-going, face-to-face contacts are called for with teachers.

Second, the lack of adequate attention to teachers by psychologists helps to explain why many behavioral interventions, despite their proven efficacy, are not more commonly implemented in schools. For optimal effectiveness, parents and teachers must be motivated to use behavioral strategies and informed as to their correct application. Obviously, the tasks of motivating and instructing teachers and parents are indirect services to children, but ones that *must* occur if the potency of behavioral interventions is to be realized. Ignoring these indirect activities invites consistent failure and, ironically, violates the tenets of the behavioral model. Teachers and parents often must develop new behaviors to cooperate with the psychologist. Psychologists trained in behavioral principles should be able to analyze what caregivers need to facilitate behavioral changes as expertly as they use applied behavioral analysis with children (Piersel & Gutkin, 1983). In other words, the principles of behavior change must be applied with caregivers as intensively as with clients. This knowledge, however, apparently has not been applied consistently as psychologists repeatedly report resistance to behavioral interventions from teachers (Abidin, 1975).

Failure to conceptualize current school psychological services within a framework of indirect service delivery has, thus, contributed to the dilemma of having potent intervention technologies and ideas that many direct service providers such as parents and teachers avoid using (Elliott, Witt, Galvin, & Peterson, 1984; Witt & Elliott, 1985; Witt, Elliott, & Martens, 1984; Witt, Martens, & Elliott, 1984). Only by increasing school psychologists' attention to those adults who, in fact, provide psychological services to children will these difficulties be overcome.

Nontraditional Work Roles Taking More Complete Advantage of Indirect Service Delivery

Use of an indirect service delivery model would expand the client population of school psychologists (see, Hyman, 1983; Kicklighter, 1983; Pantaleno, 1983). In addition to having some continuing direct therapeutic involvement with children, psychologists would routinely consult and collaborate with teachers, administrators, support staff, and parents. Therapy interventions would be broadened to include family therapy. Consultation service would grow from a reliance on case centered work to a case manager role in which the psychologist acted to coordinate services available to children from schools and other community agencies. Such coordination of services has been found to be more critical than the actual content of the particular service (Lewis, 1982).

Organization Development

From an indirect service delivery perspective, the logic of substantial attention to organization development activities by school psychologists is inescapable. Although there are data indicating the difficulty of successfully mounting organization development efforts in school cultures (Blumberg, 1976; Blumberg & Schmuck, 1972; Schmuck, 1968), these data are best seen as indications of the tremendous need for such services and the need for the continued development of techniques more consonant with existing school climates, task, and maintenance needs. A detailed review of the literature concluded that approximately 1% of the schools in North America have undertaken major organization development projects (Fullen, Miles, & Taylor, 1980).

To be useful, organizational change need not occur on the grand scales reported by consultants to business organizations (Bowers, 1973). From a systems perspective, psychologists can expect ripple effects from all of their activities and so should be encouraged to target manageable processes. For example, the psychologist might begin to promote more equal decision making among all the members of the multidisciplinary assessment and placement teams. If team members would meet to understand more thoroughly the complex ecology of problems facing referred children rather than simply to assign them to placements, the percentage of children in special education might be greatly reduced (Ysseldyke, Algozzine, Regan, & McGue, 1981). Such a process would necessitate a careful observation of the child's classroom situation, the attempts being made by current teachers to alleviate problems, the actual needs of the child rather than simple psychometric generalities, and continued involvement by all team members to validate prognostic statements.

The recent national scrutiny of education (e.g. Darling-Hammond, 1984) presents an opportunity for school psychologists to involve themselves and their districts in significant organizational change. Predictably, individuals are being blamed for failures that are systemic in nature. Teachers are seen as poorly prepared and students as coming from uncaring homes. Psychologists may be in the best position, because of their relative mastery of social psychology and organizational theory, to begin analyses at more productive levels.

For teachers to be excellent mentors for children, what must happen in the way of administrative support, reorganization of daily schedules, control over important decisions, access to consultative and other resources, rewards for excellence, meaningful feedback and many other processes? How can the school building be a community resource that invites busy, economically pressed parents to use it for their continued education, child-care services, recreation, and problem-solving activities concerning their children? What social groupings encourage learning—peer tutors, cooperative work groups, individual accelerated curriculas—for the unique needs of children? What staffing patterns in classrooms are most effective—teams, aides, volunteers, departmentalization (Aronson et al. 1978)? How must levels of and priorities in funding change to accomplish educational excellence in the United States? Examples available from industry and education suggest that these are the questions that must be addressed (Cummings, 1980; Sheldon, 1980).

Other Indirect Service Roles. Other useful indirect services would be inservice training for teachers, supervision of school counselors' handling of group therapy and difficult individual cases, monitoring of parent education groups, program development, and supervision and training of paraprofessional and peer tutors. Psychologists might spend more time acting as process consultants to administrators or as personal counselors for teachers to prevent burnout and to promote holistic wellness programs in districts. The specifics of an adult-focused service delivery system are limited only by the creativity of psychologists. The common denominator is an attempt to influence those who have high-intensity and high-duration contact with children or who have the administrative power to improve the educational environments significantly.

Another, more subtle aspect of an adult-focused service delivery model is based on information reported earlier regarding the importance of interpersonal influence factors. To make their indirect service activities more successful, psychologists, like physicians, must develop persuasive, powerful positions vis-à-vis the other adults in children's environments. This is no simple task. Because the goals of psychological treatment include the enhancement of adaptive autonomy and development of indigenous social support networks to buffer the effects of life stress (Cowen, 1982; Gottlieb, 1981; Tyler, Pargament, & Gatz, 1983), it may be inappropriate for psychologists to seek superior status in relation to the primary caregivers for their clients. A more congruent position might be the one described by Tyler et al. (1983) as the resource collaborator role of the psychologist. In this model, the influence process is seen as reciprocal, with both psychologist and caregiver benefiting from the interactions. Both parties are seen as having resources useful in solving current problems. School psychologists who are good consultants will recognize that consultation is an indirect service congruent with notions of mutual enhancement.

Expanded indirect service roles for school psychologists will depend on their abilities to maximize their expert and referent power with caregivers. Credibility is enhanced when psychologists are well prepared in both the direct and indirect service domains of knowledge. Of perhaps even greater importance, however, are psychologists' skills in building rapport with caregivers, generating plans that match the entry skills and styles of consultees, willingness to follow through and follow up on cases, and sensitivity to the wide range of driving and inhibiting forces in the life spaces of the adults and children they encounter professionally. As mentioned previously, there are some indications that physicians' reliance on only expert power is resulting in increasing resistance and noncompliance among patients. As individuals become better informed about health matters, they are questioning the once sacrosanct injunctions made by physicians. Psychologists can avoid such a dilemma by routinely involving caregivers in problem definition, strategy development, and evaluation aspects of any intervention.

Shifting Job Roles to Achieve Competent Indirect Service

To effect the full potential of school psychology as an indirect service profession, considerable psychologist apathy, hopelessness, and insecurity must be overcome. Paradigmatic and ideological shifts create discomfort and resistance (Kuhn, 1970). Fortunately, the skills and information needed to begin such a shift are available, at least in beginning forms, from the psychology literature and from observations of the activities of other professions.

Many forces operate within and around systems that affect service delivery (Fig. 14.3). Organizations must be entered and assessed as carefully as clients are met and diagnosed. Entry issues include learning and matching organizational norms, negotiating flexible but clear contracts, establishing access to all subsystems, proving credibility, collaboratively involving caregivers, and nurturing of valid feedback mechanisms. When the system is understood, the psychologist can begin a process of educating it to the benefits of indirect service. The shift may occur only after several years. It will probably not occur unless psychologists simultaneously build supportive networks for themselves.

The following are some basic guidelines for moving beyond the barriers inherent in current traditional school psychology job roles.

1. Psychologists must establish goals for themselves and the organizations in which they work. Initially, almost all the energy and thrust to attain

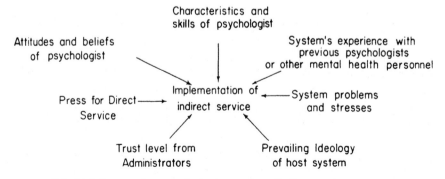

FIG. 14.3 Forces acting upon the implementation of indirect services.

these goals must come from the psychologist. The organization will not planfully change itself.
2. Establish proximity with caregivers. "Hang out" with adults in the system and establish interpersonal relationships with them.
3. Emphasize interactional styles that promote social influence. Behaviors that lend the psychologist credibility and attractiveness are as important as the actual command of a knowledge domain. Knowing something is not enough. Establishing an image of professional competence is of equal importance.
4. "Meet the system where it's at." Find ways to provide desired services to key members of the organization.
5. Schedule planning meetings with caregivers before any activities or direct services are done for children.
6. Utilize other adults in the assessment process and in the plans developed for children.
7. Offer such indirect activities as training, case management, and family consultations that may be needed by a particular system.
8. Keep decision makers informed as to the results of indirect activities in a language that is meaningful to them. This may mean an emphasis on cost/benefit analyses rather than only reports on the psychological benefits accruing to children.
9. Encourage recipients of indirect services to make their responses to such services known to decision makers.
10. Consider new "markets" for psychological interventions. For example, can school psychologists associate with the growing movement of employee assistance programs and teacher wellness programs? How would such associations be implemented?
11. Be patient. Meaningful organization change is always slow.

RESEARCH IMPLICATIONS

Conceptualizing school psychology as an indirect service delivery profession has profound implications for the types of research needed to promote the well being of children. Currently, psychological testing and its associated topics dominate the school psychology literature (Reynolds & Clark, 1984). Although new information regarding assessment is needed and questions regarding tests and testing are valid topics for school psychological research, this domain of knowledge is much too narrowly construed to warrant the quantity of attention it receives in the school psychology journals. As Reynolds and Clark (1984) note: "Perhaps the role of the school psychologist has not changed as rapidly as we would like due at least in part to our failure to provide the necessary empirical base for these changes" (p. 51).

Viewing school psychology from an indirect service delivery perspective highlights the need for research that addresses the ecological complexities that are inherent to the field. The following discussion briefly presents some areas of needed research that appear to be most cogent.

Consultation and Interpersonal Influence.

There is a tremendous need for research exploring processes of consultation and interpersonal influence in relationship to the practice of school psychology. Unless school psychologists gain increased skill in working with the adults that occupy the life spaces of school children, most of their work will be futile. Special education directors, principals, teachers, and parents are the key targets for the school psychologist. These are the people who actually control the quality of a child's life.

It may be instructive to consider the work of other mental health specialists in this regard. Family therapists theorize and intervene using a general systems theory framework (Dell, 1980; Hoffman, 1981; Minuchin, 1974). They tend to intervene with the parent subsystem in order to facilitate change for the children. They do so believing that the parents as the executive subsystem will be most influential in creating and maintaining adaptive changes that affect the children. In fact, in the family therapy literature it is common to see the term *identified patient*. This term suggests that the symptom shown by a member of a system is illustrative of problems in the entire system. If school psychologists would reframe children's learning and behavioral problems as indications of systemic issues, the need to gain influence with adults would be obvious.

Family therapists are already aware of the inescapable need to align with the powerful members of the family. The therapist gains power by such alliances. They write of "joining" with a family, that is, matching its language, norms, and expectations before attempting to introduce change. This literature may be fertile ground for school psychology researchers. A refinement and operationalization of the joining process of school psychologists and other influential adults would greatly facilitate competent and effective school psychological services.

Acceptability of Classroom Interventions

School psychologists must have a command of classroom techniques that facilitate learning and reduce behavioral deviancy. An enormous literature is already extant in this area (Emmer & Evertson, 1982). If school psychology were a direct service profession, this type of knowledge might be sufficient to guide professional practice. However, the reality of indirect service points out the need for additional categories of information. Above and beyond knowing which classroom interventions work best for which types of problems and which types of children, it is most important that we also discern what makes an intervention either acceptable or unacceptable to classroom teachers. After all, a potentially effective treatment that is not implemented by a classroom teacher is no treatment at all.

Initial research efforts by Kazdin (1980a, 1980b, 1981) and Witt et al. (1984) point out the complexity of the acceptability dimension. According to Reynolds et al. (1984), "Research indicates that teachers are concerned about how much time an intervention will require, the risks it poses to the child, the amount of training required to implement an intervention, and the possible deleterious effects that the interventon might have on other children" (p. 219). These and a multitude of other variables (e.g., cost, the consequences of failure, severity of the presenting problem, parental and student attitudes) combine in ways that are currently unknown to determine whether or not a teacher will choose to implement a school psychologist's treatment recommendation. Most of the current school psychology research addresses only the effectiveness of an intervention and is thus conceptually inadequate because it ignores the acceptability aspects of interventions and how these affect decision making by third party adults. Recognizing the indirect service delivery nature of school psychology calls attention to the need for additional study in these critical areas.

Isolation of Key Intervention Elements

For indirect services to be welcomed in the schools, psychologists need information concerning the maximizing of positive outcomes from these services. For example, work in consultation indicating the importance of follow-up services informs the practitioner that expertly done consultation interviews will not receive high teacher praise unless follow-up interviews or other contacts occur (White & Fine, 1976). Another example is provided by Bergan and Tombari (1976) who show that successful problem identification between the psychologist and teacher predict successful outcomes using consultation. Failure to achieve a mutually understood target problem predicted that indirect service would not be successful.

Further work of this sort is needed in consultation, inservice training and program evaluation. How much follow-up consultation is necessary to promote behavior change after an inservice program? When a single psychologist is evaluating a school building program, what are optimal amounts of data collection, statistical treatments that promote understanding, and techniques to involve administrators?

Assessing Organizational Environments

Straightforward, heuristic measures of organizational environments, routinely used by school psychologists (as routinely as intellectual assessments of children), are called for by the indirect service delivery model. There is already evidence that different organizational climates promote different levels of openness to mental health services (Bossard & Gutkin, 1983; Gutkin & Bossard, 1984; Kuehnel, 1975). This fact has important implications for service delivery. A possible analogy is that of the physiological host organism's ability to tolerate the "invasion" of a new organ in transplant surgery. No matter how perfect the new organ may be, it will be useless to the host if attention to readying the host for acceptance is neglected. So, too, organizations are more or less ready to tolerate innovation. Failure to determine the history of change, the key leverage sites within the organization and the procedures acceptable to the host organization will undercut the most expert attempts at planned change in organization.

The identification of driving and inhibiting organizational processes vis-à-vis utilization of mental health services depends on the development of an efficient measurement technology. There are existing measures in school, industrial/organizational, and social psychology. But, these are known to few school psychologist practitioners, are unwieldy to complete and of unknown reliability and validity in school settings, and are not closely related to actual service delivery outcomes in carefully done empirical research. Assessing only the child in a school system is much like examining a single cell in the human body and then drawing conclusions about the entire organism. There is an urgent need for research efforts leading to more effective and efficient instruments for assessing organizations.

Feasible Organizational Interventions

It may be that psychologists reading the organizational change literature in school or organizational psychology recognize its importance to their service delivery, but cannot conceptualize manageable projects. Research in the form of case studies, or $N = 1$ designs, illustrating potent organizational change strategies done by a single psychologist might provide the impetus for such activity (Illback & Maher, 1984). Also, such research would provide an empirical ground for training endeavors that emphasize organization development activities.

Research reporting on classroom interventions should highlight the ways in which the experimental treatments were institutionalized into the daily classroom processes at the completion of the study. What organizational tactics were necessary both to introduce the change and to maintain it after the direct activities of the psychologists were suspended? These issues are related to social influence and have the added dimension of conceptualizing the person-in-the-environment as a total indivisible unit for intervention.

Marketing

A final suggestion is that for school psychologists to maximize their service potential, significant attention must be paid to marketing strategies. What new markets exist that would benefit from the services of school psychologists? What techniques are most successful in selling psychological services to new markets? How must service delivery change in diverse markets? What new skills are demanded by new populations?

Some of these new markets may be Health Maintenance Organizations (or analogous Preferred Provider Groups) developing to deliver health care services. School psychologists would benefit from information about their potential role in such organizations and about successful ways of gaining access to or developing them. Company day care centers and schools, adult education, employee assistance programs, assistance to college students with learning difficulties, and private schools are examples of other potential markets.

Another important aspect of marketing research includes careful analyses of the costs and benefits of having internally or externally based school psychologists. What are some ways that psychologists could describe their worth to a district in terms of improvements in student learning or attendance, promotion of teacher wellness, reduction in behavioral deviancy, promotion of positive school family interactions, and contributions to low turnover rates among special education teachers? These are just a few possibilities. They are based, however, on the potential benefits to a school district that is receiving high quality indirect and direct services from psychologists.

SUMMARY AND CONCLUSIONS

This chapter has examined the profession of school psychology in relationship to the direct-indirect continuum of service delivery models. Three major conclusions have emerged. First, despite popular opinion to the contrary, school psychology *is* an indirect service delivery profession. If the analysis in this chapter is accurate, it is no longer necessary to debate how to become more closely affiliated with indirect service methodologies. The field has already arrived! The correct categorization of the assessment/diagnosis job function of psychologists has caused some confusion on this point. It should be clear, however, that these functions are activities rather than services per se, and that in school psychology these activities lead almost exclusively to indirect rather than direct service.

Second, indirect service delivery provides the profession of school psychology with excellent methodologies for serving children. On balance, the advantages of indirect service delivery approaches seem to far outweigh the disadvantages. The profession is, in fact, quite fortunate that this is true because the objective logistical reality seems to be that primary reliance on direct service methods is virtually impossible. There are too many problems and too few psychologists, making anything other than indirect service approaches extremely impractical and ineffective.

Finally, the principal issue facing school psychology today is: How can indirect services be delivered most effectively? Little progress toward answering this question is possible, however, until school psychologists recognize the indirect service nature of their roles. A different mindset, body of knowledge, and set of behaviors are required in an indirect versus a direct service environment. The paradox with which school psychologists must grapple is that their power to improve the lives of children is a direct function of their ability to affect the behavior and attitudes of adults. The direction of school psychology theory, practice, and research must shift if we are to develop sophisticated technologies for achieving success in light of this reality.

The significant attention paid by researchers and practitioners to assessment and intervention technologies and the scant attention directed at how services are best delivered contribute to the current dilemmas facing school psychologists. Many school psychologists are unable to contribute what they know to the lives of children, families, and school personnel. The self-conscious development and application of indirect service will address this problem by aligning psychologist with teachers, principals, and parents in a working, collaborative partnership. Membership on this team will assure the viability of the school psychologist role and will create enabling environments for children.

REFERENCES

Abidin, R. R. (1975). Negative effects of behavioral consultation: "I know I ought to, but it hurts too much." *Journal of School Psychology, 13*(1), 51–57.

Albee, G. W. (1968). Conceptual models and manpower requirements in psychology. *American Psychologist, 23,* 317–320.

Albee, G. W. (1982). Preventing psychopathology and promoting human potential. *American Psychologist, 37,* 1043–1050.

Allen, G. J., Chinsky, J. M., Larcen, S. W., Lochman, J. E., & Selinger, H. V. (1976). *Community psychology and the schools.* Hillsdale, NJ: Lawrence Erlbaum Associates.

Alpert, J. L. (1982). *Psychological consultation in educational settings.* San Francisco: Jossey-Bass.

American Psychological Association (1981). Specialty guidelines for the delivery of services by school psychologists. *American Psychologist, 36,* 670–681.

Apter, S. J. (1982). *Troubled children: Troubled systems.* New York: Pergamon Press.

Apter, S. J., & Conoley, J. C. (1984). *Childhood behavior disorders and emotional disturbance: Teaching troubled children.* Englewood Cliffs, NJ: Prentice-Hall.

Aronson, E., Blaney, N., Stephan, C., Sikes, J., & Snapp, M. (1978). *The jigsaw classroom.* Beverly Hills, CA; Sage Publications.

Asch, S. (1956). Studies of independence and conformity: A minority of one against a unanimous majority. *Psychological Monographs, 70,9.*

Bales, R. F., & Cohen, S. P. (1979). *SYMLOG: A system for the multiple level observation of groups.* New York: Free Press.

Bandura, A., & Walters, R. H. (1963). *Social learning and personality development.* New York: Holt, Rinehart & Winston.

Bardon, J. I. (1982). School psychology's dilemma: A proposal for its resolution. *Professional Psychology, 13,* 955–968.

Bassin, M., & Gross, T. (1978, March). *Organization development, a viable method of change for urban secondary schools: Assessment of a pragmentic model, high school self renewal.* Paper presented at the annual meetings of the American Educational Research Association, Toronto.

Bergan, J. R., & Tombari, M. L. (1976). Consultant skill and efficiency and the implementation and outcome of consultation. *Journal of School Psychology, 14,* 3–14.

Bertalanffy, von, L. (1966). General systems theory and psychiatry. In S. Arieti (Ed.), *American handbook of psychiatry*. Vol. III. New York: Basic Books.
Bertalanffy, von, L. (1967). *Robots, man and minds*. New York: Braziler.
Bertalanffy, von, L. (1968). *General systems theory*. New York: Braziller.
Bijou, S. W., and Baer, D. M. (1966). Operant methods in child behavior and development. In W. K. Honig (Ed.), *Operant behavior: Areas of research and application* (pp. 718–789). New York: Appleton-Century-Crofts.
Blumberg, A. (1976). ODs future in schools—Or is there one? *Education and Urban Society, 8*, 213–226.
Blumberg, A., & Schmuck, R. A. (1972). Barriers to organization development for schools. *Educational Technology, 12*(10), 30–34.
Bossard, M. D., & Gutkin, T. B. (1983). The relationship of consultant skill and school organizational characteristics with teacher use of school based consultation services. *School Psychology Review, 12*, 50–56.
Bowers, D. (1973). Techniques and their results in 23 organizations: The Michigan ICL Study. *Journal of Applied Behavioral Science, 9*, 21–43.
Brickman, P., Rabinowitz, V. C., Karuza, J., Jr., Coates, D., Cohn, E., & Kidder, L. (1982). Models of helping and coping. *American Psychologist, 37*, 368–384.
Bronfenbrenner, U. (1979). *The ecology of human development:* Cowen, E. L. (1973). Social and community interventions. *Annual Review of Psychology, 24*, 423–472.
Casey, R. J., & Berman, J. S. (1985). The outcome of psychotherapy with children. *Psychological Bulletin, 98*, 388–400.
Chambliss, C., & Murray, E. J. (1979). Cognitive procedures for smoking reduction: Symptom attribution versus efficacy attribution. *Cognitive Therapy and Research, 3*, 91–95.
Cienke, J. A. (1982). Teachers' perception of consultation as a function of consultants' use of expert and referent power. *Dissertation Abstracts International, 43* (3-A), 725.
Conoley, J. C., & Conoley, C. W. (1982). The effects of two conditions of client-centered consultation on student teacher problem description and remedial plans. *Journal of School Psychology, 20*, 323–328.
Cowen, E. L. (1982). Help is where you find it: Four informal helping groups. *American Psychologist, 37*, 385–395.
Cowen, E. L., & Gesten, E. L. (1978). Community approaches to intervention. In B. B. Wolman, J. Egan, & A. O. Ross (Eds.), *Handbook of treatment of mental disorders in childhood and adolescence* (pp. 102–125). Englewood Cliffs, NJ: Prentice-Hall.
Cowen, E. L., Pederson, A., Babigian, H., Izzo, L. D., & Trost, M. A. (1973). Long-term follow-up of early detected vulnerable children. *Journal of Consulting and Clinical Psychology, 41*, 438–446.
Cowen, E. L., Trost, M. A., Lorion, R. P., Dorr, D., Izzo, L. D., & Isaacson, R. V. (1975). *New ways in school mental health: Early detection and prevention of school maladaption*. New York: Human Sciences Press.
Cummings, T. G. (1980). *Systems theory for organization development*. New York: Wiley.
Curtis, M. J., & Watson, J. L. (1980). Changes in consultee problem clarification skills following consultation. *Journal of School Psychology, 18*, 210–221.
Cutts, N. E. (Ed.). (1955). *School psychologists at mid-century*. Washington, DC: American Psychological Association.
Darling-Hammond, L. (1984). *Beyond the commission reports: The coming crisis in teaching*. New York: Rand Corporation.
Davison, G. C., & Valins, S. (1969). Maintenance of self-attributed and drug-attributed behavior change. *Journal of Personality and Social Psychology, 11*, 25–33.
deCharms, R. (1976). *Enhancing motivation: Change in the classroom*. New York: Irvington.
Deci, E. L., Nezlek, J., & Sheinman, L. (1981). Characteristics of the rewarder and intrinsic motivation of the rewardee. *Journal of Personality and Social Psychology, 40*, 1–10.

Dell, P. (1980). Researching the family theories of schizophrenia: An exercise in epistemological confusion. *Family Process, 19,* 321-335.
Deutsch, M., Krauss, R. M. (1962). Studies of interpersonal bargaining. *Journal of Conflict Resolution, 6,* 52-76.
Durlak, J. A. (1973). Myths concerning the nonprofessional therapist. *Professional Psychology, 4,* 300-304.
Edelman, M. W. (1981). Who is for children? *American Psychologist, 36,* 109-116.
Elliott, S. N., Witt, J. C., Galvin, G., & Peterson, R. (1984). Acceptability of behavioral interventions: Factors that influence teacher's decisions. *Journal of School Psychology, 22,* 353-360.
Emmer, E. T., & Evertson, C. M. (1982). Synthesis of research on classroom management. *Focus on Behaviorally Impaired, 2,* 342-347.
French, J. R. P., & Raven, B. (1959). The bases of social power. In D. Cartwright (Ed.), *Studies in social power* (pp. 230-301). Ann Arbor: University of Michigan Press.
Freud, S. (1949). *Collected papers.* New York: Basic Books.
Freudenberger, H. J. (1974). Staff burn-out. *Journal of Social Issues, 30*(1), 159-165.
Frieze, I. H., & Snyder, H. N. (1980). Children's beliefs about the causes of success and failure in school settings. *Journal of Educational Psychology, 72,* 186-196.
Fullen, M., Miles, M. B., & Taylor, G. (1980). Organization development in schools: The state of the art. *Review of Educational Research, 50,* 121-183.
Gallessich, J. (1973). Organizational factors influencing consultation in schools. *Journal of School Psychology, 11,* 57-65.
Gallessich, J. (1982). *The profession and practice of consultation.* San Francisco: Jossey-Bass.
Garfield, S. L., & Bergin, A. E. (Eds.). (1978). *Handbook of psychotherapy and behavior change: An empirical analysis.* New York: Wiley.
Gilmore, G. E. (1974). Models for school psychology: Dimensions, barriers, and implications. *Journal of School Psychology, 12,* 95-101.
Goldenberg, I. I. (Ed.). (1973). *The helping professions in the world of action.* Lexington, MA: Lexington Books.
Goldstein, A. P. & Kanfer, F. H. (1979). *Maximizing treatment gains.* New York: Academic Press.
Gottfredson, G. D., Gottfredson, D. C., & Cook, M. S.1983). *The school action effectiveness study: Second interim report.* (Report No. 342). Baltimore: The Johns Hopkins University, Center for Social Organization of Schools.
Gottlieb, B. (1981). *Social support systems.* Beverly Hills, CA: Sage Publications.
Gutkin, T. B. (1980). Teacher perceptions of consultative services provided by school psychologists. *Professional Psychology, 11,* 637-642.
Gutkin, T. B., & Bossard, M. D. (1984). The impact of consultant, consultee, and organizational variables on teacher attitudes toward consultation services. *Journal of School Psychology, 22,* 251-258.
Gutkin, T. B., Singer, J. H., & Brown, R. (1980). Teacher reactions to school based consultation services: A multivariate analysis. *Journal of School Psychology, 18,* 126-134.
Haire, D. (1982). *How the F.D.A. determines the "safety" of drugs—just how safe is "safe"?.* Washington, DC: Women's Health Network.
Haley, J. (1976). *Problem solving therapy.* San Francisco: Jossey-Bass.
Heider, F. (1958). *The psychology of interpersonal relations.* New York: Wiley.
Heller, K., Price, R. H., Reinharz, S., Riger, S., Wandersman, A. (1984). *Psychology and community change.* Homewood, IL: Dorsey Press.
Heppner, P., & Dixon, D. N. (1981). A review of the interpersonal influence process in counseling. *Personnel & Guidance Journal, 59,* 542-550.
Hinkle, A., Silverstein, B., & Walton, D. M. (1977). A method for the evaluation of mental health consultation to the public schools. *Journal of Community Psychology, 5,* 262-265.
Hobbs, N. (1966). Helping disturbed children: Psychological and ecological strategies. *American Psychologist, 21,* 1105-1115.

Hobbs, N. (1982). *The troubled and troubling child.* San Francisco: Jossey-Bass.
Hoffman, L. (1981). *Foundations of family therapy: A conceptual framework for systems change.* New York: Basic Books.
Hughes, J. M. (1983). The application of cognitive dissonance theory to consultation. *Journal of School Psychology, 21,* 349-358.
Hughes, J., & Falk, R. S. (1981). Resistance, reactance, and consultation. *Journal of School Psychology, 19,* 134-142.
Hyman, I. (1983). We are here for the kids: A reply to Pantaleno. *Journal of School Psychology, 21,* 115-118.
Illback, R. J., & Maher, C. A. (1984). The school psychologist as an organizational boundary role professional. *Journal of School Psychology, 22,* 63-72.
Jason, L. A., & Ferone, L. (1978). Behavioral versus process consultation interventions in school settings. *American Journal of Community Psychology, 6,* 531-543.
Kazdin, A. E. (1980a). Acceptability of alternative treatment for deviant child behavior. *Journal of Applied Behavior Analysis, 13,* 259-273.
Kazdin, A. E. (1980b). Acceptability of timeout from reinforcement procedures for disruptive child behavior. *Behavior Therapy, 11,* 329-344.
Kazdin, A. E. (1981). Acceptability of child treatment techniques: The influence of treatment efficacy and adverse side effects. *Behavior Therapy, 12,* 493-506.
Kelley, H. H. (1972). *Causal schemata and the attribution process.* Morristown, NJ: General Learning Press.
Kicklighter, R. H. (1983). Clients all. *Journal of School Psychology, 21,* 119-122.
Kinsala, M. G. (1984). *A utilization of expert and referent power framework.* Unpublished dissertation, Texas Women's University, Denton, TX.
Knoff, H. M., & Smith, C. R. (1981). A comparison of school psychology and special education students' placement decisions: IQ tips the scale. *Journal of Special Education, 15,* 55-64.
Kuehnel, J. (1975). Faculty, school, and organizational characteristics and schools' openness to mental health resources. *Dissertation Abstracts International, 36,* 2716A.
Kuhn, T. S. (1970). *The structure of scientific revolutions* 2nd ed. International encyclopedia of unified science. Vol. 2(2), Chicago: University of Chicago Press.
LaCross, M. B. (1980). Perceived counselor social influence and counseling outcomes: Validity of the Counselor Rating Form. *Journal of Counseling Psychology, 27,* 320-327.
Lepper, J. R., & Greene, D. (1978). *The hidden costs of reward.* Hillsdale, NJ: Lawrence Erlbaum Associates.
Lewin, K. (1935). *Dynamic theory of personality.* New York: McGraw-Hill.
Lewin, K. (1948). *Resolving social conflicts.* New York: Harper & Row.
Lewin, K. (1951). *Field theory and social science.* New York: Harper.
Lewis, W. W. (1982). Ecological factors in successful residential treatment. *Behavioral Disorders, 7*(3), 149-156.
Liberman, B. L. (1978). The role of mastery in psychotherapy: Maintenance of improvement and prescriptive change. In J. D. Frank, R. Hoehn-Saric, D. D. Imber, B. L., Liberman, & A. R. Stone (Eds.), *The effective ingredients of successful psychotherapy* (pp. 35-72). New York: Brunner/Mazel.
Lorion, R. P. (1978). Research on psychotherapy and behavior change with the disadvantaged. In S. L. Garfield & A. E. Bergin *Handbook of psychotherapy and behavior change* (pp. 903-938). New York: Wiley.
Martin, R. (1978). Expert and referent power: A framework for understanding and maximizing consultation effectiveness. *Journal of School Psychology, 16,* 49-55.
Martin, R., & Curtis, M. (1981). Consultant's perceptions of causality for success and failure of consultation. *Professional Psychology, 12,* 670-676.
Maslach, C. (1978). The client role in staff burn-out. *Journal of Social Issues, 34*(4), 111-124.
Meacham, M., & Peckham, P. S. (1978). School psychologists at three-quarter century: Congruence between training, practice, preferred role, and competence. *Journal of School Psychology, 16,* 195-206.

Meichenbaum, D. H. (1973). Cognitive factors in behavior modification: Modifying what clients say to themselves. In R. S. Rubin, J. P. Brady, & J. D. Henderson (Eds.), *Advances in behavior therapy*, (Vol. 4, pp. 21–36). New York: Academic Press.
Meyers, J. (1975). Consultee centered consultation with a teacher as a technique in behavior management. *American Journal of Community Psychology, 3,* 111–121.
Milgram, S. (1974). *Obedience to authority: An experimental view.* New York: Harper & Row.
Miller, G. A. (1969). Psychology as a means of promoting human welfare. *American Psychologist, 24,* 1063–1075.
Minuchin, S. (1974). *Families and family therapy.* Cambridge, MA: Harvard University Press.
Monroe, V. (1979). Roles and status of school psychology. In G. D. Phye & D. J. Reschley (Eds.), *School psychology: Perspectives and issues* (pp. 25–47). New York: Academic Press.
National Association of School Psychologists. (1978). *Standards for the provision of school psychological services.* Washington, DC: Author.
O'Dell, S. (1974). Training parents in behavior modification: A review. *Psychological Bulletin, 81,* 418–433.
O'Leary, K. D., & O'Leary, S. G. (Eds.). (1976). *Classroom management: The successful use of behavior modification.* (Rev. ed.). New York: Pergamon Press.
O'Neill, P., & Trickett, E. J. (1982). *Community consultation.* San Francisco: Jossey-Bass.
Pantaleno, A. P. (1983). Parents as primary clients of the school psychologist; or, Why is it we are here? *Journal of School Psychology, 21,* 107–114.
Parloff, M. B., Waskow, I. E., & Wolfe, B. E. (1978). Research on therapist variables in relation to process and outcome. In S. L. Garfield & A. E. Bergin (Eds.), *Handbook of psychotherapy and behavior change* (2nd ed., pp. 233–282). New York: Wiley.
Pavlov, I. P. (1927). *Conditioned reflexes: An investigation of the physiological activity of the cerebral cortex.* (B. V. Anrep, Ed. and Trans.). London: Oxford University Press.
Piaget, J. (1965). *The moral judgment of the child.* New York: Free Press.
Piersel, W. C., & Gutkin, T. B. (1983). Resistance to school-based consultation: A behavioral analysis of the problem. *Psychology in the Schools, 20,* 311–326.
Price, R. H., & Politser, P. E. (Eds.). (1980). *Evaluation and action in the social environment.* New York: Academic Press.
Ramage, J. (1979). National survey of school psychologists: Update. *The School Psychology Digest, 8,* 153–161.
Raven, B. H., & Haley, R. W. (1980). Social influence in a medical context. In L. Bickman (Ed.), *Applied social psychology annual.* (Vol. I, pp. 255–277). Beverly Hills, CA: Sage Publications.
Repucci, N. D., & Saunders, J. T. (1974). The social psychology of behavior modification: Problems of implementation in natural settings. *American Psychologist, 29,* 649–660.
Reynolds, C. R., & Clark, J. H. (1984). Trends in school psychology research: 1974–1980. *Journal of School Psychology, 22,* 43–52.
Reynolds, C. R., Gutkin, T. B., Elliott, S., & Witt, J. (1984). *School psychology: Essentials of theory and practice.* New York: Wiley.
Ritter, D. R. (1978). Effects of a school consultation program upon referral patterns of teachers. *Psychology in the Schools, 15,* 239–243.
Rosenthal, R., & Jacobson, L. (1968). *Pygmalion in the classroom.* New York: Holt, Rinehart & Winston.
Sarason, S. B. (1973). Social action as a vehicle for learning. In I. I. Goldenberg (Ed.), *The helping professions in the world of action* (pp. 257–283). Lexington, MA: Lexington Books.
Sarason, S. B. (1982). *The culture of the school and the problem of change* (2nd ed.). Boston: Allyn & Bacon.
Sarason, S. B. (1983). *Schooling in America.* New York: Free Press.
Schachter, S., & Singer, J. E. (1962). Cognitive, social, and physiological determinants of emotional states. *Psychological Review, 69,* 379–399.
Schmuck, R. A. (1968). Helping teachers improve classroom group process. *Journal of Applied Behavioral Science, 4*(4), 401–435.

Schmuck, R. A., & Miles, M. B. (1971). *Organization development in the schools*. Palo Alto, CA: National Press Books.

Schneider, R. G. (1982). *When to say no to surgery*. Englewood Cliffs, NJ: Prentice-Hall.

Sheldon, A. (1980). Organizational paradigms: A theory of organizational change. *Organizational Dynamics, 8*(3), 61–80.

Sherif, M., Harvey, O. J., White, B. J., Hood, W. R., & Sherif, C. W. (1961). *Intergroup conflict and cooperation: The Robber's Cave experiment*. Norman: University of Oklahoma, Institute of Group Relations.

Simpson, R. L., & Poplin, M. S. (1981). Parents as agents of change. *School Psychology Review, 10*, 15–25.

Skinner, B. F. (1938). *The behavior of organisms*. New York: Appleton-Century-Crofts.

Skinner, B. F. (1953). *Science and human behavior*. New York: Macmillan.

Skinner, B. F. (1957). *Verbal behavior*. New York: Appleton-Century-Crofts.

Smith, M. L., & Glass, G. V. (1977). Meta-analysis of psychotherapy outcome studies. *American Psychologist, 32*, 752–760.

Strong, S. R. (1968). Counseling: An interpersonal influence process. *Journal of Counseling Psychology, 15*, 215–224.

Strong, S. R., & Claiborn, C. D. (1982). *Change through interaction*. New York: Wiley.

Takanishi, R., DeLeon, P. H., & Pallak, M. S. (1983). Psychology and education: A continuing, productive partnership. *American Psychologist, 38*, 996–1000.

Thibaut, J. W., & Kelley, H. H. (1959). *The social psychology of groups*. New York: Wiley.

Tyler, F. B., Pargament, K. I., & Gatz, M. (1983). The resource collaborator role: A model for interactions involving psychologists. *American Psychologist, 38*, 388–398.

Van Egeren, L. F. (1979). Cardiovascular changes during social competition in a mixed-motive game. *Journal of Personality and Social Psychology, 37*, 858–864.

Wahrman, R., & Pugh, M. D. (1974). Sex, nonconformity, and influence. *Sociometry, 34*, 137–147.

Watson, J. B. (1930). *Behaviorism*. New York: Norton.

Weissberg, R. P., Cowen, E. L., Lotyczewski, B. S., & Gesten, E. L. (1983). The Primary Mental Health Project: Seven consecutive years of program outcome research. *Journal of Consulting and Clinical Psychology, 51*, 100–107.

Weitz, M. (198). *Health schock*. Englewood Cliffs, NJ: Prentice-Hall.

White, P. O. & Fine, M. J. (1976). The effects of three schools' psychological consultation modes on selected teacher and pupil outcomes. *Psychology in the Schools, 13*, 414–420.

Witt, J. C., & Elliott, S. N. (1985). Acceptability of classroom intervention strategies. In T. R. Kratochwill (Ed.), *Advances in school psychology* (Vol. 4, pp. 251–288). Hillsdale, NJ: Lawrence Erlbaum Associates.

Witt, J. C., Elliott, S. N., & Martens, B. K. (1984). Acceptability of behavioral interventions used in classrooms: The influence of teacher time, severity of behavior problem, and type of intervention. *Behavioral Disorders*.

Witt, J. C., Martens, B. K., & Elliott, S. N. (1984). Factors affecting teachers' judgments of the acceptability of behavioral interventions: Time involvement, behavior problem severity, and type of intervention. *Behavior Therapy, 15*, 204–209.

Wong, P. J., & Weiner, B. (1981). When people ask why questions and the heuristics of attributional research. *Journal of Personality and Social Psychology, 40*, 650–653.

Ysseldyke, J. E. (1978). Who's calling the plays in school psychology? *Psychology in the School, 15*, 373–378.

Ysseldyke, J., Algozzine, B., Regan, R., & McGue, M. (1981). The influence of test scores and naturally occurring pupil characteristics on psychoeducational decision making with children. *Journal of School Psychology, 19*, 167–177.

Zimbardo, P. G. (1969). The human choice: Individualization, reason, and order versus deindividualization, impulse and chaos. In W. J. Arnold & D. Levine (Eds.), *Nebraska Symposium on Motivation, 17*, 237–307.

Author Index

A

Abidin, R. R., 87, 146, 149, 150, 410
Abnate, L., 376
Abt, C. C., 260
Adams, H. E., 282
Agin, T. C., 179
Agyris, C., 67
Albee, G. W., 73, 397
Alessi, G. J., 150, 282
Alevizos, P., 282
Algozzine, B., 35, 36, 44, 45, 56, 76, 190, 230, 240, 411
Allen, G. J., 15, 407
Allen, J. R., 233
Alpert, J. L., 15, 146, 147, 251, 265, 270, 407
Alwin, D. G., 344
Anastasi, A., 241
Anderegg, T., 274, 287, 290, 292
Anderson, C., 219, 362, 367, 376
Anderson, D., 140, 253, 255, 262-3
Andrews, L., 8
Antaki, C., 56
Apter, S. J., 363, 377, 381, 402
Arenas, S., 231
Argulewicz, E. N., 227, 229, 230, 237, 239
Argyris, C., 152
Armer, B., 377
Arnalde, M. A., 233, 235
Aronson, E., 403, 412

Arter, J. A., 155
Asbury, C. A., 189
Asch, S., 404
Ashton, P., 305, 306, 309
Austin, G. R., 320, 322
Avila, V., 240

B

Babigian, H., 407
Baer, D. M., 293-4, 355, 401
Bagarozzi, D. A., 203
Bailey, S., 70
Baker, F., 73, 74, 148
Baker, R. G., 83
Baker, R. L., 236
Balch, P., 149
Bales, R. F., 403
Bandura, A., 7, 28, 29, 30, 48, 54, 55, 57, 58, 83, 149, 361, 362, 401
Bannister, D., 55
Barbanel, L., 18, 27
Barclay, J. R., 63, 276
Bardon, J. I., 1, 31, 54, 61, 64, 66, 69, 71, 72, 144, 146, 147, 162, 207, 208, 346, 350, 351, 358, 362, 394
Barik, H. C., 236
Barker, R. G., 6, 220
Barlow, D. H., 251, 273, 278, 305, 307
Bassin, M., 407

425

AUTHOR INDEX

Beam, R. D., 65, 66, 68, 71
Beare, P. L., 220
Becker, L. D., 27, 123, 140
Bellack, A. A., 278, 282
Bennett, V. C., 61, 66, 207, 208
Benson, A. J., 15, 203, 213
Bentler, P. M., 253, 342, 344
Bergan, J. R., 20, 86, 240, 252-256, 260-263, 265, 269-70, 286-9, 293, 416
Bergin, A. E., 401
Berk, R. A., 241
Berkowitz, H., 358
Berliner, D. C., 263, 318
Bernauer, M., 154, 181, 186
Bernstein, D. A., 251, 277, 278
Bersoff, D. N., 28, 96, 98, 99, 100, 102, 103, 104, 115, 146, 150, 227, 353
Bertalanffy, L., 360, 374, 402
Bevan, W., 32, 33
Bickel, W. E., 321, 322
Biddle, B. J., 305
Bijour, S. W., 43, 318, 401
Biklen, D., 103
Billings, R. S., 344
Bins, M., 171
Bischoff, H. G., 213
Blaney, N., 403, 412
Blankenship, C., 209
Blatt, M., 314
Block, J. H., 197
Blumberg, A., 411
Boehm, A. E., 369
Boersma, F., 236
Boland, P. A., 213
Bolster, A. S., 305
Bond, L., 252, 253
Bornstein, P. H., 291
Bossard, M. D., 407, 417
Bossert, S. T., 322
Bower, E. M., 146, 147, 148
Bowers, D., 411
Boyer, E. L., 307, 317
Braddock, J. H., II, 311
Bradley, R. H., 370
Brantley, J. C., 64, 139, 143
Breger, L., 360
Bretzing, B. H., 53, 118, 140
Breyer, N. L., 150
Brickman, P., 404
Bronfenbrenner, U., 55, 361, 362, 367, 402
Brooks, R., 145, 155

Brophy, J., 319
Broskowski, A., 73, 74, 148
Brown, A. L., 318
Brown, D. K., 289, 2922
Brown, D. T., 28, 30, 123
Brown, R., 54, 398
Bry, B. H., 65
Bryant, B. I., 88, 155, 156
Buchanan, B., 229
Buckley, W., 374
Buriel, R., 229
Burke, J. P., 64, 143
Burke, W. W., 153
Bushell, J. D., 355
Buxton, E. B., 203
Byrnes, I. M., 286-7

C

Cahan, L. S., 263
Calchera, D. J., 150
Caldwell, B. M., 370
Calhoun, K. S., 282
Callahan, E., 282
Callenbach, C., 236
Cameron, E., 203
Cameron, H. K., 189
Cameron, W. F., 189
Campbell, D. T., 269, 272, 276, 277, 279
Cancelli, A. A., 254, 289
Cann, C., 150
Caplan, G., 86, 146, 265, 358, 363
Cardon, B. W., 28, 30
Carkhuff, R. R., 65
Carlberg, C., 265, 267
Carlos, M. L., 228, 230, 231
Carroll, J. L., 53, 118, 140
Carroll, R., 356
Carter, B. D., 19
Carter, W. E., 252
Cartwell, B., 230
Case, R., 312
Castaneda, A., 233
Catterall, C. D., 16, 18, 20, 155, 156
Chambliss, J., 404
Chandler, G. E., 357
Chandler, M. J., 370
Chandy, J., 28, 141
Chesler, M. A., 88, 155, 156
Chiang, B., 46
Childs, A. W., 203, 204

Chin, J. L., 73
Chinsky, J. M., 14, 407
Choca, P. R., 229
Chrin, M., 28, 141
Christenson, S., 27, 30, 39, 44, 47, 209, 222, 230, 349, 350, 352, 354, 377
Christenson, W., 84
Ciminero, A. R., 282
Claiborn, C D., 405
Clancy, B., 28, 141
Clarizio, H. F., 15, 16, 84
Clark, J. H., 393, 414
Clark, K. B., 310
Clark, R. D., 203, 205, 211, 213
Cleveland, S. E., 145
Coates, D., 404
Coates, T. J., 150, 281
Cohen, R., 72
Cohen, S. P., 403
Cohn, E., 404
Colby, A., 313
Coleman, J. S., 70, 320, 321, 322, 363, 374
Collins, R. C., 253
Cone, J. D., 277, 278, 279, 280, 282, 285
Conger, R. E., 282
Conoley, C. W., 87, 88
Conoley, J. C., 87, 88, 151, 393, 402
Conyne, R. K., 73
Cook, M. S., 407
Cook, T. D., 266, 269, 272, 276, 277
Cook, V. J., 27, 140, 358
Cooley, W. W., 252, 253, 309, 312, 344
Cooper, H. M., 265
Copeland, E., 240
Corder, R., 90
Costanzo, J. P., 376
Cotterell, J. L., 63
Coulter, W. A., 28, 30
Cowen, E. L., 15, 84, 116, 146, 397, 398, 399, 407, 412
Cozens, J. A., 234
Crain, R., 311
Crapanzano, V., 231
Cronbach, L. J., 63, 69, 281, 307, 346
Cross, H., 231
Crowfoot, J. E., 88, 155, 156
Cuban, L., 197
Cuellar, I., 235
Culbertson, F. M., 141
Cummings, T. G., 406, 412
Cummins, J., 232, 236, 237

Curtis, M. J., 11, 109, 110, 119, 122, 131, 251, 265, 358, 394, 398, 405
Cutts, N. E., 1, 10, 81, 132, 135, 351, 358, 362, 394

D

Daniels, D. N., 203
Dappen, L., 54
Darcy, N. T., 236
Darling-Hammond, L., 411
Das, J. P., 144
Dauphinais, P., 229
Davidson, J. L., 5
Davis, L. T., 139, 144
Davis, R. A., 293
Davison, G. C., 404
DeBlassie, R. R., 240, 241
DeCharm, R., 55, 56, 404
DeLeon, P. H., 393
DeRisisi, W., 282
Deci, E. L., 404
Dell, P., 415
Deno, S. L., 46, 47
Detmer, M., 181
Deutsch, M., 403
Dewey, J., 23
Diament, C., 285
Dick, W., 317
Dickinson, D. J., 154
Dietz, A. T., 282
Dishaw, M. M., 263
Dixon, D. N., 405
Docherty, E. M., 143
Doerksen, H., 203
Doris, J., 44
Dorr, D., 116, 398, 407
Drabman, R. S., 293-5
Dreisbach, M., 235, 236
Duffey, J., 356
Duker, J., 70, 172
Duley, S. M., 289
Duncanis, A. J., 356
Durlak, J. A., 398
Dwyer, D. C., 322
Dyer, C. O., 290
Dyson, E., 363, 374

E

Ebaugh, F. S., 203
Eberst, N. D., 123, 126

AUTHOR INDEX

Eckman, T., 282
Edelman, M. W., 398
Edgerton, R. B., 231
Edinger, J. A., 68
Edmonds, R. R., 322
Ehrlich, M. L., 363, 374
Eiserer, P. E., 213
Elam, S. M., 33
Elkin, V. B., 1, 13, 14, 217
Ellena, W. J., 305
Elliott, S. N., 2, 8, 16, 22, 24, 54, 95, 117, 123, 136, 195, 229, 230, 361, 362, 363, 393, 395, 396, 410, 416
Ellis, J. L., 203, 220
Emmer, E. T., 415
Epps, S., 36, 45
Erikson, E. H., 360
Erikson, J. G., 238
Erlbaum, V., 353
Esterson, H., 363
Estes, W. K., 57
Eubanks, E. E., 197
Everett, F., 230
Evertson, C. M., 415

F

Fagan, T. K., 82, 92, 206
Fairchild, H. N., 234
Fairchild, T. N., 144, 146
Falk, R. S., 404
Fanibanda, D. K., 87
Farber, H., 292
Farge, E. J., 231
Farley, F. H., 305
Farley, G. K., 193
Farling, W. H., 27
Fein, L. G., 144
Feistritzer, C. E., 307
Feld, J. K., 249, 252, 253, 255, 256, 262, 263
Feldman, C., 363
Fennessey, J., 197
Fenton, K. S., 96
Fernandes, I., 231
Ferone, L., 274, 287-8, 290, 292, 398
Feuerstein, R., 154
Figueroa, R. A., 235
Filby, W. W., 263
Fine, M. J., 66, 141, 363, 374, 416
Fishbein, J., 182
Fisher, C. W., 263

Fishhaut, E. H., 386
Fishman, D. B., 94
Fishman, H. C., 376
Fiske, D. W., 266, 279
Flanagan, D., 88, 151, 152, 153
Flavell, J. H., 318
Flax, J. E., 203
Flax, M., 140
Fleischman, D., 288
Fleming, D. D., 131, 195
Fleming, E. R., 131, 195
Flynn, D. L., 28, 90
Foley, W. J., 252, 259
Ford, J. D., 28, 89, 141, 268
Forehand, R. L., 8, 291
Forness, S. R., 153, 154
Foster, G. G., 56
Foster, S. L., 285
Franco, J. N.
Franzoni, J. B., 98
Freeman, H. E., 259, 269
French, J. L., 144
French, J. R. P., 404, 405
Freud, S., 400
Freudenberger, H. J., 404
Freund, J. G., 370
Frieze, I. H., 403
Frinfrock, S. R., 292
Fry, M. A., 305
Fulcher, R., 174, 227
Fullan, M., 59, 261, 411

G

Gaffney, P. D., 240
Gage, N. L., 306, 309, 317
Gagne, R. M., 154, 317
Gallessich, J., 89, 151, 152, 406
Galvin, G. A., 8, 54, 195, 410
Gandara, P., 241
Garbarino, J., 360, 361, 364, 367, 368
Garcia, E. E., 232, 237
Garcia, M., 238
Gardener, R. C., 232
Garfield, S. L., 9, 250, 289, 291, 401
Garmezy, N., 352
Garrison, V., 231
Garvey, W. P., 276
Garza, B. M., 240
Gast-Rosenberg, I., 337
Gatz, M., 412

Gelinas, P. J., 213
Gelinas, R. P., 213
Genshaft, J., 240
Gephart, W. J., 252, 259
Gerken, K. C., 141, 203, 213, 215
Germann, G., 46
Gershaw, N. J., 116, 288
Gesten, E. L., 397, 407
Gettone, V. G., 189
Gibbs, J., 313
Giebink, J. W., 27
Gilbert, M. J., 234
Gilmore, G. E., 28, 141, 146, 153, 154, 157, 160, 394
Glaser, G. C., 281
Glass, G. V., 250, 265, 266, 306, 398
Goebes, D. D., 233
Goetz, E., 203
Goh, D. S., 308, 310
Goldenberg, I. I., 407
Goldman, L., 102
Goldstein, A. P., 66, 116, 288, 399
Goldwasser, E., 27, 30, 84, 209, 222, 350, 352, 354
Golin, A. K., 356
Gonzalez, G., 232, 237
Good, T. L., 318, 319, 320
Goodenough, W. H., 228
Goodlad, J. I., 69
Goodman, L. A., 253
Goodwin, D. L., 150, 276
Gottfredson, D. C., 407
Gottfredson, G. D., 407
Gottlieb, B., 412
Gottsegen, M. G., 144
Graden, J., 27, 30, 39, 45, 47, 84, 209, 222, 350, 352, 354, 377
Graham, S., 55
Granowsky, S., 139, 144
Gray, S. W., 151, 358
Green, G., 208, 210, 213
Green, K., 363, 374
Green, M., 1, 16
Greene, D., 404
Greenwood, C., 288
Greiger, R. M., 146, 149, 150
Gresham, F. M., 8, 19, 270-72, 292
Grieger, R. N., 353
Grimes, J., 22
Grimley, L. K., 53
Grinker, R. R., Sr., 359, 361

Gross, T., 407
Grubb, R. D., 28, 90
Guba, E. G., 252, 259
Guild, J., 288
Guild, M., 1, 16, 208, 210, 213
Gumperz, J. J., 232
Gutkin, T. B., 2, 8, 11, 16, 22, 54, 95, 115, 117, 119, 123, 136, 250, 251, 265, 358, 361, 362, 363, 393, 395, 396, 398, 407, 410, 416, 417
Guydish, J., 207

H

Hadley, S. W., 250
Haertel, E., 306
Haire, D., 409
Haley, J., 400
Haley, R. W., 404
Hall, C. S., 359
Hall, M. D., 376
Hall, R., 229
Hamblin, A., 203, 213, 214, 215
Hammer, D. C., 293-5
Hammond, R. L., 252, 259
Hannafin, M. J., 151
Hapworth, C. E., 143
Hare, A. P., 61, 62, 65
Hargrove, D. S., 221
Harper, R., 149
Harre, R., 55
Harrell, J. E., 363
Harris, J. D., 53, 118, 140
Harris, L. C., 235
Harris, M. W., 2, 144, 149
Hartmann, D. P., 265, 266, 282-5
Harvey, O. J., 403
Harwood, A., 231
Hauser, G., 45
Hauser, R. M., 344
Hawkins, R. P., 277, 282
Haworth, C. C., 64
Hay, W. D., 281
Hayes, S. C., 251, 273, 281
Haynes, S. N., 282, 285
Hazel, J. S., 288
Heaston, P., 184
Hebb, D., 145
Heider, F., 54, 403
Helge, D. I., 203, 205, 206, 121, 213, 220

Heller, H., 203
Heller, K. A., 323, 407
Henderson, R. W., 253, 255, 262-3, 241
Henggeler, S. W., 219, 220
Henry, S. A., 73
Heppner, P., 405
Herrera, J., 228
Herron, W. G., 1, 10, 16, 208, 210, 213
Hersen, M., 278, 282
Hersh, R. H., 315
Herstein, R. J., 372
Hertlein, W., 45
Hessler, G. L., 63
Hetherington, E. M., 363, 374
Hiesberger, J., 219
Hildreth, G. H., 10
Hinds, R., 155, 156
Hinkle, A., 398
Hobbs, N., 219, 361, 363, 374, 386, 398, 402
Hodge, M. V., 181
Hoedt, K. C., 27
Hoff, M. K., 96
Hoffenberg-Rutman, J., 27
Hoffer, T., 320, 321, 322
Hoffman, L., 415
Hogenson, D., 356
Holland, W. R., 240
Holtzman, W. H., 323
Homer, A. L., 287
Homme, L., 45
Honigfeld, G., 144, 145
Hood, W. R., 403
Hoover, T., 181
Hops, H., 288, 292
House, A. E., 282
Houston, W. B., 240
Howard, J. S., 220
Howell, K., 53
Huessy, H. R., 203, 206, 220
Hughes, J. N., 15, 28, 119, 141, 203, 205, 211, 213, 404
Humes, C. W., 1, 94
Hummel, D. L., 1
Hunt, D. E., 63
Hunt, J. M., 6
Hunter, C. P., 282, 341
Hunter, J. E., 335, 336, 337
Hyman, I., 95, 101, 102, 151, 155, 156, 157, 356, 358, 362, 410
Hynd, G. W., 144

I

Illback, R. J., 124, 125, 203, 220, 417
Isaacson, R. V., 116, 398, 407
Ivens, R. E., 203
Izzo, L. D., 116, 398, 407

J

Jackson, A. M., 193
Jackson, D. A., 288
Jackson, J. H., 154, 171-2, 174-5, 181-2, 186, 196
Jackson, N. F., 288
Jackson, T. T., 207, 209
Jaco, E. G., 230
Jacobson, L., 403
Jacobson, L., 56
James, L. R., 344
Jarman, R. F., 144
Jason, L. A., 274, 287-8, 290, 292, 398
Jason, L. D., 116
Jasso, R., 235
Jenkins, J. R., 155
Jensen, A. R., 235, 239, 241, 372
Jilek-Aall, L., 231
Johnson, D. M., 253, 255, 262-3
Johnson, E. L., 307
Johnston, J., 282
Jones, R. R., 281, 282
Jones, R. W., 98
Jones, W. R., 236
Joreskog, K. G., 253
Judge, H., 308
Justiz, M. J., 321, 322

K

Kahl, L. J., 141
Kamin, L. J., 372
Kanfer, F. H., 399
Kantor, R. E., 1, 16, 208, 210, 213
Kaplan, L., 375
Kaplan, M. S., 28, 141
Karazu, J., Jr., 404
Karno, M., 231
Kass, R. E., 282
Kaufman, A. S., 190, 353
Kaufman, M. J., 96
Kaufman, N. L., 190
Kavale, K., 265, 267

Kazandkian, A., 292
Kazdin, A. E., 8, 19, 149, 150, 250-1, 266, 270-72, 277, 281, 285-6, 288-9, 290-3, 355, 416
Keefe, S. E., 228, 230, 231
Keller, E. F., 308
Keller, H. R., 86, 282
Kelley, H. H., 403
Kent, R. N., 285
Keogh, B. K., 27, 123, 140, 235, 236, 242
Kicklighter, R. H., 95, 102, 410
Kidder, L., 404
Kiesler, C. A., 291
Kilgore, S., 320, 321, 322
Kindall, L. M., 288
Kinsala, M. G., 405
Kirby, J. R., 144
Kirschenbaum, P. S., 15
Kirschner-Stone, M., 181
Klein, P., 116, 288
Kliegl, R. M., 266
Knitzer, J., 33
Knoff, H. M., 405
Kohlberg, L., 307, 309, 313, 314
Korman, M., 227, 329
Kozloff, M. A., 363
Kramer, J. J., 118, 203
Krasner, L., 6, 355
Kratochwill, T. R., 149, 249-52, 254, 258-62, 264-5, 272-5, 278-9, 282, 286-9, 290, 292
Krauss, R. M., 403
Krigsman, S. W., 363
Kuehnle, K., 46, 120, 407, 417
Kuhn, A., 71
Kuhn, T. S., 359, 413
Kukic, L. D., 27
Kukic, M. B., 27, 123, 140
Kukic, S. J., 123, 140
Kurtines, W., 233, 235

L

La Fromboise, T., 229
LaCross, M. B., 405
Labin, B., 377
Lacayo, N., 53, 140
Lambert, N. M., 5, 20, 73, 90, 268, 340
Lambert, W. E., 232, 236
Lamprecht, M. J., 56
Landau, S. E., 141
Lane, S., 253, 255, 262-3

Lang, P. J., 277, 279
Laosa, L. M., 229
Larcen, S. W., 15, 407
Larson, N., 376
LeBlanc, C. P., 292
Lee, W. S., 151
Lennox, N., 88, 151, 152, 153
Leonard, J., 376, 384
Lepper, J. R., 404
Lesiak, W. J., 28
Lessing, E. E., 234
Levine, A., 367
Levine, D. U., 197
Levine, M., 367
Levinson, H. H., 153
Leviton, L. C., 266
Lewin, K., 6, 152, 361, 367, 402, 406
Lewis, J. F., 190, 235, 239
Lewis, W. W., 411
Lewontin, R. C., 372
Liberman, B. L., 404
Liberman, R., 282
Lieberman, M., 313
Lily, M., 209
Lindholm, K. J., 232
Lindzey, G., 359
Litz, C., 155
Lloyd, M. E., 260
Lloyd, R., 203
Lochman, J. E., 15, 407
Lockhart, B., 229
Locklear, H. H., 230
Lohnes, P., 312
Longshore, D., 234
Lorion, R. P., 116, 146, 398, 407
Lotyczewski, B. S., 407
Lounsbury, E., 28
Loven, M. D., 376
Lovitt, T. C., 307
Lowry, L., 46
Luiten, J., 289
Luria, A. R., 144
Lutey, C., 240
Lynch, E. C., 220
Lynch, W. W., 282

M

MacDonald, K. I., 344
MacKenzie, D. E., 322

AUTHOR INDEX

Macdonald, J. B., 69
Mace, B. J., 237
Maez, L., 232, 237
Maher, C. A., 59, 76, 116, 124, 125, 153, 220
Maher, C. A., 251-253, 257-262, 275, 417
Mahoney, M. J., 150
Manley, E. T., 119, 141
Manley, T. R., 119, 141
Manni, J., 356
Mao, B. J., 252, 253
Marjoribanks, K., 363
Markley, R. P., 207
Marliave, R. S., 263
Marston, D., 46
Martens, B. K., 8, 410, 416
Martin, B., 358, 362, 363, 374
Martin, H. W., 231
Martin, R. P., 19, 20, 27, 67, 97, 151, 265, 405
Martinez, C., 231
Martinez, J. L., 235
Martinez, S. R., 235
Maslach, C., 404
Mason, E. J., 119
Masters, J. C., 355
Matarazzo, R. G., 289
Matluck, J. H., 237
Matuszek, P., 190
May, J. V., 91, 92, 93, 97
Mayer, G. R., 292, 355
McCartney, K., 362, 373
McGaw, B., 265, 306
McGue, M., 36, 45, 190, 411
McKenzie, R., 335
McLaughlin, B., 232
McLoughlin, R. J., 27, 123, 140
McMahon, R. J., 8, 291
McPartland, J. M., 311
Meacham, M. L., 27, 140, 211, 213, 310, 338, 358, 395
Mearig, J. S., 89, 155, 156, 357, 376, 377
Medway, F. J., 19, 28, 90, 118, 151, 163, 251, 265, 291
Meichenbaum, D. H., 401
Melton, G. B., 103, 203, 204
Mercer, J. R., 190, 235, 239
Meredith, K. E., 289
Merino, B., 235
Merriman, H. O., 252, 259
Messick, S., 315, 316, 323
Meyer, W. V., 55
Meyers, J., 19, 20, 27, 28, 30, 39, 47, 84, 86, 88, 119, 146, 147, 151, 152, 153, 163, 209, 222, 265, 350, 352, 353, 354, 358, 362, 398
Migles, M., 28, 89, 141, 268
Miles, M. B., 59, 151, 407, 411
Milgram, S., 404
Miller, A., 63
Miller, G. A., 397
Miller, J. G., 110
Miller, J. N., 141
Miller, T. I., 250
Miller, T. L., 290
Minke, K. M., 123
Minor, M. W., 351
Mintz, J., 266
Minuchin, S., 376, 415
Mirkin, P. K., 46
Miron, D., 315
Mischel, W., 55, 146, 361
Mitchell, J. V., 44, 76
Moe, G., 8
Moll, L. C., 228
Monroe, C., 288
Monroe, V., 1, 12, 85, 89, 394, 395
Moore, J. C., 236
Moore, S., 386
Moracco, J., 292
Morris, J., 140
Morris, R. J., 278, 279
Morrow, L., 154
Mosher, R. L., 315
Mott, S. E., 253, 255, 262-3
Muldrow, T., 335
Mullen, F. A., 182
Mullen, Y., 376
Murphy, G., 2
Murray, 404

N

Nada, H., 281
Nagle, R. J., 118, 270-72
Nantume, G., 181
Neigher, W. D., 94
Nelson, B. H., 233
Nelson, R. O., 251, 273, 281
New, P. K., 61
Nezlek, J., 404
Nichols, J. G., 55
Nisbett, R. C., 55
Nugaris, J., 193

O

O'Connor, W. A., 377
O'Dell, S., 398
O'Leary, K. D., 282, 285, 401
O'Leary, S. G., 401
O'Neill, P., 407
Oakland, T., 190, 236, 239
Obrzut, J. E., 144
Oksman, P. F., 131
Olmedo, E. L., 174, 227, 233, 235
Omark, D. R., 238
Oplesch, M., 240
Oren, D. L., 236
Orlich, D. C., 308
Ornstein, A. C., 181
Osguthorpe, R. T., 154
Overcast, T. D., 94, 95

P

Packard, V., 33, 34, 35
Padilla, A. M., 228, 230, 231, 232, 240
Paine, S., 288
Pallak, M. S., 393
Palmer, D. J., 56
Palmer, M., 240
Pantaleno, A. P., 97, 100, 101, 362, 410
Paolitto, D. P., 315
Pargament, K. I., 412
Parham v. J. L., 115
Parloff, M. B., 291, 398
Parra, E. B., 240, 253, 255, 262-3
Parsons, R. D., 19, 20, 265, 358
Passow, A. H., 1998
Patterson, G. R., 281, 282
Patterson, J. G., 27, 140, 358
Patterson, M., 68
Paul, G. P., 9, 250, 251, 277, 278, 353
Pavlov, I. P., 401
Peal, E., 236
Pearce, D., 311
Pearlman, K., 336, 337
Peckham, P. D., 27, 140, 211, 213, 310, 338, 358, 395
Pederson, A., 407
Pennypacker, H. S., 282
Perry, N. W., Jr., 330
Pervin, L. A., 359
Peter, L. J., 154
Peters, G. J., 203

Peterson, D. R., 44, 65
Peterson, L., 287
Peterson, P. E., 33
Peterson, R., 410
Petrie, P., 292
Petty, S. Z., 28, 90
Pfeffer, J., 353
Pfeiffer, S. I., 59, 76, 356, 376
Phillips, B. N., 13, 14, 63, 305, 306, 307, 329, 330, 331, 332, 338, 339, 340, 344, 345, 346
Phillips, M. A., 287
Photiadis, J. D., 205
Piaget, J., 404
Pianta, B., 44
Pielstick, N. L., 153
Piersel, W. C., 54, 195, 273, 274, 290, 292, 410
Plas, J. M., 376
Poggio, J. P., 66
Politser, P. E., 407
Poll, B. G., 187
Poplin, M. S., 87, 398
Porter, P., 45
Potter, M., 240, 377
Prasse, D., 99, 186
Price, R. H., 407
Prieto, A. G., 230
Proctor, N., 230
Provus, M. M., 252, 259
Pryzwansky, W. B., 96, 182, 356
Pugh, M. D., 403

R

Rabinowittz, V. C., 404
Rachman, S. J., 266, 289
Radonovich, J., 45
Rainey, V. C., 329
Rajaratman, N., 281
Ralph, J. H., 197
Ramage, J., 27, 53, 82, 86, 89, 90, 395
Ramirez, M., 233
Ramsey, S., 45
Rankin, R. J., 241
Rappaport, J., 364
Raven, B. H., 404, 405
Raven, J., 70
Ravitch, D., 324
Redner, R., 287
Reese, T. A., 209, 213
Regan, R., 44, 45, 190, 240, 411
Reger, R., 1, 6, 83, 143, 144, 146, 148, 153

Reid, J. B., 281, 282, 285
Reilly, D. H., 6, 139, 162
Reimer, J., 315
Reinharz, S., 407
Remer, R., 119
Repucci, N. D., 399
Reschly, D. J., 22, 56, 145, 148, 152, 153, 228, 239, 240, 316, 323
Resnick, L. B., 307
Rettke, G. H., 1
Reynolds, C. R., 2, 16, 22, 95, 117, 123, 136, 228, 235, 241, 250, 361, 362, 363, 393, 395, 396, 414, 416
Reynolds, M. C., 3, 9, 36
Reza, R., 228
Richey, L., 45
Riger, S., 407
Rimm, D. C., 355
Ringers, J., Jr., 363
Ringness, T. A., 27
Rist, R. C., 363
Ritter, D. R., 267, 292, 398
Roach, K. S., 131
Robbins, J., 8
Roberts, R. D., 28
Robinson, L., 253, 255, 262-3
Rogers, C., 56, 69
Rogers, E. M., 58, 361
Rogers, R. A., 58
Romancyzk, R. G., 282, 285
Rosenbaum, M. S., 293-5
Rosenshine, B., 319
Rosenthal, R., 56, 266, 403
Ross, A. O., 73
Rossi, P. H., 269
Rowan, B., 322
Rowe, W., 229
Rudin-Hay, L., 281
Rueda, R. S., 228
Ruiz, R. A., 228, 318
Russo, N., 174, 227
Rychtarik, R. C., 291
Rzepski, B., 356

S

Sabatino, D. A., 20
Sales, B. D., 94, 95
Salmon, P., 55
Salmon-Cox, L., 254
Salvia, J., 239
Sameroff, A. J., 370, 374
Sanchez, D. T., 230, 237, 239
Sandoval, J., 90, 139, 235, 268
Sandoval, M. C., 231
Santogrossi, D., 282
Sarason, S. B., 44, 70, 120, 353, 363, 406, 407
Sashkin, M., 153
Sattler, J. M., 235, 240, 316
Saunders, J. T., 399
Scarr, S., 362, 372, 373
Schachter, S., 403
Scharf, P., 314, 315
Schelble, M., 282
Schmidt, F. L., 335, 336, 337
Schmuck, R. A., 88, 151, 152, 265, 407, 411
Schnaps, A., 253, 255, 262-3
Schneider, K. C., 143
Schneider, R. G., 409
Schowengerdt, R. V., 66
Schreiber, K., 95, 155, 156, 157
Schumaker, J. B., 288
Schutz, R. E., 236, 309
Scopeta, M. H., 233, 235
Scriven, M. S., 258, 260, 309
Sebso, M., 132
Sechrest, L., 287
Secord, P., 55
Seligman, M., 363
Selinger, H. V., 15, 407
Senft, L. B., 54
Shanahan, T., 321
Shapiro, D. A., 266
Shapiro, E. S., 19
Shavelson, R. J., 264
Sheinman, L., 404
Sheldon, A., 412
Sheldon-Wildgren, J., 288
Shellenberger, S., 240
Shepard, L., 36
Sher, J. P., 206
Sherif, C. W., 403
Sherif, M., 403
Sherman, J. A., 288
Sherwood, G., 53, 140
Shinn, M. R., 36, 45
Shore, M. F., 233
Sikes, J., 403, 412
Silverstein, B., 398
Simoni, J. J., 205
Simpson, R. A., 87
Simpson, R. L., 398

Singer, J. E., 403
Singer, J. H., 54, 398
Skinner, B. F., 6, 83, 401
Slater, R., 207
Slaughter, E. L., 228
Slenkovich, J. E., 187
Sloves, R. E., 143
Smith, A., 1, 16, 208, 210, 213, 363, 374
Smith, C. R., 405
Smith, D. K., 15, 36, 59, 250, 265, 306, 398
Snapp, B., 54
Snider, B., 54
Snow, R. E., 63, 307
Snyder, H. N., 403
Solomon, G., 219
Sorbom, D., 253
Sosnowsky, W. P., 53
Sperber, R., 315
Sprafkin, R. P., 116, 288
Sroufe, L. A., 360, 364
Stambaugh, E. E., 282
Stapp, J., 174, 227
Starkman, S., 148
Steinberg, M. A., 357
Stephan, C., 403, 412
Stehpens, T. M., 69, 288
Stern, P., 264
Stewart, K. J., 81, 89, 90
Stewart-Lester, K. J., 90
Stokes, T. F., 293-4
Stone, C. A., 252, 253, 255, 256, 262, 263
Street, A., 288
Strong, S. R., 405, 406
Strossen, R. J., 281
Strube, M. J., 265, 266
Strupp, H. H., 250
Stuart, R. B., 6
Stufflebeam, D. J., 252, 259
Sulek-Dommis, B., 45
Sulzer,-Azaroff, B., 355
Suppes, P., 317
Swain, M. A., 236
Swanson, E. N., 240
Swarner, J. C., 253, 255, 262-3
Szapocznik, J., 233, 235
Szasz, T. S., 6

T

Takanishi, R., 393
Taplin, P. S., 285

Taylor, G., 59, 411
Taylor, J., 377
Taylor, R. B., 355
Taylor, S. E., 55
Teske, R. H. C., 233
Thibaut, J. W., 403
Thomas, B. K., 377
Thomas, J., 45
Thomas, P. J.
Thoresen, C. E., 150, 281
Thurlow, M., 240
Tieger, A. G., 115
Tindal, G., 46
Tindall, R. H., 207
Tittler, B. I., 356, 376
Tombari, M. L., 86, 269, 270, 293, 416
Toney, D. H., 240
Torrey, E. F., 228, 231
Trachtman, G. M., 81, 95, 102, 155, 157, 162, 355, 357, 362
Trenary, D. S., 213, 215
Trickett, E. J., 403, 407
Trickett, P. K., 361
Trost, M. A., 116, 398, 407
Truax, C. B., 65
Tucker, B. Z., 363, 374
Tucker, J. A., 190, 240
Turco, T. L., 8
Turnbull, A. P., 374, 376, 384
Turnbull, H. R., III, 364
Tuthill, D., 305, 306, 309
Tyler, F. B., 412
Tyler, V. O., 292

U

Ullman, L. P., 6, 355

V

Valencia, R. R., 241
Valett, R. E., 1, 154
Valins, S., 55, 404
Van Egeren, L. F., 403
VanSomeren, K. R., 249, 251, 265, 270, 287
Vasquez, L. P., 228
Vontress, C. E., 193

W

Wagenfeld, M. O., 203
Wagner, D. I., 116

Wahler, R. G., 282
Wahlstrom, M., 236
Wahrman, R., 403
Walberg, H., 306, 321
Walker, H. M., 288
Walker, J., 171
Walters, R. H., 149, 401
Walton, D. M., 398
Walton, S., 317
Wandersman, A., 407
Wang, J. J., 44
Wang, M. C., 36
Warburton, A. A., 208
Warren, R. C., 193
Waskow, I. E., 398
Waters, E., 360, 364
Waters, L. G., 119, 141, 163
Watson, J. B., 401
Watson, J. L., 398
Weick, K. E., 60
Weinberg, R. A., 1, 3, 9, 28, 349, 358, 369, 372, 373, 386
Weiner, B., 55, 56, 403
Weiner, I. B., 249
Weiss, R. J., 203
Weissberg, R. P., 407
Weitz, M., 409
Welfel, E. R., 65
Wellman, H. M., 318
Wesson, C., 46
West, S. G., 287
White, B. J., 403
White, B. L., 73
White, M. A., 2, 70, 144, 149, 172
White, P. O., 416
Whitman, J., 149, 150, 151
Whitman, M., 149, 150, 151
Willard, W., 231
Williams, R. L., 239, 288
Wilson, C. C., 282, 285
Wilson, G. T., 250, 266, 289, 290-2

Wine, J. D., 350, 351, 353
Winett, R. A., 150
Winikur, D., 356
Winkler, D., 356
Wise, A. E., 181
Witt, J. C., 2, 8, 16, 22, 95, 117, 123, 136, 151, 230, 361, 362, 363, 393, 395, 396, 410, 416
Wolf, M. M., 8, 289, 290
Wolfe, B. E., 398
Wonderlich, S. A., 287
Wong, P. J., 403
Wood, D. D., 282
Woody, R. H., 149, 150
Workman, E. A., 288
Wright, S. R., 369
Wroten, S. P., 344

Y

Yager, G. G., 110
Yammer, M. D., 251, 265, 270
Yanowitz, B., 377
Yeaton, W. H., 287
Yoshida, R. K., 96
Yoshioka-Maxwell, B., 241
Ysseldyke, J. E., 1, 3, 9, 28, 35, 36, 39, 44, 45, 47, 56, 76, 140, 190, 212, 230, 239, 240, 358, 377, 393, 411

Z

Zagorin, S. W., 234
Zander, A., 62
Zax, M., 84
Zelhart, P. F., 207
Zigler, E., 361
Zimbardo, P. G., 404
Zins, J. E., 116, 119, 122, 124, 125, 131
Zubin, J., 6
Zucker, S. H., 230
Zwald, L., 292

Subject Index

A

ABAB research design, 270
Abilities testing, 350
Accountability of school psychologists, 131, 220-222, 249-303
Accreditation of training programs, 329
Activities of school psychologists, 27, 89, 122, 139, 410
Administration of school psychological services, 130-134
Advocacy consultation, 88-89
American Psychological Association (APA)
  ethical principles, of 97-100
  specialty guidelines of 2, 116
Analogue research, 285
APA, see American Psychological Association (APA)
Aptitude treatment interactions (ATIs), 62-64
Assessment, 17-18, 185
  approaches to, 6, 151, 354
  behavioral, 54
  cultural bias in, 237-239
  decision making in, 349, 393
  ethical guidelines for, 98-100
  foci of, 349, 393
  of internal characteristics of individuals, 6, 350, 400
  of language, 236-238
  legal regulation of, 94
  of minority group members, 190-191, 235-242
  research into, 315
ATIs (aptitude treatment interactions), 62-63
Attribution theory, 54-57

B

Bandura, Albert, 6, 28, See also specific reciprocal determinism entries
Behavioral consultation 86-87
Behavioral model of behavior, 6-8, 151, 354, 401
Between-group research designs, 274
Biculturalism, 190-191, 227-247
Buckley Amendment (Family Educational Rights and Privacy Act of 1976—FERPA), 94-97

C

Case study research strategy, 270-272
Causal modeling, 252-254
Certification of school psychologists, 329
Centralized school psychological services, 13-14, 16, 128, 191-192, 217
  see also Family Educational Rights and Privacy Act of 1976 (FERPA); Public Law 94-142 (Education of All Handicapped Children Act of 1975)
Child advocacy, 103-104, 155-157

437

SUBJECT INDEX

Child advocacy model of school psychological services, 155-157
Classes, special, 349
Clients of school psychologists, 4-5, 81-107, 117-118, 143-162, 362
  conceptualizations of, 82-94
  legal issues, 94-96
Communications, confidentiality of
  see Confidentiality (privacy)
Competence, ethical staandards for, 329
Conferences of school psychology, 1, 9
Confidentiality (privacy):
  ethical standards for, 98-100
  legal right to, 94-97
  see also Educational records; Family Educational Rights and Privacy Act of 1976 (FERPA)
Consent, legal rights involving, 94-97
Consultation, 19, 393
  approaches to, 86-88
  advocacy, 88
  ecological (behavioral, problem-solving), 86-87
  in indirect delivery of school psychological services, 393
  organizational (organization development), 71-72
  process, 88-89
Consultation model of evaluation, 261-265
Contractual services, 180, 189-190
Cost-benefit analysis in research-in-action perspective, 293
Cultural bias in tests, 227-247

D

Decentralized school psychological services, 13-14, 16, 128, 217
Developmental model of behavior, 349-391
Developmental research, 310
Diagnostic model of school psychological service delivery, 143-146
Direct delivery of school psychological services, 11-13, 394-395
Direct evaluation of school psychologist performance, 249
Discrimination, minority group, 227

E

Ecological model of behavior, 6-8, 349, 367, 402

Education of school psychologists, 329
  see also Training, of school psychologists
Educational records
  parental rights in, 94-97
  inspection of, parental rights in, 94-97
  legal treatment of, 94-97
Education for All Handicapped Children Act of 1975
  see Public Law 94-142
Effectiveness of school psychological services, 249-302, 336-337
Ethical issues and guidelines, 94-97, 98-100
Evaluation
  of school psychological services, 249-302
  of school psychologist performance, 249-302
Experimental research designs, 274

F

Family Educational Rights and Privacy Act of 1976 (FERPA), 94-97
Feedback systems for school psychological services, 249
FERPA (Family Educational Rights and Privacy Act of 1976), 94-97
Follow-up of school psychological services, 249
  see also Evaluation, of school psychological services
Forrest v. Amback, 97-98
Functions of school psychologists, 27, 89, 122, 139, 410

G

Generalization of treatment effects, 249-302
Generic model of school psychology services delivery, 21
Group research designs, 274-277

I

Indirect delivery of school psychological services, 11-13, 393-394
Informed consent, legal rights involving, 94-97
Inservice education, 89
Integrity of interventions, 287
Interventions, 18-19, 416-418
  acceptability of, research on, 290, 415
  assumptions about, 85-86

SUBJECT INDEX 439

effectiveness of, 249
legal constraints, on, 94–97: *see also* Public Law 92-142 (Education for All Handicapped Children Act of 1975)

L

Labor unions, 179
Larry P. v. Riles, 115
Learning research, 317
Legal issues and guidelines, 94–97
Legal regulation
  of educational access, 94–97, 427, 432–433
  of school psychology, 226–228, 248–261, 264
  see also Family Educational Rights and Privacy Act of 1976 (FERPA); Public Law 94-142 (Education for All Handicapped Children Act of 1975); Legal rights of children (students), 94–97, 208–210
Licensing of school psychologists, 329

M

Medical model of behavior, 6–8, 350, 358, 400
Mental health consultation model, 86
Minority groups, 192–194
  educational access deprivation of, 227–247
  in urban schools, 174–175
  test bias affecting, 190–191, 227–247
Multidisciplinary teams in assessment and decision making, 44–45, 135–136

N

National Association of School Psychologists, 37–38, 379
Nature-nurture, 371

O

Organizational consultation model, 411
Organizational development model of school psychological services, 151–153
Organization of school psychological services, 109–138
Organization theory, 58–62, 406

P

Parents, rights of
  to amend educational records, 94–97
  to inspect educational records, 94–97
Pine County model of school psychology services, 47–48
PATH-referenced program evaluation, 254–256
Prescriptive intervention model of school psychological services, 153–155
Prevention-promotion model of school psychological services, 146–149
Preventive (proactive) school psychological services, 15–16, 71–75, 84–85, 146–149
Prior notice and consent
  legal rights involving, 94–97
Privacy, see Confidentiality (privacy)
Proactive (preventive) school psychological services, 15–16, 353
Process consultation, 88
Professional activities of school psychologists, 31–40, 53–54
Professional ethics
  see Ethical issues and guidelines; Legal issues and guidelines
Professional school psychologists in American Psychological Association guidelines, 2, 116–118
Program evaluation, 249–302
Provider guidelines of American Psychological Association, 2, 116–118
Psychological services
  see School psychological services
Public Law 94-142 (Education for All Handicapped Children Act of 1975), 83–84, 95–96, 114–116, 177–178, 186–189, 208–210, 311–312, 351
  assessment in, 94–97
  impact of, 11
  provisions of, 94–97
  school psychological service extension by, 94–97

Q

Qualifications of school psychologists, 329
Quasi-experimental research designs, 272

R

Reactive school psychological services, 15–16, 363
Reciprocal determinism model of behavior, 6–8, 12–13, 28–30
Regulations
  see Legal regulation

SUBJECT INDEX

Research
  in school psychology, 19, 189, 305-327
  on consultation, 415
  on intervention acceptability, 415
Research centers (institutions) in school psychology, 289-292, 302
Resistance in consultation, 107-108
Responsibility, ethical standards for, 262-263, 411, 422-423
Reversal design for research, 286
Reverse due process hearings, 258
Role models for school psychologists, 21-22
Roles of school psychologists, 9-15, 20-25, 51
  see also School psychologists, roles of
Rural school psychological services, 16, 203-225
Rural schools
  characteristics of, 204-207

S

Salaries of school psychologists, 67-68
Schools, 35-36, 69-71
School psychological associations, 10-11, 17-20, 333-335
  see also American Association on Mental Deficiency (AAMD); American Psychological Association (APA); National Association of School Psychologists (NASP)
School psychological services
  accountability of, 131, 220-222, 249-302
  administration of, 131-133
  characteristics of, 62-68
  classifications of, 48-53, 58-62
  conceptual continuums, 11-17
  delivery of, 29-76
  effectiveness of, 9-10, 249-302
  focus of, on children vs. adults, 328-330
  fundamental questions about, 30-40
  generic model of, 20-22
  goals of, 2-3, 12, 37, 142-162
  influences on, 114
  models of, 20-23, 82-84, 139-169, 349-378
  organization of, 10-11, 109-121
  priorities in, 59
  standards for, 116-117, 377-378
  supervision of, 129-131
  systems for, 20-23, 114-138
  taxonomy of, 16-18
School psychologists
  credibility of, 38, 66
  force of, 2, 37, 65-68
  ratios of, to students, 90-91, 125-126, 195-196
  roles of, 27-28, 89-91, 122-123, 139-141, 151-153, 161, 376-377, 380-384, 395-396, 410
  training of, 37-38, 91, 119-120, 329-348
  see also specific entries, e.g., Accountability of school psychologists; Clients of school psychologists; Psychologists
School psychology
  blueprint for training, 3
  challenges facing, 40-44, 114-118
  current practices in, 27-51
  defining (synthesizing) 42-43
  external influences on, 114-120
  internal influences, 120-124
  legal influences, 114-115
Schools
  professiooonal relationships with, 53-70
Self-efficacy, 57-58
Social validity, 8-10
Social learning model of school psychologidcal services, 149-151
Social policy, 32-43, 310, 378
Social psychology, 403
Social validity, 8-9
Special education, 36
Specialists in school psychology
  American Psychological Association guidelines for, 2, 116-118, 332-334
Specialty guidelines of American Psychological Association, 2, 116-117, 332-334
Spring Hill Symposium on the Future of Psychology in the Schools, 1
Structure
  of school psychological services, 16-20, 40-42
Synoptic program evaluation, 257-261
System level influences, 31-32, 58-62
Systems theory, 110-114, 374-376

T

Taxonomy of school psychological services, 16-20

SUBJECT INDEX 441

Teaching
 improvement of, 53-60, 318
 research on, 318
Thayer Conference, 1, 10
Theory and research in practice of school
  psychology, 5-8, 53-60
Time series design and analysis, 272
Training
 doctoral-nondoctoral issues, 333
 of school psychologists, 37-38, 329-348,
  379-380
Urban school psychological services, 16,
  171-202
Urban schools,
 characteristics of, 172-181